PROSE AND POETRY OF THE AMERICAN WEST

EDITED BY JAMES C. WORK

PROSE & POETRY

OF THE

AMERICAN

WEST

University of Nebraska Press

Lincoln & London

Copyright © 1990 by the University of Nebraska Press
All rights reserved
Manufactured in the United States of America

The paper in this book meets the minimum requirements
of American National Standard for Information Sciences –
Permanence of Paper for Printed Library Materials,
ANSI Z39.48-1984.

Library of Congress Cataloging-in-Publication Data
Prose and poetry of the American west /
edited by James C. Work.
p.   cm.
ISBN 0-8032-4744-3 (alkaline paper). –
ISBN 0-8032-9718-1 (pbk. : alkaline paper)
1. West (U.S.) – Literary collections.
2. American literature – West (U.S.)
I. Work, James C.
PS561.P76   1990
810.8'03278—dc20   90-32944   CIP

This volume was made possible in part by
generous grants from the Office of the
Academic Vice President and the
College of Arts, Humanities
and Social Sciences,
Colorado State University.

Contents

—

Preface

—

PEOPLE have been talking about *the West* for so long that we've begun to think of it as something tangible, something that can actually be defined, something with distinct limits and denotable characteristics. But it's not. *The West* is an abstraction, a term that summarizes, not one that characterizes. It's a concept that ultimately defies all defining. It's too comprehensive, too compendious. Geographically, the West means a thousand or more different places. Chronologically, it stretches from a prologue in the dim past to a finis somewhere in the future—taking in, so far, at least four hundred years. It's a sociological way to lump millions of unique individuals together under the heading of *westerners*. Artistically speaking, it's a generic tag for a kind of literature that has been called *regional*— probably the most widespread case of regional literature that ever existed. Anywhere.

Some have said that the American West is all the land found on the arid side of the 100th meridian, the north-south survey line that neatly bisects the Dakotas and Nebraska and slices off considerable chunks of Kansas, Oklahoma, and Texas. Some argue that the West also includes Alaska; some even argue that the West does *not* include California. The West is a comprehension of forested mountain ranges reaching two miles high and of shadeless deserts lying below the level of the sea. The term takes in prairie land so open and featureless that the eye sees it as a greenish-brown disk resting beneath a blue bowl. And whether the terrain includes mountains, seashores, deserts, or prairies, it is also a maze of canyons, valleys, gorges, arroyos, ditches, and draws.

And then there are the peopled places. Some are tight little one-street towns weathering the summers and winters of Kansas, Idaho, Nevada . . . others are sprawling acres of concrete chessboards set about with glass and cinder-block buildings. Just outside the shadows of the skyscrapers, suburbs spread like tendrils of fungi. Elsewhere, towns that are merely large strain to attract what their college-trained city managers call *development*. Whether tiny, megapolitan, or just growing, the majority of the West's peopled places can be found squatting on sites formerly occupied by fur-trading forts or by Spanish pueblos, by army posts or by pioneer townsites, by railroad sidings, fishing ports, logging camps, or steamboat landings . . . each of them a rough-sawn monument to the aspirations of America's westward people.

You and I, in our conversation, can point to an infinite number of people, places, and things and say, "Now, *that's* western." But neither of us can say why. One of those things that people all over the world recognize as western is a style of writing—the Western. This persistent brand of formalized folklore is disseminated through inexpensive novels and low-budget horse operas, tends to be written according to familiar patterns, and generally involves the cattle industry. Because the Western is so popular, and because it is usually a perennial source of confusion in the discussion of western American literature, it is the first topic we need to clarify before going on. The fact is, this book has almost nothing to do with Westerns. In the entire volume there are only four or five stories about cowboys. There are no ex-Confederates trailing stolen cattle in Texas, no marshals playing stud poker in Arizona, and no horses names Cherokee or Comanche or Blue Boy. In deference to serious literature of the American West, I have seriously avoided anthologizing the Western.

This anthology is a gallery of artists who work in various literary media. It exhibits literature that I consider to be of lasting interest and artistic value. Nor is my *gallery* metaphor simply a nifty figure of speech: a gallery is what I mean the book to be. I did not call it a *collection* because that term makes me think of specimens that have been labeled and impaled on pins. Nor did I want it to be a *showcase* because these aren't the kind of works that need to be kept under glass and handled with kid gloves. And I don't see it as a *catalog* or *index* or *guide* to western literature. My selection process is not nearly as comprehensive as such terms would suggest. Some authors in this gallery are, as yet, relatively obscure. Some have only one or two works in print. Some have even written better material than you will find here. And finally, many works and many deserving writers have been left out. So, if you have a favorite western work at home and you are disappointed that it has not been included in this anthology, well . . . I'm delighted you have it at home.

Probably the best-known western anthology to date is J. Golden Taylor's *The Literature of the American West*, now out of print; another popular one, *The Western Story* by Philip Durham and Everett L. Jones, is also off the market. Others, such as Laurence Ivan Seidman's *Once in the Saddle* or Winfred Blevins's *Give Your Heart to the Hawks*, limit themselves to single topics—cowboys and mountain men, in these instances—whereas collections like *Writers of the Purple Sage* by Russell Martin and Marc Barasch, or Alex Blackburn's *The Interior Country*, stick to the contemporary writers. Don Graham's Texas anthology, *South by Southwest*, is an example of some of the fine regional collections that are available.

One such collection, *The Literature of the Rocky Mountain West, 1803–1903*, published in 1939, includes a prefatory comment that reminds us how young the literature of the American West really is, and how the literary climate has changed in the last fifty years. "No literary master has yet arisen to portray in adequate and lasting words either the magnificent scenery of the Rocky Mountain West or the colorful life that has existed in this region from those early times when the Indians held undisputed dominion over it down to our own day. . . . nearly all of the hundreds of books inspired by this section of the United States have been produced by amateurs, minor authors, or journalists, [reflecting] a lack of conspicuous literary expression by native authors."[1]

Prose and Poetry of the American West brings together many native authors who are literary professionals; their portrayals of the scenery and the life of the West are wholly "adequate and lasting." And far from there being a "lack of conspicuous literary expression," there is now such an abundance of material that choosing which of it to use was the biggest problem in compiling this book.

Four principal considerations, in addition to my personal preferences, guided the selection of these pieces. I am against the practice of anthologizing chapters from longer books; therefore, I have avoided excerpts whenever possible. I have chosen certain works that acknowledge the Hispanic tradition, an influence in western culture since 1540. Gender was a third consideration; the two most popular anthologies to date contain a combined total of seventy-seven writers. Willa Cather is the only female among them. By including numerous examples of poetry, travel writing, letters, and fiction by women, I hope *Prose and Poetry of the American West* more accurately represents the indispensable contributions made by women to the growth of the culture, to the integrity of the civilization, and to the

---

1. Levett Jay Davidson and Prudence Bostwick, eds., *The Literature of the Rocky Mountain West, 1803–1903* (Caldwell, Idaho: Caxton Printers, 1939), p. 6.

quality of literature. My final consideration was to choose writers who could exemplify the many different facets of western literature and who could thereby act as spokespersons for the hundreds not included.

For the most part, I have tried to let the writers speak for themselves, instead of adding extensive annotations. Wherever practical, the text preserves any footnotes found in the original manuscripts. Wherever a piece of slang, an allusion, or a non-English word seems to be beyond the everyday vocabulary of an average speaker, a definition is given. Footnotes are *not* supplied when the word in question is not germane to the context. I have also added a few historical facts in the footnotes when such information seemed important to understanding the selection.

In accord with common practice, this anthology presents authors in the order in which they were born. I have also established four periods of western American literature, using a comment by Victor Hugo as my precedent: "Whether you examine one literature in particular or all literatures en masse, you always must arrive at the same conclusion: the lyric poets before the epic poets, the epic poets before the dramatic poets. . . . Indeed, a society begins by singing about its dreams, then narrates what it has done, and finally begins describing what it thinks."[2] In *Prose and Poetry of the American West*, the selections in part 1 celebrate the land and its promise; those in parts 2 and 3 narrate the era of discovery and growth, and those in part 4 reflect the ways in which the land has shaped the creative consciousness.

As for my belief in the centrality of myth in western American literature, I cite one of America's most respected thinkers, I. A. Richards. In *Coleridge on Imagination*, Richards writes:

> Make-belief is an enervating exercise of fancy not to be confused with imaginative growth. The saner and greater mythologies are not fancies; they are the utterance of the whole soul of man and, as such, inexhaustible to meditation. They are no amusement or diversion to be sought as relaxation and an escape from the hard realities of life. They are these hard realities in projection, their symbolic recognition, coordination and acceptance. Through such mythologies our will is collected, our powers unified, our growth controlled. Through

---

2. "Qu'on examine une littérature en particulier, ou toutes les littératures en masse, on arrivera toujours au même fait: les poëtes lyriques avant les poëtes épiques, les poëtes épiques avant les poëtes dramatiques. . . . La société, en effet, commence par chanter ce qu'elle rêve, puis raconte ce qu'elle fait, et enfin se met à peindre ce qu'elle pense" (translation is mine). Victor Hugo, Preface to *Cromwell*, in *Théâtre Complet de Victor Hugo* (Paris: Éditions Gallimard, 1963), 1: 423.

them the infinitely divergent strayings of our being are brought into "balance or reconciliation." . . .

Without his mythologies man is only a cruel animal without a soul—for a soul is a central part of his governing mythology—he is a congeries of possibilities without order and without aim.[3]

I invite visitors to the gallery to carry this quotation along with them so that they may use it to evaluate the exhibits. Judge for yourself whether this book offers "hard realities in projection" and stimulates your meditation on the "whole soul" of the American West. Evaluate each selection's contribution to the "imaginative growth" of the West's collective soul. Behind the Western's fanciful amusements, deep under a make-believe world of six-guns and schoolma'ams, is a central mythology "inexhaustible to meditation," given voice in this book by a few gifted interpreters.

3. I. A. Richards, *Coleridge on Imagination* (Bloomington: Indiana University Press, 1960), pp. 171–72.

PART I
The Emergence Period
1540-1832

Introduction

—

Wherever a civilization has evolved an awareness of itself, mythic accounts of its origin have also evolved. Native American cultures preserve stories of ancient dark worlds and of journeying into new and brighter worlds. The transformation from darkness into light symbolizes awareness or enlightenment, two characteristics enabling a "new" people to arise. The landscape is an essential influence in this metamorphosis. The land possesses a personality all its own, with the power to change its human inhabitants.

Collectively, these accounts are called emergence myths. Ethnologists and others, who have collected hundreds of such stories, find that there are certain features common to all of them. The "old" place is confining and without order; the new place has more light, and life forms that are more clearly structured; some of the people have to be left behind during the emergence; and those who make it to the new place undergo changes in their lives and in their awareness of themselves.

In a sense, this pattern of experience also applies to the first Europeans to reach the American West, the Spanish explorers and colonists of the Southwest. Their expeditions were known as *entradas* ("entrances," or "coming out"). At first they called the country New Spain, as if it were just an extension of the old country; but as they colonized farther and farther north and adapted to the land, they became Mexican rather than New Spanish. Even farther north, they became known as New Mexicans. Their life had changed, and they knew it.

Other European newcomers had already adopted the name *Americans* even before starting their explorations west of the seaboard mountains. As they emerged from the forested ranges and stepped out onto the Great Plains, they began calling themselves pioneers. Their symbols were the shovel, the ax, and the rifle. They too were the first wave of a new breed, a different kind of people. They left families and acquaintances behind, back in the "states" or back in the "old country"; they felt re-created in the vast new environment; and they preserved stories about their immigration.

In the American and Spanish writings, as in the oral literature of the Native Americans, the theme of an emerging people is predominant until the 1830s or thereabouts. In calling this the Emergence Period, therefore, we make the term do double duty for us: it refers to the theme of coming forth into the West, and it refers also to the era in which the first written literature of the West came into being.

Native
American
Emergence
Myths

—

EUROPEAN interest in recording the ethnography of American Indians began as early as Columbus's second voyage, when Fray Ramon Pane collected folklore of the Tainos. Spanish priests too recorded a significant number of New World folktales, especially among the Aztecs. Later, New England missionaries wrote down accounts told to them by Native Americans. In the writings of Benjamin Franklin we find a detailed creation story from a member of the Susquehanna tribe.

Although the interest existed, there were many problems in transferring the oral literature of one language into the written format of another language. Because there were no reliable linguistic methodologies and cultural studies, and no means of making accurate transcriptions, a great deal of information was lost or misconstrued. Early recorders even found it difficult, if not impossible, to differentiate between narratives, songs, and prayers. In many cases, the difference between a myth and a simple story was overlooked or misunderstood. Before photography and sound recordings, recorders could not take into account the important gestures and vocal characteristics involved in oral performances.

The cultural context also posed a problem. A story may have a serious function in one layer of a culture but may simply be entertainment in another layer; intricacies of literary purpose are usually obliterated by inexpert transcription. One authority on the subject, Barre Toelken, suggests that our own literacy is the problem: translators from the European tradition tend to *see* stories as formal arrangements of words rather than *hear* them as performances.[1]

Nevertheless, we are indebted to a number of people for preserving oral literature of Native Americans. One is Henry Rowe Schoolcraft (1793–1864). Between 1851 and 1857 he produced the impressively comprehensive six-volume *Historical and Statistical Information Respecting the History, Condition, and Prospects of the Indian Tribes of the United States*. Another is Franz Boas (1858–1942), who wrote more than seven hundred books, articles, and reviews in anthropology, many of them on the language and literature of tribes found all the way from the Northwest Coast to New Mexico. More recently, we find Native American literature in the works of such anthropologists as Margot Astrov (*The Winged Serpent*, 1946), Melville Jacobs (*The Content and Style of an Oral Literature*, 1959), and Claude Levi-Strauss (*Structural Anthropology*, 1963).

The development of Native American writers was severely hampered in the early phases of United States history. Efforts by President Jefferson and then by President Jackson to remove Indians to Indian Territory were followed by periods of confinement. The frontier continued to move west, a harassment to the American Indians who stood in the way, and the end of the Civil War meant an increase in western militarization and Indian conflicts. Few Native Americans managed to become educated in this time of trouble, and fewer still became published writers.

Probably the first Native American autobiography to be published was *A Son of the Forest*, by William Apes (born 1798). Apes tells of his early life as an abused child, then of his being educated to fear the Native Americans—a term he used rather than *Indians*. The 1829 autobiography served as a prototype for other personal histories by Native Americans in that it showed education and Christianity as the forces that liberate Native Americans from tribalism and set them on the road to civilization.

Black Hawk, however, was a different case. It was Black Hawk, in 1832, who refused to remove his Sauk people to the west side of the Mississippi River, thus precipitating what became known as the Black Hawk War. He told his story to a newspaper editor, John Patterson, and it was published in 1833 as *Black Hawk: An Autobiography*.

George Copway's autobiography, which went through several printings, came out in 1847 as *The Life, History, and Travels of Kah-ge-ga-bowh, a Young*

---

1. Barre Toelken and Tacheeni Scott, "Poetic Retranslation and the 'Pretty Languages' of Yellowman," in *Traditional Literatures of the American Indian*, comp. and ed. Karl Kroeber (Lincoln: University of Nebraska Press, 1981), p. 65.

Indian Chief of the Ojebwa Nation. In 1887, Andrew Blackbird wrote his *History of the Ottawa and Chippewa Indians of Michigan.* Neither book did as much to popularize Native American autobiography as the works of Charles Eastman. Eastman's *Indian Boyhood* (1902), *The Soul of the Indian* (1911), and *From the Deep Woods to Civilization* (1916) proved to be extremely popular, especially with citybound Anglo youth, and had extraordinary influence in the Boy Scout and the Indian hobbyist movements. His versions of vision quests and mystic ceremonies were generally understood to be accurate depictions of a universal Indian religion.

Following Eastman's success, and taking his works as a model, writers such as Luther Standing Bear, James Paytiamo, Don Talayesva, and John J. Mathews produced similar autobiographical accounts. The longevity of Eastman's influence may be seen in the fact that N. Scott Momaday won the Pulitzer Prize in literature for his autobiography, *The Way to Rainy Mountain*, in 1969.

One last form of Native American authorship needs to be mentioned. In his study *Native American Literature*, Andrew Wiget terms this the "as-told-to" form of autobiography.[2] The most famous example is *Black Elk Speaks*, subtitled *Being the Life Story of a Holy Man of the Oglala Sioux, as told through John G. Neihardt* (1932).

* * *

The following samples are in no way intended to show a chronological progression of the emergence myth, nor are they presented to chart the beginnings of Native American literature. Readers should imagine themselves in the role of ethnologists, discovering a body of literature. The dates and authors are unverifiable; the original language, together with the gestures and vocal inflections, is lost; the relationship of speaker to audience is uncertain; and finally, some versions have been influenced by the attitudes of a translator who may not be of the tribe or even the race in question.

Earth-emergence is only one motif, or theme, in the many versions of how people came into being, but in the study of western American literature it is particularly important for three reasons. First, the literature of the West is markedly landscape-related; the vast expanses and monumental features of the land are essential factors in the novels, stories, and poems of the West. Consider, now, how a Native American emergence myth clarifies the individual's relationship to the land. The people were not "given" the earth to rule, nor were they brought to it as wandering immigrants. Instead, they rose out of it like plants from the soil, or like infants from the womb.

2. Andrew Wiget, *Native American Literature* (Boston: Twayne, 1985), p. 50.

Second, the emergence myth interprets basic life cycles that are, like the landscape, inescapable. The hot, brilliant sunshine of day always yields to the cool depth of black night, the power of thunder and flood comes to banish silent drought, and the seed placed in the ground becomes a plant again. Life is an endless series of cycles. These life cycles—not inherently evil yet not always beneficial—are constant reminders of the people's relationship to the creative force.

Finally, the emergence myth is significant because it anticipates Carl Jung's theory of a single collective unconsciousness. Emergence begins, as Frank Waters says of the Hopi version,

> in a time that is being continually pushed back to the edge of the one great mystery of life. . . . The great myth of their Emergence . . . is the dramatized story of the emergence of consciousness from the great pool of the unconscious—the evolution of that consciousness of object and self which has enabled man alone to distinguish himself from the rest of nature. It is one of the great awakenings along the Road of Life. By it man gives the world its objective existence and so partakes himself in the process of Creation.
>
> . . . So upon their arrival they first asked permission to live upon [the earth] from its guardian spirit and protector. The spirit gave his permission, telling them, however, that they were not free to wander over it rampantly, using it as they wished. They were to make ordered migrations, north, south, east, and west, to the four *pasos* where the land met the sea, before settling in the place prescribed for their permanent home. There they were to establish those annual ceremonies which would recapitulate their wanderings and reclaim the land for its Creator.
>
> The meaning of the myth is clear. The emergence of consciousness does not set man entirely free. He is still obligated to the dictates of the unconscious which embodies all his primordial past. He may travel to the limits of his mind and will, but he must always observe those thaumaturgical rites which acknowledge his arising from the one great origin of all life and which keep him whole.[3]

---

3. Frank Waters, *Pumpkin Seed Point* (Chicago: Swallow Press, 1969), p. 63.

Mandan

*George Catlin (1796–1872) went up the Missouri River on the maiden voyage
of the steamboat* Yellowstone *in 1832. He traveled among the Mandans, and
later entered the territory of the Pawnees and the Comanches, studying Indian
customs and painting portraits of Indian life. In 1867, he published his account
of Mandan religious rituals, including a version of the Mandan emergence myth.*

*Catlin claims that all 120 tribes he visited in North and South America have
versions of a myth that tells of the Great Flood. But he refutes those scientists
who use this as proof that the Indians had migrated from other lands where flood
stories are found, such as Egypt or Asia. Instead, Catlin maintains, the tribes are
"American,—indigenous, and not exotic." Catlin continues:*

If it were shown that inspired history of the Deluge and of the
Creation restricted those events to one continent alone, then it might
be that the American races came from the Eastern continent, bringing
these traditions with them; but until that is proved, the American traditions of the Deluge are no evidence whatever of an Eastern origin.
If it were so, and the aborigines of America brought their traditions
of the Deluge from the East, why did they not bring inspired history
of the *Creation*?

Though there is not a tribe in America but what have some theory
of man's creation, there is not one amongst them all that bears the
slightest resemblance to the Mosaic account. How strange is this if
these people came from the country where inspiration was prior to all
history! The Mandans believed they were created under the ground,
and that a portion of their people reside there yet. The Choctaws
assert that "they were created *craw-fish*, living alternately under the
ground and above it, as they chose; and coming out at their little
holes in the earth to get the warmth of the sun one sunny day, a portion of the tribe was driven away and could not return; they built the
Choctaw village, and the remainder of the tribe are still living under
the ground."

Other tribes were created under the water; and at least one half of the tribes in America represent that man was first created under the ground, or in the rocky caverns of the mountains. Why this diversity of theories in the *Creation*, if these people brought their tradition of the Deluge from the land of inspiration?[4]

Ácoma

Sky City, the Ácoma pueblo that sits atop a high mesa in New Mexico, has frequently been described in the history and literature of the West, ever since Francisco Vásquez de Coronado's expedition came upon it in 1540—the same expedition that searched for the golden cities of Cíbola and found Zuñi. The Ácoma creation tale has been recorded by numerous ethnologists. It is a long and complex story; the excerpts provided here give only a few basic episodes from the emergence portion. One feature of interest to researchers is that the Ácoma creation does not begin with a man and a woman (nor with a ready-made race), but with two females. One of these, later in the story, violates an injunction of the gods and becomes impregnated by rain, thus beginning the birth cycle.

How the Ácoma Entered the World of Uchtsiti

IN THE beginning two female human beings were born. These two children were born underground at a place called *Shipapu*. As they grew up, they began to be aware of each other. There was no light and they could only feel each other.

After they had grown large enough to think for themselves, they spoke to the Spirit (*Tsichtinako*) and asked it to make itself known to them. But it only replied that it was not allowed to meet with them. They then asked why they were living in the dark without knowing each other. The Spirit replied that they were under the earth, and must wait patiently until the time came to go up into the light.

While waiting, the two girls were given baskets of seeds. Some of these sprouted and slowly grew into trees. The tree *lanye* grew faster than the others, and pushed a hole in the earth, letting in a little light. But it was

From Matthew W. Sterling, *The Origin Myth of Ácoma and Other Records*, Bureau of American Ethnology Bulletin no. 135 (Washington, D.C.: Smithsonian Institution, 1942).

4. George Catlin, *O-Kee-Pa, a Religious Ceremony*, ed. John C. Ewers (New Haven: Yale University Press, 1967), pp. 40–41.

not large enough to pass through, and so the girls looked into the baskets again and found the badger.

Tsichtinako spoke to them again, instructing them to tell Badger to climb the pine tree, to bore a hole large enough for them to crawl up, cautioning him not to go out into the light, but to return when the hole was finished. Badger climbed the tree and, after he had dug a hole large enough, returned saying that he had done his work. They thanked him and said, "As a reward you will come up with us to the light and thereafter you will live happily. You will always know how to dig and your home will be in the ground where you will be neither too hot nor too cold."

Tsichtinako now spoke again, telling them to look in the basket for Locust, giving it life and asking it to smooth the hole by plastering. It, too, was to be cautioned to return. This they did and Locust smoothed the hole but, having finished, went out into the light. When it returned, reporting that it had done its work, they asked it if it had gone out. Locust said no, and every time he was asked he replied no, until the fourth time when he admitted that he had gone out. They asked Locust what it was like outside. Locust replied that it was just *tsi iti* (laid out flat). They said, "From now on you will be known as *Tsi-k'a*. You will also come up with us, but you will be punished for disobedience by being allowed out only a short time. Your home will be in the ground and you will have to return when the weather is bad. You will soon die but you will be reborn each season."

The hole now let light into the place where the two sisters were, and Tsichtinako spoke to them, "Now is the time you are to go out. You are able to take your baskets with you. In them you will find pollen and sacred corn meal. When you reach the top, you will wait for the sun to come up and that direction will be called *ha'nami* (east). With the pollen and the sacred corn meal you will pray to the Sun. You will thank the Sun for bringing you to light, ask for a long life and happiness, and for success in the purpose for which you were created."

When the sun came up and they prayed, their eyes hurt for they were not accustomed to the strong light. For the first time they asked Tsichtinako why they were on earth and why they were created. Tsichtinako replied, "I did not make you. Your father, Uchtsiti, made you, and it is he who has made the world, the sun, and many other things you will see. But Uchtsiti says the world is not yet completed, not yet satisfactory as he wants it. This is the reason he has made you. You will rule and bring to life the rest of the things he has given you in the basket. . . . Everything in the baskets is to be created by your word, for you are made in the image of Uchtsiti and your word will be as powerful as his word. He has created you to help him complete the world. You are to plant the seeds of the different plants to be used when anything is needed. I shall always be ready to point out to you the various plants and animals."

[In the Ácoma account, there is no tribe, just the two sisters. As they go about their work of creating the animals and plants, they begin to quarrel more and more. Finally a serpent appears—although they cannot remember having brought the serpent to life—and tempts one of the sisters to allow the rain to impregnate her so that she will have someone like herself to be with. This transgression causes Uchtsiti to take Tsichtinako away from the sisters. They separate, each taking one of the twins that resulted from the transgression and each forming her own tribe.]

—

Zuñi

When Frank Hamilton Cushing (1857–1900) went among the Zuñis of New Mexico as an ethnologist in 1879, he became so interested in their lifestyle that his intended "visit" lasted for four and a half years. During that time he was initiated as a member of the Bow fraternity, became a war chief, and was adopted into the Macaw clan. His publications, including Zuñi Breadstuff *and* Zuñi Folk Tales, *are still used as standard source materials on the Zuñis.*

In the Zuñi account, the people emerged from the darkness into the light in several stages, much like the stages that Plato used as an analogy for the gaining of wisdom. The wisdom (or power) gained in the Zuñi myth, however, is an awareness of the people's responsibility for keeping essential elements of nature sacred. Unlike Adam and Eve in the story of Eden, the Zuñi people do not have dominion over anything, and there is no "lower" form of life. The Zuñi's have a sacred obligation to respect all creation. They make their epic migration in order to find the center of Unity, not to claim a promised land. And in the Zuñi emergence, as well as the migration toward the center, there are some who become a "lost tribe" because they were left behind, in the darkness of the former world, or because they took a wrong road after reaching the sun-world.

From Frank Hamilton Cushing, *Zuñi: Selected Writings of Frank Hamilton Cushing*, ed. Jesse Green (Lincoln: University of Nebraska Press, 1979), pp. 346–54. Copyright © 1979 by the University of Nebraska Press.

Creation and the Origin of Corn

I ONCE heard a Zuñi priest say: "Five things alone are necessary to the sustenance and comfort of the 'dark ones' [Indians] among the children of earth."

"The sun, who is the Father of all.

"The earth, who is the Mother of men.

"The water, who is the Grandfather.

"The fire, who is the Grandmother.

"Our brothers and sisters the Corn, and seeds of growing things."

This Indian philosopher explained himself somewhat after the following fashion:

"Who among men and the creatures could live without the Sun-father? for his light brings day, warms and gladdens the Earth-mother with rain which flows forth in the water we drink and that causes the flesh of the Earth-mother to yield abundantly seeds, while these—are they not cooked by the brand of fire which warms us in winter?"

That he reasoned well, may be the better understood if we follow for a while the teachings which instructed his logic. These relate that:

First, there was sublime darkness, which vanished not until came the "Ancient Father of the Sun," revealing universal waters. These were, save him, all that were.

The Sun-father thought to change the face of the waters and cause life to replace their desolation.

He rubbed the surface of his flesh, thus drawing forth *yep'-na*.[5]

The *yep'-na* he rolled into two balls. From his high and "ancient place among the spaces," (*Te'-thlä-shi-na-kwin*) he cast forth one of these balls and it fell upon the surface of the waters. There, as a drop of deer suet on hot broth, so this ball melted and spread far and wide like scum over the great waters, ever growing, until it sank into them.

Then the Sun-father cast forth the other ball, and it fell, spreading out

5. Or the "substance of living flesh." This is exemplified as well as may be by the little cylinders of cuticle and fatty-matter that may be rubbed from the person after bathing. [Cushing's note]

and growing even larger than had the first, and dispelling so much of the waters that it rested upon the first. In time, the first became a great being— our Mother, the Earth; and the second became another great being—our Father, the Sky. Thus was divided the universal fluid into the "embracing waters of the World" below, and the "embracing waters of the Sky" above. Behold! this is why the Sky-father is blue as the ocean which is the home of the Earth-mother, blue even his flesh, as seem the far-away mountains— though they be the flesh of the Earth-mother.

Now while the Sky-father and the Earth-mother were together, the Earth-mother conceived in her ample wombs—which were the four great underworlds or caves—the first of men and creatures. Then the two entered into council that they might provide for the birth of their children.

"How shall it be?" said the one to the other. "How, when born forth, shall our children subsist, and who shall guide them?"

"Behold!" said the Sky-father. He spread his hand high and abroad with the hollow palm downward. Yellow grains like corn he stuck into all the lines and wrinkles of his palm and fingers. "Thus," said he, "shall I, as it were, hold my hand ever above thee and thy children, and the yellow grains shall represent so many shining points which shall guide and light these, our children, when the Sun-father is not nigh."

Gaze on the sky at night-time! Is it not the palm of the Great Father, and are the stars not in many lines of his hand yet to be seen?

"Ah yes!" said the Earth-mother, "yet my tiny children may not wander over my lap and bosom without guidance, even in the light of the Sun-father; therefore, behold!"

She took a great terraced bowl into which she poured water; upon the water she spat, and whipping it rapidly with her fingers it was soon beaten into foam as froths the soap-weed, and the foam rose high up around the rim of the bowl. The Earth-mother blew the foam. Flake after flake broke off, and bursting, cast spray downward into the bowl.

"See," said she, "this bowl is, as it were, the world, the rim its farthest limits, and the foam-bounden terraces round about, my features, which they shall call mountains whereby they shall name countries and be guided from place to place, and whence white clouds shall rise, float away, and, bursting, shed spray, that my children may drink of the water of life, and from my substance add unto the flesh of their being. Thou has said thou wilt watch over them when the Sun-father is absent, but thou art the cold being; I am the warm. Therefore, at night, when thou watchest, my children shall nestle in my bosom and find there warmth, strength and length of life from one day light to another."

Is not the bowl the emblem of the Earth, our mother? for from it we draw both food and drink, as a babe draws nourishment from the breast of its mother, and round, as is the rim of a bowl, so is the horizon, terraced with mountains, whence rise the clouds. Is not woman the warm, man the cold being? For while woman sits shivering as she cooks by the fire in the house-room, man goes forth little heeding the storms of winter, to hunt the feed and gather pine-faggots.

Yet alas! men and the creatures remained bounden in the lowermost womb of the Earth-mother, for she and the Sky-father feared to deliver them as a mother fears for the fate of her first offspring.

Then the Ancient Sun pitied the children of Earth. That they might speedily see his light, he cast a glance upon a foam cap floating abroad on the great waters. Forthwith the foam cap became instilled with life, and bore twin children, brothers one to the other, older and younger, for one was born before the other. To these he gave the *k'ia´-al-lan,* or "water-shield," that on it they might fly over the waters as the clouds—from which it was spun and woven—float over the ocean; that they might blind with its mists the sight of the enemy as the clouds darken the earth with rain-drops. He gave them for their bow, the rainbow, that with it they might clear men's trails of enemies, as the rain-bow clears away the storm-shadows; and for their arrows gave he them the thunder-bolts, that they might rive open the mountains, as the lightning cleaves asunder the pine trees; and then he sent them abroad to deliver, guide and protect the children of earth and the Sky-father. With their bow they lifted from his embraces the Sky-father from the bosom of the Earth-mother, "for," said they, "if he remain near, his cold will cause men to be stunted and stooped with shivering and to grovel in the earth," as stunted trees in the mountains delve under the snow to hide from the cold of the Sky-father. With their thunder-bolts they broke open the mountain which gave entrance to the cave-wombs of the Earth-mother, and upon their water-shields they descended into the lowermost of the caves, where dwelt the children of earth—men and all creatures.

Alas! It was dark as had been the world before the coming of the Sun, and the brothers found men and the beings sadly bewailing their lot. When one moved it was but to jostle another, whose complaints wearied the ears of yet others; hence the brothers called a council of the priest-chiefs—even ere the coming forth of men such lived—and they made a ladder of tall canes which they placed against the roof of the cavern. Up this rushed the children of earth. Some, climbing out before of their own wills, found deliverance from the caves above and, wandering away, became the ancestors of nations unknown to us; but our fathers followed in the footsteps of the older and younger brothers. Does not the cane grow jointed to-day, showing thus the notches which men traversed to day-light?

In the second cave all was still dark, but like starlight through cloud rifts, through the cleft above showed the twilight. After a time the people murmured again, until the two delivered them into the third world where they found light like that of early dawn. Again they grew discontented, again were guided upward, this time into the open light of the Sun—which was the light of this world. But some remained behind, not escaping until afterward; and these were the fathers of the Western nations whom our ancients knew not.

Then indeed for a time the people complained bitterly, for it was then that they *first* saw the light of the Sun-father, which, in its brilliancy, smote them so that they fell grasping their eye-balls and moaning. But when they became used to the light they looked around in joy and wonderment; yet they saw that the earth seemed but small, for everywhere rolled about the great misty waters.

The two brothers spread open the limbs of the Earth-mother, and cleft the western mountains with their shafts of lightning and the waters flowed down and away from the bosom of the Earth-mother, cutting great cañons and valleys which remain to this day. Thus was widened the land, yet the earth remained damp. Then they guided the people eastward.

Already before men came forth from the lower worlds with the priest-chiefs, there were many gods and strange beings. The gods gave to the priests many treasures and instructions, but the people knew not yet the meaning of either. Thus were first taught our ancients incantations, rituals and sacred talks (prayer), each band of them according to its usefulness. These bands were the "Priesthood"—*Shi´-wa-na-kwe;* the "Hunter-band" —*Sa´-ni-a-k'ia-kwe;* the "Knife-band"—*A'tchi-a-k'ia-kwe* or Warrior, and the *Ne´-we-kwe,* or Band of Wise Medicine Men. The leaders of each band thus came to have wonderful knowledge and power—even as that of the gods! They summoned a great council of their children—for they were called the "Fathers of the People"—and asked them to choose such things as they would have for special ownership or use. Some chose the macaw, the eagle, or the turkey; others chose the deer, bear, or coyote; others the seeds of earth, or *a´-tâ-a,* the spring vine, tobacco, and the plants of medicine, the yellow-wood and many other things. Thus it came about that they and their brothers and sisters and their children, even unto the present day, were named after the things they chose in the days when all was new, and thus was divided our nation into many clans, or gentes (*A´-no-ti-we*) of brothers and sisters who may not marry one another but from one to the other. To some of the elders of these bands and clans was given some thing which should be, above all other things, precious. For instance, the clans of the Bear and Crane were given the *Mu´-et-ton-ne,* or medicine seed of hail and snow. For does not the bear go into his den, and appears not the crane when come storms of hail and snow?

When more than one clan possessed one of these magic medicines they formed a secret society—like the first four—for its keeping and use. Thus the Bear and Crane peoples became the "Holders of the Wand"—who bring the snow of winter and are potent to cure the diseases which come with them. In time they let into their secret council others, whom they had cured, that the precious secrets of their band might not be wasted. Thus it was that one after another were formed the rest of our medicine bands, who were and are called the finishers of men's trails, because, despite disease and evil, they guard and lengthen our lives; but in the "days of the new" there were only four bands.[6]

To the Eagle, Deer and Coyote peoples was given the *Nal´-e-ton,* or "Deer Medicine Seed," which the Hunter-band still guards; and to the Macaw, Sun and Frog peoples the *Kia´-et-ton,* or the "Medicine Seed of Water," which the priesthood and the Sacred Dance, or *Kâ´-kâ,* still hold—without the administration of which the world would dry up and even the insects of the mountains and hollows of earth grow thirsty and perish. Yet, not less precious was the gift to the "Seed-people," or *Ta´-a-kwe.* This was the *Tchu´-et-ton,* or the "Medicine Seed of Corn"—for from this came the parents of flesh and beauty, the solace of hunger, the emblems of birth, mortal life, death and immortality. To the Badger people was given the knowledge of Fire, for in the roots of all trees, great and little—which the badger best knows how to find—dwells the essence of fire.[7]

To all of these peoples it was told that they should wander for many generations toward the land whence the Sun brings the day-light (Eastward) until at last they would reach the "middle of the world," where their children should dwell forever over the heart of our Earth-mother until their days should be numbered and the light of Zuñi grow dark.

6. It may be seen that the Zunis have here their own way of accounting for their primitive social organization into *Gentes* [clans] and *Phratries* [associations of clans]— organizations well nigh universal in the ancient world, as with the society of the early Greeks and Romans, and still prevalent amongst savage tribes of today. [Cushing's note]

7. In ancient times when desirous of making fire, and even today when kindling the sacred flame, the Zunis produced and still produce, the first spark by drilling with a hard stick like an arrow-shaft into a dry piece of soft root. An arrow-shaft is now used by preference, as it is the emblem of lightning. [Cushing's note]

Toward this unknown country the "twin brothers of light" guided them. In those times a day meant a year, and a night another, so that four days and nights meant eight years. Many days the people wandered eastward, slaying game for their flesh-food, gathering seeds from grasses and weeds for their bread-food, and binding rushes about their loins for their clothing; they knew not until afterward, the flesh of the cotton and yucca-mothers.

The earth was still damp. Dig a hole in a hill-side, quickly it filled with water. Drop a seed on the highest table-land and it without waiting shot forth green sprouts. So moist, indeed, was the soil, that even foot-prints of men and all creatures might be traced whithersoever they tended. The beings and strange creatures increased with men, and spread over the world. Many monsters lived, by whose ferocity men perished.

Then said the twin brothers: "Men, our children, are poorer than the beasts, their enemies; for each creature has a special gift of strength or sagacity, while to men has been given only the power of guessing. Nor would we that our children be web-footed like the beings that live over the waters and damp places."

Therefore, they sent all men and harmless beings to a place of security; then laid their water shield on the ground. Upon it they placed four thunder-bolts, one pointed north, another west, another south, and the other eastward. When all was ready they let fly the thunder-bolts. Instantly the world was covered with lurid fire and shaken with rolling thunders, as is a forest to-day burned and blasted where the lightning has fallen. Thus as the clay of vessels is burned to rock, and the mud of the hearth crackled and reddened by fire, so the earth was mottled and crackled and hardened where now we see mountains and masses of rock. Many of the great monsters and prey-beings were changed in a twinkling to enduring rock or shriveled into twisted idols which the hunter and priest-warrior know best how to prize. Behold, their forms along every mountain side and ravine, and in the far western valleys and plains, still endure the tracks of the fathers of men and beings, the children of earth. Yet some of the beings of prey were spared, that the world might not become over-filled with life, and starvation follow, and that men might breathe of their spirits and be inspired with the hearts of warriors and hunters.

Often the people rested from their wanderings, building great houses of stone which may even now be seen, until the Conch of the Gods sounded, which lashed the ocean to fury and beat the earth to trembling. Then the people started up, and gathering the few things they could, again commenced their wanderings; yet often those who slept or lingered were buried beneath their own walls, where yet their bones may sometimes be found.

Marvelous both of good and evil were the works of the ancients. Alas! there came forth with others, those impregnated with the seed of sorcery. Their evil works caused discord among men, and, through fear and anger, men were divided from one another. Born before our ancients, had been other men, and these our fathers sometimes overtook and looked not peacefully upon them, but challenged them—though were they not their older brothers? It thus happened when our ancients came to their fourth resting place on their eastward journey, that which they named *Shi-po-lo-lon-K'ai-a,* or "The Place of Misty Waters," there already dwelt a clan of people called the *A´-ta-a,* or Seed People, and the seed clan of our ancients challenged them to know by what right they assumed the name and attributes of their own clan. "Behold," said these stranger-beings, "we have power with the gods above yours, yet can we not exert it without your aid. Try, therefore, your own power first, then we will show you ours." At last, after much wrangling, the Seed clan agreed to this, and set apart eight days for prayer and sacred labors. First they worked together cutting sticks, to which they bound the plumes of summer birds which fly in the clouds or sail over the waters. "Therefore," thought our fathers, "why should not their plumes waft our beseechings to the waters and clouds?" These plumes, with prayers and offerings, they planted in the valleys, and there, also, they placed their *Tchu´-e-ton-ne.* Lo! for eight days and nights it rained and there were thick mists; and the waters from the mountains poured down bringing new soil and spreading it over the valleys where the plumed sticks had been planted. "See!" said the fathers of the seed clan, "water and new earth bring we by our supplications."

"It is well," replied the strangers, "yet *life* ye did not bring. Behold!" and they too set apart eight days, during which they danced and sang a beautiful dance and prayer song, and at the end of that time they took the people of the seed clan to the valleys. Behold, indeed! Where the plumes had been planted and the *tchu´-e-ton* placed grew seven corn-plants, their tassels waving in the wind, their stalks laden with ripened grain. "These," said the strangers, "are the severed flesh of seven maidens, our own sisters and children. The eldest sister's is the yellow corn; the next, the blue; the next, the red; the next, the white; the next, the speckled; the next, the black, and the last and youngest is the sweet-corn, for see! even ripe, she is soft like the young of the others. The first is of the North-land, yellow like the light of winter; the second is of the West, blue like the great world of waters; the third is of the South, red like the Land of Everlasting Summer; the fourth is of the East, white like the land whence the sun brings the daylight; the fifth is of the upper regions, many-colored as are the clouds of morning and evening, and the sixth is of the lower regions, black as are the caves whence came we, your older, and ye, our younger brothers." "Brothers indeed be we, each one to the other," said the people to the strangers, "and may we not journey together seeking the middle of the world?" "Aye, we may," replied the strangers, "and of the flesh of our maidens ye may eat, no more seeking the seeds of the grasses and of your water we may drink, no more wondering whither we shall find it; thus shall each help the other to life and contentment. Ye shall pray and cut prayer-plumes, we shall sing, and dance shall our maidens that all may be delighted and that it may be for the best. But beware! no mortal must approach the persons of our maidens."

Thenceforward, many of the *A´-ta-a* and the seed clan journeyed together, until at last the Sun, Macaw, and some other clans-people found the middle of the world; while others yet wandered in search of it, not for many generations to join their brothers, over the heart of the Earth-mother, which is *Shi-wi-na-kwin,* or the "Land of the Zuñis."

Navajo

In their own language the Navajos call themselves Diné, "The People." Their ancestral homeland in the American Southwest is called Diné't'a, "Land of the People." The Navajo emergence myth is directly connected with specific geographical points within this area. Near Silverton, Colorado, is the Place of Emergence; it was here that the First People finally emerged after going through a long series of ascents through three worlds beneath this one. The first house of the gods, a pyramid-shaped hogan, turned into stone and is now Cabezon Peak, lying northwest of modern-day Albuquerque. Each of the underground worlds was marked, at the corners, with four peaks; and so, with materials that they had brought up with them during their Emergence, the First People placed mountains at the proper corners of the new world. The East mountain, of white shell, had a dark streak across it; this is either Blanco Peak in Colorado or Pelado Peak in New Mexico. The South mountain, of turquoise, is New Mexico's Mount Taylor. The San Francisco Peaks in Arizona, with their perpetual covering of snow, are the abalone West peaks. North is the black direction, signified by the dark range of the La Platas above Mesa Verde in Colorado. The boundaries differ in other versions of the myth, but they are always linked to specific mountains that correspond in color to the Diné sacred directions.

The emergence of the Diné occurred in four stages, through four successive worlds. First, the Diné were in a Dark World, where there was no light at all. The second world was the Blue World, partially illuminated in bluish light. The light did not come from the sun or the moon but came, according to the myth, from the Shining Mountains. In the third world they found yellow light—the reflection of the sun—and after a long time there, the Diné ascended through a huge hollow reed and emerged in the White World, where they have lived ever since. According to Ruth Underhill's version of the myth, the Diné had the help of the badger in making a hole large enough for them to get into this world.[8]

It is not known how evil powers—monsters—came to live in the world, but there were many of them, threatening the Diné. The people were saved from the constant threat, however, through Ever-Changing Woman. She was found as a baby, on Pedernal Peak, wrapped in a rainbow of light, and the people took her to live on Huerfano Mesa (a Spanish name, but suitably meaning "orphan mesa"). There she was safe from the monsters, even the climbing ones. Ever-Changing Woman matured quickly and then was married twice, once to the Sun and once to the Water, and gave birth to twin boys. The boys grew into warriors and went throughout Diné't'a killing the monsters. But they did not kill all the evil powers: four—Age, Poverty, Sickness, and Death—were left alive to keep mankind from becoming lazy and forgetting that nature is more powerful than the people. Having done their work, all of the good spirits went to live in homes on the tops of the sacred mountains. For ceremonies and festivals, they come down from the mountains in the form of masked figures.

Kiowa

When N. Scott Momaday wrote an autobiographical account of his Kiowa heritage, he organized his series of tales to reflect the legend, the known history, and his personal feeling for each episode. In the first section of The Way to Rainy Mountain, *called "The Setting Out," Momaday relates that somewhere in the northern Rocky Mountains, the Kiowas first entered the world through a hollow log.*

You know, everything had to begin, and this is how it was: the Kiowas came one by one into the world through a hollow log. They were many more than now, but not all of them got out. There was a woman whose body was swollen up with child, and she got stuck in the log. After that, no one could get through, and that is why

8. Ruth Underhill, *Here Come the Navajo!* (Washington, D.C.: United States Department of the Interior, Bureau of Indian Affairs, 1953), pp. 16–20. See also Frank Waters, *The Colorado* (New York: Rinehart and Co., 1946), pp. 164–65.

the Kiowas are a small tribe in number. They looked all around and saw the world. It made them glad to see so many things. They called themselves *Kwuda*, "coming out."[9]

*In time, the Kiowas left the mountains and emerged onto the Great Plains, slowly migrating along a route that eventually ended at Rainy Mountain in Oklahoma. As they moved farther away from the Rockies, they adopted another name for themselves—*Tepda, *which, like* Kwuda, *means "those who are coming out."*

One account in The Way to Rainy Mountain *tells of a disagreement over the sharing of some antelope meat. The quarrel caused some of the Kiowas to walk away from the rest of the tribe, never to be seen again. There is also a story about a woman who marries the sun. After bearing a male child, she is killed by the sun for attempting to rejoin her people in the lower world. Her son is later split in half, becoming a pair of twins.*

Momaday wrote that on reaching the prairie, "the Kiowas paused on their way; they had come to the place where they must change their lives. The sun is at home on the plains. Precisely there does it have the certain character of a god." The tribe took up the religious ceremony of the Sun Dance, which they adhered to until the United States government declared the dance illegal. In 1887, government soldiers from Fort Sill, Oklahoma, broke up the last Kiowa Sun Dance. The tribe went into decline, having been "forbidden without cause the essential act of their faith."[10]

9. N. Scott Momaday, *The Way to Rainy Mountain* (Albuquerque: University of New Mexico Press, 1969), p. 16.
10. Ibid., pp. 7, 10.

The Coming of
Europeans

—

THE EARLIEST recorded visit of Europeans to western America began in 1528, when Alvar Núñez Cabeza de Vaca, Alonso del Castillo Maldonado, Andrés Dorantes de Carranca, and an Arab slave named Estevanito came ashore somewhere in the vicinity of Galveston Island. With approximately three hundred other men, led by Pánfilo de Narváez, they had been on an expedition into northern Florida. After a series of disasters, less than a hundred men made it back to the Gulf of Mexico, where they built crude boats and attempted to follow the coastline. Hunger, thirst, and hostile Indian attacks gradually weakened the group, and finally storms wrecked the boats off the Texas coast. There were eighty or ninety survivors, but by the year 1530 de Vaca and his three companions were the only ones left.

In 1532, the four men began wandering westward and probably walked across a region that today includes Texas, New Mexico, Arizona, and some of the northern Mexican states. Eventually, in 1536, they arrived at the Spanish outpost of Culiacán.

Francisco Vásquez de Coronado heard the stories about the strange people and wealthy cities de Vaca had seen in his eight-year sojourn. Coronado raised money, gathered up a large force—over a thousand men—and in 1540 launched an expedition in search of the Seven Golden Cities of Cíbola. In advance of Coronado's columns went the Arab slave Estevanito and Fray Marcos, a priest, to scout the way to the treasure. The army came to Zuñi and went on to the pueblo of Pecos, in central New Mexico. There the Spaniards made slaves of some of the natives, stole whatever silver ornaments they could, and then marched northeastward. One of the Indians had convinced Coronado that there were rich cities out on the plains to the northeast, and so managed to lead the expedition away from Pecos. When

Coronado's credulity—and patience—finally came to an end, he and his followers had crossed not only New Mexico, but Kansas as well. They were standing, probably, in what is now south-central Nebraska.

Coronado and his successors failed to discover any golden cities, but they opened the way for a steady stream of Spanish missionaries and colonists who flowed into the northern territory. In 1598, Juan de Oñate led the establishment of New Mexico's first permanent settlement, the town of San Gabriel.

The year 1540 was when the Spanish entrada really began. The year of disaster was 1680, when the Pueblo Indians followed a Tewa medicine man, Popé, in massive revolt. Altogether, the Pueblos killed four or five hundred Spaniards, including twenty-one priests. The survivors fled southward, and it was not long until the Indians could boast—with reasonable accuracy—that no living Spaniard could be found north of the Rio Grande. Churches and any other reminders of the Spanish invasion were destroyed. Indians who had been baptized into the Christian faith were subjected to rituals of cleansing and purification.

Meanwhile, far to the north and east, Jamestown had been struggling along, and the American colonies had been growing. By 1776, the year of the American Revolution, the Spanish territorial settlers had returned to reestablish authority over the Pueblos. But Spain's European difficulties had grown steadily worse, and in 1800 the Spanish government transferred its North American territory to France.

Napoleon Bonaparte sold the Louisiana Territory to the United States in 1803. Thomas Jefferson had always been intrigued by the idea of an immense area of open land to the west. His journals and letters relay his plans to explore it: two young men, Meriwether Lewis and William Clark, would make the epic journey up the Missouri River, across the Rocky Mountains, and on to the Pacific coast. They came back in 1806 with reports that the territory was rich in open land, wild game, and mineral wealth. Among other riches, according to the adventurers, was an abundance of beaver and other fur-bearing animals.

The European demand for good fur, especially beaver, was very heavy. Prices were high, and men were looking for new places to trap. In 1822, St. Louis newspapers carried a brief advertisement, one that marked the start of the glorious years of the mountain men.

To

ENTERPRISING YOUNG MEN

The subscriber wishes to engage ONE HUNDRED MEN, to ascend the river Missouri to its source, there to be employed for one, two, or three years. For Particulars enquire of Major Andrew Henry . . . (who will ascend with, and command the party) or to the subscriber at St. Louis.

Wm. H. Ashley

There are two ways to appreciate the mountain man image in American literature and myth. One is to read the actual accounts of travelers such as Jim Beckwourth, Washington Irving, George F. Ruxton, James Clyman, Jedediah Smith, or Osborne Russell. These firsthand accounts have been used as the basis for such works as LeRoy Hafen's *The Mountain Men and the Fur Trade of the Far West*, Robert Cleland's *This Reckless Breed of Men*, Don Berry's *A Majority of Scoundrels*, and Winfred Blevins's *Give Your Heart to the Hawks*. The legends are also preserved in fiction. Among the classic novels of the fur trade are *The Long Rifle*, by Stewart Edward White; *Wolf Song*, by Harvey Fergusson; *Mountain Man*, by Vardis Fisher; *Lord Grizzly*, by Frederick Manfred; and, perhaps the best known of all mountain man novels, *The Big Sky*, by A. B. Guthrie, Jr.

It was Major William Henry Ashley, the advertiser in the St. Louis newspapers, who organized the rendezvous system, aided by Jedediah Smith's rediscovery of South Pass. Stories of these annual mountain reunions rival the tales told of the Greeks' celebrations at Troy. The first rendezvous was held in 1825, the year before Jedediah Smith left on his odyssey across the deserts and Death Valley and into California. The last rendezvous took place in 1840, signalling the end of the mountain man era.

Smith's explorations did much to fill in the remaining blanks on the map of the West, and his mountain colleagues, finding fewer beaver and less demand for pelts, began to do more exploring for the settlers who wanted to move westward. The mountain men had had a brief period of unique glory before the time of the "companyero" and the age of the free trapper ended.

A set of connected events, beginning in 1831, marked the closure of the emergence era for all the western peoples. Jedediah Smith, the "Knight in Buckskins," was killed while leading a wagon train on the Santa Fe trail. A week behind Smith's train came another trading caravan, and in that caravan was a man named Josiah Gregg. Gregg spent the next eight years as a Santa Fe trader and in 1844 published *The Commerce of the Prairies*. That book, which Gregg began writing in 1832, became an indispensable travel guide for eighteen-year-old Susan Shelby Magoffin, who in 1846 became the first white woman to make the trip on the Santa Fe trail. Other women from the civilized East soon followed, and their presence in the West led directly to the establishment of schools, churches, and law.

In 1832 the *Yellowstone* became the first steamboat to make it up the

Missouri, all the way to Fort Union near the mouth of the Yellowstone River. Traveling on it were artists to paint the dying tribes of Indians, government agents to introduce the Indians to bureaucracy, surveyors to mark the land into squares and to plan the roads, soldiers to protect all of these enterprising citizens from the Indians and each other, and missionaries to protect everyone from the evils that were rampant way out West in Satan's backyard.

Emergence Period
Literature

—

THE FIRST significant literature about the American West was written in Spanish, not English, and recounts *entradas* into the West made between 1528 and 1540. Another sixty years would pass before there were historical parallels with settlement on the eastern coast. Jamestown was not settled until 1607; by that time, Juan de Oñate had decided to resign as governor of the ten-year-old settlement of San Gabriel in what is now New Mexico, leaving his successor to establish the province's capital, Santa Fe, in 1610.

That any literature of the Spanish explorations has survived is something of a wonder. First, money and men and equipment had to be found to chase the dream of extending Spain's dominion into the New World. Then one of the conquistadores had to be literate enough to keep a journal and to expand it into a "History" and influential enough to have it copied by hand—generally in a religious establishment—and to have it preserved in some sort of library or government record office. There the manuscript copies had to survive three hundred years of mold, fire, mishandling, vermin, revolutionaries, and the general havoc of war.

This is not artistic literature by any means, but in the accounts of Pedro de Castañeda, we find an author who senses that he has indeed witnessed an "emergence" into a totally new land. He describes a land in which strange animals roam by the millions, a land so vast and so empty that it gives a man the sensation of standing within a gigantic bowl, with the horizon curving in all directions. To Castañeda, it is a land of such enormous and deceptive proportions that he estimates the width of the Colorado River, seen from the rim of the Grand Canyon, to be six feet. No accounts existed to prepare Castañeda for what he would see; he had no way to describe the land adequately, since he had no comparable references, only such things as a large mixing bowl or a 275-foot tower in Seville.

Their progress halted by the Grand Canyon and the unmeasurable expanse of the Great Plains, the Spanish drew back and established their church and trading networks in California and the Southwest. English-speaking settlers came ashore in Virginia and gradually began to make explorations westward. They too came to the great treeless lands of the Mississippi and Missouri basins. They too experienced the feeling that they had emerged into a wholly new land, and sought ways of recording the experience. J. Hector St. John de Crèvecoeur, a Frenchman determined to be a frontier farmer, wrote his impressions of the people who lived at the western edge of America. "What Is an American?" he asked, and answered that it was a new breed of person finding a new home in a new land, a person emerging with a fervent allegiance for the only country to ever offer people land of their own.

President Thomas Jefferson sent Meriwether Lewis and William Clark to follow the Missouri River to wherever it led. And it led them, just as the Río Colorado and its tributaries had led the Spanish, into the land of endless horizons. As William Cullen Bryant tells us in his poem, there was not even a word in the English language for *prairie*. The term had to be borrowed from the French word, meaning simply "meadow." Walt Whitman traveled briefly into the Great American Desert and went back East to romanticize the emigrants, the pioneers of the new land. The literary West had begun.

Pedro de Castañeda
1510?-54?

—

c. 1565: *The Journey of Coronado, 1540–1542, from the
City of Mexico to the Grand Cañon of the
Colorado and the Buffalo Plains of Texas,
Kansas, and Nebraska*

—

SPURRED *by the reports of Alvar Núñez Cabeza de Vaca and Fray
Marcos, Francisco Vásquez de Coronado set out in 1540 in search of the
golden cities of Cíbola. He and three hundred Spaniards, and up to eight
hundred Indians, left the Mexican province of New Galicia, crossed the border,
and rode into history as the first Europeans to invade the American West. Among
the crowd of fortune seekers was a soldier called Pedro de Castañeda. When he
returned to Spain, Castañeda wrote his memoirs about the fabled expedition of
Coronado.*

*Moving north out of Mexico, following a line approximately the same as today's
Arizona–New Mexico border, the expedition found the pueblos of Zuñi, called
them "Cíbola," and conquered them in the name of Spain. Coronado then sent
some of his officers north and west to reconnoiter; one of these officers and his men
captured the villages of the Hopis, and one of the other leaders, García López
de Cárdenas, became the first European to see the Grand Canyon.*

*Still hoping to find cities of gold, Coronado and his followers tracked down some
Indian reports of a place called Quivira. The rumors and the quest led them to
turn gradually eastward, across the Texas and Oklahoma panhandle country. As
the spring of 1541 arrived on the Great Plains, Coronado's columns made their
way up through the area of Kansas and into the lower part of Nebraska. They
saw what seemed to be endless empty grasslands, and vast herds of buffalo, but no
golden cities. Quivira turned out to be only a poor collection of huts, baking in the
heat of the prairie sun.*

Coronado's failure to find gold became the subject of an official government investigation, which created a great deal of public interest throughout Europe. In the introduction to his account of Coronado's journey, Castañeda wrote that he was often approached by inquisitive people who often bothered him "not a little with their requests" that he resolve for them "some doubts which they . . . had about different things . . . commonly related concerning the events and occurrences that took place during the expedition to Cíbola."[1] His narrative can hardly be called literary or artistic, but it is almost certainly the first document in a long line of journals, essays, poems, and novels about the mysterious region of the American West.

━━

On the Rim of the Grand Canyon

Chapter 11, of how Don Pedro de Tovar discovered
Tusayan or Tutahaco and Don Garcia Lopez de Cardenas saw the
Firebrand river and the other things that had happened.

WHILE the things already described were taking place, Cibola being at peace, the General Francisco Vazquez found out from the people of the province about the provinces that lay around it, and got them to tell their friends and neighbors that Christians had come into the country, whose only desire was to be their friends, and to find out about good lands to live in, and for them to come to see the strangers and talk with them. They did this, since they know how to communicate with one another in these regions, and they informed him about a province with seven villages of the same sort as theirs, although somewhat different. They had nothing to do with these people. This province is called Tusayan. It is twenty-five leagues from Cibola. The villages are high and the people are warlike.

The general had sent Don Pedro de Tovar to these villages with seventeen horsemen and three or four foot soldiers. Juan de Padilla, a Franciscan friar, who had been a fighting man in his youth, went with them. When they reached the region, they entered the country so quietly that nobody

This and the following selection are from Pedro de Castañeda, *The Coronado Expedition, 1540–1542*, trans. George Parker Winship, in *Fourteenth Annual Report of the Bureau of Ethnology to the Secretary of the Smithsonian Institution, 1892–93* (Washington, D.C.: GPO, 1896), pp. 487–90, 541–44.

1. Pedro de Castañeda, *The Journey of Coronado, 1540–1542*, trans. and ed. George Parker Winship (1907; reprint, New York: Allerton Book Co., 1965), p. xxix.

observed them, because there were no settlements or farms between one village and another and the people do not leave the villages except to go to their farms, especially at this time, when they had heard that Cibola had been captured by very fierce people, who traveled on animals which ate people. This information was generally believed by those who had never seen horses, although it was so strange as to cause much wonder. Our men arrived after nightfall and were able to conceal themselves under the edge of the village, where they heard the natives talking in their houses. But in the morning they were discovered and drew up in regular order, while the natives came out to meet them, with bows, and shields, and wooden clubs, drawn up in lines without any confusion. The interpreter was given a chance to speak to them and give them due warning, for they were very intelligent people, but nevertheless they drew lines and insisted that our men should not go across these lines toward their village. While they were talking, some men acted as if they would cross the lines, and one of the natives lost control of himself and struck a horse a blow on the cheek of the bridle with his club. Friar Juan, fretted by the time that was being wasted in talking with them, said to the captain: "To tell the truth, I do not know why we came here." When the men heard this, they gave the Santiago so suddenly that they ran down many Indians and the others fled to the town in confusion. Some indeed did not have a chance to do this, so quickly did the people in the village come out with presents, asking for peace. The captain ordered his force to collect, and, as the natives did not do any more harm, he and those who were with him found a place to establish their headquarters near the village. They had dismounted here when the natives came peacefully, saying that they had come to give in the submission of the whole province and that they wanted him to be friends with them and to accept the presents which they gave him. This was some cotton cloth, although not much, because they do not make it in that district. They also gave him some dressed skins and corn meal, and pine nuts and corn and birds of the country. Afterward they presented some turquoises, but not many. The people of the whole district came together that day and submitted themselves, and they allowed him to enter their villages freely to visit, buy, sell, and barter with them.

It[2] is governed like Cibola, by an assembly of the oldest men. They have

2. "It" refers to the pueblo called Awatobi, in northeastern Arizona. This was the southernmost Hopi pueblo; other Hopi pueblos destroyed it in 1700 because the people of Awatobi wanted to reestablish the Spanish mission there. The mission had been destroyed in the 1680 Pueblo revolt.

their governors and generals. This was where they obtained the information about a large river, and that several days down the river there were
some people with very large bodies.

As Don Pedro de Tovar was not commissioned to go farther, he returned
from there and gave this information to the general, who dispatched Don
Garcia Lopez de Cardenas with about twelve companions to go to see this
river. He was well received when he reached Tusayan and was entertained
by the natives, who gave him guides for his journey. They started from
here loaded with provisions, for they had to go through a desert country
before reaching the inhabited region, which the Indians said was more than
twenty days' journey. After they had gone twenty days they came to the
banks of the river, which seemed to be more than 3 or 4 leagues above the
stream which flowed between them.[3] This country was elevated and full of
low twisted pines, very cold, and lying open toward the north, so that, this
being the warm season, no one could live there on account of the cold.
They spent three days on this bank looking for a passage down to the river,
which looked from above as if the water was 6 feet across, although the
Indians said it was half a league wide. It was impossible to descend, for after
these three days Captain Melgosa and one Juan Galeras and another companion, who were the three lightest and most agile men, made an attempt
to go down at the least difficult place, and went down until those who were
above were unable to keep sight of them. They returned about 4 oclock
in the afternoon, not having succeeded in reaching the bottom on account
of the great difficulties which they found, because what seemed to be easy
from above was not so, but instead very hard and difficult. They said that
they had been down about a third of the way and that the river seemed very
large from the place which they reached, and that from what they saw they
thought the Indians had given the width correctly. Those who stayed above
had estimated that some huge rocks on the sides of the cliffs seemed to be
about as tall as a man, but those who went down swore that when they
reached these rocks they were bigger than the great tower of Seville. They
did not go farther up the river, because they could not get water. Before
this they had had to go a league or two inland every day late in the evening
in order to find water, and the guides said that if they should go four days
farther it would not be possible to go on, because there was no water within
three or four days, for when they travel across this region themselves they
take with them women loaded with water in gourds, and bury the gourds

3. A league is approximately three miles. Don Garcia and his men were looking down
into the Grand Canyon, evidently the first Europeans to do so.

of water along the way, to use when they return, and besides this, they travel in one day over what it takes us two days to accomplish.

This was the Tison (Firebrand) river, much nearer its source than where Melchior Diaz and his company crossed it. These were the same kind of Indians, judging from what was afterward learned. They came back from this point and the expedition did not have any other result. On the way they saw some water falling over a rock and learned from the guides that some bunches of crystals which were hanging there were salt. They went and gathered a quantity of this and brought it back to Cibola, dividing it among those who were there. They gave the general a written account of what they had seen, because one Pedro de Sotomayor had gone with Don Garcia Lopez as chronicler for the army. The villages of that province remained peaceful, since they were never visited again, nor was any attempt made to find other peoples in that direction.

The Bison of the Great Plains

Chapter 8, which describes some remarkable things that were seen on the plains, with a description of the bulls.

MY SILENCE was not without mystery and dissimulation when, in chapter 7 of the second part of this book, I spoke of the plains and of the things of which I will give a detailed account in this chapter, where all these things may be found together; for these things were remarkable and something not seen in other parts. I dare to write of them because I am writing at a time when many men are still living who saw them and who will vouch for my account. Who could believe that 1,000 horses and 500 of our cows and more than 5,000 rams and ewes and more than 1,500 friendly Indians and servants, in traveling over those plains, would leave no more trace where they had passed than if nothing had been there—nothing—so that it was necessary to make piles of bones and cow dung now and then, so that the rear guard could follow the army. The grass never failed to become erect after it had been trodden down, and, although it was short, it was as fresh and straight as before.

Another thing was a heap of cow bones, a crossbow shot long, or a very little less, almost twice a man's height in places, and some 18 feet or more wide, which was found on the edge of a salt lake in the southern part, and this in a region where there are no people who could have made it. The only explanation of this which could be suggested was that the waves which the north winds must make in the lake had piled up the bones of the cattle which had died in the lake, when the old and weak ones who went into the water were unable to get out. The noticeable thing is the number of cattle that would be necessary to make such a pile of bones.

Now that I wish to describe the appearance of the bulls, it is to be noticed first that there was not one of the horses that did not take flight when he saw them first, for they have a narrow, short face, the brow two palms across from eye to eye, the eyes sticking out at the side, so that, when they are running, they can see who is following them. They have very long beards, like goats, and when they are running they throw their heads back with the beard dragging on the ground. There is a sort of girdle round the middle of the body. The hair is very woolly, like a sheep's, very fine, and in front of the girdle the hair is very long and rough like a lion's. They have a great hump, larger than a camel's. The horns are short and thick, so that they are not seen much above the hair. In May they change the hair in the middle of the body for a down, which makes perfect lions of them. They rub against the small trees in the little ravines to shed their hair, and they continue this until only the down is left, as a snake changes his skin. They have a short tail, with a bunch of hair at the end. When they run, they carry it erect like a scorpion. It is worth noticing that the little calves are red and just like ours, but they change their color and appearance with time and age.

Another strange thing was that all the bulls that were killed had their left ears slit, although these were whole when young. The reason for this was a puzzle that could not be guessed. The wool ought to make good cloth on account of its fineness, although the color is not good, because it is the color of buriel.[4]

Another thing worth noticing is that the bulls traveled without cows in such large numbers that nobody could have counted them, and so far away from the cows that it was more than 40 leagues from where we began to see the bulls to the place where we began to see the cows. The country they traveled over was so level and smooth that if one looked at them the sky could be seen between their legs, so that if some of them were at a distance they looked like smooth-trunked pines whose tops joined, and if there was only one bull it looked as if there were four pines. When one was near them, it was impossible to see the ground on the other side of them. The reason for all this was that the country seemed as round as if a man should

4. A heavy gray cloth of coarse wool.

imagine himself in a three-pint measure, and could see the sky at the edge of it, about a crossbow shot from him, and even if a man only lay down on his back he lost sight of the ground.

I have not written about other things which were seen nor made any mention of them, because they were not of so much importance, although it does not seem right for me to remain silent concerning the fact that they venerate the sign of the cross in the region where the settlements have high houses. For at a spring which was in the plain near Acuco they had a cross two palms high and as thick as a finger, made of wood with a square twig for its crosspiece, and many little sticks decorated with feathers around it, and numerous withered flowers, which were the offerings. In a graveyard outside the village at Tutahaco there appeared to have been a recent burial. Near the head there was another cross made of two little sticks tied with cotton thread, and dry withered flowers. It certainly seems to me that in some way they must have received some light from the cross of Our Redeemer, Christ, and it may have come by way of India, from whence they proceeded.

J. Hector St. John
de Crèvecoeur
1735-1813

—

1782: *Letters from an American Farmer*
1801: *Voyage dans la Haute Pensylvanie et dans l'État
de New York*
1925: *Sketches of Eighteenth Century America*

—

MICHEL GUILLAUME JEAN DE CRÈVECOEUR, *who pub-
lished his popular* Letters from an American Farmer *under the pen
name of Hector St. John, was at various times a farmer, a restless
traveler, a soldier, a surveyor/mapmaker, an author, and, according to some, a
Tory spy.*

*With a survey party, he made a journey down the Ohio River to its conflu-
ence with the Mississippi. After a stopover in St. Louis, the group went up the
Mississippi and on to the Great Lakes. They returned to New York by a route
that took him through the Mohawk Valley, the home of the Oneida Indians. His
farm in New York was close to what was then the frontier: in 1783 he returned
from a "diplomatic mission" in Europe to find his farm burned, his wife dead, and
his children missing. His "frontier" was certainly not the West by any modern
definition, but de Crèvecoeur offers us, through his classic* Letters, *the first truly
literate insight into the American character, describing traits that would merge
and interact with the forces of the New Land and that would eventually become
the trademarks of the Anglo-American westerner.*

—

What Is an American?

I wish I could be acquainted with the feelings and thoughts which must agitate the heart and present themselves to the mind of an enlightened Englishman, when he first lands on this continent. He must greatly rejoice that he lived at a time to see this fair country discovered and settled; he must necessarily feel a share of national pride, when he views the chain of settlements which embellishes these extended shores. When he says to himself, this is the work of my countrymen, who, when convulsed by factions, afflicted by a variety of miseries and wants, restless and impatient, took refuge here. They brought along with them their national genius, to which they principally owe what liberty they enjoy, and what substance they possess. Here he sees the industry of his native country displayed in a new manner, and traces in their works the embrios of all the arts, sciences, and ingenuity which flourish in Europe. Here he beholds fair cities, substantial villages, extensive fields, an immense country filled with decent houses, good roads, orchards, meadows, and bridges, where an hundred years ago all was wild, woody and uncultivated! What a train of pleasing ideas this fair spectacle must suggest; it is a prospect which must inspire a good citizen with the most heartfelt pleasure. The difficulty consists in the manner of viewing so extensive a scene. He is arrived on a new continent; a modern society offers itself to his contemplation, different from what he had hitherto seen. It is not composed, as in Europe, of great lords who possess every thing, and of a herd of people who have nothing. Here are no aristocratical families, no courts, no kings, no bishops, no ecclesiastical dominion, no invisible power giving to a few a very visible one; no great manufacturers employing thousands, no great refinements of luxury. The rich and the poor are not so far removed from each other as they are in Europe. Some few towns excepted, we are all tillers of the earth, from Nova Scotia to West Florida. We are a people of cultivators, scattered over an immense territory, communicating with each other by means of good roads

From J. Hector St. John de Crèvecoeur, *Letters from an American Farmer* (1782; reprint, New York: Fox, Duffield and Co., 1904), pp. 48–61.

and navigable rivers, united by the silken bands of mild government, all respecting the laws, without dreading their power, because they are equitable. We are all animated with the spirit of an industry which is unfettered and unrestrained, because each person works for himself. If he travels through our rural districts he views not the hostile castle, and the haughty mansion, contrasted with the clay-built hut and miserable cabbin, where cattle and men help to keep each other warm, and dwell in meanness, smoke, and indigence. A pleasing uniformity of decent competence appears throughout our habitations. The meanest of our log-houses is a dry and comfortable habitation. Lawyer or merchant are the fairest titles our towns afford; that of a farmer is the only appellation of the rural inhabitants of our country. It must take some time ere he can reconcile himself to our dictionary, which is but short in words of dignity, and names of honour. There, on a Sunday, he sees a congregation of respectable farmers and their wives, all clad in neat homespun, well mounted, or riding in their own humble waggons. There is not among them an esquire, saving the unlettered magistrate. There he sees a parson as simple as his flock, a farmer who does not riot on the labour of others. We have no princes, for whom we toil, starve, and bleed: we are the most perfect society now existing in the world. Here man is free as he ought to be; nor is this pleasing equality so transitory as many others are. Many ages will not see the shores of our great lakes replenished with inland nations, nor the unknown bounds of North America entirely peopled. Who can tell how far it extends? Who can tell the millions of men whom it will feed and contain? for no European foot has as yet travelled half the extent of this mighty continent![1]

The next wish of this traveller will be to know whence came all these people? they are a mixture of English, Scotch, Irish, French, Dutch, Germans, and Swedes. From this promiscuous breed, that race now called Americans have arisen. The eastern provinces must indeed be excepted, as being the unmixed descendents of Englishmen. I have heard many wish that they had been more intermixed also: for my part, I am no wisher, and think it much better as it has happened. They exhibit a most conspicuous figure in this great and variegated picture; they too enter for a great share

---

1. De Crèvecoeur not only overlooks the far-ranging travels of the Spanish but also is apparently ignorant of the journey from Canada to Santa Fe made by Pierre and Paul Mallet and six other men in 1739. Although two hundred years had passed since the Spanish explorers, people—including the Mallets—believed that Santa Fe could be reached by following the Missouri. The Mallets, after leaving the Missouri at the Niobrara junction and crossing a river they named the Platte, eventually did reach Taos and Santa Fe. From there they made their way to New Orleans.

in the pleasing perspective displayed in these thirteen provinces. I know it is fashionable to reflect on them, but I respect them for what they have done; for the accuracy and wisdom with which they have settled their territory; for the decency of their manners; for their early love of letters; their ancient college,[2] the first in this hemisphere; for their industry; which to me who am but a farmer, is the criterion of everything. There never was a people, situated as they are, who with so ungrateful a soil have done more in so short a time. Do you think that the monarchical ingredients which are more prevalent in other governments, have purged them from all foul stains? Their histories assert the contrary.

In this great American asylum, the poor of Europe have by some means met together, and in consequence of various causes; to what purpose should they ask one another what countrymen they are? Alas, two thirds of them had no country. Can a wretch who wanders about, who works and starves, whose life is a continual scene of sore affliction or pinching penury; can that man call England or any other kingdom his country? A country that had no bread for him, whose fields procured him no harvest, who met with nothing but the frowns of the rich, the severity of the laws, with jails and punishments; who owned not a single foot of the extensive surface of this planet? No! urged by a variety of motives, here they came. Every thing has tended to regenerate them; new laws, a new mode of living, a new social system; here they are become men: in Europe they were as so many useless plants, wanting vegitative mould, and refreshing showers; they withered, and were mowed down by want, hunger, and war; but now by the power of transplantation, like all other plants they have taken root and flourished! Formerly they were not numbered in any civil lists of their country, except in those of the poor; here they rank as citizens. By what invisible power has this surprising metamorphosis been performed? By that of the laws and that of their industry. The laws, the indulgent laws, protect them as they arrive, stamping on them the symbol of adoption; they receive ample rewards for their labours; these accumulated rewards procure them lands; those lands confer on them the title of freemen, and to that title every benefit is affixed which men can possibly require. This is the great operation daily performed by our laws. From whence proceed these laws? From our government. Whence the government? It is derived from the original genius and strong desire of the people ratified and confirmed by the crown. This is the great chain which links us all, this is the picture which every province exhibits, Nova Scotia excepted. There the crown has done all; either there were no

2. Harvard, founded in 1636.

people who had genius, or it was not much attended to: the consequence is, that the province is very thinly inhabited indeed; the power of the crown in conjunction with the musketos has prevented men from settling there. Yet some parts of it flourished once, and it contained a mild harmless set of people. But for the fault of a few leaders, the whole were banished. The greatest political error the crown ever committed in America, was to cut off men from a country which wanted nothing but men!

What attachment can a poor European emigrant have for a country where he had nothing? The knowledge of the language, the love of a few kindred as poor as himself, were the only cords that tied him: his country is now that which gives him land, bread, protection, and consequence: *Ubi panis ibi patria*,[3] is the motto of all emigrants. What then is the American, this new man? He is either an European, or the descendant of an European, hence that strange mixture of blood, which you will find in no other country. I could point out to you a family whose grandfather was an Englishman, whose wife was Dutch, whose son married a French woman, and whose present four sons have now four wives of different nations. *He* is an American, who leaving behind him all his ancient prejudices and manners, receives new ones from the new mode of life he has embraced, the new government he obeys, and the new rank he holds. He becomes an American by being received in the broad lap of our great *Alma Mater*. Here individuals of all nations are melted into a new race of men, whose labours and posterity will one day cause great changes in the world. Americans are the western pilgrims, who are carrying along with them that great mass of arts, sciences, vigour, and industry which began long since in the east; they will finish the great circle. The Americans were once scattered all over Europe; here they are incorporated into one of the finest systems of population which has ever appeared, and which will hereafter become distinct by the power of the different climates they inhabit. The American ought therefore to love this country much better than that wherein either he or his forefathers were born. Here the rewards of his industry follow with equal steps the progress of his labour; his labour is founded on the basis of nature, *self-interest;* can it want a stronger allurement? Wives and children, who before in vain demanded of him a morsel of bread, now, fat and frolicsome, gladly help their father to clear those fields whence exuberant crops are to arise to feed and to clothe them all; without any part being claimed, either by a despotic prince, a rich abbot, or a mighty lord. Here religion demands but little of him; a small voluntary salary to the minister, and

3. "Where a person has his bread, there he has his fatherland."

gratitude to God; can he refuse these? The American is a new man, who acts upon new principles; he must therefore entertain new ideas, and form new opinions. From involuntary idleness, servile dependence, penury, and useless labour, he has passed to toils of a very different nature, rewarded by ample subsistence.—This is an American.

British America is divided into many provinces, forming a large association, scattered along a coast 1500 miles extent and about 200 wide. This society I would fain examine, at least such as it appears in the middle provinces; if it does not afford that variety of tinges and gradations which may be observed in Europe, we have colours peculiar to ourselves. For instance, it is natural to conceive that those who live near the sea, must be very different from those who live in the woods; the intermediate space will afford a separate and distinct class.

Men are like plants; the goodness and flavour of the fruit proceeds from the peculiar soil and exposition in which they grow. We are nothing but what we derive from the air we breathe, the climate we inhabit, the government we obey, the system of religion we profess, and the nature of our employment. Here you will find but few crimes; these have acquired as yet no root among us. I wish I were able to trace all my ideas; if my ignorance prevents me from describing them properly, I hope I shall be able to delineate a few of the outlines, which are all I propose.

Those who live near the sea, feed more on fish than on flesh, and often encounter that boisterous element. This renders them more bold and enterprising; this leads them to neglect the confined occupations of the land. They see and converse with a variety of people; their intercourse with mankind becomes extensive. The sea inspires them with a love of traffic, a desire of transporting produce from one place to another; and leads them to a variety of resources which supply the place of labour. Those who inhabit the middle settlements, by far the most numerous, must be very different; the simple cultivation of the earth purifies them, but the indulgences of the government, the soft remonstrances of religion, the rank of independent freeholders, must necessarily inspire them with sentiments, very little known in Europe among people of the same class. What do I say? Europe has no such class of men; the early knowledge they acquire, the early bargains they make, give them a great degree of sagacity. As freemen they will be litigious; pride and obstinacy are often the cause of law suits; the nature of our laws and governments may be another. As citizens it is easy to imagine, that they will carefully read the newspapers, enter into every political disquisition, freely blame or censure governors and others. As farmers they will be carful and anxious to get as much as they can, because what they get is their own. As northern men they will love the chearful cup. As Christians, religion curbs them not in their opinions; the general indulgence leaves every one to think for themselves in spiritual matters; the laws inspect our actions, our thoughts are left to God. Industry, good living, selfishness, litigiousness, country politics, the pride of freemen, religious indifference, are their characteristics. If you recede still farther from the sea, you will come into more modern settlements; they exhibit the same strong lineaments, in a ruder appearance. Religion seems to have still less influence, and their manners are less improved.

Now we arrive near the great woods, near the last inhabited districts; there men seem to be placed still farther beyond the reach of government, which in some measure leaves them to themselves. How can it pervade every corner; as they were driven there by misfortunes, necessity of beginnings, desire of acquiring large tracks of land, idleness, frequent want of œconomy, ancient debts; the re-union of such people does not afford a very pleasing spectacle. When discord, want of unity and friendship; when either drunkenness or idleness prevail in such remote districts; contention, inactivity, and wretchedness must ensue. There are not the same remedies to these evils as in a long established community. The few magistrates they have, are in general little better than the rest; they are often in a perfect state of war; that of man against man, sometimes decided by blows, sometimes by means of the law; that of man against every wild inhabitant of these venerable woods, of which they are come to dispossess them. There men appear to be no beter than carnivorous animals of a superior rank, living on the flesh of wild animals when they can catch them, and when they are not able, they subsist on grain. He who would wish to see America in its proper light, and have a true idea of its feeble beginnings and barbarous rudiments, must visit our extended line of frontiers where the last settlers dwell, and where he may see the first labours of settlement, the mode of clearing the earth, in all their different appearances; where men are wholly left dependent on their native tempers, and on the spur of uncertain industry, which often fails when not sanctified by the efficacy of a few moral rules. There, remote from the power of example, and check of shame, many families exhibit the most hideous parts of our society. They are a kind of forlorn hope, preceding by ten or twelve years the most respectable army of veterans which come after them. In that space, prosperity will polish some, vice and the law will drive off the rest, who uniting again with others like themselves will recede still farther; making room for more industrious people, who will finish their improvements, convert the loghouse into a convenient habitation, and rejoicing that the first heavy labours are finished, will change in a few years that hitherto barbarous country into a fine fertile, well regulated district. Such is our progress, such is the march of the Europeans toward the interior parts of this continent. In all societies there are off-casts; this impure part serves as our precursors or pioneers; my father himself was one of that class, but he came upon honest principles, and was therefore one of the few who held fast; by good conduct and temperance, he transmitted to me his fair inheritance, when not above one in fourteen of his contemporaries had the same good fortune.

Forty years ago this smiling country was thus inhabited; it is now purged, a general decency of manners prevails throughout, and such has been the fate of our best countries.

Exclusive of those general characteristics, each province has its own, founded on the government, climate, mode of husbandry, customs, and peculiarity of circumstances. Europeans submit insensibly to these great powers, and become, in the course of a few generations, not only Americans in general, but either Pensylvanians, Virginians, or provincials under some other name. Whoever traverses the continent must easily observe those strong differences, which will grow more evident in time. The inhabitants of Canada, Massachuset, the middle provinces, the southern ones will be as different as their climates; their only points of unity will be those of religion and language.

Meriwether Lewis
1774-1809

and William Clark
1770-1838

▬

1893: *Journals of the Lewis and Clark Expedition,*
May 14, 1804–September 23, 1806

▬

MERIWETHER *Lewis and William Clark were both born near Charlottesville, Virginia, not far from Monticello, the home of Thomas Jefferson. Lewis grew up on his family's plantation, Locust Hill, enlisting in the Virginia militia when he was twenty years old. A year later, he earned an ensign appointment in the First United States Infantry Regiment. During his tour of duty, Lewis gained valuable experience in wilderness and frontier travel.*

Shortly after Lewis's promotion to captain in 1800, President-elect Thomas Jefferson chose the young officer as his private secretary. And shortly after being inaugurated, President Jefferson decided to let the captain lead a "Corps of Discovery" to explore the continent's interior. Lewis soon found himself in Philadelphia, improving and expanding his knowledge of cartography, natural science, astronomy, and ethnology and arranging men, supplies, and transportation for the journey.

The eight-thousand-mile trek took twenty-eight months. When it was over, Jefferson made Lewis governor of Louisiana Territory. Months of quarrels and difficulties followed; then, in 1809, while traveling the Natchez Trace in Tennessee on his way to Washington, D.C., Lewis apparently took his own life.

William Clark, like Lewis, began his military service in the militia. He was probably nineteen at the time of his first battle with the Indians, in one of the Ohio River campaigns. His commission as lieutenant in the regular army came in 1792; two years later, he fought at the battle of Fallen Timbers under the command of General Anthony Wayne. Resigning in 1796, with honor, Clark returned home to supervise the family plantation.

Asked by Jefferson to find a suitable second-in-command for the Corps of Discovery, Lewis chose Clark, under whom he had previously served. Jefferson asked that Clark's commission as captain be reinstated for the mission, but army foul-ups caused a second-lieutenant commission to be sent instead. The other men on the expedition were never told of this, and all records refer to each leader as "captain."

Following the expedition, Clark held various posts in the militia and in Indian affairs. In 1813, he was appointed governor of Missouri Territory (the new name of Louisiana Territory), and in 1822 he became superintendent of Indian affairs in St. Louis, a post he held until his death.

The historic trip began with Lewis's departure from Pittsburgh, where he had supervised the building of the keelboat for the journey. Setting out on August 31, 1803, Lewis traveled down the Ohio River, picking up Clark and a few additional men along the way. They stayed the winter at Camp Dubois, near St. Louis, and in May 1804 set out upon the spring floods of the Missouri River. By November they were at the Mandan villages, in the middle of present-day North Dakota, where they built a small fort, called Fort Mandan, and settled down to wait for the spring thaw.

When that thaw finally arrived, in April 1805, the captains sent a portion of the party back downriver with the keelboat and proceeded by canoe and pirogue. In four months, they were on foot, crossing one of the most rugged parts of the northern Rockies just ahead of dangerous winter snows. Reaching the mouth of the Columbia River in November, they built Fort Clatsop and once again prepared to wait out the freezing weather. The return trip began in March 1806, by canoe and horseback; after passing over the Bitterroots, the captains split the corps into two parties and explored different routes, rejoining before arriving back at the Mandan villages. The summer was spent canoeing down the Missouri; they arrived in St. Louis on September 23, 1806, to the surprise of almost everyone, since the corps had been given up as lost.

Thomas Jefferson had issued explicit instructions to Lewis; the captains were to gather information about topography, climate, minerals, plants, animals, major landmarks, strategic sites for forts and for trading, and the Missouri's tributaries. In addition, they were to keep records of the people they encountered, including observations about tribal histories, lore, customs, religions, languages, territories, alliances, food, clothing, weapons, and manufactures. All of this data, moreover, was to be recorded in duplicate. Not only did Lewis and Clark keep journals, but so did others on the journey, men such as John Ordway, Charles Floyd, Joseph Whitehouse, and Patrick Gass.

Altogether, more than four dozen separate notebooks, journals, and bundles of loose notes, letters, and miscellaneous records of the Lewis and Clark expedition have survived. Some records contain commonplace details such as lists of men assigned to the various mess details, inventories of supplies, daily weather notes, and accounts of disciplinary procedures. But some parts of the journals include very detailed descriptions of people, places, plants, and animals; some of these, such as Clark's description of prairie dogs and pronghorns, are the first recordings of various phenomena.

Clark had limited skill when it came to writing, and was aware of it; Lewis, on the other hand, occasionally ventured into the travel-essay, or travel-narrative style, a literary tradition in Europe as well as in the new country. Lewis's style is reminiscent of James Boswell's Journal of a Tour to the Hebrides with Samuel Johnson, LL. D. *(1785), for instance, or of the early American* Travels, *by William Bartram (1791), and* Letters from an American Farmer, *by J. Hector St. John de Crèvecoeur (1782). Gary Moulton, editor of* The Journals of the Lewis and Clark Expedition, *notes:*

> Jefferson wanted a full record of their findings to present to the world as soon as possible in a multivolume work, including a narrative of the journey and a full exposition of their scientific and geographic discoveries, with appropriate maps and illustrations. The published accounts of Captain Cook's voyages and the journals of American naturalist William Bartram probably provided models of what Jefferson had in mind. Certainly he did not intend to have the journals published in their original, rough form; the convention of the time demanded that someone should produce a polished, literary version. Jefferson intended that Lewis, who had the sort of literary style admired at the time, should do the writing.[1]

Publication was delayed, however. In 1814, Nicholas Biddle, with Clark's cooperation, published an expedition history that was more a paraphrase than anything else, emphasizing the romantic aspects and practically ignoring the scientific and other practical data. Elliott Coues edited the Biddle work, and his 1893 version of the History of the Expedition under the Command of Captains Lewis and Clark *(Biddle's title) brought to light a great deal of ignored information and expanded the public knowledge of the corps's accomplishment.*

---

1. Gary E. Moulton, ed., *The Journals of the Lewis and Clark Expedition* (Lincoln: University of Nebraska Press, 1987), vol. 3, p. 35.

For years, the standard edition of the journals was that of Reuben Gold Thwaites, The Original Journals of the Lewis and Clark Expedition, 1804– 1806, *eight volumes published in 1904–5. Subsequent scholarship, together with recently rediscovered documents, has led the University of Nebraska Press to under- take a new, thorough edition. Under the editorial guidance of Gary E. Moulton and with the help of a battery of experts in western history, natural science, and ethnology, the new edition was inaugurated in 1983.*

The following entry in the journals, written by Meriwether Lewis, describes Lewis's impressions of a town at the edge of the American frontier. Like Hector St. John de Crèvecoeur before him, and like such successive sociological reporters as John Mason Peck and Frederick Jackson Turner, Lewis is interested in the char- acter of these people who inhabit the frontier and who seem to represent, for better or for worse, notable traits of the American personality. At St. Charles, Lewis will join Clark, who left St. Louis with the keelboat and pirogues some six days earlier. The great expedition to the Pacific has begun.

The Departure

[Lewis]   *Sunday May 20th 1804*

The morning was fair, and the weather pleasent; at 10 oCk A M. agreably to an appointment of the preceeding day, I was joined by Capt. Stod- dard, Lieuts. Milford[2] & Worrell[3] together with Messrs. A. Chouteau, C. Gratiot, and many other respectable inhabitants of St. Louis, who had engaged to accompany me to the Vilage of St. Charles; accordingly at 12 Oclk after bidding an affectionate adieu to my Hostis, that excellent woman the spouse of Mr. Peter Chouteau,[4] and some of my fair friends of St. Louis, we set forward to that village in order to join my friend compan- ion and fellow labourer Capt. William Clark who had previously arrived at

This and the following two selections are from Gary E. Moulton, ed., *The Journals of the Lewis and Clark Expedition* (Lincoln: University of Nebraska Press, 1986, 1987), 2:240–42, 243; 3:80–86; and 3:362–65. Copyright © 1986 (vol. 2), 1987 (vol. 3) by the University of Nebraska Press.

2. "Milford" to Lewis and "Minford" to Clark, he was Clarence Mulford, first com- missioned in 1800, from the state of New Jersey. In 1804 he was a lieutenant in Captain Amos Stoddard's artillery company; he resigned in 1811. Heitman, 482. [Moulton's note]

3. Stephen Worrell, of Pennsylvania, was another of Stoddard's junior officers. He was appointed in 1801 and resigned in 1806. Ibid., 713. [Moulton's note]

4. Lewis's hostess was Pierre Chouteau's second wife, Brigitte Saucier Chouteau. [Moulton's note]

that place with the party destined for the discovery of the interior of the continent of North America   the first 5 miles of our rout laid through a beatifull high leavel and fertile prarie which incircles the town of St. Louis from N. W. to S. E.   the lands through which we then passed are somewhat broken up fertile   the plains and woodlands are here indiscriminately interspersed untill you arrive within three miles of the vilage when the woodland commences and continues to the Missouri   the latter is extreamly fertile. At half after one P. M. our progress was interrupted [*hole*]   the near approach of a violent thunder storm from the N. W. and concluded to take shelter in a little cabbin hard by untill the rain should be over; accordingly we alighted and remained about an hour and a half and regailed ourselves with a could collation which we had taken the precaution to bring with us from St. Louis.

The clouds continued to follow each other in rapaid succession, insomuch that there was but little prospect of it's ceasing to rain this evening; as I had determined to reach St. Charles this evening and knowing that there was now no time to be lost I set forward in the rain, most of the gentlemen continued with me, we arrived at half after six and joined Capt Clark, found the party in good health and sperits.   suped this evening with Monsr. Charles Tayong a Spanish Ensign & late Commandant of St. Charles   at an early hour I retired to rest on board the barge— St. Charles is situated on the North bank of the Missouri 21 Miles above it's junction with the Mississippi, and about the same distance N. W. from St. Louis; it is bisected by one principal street about a mile in length running nearly parrallel with the river, the plain on which it stands—is narrow tho' sufficiently elivated to secure it against the annual inundations of the river, which usually happen in the month of June, and in the rear it is terminated by a range of small hills, hence the appellation of *petit Cote,* a name by which this vilage is better known to the French inhabitants of the Illinois than that of St. Charles. The Vilage contains a Chappel, one hundred dwelling houses, and about 450 inhabitants; their houses are generally small and but illy constructed; a great majority of the inhabitants are miserably pour, illiterate and when at home excessively lazy, tho' they are polite hospitable and by no means deficient in point of natural genious, they live in a perfect state of harmony among each other; and plase as implicit confidence in the doctrines of their speritual pastor, the Roman Catholic priest, as they yeald passive obedience to the will of their temporal master the commandant.   a small garden of vegetables is the usual extent of their cultivation, and this is commonly imposed on the old men and boys; the men in the vigor of life consider the cultivation of the earth a degrading occupation, and in order to gain the necessary subsistence for themselves and families, either undertake hunting voyages on their own account, or engage themselves as hirelings to such persons as possess sufficient capital to extend their traffic to the natives of the interior parts of the country; on those voyages in either case, they are frequently absent from their families or homes the term of six twelve or eighteen months and alwas subjected to severe and incessant labour, exposed to the ferosity of the lawless savages, the vicissitudes of weather and climate, and dependant on chance or accident alone for food, raiment or relief in the event of malady. These people are principally the descendants of the Canadian French, and it is not an inconsiderable proportian of them that can boast a small dash of the pure blood of the aboriginees of America. On consulting with my friend Capt. C. I found it necessary that we should pospone our departure untill 2 P M. the next day and accordingly gave orders to the party to hold themselves in readiness to depart at that hour.—

Captn. Clark now informed me that having gotten all the stores on board the Barge and perogues on the evening of the 13th of May he determined to leave our winter cantainment at the mouth of River Dubois the next day, and to ascend the Missouri as far as the Vilage of St. Charles, where as it had been previously concerted between us, he was to wait my arrival; this movement while it advanced us a small distance on our rout, would also enable him to determine whether the vessels had been judiciously loaded and if not timely to make the necessary alterations; accordingly at 4 P.M. on Monday the 14th of May 1804, he embarked with the party in the presence of a number of the neighbouring Citizens who had assembled to witness his departure during the fore part of this day it rained excessively hard. In my last letter to the President dated at St. Louis I mentioned the departure of Capt. Clark from River Dubois on the 15th Inst,[5] which was the day that had been calculated on, but having completed the arrangements a day earlyer he departed on the 14th as before mentioned. On the evening of the 14th the party halted and encamped on the upper point of the first Island which lyes near the Larbord shore,[6] on the same side and nearly opposite the center of this Island a small Creek disimbogues called Couldwater.

5. Lewis's last known letter to Jefferson before leaving St. Louis does not mention the date of departure; it is simply a list of goods shipped to Jefferson and is largely in Clark's hand. Possibly the list was an enclosure with the letter referred to by Lewis. Lewis to Jefferson, May 18, 1804, Jackson (LLC), 1: 192–94 and headnote. [Moulton's note]

6. The first letter of the word appears to be "*L*," but Clark's entries for May 14 clearly locate the island on the starboard side. [Moulton's note]

The course and distance of this day was West 4 Miles the Wind from
N. E.

✳ ✳ ✳

By autumn of 1804, the corps had reached what is now South Dakota; by mid-November they would be at the Mandan villages, where they would spend the winter. Lewis's entry for September 17 is of the travel-narrative type, whereas Clark's is more typical of the notebook style of entry. Taken together, all of the entries for September 17 offer insight into the manner in which both men took notes and then used their own and each other's notes to write journal narratives; also notable is their interest in species wholly unknown in the eastern states, species such as the coyote and the "barking squril," or the prairie dog.

▬

Specimens of Natural History

[Lewis]   *Monday September 17th 1804.*

Having for many days past confined myself to the boat, I determined to devote this day to amuse myself on shore with my gun and view the interior of the country lying between the river and the Corvus Creek—   accordingly before sunrise I set out with six of my best hunters,[7] two of whom I dispatched to the lower side of Corvus creek, two with orders to hunt the bottoms and woodland on the river, while I retained two others to acompany me in the intermediate country.   one quarter of a mile in rear of our camp which was situated in a fine open grove of cotton wood passed a grove of plumb trees loaded with fruit and now ripe.   observed but little difference between this fruit and that of a similar kind common to the Atlantic States.[8]   the trees are smaller and more thickly set.   this forrest of plumb trees garnish a plain about 20 feet more lelivated than that on which we were encamped; this plain extends back about a mile to the foot of the hills one mile distant and to which it is gradually ascending   this plane extends with the same bredth from the creek below to the distance of near three miles above parrallel with the river, and is intirely occupied by the burrows of the *barking squril* hertefore discribed; this anamal appears here in infinite numbers, and the shortness and virdue [verdure] of grass gave the plain the appearance throughout it's whole extent of beatifull bowlinggreen in fine

7. They may have included Colter (see Clark's entry, below), and probably Drouillard, the premier hunter of the party. [Moulton's note]
    8. These plums are the same species, the common wild plum. [Moulton's note]

order. it's aspect is S. E. a great number of wolves of the small kind, halks and some pole-cats[9] were to be seen. I presume that those anamals feed on this squirril.— found the country in every direction for about three miles intersected with deep revenes and steep irregular hills of 100 to 200 feet high; at the tops of these hills the country breakes of as usual into a fine leavel plain extending as far as the eye can reach. from this plane I had an extensive view of the river below, and the irregular hills which border the opposite sides of the river and creek. the surrounding country had been birnt about a month before and young grass had now sprung up to hight of 4 Inches presenting the live green of the spring. to the West a high range of hills,[10] strech across the country from N. to S and appeared distant about 20 miles; they are not very extensive as I could plainly observe their rise and termination no rock appeared on them and the sides were covered with virdue similar to that of the plains this senery already rich pleasing and beatiful, was still farther hightened by immence herds of Buffaloe deer Elk and Antelopes which we saw in every direction feeding on the hills and plains. I do not think I exagerate when I estimate the number of Buffaloe which could be compreed at one view to amount to 3000. my object was if possible to kill a female Antelope having already procured a male; I pursued my rout on this plain to the west flanked by my two hunters untill eight in the morning when I made the signal for them to come to me which they did shortly after. we rested our selves about half an hour, and regailed ourselves on half a bisquit each and some jirk of Elk which we had taken the precaution to put in our pouches in the morning before we set out, and drank of the water of a small pool which had collected on this plain from the rains which had fallen some days before. We had now after various windings in pursuit of several herds of antelopes which we had seen on our way made the distance of about eight miles from our camp. we found the Antelope extremly shye and watchfull insomuch that we had been unable to get a shot at them; when at rest they generally seelect the most elivated point in the neighbourhood, and as they are watchfull and extreemly quick of sight and their sense of smelling very accute it is almost impossible to approach them within gunshot; in short they will frequently discover and flee from you at the distance of three miles. I had this day an opportunity of witnessing the agility and superior fleetness of this anamal which was to me really astonishing. I had pursued and twice surprised a small herd of seven, in the first instance they did not discover me distinctly and therefore

9. Skunks, *Mephitis mephitis*. Cutright (LCPN), 93. [Moulton's note]
10. These may include the later Red Butte. *South Dakota Guide*, 403. [Moulton's note]

did not run at full speed, tho' they took care before they rested to gain an elivated point where it was impossible to approach them under cover except in one direction and that happened to be in the direction from which the wind blew towards them; bad as the chance to approach them was, I made the best of my way towards them, frequently peeping over the ridge with which I took care to conceal myself from their view   the male, of which there was but one, frequently incircled the summit of the hill on which the females stood in a group, as if to look out for the approach of danger. I got within about 200 paces of them when they smelt me and fled; I gained the top of the eminece on which they stood, as soon as possible from whence I had an extensive view of the country   the antilopes which had disappeared in a steep revesne now appeared at the distance of about three miles on the side of a ridge which passed obliquely across me and extended about four miles.   so soon had these antelopes gained the distance at which they had again appeared to my view I doubted at ferst that they were the same that I had just surprised, but my doubts soon vanished when I beheld the rapidity of their flight along the ridge before me   it appeared reather the rappid flight of birds than the motion of quadrupeds. I think I can safely venture the asscertion that the speed of this anamal is equal if not superior to that of the finest blooded courser.—   this morning I saw [11]

[Clark] [12]

17th of Septr. Monday 1804   above White river   Dried all those articles which had got wet by the last rain, a fine day   Capt Lewis went hunting with a vew to see the Countrey & its productions, he was out all Day   Killed a Buffalow & a remarkable bird of the Spicies of Corvus, long tail of a Greenish Purple, Varigated   a Beck like a Crow   white round its neck comeing to a point on its back, its belley white   feet like a Hawk   abt. the size of a large Pigeon [13]   Capt Lewis returned at Dark. I took the Meridian & equal altitudes to day   made the Lattitude.

Colter Killed a Goat, & a Curious kind of Deer, a Darker grey than Common   the hair longer & finer, the ears verry large & long   a Small

11. Codex Ba ends abruptly at this point. [Moulton's note]

12. Biddle has the notation "and 20" at the top of this document 55 of the Field Notes, indicating that the entries on this sheet go through that date. [Moulton's note]

13. Clark's, and Lewis's longer account in Codex Q for this date, are the first descriptions of the black-billed magpie. Magpies had not previously been known to exist in the New World; the American bird is a subspecies of the European magpie. They named Corvus Creek for this bird, one of the few uses of a Latin zoological term in the journals. Cutright (LCPN), 84–85. [Moulton's note]

resepitical under its eye   its tail round and white to near the end which is black & like a Cow   in every other respect like a Deer, except it runs like a goat.   large.[14]

The hunters brought in 8 fallow Deer & 5 Common Deer to day, Great numbers of Buffalow in the Praries, also a light Coloured woolf Covered with hair & corse fur, also a Small wolf with a large bushey tail—[15]   Some Goats of a Different Kind Seen to day,—   Great many Plumbs, rabits, Porcupines & barking Squrels, Capt Lewis Killed a rattle Snake in a village of the Squirel's and Saw a Hair to day. Wind from the S. W.   we finished Drying our Provisions   Some of which was wet and Spoiled,[16]

White River 17th Septr. *Plomb Camp*
Course Distance & reffurence

[Clark]   *17th September* Monday 1804

Dried all our wet articles this fine Day, Capt Lewis went out with a View to see the Countrey and its productions, he was out all day   he killed a Buffalow and a remarkable *Bird* [*WC: Magpy*] of the *Corvus* Species long tail the upper part of the feathers & also the wing is of a purplish variated Green, the black, [*X: back &*] a part of the wing feather are white edjed with black, white belley, white from the root of the wings to Center of the back is white, the head nake [neck] breast & other parts are black the Becke like a Crow. abt. the Size of a large Pigion. a butifull thing (See Suplement in No. 3)[17]

I took equal altitudes and a meridian altitude. Capt. Lewis returned at Dark, Colter Killed a Goat like the one I killed and a curious kind of deer [*WC: Mule Deer*][18] of a Dark gray Colr. more so than common, hair long

14. The mule deer. [Moulton's note]

15. The latter was apparently their first specimen of the coyote, described in more detail on September 18. Cutright (LCPN), 85. [Moulton's note]

16. Clark evidently combined his September 17 and 18 entries in the Field Notes at this point. They are separated here and brought together in regular order. [Moulton's note]

17. Clark's "No. 3" is the notebook now called Codex C, but the reference here is probably to Lewis's lengthy description of the magpie in Codex Q under this date. [Moulton's note]

18. Clark probably inserted the phrase "Mule Deer" later, when the captains had adopted that name for *Odocoileus hemionus,* based on its large ears. He used red ink for this and the previous emendation. Clark may also have lined out in red the passage about the magpie. Lewis's use of the term on April 23, 1805, is the first written use of today's common name of the animal, which Lewis and Clark were the first to describe. [Moulton's note]

& fine, the ears large & long, a Small reseptical under the eyes; like an Elk, the Taile about the length of Common Deer, round (like a Cow) a tuft of black hair about the end, this Speces of Deer jumps like a goat or Sheep

8 fallow Deer 5 Common & 3 buffalow killed to day, Capt. Lewis Saw a *hare* & Killed a Rattle Snake in a village of B. squerels The wind from S. W. Dryed our provisions, Some of which was much Damaged.

[Lewis]   Sept. 17th[19]

one of the hunters killed a bird of the *Corvus genus* [EC: *Pica pica hudsonica*] and order of the pica & about the size of a jack-daw with a remarkable long tale. beautifully variagated. it ⟨has an agreeable note something like goald winged Blackbird⟩ note is not disagreeable though loud—it is twait twait twait, twait; twait, twait twait, twait.

	F	I
from tip to tip of wing	1	10
Do. beak to extremity of tale	1	8½
of which the tale occupys		11
from extremity of middle toe to hip		5½

it's head, beak, and neck are large for a bird of it's size; the beak is black, and of a convex and cultrated figure, the chops nearly equal, and it's base large and beset with hairs— the eyes are black encircled with a ⟨small⟩ narrow ring of yellowish black it's head, neck, brest & back within one inch of the tale are of a fine glossey black, as are also the short fathers of the under part of the wing, the thies and those about the root of the tale. the ⟨body⟩ belly is of a beatifull white which passes above and arround the but of the wing, where the feathers being long reach to a small white spot on the rump one inch in width— the wings have nineteen feathers, of which the ten first have the longer side of their plumage white in the midde of the feather and occupying unequal lengths of the same from one to three inches, and forming when the wing is spead a kind [of] triangle the upper and lower part of these party coloured feathers on the under side of the wing being of dark colour but not jut or shining black. the under side of

---

19. Lewis's natural history notes from Codex Q. The bird is the black-billed magpie and the turkey may be the wild turkey, *Meleagris gallopavo* [A O U, 310], which Coues (in his interlineation) calls a rare bird in the area described. One authority suggests other possibilities, including the white-tailed ptarmigan, *Lagopus leucurus* [A O U, 304]. Holmgren, 34. The gold-winged blackbird mentioned for comparison of the magpie may be the red-winged blackbird, *Agelaius phoeniceus* [A O U, 498], or possibly some type of oriole (*Icterus* sp.). [Moulton's note]

the remaining feathers of the wing are darker. the upper side of the wing, as well as the short side of the plumage of the party coloured feathers is of a dark blackis or bluish green sonetimes presenting as light orange yellow or bluish ⟨tinge⟩ tint as it ⟨rise⟩ happens to be presented to different exposures of ligt— the plumage of the tale consits of 12 feathers of equal lengths by pai[r]s, those in the center are the longest, and the others on each side deminishing about an inch each pair— the underside of the feathers is a pale black, the upper side is a dark blueish green which like the ⟨upper and⟩ outer part of the wings is changable as it reflects different portions of light. towards the the extremety of these feathers they become of an orrange green, then shaded pass to a redish indigo blue, and again at the extremity assume the predominant colour of changeable green— the tints of these feathers are very similar and equally as beatiful and rich as the tints of blue and green of the peacock— it is a most beatifull bird.— the legs and toes are black and imbricated. it has four long toes, three in front and one in rear, each terminated with a black sharp tallon from ⅜ths to ½ an inch in length.— these birds are seldom found in parties of more than three or four and most usually at this season single as the halks ⟨ravens⟩ and other birds of prey usually are— ⟨from it's appearance I believe to⟩ it's usual food is flesh— this bird dose not spread it's tail when it flys and the motion of it's wings when flying is much like that of a Jay-bird— ⟨it's note— tah, tah, tah, tah tah, tah, tah, tah⟩

The White turkey of the black hills from information of a french lad who wintered with the Chien Indians [*EC: rara avis in terris!*] About the size of the common wild turkey the plumage perfectly white— this bird is booted as low as the toes—

Point of Obstn. No. 42.

[Lewis]   *Monday* September 17th 1804.

On the Lard. shore, one mile and a haf above the mouth of Corvus Creek observed equal Altitudes of ☉ with Sextant.—

	h	m	s		h	m	s
A. M.	7	46	49	P. M.	2	59	50
"		47	25		3	1	30
"		49	12	"		3	3

Altd. by sextant at the time of Observatn. 53° 17′ 45″

Observed meridian Altitude of ☉'s L. L. with Octant by the back Observation 87° 31′ 00″

✳ ✳ ✳

During the 1804–5 winter layover at Fort Mandan, the explorers had time to review their journals and notes and to prepare materials to be sent back to President Jefferson by means of a group of men selected to return downriver. In this miscellany of narrative and statistics, we find a detailed account of what Lewis expects to find farther upstream. Other travelers, mostly trappers, had been as far as the Mandan villages, but when spring came, Lewis and Clark would be setting out into wholly new territory.

Lewis's narrative not only demonstrates the care with which he gathered his intelligence—much of it told to him by Indians through interpreters—but also underlines the political importance of this first American visit to the newly acquired Louisiana Purchase.

The Missouri Tributaries

A s WE have only ascended the Missouri, a few miles above the Mouth of Knife river, the subsequent discription of this river, and it's subsidiary streams are taken altogether from Indian Information. the existence of these rivers, their connection with each other, and their relative positions with rispect to the Missouri, I conceive are entitled to some confidence. information has been obtained on this subject, in the course of the winter, from a number of individuals, questioned seperately and at different times. the information thus obtained has been carefully compared, and those points only, in which they generally agreed, have been retained, their distances they give, by days travel, which we have estimated at 25 miles pr. day.— [20]

20. At Fort Mandan both Lewis and Clark made up lists from Indian information giving tributaries and other points on the Missouri above the fort and on the Yellowstone. The present names of the streams are given in the pages immediately preceding these notes. Here the Indian words are given transliterations and translations as far as possible. The following are in Hidatsa (the word *awáaʰi*, "river," was their name for the Missouri River:
  E-pe,-Âh-zhan (*apée áaši*, "coiling creek")
  E-mâh-tark',-Ah'-zhah (*awáaʰi áaši*, "[Missouri] river creek")
  Ok-hah-,Âh-zhâh (*oxáati áaši*, "white creek")
  Meé,ah'-zah (*mí'i áaši*, "stone creek")
  Ah-mâh-tâh, ru-shush-sher (*awáaʰi arušaša*, "[Missouri] river forks")
  Mah-tush,-ah-zhah (*matóoki áaši*, "mussel shell creek")
  Mah-pah-pah, ah-zhah (*máapiwiri áaši*, "sun creek")
The remaining names are in Mandan (only part of them have been identified):
  Oke-tar-pas-ah-ha (*pasáŋh*, "creek"); the meaning of oke-tar is not known.
  War-rah-sah (*wᵈašuŋte*, "powder")

About fifteen miles above the mouth of Knife river, the *E-pe,-Âh-zhah*, or *Miry river* discharges itself on the N. Side.   it is but an inconsiderable stream as to width, but extends itself through level and open plains about 30 miles N. E. of it's entrance, taking it's rise in some small lakes, strongly impregnated with Glauber Salts.   not navigable.[21]

Ascending the Missouri about one hundred miles further, the *E-mâh-tark', Ah'-zhah* or Little Missouri discharges itself on the S. side.   about the width of Knife river.   takes it's rise in the Nothern extremity of the Blackhills.   and passes through a broken country with but little timber.   it passes near the turtle mountain in it's course to the Missouri.   it is said not to be navigable in consequence of it's rappidity and shoals.—

About 117 miles higher up, the *Ok-hah-Âh-zhâh*, or *White earth river*, discharges itself on the N. side.   it is said to be about the size of the Cannonball river; takes it's rise N. Westwardly from it's mouth in level open plains with the waters of the S. fork of the Saskashawin river, and passes through an open and level country generally without timber some timber on the borders of this stream.   it is navigable nearly to it's source, which is said not to be very distant, from the establishment of the N. West Company on the S. branch of the Saskashawin.   if this information be correct it is highly probable that a line drawn due West from the lake of the Woods, in conformity to our treaty with Great Britain; would intersect the waters of this river, if so the boundary of the United States would pass Red river between the entrance of the Assinniboin and Lake Winnipic, including those rivers almost entirely, and with them the whole of the British trading establishments on the red Lake, Red river and the Assinniboin.   should the portage between the Saskashawin and *White earth* river, prove not to be very distant or difficult, it is easy to conceive the superior advantages, which the Missouri offers as a rout to the Athabasca country, compared with that commonly traveled by the traders of Canada.—

About 3 miles above the mouth of *White Earth* river the Meé,-ah'-zah, or *Yellowstone river* discharges itself on the S. side.   this river is said to be nearly as large as the Missouri, but is more rappid.   it takes it's rise in the Rocky mountains, with the waters of a river on which the Spaniards reside; but whether this stream be the N. *river*, or the waters of the Gulph of Cali-

---

Le-ze-ke (*résik,* "tongue")

Ar-sar-ta (*áŋsexte,* "bighorn") [Moulton's note]

21. Clark's No. 3 breaks its duplication of Lewis's summary here and then ends after summarizing the area to the north of the Mandan-Hidatsa villages. From this point Clark's No. 1 follows Lewis's summary, but giving distances in leagues rather than miles. [Moulton's note]

fornia, our information dose not enable us to determine. from it's source it takes it's course for many miles through broken ranges of the Rocky mountains, principally broken, and stoney, and thickly timbered. the vallies said to be wide in many places and the lands fertile. after leaving the Rocky mountains it descends into a country more level, tho' still broken, fertile and well timbered. this discription of country continues as far down as the *Oke-tar-pas-ah-ha,* where the river enters an open level and fertile country through which it continues it's rout to the Missouri; even in this open country it possesses considerable bodies of well timbered land. there are no stream[s] worthy of notice which discharge themselves into this river on the N. side, the country between this river, and the Missouri being watered by the *Mussle shell* river. the yellow Stone river is navigable at all seasons of the year, for boats or perogues to the foot of the Rocky Mountains, near which place, it is said to be not more than 20 miles distant from the most southernly of the three forks of the Missouri, which last is also navigable to this point. if Indian information can be relied on, this river waters one of the fairest portions of Louisiana, a country not yet hunted, and abounding in animals of the fur kind. The bed of this river is formed of sand gravel and yellow rock. from the great rapidity of this stream after it enters the rocky mountains, it is said not be navigable. we are informed that there is a sufficiency of timber near the mouth of this river for the purpose of erecting a fortification, and the necessary buildings. in point of position, we have no hesitation in declaring our belief, of it's being one of the most eligible and necessary, that can be chosen on the Missouri, as well in a governmental point of view, as that of affording to our citizens the benefit of a most lucrative fur trade. this establishment might be made to hold in check the views of the British N. West Company on the fur-trade of the upper part of the Missouri, which we believe it is their intention to panopolize if in their power. They have for several years maintained a partial trade with the Indian nations on the Missouri near this place, over land from their establishment at the entrance of Mouse river on the Assinniboin, unlicenced by the Spanish government, then the sovereigns of the country. But since the U' States have acquired Louisiana, we are informed, that relying on the privilege extended to them by our treaty with Great Britain, they intend fixing a permanent establishment on the Missouri near the mouth of Knife river, in the course of the present summer. if this powerfull and ambitious company, are suffered uninterruptedly to prosecute their trade with the nations inhabiting the upper portion of the Missouri, and thus acquire an influence with those people; it is not difficult to conceive the obstructions, which they might hereafter through the medium of that influence, oppose to the will of our government, or the navigation of the Missouri.   whether the privileges extended to British subjects, under existing treaties with that power, will equally effect a territory not in our possession at the time those treaties were entered into, is not for me to determine; but it appears to me, that in this rispect Liouisiana is differently situated, from the other territory of the United States.—

* * *

Returning toward St. Louis, Clark and his detachment came down the Yellow-stone River and reached the Missouri on August 3. About a week later, on August 12, they met up with Lewis and his group. Clark learned of Lewis's dif-ficulty with the Blackfeet, during which two of the Indians were killed.

In this selection, Clark records the departure of John Colter, who requested per-mission to go back up into the mountains with a pair of trappers, Joseph Dickson and Forrest Hancock. Colter stayed in the Rocky Mountains until 1810, explor-ing and trapping; among his adventures was his famous capture by the Blackfoot Indians and his life-or-death footrace. The story of that escape was widely repeated in the West and was the basis for the classic short story "Mountain Medicine," by A. B. Guthrie, Jr.

John Colter Takes His Leave

Thursday August 15ᵗʰ 1806 (continued)
Mandans Vilg.

after assembling the Chiefs and Smokeing one pipe, I informed them that I still Spoke the Same words which we had Spoken to them when we first arived in their Country in the fall of 1804.   we then envited them to visit their great father the president of the U. States and to hear his own Councils and recieve his Gifts from his own hands as also See the popula-tion of a government which can at their pleasure protect and Secure you from all your enimies, and chastize all those who will shut their years to his Councils.   we now offer to take you at the expense of our Government and Send you back to your Country again with a considerable present in Merchendize which you will receive of your great Father.   I urged the necessity of their going on with us as it would be the means of hastening those Suppl[i]es of Merchindize which would be Sent to their Country

This and the following selection are from Reuben Gold Thwaites, ed., *The Original Jour-nals of the Lewis and Clark Expedition, 1804–1806,* 8 vols. (New York: Dodd, Mead and Co., 1904–5), 5:339–42 and 5:346–48.

and exchanged as before mentioned for a moderate price in Pelteries and furs &c.   the great chief of the Menetaras Spoke, he Said he wished to go down and see his great father very much, but that the Scioux were in the road and would most certainly kill him or any others who should go down   they were bad people and would not listen to any thing which was told them.   when he Saw us last we told him that we had made peace with all the nations below, Since that time the Seioux had killed 8 of their people and Stole a number of their horses.   he Said that he had opened his ears and followed our Councils, he had made peace with the Chyennes and rocky Mountains indians, and repieted the same objecctions as mentioned. that he went to war against none and was willing to recieve all nations as friends.   he Said that the Ricaras had Stolen from his people a number of horses at different times and his people had killed 2 Ricaras.   if the Sieoux were at peace with them and could be depended on he as also other Chiefs of the villages would be glad to go and See their great father, but as they were all afraid of the Sieoux they should not go down &c.

The Black Cat Chief of the Mandans Village on the North Side of the Missouri sent over and requested me to go over to his village which invertation I axcept^d and crossed over to his Village.   he had a parcel of corn about 12 bushels in a pile in his lodge.   he told me that his people had but little corn part of which they had given me.   after takeing a Smoke he informed me that as the Scioux were very troublesom and the road to his great father dangerous none of this village would go down with us.   I told the Cheifs and wariers of the village who were then present that we were anxious that some of the village Should go and See their great father and hear his good words & receve his *bountifull gifts* &c. and told them to pitch on Some Man on which they could rely on and Send him to see their Great father, they made the same objections which the Chief had done before.   a young man offered to go down, and they all agreed for him to go down   the charactor of this young man I knew as a bad one and made an objection as to his age and Chareckter   at this time Gibson who was with me informed me that this young man had Stole his knife and had it then in his possession,   this I informed the Chief and directed him to give up the knife   he delivered the knife with a very faint apology for his haveing it in his possession.   I then reproached those people for wishing to send such a man to See and hear the words of so great a man as their great father,   they hung their heads and said nothing for some time when the Cheif spoke and Said that they were afraid to Send any one for fear of their being killed by the Sieux. after smoking a pipe and relateing some passages I recrossed to our Camp. being informed by one of our enterpreters that the 2^d Chief of the Mandans comonly called the little crow[22] intended to accompany us down,   I took Charbono and walked to the Village to see this Chief and talk with him on the subject   he told me he had deturmined to go down, but wished to have a council first with his people which would be in the after part of the day. I smoked a pipe with the little Crow and returned to the boat. Colter one of our men expressed a desire to join Some trappers [*the two Illinois Men we met, & who now came down to us*] who offered to become shearers with [him] and furnish traps &c.   the offer [was] a very advantagious one, to him, his services could be dispenced with from this down and as we were disposed to be of service to any one of our party who had performed their duty as well as Colter had done,   we agreed to allow him the privilage provided no one of the party would ask or expect a Similar permission to which they all agreed that they wished Colter every suckcess and that as we did not wish any of them to Seperate untill we Should arive at St. Louis they would not apply or expect it &c.   The Maharha Chief brought us Some Corn, as did also the Chief of the little village of the Menetarras on mules of which they have Several.   [*bought from the Crow. Ind* *who get or Steal them from the Spaniards*]   The evening is cool and windy.   great number of the nativs of the different villages came to view us and exchange robes with our men for their Skins   we gave Jo Colter Some Small articles which we did not want and some powder & lead.   the party also gave him several articles which will be usefull to him on his expedittion.   This evening Charbono informed me that our back was scercely turned before a war party from the two menetarry villages followed on and attacked and killed the Snake Indians whome we had seen and in the engagement be- tween them and the Snake indians they had lost two men one of which was the Son of the principal Chief of the little village of the Menitarras.   that they had also went to war from the Menetarras and killed two Ricaras.   he further informed me that a missunderstanding had taken place between the Mandans & Minetarras and had very nearly come to blows about a woman, the Menitarres at length presented a pipe and a reconsilliation took place between them.   * * *

Lewis and Clark now take leave of the Mandan villages; in five weeks they will arrive in St. Louis. Still mindful of Jefferson's instructions to record the history and lore of the Indians they encounter, Clark writes down a story told to him by the Mandan chief who accompanies them back to civilization.

22. This is the chief Kagohanis, or Little Raven. [Thwaites's note]

How the Mandans Came into the World

Monday 18th *August* 1806

moderate rain last night, the wind of this morning from the S.E. as to cause the water to be so rough that we could not proceed on untill 8 a.m. at which time it fell a little & we proceeded on tho' the waves were yet high and the wind Strong. Saw Several Indians on either side of the river. at 9 A.M. I saw an Indian running down the beech and app^d to be anxious to Speak to us I derected the Canoes to land. this Indian proved to be the brother of the Chief we had on board and came down from his Camp at no great distance to take his leave of his brother. the Chief gave him a par of Legins and took an effectunate leave of his brother and we procedeed on haveing previously sent on 2 canoes with hunters to kill some meat at 2 P.M. we overtook the Canoe hunters, they had killed three deer which was divided and we halted and cooked some dinner on the Sandbar. wind still high and from the same point. The Chief pointed out Several places where he Said his nation formerly lived and related some extroadinary Stories of their tredition. after Dinner we proceeded on to a point on the NE. side opposit the remains of an old Mandan village a little below the enterance of *Chiss-che-tor* [Heart] River and the place we Encamped as we assended this river 20th of October 1804 haveing come 40 miles to day. after landing which was a little before night the hunters run out into the bottom and Killed four deer. The winds blew hard from the S.E. all day which retarded our progress very much after the fires were made I set my self down with the bigwhite man Chiefe and made a number of enquiries into the tredition of his nation as well as the time of their inhabiting the number of villages the remains of which we see on different parts of the river, as also the cause of their evacuation. he told me his nation first came out of the ground where they had a great village. a grape vine grew down through the Earth to their village and they Saw light Some of their people assended by the grape vine upon the earth, and saw Buffalow and every kind of animal also Grapes plumbs &c. they gathered some grapes & took down the vine to the village, and they tasted and found them good, and deturmined to go up and live upon earth, and great numbers climbed the vine and got upon earth men womin and children.   at length a large big bellied woman in climbing broke the vine and fell and all that were left in the village below has remained there ever since (The Mandans beleive when they die that they return to this village)   Those who were left on earth made a village on the river below and were very noumerous &c.   he said that he was born [*about 40 years*] [ago] in the Village Opposit to our camp and at that time his nation inhabited 7 villages as large as that and were full of people,   the Sieoux and Smallpox killed the greater part of them and made them so weak that all that were left only made two small villages when collected, which were built near the old Ricaras village above.   their troubles with the Seeoux & Pawnees or Ricaras Compelled them to move and build a village where they now live.   [*Qu: The Village of the Mandans on the North East side was formed of two villages* [who] *formerly lived on the East side opposite the 7. War & Small pox reduced them to one vill which crossed & joined the 2 vill*[s] *near ricaras haveing first settled (before the 7 came into 2) on East side   Then they moved with the 2 to where they now live, so that the vill*[s] *originally was of 9 vill*[s] *(See Note)*]   he Said that the Menitarras Came out of the water to the East and came to this country and built a village near the mandans from whome they got corn beens &c.   they were very noumerous and resided in one village a little above this place on the opposit side.   they quarreled about a buffalow, and two bands left the village and went into the plains, (those two bands are now known bye the title Pounch, and Crow Indians.   the ballance of the Menetaras moved their village to where it now Stands where they have lived ever Since

William Cullen Bryant
1794-1878

▬

1817: "Thanatopsis"
1832: *Collected Poems*
1833: "The Prairies"

▬

AMERICAN *writers, confronted with a wilderness of unprecedented vastness, often based their images on religious metaphors grounded in doctrines that dictated the relationship of the people to the land, the people's role among the natives living in the land, and their "mission" as newly arrived people. In one such metaphor, the American wilderness is seen as a latter-day Eden; it is a garden in which the people have dominion and by which they will be fed and clothed and sheltered if they remain faithful to their God. From a second viewpoint, the West is a Promised Land in which it is the destiny of the new people to work and to prosper; they will subdue the primitive and cultivate the soil and build the cities. And to the more pessimistic pioneers, or to those who stayed back East, the West represented Satan's own wilderness, an unholy place to which humans were sent to be tempted, tested, and punished.*

William Cullen Bryant did not regard poetry as his principal occupation, yet he is acknowledged as one of our first national poets of note. Nor was Bryant a westerner. However, he belonged to a certain group of widely traveled and well-educated new Americans, observers who were qualified to compare the American West with other regions. His literary background and his fresh perspective give us a valuable extension of our own perspective of the prairie country as it looked to people during the period of American emergence.

In 1832, Bryant visited his brothers in Illinois, where he first saw the unbroken and seemingly endless oceans of grass. To commemorate their effect on him, he wrote "The Prairies." Educated in European and ancient literature, and being a conservatively religious man, Bryant ornamented his pastoral Promised Land metaphor with allusions to the classics, with a sense of mythic history, and with obviously romantic imagery.

The Prairies

These are the gardens of the Desert, these
The unshorn fields, boundless and beautiful,
For which the speech of England has no name—
The Prairies. I behold them for the first,
And my heart swells, while the dilated sight
Takes in the encircling vastness. Lo! they stretch,
In airy undulations, far away,
As if the ocean, in his gentlest swell,
Stood still, with all his rounded billows fixed,
And motionless forever.—Motionless?—
No—they are all unchained again. The clouds
Sweep over with their shadows, and, beneath,
The surface rolls and fluctuates to the eye;
Dark hollows seem to glide along and chase
The sunny ridges. Breezes of the South!
Who toss the golden and the flame-like flowers,
And pass the prairie-hawk that, poised on high,
Flaps his broad wings, yet moves not—ye have played
Among the palms of Mexico and vines
Of Texas, and have crisped the limpid brooks
That from the fountains of Sonora glide
Into the calm Pacific—have ye fanned
A nobler or a lovelier scene than this?
Man hath no power in all this glorious work:
The hand that built the firmament hath heaved
And smoothed these verdant swells, and sown their slopes
With herbage, planted them with island groves,
And hedged them round with forests. Fitting floor
For this magnificent temple of the sky—
With flowers whose glory and whose multitude

From William Cullen Bryant, *The Poetical Works of William Cullen Bryant* (New York: D. Appleton and Co., 1903), pp. 130–33.

Rival the constellations! The great heavens
Seem to stoop down upon the scene in love,—
A nearer vault, and of a tenderer blue,
Than that which bends above our eastern hills.

As o'er the verdant waste I guide my steed,
Among the high rank grass that sweeps his sides
The hollow beating of his footstep seems
A sacrilegious sound. I think of those
Upon whose rest he tramples. Are they here—
The dead of other days?—and did the dust
Of these fair solitudes once stir with life
And burn with passion? Let the mighty mounds
That overlook the rivers, or that rise
In the dim forest crowded with old oaks,
Answer. A race, that long has passed away,
Built them;—a disciplined and populous race
Heaped, with long toil, the earth, while yet the Greek
Was hewing the Pentelicus[1] to forms
Of symmetry, and rearing on its rock
The glittering Parthenon. These ample fields
Nourished their harvests, here their herds were fed,
When haply by their stalls the bison lowed,
And bowed his manèd shoulder to the yoke.
All day this desert murmured with their toils,
Till twilight blushed, and lovers walked, and wooed
In a forgotten language, and old tunes,
From instruments of unremembered form,
Gave the soft winds a voice. The red man came—
The roaming hunter tribes, warlike and fierce,
And the mound-builders vanished from the earth.
The solitude of centuries untold
Has settled where they dwelt. The prairie-wolf
Hunts in their meadows, and his fresh-dug den
Yawns by my path. The gopher mines the ground
Where stood their swarming cities. All is gone;
All—save the piles of earth that hold their bones,

---

1. Pentelicus—a mountain in Greece, from which was quarried the marble for Athenian buildings such as the Parthenon.

The platforms where they worshipped unknown gods,
The barriers which they builded from the soil
To keep the foe at bay—till o'er the walls
The wild beleaguerers broke, and, one by one,
The strongholds of the plain were forced, and heaped
With corpses. The brown vultures of the wood
Flocked to those vast uncovered sepulchres,
And sat unscared and silent at their feast.
Haply some solitary fugitive,
Lurking in marsh and forest, till the sense
Of desolation and of fear became
Bitterer than death, yielded himself to die.
Man's better nature triumphed then. Kind words
Welcomed and soothed him; the rude conquerors
Seated the captive with their chiefs; he chose
A bride among their maidens, and at length
Seemed to forget—yet ne'er forgot—the wife
Of his first love, and her sweet little ones,
Butchered, amid their shrieks, with all his race.

Thus change the forms of being. Thus arise
Races of living things, glorious in strength,
And perish, as the quickening breath of God
Fills them, or is withdrawn. The red man, too,
Has left the blooming wilds he ranged so long,
And, nearer to the Rocky Mountains, sought
A wilder hunting-ground. The beaver builds
No longer by these streams, but far away,
On waters whose blue surface ne'er gave back
The white man's face—among Missouri's springs,
And pools whose issues swell the Oregon—[2]
He rears his little Venice. In these plains
The bison feeds no more. Twice twenty leagues
Beyond remotest smoke of hunter's camp,
Roams the majestic brute, in herds that shake
The earth with thundering steps—yet here I meet
His ancient footprints stamped beside the pool.

2. The Columbia River.

Still this great solitude is quick with life.
Myriads of insects, gaudy as the flowers
They flutter over, gentle quadrupeds,
And birds, that scarce have learned the fear of man,
Are here, and sliding reptiles of the ground,
Startlingly beautiful. The graceful deer
Bounds to the wood at my approach. The bee,
A more adventurous colonist than man,
With whom he came across the eastern deep,
Fills the savannas with his murmurings,
And hides his sweets, as in the golden age,
Within the hollow oak. I listen long
To his domestic hum, and think I hear
The sound of that advancing multitude
Which soon shall fill these deserts. From the ground
Comes up the laugh of children, the soft voice
Of maidens, and the sweet and solemn hymn
Of Sabbath worshippers. The low of herds
Blends with the rustling of the heavy grain
Over the dark brown furrows. All at once
A fresher wind sweeps by, and breaks my dream,
And I am in the wilderness alone.

Jedediah S. Smith
1799-1831

███

1977: *The Southwest Expedition of Jedediah S. Smith:*
His Personal Account of the
Journey to California, 1826–1827

███

WHEN NOVELISTS *portray the extraordinary daring and endurance of the American mountain man, the characterizations seem to be exaggerations. In the case of Jedediah Smith, such a portrayal might be an understatement. As a leader, entrepreneur, trader, and fighter, Smith is the epitome of the fur trappers and explorers who opened the Rocky Mountain West to American settlement. In 1822, he accompanied William H. Ashley's first expedition up the Missouri. In the following year he was with Ashley's second party when it was attacked by the Arikara Indians. Surviving that near massacre, Smith, in command of yet another force, set out overland to explore the Black Hills. On this trip he was seized in the jaws of a large grizzly bear and badly mauled. Smith rediscovered South Pass in the wilds of Wyoming, thus opening the way for wagons to cross the Rocky Mountain barrier, and he explored the unknown territory between the Salt Lake and southern California. He and his men faced death on an almost daily basis, whether from freezing, thirst, wild animals, starvation, accident, Indians, or Spanish soldiers.*

An example of one of Smith's experiences is found in the following paragraph from the journal of his "companyero" James Clyman (1792–1881), who described the aftermath of the grizzly attack.

I asked the captain [Smith, who had been heading the column when the bear seized him] what was best, he said one or two [of you go] for water and if you have a needle and thread git it out and sew up my wounds around my head which was bleeding freely. I got a pair of scissors and cut off his hair and then began my first job of dressing wounds. Upon examination I [saw that] the bear had taken nearly all of his head in his capacious mouth close to his left eye on one side and close to his right ear on the other and laid the skull bare to near the crown of the head leaving a white streak where his teeth passed. One of his ears was torn from his head out to the outer rim. After stitching on the other wounds in the best way I was capable and according to the captain's directions, the ear being the last, I told him I could do nothing for his ear. "Oh you must try to stitch it up some way or other," said he. Then I put in my needle stitching it through and through and over and over laying the lacerated parts together as nice as I could with my hands.[1]

Smith also kept journals, which contain invaluable material for historians and novelists alike. Some of his journals, in fact, may still lie undiscovered somewhere; one was not found until 1967, when a historian, George R. Brooks, was given a cardboard box containing some old manuscripts. One of the manuscripts turned out to be by Jedediah Smith. It was the record of his 1826 expedition to California—the firsthand account of the first American to travel that route.

In 1831, while scouting out ahead of a wagon train on the Santa Fe trail, Smith was killed, probably by Comanches. But in spite of his early death—he was barely thirty-two—Jedediah Smith left future generations a remarkably rich store of information about the life of fur traders and trappers in the Rocky Mountains.

———

The Great Salt Lake

[June 20, 1827]   NE 20 miles along a valley sandy as usual and just at night found water. In this part of the plain almost all the high hills have snow on their tops. But for these snowy Peaks the country would be utterly impassible as they furnish almost the only grass or water of this unhospitable land. They are to this plain like the islands of the Ocean. Rising but a short distance from the sandy base the snowy region commences which is an evidence of the great elevation of this plain.

From Jedediah S. Smith, *The Southwest Expedition of Jedediah S. Smith, 1826–1827*, ed. George R. Brooks (1977; reprint, Lincoln: University of Nebraska Press, 1989), pp. 184–97. Copyright © 1989 by the University of Nebraska Press.

1. James Clyman, "Colonel James Clyman's Narrative of 1823–24," in *James Clyman, American Frontiersman, 1792–1881*, ed. Charles L. Camp (Cleveland: Arthur H. Clark Co., 1928), p. 25.

[The]re after encamping some Indians came to me. They appeared verry friendly. These as well as those last mentioned I supposed were somewhat acquainted with whites as I saw among them some Iron arrow points and some Beads. They gave me some squirrels and in return I gave them presents of such little things as I had after which they went to their camp and we our rest.

21st   25 miles North. Early this morning the indians that were at the camp last night returned and with them several others. They seemed to have come out of mere curiosity and as I was ready for starting they accompanied me a short distance. Some of them I presume had never before seen a white man and as they were handling and examining almost every thing I fired off my gun as one of them was fingering about the double triggers. At the sound some fell flat on the ground and some sought safety in flight. The indian who had hold of the gun alone stood still although he appeared at first thunder struck yet on finding that he was not hurt he called out to his companions to return. I endeavored to learn from those indians by signs something in relation to the distance and course to the Salt Lake But from them I could get no satisfaction whatever for instead of answering my signs they would imitate them as nearly as possible. After vexing myself for some time with those children of nature I left them and continued on my way. All the indians I had seen since leaving the Lake had been the same unintelligent kind of beings. Nearly naked having at most a scanty robe formed from the skin of the hare peculiar to this plain which is cut into narrow strips and interwoven with a kind of twine or cord made apparently from wild flax or hemp. They form a connecting link between the animal and intelectual creation and quite in keeping with the country in which they are located. In the course of the day I passed water several times. It came out from a range of hills on the west on the top of which was some snow. I encamped on the bank of a Salt Lake. The water was verry salt and a good deal of salt was formed along the beach. In crossing a mirey place just before encamping one of my horses was mired. After some considerable exertion I found it impossible to get him out   I therefore killed him and took a quarter of his flesh which was a seasonable replenishment for our stock of provision as the little I took of the horse I killed last was at that time exhausted.

22nd June 1827   North 25 Miles. My course was parallel with a chain of hills on the west on the tops of which was some snow and from which ran a creek to the north east. On this creek I encamped. The Country in the vicinity so much resembled that on the south side of the Salt Lake that for a while I was induced to believe that I was near that place. During the day I saw a good many Antelope but could not kill any. I however killed 2 hares which when cooked at night we found much better than horse meat.

June 23d   N E 35 Miles. Moving on in the morning I kept down the creek on which we had encamped until it was lost in a small Lake. We then filled our horns and continued on our course, passing some brackish as well as some verry salt springs and leaving on the north of the latter part of the days travel a considerable Salt Plain. Just before night I found water that was drinkable but continued on in hopes of find better and was obliged to encamp without any.

June 24th   N E 40 Miles   I started verry early in hopes of soon finding water. But ascending a high point of a hill I could discover nothing but sandy plains or dry Rocky hills with the Exception of a snowy mountain off to the N E at the distance of 50 or 60 Miles. When I came down I durst not tell my men of the desolate prospect ahead. but framed my story so as to discourage them as little as possible. I told them I saw something black at a distance near which no doubt we would find water. While I had been up on the one of the horses gave out and had been left a short distance behind. I sent the men back to take the best of his flesh for our supply was again nearly exhausted whilst I would push forward in search of water. I went on a short distance and waited until they came up. They were much discouraged with the gloomy prospect but I said all I could to enliven their hopes and told them in all probability we would soon find water. But the view ahead was almost hopeless. With our best exertion we pushed forward walking as we had been for a long time over the soft sand. That kind of traveling is verry tiresome to men in good health who can eat when and what they choose and drink as often as they desire. and to us worn down with hunger and fatigue and burning with thirst increased by the blazing sands it was almost insurportable. At about 4 O Clock we were obliged to stop on the side of a sand hill under the shade of a small Cedar. We dug holes in the sand and laid down in them for the purpose of cooling our heated bodies. After resting about an hour we resumed our wearysome journey and traveled until 10 O Clock at night when we laid down to take a little repose. Previous to this and a short time after sun down I saw several turtle doves and as I did not recollect of ever having seen them more than 2 or 3 miles from water I spent more than an hour in looking for water but it was in vain. Our sleep was not repose for tormented nature made us dream of things we had not and for the want of which it then seemed possible and even probable we might perish in the desert unheard of and unpitied. In those moments how trifling were all those things that hold such an absolute sway over the busy and the prosperous world. My dreams were not of Gold or ambitious honors but of my distant quiet home of murmuring brooks of cooling cascades. After a short rest we continued our march and traveled all night. The murmur of falling waters still sounding in our ears and the apprehension that we might never live to hear that sound in reality weighed heavily uppon us.

June 25th   When morning came it saw us in the same unhappy situa- tion pursuing our journey over the desolate waste now gleming in the sun and more insuportably tormenting than it had been during the night. At 10 O Clock Robert Evans laid down in the plain under the shade of a small cedar being able to proceed no further. The Mountain of which I have before spoken was apparently not far off and we left him and proceeded onward in the hope of finding water in time to return with some in season to save his life. After traveling about three Miles we came to the foot of the Mt and then to our inexpressible joy we found water. Goble plunged into it at once and I could hardly wait to bath my burning forehead be- fore I was pouring it down regardless of the consequences. Just before we arrived at the spring I saw two indians traveling in the direction in which Evans was left and soon after the report of two guns was heard in quick succession. This considerably increased our apprehension for his safety but shortly after a smoke was seen back on the trail and I took a small kettle of water and some meat and going back found him safe. he had not seen the indians and had discharged his gun to direct me where he lay and for the same purpose had raised a smoke. He was indeed far gone being scarcely able to speak. When I came the first question he asked me was have you any water! I told him I had plenty and handed the kettle which would hold 6 or 7 quarts in which there was some meat mixed with the water. O says he why did you bring the meat and putting the kettle to his mouth he did not take it away untile he had drank all the water of which there was at least 4 or 5 quarts and then asked me why I had not brought more. This however revived him so much that he was able to go on to the spring. I cut the horse meat and spread it out to dry and determined to remain for the rest of the day that we might repose our wearied and emaciated bodies. I have at dif- ferent times suffered all the extremes of hunger and thirst. Hard as it is to bear for succesive days the knawings of hunger yet it is light in comparison to the agony of burning thirst, and [o]n the other hand I have observed that a man reduced by hunger is some days in recovering his strength. A man equally reduced by thirst seems renovated almost instantaneneously. Hunger can be endured more than twice as long as thirst. To some it may appear surprising that a man who has been for several days without eating has a most incessant desire to drink and although he can drink but a little at a time yet he wants it much oftener than in ordinary circumstances. In the course of the day several indians showed themselves on the high points of the hills but would not come to my camp.

26th June N 10 miles along a valley and encamped at some brackish water having passed during the day several salt springs and one Indian Lodge. The lodge was occupied by 2 indians one squaw and 2 children. They were somewhat alarmed but friendly and when we made signs to them of being hungry they cheerfully divided with us some antelope meat. They spoke like the snake Indians and by enquiry I found they were Panakhies from Lewis's River. They had some pieces of Buffalo Robes and told me that a few days travel to the North E. Buffalo were plenty. Although they knew the shoshones I could not learn any thing from them in relation to the Salt Lake. In the evening I discovered from a high piece of ground what appeared to be a large body of water.

June 27th North 10 Miles along a valley in which were many salt springs. Coming to the point of the ridge which formed the Eastern boundary of the valley I saw an expanse of water Extending far to the North and East. The Salt Lake a joyful sight was spread before us. Is it possible said the companions of my sufferings that we are so near the end of our troubles. For myself I durst scarcely believe that it was really the Big Salt Lake that I saw. It was indeed a most cheering view for although we were some distance from the depo yet we knew we would soon be in a country where we would find game and water which were to us objects of the greatest importance and those which would contribute more than any others to our comfort and happiness. Those who may chance to read this at a distance from the scene may perhaps be surprised that the sight of this lake surrounded by a wilderness of more than 2000 miles diameter excited in me these feelings known to the traveler who after long and perilous journeying comes again in view of his home. But so it was with me for I had traveled so much in the vicinity of the Salt Lake that it had become my home of the wilderness. After coming in view of the lake I traveled East keeping nearly paralel with the shore of the lake. At about 25 miles from my last encampment I found a spring of fresh water and encamped. The water during the day had been generally Salt. I saw several antelope but could not get a shot at them.

28th East 20 miles traveling nearly parallel with the shore of the Lake. When I got within a mile of the outlet of the Uta Lake which comes in from the south East I found the ground which is thick covered with flags and Bulrushes overflowed to a considerable distance from the channel and before I got to the current the water had increased to between 2 & 3 feet and the cain grass and Bulrushes were extremely thick. The channel was deep and as the river was high was of course rapid and about 60 yards wide. As I would have to wade a long distance should I attempt to return before I would find dry land I determined to make a raft and for this purpose cut a quantity of Cain Grass for of this material there was no want. The grass I tied into Bundles and attaching them together soon formed a raft sufficiently strong to bear my things. In the first place I swam and lead my horse over the mule following to the opposite bank which was also overflowed. I then returned and attaching a cord to the raft and holding the end in my mouth I swam before the raft while the two men swam behind. Unfortunately neither of my men were good swimmers and the current being strong we were swept down a considerable distance and it was with great difficulty that I was enabled to reach the shore as I was verry much strangled. When I got to the shore I put my things on the mule and horse and endeavored to go out to dry land but the animals mired and I was obliged to leave my things in the water for the night and wade out to the dry land. We made a fire of sedge and after eating a little horse flesh we laid down to rest.

29th 15 Miles North Early in the morning I brought my things out from the water and spread them out to dry. We were verry weak and worn down with suffering and fatigue but we thought ourselves near the termination of our troubles for it was not more than four days travel to the place where we expected to find my partners. At 10 O Clock we moved onward and after traveling 15 miles encamped. Just before encamping I got a shot at a Bear and wounded him badly but did not kill him. At supper we ate the last of our horse meat and talked a little of the probability of our suffering being soon at an end. I say we talked a little for men suffering from hunger never talk much but rather bear their sorrows in moody silence which is much preferable to fruitless compaint.

30th North 15 miles. I Started early and as Deer were tolerably plenty I went on ahead and about 8 O Clock got a shot at a Deer. he ran off I followed him and found a good deal of blood and told the men to stop while I should look for him. I soon found him laying in a thicket. As he appeared nearly dead I went up to him took hold of his horns when he sprang up and ran off. I was vexed at myself for not shooting him again when it was in my power and my men were quite discouraged. However I followed on and in a short time found him again. I then made sure of him by cutting his ham strings It was a fine fat Buck and it was not long before we struck up a fire and had some of his meat cooking. We then employed ourselves most pleasantly in eating for about two hours and for the time being forgot that we were not the happiest people in the world or at least thought but of our feast that was eaten with a relish unknown to a palace. So much do we make our estimation of happiness by a contrast with our situation that we were as much pleased and as well satisfied with our fat venison on the bank of the Salt Lake as we would have been in the possession of all the Luxuries and enjoyments of civilized life in other circumstances. These things may perhaps appear trifling to most readers but let any one of them travel over the same plain as I did and they will consider the killing of a buck a great achievement and certainly a verry useful one. After finishing our repast the meat of the Deer was cut and dried over the fire.

July 1st   25 miles North along the shore of the Lake. Nothing material occured.

2nd   20 Miles North East made our way to the Cache. But just before arriving there I saw some indians on the opposite side of a creek. It was hardly worth while as I thought to be any wise careful so I went directly to them and found as near as I could judge by what I knew of the language to be a band of the snakes. I learned from them that the whites as they term our parties were all assembled at the little Lake a distance of about 25 miles. There was in this camp about 200 Lodges of indians and as the[y] were on their way to the rendezvous I encamped with them.

3d   I hired a horse and a guide and at three O Clock arrived at the rendez-vous   My arrival caused a considerable bustle in camp for myself and party had been given up as lost. A small Cannon brought up from St Louis was loaded and fired for a salute.

Walt Whitman
1819-92

—

WALT WHITMAN'S *imagination, like his artistic ambition, was fired by the epic possibilities inherent in America's quick and turbulent history. In "Passage to India," written almost ten years before Whitman saw the West, he described the Americans as a God-chosen race, surmounting all obstacles on their headlong migration to the Pacific. His epic catalogue of natural barriers included the Platte River, the Laramie plains, the Wind River and Wasatch mountains, Monument Mountain, Eagle's Nest, the Sierra Nevada, and the Humboldt Range. In "Song of Myself," Whitman adopted the persona of an Alamo martyr, one of the buckskin warriors who were the "glory of the race of rangers."*

"Pioneers! O Pioneers!" is a later poem, written after Whitman's brief visit to the West. On September 10, 1879, he left New Jersey and went by way of St. Louis through Kansas and into Colorado as far as South Park. Retracing the same basic route in reverse, he arrived in Philadelphia on January 5, 1880. Although Whitman's western experience was very limited, his poem still captures the spirit of the restless westward movement. He saw a vigorous new race of people emerging from a new land. In the style of the classic epic poets, he catalogued their tools, weapons, places, trades, and accomplishments; in lofty-sounding but distinctly "American" epic language, Whitman immortalized the sense of movement and Manifest Destiny.

—

Pioneers! O Pioneers!

Come my tan-faced children,
Follow well in order, get your weapons ready,
Have you your pistols? have you your sharp-edged axes?
    Pioneers! O pioneers!

For we cannot tarry here,
We must march my darlings, we must bear the brunt of danger
We the youthful sinewy races, all the rest on us depend,
    Pioneers! O pioneers!

O you youths, Western youths,
So impatient, full of action, full of manly pride and friendship,
Plain I see you Western youths, see you tramping with the
    foremost,
    Pioneers! O pioneers!

Have the elder races halted?
Do they droop and end their lesson, wearied over there beyond
    the seas?
We take up the task eternal, and the burden and the lesson,
    Pioneers! O pioneers!

All the past we leave behind,
We debouch upon a newer mightier world, varied world,
Fresh and strong the world we seize, world of labor and the
    march,
    Pioneers! O pioneers!

We detachments steady throwing,
Down the edges, through the passes, up the mountains steep,

From Walt Whitman, *Leaves of Grass*, vol. 1 (New York: G. P. Putnam's Sons, 1902), pp. 279–84.

Conquering, holding, daring, venturing as we go the unknown
    ways,
    Pioneers! O pioneers!

We primeval forests felling,
We the rivers stemming, vexing we and piercing deep the mines
    within,
We the surface broad surveying, we the virgin soil upheaving,
    Pioneers! O pioneers!

Colorado men are we,
From the peaks gigantic, from the great sierras and the high
    plateaus,
From the mine and from the gully, from the hunting trail we
    come,
    Pioneers! O pioneers!

From Nebraska, from Arkansas,
Central inland race are we, from Missouri, with the continental
    blood intervein'd,
All the hands of comrades clasping, all the Southern, all the
    Northern,
    Pioneers! O pioneers!

O resistless restless race!
O beloved race in all! O my breast aches with tender love for all!
O I mourn and yet exult, I am rapt with love for all,
    Pioneers! O pioneers!

Raise the mighty mother mistress,
Waving high the delicate mistress, over all the starry mistress,
    (bend your heads all,)
Raise the fang'd and warlike mistress, stern, impassive, weapon'd
    mistress,
    Pioneers! O pioneers!

See my children, resolute children,
By those swarms upon our rear we must never yield or falter,
Ages back in ghostly millions frowning there behind us urging,
    Pioneers! O pioneers!

On and on the compact ranks,
With accessions ever waiting, with the places of the dead quickly
　　　fill'd,
Through the battle, through defeat, moving yet and never
　　　stopping,
　　Pioneers! O pioneers!

O to die advancing on!
Are there some of us to droop and die? has the hour come?
Then upon the march we fittest die, soon and sure the gap is
　　　fill'd,
　　Pioneers! O pioneers!

All the pulses of the world,
Falling in they beat for us, with the Western movement beat,
Holding single or together, steady moving to the front, all for us,
　　Pioneers! O pioneers!

Life's involv'd and varied pageants,
All the forms and shows, all the workmen at their work,
All the seamen and the landsmen, all the masters with their
　　　slaves,
　　Pioneers! O pioneers!

All the hapless silent lovers,
All the prisoners in the prisons, all the righteous and the wicked,
All the joyous, all the sorrowing, all the living, all the dying,
　　Pioneers! O pioneers!

I too with my soul and body,
We, a curious trio, picking, wandering on our way,
Through these shores amid the shadows, with the apparitions
　　　pressing,
　　Pioneers! O pioneers!

Lo, the darting bowling orb!
Lo, the brother orbs around, all the clustering suns and planets,
All the dazzling days, all the mystic nights with dreams,
　　Pioneers! O pioneers!

These are of us, they are with us,
All for primal needed work, while the followers there in embryo
      wait behind,
We to-day's procession heading, we the route for travel clearing,
      Pioneers! O pioneers!

O you daughters of the West!
O you young and elder daughters! O you mothers and you
      wives!
Never must you be divided, in our ranks you move united,
      Pioneers! O pioneers!

Minstrels latent on the prairies!
(Shrouded bards of other lands, you may rest, you have done
      your work,)
Soon I hear you coming warbling, soon you rise and tramp
      amid us,
      Pioneers! O pioneers!

Not for delectations sweet,
Not the cushion and the slipper, not the peaceful and the
      studious
Not the riches safe and palling, not for us the tame enjoyment,
      Pioneers! O pioneers!

Do the feasters gluttonous feast?
Do the corpulent sleepers sleep? have they lock'd and bolted
      doors?
Still be ours the diet hard, and the blanket on the ground,
      Pioneers! O pioneers!

Has the night descended?
Was the road of late so toilsome? did we stop discouraged
      nodding on our way?
Yet a passing hour I yield you in your tracks to pause oblivious,
      Pioneers! O pioneers!

Till with sound of trumpet,
Far, far off the daybreak call—hark! how loud and clear I hear it
      wind,
Swift! to the head of the army!—swift! spring to your places,
      Pioneers! O pioneers!

PART 2

The Mythopoeic Period

1833-89

Introduction

—

mythos (mi´thos): the beliefs and social values, expressed through the
arts, which reflect the character and identity of a race of people

✳

mythopoeia (mith-uh-pe´-uh): the invention and expression of a new
system of values and beliefs; an artistic reaction to new experiences
which do not fit traditional frames of thought and/or behavior
(*poiein,* to create)

—

Where the Storied West Begins

THE SMOKE of steamboats churning along the upper Missouri and
the rumble of the first wagon wheels crossing South Pass signaled
the coming of the settlement generation. This was the generation
that built roads where mountain men had walked and towns where Indian
lodges had stood. The members of this generation saw the West as the
home of a new culture; they were westerners, not colonists of the seaboard
United States, and they quickly began to establish their own identity, their
own histories, and their own aspirations and standards.

It took slightly less than fifty years for the West's new civilization to
form its most characteristic myths; but before that new era could come into
being, the old era of nomadic Indians and wild mountain men had to come
to an end. The mountain men were already writing the last chapter to their
own way of life. The seemingly simple event of wagons being taken across
the Rockies to rendezvous in 1830 meant that settlers could now go where
only the Indians and mountain men had gone before. On the Missouri,
the early traders and explorers had found the Mandan Indians to be hospitable, and had enjoyed the "free livin'" among them. But in 1837 smallpox
struck the tribes of the Upper Missouri, with disastrous consequences for
the Mandans and other tribes of the region.

The 1830s also saw the beginnings of public education in the West, a sure sign that civilization was on its way. And the United States reelected, for a second term, a legendary fighter and frontiersman as president; Andrew Jackson seemed to be the embodiment of western beliefs in political equality and in equal opportunity. Frontier values had gained public attention, and Americans began to realize that the American identity, the American character, was being reformed and redefined out there in the Far West.

On came the Americans, opening up the country, bringing in the new society. One of the favorite western myths tells of pioneers in wagon trains moving unceasingly westward, people following their Manifest Destiny, stern-looking men and women who bravely faced Indians, deserts, mountain passes, and swollen rivers. Their values were faith, honesty, fortitude, and free enterprise. Theirs was the myth of the Oregon Trail, made possible by the opening of a westward route over South Pass, a way across the Rocky Mountains. Although Robert Stuart and his Astorians had discovered South Pass in 1812, it remained unknown and had to be rediscovered by Jedediah Smith in 1824. Captain B.L.E. Bonneville took wagons through in 1832, and in 1836 Eliza Spalding and Narcissa Whitman became the first American women to cross South Pass. John Bedwell brought the first full-scale emigrant wagon train in 1841; eventually, an estimated 150,000 people had made the long trek to Utah, California, and Oregon.

The image of the United States Cavalry riding against the "hostiles" was also created in the period from the 1830s through the 1880s. The battles were many and varied, of course, with the most commonly portrayed ones being against the Sioux. Those troubles started in 1854. In 1876 the Sioux and allied tribes had their moment of triumph at the Little Big Horn River, but when the smoke cleared at Wounded Knee in 1890, the time of the fighting Sioux was over. Wounded Knee was the final episode in four decades of Indian wars, but the myth would go on.

This was the gold rush time too. The prospector with his long-handled shovel and burro became a familiar image starting with the forty-niner, on his way to see if he could find some easy gold in California. Right behind him came the gamblers, the saloon girls, the whiskey merchants, the storekeepers, and the land lawyers—all of them urging the forty-niner to hurry up with that gold.

The Homestead Act, chief among many attempts by the government to populate the West, was passed by Congress in 1862, and suddenly the country had a subculture of people living in sod huts and plowing up the prairies. They fought the drought and locusts, the Indians and land crooks, the blizzards and loneliness. Some were the same people who had hired mountain men to guide them across the mountains, who had looked for gold in California, and who had come at last to the Promised Land of the Great Plains. Or so the myth says.

The cowboy, that indelible western symbol frequently declared extinct by eastern journalists, had his mythic heyday now too. Many cowboys were ranch hands, but it was the trail-drive cowboy who became the real-life basis of the mythic horseman—young, brave, recklessly independent, and chivalrous. These cowboys got their start through such entrepreneurs as Joseph McCoy. In 1867, McCoy observed that the new transcontinental railroad was going to go straight through a little place in Kansas called Abilene. So he bought Abilene and advertised for Texas cattle, f.o.b. Kansas; the herds beat a path to his door, a path called the Chisholm Trail. Soon there were other trails going north out of Texas and one, the legendary Goodnight-Loving, heading to New Mexico. Along those trails came the cowboys.

Abilene and other towns of the cattle industry gave rise to a body of stories centered on variations of the sheriff-gunfighter myth. This myth is sprinkled with town names like Dodge City, Ogallala, and Deadwood, and names of places where Col. Colt and Judge Lynch settled local disputes— places like the O.K. Corral, Lincoln County, and Johnson County. Heroes in the myth were named Garrett, Holliday, James, Masterson, Hickok, Earp, and the Kid.

The New Myth-Makers

BETWEEN 1830 and 1881, writers were born who would be the first to witness and popularize the new mythos of the western people. These writers were the ones who, according to Wallace Stegner, made a new literature founded on six basic elements of the West: a romantic past, a realistic present, a picturesque and fleeting social order, a remarkable country, new ideas and dreams, and the common man as a hero for the native literature of mass America.[1]

In some cases, that "hero" was none other than the writer himself—or herself. Readers perceived Major John Wesley Powell as the hero of his own story, for example, even though doing so required that they read between the lines of his matter-of-fact accounts. Here was a one-armed man climb-

---

1. Wallace Stegner, "Western Record and Romance," in *Literary History of the United States*, ed. Robert E. Spiller, Willard Thorp, et al., 3d ed. (New York: Macmillan, 1963), pp. 863–65.

ing cliffs, riding the wildly lunging deck of a fragile rowboat, leading his tiny party of explorers down through the ominous unknown of the Colorado River's canyons. People who have not even read Powell's accounts still think of him as one of the picturesque, romantic characters in the western chronicle. Arizona readers saw Sharlot Hall as a true heroine. Her poems and her stories, like the journals of Major Powell, are rather matter-of-fact; but her personal life was a model of western independence and endurance. John Muir led a life of enviable exploits and was the embodiment of all the values he wrote about, the hero of his own essays.

Some western fiction writers born during this period—Mark Twain, Bret Harte, and Willa Cather, to name three prominent examples—were later idolized by enthusiasts who knew more about the authors' lives than about the authors' writings. The writers were perpetually expected to show up in their own books. *My Ántonia*, readers believed, had to be about Cather and about the people she knew in Nebraska; surely Twain was the one who really owned the jumping frog; and Harte must have used himself as a model for dozens of his California characters. It was a new kind of myth, and a very romantic one: you could put your own experiences into the form of fiction, and soon people could not tell the "real" person from the fictional narrator.

Either version of the writer-as-hero idea is in keeping with Theodore Roosevelt's assessment of those who were creating a unique American tradition.

> The men who actually do the things best worth doing in American life are, as they always have been, purely, and usually quite unconsciously, American. The paths in which we have done the best work are precisely those where our work has been most original and our workers least hampered by Old World conventions and ideas. Our statesmen and soldiers, our pioneers and commonwealth-builders, and the architects of our material prosperity have struck out on their own lines, and during the last century have done more than has ever been elsewhere accomplished in the same space of time. These men live for their work. They strive mightily, and they fail or succeed as chance and their own strength direct; but whether they succeed or fail, they live in and for their own land, their work is indissolubly connected with her well or ill being, and the praise which gives them heart, and the blame which may or may not cast them down, come from their own countrymen.[2]

2. Theodore Roosevelt, *American Ideals* (New York: G. P. Putnam's Sons, 1897), pp. 21–22.

Roosevelt's ideals apply to the protagonists created by our mythopoeic writers. First, the heroes and heroines have characteristics that are recognizably western. Second, there is a definite relationship between the characters and the natural setting; the setting is often important enough to be seen as an active participant in the story.

What are the essential characteristics of the western protagonists? Unlike other mythological figures, those in western literature have no supernatural or superhuman powers, carry no magical weapons, and have no hereditary rank or prestige. More often than not, their personal history is obscure or is altogether unknown. What they *do* have is some attribute or talent in which they are superior to their peers. Mary Austin's Walking Woman has a quiet sort of endurance that goes beyond normal experience; Owen Wister's cowboy, Dean Drake, has a keener sense of humor, more ingenuity, and more sensitivity than we expect from the average cowpuncher; the man spinning the story in Andy Adams's "The Double Trail" is exactly that: a highly talented spinner of stories.

Second, characters in western fiction are not always morally perfect—usually the opposite. But their writers are prepared to forgive them their sins. Mark Twain sees the nobility of his stage driver and overlooks any faults; Bret Harte knows that his outcasts are better persons than they appear to be; and John Neihardt treats even the vicious Mike Fink as a man who has been misunderstood.

In Major John Wesley Powell and Mary Austin, in John Muir and in Owen Wister's Virginian, to name a few, we see a third trait common among western literary protagonists. On their own, they attained impressive educations well beyond their formal schooling. Most of their knowledge and talent was acquired through independent curiosity, keenness of mind, and a willingness to learn.

Fourth, these characters are shown as people who are capable of leadership, even though they have a tendency to be individualists. They do not usually put themselves forward as leaders, yet neither do they shirk from leadership when it is put upon them. Owen Wister's "Jimmyjohn Boss" exemplifies this, and so does Isabella Bird's picturesque "Mountain Jim."

Finally, the characters have an insatiable appetite for movement, for experience, for discovery. They prefer physical experience to the intellectual, almost every time. The cowboys of Emerson Hough and Owen Wister would rather ride a bronc or rope a grizzly than sit down to a discussion. Isabella Bird, like John Muir, would rather keep moving than stop to meditate. Those boys of Willa Cather's "The Enchanted Bluff" dream not of making great intellectual discoveries but of finding a way to scale that mysterious mesa.

In western literature, Wallace Stegner's "remarkable country" interacts with the human protagonists, playing a major role. Sometimes its role is to offer benevolent protection to the human characters, providing food, shelter, and contentment. Native American writers frequently give us this enviable ideal, a world in which man and nature are united, in which there is no notion of "wilderness." Closely related is the European ideal that the human mind can reach a transcendent understanding of nature, an understanding that will in turn lead to harmony between the characters and the setting. Sometimes, as Mary Austin shows us, the characters can even feel the "spirit of place" that lives in the landscape.

The boys of Willa Cather's "The Enchanted Bluff" see the landscape more as a curiosity, as scenery. They do not realize that the bluff was an essential part of the Anasazi culture's personality, just as surely as their Nebraska sandbar has become a part of their own. We frequently see this "spectator" sort of character in western literature, one who at first appreciates only the panoramic aspect but later realizes that nature is an active force in his or her whole development.

In the literature of the American West, nature can also be an antagonist. As such, the landscape is generally inhospitable and threatening, but not malevolent—although the author may at times make it appear that way, as in O. E. Rölvaag's *Giants in the Earth* (1927). The human conflict focuses on either endurance or conquest of the natural surroundings. The human characters cannot feel that they are in harmony with nature, nor can they see the physical environment from a detached point of view, as if it is only scenery. This man-versus-nature conflict makes the mythic hero seem all the larger, all the more dramatic: a mountain man in a life-and-death struggle with the elements appears far more heroic than a Native American or naturalist attempting to bond with the spirit of place.

Although noted for being independent, the western mythic character is inevitably identified with a social group of some form or another, and with that society's values. The group respects the individual's personal achievement, independence, and strength (and sometimes approves of fighting, lying, and even attempts to thwart its own system). The society in which the myth takes place shares with the mythic character a strong love for growth and movement; it prefers to work with physical problems rather than intellectual ones; it may at times show a disregard for organized education, religion, and government.

All of the essential western myths, from the explorers to the cowboys, had one thing in common: they required vast expanses of open land. Without all that country to roam around in, no new heroes could be invented and made into myth. The people took the heroes they had, therefore, and raised them to the level of romance and idealism.

Just as steam on the Missouri signaled the opening of the Mythopoeic Period, steel on the Great Plains marked its closure, bound it with rails and wire. Barbed wire, between 1874 and 1880, made ranch hands out of trail drivers, made sedentary farmers out of westering pioneers, and made section-line surveyors out of explorers. Across the southern edge of the plains, the Atchison, Topeka and Santa Fe Railroad linked up with the Southern Pacific—the "octopus" of Frank Norris—in 1881. Across the northern regions, between 1878 and 1893, James J. Hill's Great Northern Railway went clear to the Pacific coast. The West was contained within a box of steel, webbed with barbed wire. Gone were the wagon trains, gone were the trail herds; gone too were the battles between the cavalry and the Indians. What remains is the literature, expressing the fundamentals of the American personality in all of its variety and scope.

Helen Hunt Jackson
1830-85

—

1870: *Verses*
1881: *A Century of Dishonor*
1884: *Ramona*
1890: *Saxe Holm's Stories*
1892: *Poems*

—

H ELEN HUNT JACKSON'S *mother once wrote to a friend that the young Helen "learns very well, but I do not drive her very much to make her literary—she is quite inclined to question the author of everything; the Bible she says does not feel as if it were true."* [1]

Jackson was born in Amherst, Massachusetts, to Nathan and Deborah Fiske. By the time she was seventeen, she had lost both parents. At nineteen, Jackson discovered New York, her lifelong mecca of friendships, literary contacts, culture, and renewal. In Albany, New York, Helen met Edward Hunt, an army engineer and a promising scientist and professor at West Point Academy. She married him at twenty-two, and was widowed at thirty-three. Her first son died in infancy; her second son died when she was thirty-five. As an outlet for overwhelming grief, Jackson began to write poetry. Her poem "Lifted Over" brought public recognition and acclaim.

Jackson's literary guide and mentor, Colonel Thomas Wentworth Higginson, introduced her to literary circles in Boston and New York. She aggressively began supporting herself through writing; she traveled throughout New England and took the "grand tour" of Europe, publishing travel stories about the journeys. Some of these took the form of letters to her sister. Of several pen names, the one she preferred was the simple "H. H."

1. Evelyn I. Banning, *Helen Hunt Jackson* (New York: Vanguard Press, 1973), p. 11.

Jackson's poetry is romantic and highly stylized. Its themes of death, honor, immortality, and love echo with chivalrous images, pastoral scenes, and exalted personifications of nature. Colonel Higginson called Jackson "the woman who has come nearest in our day and tongue to the genius of Elizabeth Barrett Browning." [2] *Jackson's lifelong acquaintance with Emily Dickinson developed into a strong and supportive exchange of letters and poems. Jackson believed in Dickinson's unique genius and begged her to publish, but to no avail.*

Jackson wrote two novels and numerous short stories, the latter under the pen name of Saxe Holm. The short stories seem extensions of her poetry in theme and style, with women figures who are highly idealized, intelligent, and totally centered in family obligations and devotion. Speculation arose as to the identity of the silent author; Jackson more than once denied the Saxe Holm authorship.

In October 1875 she married William Jackson of Colorado Springs. From her home in the West she traveled extensively in the Southwest and elsewhere. While visiting Boston in 1879, Jackson attended lectures by Chief Standing Bear and Bright Eyes; outraged by accounts of how the Ponca Indians of Nebraska had been treated under United States administration, she made it her ambition to call the public's attention to what she perceived as the government's destruction of the Indians. At the Astor Library in New York City, Jackson pored over official records of Indian affairs, and as she came across evidence of broken treaties or unjust treatment, she wrote up and published her findings. In a whirlwind of activity, she became a veritable one-person reform movement, circulating petitions and tracts, rebuking editors, army officers, clergymen, college presidents, and congressmen, and filling the columns of the Independent, *the* New York Tribune, *and the* New York Times *with stinging letters.* [3]

In the introduction to A Century of Dishonor, *Jackson wrote: "There is but one hope in righting this wrong. It lies in appeal to the heart and the conscience of the American People. What the people demand, Congress will do. It has been— to our shame be it spoken—at the demand of part of the people that these wrongs have been committed, these treaties broken, these robberies done, by the Government. . . . The only thing that can stay this is a mighty outspoken sentiment and purpose of the great body of the people." She hoped that her revelations in* A Century of Dishonor *would move the Congress of 1880 to be "the first to attempt to redeem the name of the United States from the stain of a century of dishonor."* [4] *To her disappointment, the book had little effect on Congress. In one more attempt*

2. Thomas Wentworth Higginson, *Short Studies of American Authors* (Boston: Lee and Shepard, 1888), p. 41.

3. Francis Paul Prucha, *American Indian Policy in Crisis: Christian Reformers and the Indian, 1865–1900* (Norman: University of Oklahoma Press, 1976), p. 162.

4. Helen Hunt Jackson, *A Century of Dishonor* (New York: Harper, 1881), pp. 30–31.

to reach the American people, she wrote the novel Ramona, *a story calculated to do for the American Indians what* Uncle Tom's Cabin *had done for the blacks. However, it was and still is viewed as little more than a romance novel.*

Shortly before her death, Jackson wrote Colonel Higginson: "My Century of Dishonor *and* Ramona *are the only things I have done for which I am glad now. The rest is of no moment. They will live on and bear fruit. They have already." Her last letter to President Grover Cleveland was a plea. "I ask you to read my* Century of Dishonor. *I am dying happier in the belief I have that it is your hand that is destined to strike the first blow toward lifting the burden of infamy from our country and righting the wrongs of the Indian race."* [5]

After Jackson's death, Emily Dickinson wrote: "Helen of Troy may die, but Helen of Colorado, never. 'Dear friend, can you walk' were the last words I wrote her—'Dear friend, I can fly'—her immortal reply." [6]

——

Conclusion of
A Century of Dishonor

T HERE ARE within the limits of the United States between two hundred and fifty and three hundred thousand Indians, exclusive of those in Alaska. The names of the different tribes and bands, as entered in the statistical tables of the Indian Office Reports, number nearly three hundred. One of the most careful estimates which have been made of their numbers and localities gives them as follows: "In Minnesota and States east of the Mississippi, about 32,500; in Nebraska, Kansas, and the Indian Territory, 70,650; in the Territories of Dakota, Montana, Wyoming, and Idaho, 65,000; in Nevada and the Territories of Colorado, New Mexico, Utah, and Arizona, 84,000; and on the Pacific slope, 48,000."

Of these, 130,000 are self-supporting on their own reservations, "receiving nothing from the Government except interest on their own moneys, or annuities granted them in consideration of the cession of their lands to the United States." [7]

From Helen Hunt Jackson, *A Century of Dishonor: A Sketch of the United States Government's Dealings with Some of the Indian Tribes* (New York: Harper and Brothers, 1881), pp. 336–42.

5. Banning, *Jackson*, p. 224.
6. Ibid., p. 225.
7. Annual Report of Indian Commissioner for 1872. [Jackson's note]

This fact alone would seem sufficient to dispose forever of the accusation, so persistently brought against the Indian, that he will not work.

Of the remainder, 84,000 are partially supported by the Government—the interest money due them and their annuities, as provided by treaty, being inadequate to their subsistence on the reservations where they are confined. In many cases, however, these Indians furnish a large part of their support—the White River Utes, for instance, who are reported by the Indian Bureau as getting sixty-six per cent. of their living by "root-digging, hunting, and fishing;" the Squaxin band, in Washington Territory, as earning seventy-five per cent., and the Chippewas of Lake Superior as earning fifty per cent. in the same way. These facts also would seem to dispose of the accusation that the Indian will not work.

There are about 55,000 who never visit an agency, over whom the Government does not pretend to have either control or care. These 55,000 "subsist by hunting, fishing, on roots, nuts, berries, etc., and by begging and stealing;" and this also seems to dispose of the accusation that the Indian will not "work for a living." There remains a small portion, about 31,000, that are entirely subsisted by the Government.

There is not among these three hundred bands of Indians one which has not suffered cruelly at the hands either of the Government or of white settlers. The poorer, the more insignificant, the more helpless the band, the more certain the cruelty and outrage to which they have been subjected. This is especially true of the bands on the Pacific slope. These Indians found themselves of a sudden surrounded by and caught up in the great influx of gold-seeking settlers, as helpless creatures on a shore are caught up in a tidal wave. There was not time for the Government to make treaties; not even time for communities to make laws. The tale of the wrongs, the oppressions, the murders of the Pacific-slope Indians in the last thirty years would be a volume by itself, and is too monstrous to be believed.

It makes little difference, however, where one opens the record of the history of the Indians; every page and every year has its dark stain. The story of one tribe is the story of all, varied only by differences of time and place; but neither time nor place makes any difference in the main facts. Colorado is as greedy and unjust in 1880 as was Georgia in 1830, and Ohio in 1795; and the United States Government breaks promises now as deftly as then, and with an added ingenuity from long practice.

One of its strongest supports in so doing is the wide-spread sentiment among the people of dislike to the Indian, of impatience with his presence as a "barrier to civilization," and distrust of it as a possible danger. The old tales of the frontier life, with its horrors of Indian warfare, have gradually,

by two or three generations' telling, produced in the average mind something like an hereditary instinct of unquestioning and unreasoning aversion
which it is almost impossible to dislodge or soften.

There are hundreds of pages of unimpeachable testimony on the side
of the Indian; but it goes for nothing, is set down as sentimentalism or
partisanship, tossed aside and forgotten.

President after president has appointed commission after commission to
inquire into and report upon Indian affairs, and to make suggestions as to
the best methods of managing them. The reports are filled with eloquent
statements of wrongs done to the Indians, of perfidies on the part of the
Government; they counsel, as earnestly as words can, a trial of the simple
and unperplexing expedients of telling truth, keeping promises, making fair
bargains, dealing justly in all ways and all things. These reports are bound
up with the Government's Annual Reports, and that is the end of them. It
would probably be no exaggeration to say that not one American citizen
out of ten thousand ever sees them or knows that they exist, and yet any
one of them, circulated throughout the country, read by the right-thinking,
right-feeling men and women of this land, would be of itself a "campaign
document" that would initiate a revolution which would not subside until
the Indians' wrongs were, so far as is now left possible, righted.

In 1869 President Grant appointed a commission of nine men, representing the influence and philanthropy of six leading States, to visit the
different Indian reservations, and to "examine all matters appertaining to
Indian affairs."

In the report of this commission are such paragraphs as the following:
"To assert that 'the Indian will not work' is as true as it would be to say that
the white man will not work.

"Why should the Indian be expected to plant corn, fence lands, build
houses, or do anything but get food from day to day, when experience has
taught him that the product of his labor will be seized by the white man
to-morrow? The most industrious white man would become a drone under
similar circumstances. Nevertheless, many of the Indians" (the commis-
sioners might more forcibly have said 130,000 of the Indians) "are already
at work, and furnish ample refutation of the assertion that 'the Indian will
not work.' There is no escape from the inexorable logic of facts.

"The history of the Government connections with the Indians is a
shameful record of broken treaties and unfulfilled promises. The history of
the border white man's connection with the Indians is a sickening record
of murder, outrage, robbery, and wrongs committed by the former, as the

rule, and occasional savage outbreaks and unspeakably barbarous deeds of retaliation by the latter, as the exception.

"Taught by the Government that they had rights entitled to respect, when those rights have been assailed by the rapacity of the white man, the arm which should have been raised to protect them has ever been ready to sustain the aggressor.

"The testimony of some of the highest military officers of the United States is on record to the effect that, in our Indian wars, almost without exception, the first aggressions have been made by the white man; and the assertion is supported by every civilian of reputation who has studied the subject. In addition to the class of robbers and outlaws who find impunity in their nefarious pursuits on the frontiers, there is a large class of professedly reputable men who use every means in their power to bring on Indian wars for the sake of the profit to be realized from the presence of troops and the expenditure of Government funds in their midst. They proclaim death to the Indians at all times in words and publications, making no distinction between the innocent and the guilty. They irate the lowest class of men to the perpetration of the darkest deeds against their victims, and as judges and jurymen shield them from the justice due to their crimes. Every crime committed by a white man against an Indian is concealed or palliated. Every offence committed by an Indian against a white man is borne on the wings of the post or the telegraph to the remotest corner of the land, clothed with all the horrors which the reality or imagination can throw around it. Against such influences as these the people of the United States need to be warned."

To assume that it would be easy, or by any one sudden stroke of legislative policy possible, to undo the mischief and hurt of the long past, set the Indian policy of the country right for the future, and make the Indians at once safe and happy, is the blunder of a hasty and uninformed judgment. The notion which seems to be growing more prevalent, that simply to make all Indians at once citizens of the United States would be a sovereign and instantaneous panacea for all their ills and all the Government's perplexities, is a very inconsiderate one. To administer complete citizenship of a sudden, all round, to all Indians, barbarous and civilized alike, would be as grotesque a blunder as to dose them all round with any one medicine, irrespective of the symptoms and needs of their diseases. It would kill more than it would cure. Nevertheless, it is true, as was well stated by one of the superintendents of Indian Affairs in 1857, that, "so long as they are not citizens of the United States, their rights of property must remain insecure against invasion. The doors of the federal tribunals being barred against them while wards and dependents, they can only partially exercise the rights of free government, or give to those who make, execute, and construe the few laws they are allowed to enact, dignity sufficient to make them respectable. While they continue individually to gather the crumbs that fall from the table of the United States, idleness, improvidence, and indebtedness will be the rule, and industry, thrift, and freedom from debt the exception. The utter absence of individual title to particular lands deprives every one among them of the chief incentive to labor and exertion—the very mainspring on which the prosperity of a people depends."

All judicious plans and measures for their safety and salvation must embody provisions for their becoming citizens as fast as they are fit, and must protect them till then in every right and particular in which our laws protect other "persons" who are not citizens.

There is a disposition in a certain class of minds to be impatient with any protestation against wrong which is unaccompanied or unprepared with a quick and exact scheme of remedy. This is illogical. When pioneers in a new country find a tract of poisonous and swampy wilderness to be reclaimed, they do not withhold their hands from fire and axe till they see clearly which way roads should run, where good water will spring, and what crops will best grow on the redeemed land. They first clear the swamp. So with this poisonous and baffling part of the domain of our national affairs—let us first "clear the swamp."

However great perplexity and difficulty there may be in the details of any and every plan possible for doing at this late day anything like justice to the Indian, however hard it may be for good statesmen and good men to agree upon the things that ought to be done, there certainly is, or ought to be, no perplexity whatever, no difficulty whatever, in agreeing upon certain things that ought not to be done, and which must cease to be done before the first steps can be taken toward righting the wrongs, curing the ills, and wiping out the disgrace to us of the present condition of our Indians.

Cheating, robbing, breaking promises—these three are clearly things which must cease to be done. One more thing, also, and that is the refusal of the protection of the law to the Indian's rights of property, "of life, liberty, and the pursuit of happiness."

When these four things have ceased to be done, time, statesmanship, philanthropy, and Christianity can slowly and surely do the rest. Till these four things have ceased to be done, statesmanship and philanthropy alike must work in vain, and even Christianity can reap but small harvest.

October's Bright Blue Weather[8]

O suns and skies and clouds of June,
    And flowers of June together,
Ye cannot rival for one hour
    October's bright blue weather,

When loud the bumble-bee makes haste,
    Belated, thriftless vagrant,
And Golden-Rod is dying fast,
    And lanes with grapes are fragrant;

When Gentians roll their fringes tight
    To save them for the morning,
And chestnuts fall from satin burrs
    Without a sound of warning;

When on the ground red apples lie
    In piles like jewels shining,
And redder still on old stone walls
    Are leaves of woodbine twining;

When all the lovely wayside things
    Their white-winged seeds are sowing,
And in the fields, still green and fair,
    Late aftermaths are growing;

When springs run low, and on the brooks,
    In idle golden freighting,
Bright leaves sink noiseless in the hush
    Of woods, for winter waiting;

The selections of Helen Hunt Jackson's verse included here are from *Poems* (Boston: Roberts Brothers, 1892), pp. 254–55, 116–17, 175, and 45–49, respectively.

8. This poem was written in the month of Helen Hunt's marriage to William Jackson.

When comrades seek sweet country haunts,
  By twos and twos together,
And count like misers hour by hour,
  October's bright blue weather.

O suns and skies and flowers of June,
  Count all your boasts together,
Love loveth best of all the year
  October's bright blue weather.

———

Shadows of Birds

In darkened air, alone with pain,
I lay. Like links of heavy chain
The minutes sounded, measuring day,
And slipping lifelessly away.
Sudden across my silent room
A shadow darker than its gloom
Swept swift; a shadow slim and small
Which poised and darted on the wall,
And vanished quickly as it came;
A shadow, yet it lit like flame;
A shadow, yet I heard it sing,
And heard the rustle of its wing,
Till every pulse with joy was stirred;
It was the shadow of a bird!

Only the shadow! Yet it made
Full summer everywhere it strayed;
And every bird I ever knew
Back and forth in the summer flew;
And breezes wafted over me
The scent of every flower and tree;
Till I forgot the pain and gloom
And silence of my darkened room.
Now, in the glorious open air,
I watch the birds fly here and there;
And wonder, as each swift wing cleaves
The sky, if some poor soul that grieves

In lonely, darkened, silent walls
Will catch the shadow as it falls!

Danger

With what a childish and short-sighted sense
Fear seeks for safety; reckons up the days
Of danger and escape, the hours and ways
Of death; it breathless flies the pestilence;
It walls itself in towers of defence;
By land, by sea, against the storm it lays
Down barriers; then, comforted, it says:
"This spot, this hour is safe." Oh, vain pretence!
Man born of man knows nothing when he goes;
The winds blow where they list, and will disclose
To no man which brings safety, which brings risk.
The mighty are brought low by many a thing
Too small to name. Beneath the daisy's disk
Lies hid the pebble for the fatal sling.

A Ballad of the Gold Country[9]

Deep in the hill the gold sand burned;
    The brook ran yellow with its gleams;
Close by, the seekers slept, and turned
    And tossed in restless dreams.

At dawn they waked. In friendly cheer
    Their dreams they told, by one, by one;

---

9. The story partly parallels what happened to James Marshall, who discovered gold in 1848 while building a sawmill for John Sutter near Sacramento, California. Claim jumpers robbed Marshall of everything he had, including his 640-acre claim, and after ten years of wandering poverty, he began growing grapes and started a small winery. Unlike the character in Jackson's ballad, however, Marshall went bankrupt; following his death in 1885, the state of California buried him near the site of Sutter's Fort and provided an expensive monument to the man who had discovered California's gold.

And each man laughed the dreams to hear,
　　But sighed when they were done.

Visions of golden birds that flew,
　　Of golden cloth piled fold on fold,
Of rain which shone, and filtered through
　　The air in showers of gold;

Visions of golden bells that rang,
　　Of golden chariots that rolled,
Visions of girls that danced and sang,
　　With hair and robes of gold;

Visions of golden stairs that led
　　Down golden shafts of depths untold,
Visions of golden skies that shed
　　Gold light on seas of gold.

"Comrades, your dreams have many shapes,"
　　Said one who, thoughtful, sat apart:
"But I six nights have dreamed of grapes,
　　One dream which fills my heart.

"A woman meets me, crowned with vine;
　　Great purple clusters fill her hands;
Her eyes divinely smile and shine,
　　As beckoning she stands.

"I follow her a single pace;
　　She vanishes, like light or sound,
And leaves me in a vine-walled place,
　　Where grapes pile all the ground."

The comrades laughed: "We know thee by
　　This fevered, drunken dream of thine."
"Ha, ha," cried he, "never have I
　　So much as tasted wine!

"Now, follow ye your luring shapes
　　Of gold that clinks and gold that shines;

I shall await my maid of grapes,
    And plant her trees and vines."

All through the hills the gold sand burned;
    All through the lands ran yellow streams;
To right, to left, the seekers turned,
    Led by the golden gleams.

The ruddy hills were gulfed and strained;
    The rocky fields were torn and trenched;
The yellow streams were drained and drained,
    Until their sources quenched.

The gold came fast; the gold came free:
    The seekers shouted as they ran,
"Now let us turn aside, and see
    How fares that husbandman!"

"Ho here! ho there! good man," they cried,
    And tossed gold nuggets at his feet;
"Serve us with wine! Where is thy bride
    That told thee tales so sweet?"

"No wine as yet, my friends, to sell;
    No bride to show," he smiling said:
"But here is water from my well;
    And here is wheaten bread."

"Is this thy tale?" they jeering cried;
    "Who was it followed luring shapes?
And who has won? It seems she lied,
    Thy maid of purple grapes!"

"When years have counted up to ten,"
    He answered gayly, smiling still,
"Come back once more, my merry men,
    And you shall have your fill

"Of purple grapes and sparkling wine,
    And figs, and nectarines like flames,

And sweeter eyes than maids' shall shine
    In welcome at your names."

In scorn they heard; to scorn they laughed
    The water and the wheaten bread;
"We'll wait until a better draught
    For thy bride's health," they said.

The years ran fast. The seekers went
    All up, all down the golden lands:
The streams grew pale; the hills were spent;
    Slow ran the golden sands.

And men were beggars in a day,
    For swift to come was swift to go;
What chance had got, chance flung away
    On one more chance's throw.

And bleached and seamed and riven plains,
    And tossed and tortured rocks like ghosts,
And blackened lines and charred remains,
    And crumbling chimney-posts,

For leagues their ghastly records spread
    Of youth, and years, and fortunes gone,
Like graveyards whose sad living dead
    Had hopeless journeyed on.

The years had counted up to ten:
    One night, as it grew chill and late,
The husbandman marked beggar-men
    Who leaned upon his gate.

"Ho here! good men," he eager cried,
    Before the wayfarers could speak;
"This is my vineyard. Far and wide,
    For laborers I seek.

"This year had doubled on last year;
    The fruit breaks down my vines and trees;

Tarry and help, till wine runs clear,
    And ask what price you please."

Purple and red, to left, to right,
    For miles the gorgeous vintage blazed;
And all day long and into night
    The vintage song was raised.

And wine ran free all thirst beyond,
    And no hand stinted bread or meat;
And maids were gay, and men were fond,
    And hours were swift and sweet.

The beggar-men they worked with will;
    Their hands were thin and lithe and strong;
Each day they ate good two days' fill,
    They had been starved so long.

The vintage drew to end. New wine
    From thousand casks was dripping slow,
And bare and yellow fields gave sign
    For vintagers to go.

The beggar-men received their pay,
    Bright yellow gold,—twice their demand;
The master, as they turned away,
    Held out his brawny hand,

And said: "Good men, this time next year
    My vintage will be bigger still;
Come back, if chance should bring you near,
    And it should suit your will."

The beggars nodded. But at night
    They said: "No more we go that way:
He did not know us then; he might
    Upon another day!"

Isabella L. Bird
1831-1904

—

1856: The Englishwoman in America
1875: The Hawaiian Archipelago
1879: A Lady's Life in the Rocky Mountains
1891: Journeys in Persia and Kurdistan
1899: The Yangtze Valley and Beyond

—

W*IDELY traveled and unwaveringly British, Isabella Bird is known today principally for her contributions to western landscape writing, especially for her descriptions of the "sublime" beauty—and terror— to be found in the newly settled region. In spite of a painful spinal condition, she traveled to the United States in 1854, in 1857, and in 1873. Her 1873 visit to the Rocky Mountains was the final segment of an eighteen-month tour of Australia, New Zealand, the Sandwich Islands (now Hawaii), and America. In addition to being an accomplished horsewoman, she had courage and curiosity and an eagerness to experience all the land had to offer, even when that meant eating coarse food and traveling with men who had "little idea of . . . even ordinary civilities." She wrote her adventurous accounts as letters to her sister; the majority of the chapters in* A Lady's Life in the Rocky Mountains *come from those letters.*

The incongruities in her account speak for themselves. Here she is, a genteel lady and a veteran traveler, placing herself in the hands of that "awful-looking ruffian," the provincial "Mountain Jim" Nugent. She is ill, in pain from her spinal affliction, riding a horse on 14,000-foot Long's Peak. Her attire is her "Hawaiian riding dress." She is an educated and religious lady, the daughter of a minister, camping alone with three males in the wilderness.

Western American literature is crisscrossed with travel narratives. Most of our material in that genre comes, like A Lady's Life in the Rocky Mountains, *from nonwesterners. Bird's style is conversational and easy; it is sometimes difficult to follow the continuity of her description of the ride and the climb, but her details tend to be precise and open-minded, flavored with a romanticist's subtle sense of the sublime, the ironic, and the magnificent. We find here more influence of William Wordsworth than of Walden, but with sharper images: sometimes her prose is as bold as the journey itself, as in "snow patches, snow slashes, snow abysses, snow for-lorn and soiled looking, snow pure and dazzling, snow glistening above the purple robe of pine."*

Isabella Bird's travel accounts and photographs earned her election to the Royal Scottish Geographical Society in 1891, and in 1892 she became the first woman to be made a fellow of the Royal Geographical Society. In 1900, at the age of seventy, she traveled to Morocco, and even during the severe illness that led to her death, she was planning a trip to China.

——

Letter VII

Estes Park, Colorado, October

A S THIS account of the ascent of Long's Peak could not be written at the time, I am much disinclined to write it, especially as no sort of description within my powers could enable another to realize the glorious sublimity, the majestic solitude, and the unspeakable awfulness and fascination of the scenes in which I spent Monday, Tuesday, and Wednesday.

Long's Peak, 14,700 feet high, blocks up one end of Estes Park, and dwarfs all the surrounding mountains. From it on this side rise, snow-born, the bright St. Vrain, and the Big and Little Thompson. By sunlight or moonlight its splintered grey crest is the one object which, in spite of wapiti and bighorn, skunk and grizzly, unfailingly arrests the eyes. From it come all storms of snow and wind, and the forked lightnings play round its head like a glory. It is one of the noblest of mountains, but in one's imagination it grows to be much more than a mountain. It becomes invested with a personality. In its caverns and abysses one comes to fancy that it generates and chains the strong winds, to let them loose in its fury. The thunder becomes its voice, and the lightnings do it homage. Other summits blush under the morning kiss of the sun, and turn pale the next moment; but it detains the

From Isabella Bird, *A Lady's Life in the Rocky Mountains* (London: John Murray, 1879), pp. 83–101.

first sunlight and holds it round its head for an hour at least, till it pleases to change from rosy red to deep blue; and the sunset, as if spell-bound, lingers latest on its crest. The soft winds which hardly rustle the pine needles down here are raging rudely up there round its motionless summit. The mark of fire is upon it; and though it has passed into a grim repose, it tells of fire and upheaval as truly, though not as eloquently, as the living volcanoes of Hawaii. Here under its shadow one learns how naturally nature worship, and the propitiation of the forces of nature, arose in minds which had no better light.

Long's Peak, "the American Matterhorn," as some call it, was ascended five years ago for the first time. I thought I should like to attempt it, but up to Monday, when Evans left for Denver, cold water was thrown upon the project. It was too late in the season, the winds were likely to be strong, etc.; but just before leaving, Evans said that the weather was looking more settled, and if I did not get farther than the timber line it would be worth going. Soon after he left, "Mountain Jim" came in, and he would go up as guide, and the two youths who rode here with me from Longmount and I caught at the proposal. Mrs. Edwards at once baked bread for three days, steaks were cut from the steer which hangs up conveniently, and tea, sugar, and butter were benevolently added. Our picnic was not to be a luxurious or "well-found" one, for, in order to avoid the expense of a pack mule, we limited our luggage to what our saddle horses could carry. Behind my saddle I carried three pair of camping blankets and a quilt, which reached to my shoulders. My own boots were so much worn that it was painful to walk, even about the park, in them, so Evans had lent me a pair of his hunting boots, which hung to the horn of my saddle. The horses of the two young men were equally loaded, for we had to prepare for many degrees of frost. "Jim" was a shocking figure; he had on an old pair of high boots, with a baggy pair of old trousers made of deer hide, held on by an old scarf tucked into them; a leather shirt, with three or four ragged unbuttoned waistcoats over it; an old smashed wideawake, from under which his tawny, neglected ringlets hung; and with his one eye, his one long spur, his knife in his belt, his revolver in his waistcoat pocket, his saddle covered with an old beaver skin, from which the paws hung down; his camping blankets behind him, his rifle laid across the saddle in front of him, and his axe, canteen, and other gear hanging to the horn, he was as awful-looking a ruffian as one could see. By way of contrast he rode a small Arab mare, of exquisite beauty, skittish, high spirited, gentle, but altogether too light for him, and he fretted her incessantly to make her display herself.

Heavily loaded as all our horses were, "Jim" started over the half-mile of level grass at a hard gallop, and then throwing his mare on her haunches, pulled up alongside of me, and with a grace of manner which soon made me forget his appearance, entered into a conversation which lasted for more than three hours, in spite of the manifold checks of fording streams, single file, abrupt ascents and descents, and other incidents of mountain travel. The ride was one series of glories and surprises, of "park" and glade, of lake and stream, of mountains on mountains, culminating in the rent pinnacles of Long's Peak, which looked yet grander and ghastlier as we crossed an attendant mountain 11,000 feet high. The slanting sun added fresh beauty every hour. There were dark pines against a lemon sky, grey peaks reddening and etherealizing, gorges of deep and infinite blue, floods of golden glory pouring through canyons of enormous depth, an atmosphere of absolute purity, an occasional foreground of cotton-wood and aspen flaunting in red and gold to intensify the blue gloom of the pines, the trickle and murmur of streams fringed with icicles, the strange *sough* of gusts moving among the pine tops—sights and sounds not of the lower earth, but of the solitary, beast-haunted, frozen upper altitudes. From the dry, buff grass of Estes Park we turned off up a trail on the side of a pine-hung gorge, up a steep pine-clothed hill, down to a small valley, rich in fine, sun-cured hay about eighteen inches high, and enclosed by high mountains whose deepest hollow contains a lily-covered lake, fitly named "The Lake of the Lilies." Ah, how magical its beauty was, as it slept in silence, while *there* the dark pines were mirrored motionless in its pale gold, and *here* the great white lily cups and dark green leaves rested on amethyst-colored water!

From this we ascended into the purple gloom of great pine forests which clothe the skirts of the mountains up to a height of about 11,000 feet, and from their chill and solitary depths we had glimpses of golden atmosphere and rose-lit summits, not of "the land very far off," but of the land nearer now in all its grandeur, gaining in sublimity by nearness—glimpses, too, through a broken vista of purple gorges, of the illimitable Plains lying idealized in the late sunlight, their baked, brown expanse transfigured into the likeness of a sunset sea rolling infinitely in waves of misty gold.

We rode upwards through the gloom on a steep trail blazed through the forest, all my intellect concentrated on avoiding being dragged off my horse by impending branches, or having the blankets badly torn, as those of my companions were, by sharp dead limbs, between which there was hardly room to pass—the horses breathless, and requiring to stop every few yards, though their riders, except myself, were afoot. The gloom of the dense, ancient, silent forest is to me awe inspiring. On such an evening it is soundless, except for the branches creaking in the soft wind, the frequent snap of decayed timber, and a murmur in the pine tops as of a not distant waterfall, all tending to produce *eeriness* and a sadness "hardly akin to pain." There no lumberer's axe has ever rung. The trees die when they have attained their prime, and stand there, dead and bare, till the fierce mountain winds lay them prostrate. The pines grew smaller and more sparse as we ascended, and the last stragglers wore a tortured, warring look. The timber line was passed, but yet a little higher a slope of mountain meadow dipped to the south-west towards a bright stream trickling under ice and icicles, and there a grove of the beautiful silver spruce marked our camping ground. The trees were in miniature, but so exquisitely arranged that one might well ask what artist's hand had planted them, scattering them here, clumping them there, and training their slim spires towards heaven. Hereafter, when I call up memories of the glorious, the view from this camping ground will come up. Looking east, gorges opened to the distant Plains, then fading into purple grey. Mountains with pine-clothed skirts rose in ranges, or, solitary, uplifted their grey summits, while close behind, but nearly 3,000 feet above us, towered the bald white crest of Long's Peak, its huge precipices red with the light of a sun long lost to our eyes. Close to us, in the caverned side of the Peak, was snow that, owing to its position, is eternal. Soon the afterglow came on, and before it faded a big half-moon hung out of the heavens, shining through the silver blue foliage of the pines on the frigid background of snow, and turning the whole into fairyland. The "photo" which accompanies this letter is by a courageous Denver artist who attempted the ascent just before I arrived, but, after camping out at the timber line for a week, was foiled by the perpetual storms, and was driven down again, leaving some very valuable apparatus about 3,000 feet from the summit.

Unsaddling and picketing the horses securely, making the beds of pine shoots, and dragging up logs for fuel, warmed us all. "Jim" built up a great fire, and before long we were all sitting around it at supper. It didn't matter much that we had to drink our tea out of the battered meat tins in which it was boiled, and eat strips of beef reeking with pine smoke without plates or forks.

"Treat Jim as a gentleman and you'll find him one," I had been told; and though his manner was certainly bolder and freer than that of gentlemen generally, no imaginary fault could be found. He was very agreeable as a man of culture as well as a child of nature; the desperado was altogether out of sight. He was very courteous and even kind to me, which was fortunate, as the young men had little idea of showing even ordinary civilities. That night I made the acquaintance of his dog "Ring," said to be the best hunting dog in Colorado, with the body and legs of a collie, but a head approaching that of a mastiff, a noble face with a wistful human expression, and the most truthful eyes I ever saw in an animal. His master loves him if he loves anything, but in his savage moods ill-treats him. "Ring's" devotion never swerves, and his truthful eyes are rarely taken off his master's face. He is almost human in his intelligence, and, unless he is told to do so, he never takes notice of any one but "Jim." In a tone as if speaking to a human being, his master, pointing to me, said, "Ring, go to that lady, and don't leave her again to-night." "Ring" at once came to me, looked into my face, laid his head on my shoulder, and then lay down beside me with his head on my lap, but never taking his eyes from "Jim's" face.

The long shadows of the pines lay upon the frosted grass, an aurora leaped fitfully, and the moonlight, though intensely bright, was pale beside the red, leaping flames of our pine logs and their red glow on our gear, ourselves, and Ring's truthful face. One of the young men sang a Latin student's song and two Negro melodies; the other "Sweet Spirit, hear my Prayer." "Jim" sang one of Moore's melodies in a singular falsetto, and all together sang, "The Star-spangled Banner" and "The Red, White, and Blue." Then "Jim" recited a very clever poem of his own composition, and told some fearful Indian stories. A group of small silver spruces away from the fire was my sleeping place. The artist who had been up there had so woven and interlaced their lower branches as to form a bower, affording at once shelter from the wind and a most agreeable privacy. It was thickly strewn with young pine shoots, and these, when covered with a blanket, with an inverted saddle for a pillow, made a luxurious bed. The mercury at 9 P.M. was 12° below the freezing point. "Jim," after a last look at the horses, made a huge fire, and stretched himself out beside it, but "Ring" lay at my back to keep me warm. I could not sleep, but the night passed rapidly. I was anxious about the ascent, for gusts of ominous sound swept through the pines at intervals. Then wild animals howled, and "Ring" was perturbed in spirit about them. Then it was strange to see the notorious desperado, a red-handed man, sleeping as quietly as innocence sleeps. But, above all, it was exciting to lie there, with no better shelter than a bower of pines, on a mountain 11,000 feet high, in the very heart of the Rocky Range, under twelve degrees of frost, hearing sounds of wolves, with shivering stars looking through the fragrant canopy, with arrowy pines for bed-posts, and for a night lamp the red flames of a camp-fire.

Day dawned long before the sun rose, pure and lemon colored. The rest were looking after the horses, when one of the students came running to tell me that I must come farther down the slope, for "Jim" said he had never seen such a sunrise. From the chill, grey Peak above, from the everlasting snows, from the silvered pines, down through mountain ranges with their depths of Tyrian purple, we looked to where the Plains lay cold, in blue-grey, like a morning sea against a far horizon. Suddenly, as a dazzling streak at first, but enlarging rapidly into a dazzling sphere, the sun wheeled above the grey line, a light and glory as when it was first created. "Jim" involuntarily and reverently uncovered his head, and exclaimed, "I believe there is a God!" I felt as if, Parsee-like, I must worship. The grey of the Plains changed to purple, the sky was all one rose-red flush, on which vermilion cloud-streaks rested; the ghastly peaks gleamed like rubies, the earth and heavens were new created. Surely "the Most High dwelleth not in temples made with hands!" For a full hour those Plains simulated the ocean, down to whose limitless expanse of purple, cliff, rocks, and promontories swept down.

By seven we had finished breakfast, and passed into the ghastlier solitudes above, I riding as far as what, rightly or wrongly, are called the "Lava Beds," an expanse of large and small boulders, with snow in their crevices. It was very cold; some water which we crossed was frozen hard enough to bear the horse. "Jim" had advised me against taking any wraps, and my thin Hawaiian riding dress, only fit for the tropics, was penetrated by the keen air. The rarefied atmosphere soon began to oppress our breathing, and I found that Evans's boots were so large that I had no foothold. Fortunately, before the real difficulty of the ascent began, we found, under a rock, a pair of small overshoes, probably left by the Hayden exploring expedition, which just lasted for the day. As we were leaping from rock to rock, "Jim" said, "I was thinking in the night about your traveling alone, and wondering where you carried your Derringer, for I could see no signs of it." On my telling him that I traveled unarmed, he could hardly believe it, and adjured me to get a revolver at once.

On arriving at the "Notch" (a literal gate of rock), we found ourselves absolutely on the knifelike ridge or backbone of Long's Peak, only a few feet wide, covered with colossal boulders and fragments, and on the other side shelving in one precipitous, snow-patched sweep of 3,000 feet to a picturesque hollow, containing a lake of pure green water. Other lakes, hidden among dense pine woods, were farther off, while close above us rose the Peak, which, for about 500 feet, is a smooth, gaunt, inaccessible-looking pile of granite. Passing through the "Notch," we looked along the nearly inaccessible side of the Peak, composed of boulders and *débris* of all shapes and sizes, through which appeared broad, smooth ribs of reddish-colored granite, looking as if they upheld the towering rock mass above. I usually dislike bird's-eye and panoramic views, but, though from a mountain, this was not one. Serrated ridges, not much lower than that on which we stood, rose, one beyond another, far as that pure atmosphere could carry the vision, broken into awful chasms deep with ice and snow, rising into pinnacles piercing the heavenly blue with their cold, barren grey, on, on for ever, till the most distant range upbore unsullied snow alone. There were fair lakes mirroring the dark pine woods, canyons dark and blue-black with unbroken expanses of pines, snow-slashed pinnacles, wintry heights frowning upon lovely parks, watered and wooded, lying in the lap of summer; North Park floating off into the blue distance, Middle Park closed till another season, the sunny slopes of Estes Park, and winding down among the mountains the snowy ridge of the Divide, whose bright waters seek both the Atlantic and Pacific Oceans. There, far below, links of diamonds showed where the Grand River takes its rise to seek the mysterious Colorado, with its still unsolved enigma,[1] and lose itself in the waters of the Pacific; and nearer the snow-born Thompson bursts forth from the ice to begin its journey to the Gulf of Mexico. Nature, rioting in her grandest mood, exclaimed with voices of grandeur, solitude, sublimity, beauty, and infinity, "Lord, what is man, that Thou art mindful of him? or the son of man, that Thou visitest him?" Never-to-be-forgotten glories they were, burnt in upon my memory by six succeeding hours of terror.

You know I have no head and no ankles, and never ought to dream of mountaineering; and had I known that the ascent was a real mountaineering feat I should not have felt the slightest ambition to perform it. As it is, I am only humiliated by my success, for "Jim" dragged me up, like a bale of goods, by sheer force of muscle. At the "Notch" the real business of the ascent began. Two thousand feet of solid rock towered above us, four thousand feet of broken rock shelved precipitously below; smooth granite ribs, with barely foothold, stood out here and there; melted snow refrozen several times, presented a more serious obstacle; many of the rocks were loose, and tumbled down when touched. To me it was a time of extreme terror. I was roped to "Jim," but it was of no use; my feet were paralyzed and slipped on the bare rock, and he said it was useless to try to go that way, and we retraced our steps. I wanted to return to the "Notch," knowing that my incompetence would detain the party, and one of the young men said almost plainly that a woman was a dangerous encumbrance, but the trapper

1. Actually, the "enigma" of the "mysterious Colorado" was solved by Major John Wesley Powell's expeditions down through the Grand Canyon in 1869 and 1871. His report was published in 1875.

replied shortly that if it were not to take a lady up he would not go up at all. He went on the explore, and reported that further progress on the correct line of ascent was blocked by ice; and then for two hours we descended, lowering ourselves by our hands from rock to rock along a boulder-strewn sweep of 4,000 feet, patched with ice and snow, and perilous from rolling stones. My fatigue, giddiness, and pain from bruised ankles, and arms half pulled out of their sockets, were so great that I should never have gone halfway had not "Jim," *nolens volens,*[2] dragged me along with a patience and skill, and withal a determination that I should ascend the Peak, which never failed. After descending about 2,000 feet to avoid the ice, we got into a deep ravine with inaccessible sides, partly filled with ice and snow and partly with large and small fragments of rock, which were constantly giving away, rendering the footing very insecure. That part to me was two hours of painful and unwilling submission to the inevitable; of trembling, slipping, straining, of smooth ice appearing when it was least expected, and of weak entreaties to be left behind while the others went on. "Jim" always said that there was no danger, that there was only a short bad bit ahead, and that I should go up even if he carried me!

Slipping, faltering, gasping from the exhausting toil in the rarefied air, with throbbing hearts and panting lungs, we reached the top of the gorge and squeezed ourselves between two gigantic fragments of rock by a passage called the "Dog's Lift," when I climbed on the shoulders of one man and then was hauled up. This introduced us by an abrupt turn round the southwest angle of the Peak to a narrow shelf of considerable length, rugged, uneven, and so overhung by the cliff in some places that it is necessary to crouch to pass at all. Above, the Peak looks nearly vertical for 400 feet; and below, the most tremendous precipice I have ever seen descends in one unbroken fall. This is usually considered the most dangerous part of the ascent, but it does not seem so to me, for such foothold as there is is secure, and one fancies that it is possible to hold on with the hands. But there, and on the final, and, to my thinking, the worst part of the climb, one slip, and a breathing, thinking, human being would lie 3,000 feet below, a shapeless, bloody heap! "Ring" refused to traverse the Ledge, and remained at the "Lift" howling piteously.

From thence the view is more magnificent even than that from the "Notch." At the foot of the precipice below us lay a lovely lake, wood embosomed, from or near which the bright St. Vrain and other streams take their rise. I thought how their clear cold waters, growing turbid in the afflu-

2. Unwilling or willing.

ent flats, would heat under the tropic sun, and eventually form part of that great ocean river which renders our far-off islands habitable by impinging on their shores. Snowy ranges, one behind the other, extended to the distant horizon, folding in their wintry embrace the beauties of Middle Park. Pike's Peak, more than one hundred miles off, lifted that vast but shapeless summit which is the landmark of southern Colorado. There were snow patches, snow slashes, snow abysses, snow forlorn and soiled looking, snow pure and dazzling, snow glistening above the purple robe of pine worn by all the mountains; while away to the east, in limitless breadth, stretched the green-grey of the endless Plains. Giants everywhere reared their splintered crests. From thence, with a single sweep, the eye takes in a distance of 300 miles—that distance to the west, north, and south being made up of mountains ten, eleven, twelve, and thirteen thousand feet in height, dominated by Long's Peak, Gray's Peak, and Pike's Peak, all nearly the height of Mont Blanc! On the Plains we traced the rivers by their fringe of cottonwoods to the distant Platte, and between us and them lay glories of mountain, canyon, and lake, sleeping in depths of blue and purple most ravishing to the eye.

As we crept from the ledge round a horn of rock I beheld what made me perfectly sick and dizzy to look at—the terminal Peak itself—a smooth, cracked face or wall of pink granite, as nearly perpendicular as anything could well be up which it was possible to climb, well deserving the name of the "American Matterhorn."[3]

Scaling, not climbing, is the correct term for this last ascent. It took one hour to accomplish 500 feet, pausing for breath every minute or two. The only foothold was in narrow cracks or on minute projections on the granite. To get a toe in these cracks, or here and there on a scarcely obvious projection, while crawling on hands and knees, all the while tortured with thirst and gasping and struggling for breath, this was the climb; but at last the Peak was won. A grand, well-defined mountain top it is, a nearly level acre of boulders, with precipitous sides all round, the one we came up being the only accessible one.

It was not possible to remain long. One of the young men was seriously alarmed by bleeding from the lungs, and the intense dryness of the day and the rarefication of the air, at a height of nearly 15,000 feet, made respiration very painful. There is always water on the Peak, but it was frozen as

3. Let no practical mountaineer be allured by my description into the ascent of Long's Peak. Truly terrible as it was to me, to a member of the Alpine Club it would not be a feat worth performing. [Bird's note]

hard as a rock, and the sucking of ice and snow increases thirst. We all suffered severely from the want of water, and the gasping for breath made our mouths and tongues so dry that articulation was difficult, and the speech of all unnatural.

From the summit were seen in unrivalled combination all the views which had rejoiced our eyes during the ascent. It was something at last to stand upon the storm-rent crown of this lonely sentinel of the Rocky Range, on one of the mightiest of the vertebrae of the backbone of the North American continent, and to see the waters start for both oceans. Uplifted above love and hate and storms of passion, calm amidst the eternal silences, fanned by zephyrs and bathed in living blue, peace rested for that one bright day on the Peak, as if it were some region

> *Where falls not rain, or hail, or any snow,*
> *Or ever wind blows loudly.*[4]

We placed our names, with the date of ascent, in a tin within a crevice, and descended to the Ledge, sitting on the smooth granite, getting our feet into cracks and against projections, and letting ourselves down by our hands, "Jim" going before me, so that I might steady my feet against his powerful shoulders. I was no longer giddy, and faced the precipice of 3,500 feet without a shiver. Repassing the Ledge and Lift, we accomplished the descent through 1,500 feet of ice and snow, with many falls and bruises, but no worse mishap, and there separated, the young men taking the steepest but most direct way to the "Notch," with the intention of getting ready for the march home, and "Jim" and I taking what he thought the safer route for me—a descent over boulders for 2,000 feet, and then a tremendous ascent to the "Notch." I had various falls, and once hung by my frock, which caught on a rock, and "Jim" severed it with his hunting knife, upon which I fell into a crevice full of soft snow. We were driven lower down the mountains than he had intended by impassable tracts of ice, and the ascent was tremendous. For the last 200 feet the boulders were of enormous size, and the steepness fearful. Sometimes I drew myself up on hands and knees, sometimes crawled; sometimes "Jim" pulled me up by my arms or a lariat, and sometimes I stood on his shoulders, or he made steps for me of his feet and hands, but at six we stood on the "Notch" in the splendor of the sinking sun, all color deepening, all peaks glorifying, all shadows purpling, all peril past.

"Jim" had parted with his *brusquerie* when we parted from the students,

4. From Alfred, Lord Tennyson's *Morte d'Arthur*, line 424.

and was gentle and considerate beyond anything, though I knew that he must be grievously disappointed, both in my courage and strength. Water was an object of earnest desire. My tongue rattled in my mouth, and I could hardly articulate. It is good for one's sympathies to have for once a severe experience of thirst. Truly, there was

> *Water, water, everywhere,*
> *But not a drop to drink.*[5]

Three times its apparent gleam deceived even the mountaineer's practised eye, but we found only a foot of "glare ice." At last, in a deep hole, he succeeded in breaking the ice, and by putting one's arm far down one could scoop up a little water in one's hand, but it was tormentingly insufficient. With great difficulty and much assistance I recrossed the "Lava Beds," was carried to the horse and lifted upon him, and when we reached the camping ground I was lifted off him, and laid on the ground wrapped up in blankets, a humiliating termination of a great exploit. The horses were saddled, and the young men were all ready to start, but "Jim" quietly said, "Now, gentlemen, I want a good night's rest, and we shan't stir from here tonight." I believe they were really glad to have it so, as one of them was quite "finished." I retired to my arbor, wrapped myself in a roll of blankets, and was soon asleep.

When I woke, the moon was high shining through the silvery branches, whitening the bald Peak above, and glittering on the great abyss of snow behind, and pine logs were blazing like a bonfire in the cold still air. My feet were so icy cold that I could not sleep again, and getting some blankets to sit in, and making a roll of them for my back, I sat for two hours by the camp-fire. It was weird and gloriously beautiful. The students were asleep not far off in their blankets with their feet towards the fire. "Ring" lay on one side of me with his fine head on my arm, and his master sat smoking, with the fire lighting up the handsome side of his face, and except for the tones of our voices, and an occasional crackle and splutter as a pine knot blazed up, there was no sound on the mountain side. The beloved stars of my far-off home were overhead, the Plough and Pole Star, with their steady light; the glittering Pleiades, looking larger than I ever saw them, and "Orion's studded belt" shining gloriously. Once only some wild animals prowled near the camp, when "Ring," with one bound, disappeared from my side; and the horses, which were picketed by the stream, broke their lariats, stampeded, and came rushing wildly towards the fire, and it was

---

5. From Samuel Taylor Coleridge's *The Rime of the Ancient Mariner*, part 2, line 119.

fully half an hour before they were caught and quiet was restored. "Jim," or Mr. Nugent, as I always scrupulously called him, told stories of his early youth, and of a great sorrow which had led him to embark on a lawless and desperate life. His voice trembled, and tears rolled down his cheek. Was it semi-conscious acting, I wondered, or was his dark soul really stirred to its depths by the silence, the beauty, and the memories of youth?

We reached Estes Park at noon of the following day. A more successful ascent of the Peak was never made, and I would not now exchange my memories of its perfect beauty and extraordinary sublimity for any other experience of mountaineering in any part of the world. Yesterday snow fell on the summit, and it will be inaccessible for eight months to come.

John Wesley Powell
1834-1902

▬

1875: *Exploration of the Colorado River*
1878: *Report on the Lands of the Arid Region
of the United States*
1895: *Canyons of the Colorado*

▬

J OHN WESLEY POWELL'S *father, a Methodist minister, brought the
family to the United States from England in 1830. Like many new American families, the Powells tried living in several communities before settling
down, always traveling west. When Powell was born, the family was living
in Mount Morris, New York. He had his first informal education in Jackson,
Ohio. He labored on family farms in Wisconsin and Illinois. The first explorer of
the Colorado River was a man who was born and raised to be on the move.*

*Powell also had an eagerness for self-improvement. Typical of the young men
in the settlement wave, he was mostly self-educated, supplementing his reading
and study with a few years of schooling whenever possible. By the time he was
eighteen, Powell was teaching in an elementary school, and until the outbreak
of the Civil War he continued to teach in various country schools. When he had
free time, he took college courses in natural history. Eventually, Powell became a
highly respected biologist in Illinois, even though he had no diploma.*

*When he enlisted in the Union army, Powell was able to educate himself in
military tactics and procedures and thus rise in the ranks as an officer. He lost his
right arm at the battle of Shiloh, recuperated quickly, was promoted to the rank
of major, and went on to command with distinction at Vicksburg in 1863. After
the war, he taught science in several Illinois colleges.*

*Powell's determination, courage, and scientific curiosity found a challenging
outlet in the summer of 1867. While on a Colorado field trip with some students
and naturalists, Powell began considering the idea of exploring "the Canyons of*

the Grand, Green, and Colorado Rivers." On May 24, 1869, his expedition of ten men and four boats set out from Green River, Wyoming, to fill in the last remaining blank spot on the North American map: the unknown depths of the Grand Canyon. A week after Powell's group started down the river, newspapers printed a story that the expedition had already been given up for lost. But six of the explorers did make it through the canyon, reaching the Virgin River on August 30.

In contrast to the sometimes flowery, romantic quality of Isabella Bird's narrative, Powell's writing has a rather plain style. It is hard, largely unadorned, and frequently understated. Other western American naturalists—John Muir, John Burroughs, and Joseph Wood Krutch—used a similar style to characterize the new mythic American landscape, making this manner of writing familiar to readers of nature essays. The use of the present tense intensifies the suspense of the narrative, an effect that Powell frequently exploited in his writing. His account reads like an on-the-spot journal, partly because it is based on such a journal. The fact is, however, that Powell thoroughly polished and revised his account years after the journey took place. To the dismay of some historians, he also added details from his second expedition down the river and did not bother to distinguish between the two trips in his writing.

Powell was regarded as a hero for running the Grand Canyon, and so became part of the West's growing myth. He was one of a new race of men who turned their backs on cities, who exuberantly challenged the deadly unknown, and who mastered that unknown through strength, ingenuity, and perseverance. They rose to the stature of mountains, of rivers, of the land itself. None of them exhibited timorousness or weakness, at least not in the mythic version of the West: each venture into the unknown is, like Powell's, an expedition of heroes. Places such as the Colorado River are heroes' odysseys, and man-eating torrents are their encounters with Charybdis.

From the Little Colorado to the Foot
of the Grand Canyon

AUGUST 13.—We are now ready to start on our way down the
Great Unknown.[1] Our boats, tied to a common stake, chafe each
other as they are tossed by the fretful river. They ride high and
buoyant, for their loads are lighter than we could desire. We have but
a month's rations remaining. The flour has been resifted through the
mosquito-net sieve; the spoiled bacon has been dried and the worst of it
boiled; the few pounds of dried apples have been spread in the sun and
reshrunken to their normal bulk. The sugar has all melted and gone on its
way down the river. But we have a large sack of coffee. The lightening of
the boats has this advantage: they will ride the waves better and we shall
have but little to carry when we make a portage.

We are three quarters of a mile in the depths of the earth, and the great
river shrinks into insignificance as it dashes its angry waves against the walls
and cliffs that rise to the world above; the waves are but puny ripples,
and we but pigmies, running up and down the sands or lost among the
boulders.

We have an unknown distance yet to run, an unknown river to explore.
What falls there are, we know not; what rocks beset the channel, we know
not; what walls rise over the river, we know not. Ah, well! we may conjecture many things. The men talk as cheerfully as ever; jests are bandied

From John Wesley Powell, *Canyons of the Colorado* (New York: Flood and Vincent, 1895),
pp. 247–87. Originally published as *Exploration of the Colorado River* (Washington, D.C.:
Smithsonian Institution, 1875).

1. Powell and his party set out from Green River, Wyoming, on May 24, 1869.
Through June and July, they explored down the Green River to its junction with the
Colorado and followed the Colorado the rest of the way through Utah and into Arizona.
Having already run such places as Labyrinth Canyon, Marble Canyon, Echo Canyon, and
Glen Canyon, they now prepare to enter the least known and most dangerous stretch of
the Grand Canyon.

about freely this morning; but to me the cheer is somber and the jests are ghastly.

With some eagerness and some anxiety and some misgiving we enter the canyon below and are carried along by the swift water through walls which rise from its very edge. They have the same structure that we noticed yesterday—tiers of irregular shelves below, and, above these, steep slopes to the foot of marble cliffs. We run six miles in a little more than half an hour and emerge into a more open portion of the canyon, where high hills and ledges of rock intervene between the river and the distant walls. Just at the head of this open place the river runs across a dike; that is, a fissure in the rocks, open to depths below, was filled with eruptive matter, and this on cooling was harder than the rocks through which the crevice was made, and when these were washed away the harder volcanic matter remained as a wall, and the river has cut a gateway through it several hundred feet high and as many wide. As it crosses the wall, there is a fall below and a bad rapid, filled with boulders of trap; so we stop to make a portage. Then on we go, gliding by hills and ledges, with distant walls in view; sweeping past sharp angles of rock; stopping at a few points to examine rapids, which we find can be run, until we have made another five miles, when we land for dinner.

Then we let down with lines over a long rapid and start again. Once more the walls close in, and we find ourselves in a narrow gorge, the water again filling the channel and being very swift. With great care and constant watchfulness we proceed, making about four miles this afternoon, and camp in a cave.

August 14.—At daybreak we walk down the bank of the river, on a little sandy beach, to take a view of a new feature in the canyon. Heretofore hard rocks have given us bad river; soft rocks, smooth water; and a series of rocks harder than any we have experienced sets in. The river enters the gneiss! We can see but a little way into the granite gorge, but it looks threatening.

After breakfast we enter on the waves. At the very introduction it inspires awe. The canyon is narrower than we have ever before seen it; the water is swifter; there are but few broken rocks in the channel; but the walls are set, on either side, with pinnacles and crags; and sharp, angular buttresses, bristling with wind- and wave-polished spires, extend far out into the river.

Ledges of rock jut into the stream, their tops sometimes just below the surface, sometimes rising a few or many feet above; and island ledges and island pinnacles and island towers break the swift course of the stream into chutes and eddies and whirlpools. We soon reach a place where a creek comes in from the left, and, just below, the channel is choked with boulders, which have washed down this lateral canyon and formed a dam, over which there is a fall of 30 or 40 feet; but on the boulders foothold can be had, and we make a portage. Three more such dams are found. Over one we make a portage; at the other two are chutes through which we can run.

As we proceed the granite rises higher, until nearly a thousand feet of the lower part of the walls are composed of this rock.

About eleven o'clock we hear a great roar ahead, and approach it very cautiously. The sound grows louder and louder as we run, and at last we find ourselves above a long, broken fall, with ledges and pinnacles of rock obstructing the river. There is a descent of perhaps 75 or 80 feet in a third of a mile, and the rushing waters break into great waves on the rocks, and lash themselves into a mad, white foam. We can land just above, but there is no foothold on either side by which we can make a portage. It is nearly a thousand feet to the top of the granite; so it will be impossible to carry our boats around, though we can climb to the summit up a side gulch and, passing along a mile or two, descend to the river. This we find on examination; but such a portage would be impracticable for us, and we must run the rapid or abandon the river. There is no hesitation. We step into our boats, push off, and away we go, first on smooth but swift water, then we strike a glassy wave and ride to its top, down again into the trough, up again on a higher wave, and down and up on waves higher and still higher until we strike one just as it curls back, and a breaker rolls over our little boat. Still on we speed, shooting past projecting rocks, till the little boat is caught in a whirlpool and spun around several times. At last we pull out again into the stream. And now the other boats have passed us. The open compartment of the "Emma Dean" is filled with water and every breaker rolls over us. Hurled back from a rock, now on this side, now on that, we are carried into an eddy, in which we struggle for a few minutes, and are then out again, the breakers still rolling over us. Our boat is unmanageable, but she cannot sink, and we drift down another hundred yards through breakers—how, we scarcely know. We find the other boats have turned into an eddy at the foot of the fall and are waiting to catch us as we come, for the men have seen that our boat is swamped. They push out as we come near and pull us in against the wall. Our boat bailed, on we go again.

The walls now are more than a mile in height—a vertical distance difficult to appreciate. Stand on the south steps of the Treasury building in Washington and look down Pennsylvania Avenue to the Capitol; measure this distance overhead, and imagine cliffs to extend to that altitude, and you will understand what is meant; or stand at Canal Street in New York and look up Broadway to Grace Church, and you have about the distance; or stand at Lake Street bridge in Chicago and look down to the Central Depot, and you have it again.

A thousand feet of this is up through granite crags; then steep slopes and perpendicular cliffs rise one above another to the summit. The gorge is black and narrow below, red and gray and flaring above, with crags and angular projections on the walls, which, cut in many places by side canyons, seem to be a vast wilderness of rocks. Down in these grand, gloomy depths we glide, ever listening, for the mad waters keep up their roar; ever watching, ever peering ahead, for the narrow canyon is winding and the river is closed in so that we can see but a few hundred yards, and what there may be below we know not; so we listen for falls and watch for rocks, stopping now and then in the bay of a recess to admire the gigantic scenery; and ever as we go there is some new pinnacle or tower, some crag or peak, some distant view of the upper plateau, some strangely shaped rock, or some deep, narrow side canyon.

Then we come to another broken fall, which appears more difficult than the one we ran this morning. A small creek comes in on the right, and the first fall of the water is over boulders, which have been carried down by this lateral stream. We land at its mouth and stop for an hour or two to examine the fall. It seems possible to let down with lines, at least a part of the way, from point to point, along the right-hand wall. So we make a portage over the first rocks and find footing on some boulders below. Then we let down one of the boats to the end of her line, when she reaches a corner of the projecting rock, to which one of the men clings and steadies her while I examine an eddy below. I think we can pass the other boats down by us and catch them in the eddy. This is soon done, and the men in the boats in the eddy pull us to their side. On the shore of this little eddy there is about two feet of gravel beach above the water. Standing on this beach, some of the men take the line of the little boat and let it drift down against another projecting angle. Here is a little shelf, on which a man from my boat climbs, and a shorter line is passed to him, and he fastens the boat to the side of the cliff; then the second one is let down, bringing the line of the third. When the second boat is tied up, the two men standing on the beach above spring into the last boat, which is pulled up alongside of ours; then we let down the boats for 25 or 30 yards by walking along the shelf, landing them again in the mouth of a side canyon. Just below this there is another pile of boulders, over which we make another portage. From the foot of these rocks we can climb to another shelf, 40 or 50 feet above the water.

On this bench we camp for the night. It is raining hard, and we have no shelter, but find a few sticks which have lodged in the rocks, and kindle a fire and have supper. We sit on the rocks all night, wrapped in our *ponchos,* getting what sleep we can.

August 15.—This morning we find we can let down for 300 or 400 yards, and it is managed in this way: we pass along the wall by climbing from projecting point to point, sometimes near the water's edge, at other places 50 or 60 feet above, and hold the boat with a line while two men remain aboard and prevent her from being dashed against the rocks and keep the line from getting caught on the wall. In two hours we have brought them all down, as far as it is possible, in this way. A few yards below, the river strikes with great violence against a projecting rock and our boats are pulled up in a little bay above. We must now manage to pull out of this and clear the point below. The little boat is held by the bow obliquely up the stream. We jump in and pull out only a few strokes, and sweep clear of the dangerous rock. The other boats follow in the same manner and the rapid is passed.

It is not easy to describe the labor of such navigation. We must prevent the waves from dashing the boats against the cliffs. Sometimes, where the river is swift, we must put a bight of rope about a rock, to prevent the boat from being snatched from us by a wave; but where the plunge is too great or the chute too swift, we must let her leap and catch her below or the undertow will drag her under the falling water and sink her. Where we wish to run her out a little way from shore through a channel between rocks, we first throw in little sticks of driftwood and watch their course, to see where we must steer so that she will pass the channel in safety. And so we hold, and let go, and pull, and lift, and ward—among rocks, around rocks, and over rocks.

And now we go on through this solemn, mysterious way. The river is very deep, the canyon very narrow, and still obstructed, so that there is no steady flow of the stream; but the waters reel and roll and boil, and we are scarcely able to determine where we can go. Now the boat is carried to the right, perhaps close to the wall; again, she is shot into the stream, and perhaps is dragged over to the other side, where, caught in a whirlpool, she spins about. We can neither land nor run as we please. The boats are entirely unmanageable; no order in their running can be preserved; now one, now another, is ahead, each crew laboring for its own preservation. In such a place we come to another rapid. Two of the boats run it perforce. One succeeds in landing, but there is no foothold by which to make a portage and she is pushed out again into the stream. The next minute a great reflex wave fills the open compartment; she is water-logged, and drifts unmanageable. Breaker after breaker rolls over her and one capsizes her. The men are thrown out; but they cling to the boat, and she drifts down some distance alongside of us and we are able to catch her. She is soon bailed out and the men are aboard once more; but the oars are lost, and so a pair from the "Emma Dean" is spared. Then for two miles we find smooth water.

Clouds are playing in the canyon to-day. Sometimes they roll down in great masses, filling the gorge with gloom; sometimes they hang aloft from wall to wall and cover the canyon with a roof of impending storm, and we can peer long distances up and down this canyon corridor, with its cloud-roof overhead, its walls of black granite, and its river bright with the sheen of broken waters. Then a gust of wind sweeps down a side gulch and, making a rift in the clouds, reveals the blue heavens, and a stream of sunlight pours in. Then the clouds drift away into the distance, and hang around crags and peaks and pinnacles and towers and walls, and cover them with a mantle that lifts from time to time and sets them all in sharp relief. Then baby clouds creep out of side canyons, glide around points, and creep back again into more distant gorges. Then clouds arrange in strata across the canyon, with intervening vista views to cliffs and rocks beyond. The clouds are children of the heavens, and when they play among the rocks they lift them to the region above.

It rains! Rapidly little rills are formed above, and these soon grow into brooks, and the brooks grow into creeks and tumble over the walls in innumerable cascades, adding their wild music to the roar of the river. When the rain ceases the rills, brooks, and creeks run dry. The waters that fall during a rain on these steep rocks are gathered at once into the river; they could scarcely be poured in more suddenly if some vast spout ran from the clouds to the stream itself. When a storm bursts over the canyon a side gulch is dangerous, for a sudden flood may come, and the inpouring waters will raise the river so as to hide the rocks.

Early in the afternoon we discover a stream entering from the north— a clear, beautiful creek, coming down through a gorgeous red canyon. We land and camp on a sand beach above its mouth, under a great, overspreading tree with willow-shaped leaves.

August 16.—We must dry our rations again to-day and make oars.

The Colorado is never a clear stream, but for the past three or four days it has been raining much of the time, and the floods poured over the walls have brought down great quantities of mud, making it exceedingly turbid now. The little affluent which we have discovered here is a clear, beautiful creek, or river, as it would be termed in this western country, where streams are not abundant. We have named one stream, away above, in honor of the great chief of the "Bad Angels," and as this is in beautiful contrast to that, we conclude to name it "Bright Angel."

Early in the morning the whole party starts up to explore the Bright Angel River, with the special purpose of seeking timber from which to make oars. A couple of miles above we find a large pine log, which has been floated down from the plateau, probably from an altitude of more than 6,000 feet, but not many miles back. On its way it must have passed over many cataracts and falls, for it bears scars in evidence of the rough usage which it has received. The men roll it on skids, and the work of sawing oars is commenced.

This stream heads away back under a line of abrupt cliffs that terminates the plateau, and tumbles down more than 4,000 feet in the first mile or two of its course; then runs through a deep, narrow canyon until it reaches the river.

Late in the afternoon I return and go up a little gulch just above this creek, about 200 yards from camp, and discover the ruins of two or three old houses, which were originally of stone laid in mortar. Only the foundations are left, but irregular blocks, of which the houses were constructed, lie scattered about. In one room I find an old mealing-stone, deeply worn, as if it had been much used. A great deal of pottery is strewn around, and old trails, which in some places are deeply worn into the rocks, are seen.

It is ever a source of wonder to us why these ancient people sought such inaccessible places for their homes. They were, doubtless, an agricultural race, but there are no lands here of any considerable extent that they could have cultivated. To the west of Oraibi, one of the towns in the Province of Tusayan, in northern Arizona, the inhabitants have actually built little terraces along the face of the cliff where a spring gushes out, and thus made their sites for gardens. It is possible that the ancient inhabitants of this place made their agricultural lands in the same way. But why should they seek such spots? Surely the country was not so crowded with people as to demand the utilization of so barren a region. The only solution suggested of the problem is this: We know that for a century or two after the settlement of Mexico many expeditions were sent into the country now comprising Arizona and New Mexico, for the purpose of bringing the town-building people under the dominion of the Spanish government. Many of their villages were destroyed, and the inhabitants fled to regions at that time unknown; and there are traditions among the people who inhabit the pueblos that still remain that the canyons were these unknown lands. It may be these buildings were erected at that time; sure it is that they have a much more modern appearance than the ruins scattered over Nevada, Utah, Colorado,

Arizona, and New Mexico. Those old Spanish conquerors had a monstrous greed for gold and a wonderful lust for saving souls. Treasures they must have, if not on earth, why, then, in heaven; and when they failed to find heathen temples bedecked with silver, they propitiated Heaven by seizing the heathen themselves. There is yet extant a copy of a record made by a heathen artist to express his conception of the demands of the conquerers. In one part of the picture we have a lake, and near by stands a priest pouring water on the head of a native. On the other side, a poor Indian has a cord about his throat. Lines run from these two groups to a central figure, a man with beard and full Spanish panoply. The interpretation of the picture-writing is this: "Be baptized as this saved heathen, or be hanged as that damned heathen." Doubtless, some of these people preferred another alternative, and rather than be baptized or hanged they chose to imprison themselves within these canyon walls.

August 17.—Our rations are still spoiling; the bacon is so badly injured that we are compelled to throw it away. By an accident, this morning, the saleratus was lost overboard. We have now only musty flour sufficient for ten days and a few dried apples, but plenty of coffee. We must make all haste possible. If we meet with difficulties such as we have encountered in the canyon above, we may be compelled to give up the expedition and try to reach the Mormon settlements to the north. Our hopes are that the worst places are passed, but our barometers are all so much injured as to be useless, and so we have lost our reckoning in altitude, and know not how much descent the river has yet to make.

The stream is still wild and rapid and rolls through a narrow channel. We make but slow progress, often landing against a wall and climbing around some point to see the river below. Although very anxious to advance, we are determined to run with great caution, lest by another accident we lose our remaining supplies. How precious that little flour has become! We divide it among the boats and carefully store it away, so that it can be lost only by the loss of the boat itself.

We make ten miles and a half, and camp among the rocks on the right. We have had rain from time to time all day, and have been thoroughly drenched and chilled; but between showers the sun shines with great power and the mercury in our thermometers stands at 115°, so that we have rapid changes from great extremes, which are very disagreeable. It is especially cold in the rain to-night. The little canvas we have is rotten and useless; the rubber *ponchos* with which we started from Green River City have all been lost; more than half the party are without hats, not one of us has an entire suit of clothes, and we have not a blanket apiece. So we gather driftwood and build a fire; but after supper the rain, coming down in torrents, extinguishes it, and we sit up all night on the rocks, shivering, and are more exhausted by the night's discomfort than by the day's toil.

August 18.—The day is employed in making portages and we advance but two miles on our journey. Still it rains.

While the men are at work making portages I climb up the granite to its summit and go away back over the rust-colored sandstones and greenish-yellow shales to the foot of the marble wall. I climb so high that the men and boats are lost in the black depths below and the dashing river is a rippling brook, and still there is more canyon above than below. All about me are interesting geologic records. The book is open and I can read as I run. All about me are grand views, too, for the clouds are playing again in the gorges. But somehow I think of the nine days' rations and the bad river, and the lesson of the rocks and the glory of the scene are but half conceived.

I push on to an angle, where I hope to get a view of the country beyond, to see if possible what the prospect may be of our soon running through this plateau, or at least of meeting with some geologic change that will let us out of the granite; but, arriving at the point, I can see below only a labyrinth of black gorges.

August 19.—Rain again this morning. We are in our granite prison still, and the time until noon is occupied in making a long, bad portage.

After dinner, in running a rapid the pioneer boat is upset by a wave. We are some distance in advance of the larger boats. The river is rough and swift and we are unable to land, but cling to the boat and are carried down stream over another rapid. The men in the boats above see our trouble, but they are caught in whirlpools and are spinning about in eddies, and it seems a long time before they come to our relief. At last they do come; our boat is turned right side up and bailed out; the oars, which fortunately have floated along in company with us, are gathered up, and on we go, without even landing. The clouds break away and we have sunshine again.

Soon we find a little beach with just room enough to land. Here we camp, but there is no wood. Across the river and a little way above, we see some driftwood lodged in the rocks. So we bring two boat loads over, build a huge fire, and spread everything to dry. It is the first cheerful night we have had for a week—a warm, drying fire in the midst of the camp, and a few bright stars in our patch of heavens overhead.

August 20.—The characteristics of the canyon change this morning. The river is broader, the walls more sloping, and composed of black slates that stand on edge. These nearly vertical slates are washed out in places—that is, the softer beds are washed out between the harder, which are left standing. In this way curious little alcoves are formed, in which are quiet bays of water, but on a much smaller scale than the great bays and buttresses of Marble Canyon.

The river is still rapid and we stop to let down with lines several times, but make greater progress, as we run ten miles. We camp on the right bank. Here, on a terrace of trap, we discover another group of ruins. There was evidently quite a village on this rock. Again we find mealing-stones and much broken pottery, and up on a little natural shelf in the rock back of the ruins we find a globular basket that would hold perhaps a third of a bushel. It is badly broken, and as I attempt to take it up it falls to pieces. There are many beautiful flint chips, also, as if this had been the home of an old arrow-maker.

August 21.—We start early this morning, cheered by the prospect of a fine day and encouraged also by the good run made yesterday. A quarter of a mile below camp the river turns abruptly to the left, and between camp and that point is very swift, running down in a long, broken chute and piling up against the foot of the cliff, where it turns to the left. We try to pull across, so as to go down on the other side, but the waters are swift and it seems impossible for us to escape the rock below; but, in pulling across, the bow of the boat is turned to the farther shore, so that we are swept broadside down and are prevented by the rebounding waters from striking against the wall. We toss about for a few seconds in these billows and are then carried past the danger. Below, the river turns again to the right, the canyon is very narrow, and we see in advance but a short distance. The water, too, is very swift, and there is no landing-place. From around this curve there comes a mad roar, and down we are carried with a dizzying velocity to the head of another rapid. On either side high over our heads there are overhanging granite walls, and the sharp bends cut off our view, so that a few minutes will carry us into unknown waters. Away we go on one long, winding chute. I stand on deck, supporting myself with a strap fastened on either side of the gunwale. The boat glides rapidly where the water is smooth, then, striking a wave, she leaps and bounds like a thing of life, and we have a wild, exhilarating ride for ten miles, which we make in less than an hour. The excitement is so great that we forget the danger until we hear the roar of a great fall below; then we back on our oars and are carried slowly toward its head and succeed in landing just above and find that we have to make another portage. At this we are engaged until some time after dinner.

Just here we run out of the granite. Ten miles in less than half a day, and limestone walls below. Good cheer returns; we forget the storms and the gloom and the cloud-covered canyons and the black granite and the raging river, and push our boats from shore in great glee.

Though we are out of the granite, the river is still swift, and we wheel about a point again to the right, and turn, so as to head back in the direction from which we came; this brings the granite in sight again, with its narrow gorge and black crags; but we meet with no more great falls or rapids. Still, we run cautiously and stop from time to time to examine some places which look bad. Yet we make ten miles this afternoon; twenty miles in all to-day.

August 22.—We come to rapids again this morning and are occupied several hours in passing them, letting the boats down from rock to rock with lines for nearly half a mile, and then have to make a long portage. While the men are engaged in this I climb the wall on the northeast to a height of about 2,500 feet, where I can obtain a good view of a long stretch of canyon below. Its course is to the southwest. The walls seem to rise very abruptly for 2,500 or 3,000 feet, and then there is a gently sloping terrace on each side for two or three miles, when we again find cliffs, 1,500 or 2,000 feet high. From the brink of these the plateau stretches back to the north and south for a long distance. Away down the canyon on the right wall I can see a group of mountains, some of which appear to stand on the brink of the canyon. The effect of the terrace is to give the appearance of a narrow winding valley with high walls on either side and a deep, dark, meandering gorge down its middle. It is impossible from this point of view to determine whether or not we have granite at the bottom; but from geologic considerations, I conclude that we shall have marble walls below.

After my return to the boats we run another mile and camp for the night. We have made but little over seven miles to-day, and a part of our flour has been soaked in the river again.

August 23.—Our way to-day is again through marble walls. Now and then we pass for a short distance through patches of granite, like hills thrust up into the limestone. At one of these places we have to make another portage, and, taking advantage of the delay, I go up a little stream to the north, wading it all the way, sometimes having to plunge in to my neck, in other places being compelled to swim across little basins that have been excavated at the foot of the falls. Along its course are many cascades and springs, gushing out from the rocks on either side. Sometimes a cottonwood tree grows over the water. I come to one beautiful fall, of more than 150 feet, and climb around it to the right on the broken rocks. Still going up, the canyon is found to narrow very much, being but 15 or 20 feet wide; yet the walls rise on either side many hundreds of feet, perhaps thousands; I can hardly tell.

In some places the stream has not excavated its channel down vertically through the rocks, but has cut obliquely, so that one wall overhangs the other. In other places it is cut vertically above and obliquely below, or obliquely above and vertically below, so that it is impossible to see out overhead. But I can go no farther; the time which I estimated it would take to make the portage has almost expired, and I start back on a round trot, wading in the creek where I must and plunging through basins. The men are waiting for me, and away we go on the river.

Just after dinner we pass a stream on the right, which leaps into the Colorado by a direct fall of more than 100 feet, forming a beautiful cascade. There is a bed of very hard rock above, 30 or 40 feet in thickness, and there are much softer beds below. The hard beds above project many yards beyond the softer, which are washed out, forming a deep cave behind the fall, and the stream pours through a narrow crevice above into a deep pool below. Around on the rocks in the cavelike chamber are set beautiful ferns, with delicate fronds and enameled stalks. The frondlets have their points turned down to form spore cases. It has very much the appearance of the maidenhair fern, but is much larger. This delicate foliage covers the rocks all about the fountain, and gives the chamber great beauty. But we have little time to spend in admiration; so on we go.

We make fine progress this afternoon, carried along by a swift river, shooting over the rapids and finding no serious obstructions. The canyon walls for 2,500 or 3,000 feet are very regular, rising almost perpendicularly, but here and there set with narrow steps, and occasionally we can see away above the broad terrace to distant cliffs.

We camp to-night in a marble cave, and find on looking at our reckoning that we have run 22 miles.

August 24.—The canyon is wider to-day. The walls rise to a vertical height of nearly 3,000 feet. In many places the river runs under a cliff in great curves, forming amphitheaters half-dome shaped.

Though the river is rapid, we meet with no serious obstructions and run 20 miles. How anxious we are to make up our reckoning every time we stop, now that our diet is confined to plenty of coffee, a very little spoiled flour, and very few dried apples! It has come to be a race for a dinner. Still, we make such fine progress that all hands are in good cheer, but not a moment of daylight is lost.

August 25.—We make 12 miles this morning, when we come to monuments of lava standing in the river,—low rocks mostly, but some of them shafts more than a hundred feet high. Going on down three or four miles, we find them increasing in number. Great quantities of cooled lava and many cinder cones are seen on either side; and then we come to an abrupt cataract. Just over the fall on the right wall a cinder cone, or extinct volcano, with a well-defined crater, stands on the very brink of the canyon. This, doubtless, is the one we saw two or three days ago. From this volcano vast floods of lava have been poured down into the river, and a stream of molten rock has run up the canyon three or four miles and down we know not how far. Just where it poured over the canyon wall is the fall. The whole north side as far as we can see is lined with the black basalt, and high up on the opposite wall are patches of the same material, resting on the benches and filling old alcoves and caves, giving the wall a spotted appearance.

The rocks are broken in two along a line which here crosses the river, and the beds we have seen while coming down the canyon for the last 30 miles have dropped 800 feet on the lower side of the line, forming what geologists call a "fault." The volcanic cone stands directly over the fissure thus formed. On the left side of the river, opposite, mammoth springs burst out of this crevice, 100 or 200 feet above the river, pouring in a stream quite equal in volume to the Colorado Chiquito.

This stream seems to be loaded with carbonate of lime, and the water, evaporating, leaves an incrustation on the rocks; and this process has been continued for a long time, for extensive deposits are noticed in which are basins with bubbling springs. The water is salty.

We have to make a portage here, which is completed in about three hours; then on we go.

We have no difficulty as we float along, and I am able to observe the wonderful phenomena connected with this flood of lava. The canyon was doubtless filled to a height of 1,200 or 1,500 feet, perhaps by more than one flood. This would dam the water back; and in cutting through this great lava bed, a new channel has been formed, sometimes on one side, sometimes on the other. The cooled lava, being of firmer texture than the rocks of which the walls are composed, remains in some places; in others a narrow channel has been cut, leaving a line of basalt on either side. It is possible that the lava cooled faster on the sides against the walls and that the center ran out; but of this we can only conjecture. There are other places where almost the whole of the lava is gone, only patches of it being seen where it has caught on the walls. As we float down we can see that it ran out into side canyons. In some places this basalt has a fine, columnar structure, often in concentric prisms, and masses of these concentric columns have coalesced. In some places, when the flow occurred the canyon was probably about the same depth that it is now, for we can see where the basalt has rolled out on the sands, and—what seems curious to me—the sands are not melted or metamorphosed to any appreciable extent. In places the bed of the river is of sandstone or limestone, in other places of lava, showing that it has all been cut out again where the sandstones and limestones appear; but there is a little yet left where the bed is of lava.

What a conflict of water and fire there must have been here! Just imagine a river of molten rock running down into a river of melted snow. What a seething and boiling of the waters; what clouds of steam rolled into the heavens!

Thirty-five miles to-day. Hurrah!

August 26.—The canyon walls are steadily becoming higher as we advance. They are still bold and nearly vertical up to the terrace. We still see evidence of the eruption discovered yesterday, but the thickness of the basalt is decreasing as we go down stream; yet it has been reinforced at points by streams that have come down from volcanoes standing on the terrace above, but which we cannot see from the river below.

Since we left the Colorado Chiquito we have seen no evidences that the tribe of Indians inhabiting the plateaus on either side ever come down to the river; but about eleven o'clock to-day we discover an Indian garden at the foot of the wall on the right, just where a little stream with a narrow flood plain comes down through a side canyon. Along the valley the Indians have planted corn, using for irrigation the water which bursts out in springs at the foot of the cliff. The corn is looking quite well, but it is not sufficiently advanced to give us roasting ears; but there are some nice green squashes. We carry ten or a dozen of these on board our boats and hurriedly leave, not willing to be caught in the robbery, yet excusing ourselves by pleading our great want. We run down a short distance to where we feel certain no Indian can follow, and what a kettle of squash sauce we make! True, we have no salt with which to season it, but it makes a fine addition to our unleavened bread and coffee. Never was fruit so sweet as these stolen squashes.

After dinner we push on again and make fine time, finding many rapids, but none so bad that we cannot run them with safety; and when we stop, just at dusk, and foot up our reckoning, we find we have run 35 miles again. A few days like this, and we are out of prison.

We have a royal supper—unleavened bread, green squash sauce, and strong coffee. We have been for a few days on half rations, but now have no stint of roast squash.

August 27.—This morning the river takes a more southerly direction. The dip of the rocks is to the north and we are running rapidly into lower formations. Unless our course changes we shall very soon run again into the granite. This gives some anxiety. Now and then the river turns to the west and excites hopes that are soon destroyed by another turn to the south. About nine o'clock we come to the dreaded rock. It is with no little misgiving that we see the river enter these black, hard walls. At its very entrance we have to make a portage; then let down with lines past some ugly rocks. We run a mile or two farther, and then the rapids below can be seen.

About eleven o'clock we come to a place in the river which seems much worse than any we have yet met in all its course. A little creek comes down from the left. We land first on the right and clamber up over the granite pinnacles for a mile or two, but can see no way by which to let down, and to run it would be sure destruction. After dinner we cross to examine on the left. High above the river we can walk along on the top of the granite, which is broken off at the edge and set with crags and pinnacles, so that it is very difficult to get a view of the river at all. In my eagerness to reach a point where I can see the roaring fall below, I go too far on the wall, and can neither advance nor retreat. I stand with one foot on a little projecting rock and cling with my hand fixed in a little crevice. Finding I am caught here, suspended 400 feet above the river, into which I must fall if my footing fails, I call for help. The men come and pass me a line, but I cannot let go of the rock long enough to take hold of it. Then they bring two or three of the largest oars. All this takes time which seems very precious to me; but at last they arrive. The blade of one of the oars is pushed into a little crevice in the rock beyond me in such a manner that they can hold me pressed against the wall. Then another is fixed in such a way that I can step on it; and thus I am extricated.

Still another hour is spent in examining the river from this side, but no good view of it is obtained; so now we return to the side that was first examined, and the afternoon is spent in clambering among the crags and pinnacles and carefully scanning the river again. We find that the lateral streams have washed boulders into the river, so as to form a dam, over which the water makes a broken fall of 18 or 20 feet; then there is a rapid, beset with rocks, for 200 or 300 yards, while on the other side, points of the wall project into the river. Below, there is a second fall; how great, we cannot tell. Then there is a rapid, filled with huge rocks, for 100 or 200 yards. At the bottom of it, from the right wall, a great rock projects quite halfway across the river. It has a sloping surface extending up stream, and the water, coming down with all the momentum gained in the falls and rapids above, rolls up this inclined plane many feet, and tumbles over to the left. I decide that it is possible to let down over the first fall, then run near the right cliff to a point just above the second, where we can pull out into a little chute, and, having run over that in safety, if we pull with all our power across the stream, we may avoid the great rock below. On my return to the boat I announce to the men that we are to run it in the morning. Then we cross the river and go into camp for the night on some rocks in the mouth of the little side canyon.

After supper Captain Howland asks to have a talk with me. We walk up the little creek a short distance, and I soon find that his object is to remonstrate against my determination to proceed. He thinks that we had better abandon the river here. Talking with him, I learn that he, his brother, and William Dunn have determined to go no farther in the boats. So we return to camp. Nothing is said to the other men.

For the last two days our course has not been plotted. I sit down and do this now, for the purpose of finding where we are by dead reckoning. It is a clear night, and I take out the sextant to make observation for latitude, and I find that the astronomic determination agrees very nearly with that of the plot—quite as closely as might be expected from a meridian observation on a planet. In a direct line, we must be about 45 miles from the mouth of the Rio Virgen. If we can reach that point, we know that there are settlements up that river about 20 miles. This 45 miles in a direct line will probably be 80 or 90 by the meandering line of the river. But then we know that there is comparatively open country for many miles above the mouth of the Virgen, which is our point of destination.

As soon as I determine all this, I spread my plot on the sand and wake Howland, who is sleeping down by the river, and show him where I suppose we are, and where several Mormon settlements are situated.

We have another short talk about the morrow, and he lies down again; but for me there is no sleep. All night long I pace up and down a little path, on a few yards of sand beach, along by the river. Is it wise to go on? I go to the boats again to look at our rations. I feel satisfied that we can get over the danger immediately before us; what there may be below I know not. From our outlook yesterday on the cliffs, the canyon seemed to make another great bend to the south, and this, from our experience heretofore, means more and higher granite walls. I am not sure that we can climb out of the canyon here, and, if at the top of the wall, I know enough of the country to be certain that it is a desert of rock and sand between this and the nearest Mormon town, which, on the most direct line, must be 75 miles away. True, the late rains have been favorable to us, should we go out, for the probabilities are that we shall find water still standing in holes; and at one time I almost conclude to leave the river. But for years I have been contemplating this trip. To leave the exploration unfinished, to say that there is a part of the canyon which I cannot explore, having already nearly accomplished it, is more than I am willing to acknowledge, and I determine to go on.

I wake my brother and tell him of Howland's determination, and he promises to stay with me; then I call up Hawkins, the cook, and he makes a like promise; then Sumner and Bradley and Hall, and they all agree to go on.

August 28.—At last daylight comes and we have breakfast without a word being said about the future. The meal is as solemn as a funeral. After breakfast I ask the three men if they still think it best to leave us. The elder Howland thinks it is, and Dunn agrees with him. The younger Howland tries to persuade them to go on with the party; failing in which, he decides to go with his brother.

Then we cross the river. The small boat is very much disabled and unseaworthy. With the loss of hands, consequent on the departure of the three men, we shall not be able to run all of the boats; so I decide to leave my "Emma Dean."

Two rifles and a shotgun are given to the men who are going out. I ask them to help themselves to the rations and take what they think to be a fair share. This they refuse to do, saying they have no fear but that they can get something to eat; but Billy, the cook, has a pan of biscuits prepared for dinner, and these he leaves on a rock.

Before starting, we take from the boat our barometers, fossils, the minerals, and some ammunition and leave them on the rocks. We are going over this place as light as possible. The three men help us lift our boats over a rock 25 or 30 feet high and let them down again over the first fall, and now we are all ready to start. The last thing before leaving, I write a letter to my wife and give it to Howland. Sumner gives him his watch, directing that it be sent to his sister should he not be heard from again. The records of the expedition have been kept in duplicate. One set of these is given to Howland; and now we are ready. For the last time they entreat us not to go on, and tell us that it is madness to set out in this place; that we can never get safely through it; and, further, that the river turns again to the south into the granite, and a few miles of such rapids and falls will exhaust our entire stock of rations, and then it will be too late to climb out. Some tears are shed; it is rather a solemn parting; each party thinks the other is taking the dangerous course.

My old boat left, I go on board of the "Maid of the Canyon." The three men climb a crag that overhangs the river to watch us off. The "Maid of the Canyon" pushes out. We glide rapidly along the foot of the wall, just grazing one great rock, then pull out a little into the chute of the second fall and plunge over it. The open compartment is filled when we strike the first wave below, but we cut through it, and then the men pull with all their power toward the left wall and swing clear of the dangerous rock below all right. We are scarcely a minute in running it, and find that, although it looked bad from above, we have passed many places that were worse.

The other boat follows without more difficulty. We land at the first practicable point below, and fire our guns, as a signal to the men above that we have come over in safety. Here we remain a couple of hours, hoping that they will take the smaller boat and follow us. We are behind a curve in the canyon and cannot see up to where we left them, and so we wait until their coming seems hopeless, and then push on.

And now we have a succession of rapids and falls until noon, all of which we run in safety. Just after dinner we come to another bad place. A little stream comes in from the left, and below there is a fall, and still below another fall. Above, the river tumbles down, over and among the rocks, in whirlpools and great waves, and the waters are lashed into mad, white foam. We run along the left, above this, and soon see that we cannot get down on this side, but it seems possible to let down on the other. We pull up stream again for 200 or 300 yards and cross. Now there is a bed of basalt on this northern side of the canyon, with a bold escarpment that seems to be a hundred feet high. We can climb it and walk along its summit to a point where we are just at the head of the fall. Here the basalt is broken down again, so it seems to us, and I direct the men to take a line to the top of the cliff and let the boats down along the wall. One man remains in the boat to keep her clear of the rocks and prevent her line from being caught on the projecting angles. I climb the cliff and pass along to a point just over the fall and descend by broken rocks, and find that the break of the fall is above the break of the wall, so that we cannot land, and that still below the river is very bad, and that there is no possibility of a portage. Without waiting further to examine and determine what shall be done, I hasten back to the top of the cliff to stop the boats from coming down. When I arrive I find the men have let one of them down to the head of the fall. She is in swift water and they are not able to pull her back; nor are they able to go on with the line, as it is not long enough to reach the higher part of the cliff which is just before them; so they take a bight around a crag. I send two men back for the other line. The boat is in very swift water, and Bradley is standing in the open compartment, holding out his oar to prevent her from striking against the foot of the cliff. Now she shoots out into the stream and up as far as the line will permit, and then, wheeling, drives headlong against the rock, and then out and back again, now straining on the line, now striking against the rock. As soon as the second line is brought, we pass it down to him; but his attention is all taken up with his own situation, and he does not see that we are passing him the line. I stand on a projecting rock, waving my hat to gain his attention, for my voice is drowned by the roaring of the falls. Just at this moment I see him take his knife from its sheath and step forward to cut the line. He has evidently decided that it is better to go over with the boat as it is than to wait for her to be broken to pieces. As he leans over, the boat sheers again into the stream, the stem-post breaks away and she is loose. With perfect composure Bradley seizes the great scull oar, places it in the stern rowlock, and pulls with all his power (and he is an athlete) to turn the bow of the boat down stream, for he wishes to go bow down, rather than to drift broadside on. One, two strokes he makes, and a third just as she goes over, and the boat is fairly turned, and she goes down almost beyond our sight, though we are more than a hundred feet above the river. Then she comes up again on a great wave, and down and up, then around behind some great rocks, and is lost in the mad, white foam below. We stand frozen with fear, for we see no boat. Bradley is gone! so it seems. But now, away below, we see something coming out of the waves. It is evidently a boat. A moment more, and we see Bradley standing on deck, swinging his hat to show that he is all right. But he is in a whirlpool. We have the stem-post of his boat attached to the line. How badly she may be disabled we know not. I direct Sumner and Powell to pass along the cliff and see if they can reach him from below. Hawkins, Hall, and myself run to the other boat, jump aboard, push out, and away we go over the falls. A wave rolls over us and our boat is unmanageable. Another great wave strikes us, and the boat rolls over, and tumbles and tosses, I know not how. All I know is that Bradley is picking us up. We soon have all right again, and row to the cliff and wait until Sumner and Powell can come. After a difficult climb they reach us. We run two or three miles farther and turn again to the northwest, continuing until night, when we have run out of the granite once more.

August 29.—We start very early this morning. The river still continues swift, but we have no serious difficulty, and at twelve o'clock emerge from the Grand Canyon of the Colorado. We are in a valley now, and low mountains are seen in the distance, coming to the river below. We recognize this as the Grand Wash.

A few years ago a party of Mormons set out from St. George, Utah, taking with them a boat, and came down to the Grand Wash, where they divided, a portion of the party crossing the river to explore the San Francisco Mountains. Three men–Hamblin, Miller, and Crosby—taking the boat, went on down the river to Callville, landing a few miles below the mouth of the Rio Virgen. We have their manuscript journal with us, and so the stream is comparatively well known.

To-night we camp on the left bank, in a mesquite thicket.

The relief from danger and the joy of success are great. When he who has been chained by wounds to a hospital cot until his canvas tent seems like a dungeon cell, until the groans of those who lie about tortured with probe and knife are piled up, a weight of horror on his ears that he cannot throw off, cannot forget, and until the stench of festering wounds and anæsthetic drugs has filled the air with its loathsome burthen,—when he at last goes out into the open field, what a world he sees! How beautiful the sky, how bright the sunshine, what "floods of delirious music" pour from the throats of birds, how sweet the fragrance of earth and tree and blossom! The first hour of convalescent freedom seems rich recompense for all pain and gloom and terror.

Something like these are the feelings we experience to-night. Ever before us has been an unknown danger, heavier than immediate peril. Every waking hour passed in the Grand Canyon has been one of toil. We have watched with deep solicitude the steady disappearance of our scant supply of rations, and from time to time have seen the river snatch a portion of the little left, while we were a-hungered. And danger and toil were endured in those gloomy depths, where ofttimes clouds hid the sky by day and but a narrow zone of stars could be seen at night. Only during the few hours of deep sleep, consequent on hard labor, has the roar of the waters been hushed. Now the danger is over, now the toil has ceased, now the gloom has disappeared, now the firmament is bounded only by the horizon, and what a vast expanse of constellations can be seen!

The river rolls by us in silent majesty; the quiet of the camp is sweet; our joy is almost ecstasy. We sit till long after midnight talking of the Grand Canyon, talking of home, but talking chiefly of the three men who left us. Are they wandering in those depths, unable to find a way out? Are they searching over the desert lands above for water? Or are they nearing the settlements?

August 30.—We run in two or three short, low canyons to-day, and on emerging from one we discover a band of Indians in the valley below. They see us, and scamper away in eager haste to hide among the rocks. Although we land and call for them to return, not an Indian can be seen.

Two or three miles farther down, in turning a short bend of the river, we come upon another camp. So near are we before they can see us that I can shout to them, and, being able to speak a little of their language, I tell them we are friends; but they all flee to the rocks, except a man, a woman, and two children. We land and talk with them. They are without lodges, but have built little shelters of boughs, under which they wallow in the sand. The man is dressed in a hat; the woman, in a string of beads only. At first they are evidently much terrified; but when I talk to them in their own language and tell them we are friends, and inquire after people in the Mormon towns, they are soon reassured and beg for tobacco. Of this precious article we have none to spare. Sumner looks around in the boat for something to give them, and finds a little piece of colored soap, which they receive as a valuable present,—rather as a thing of beauty than as a useful commodity, however. They are either unwilling or unable to tell us anything about the Indians or white people, and so we push off, for we must lose no time.

We camp at noon under the right bank. And now as we push out we are in great expectancy, for we hope every minute to discover the mouth of the Rio Virgen. Soon one of the men exclaims: "Yonder's an Indian in the river." Looking for a few minutes, we certainly do see two or three persons. The men bend to their oars and pull toward them. Approaching, we see that there are three white men and an Indian hauling a seine, and then we discover that it is just at the mouth of the long-sought river.

As we come near, the men seem far less surprised to see us than we do to see them. They evidently know who we are, and on talking with them they tell us that we have been reported lost long ago, and that some weeks before a messenger had been sent from Salt Lake City with instructions for them to watch for any fragments or relics of our party that might drift down the stream.

Our new-found friends, Mr. Asa and his two sons, tell us that they are pioneers of a town that is to be built on the bank. Eighteen or twenty miles up the valley of the Rio Virgen there are two Mormon towns, St. Joseph and St. Thomas. To-night we dispatch an Indian to the last-mentioned place to bring any letters that may be there for us.

Our arrival here is very opportune. When we look over our store of supplies, we find about 10 pounds of flour, 15 pounds of dried apples, but 70 or 80 pounds of coffee.

August 31.—This afternoon the Indian returns with a letter informing us that Bishop Leithhead of St. Thomas and two or three other Mormons are coming down with a wagon, bringing us supplies. They arrive about sundown. Mr. Asa treats us with great kindness to the extent of his ability; but Bishop Leithhead brings in his wagon two or three dozen melons and many other little luxuries, and we are comfortable once more.

September 1.—This morning Sumner, Bradley, Hawkins, and Hall, taking on a small supply of rations, start down the Colorado with the boats. It is their intention to go to Fort Mojave, and perhaps from there overland to Los Angeles.

Captain Powell and myself return with Bishop Leithhead to St. Thomas. From St. Thomas we go to Salt Lake City.[2]

2. Powell later learned that William Dunn and the two Howland brothers managed to climb out of the canyon but were killed by Shivwits Indians. The Indians claimed that they had been seeking revenge: they had mistaken the three men for a group of miners who had killed an Indian woman.

Mark Twain
1835-1910

━━

1869: *The Innocents Abroad*
1872: *Roughing It*
1876: *The Adventures of Tom Sawyer*
1883: *Life on the Mississippi*
1884: *The Adventures of Huckleberry Finn*

━━

CHRISTENED *Samuel Langhorne Clemens, Mark Twain grew up in Hannibal, Missouri. He began his career as a printer's apprentice and became a printer, but he grew restless and soon started on a long tour of the East, primarily New York. Returning to the Mississippi River, Clemens went into training as an apprentice river pilot. But as soon as he had earned his license, the outbreak of the Civil War closed down traffic on the Mississippi River, put a virtual end to the era of the great steamboats, and threw Clemens out of work. His brother Orion had just been appointed secretary to the new governor of the Nevada Territory; Samuel accepted an offer to become his brother's secretary and to accompany him out West. What happened on the trip, and what happened after they arrived, became the basis of* Roughing It.

There was very little pay and even less excitement in being his brother's secretary. But it was 1861, and the goldfields of Nevada were booming. Clemens tried the mining business but soon found that he could make an easier living as a newspaperman. He began writing under the name Mark Twain, first in Virginia City and then in California. In 1865 he published "The Celebrated Jumping Frog of Calaveras County," the story that launched his writing career.

Impressed with the popularity of Twain's frog story, a California newspaper hired Twain as a special traveling correspondent and put him aboard a ship bound for the Sandwich Islands. On his return he discovered that people would pay to listen to his lectures; they would also buy copies of his travel narrative. He called it The Innocents Abroad, *and it made so much money for Twain that he began to write another such narrative, this one based on his stagecoach trip with the secretary to the new governor of the Nevada Territory.*

When Roughing It *arrived in print in 1872, so did Mark Twain's reputation. Both the book and the man seemed to typify the western image.* Roughing It *was new myth about a rough, wild land and a coarse new people. To his sophisticated eastern audience, Twain even introduced a scruffy, disreputable coyote who became a hero worthy of Aesop's fables. On the passing stagecoach sat a new western mogul, the heroic stage driver. This lord of the leather reins was a dry-land version of Twain's omnipotent riverboat pilot; neither was actually a demigod, but both certainly represented the cream of democracy's self-made aristocrats.*

Although Twain wrote several western short stories and collaborated with Bret Harte on Ah Sin, *a mining camp melodrama,* Roughing It *was Twain's only western book. It gave eastern readers a fresh and entertaining view of the West. But Twain also demonstrated that there was a new literature coming out of the West, a literature with its own unique anecdotes, tall tales, fables, legends, and characters. And at the same time that* Roughing It *introduced a western style of literature, it also expanded the myth of the western storyteller: plainspoken, unpretentious, self-made, and almost unselfconsciously humorous.*

▬

The Desert Cayote

ANOTHER night of alternate tranquillity and turmoil. But morning came, by and by. It was another glad awakening to fresh breezes, vast expanses of level greensward, bright sunlight, an impressive solitude utterly without visible human beings or human habitations, and an atmosphere of such amazing magnifying properties that trees that seemed close at hand were more than three miles away. We resumed undress uniform, climbed a-top of the flying coach, dangled our legs over the side, shouted occasionally at our frantic mules, merely to see them lay their ears back and scamper faster, tied our hats on to keep our hair from blowing away, and leveled an outlook over the world-wide carpet about us for things new and strange to gaze at. Even at this day it thrills me through and through to think of the life, the gladness and the wild sense of free-

This and the following two selections are from Mark Twain, *Roughing It*, vol. 1 (New York: Harper and Brothers, 1899), pp. 47–68.

dom that used to make the blood dance in my veins on those fine overland mornings!

Along about an hour after breakfast we saw the first prairie-dog villages, the first antelope, and the first wolf. If I remember rightly, this latter was the regular *cayote* (pronounced ky-*o*-te) of the farther deserts. And if it *was,* he was not a pretty creature, or respectable either, for I got well acquainted with his race afterward, and can speak with confidence. The cayote is a long, slim, sick and sorry-looking skeleton, with a gray wolf-skin stretched over it, a tolerably bushy tail that forever sags down with a despairing expression of forsakenness and misery, a furtive and evil eye, and a long, sharp face, with slightly lifted lip and exposed teeth. He has a general slinking expression all over. The cayote is a living, breathing allegory of Want. He is *always* hungry. He is always poor, out of luck and friendless. The meanest creatures despise him, and even the fleas would desert him for a velocipede. He is so spiritless and cowardly that even while his exposed teeth are pretending a threat, the rest of his face is apologizing for it. And he is *so* homely!—so scrawny, and ribby, and coarse-haired, and pitiful. When he sees you he lifts his lip and lets a flash of his teeth out, and then turns a little out of the course he was pursuing, depresses his head a bit, and strikes a long, soft-footed trot through the sage-brush, glancing over his shoulder at you, from time to time, till he is about out of easy pistol range, and then he stops and takes a deliberate survey of you; he will trot fifty yards and stop again—another fifty and stop again; and finally the gray of his gliding body blends with the gray of the sage-brush, and he disappears. All this is when you make no demonstration against him; but if you do, he develops a livelier interest in his journey, and instantly electrifies his heels and puts such a deal of real estate between himself and your weapon, that by the time you have raised the hammer you see that you need a minie rifle, and by the time you have got him in line you need a rifled cannon, and by the time you have "drawn a bead" on him you see well enough that nothing but an unusually long-winded streak of lightning could reach him where he is now. But if you start a swift-footed dog after him, you will enjoy it ever so much—especially if it is a dog that has a good opinion of himself, and has been brought up to think he knows something about speed. The cayote will go swinging gently off on that deceitful trot of his, and every little while he will smile a fraudful smile over his shoulder that will fill that dog entirely full of encouragement and worldly ambition, and make him lay his head still lower to the ground, and stretch his neck further to the front, and pant more fiercely, and stick his tail out straighter behind, and move his furious legs with a yet wilder frenzy, and leave a broader and broader, and higher and denser cloud of desert sand smoking behind, and marking his long wake across the level plain! And all this time the dog is only a short twenty feet behind the cayote, and to save the soul of him he cannot understand why it is that he cannot get perceptibly closer; and he begins to get aggravated, and it makes him madder and madder to see how gently the cayote glides along and never pants or sweats or ceases to smile; and he grows still more and more incensed to see how shamefully he has been taken in by an entire stranger, and what an ignoble swindle that long, calm, soft-footed trot is; and next he notices that he is getting fagged, and that the cayote actually has to slacken speed a little to keep from running away from him—and *then* that town-dog is mad in earnest, and he begins to strain and weep and swear, and paw the sand higher than ever, and reach for the cayote with concentrated and desperate energy. This "spurt" finds him six feet behind the gliding enemy, and two miles from his friends. And then, in the instant that a wild new hope is lighting up his face, the cayote turns and smiles blandly upon him once more, and with a something about it which seems to say: "Well, I shall have to tear myself away from you, bub—business is business, and it will not do for me to be fooling along this way all day"—and forthwith there is a rushing sound, and the sudden splitting of a long crack through the atmosphere, and behold that dog is solitary and alone in the midst of a vast solitude!

It makes his head swim. He stops, and looks all around; climbs the nearest sand-mound, and gazes into the distance; shakes his head reflectively, and then, without a word, he turns and jogs along back to his train, and takes up a humble position under the hindmost wagon, and feels unspeakably mean, and looks ashamed, and hangs his tail at half-mast for a week. And for as much as a year after that, whenever there is a great hue and cry after a cayote, that dog will merely glance in that direction without emotion, and apparently observe to himself, "I believe I do not wish any of the pie."

The cayote lives chiefly in the most desolate and forbidding deserts, along with the lizard, the jackass-rabbit and the raven, and gets an uncertain and precarious living, and earns it. He seems to subsist almost wholly on the carcasses of oxen, mules, and horses that have dropped out of emigrant trains and died, and upon windfalls of carrion, and occasional legacies of offal bequeathed to him by white men who have been opulent enough to have something better to butcher than condemned army bacon. He will eat anything in the world that his first cousins, the desert-frequenting tribes of Indians, will, and they will eat anything they can bite. It is a curious fact that these latter are the only creatures known to history who will eat nitro-glycerine and ask for more if they survive.

The cayote of the deserts beyond the Rocky Mountains has a peculiarly hard time of it, owing to the fact that his relations, the Indians, are just as apt to be the first to detect a seductive scent on the desert breeze, and follow the fragrance to the late ox it emanated from, as he is himself; and when this occurs he has to content himself with sitting off at a little distance watching those people strip off and dig out everything edible, and walk off with it. Then he and the waiting ravens explore the skeleton and polish the bones. It is considered that the cayote, and the obscene bird, and the Indian of the desert, testify their blood kinship with each other in that they live together in the waste places of the earth on terms of perfect confidence and friendship, while hating all other creatures and yearning to assist at their funerals. He does not mind going a hundred miles to breakfast, and a hundred and fifty to dinner, because he is sure to have three or four days between meals, and he can just as well be traveling and looking at the scenery as lying around doing nothing and adding to the burdens of his parents.

We soon learned to recognize the sharp, vicious bark of the cayote as it came across the murky plain at night to disturb our dreams among the mail-sacks; and remembering his forlorn aspect and his hard fortune, made shift to wish him the blessed novelty of a long day's good luck and a limitless larder the morrow.

The Stage-Driver

OUR NEW conductor (just shipped) had been without sleep for twenty hours. Such a thing was very frequent. From St. Joseph, Missouri, to Sacramento, California, by stage-coach, was nearly nineteen hundred miles, and the trip was often made in fifteen days (the cars do it in four and a half, now), but the time specified in the mail contracts, and required by the schedule, was eighteen or nineteen days, if I remember rightly. This was to make fair allowance for winter storms and snows, and other unavoidable causes of detention. The stage company had everything under strict discipline and good system. Over each two hundred and fifty miles of road they placed an agent or superintendent, and invested him with great authority. His beat or jurisdiction of two hundred and fifty miles was called a "division." He purchased horses, mules, harness, and food for men and beasts, and distributed these things among his stage stations, from time to time, according to his judgment of what each station needed. He erected station buildings and dug wells. He attended to the paying of the station-keepers, hostlers, drivers, and blacksmiths, and discharged them whenever he chose. He was a very, very great man in his "division"—a kind of Grand Mogul, a Sultan of the Indies, in whose presence common men were modest of speech and manner, and in the glare of whose greatness even the dazzling stage-driver dwindled to a penny dip. There were about eight of these kings, all told, on the Overland route.

Next in rank and importance to the division-agent came the "conductor." His beat was the same length as the agent's—two hundred and fifty miles. He sat with the driver, and (when necessary) rode that fearful distance, night and day, without other rest or sleep than what he could get perched thus on top of the flying vehicle. Think of it! He had absolute charge of the mails, express matter, passengers, and stage-coach, until he delivered them to the next conductor, and got his receipt for them. Consequently he had to be a man of intelligence, decision, and considerable executive ability. He was usually a quiet, pleasant man, who attended closely to his duties, and was a good deal of a gentleman. It was not absolutely necessary that the division-agent should be a gentleman, and occasionally he wasn't. But he was always a general in administrative ability, and a bull-dog in courage and determination—otherwise the chieftainship over the lawless underlings of the Overland service would never in any instance have been to him anything but an equivalent for a month of insolence and distress and a bullet and a coffin at the end of it. There were about sixteen or eighteen conductors on the Overland, for there was a daily stage each way, and a conductor on every stage.

Next in *real* and official rank and importance, *after* the conductor, came my delight, the driver—next in real but not in *apparent* importance—for we have seen that in the eyes of the common herd the driver was to the conductor as an admiral is to the captain of the flag-ship. The driver's beat was pretty long, and his sleeping-time at the stations pretty short, sometimes; and so, but for the grandeur of his position his would have been a sorry life, as well as a hard and a wearing one. We took a new driver every day or every night (for they drove backward and forward over the same piece of road all the time), and therefore we never got as well acquainted with them as we did with the conductors; and besides, they would have been above being familiar with such rubbish as passengers, anyhow, as a general thing. Still, we were always eager to get a sight of each and every new driver as soon as the watch changed, for each and every day we were either anxious to get rid of an unpleasant one, or loath to part with a driver we had learned to like and had come to be sociable and friendly with. And so the first question we asked the conductor whenever we got to where we were to exchange drivers, was always, "Which is him?" The grammar was faulty, maybe, but we could not know, then, that it would go into a book some day. As long as everything went smoothly, the Overland driver was well enough situated, but if a fellow driver got sick suddenly it made trouble, for the coach *must* go on, and so the potentate who was about to climb down and take a luxurious rest after his long night's siege in the midst of wind and rain and darkness, had to stay where he was and do the sick man's work. Once in the Rocky Mountains, when I found a driver sound asleep on the box, and the mules going at the usual break-neck pace, the conductor said never mind him, there was no danger, and he was doing double duty—had driven seventy-five miles on one coach, and was now going back over it on this without rest or sleep. A hundred and fifty miles of holding back of six vindictive mules and keeping them from climbing the trees! It sounds incredible, but I remember the statement well enough.

The station-keepers, hostlers, etc., were low, rough characters, as already described; and from western Nebraska to Nevada a considerable sprinkling of them might be fairly set down as outlaws—fugitives from justice, criminals whose best security was a section of country which was without law and without even the pretense of it. When the "division-agent" issued an order to one of these parties he did it with the full understanding that he might have to enforce it with a navy six-shooter, and so he always went "fixed" to make things go along smoothly. Now and then a division-agent was really obliged to shoot a hostler through the head to teach him some simple matter that he could have taught him with a club if his circumstances and surroundings had been different. But they were snappy, able men, those division-agents, and when they tried to teach a subordinate anything, that subordinate generally "got it through his head."

A great portion of this vast machinery—these hundreds of men and coaches, and thousands of mules and horses—was in the hands of Mr. Ben Holliday. All the western half of the business was in his hands. This reminds me of an incident of Palestine travel which is pertinent here, and so I will transfer it just in the language in which I find it set down in my Holy Land note-book:

> No doubt everybody has heard of Ben Holliday—a man of prodigious energy, who used to send mails and passengers flying across the continent in his overland stage-coaches like a very whirlwind—two thousand long miles in fifteen days and a half, by the watch! But this

fragment of history is not about Ben Holliday, but about a young New York boy by the name of Jack, who traveled with our small party of pilgrims in the Holy Land (and who had traveled to California in Mr. Holliday's overland coaches three years before, and had by no means forgotton it or lost his gushing admiration of Mr. H.). Aged nineteen. Jack was a good boy—a good-hearted and always well-meaning boy, who had been reared in the city of New York, and although he was bright and knew a great many useful things, his Scriptural education had been a good deal neglected—to such a degree, indeed, that all Holy Land history was fresh and new to him, and all Bible names mysteries that had never disturbed his virgin ear. Also in our party was an elderly pilgrim who was the reverse of Jack, in that he was learned in the Scriptures and an enthusiast concerning them. He was our encyclopedia, and we were never tired of listening to his speeches, nor he of making them. He never passed a celebrated locality, from Bashan to Bethlehem, without illuminating it with an oration. One day, when camped near the ruins of Jericho, he burst forth with something like this:

"Jack, do you see that range of mountains over yonder that bounds the Jordan valley? The mountains of Moab, Jack! Think of it, my boy—the actual mountains of Moab—renowned in Scripture history! We are actually standing face to face with those illustrious crags and peaks—and for all we know" [dropping his voice impressively], *our eyes may be resting at this very moment upon the spot* WHERE LIES THE MYSTERIOUS GRAVE OF MOSES! Think of it, Jack!"

"Moses *who?*" (falling inflection).

"Moses *who!* Jack, you ought to be ashamed of yourself—you ought to be ashamed of such criminal ignorance. Why, Moses, the great guide, soldier, poet, lawgiver of ancient Israel! Jack, from this spot where we stand, to Egypt, stretches a fearful desert three hundred miles in extent—and across that desert that wonderful man brought the children of Israel!—guiding them with unfailing sagacity for forty years over the sandy desolation and among the obstructing rocks and hills, and landed them at last, safe and sound, within sight of this very spot; and where we now stand they entered the Promised Land with anthems of rejoicing! It was a wonderful, wonderful thing to do, Jack! Think of it!"

"*Forty years? Only three hundred miles?* Humph! Ben Holliday would have fetched them through in thirty-six hours!"

The boy meant no harm. He did not know that he had said anything that was wrong or irreverent. And so no one scolded him or felt offended with him—and nobody *could* but some ungenerous spirit incapable of excusing the heedless blunders of a boy.

At noon on the fifth day out, we arrived at the "Crossing of the South Platte," *alias* "Julesburg," *alias* "Overland City," four hundred and seventy miles from St. Joseph—the strangest, quaintest, funniest frontier town that our untraveled eyes had ever stared at and been astonished with.

—

Bemis and the Buffalo

I T   D I D   S E E M   strange enough to see a town again after what appeared to us such a long acquaintance with deep, still, almost lifeless and houseless solitude! We tumbled out into the busy street feeling like meteoric people crumbled off the corner of some other world, and wakened up suddenly in this. For an hour we took as much interest in Overland City as if we had never seen a town before. The reason we had an hour to spare was because we had to change our stage (for a less sumptuous affair, called a "mud-wagon") and transfer our freight of mails.

Presently we got under way again. We came to the shallow, yellow, muddy South Platte, with its low banks and its scattering flat sand-bars and pigmy islands—a melancholy stream straggling through the center of the enormous flat plain, and only saved from being impossible to find with the naked eye by its sentinel rank of scattering trees standing on either bank. The Platte was "up," they said—which made me wish I could see it when it was down, if it could look any sicker and sorrier. They said it was a dangerous stream to cross, now, because its quicksands were liable to swallow up horses, coach, and passengers if an attempt was made to ford it. But the mails had to go, and we made the attempt. Once or twice in midstream the wheels sunk into the yielding sands so threateningly that we half believed we had dreaded and avoided the sea all our lives to be shipwrecked in a "mud-wagon" in the middle of a desert at last. But we dragged through and sped away toward the setting sun.

Next morning just before dawn, when about five hundred and fifty miles from St. Joseph, our mud-wagon broke down. We were to be delayed five or six hours, and therefore we took horses, by invitation, and joined a party who were just starting on a buffalo hunt. It was noble sport galloping over the plain in the dewy freshness of the morning, but our part of the hunt ended in disaster and disgrace, for a wounded buffalo bull chased the passenger Bemis nearly two miles, and then he forsook his horse and took to a lone tree. He was very sullen about the matter for some twenty-four hours, but at last he began to soften little by little, and finally he said:

"Well, it was not funny, and there was no sense in those gawks making themselves so facetious over it. I tell you I was angry in earnest for awhile. I should have shot that long gangly lubber they called Hank, if I could have done it without crippling six or seven other people—but of course I couldn't, the old 'Allen''s so confounded comprehensive. I wish those loafers had been up in the tree; they wouldn't have wanted to laugh so. If I had had a horse worth a cent—but no, the minute he saw that buffalo bull wheel on him and give a bellow, he raised straight up in the air and stood on his heels. The saddle began to slip, and I took him round the neck and laid close to him, and began to pray. Then he came down and stood up on the other end awhile, and the bull actually stopped pawing sand and bellowing to contemplate the inhuman spectacle. Then the bull made a pass at him and uttered a bellow that sounded perfectly frightful, it was so close to me, and that seemed to literally prostrate my horse's reason, and make a raving distracted maniac of him, and I wish I may die if he didn't stand on his head for a quarter of a minute and shed tears. He was absolutely out of his mind—he was, as sure as truth itself, and he really didn't know what he was doing. Then the bull came charging at us, and my horse dropped down on all fours and took a fresh start—and then for the next ten minutes he would actually throw one handspring after another so fast that the bull began to get unsettled, too, and didn't know where to start in—and so he stood there sneezing, and shoveling dust over his back, and bellowing every now and then, and thinking he had got a fifteen-hundred dollar circus horse for breakfast, certain. Well, I was first out on his neck—the horse's, not the bull's—and then underneath, and next on his rump, and sometimes head up, and sometimes heels—but I tell you it seemed solemn and awful to be ripping and tearing and carrying on so in the presence of death, as you might say. Pretty soon the bull made a snatch for us and brought away some of my horse's tail (I suppose, but do not know, being pretty busy at the time), but *something* made him hungry for solitude and suggested to him to get up and hunt for it. And then you ought to have seen that spider-legged old skeleton go! and you ought to have seen the bull cut out after him, too—head down, tongue out, tail up, bellowing like everything, and actually mowing down the weeds, and tearing up the earth, and boosting up the sand like a whirlwind! By George, it was a hot race! I and the saddle were back on the rump, and I had the bridle in my teeth and holding on to the pommel with both hands. First we left the dogs behind; then we passed a jackass rabbit; then we overtook a cayote, and were gaining on an antelope when the rotten girths let go and threw me about thirty yards off to the left, and as the saddle went down over the horse's rump he gave it a lift with his heels that sent it more than four hundred yards up in the air, I wish I may die in a minute if he didn't. I fell at the foot of the only solitary tree there was in nine counties adjacent (as any creature could see with the naked eye), and the next second I had hold of the bark with four sets of nails and my teeth, and the next second after that I was astraddle of the main limb and blaspheming my luck in a way that made my breath smell of brimstone. I *had* the bull, now, if he did not think of *one* thing. But that one thing I dreaded. I dreaded it very seriously. There was a possibility that the bull might not think of it, but there were greater chances that he would. I made up my mind what I would do in case he did. It was a little over forty feet to the ground from where I sat. I cautiously unwound the lariat from the pommel of my saddle—"

"Your *saddle?* Did you take your saddle up in the tree with you?"

"Take it up in the tree with me? Why, how you talk. Of course I didn't. No man could do that. It *fell* in the tree when it came down."

"Oh—exactly."

"Certainly. I unwound the lariat, and fastened one end of it to the limb. It was the very best green raw-hide, and capable of sustaining tons. I made a slip-noose in the other end, and then hung it down to see the length. It reached down twenty-two feet—half way to the ground. I then loaded every barrel of the Allen with a double charge. I felt satisfied. I said to myself, if he never thinks of that one thing that I dread, all right—but if he does, all right anyhow—I am fixed for him. But don't you know that the very thing a man dreads is the thing that always happens? Indeed it is so. I watched the bull, now, with anxiety—anxiety which no one can conceive of who has not been in such a situation and felt that at any moment death might come. Presently a thought came into the bull's eye. I knew it! said I— if my nerve fails now, I am lost. Sure enough, it was just as I had dreaded, he started in to climb the tree—"

"What, the bull?"

"Of course—who else?"

"But a bull can't climb a tree."

"He can't, can't he? Since you know so much about it, did you ever see a bull try?"

"No! I never dreamt of such a thing."

"Well, then, what is the use of your talking that way, then? Because you never saw a thing done, is that any reason why it can't be done?"

"Well, all right—go on. What did you do?"

"The bull started up, and got along well for about ten feet, then slipped and slid back. I breathed easier. He tried it again—got up a little higher—slipped again. But he came at it once more, and this time he was careful. He got gradually higher and higher, and my spirits went down more and more. Up he came—an inch at a time—with his eyes hot, and his tongue hanging out. Higher and higher—hitched his foot over the stump of a limb, and looked up, as much as to say, 'You are my meat, friend.' Up again—higher and higher, and getting more excited the closer he got. He was within ten feet of me! I took a long breath,—and then said I, 'It is now or never.' I had the coil of the lariat all ready; I paid it out slowly, till it hung right over his head; all of a sudden I let go of the slack, and the slipnoose fell fairly round his neck! Quicker than lightning I out with the Allen and let him have it in the face. It was an awful roar, and must have scared the bull out of his senses. When the smoke cleared away, there he was, dangling in the air, twenty foot from the ground, and going out of one convulsion into another faster than you could count! I didn't stop to count, anyhow—I shinned down the tree and shot for home."

"Bemis, is all that true, just as you have stated it?"

"I wish I may rot in my tracks and die the death of a dog if it isn't."

"Well, we can't refuse to believe it, and we don't. But if there were some proofs—"

"Proofs! Did I bring back my lariat?"

"No."

"Did I bring back my horse?"

"No."

"Did you ever see the bull again?"

"No."

"Well, then, what more do you want? I never saw anybody as particular as you are about a little thing like that."

I made up my mind that if this man was not a liar he only missed it by the skin of his teeth. This episode reminds me of an incident of my brief sojourn in Siam, years afterward. The European citizens of a town in the neighborhood of Bangkok had a prodigy among them by the name of Eckert, an Englishman—a person famous for the number, ingenuity, and imposing magnitude of his lies. They were always repeating his most celebrated falsehoods, and always trying to "draw him out" before strangers;

but they seldom succeeded. Twice he was invited to the house where I was visiting, but nothing could seduce him into a specimen lie. One day a planter named Bascom, an influential man, and a proud and sometimes irascible one, invited me to ride over with him and call on Eckert. As we jogged along, said he:

"Now, do you know where the fault lies? It lies in putting Eckert on his guard. The minute the boys go to pumping at Eckert he knows perfectly well what they are after, and of course he shuts up his shell. Anybody might know he would. But when we get there, we must play him finer than that. Let him shape the conversation to suit himself—let him drop it or change it whenever he wants to. Let him see that nobody is trying to draw him out. Just let him have his own way. He will soon forget himself and begin to grind out lies like a mill. Don't get impatient—just keep quiet, and let me play him. I will make him lie. It does seem to me that the boys must be blind to overlook such an obvious and simple trick as that."

Eckert received us heartily—a pleasant-spoken, gentle-mannered creature. We sat in the veranda an hour, sipping English ale, and talking about the king, and the sacred white elephant, the Sleeping Idol, and all manner of things; and I noticed that my comrade never led the conversation himself or shaped it, but simply followed Eckert's lead, and betrayed no solicitude and no anxiety about anything. The effect was shortly perceptible. Eckert began to grow communicative; he grew more and more at his ease, and more and more talkative and sociable. Another hour passed in the same way, and then all of a sudden Eckert said:

"Oh, by the way! I came near forgetting. I have got a thing here to astonish you. Such a thing as neither you nor any other man ever heard of—I've got a cat that will eat cocoanut! Common green cocoanut—and not only eat the meat, but drink the milk. It is so—I'll swear to it."

A quick glance from Bascom—a glance that I understood—then:

"Why, bless my soul, I never heard of such a thing. Man, it is impossible."

"I knew you would say it. I'll fetch the cat."

He went in the house. Bascom said:

"There—what did I tell you? Now, that is the way to handle Eckert. You see, I have petted him along patiently, and put his suspicions to sleep. I am glad we came. You tell the boys about it when you go back. Cat eat a cocoanut—oh, my! Now, that is just his way, exactly—he will tell the absurdest lie, and trust to luck to get out of it again. Cat eat a cocoanut—the innocent fool!"

Eckert approached with his cat, sure enough.

Bascom smiled. Said he:

"I'll hold the cat—you bring a cocoanut."

Eckert split one open, and chopped up some pieces. Bascom smuggled a wink to me, and proffered a slice of the fruit to puss. She snatched it, swallowed it ravenously, and asked for more!

We rode our two miles in silence, and wide apart. At least I was silent, though Bascom cuffed his horse and cursed him a good deal, notwithstanding the horse was behaving well enough. When I branched off homeward, Bascom said:

"Keep the horse till morning. And—you need not speak of this ――― foolishness to the boys."

Bret Harte

1836-1902

—

1867: *The Lost Galleon and Other Tales*
1870: *The Luck of Roaring Camp
and Other Sketches*
1875: *Tales of the Argonauts*
1876: *Gabriel Conroy*
1876: *Two Men of Sandy Bar*

—

FRANCIS BRET HARTE'S *rise to fame is an American success story.
As the hero of that story, Harte has all the characteristics required by the
western myth: obscure origins, self-taught talents, boldness, restlessness,
and adaptability. He was born in Albany, New York, into a family of modest
means. His father, a schoolteacher, died when Harte was nine years old. Harte's
formal education ended when he was thirteen. In 1854, he and his sister Margaret sailed from New York to San Francisco by way of Nicaragua. They joined
their mother, who had arrived in California the previous year. We know very
little about his early years in California. Apparently he worked at a number of
different jobs—as a shotgun messenger with Wells Fargo, a teacher, a miner, and
an apprentice typesetter. And he taught himself to be a writer. He had inherited
a collection of books from his father and also had his father's love of reading. Harte
studied the great classics of literature and developed such a keen sense of style that
he could write imitations of Henry Fielding, Tobias Smollett, Washington Irving,
and Charles Dickens. During his acquaintance with Mark Twain in California,
Harte bragged that he could write Dickens's style better than Dickens could, and
Twain agreed.*

*Harte moved up from being a typesetter to being a reporter and feature writer
for various California newspapers. He quickly made a good reputation for himself,
first in San Francisco and then throughout California. In 1868, he was invited to*

become editor of the new Overland Monthly. *There he published the poems and stories that brought him national fame. The poems included "Plain Language from Truthful James" ("The Heathen Chinee"); among the stories were "The Luck of Roaring Camp" and "The Outcasts of Poker Flat." Harte took his wife and his fame on a widely publicized trip back east to Boston, to become the best-paid writer at William Dean Howells's* Atlantic Monthly. *But there Harte's luck with the eastern literary leaders ran into serious trouble. He left his wife and his creditors in 1878 to accept a consular position in Prussia. He worked for the U.S. consul in Prussia and Scotland until 1885, and then lived out the rest of his years in London, never seeing his wife again.*

In the preface to the 1870 edition of The Luck of Roaring Camp and Other Sketches, *Harte wrote that he had "abstained from any positive moral" in his stories and had tried only to "illustrate an era" of California history, "an era replete with a certain heroic Greek poetry, of which perhaps none were more unconscious than the heroes themselves." He added, "And I shall be quite content to have collected here merely the materials for the Iliad that is yet to be sung."*[1] *But there is little in Harte's material that could be called either history or epic. It is what scholars call local color, regional humor, and folklore. Harte's characters, like the models Harte found in Charles Dickens's works, can wring the tear from the eye; and to give Harte his due, those same melodramatic characters were instrumental in establishing the literary folk-heroes found in later writers' stories of miners and prostitutes, schoolmistresses and gamblers, even cowboys and immigrants.*

In calling the following story an "idyl," Harte undoubtedly realized the parallel with Theocritus, who is said to have invented the pastoral genre in the third century B.C. *Theocritus wrote idealized, romantic stories about pastoral characters and rustic situations, filling his stories with authentic details chosen for sentimental impact. Similarly, Harte used such details as the red dust, the water barrel, and the boy's new pocketknife. Both Theocritus and Harte wrote their "idyls" for the aristocratic, educated classes, not for the commoners; the "unconscious heroes" of Harte's stories would not appreciate them as much as would the eastern subscribers to the* Overland Monthly *and the* Atlantic. *Unfortunately for Harte's popularity, the local-color realism and the sentimentality became stale magazine fare; readers began to look for more substantial characterizations and complexities in their fiction.*

——

1. Francis Bret Harte, *The Luck of Roaring Camp and Other Sketches* (Boston: Fields, Osgood and Co., 1870), p. iv.

The Idyl of Red Gulch

ANDY was very drunk. He was lying under an azalea-bush, in pretty much the same attitude in which he had fallen some hours before. How long he had been lying there he could not tell, and didn't care; how long he should lie there was a matter equally indefinite and unconsidered. A tranquil philosophy, born of his physical condition, suffused and saturated his moral being.

The spectacle of a drunken man, and of this drunken man in particular, was not, I grieve to say, of sufficient novelty in Red Gulch to attract attention. Earlier in the day some local satirist had erected a temporary tombstone at Sandy's head, bearing the inscription "Effects of McCorkle's whiskey,—kills at forty rods," with a hand pointing to McCorkle's saloon. But this, I imagine, was, like most local satire, personal; and was a reflection upon the unfairness of the process rather than a commentary upon the impropriety of the result. With this facetious exception, Sandy had been undisturbed. A wandering mule, released from his pack, had cropped the scant herbage beside him, and sniffed curiously at the prostrate man; a vagabond dog, with that deep sympathy which the species have for drunken men, had licked his dusty boots, and curled himself up at his feet, and lay there, blinking one eye in the sunlight, with a simulation of dissipation that was ingenious and dog-like in its implied flattery of the unconscious man beside him.

Meanwhile the shadows of the pine-trees had slowly swung around until they crossed the road, and their trunks barred the open meadow with gigantic parallels of black and yellow. Little puffs of red dust, lifted by the plunging hoofs of passing teams, dispersed in a grimy shower upon the recumbent man. The sun sank lower and lower; and still Sandy stirred not. And then the repose of this philosopher was disturbed, as other philosophers have been, by the intrusion of an unphilosophical sex.

"Miss Mary," as she was known to the little flock that she had just dis-

From Bret Harte, *The Luck of Roaring Camp and Other Sketches* (1870; reprint, New York: P. F. Collier and Son, 1899), pp. 72–88.

missed from the log school-house beyond the pines, was taking her after-noon walk. Observing an unusually fine cluster of blossoms on the azalea-bush opposite, she crossed the road to pluck it,—picking her way through the red dust, not without certain fierce little shivers of disgust, and some feline circumlocution. And then she came suddenly upon Sandy!

Of course she uttered the little *staccata* cry of her sex. But when she had paid that tribute to her physical weakness she became overbold, and halted for a moment,—at least six feet from this prostrate monster,—with her white skirts gathered in her hand, ready for flight. But neither sound nor motion came from the bush. With one little foot she then overturned the satirical head-board, and muttered "Beasts!"—an epithet which prob-ably, at that moment, conveniently classified in her mind the entire male population of Red Gulch. For Miss Mary, being possessed of certain rigid notions of her own, had not, perhaps, properly appreciated the demonstra-tive gallantry for which the Californian has been so justly celebrated by his brother Californians, and had, as a new-comer, perhaps, fairly earned the reputation of being "stuck up."

As she stood there she noticed, also, that the slant sunbeams were heat-ing Sandy's head to what she judged to be an unhealthy temperature, and that his hat was lying uselessly at his side. To pick it up and to place it over his face was a work requiring some courage, particularly as his eyes were open. Yet she did it and made good her retreat. But she was somewhat con-cerned, on looking back, to see that the hat was removed, and that Sandy was sitting up and saying something.

The truth was, that in the calm depths of Sandy's mind he was satisfied that the rays of the sun were beneficial and healthful; that from childhood he had objected to lying down in a hat; that no people but condemned fools, past redemption, ever wore hats; and that his right to dispense with them when he pleased was inalienable. This was the statement of his inner consciousness. Unfortunately, its outward expression was vague, being lim-ited to a repetition of the following formula,—"Su'shine all ri'! Wasser maär, eh? Wass up, su'shine?"

Miss Mary stopped, and, taking fresh courage from her vantage of dis-tance, asked him if there was anything that he wanted.

"Wass up? Wasser maär?" continued Sandy, in a very high key.

"Get up, you horrid man!" said Miss Mary, now thoroughly incensed; "get up, and go home."

Sandy staggered to his feet. He was six feet high, and Miss Mary trembled. He started forward a few paces and then stopped.

"Wass I go home for?" he suddenly asked, with great gravity.

"Go and take a bath," replied Miss Mary, eying his grimy person with great disfavor.

To her infinite dismay, Sandy suddenly pulled off his coat and vest, threw them on the ground, kicked off his boots, and, plunging wildly forward, darted headlong over the hill, in the direction of the river.

"Goodness Heavens!—the man will be drowned!" said Miss Mary; and then, with feminine inconsistency, she ran back to the schoolhouse, and locked herself in.

That night, while seated at supper with her hostess, the blacksmith's wife, it came to Miss Mary to ask, demurely, if her husband ever got drunk. "Abner," responded Mrs. Stidger, reflectively, "let's see: Abner hasn't been tight since last 'lection." Miss Mary would have liked to ask if he preferred lying in the sun on these occasions, and if a cold bath would have hurt him; but this would have involved an explanation, which she did not then care to give. So she contented herself with opening her gray eyes widely at the red-cheeked Mrs. Stidger,—a fine specimen of Southwestern efflorescence,—and then dismissed the subject altogether. The next day she wrote to her dearest friend, in Boston: "I think I find the intoxicated portion of this community the least objectionable. I refer, my dear, to the men, of course. I do not know anything that could make the women tolerable."

In less than a week Miss Mary had forgotten this episode, except that her afternoon walks took thereafter, almost unconsciously, another direction. She noticed, however, that every morning a fresh cluster of azalea-blossoms appeared among the flowers on her desk. This was not strange, as her little flock were aware of her fondness for flowers, and invariably kept her desk bright with anemones, syringas, and lupines; but, on questioning them, they, one and all, professed ignorance of the azaleas. A few days later, Master Johnny Stidger, whose desk was nearest to the window, was suddenly taken with spasms of apparently gratuitous laughter, that threatened the discipline of the school. All that Miss Mary could get from him was, that some one had been "looking in the winder." Irate and indignant, she sallied from her hive to do battle with the intruder. As she turned the corner of the school-house she came plump upon the quondam drunkard,—now perfectly sober, and inexpressibly sheepish and guilty-looking.

These facts Miss Mary was not slow to take a feminine advantage of, in her present humor. But it was somewhat confusing to observe, also, that the beast, despite some faint signs of past dissipation, was amiable-looking,—in fact, a kind of blond Samson, whose corn-colored, silken beard apparently had never yet known the touch of barber's razor or Delilah's shears. So that the cutting speech which quivered on her ready tongue died upon her lips, and she contented herself with receiving his stammering apology with supercilious eyelids and the gathered skirts of uncontamination. When she re-entered the school-room, her eyes fell upon the azaleas with a new sense of revelation. And then she laughed, and the little people all laughed, and they were all unconsciously very happy.

It was on a hot day—and not long after this—that two short-legged boys came to grief on the threshold of the school with a pail of water, which they had laboriously brought from the spring, and that Miss Mary compassionately seized the pail and started for the spring herself. At the foot of the hill a shadow crossed her path, and a blue-shirted arm dexterously, but gently relieved her of her burden. Miss Mary was both embarrassed and angry. "If you carried more of that for yourself," she said, spitefully, to the blue arm, without deigning to raise her lashes to its owner, "you'd do better." In the submissive silence that followed she regretted the speech, and thanked him so sweetly at the door that he stumbled. Which caused the children to laugh again,—a laugh in which Miss Mary joined, until the color came faintly into her pale cheek. The next day a barrel was mysteriously placed beside the door, and as mysteriously filled with fresh spring-water every morning.

Nor was this superior young person without other quiet attentions. "Profane Bill," driver of the Slumgullion Stage, widely known in the newspapers for his "gallantry" in invariably offering the box-seat to the fair sex, had excepted Miss Mary from this attention, on the ground that he had a habit of "cussin' on up grades," and gave her half the coach to herself. Jack Hamlin, a gambler, having once silently ridden with her in the same coach, afterward threw a decanter at the head of a confederate for mentioning her name in a bar-room. The over-dressed mother of a pupil whose paternity was doubtful had often lingered near this astute Vestal's temple, never daring to enter its sacred precincts, but content to worship the priestess from afar.

With such unconscious intervals the monotonous procession of blue skies, glittering sunshine, brief twilights, and starlit nights passed over Red Gulch. Miss Mary grew fond of walking in the sedate and proper woods. Perhaps she believed, with Mrs. Stidger, that the balsamic odors of the firs "did her chest good," for certainly her slight cough was less frequent and her step was firmer; perhaps she had learned the unending lesson which the patient pines are never weary of repeating to heedful or listless ears. And so, one day, she planned a picnic on Buckeye Hill, and took the children with her. Away from the dusty road, the straggling shanties, the yellow ditches, the clamor of restless engines, the cheap finery of shop-windows, the deeper glitter of paint and colored glass, and the thin veneering which barbarism takes upon itself in such localities,—what infinite relief was theirs! The last heap of ragged rock and clay passed, the last unsightly chasm crossed,— how the waiting woods opened their long files to receive them! How the children—perhaps because they had not yet grown quite away from the breast of the bounteous Mother—threw themselves face downward on her brown bosom with uncouth caresses, filling the air with their laughter; and how Miss Mary herself—felinely fastidious and intrenched as she was in the purity of spotless skirts, collar, and cuffs—forgot all, and ran like a crested quail at the head of her brood, until, romping, laughing, and panting, with a loosened braid of brown hair, a hat hanging by a knotted ribbon from her throat, she came suddenly and violently, in the heart of the forest, upon— the luckless Sandy!

The explanations, apologies, and not overwise conversation that ensued, need not be indicated here. It would seem, however, that Miss Mary had already established some acquaintance with this ex-drunkard. Enough that he was soon accepted as one of the party; that the children, with that quick intelligence which Providence gives the helpless, recognized a friend, and played with his blond beard, and long silken mustache, and took other liberties,—as the helpless are apt to do. And when he had built a fire against a tree, and had shown them other mysteries of wood-craft, their admiration knew no bounds. At the close of two such foolish, idle, happy hours he found himself lying at the feet of the schoolmistress, gazing dreamily in her face, as she sat upon the sloping hillside, weaving wreaths of laurel and syringa, in very much the same attitude as he had lain when first they met. Nor was the similitude greatly forced. The weakness of an easy, sensuous nature, that had found a dreamy exaltation in liquor, it is to be feared was now finding an equal intoxication in love.

I think that Sandy was dimly conscious of this himself. I know that he longed to be doing something,—slaying a grizzly, scalping a savage, or sacrificing himself in some way for the sake of this sallow-faced, gray-eyed schoolmistress. As I should like to present him in a heroic attitude, I stay my hand with great difficulty at this moment, being only withheld from introducing such an episode by a strong conviction that it does not usually occur at such times. And I trust that my fairest reader, who remembers that, in a real crisis, it is always some uninteresting stranger or unromantic policeman, and not Adolphus, who rescues, will forgive the omission.

So they sat there, undisturbed,—the woodpeckers chattering overhead, and the voices of the children coming pleasantly from the hollow below. What they said matters little. What they thought—which might have been interesting—did not transpire. The woodpeckers only learned how Miss

Mary was an orphan; how she left her uncle's house, to come to California, for the sake of health and independence; how Sandy was an orphan, too; how he came to California for excitement; how he had lived a wild life, and how he was trying to reform; and other details, which, from a wood-pecker's view-point, undoubtedly must have seemed stupid, and a waste of time. But even in such trifles was the afternoon spent; and when the children were again gathered, and Sandy, with a delicacy which the school-mistress well understood, took leave of them quietly at the outskirts of the settlement, it had seemed the shortest day of her weary life.

As the long, dry summer withered to its roots, the school term of Red Gulch—to use a local euphuism—"dried up" also. In another day Miss Mary would be free; and for a season, at least, Red Gulch would know her no more. She was seated alone in the school-house, her cheek resting on her hand, her eyes half closed in one of those day-dreams in which Miss Mary—I fear, to the danger of school discipline—was lately in the habit of indulging. Her lap was full of mosses, ferns, and other woodland memories. She was so preoccupied with these and her own thoughts that a gentle tapping at the door passed unheard, or translated itself into the remembrance of far-off woodpeckers. When at last it asserted itself more distinctly, she started up with a flushed cheek and opened the door. On the threshold stood a woman, the self-assertion and audacity of whose dress were in singular contrast to her timid, irresolute bearing.

Miss Mary recognized at a glance the dubious mother of her anonymous pupil. Perhaps she was disappointed, perhaps she was only fastidious; but as she coldly invited her to enter, she half unconsciously settled her white cuffs and collar, and gathered closer her own chaste skirts. It was, perhaps, for this reason that the embarrassed stranger, after a moment's hesitation, left her gorgeous parasol open and sticking in the dust beside the door, and then sat down at the farther end of a long bench. Her voice was husky as she began:—

"I heerd tell that you were goin' down to the Bay to-morrow, and I could n't let you go until I came to thank you for your kindness to my Tommy."

Tommy, Miss Mary said, was a good boy, and deserved more than the poor attention she could give him.

"Thank you, miss; thank ye!" cried the stranger, brightening even through the color which Red Gulch knew facetiously as her "war paint," and striving, in her embarrassment, to drag the long bench nearer the schoolmistress. "I thank you, miss, for that! and if I am his mother, there ain't a sweeter, dearer, better boy lives than him. And if I ain't much as says it, thar ain't a sweeter, dearer, angeler teacher lives than he's got."

Miss Mary, sitting primly behind her desk, with a ruler over her shoulder, opened her gray eyes widely at this, but said nothing.

"It ain't for you to be complimented by the like of me, I know," she went on, hurriedly. "It ain't for me to be comin' here, in broad day, to do it, either; but I come to ask a favor,—not for me, miss,—not for me, but for the darling boy."

Encouraged by a look in the young schoolmistress's eye, and putting her lilac-gloved hands together, the fingers downward, between her knees, she went on, in a low voice:—

"You see, miss, there's no one the boy has any claim on but me, and I ain't the proper person to bring him up. I thought some, last year, of sending him away to 'Frisco to school, but when they talked of bringing a schoolma'am here, I waited till I saw you, and then I knew it was all right, and I could keep my boy a little longer. And O, miss, he loves you so much; and if you could hear him talk about you, in his pretty way, and if he could ask you what I ask you now, you could n't refuse him.

"It is natural," she went on, rapidly, in a voice that trembled strangely between pride and humility,—"it's natural that he should take to you, miss, for his father, when I first knew him, was a gentleman,—and the boy must forget me, sooner or later,—and so I ain't a goin' to cry about that. For I come to ask you to take my Tommy,—God bless him for the bestest, sweetest boy that lives,—to—to—take him with you."

She had risen and caught the young girl's hand in her own, and had fallen on her knees beside her.

"I've money plenty, and it's all yours and his. Put him in some good school, where you can go and see him, and help him to—to—to forget his mother. Do with him what you like. The worst you can do will be kindness to what he will learn with me. Only take him out of this wicked life, this cruel place, this home of shame and sorrow. You will; I know you will,— won't you? You will,—you must not, you cannot say no! You will make him as pure, as gentle as yourself; and when he has grown up, you will tell him his father's name,—the name that has n't passed my lips for years,— the name of Alexander Morton, whom they call here Sandy! Miss Mary!— do not take your hand away! Miss Mary, speak to me! You will take my boy? Do not put your face from me. I know it ought not to look on such as me. Miss Mary!—my God, be merciful!—she is leaving me!"

Miss Mary had risen, and, in the gathering twilight, had felt her way to the open window. She stood there, leaning against the casement, her eyes fixed on the last rosy tints that were fading from the western sky. There was still some of its light on her pure young forehead, on her white collar, on her clasped white hands, but all fading slowly away. The suppliant had dragged herself, still on her knees, beside her.

"I know it takes time to consider. I will wait here all night; but I cannot go until you speak. Do not deny me now. You will!—I see it in your sweet face,—such a face as I have seen in my dreams. I see it in your eyes, Miss Mary!—you will take my boy!"

The last red beam crept higher, suffused Miss Mary's eyes with something of its glory, flickered, and faded, and went out. The sun had set on Red Gulch. In the twilight and silence Miss Mary's voice sounded pleasantly.

"I will take the boy. Send him to me tonight."

The happy mother raised the hem of Miss Mary's skirts to her lips. She would have buried her hot face in its virgin folds, but she dared not. She rose to her feet.

"Does—this man—know of your intention?" asked Miss Mary, suddenly.

"No, nor cares. He has never even seen the child to know it."

"Go to him at once,—to-night,—now! Tell him what you have done. Tell him I have taken his child, and tell him—he must never see—see—the child again. Wherever it may be, he must not come; wherever I may take it, he must not follow! There, go now, please,—I'm weary, and—have much yet to do!"

They walked together to the door. On the threshold the woman turned. "Good night."

She would have fallen at Miss Mary's feet. But at the same moment the young girl reached out her arms, caught the sinful woman to her own pure breast for one brief moment, and then closed and locked the door.

✳ ✳ ✳

It was with a sudden sense of great responsibility that Profane Bill took the reins of the Slumgullion Stage the next morning, for the schoolmistress was one of his passengers. As he entered the high-road, in obedience to a pleasant voice from the "inside," he suddenly reined up his horses and respectfully waited, as "Tommy" hopped out at the command of Miss Mary.

"Not that bush, Tommy,—the next."

Tommy whipped out his new pocket-knife, and, cutting a branch from a tall azalea-bush, returned with it to Miss Mary.

"All right now?"

"All right."

And the stage-door closed on the Idyl of Red Gulch.

John Muir
1838-1914

▬

1894: *The Mountains of California*
1901: *Our National Parks*
1909: *Stickeen*
1911: *My First Summer in the Sierra*
1912: *The Yosemite*
(1916): *A Thousand-Mile Walk
to the Gulf*

▬

N O   B I O G R A P H E R *will ever picture John Muir's boyhood in Scotland
as a happy one. At the age of three, he was enrolled at a school in
Dunbar, where he and his young classmates were expected to memorize
lessons in French, Latin, arithmetic, spelling, and geography. They were whipped
for any forgetfulness. When John arrived home from school, his father, Daniel
Muir, would order the boy to recite selected verses from the Bible; if John had not
learned them perfectly, he could expect another whipping. One of Muir's early
biographers maintains that this sort of memory training contributed greatly to the
naturalist's prose style, later in his career.*[1]

*When Muir was eleven, his father moved the family to America. There, Muir's
formal education ended and his lessons in homesteading began. For eight years the
boy cleared stumps, split rails, built fences, plowed and hoed large fields, and harvested grain with a hand scythe. Gradually the farm took shape, but Daniel Muir
found a piece of land he liked better, four or five miles to the east, and what John
called the "stunting, heartbreaking" labors began all over again.*[2] *Daniel expected*

---

1. William F. Badè, *The Life and Letters of John Muir*, 2 vols. (Boston: Houghton
Mifflin Co., 1924), 1:27.

2. Frederick Turner, *Rediscovering America: John Muir in His Time and Ours* (New
York: Viking, 1985), p. 49.

his son to work at his tasks from the first light of day to the last; but because he knew the value of reading and education, he allowed John to study whatever books the boy might borrow—but only in his "spare time" before sunrise.

*Muir persevered in his predawn studies and was admitted to the University of Wisconsin (student population, 180) in 1861. He did not receive a degree, however, because he avoided the prescribed programs and instead picked his own course of study. College excited him, but it also made him discontent and confused about his ambitions; so in 1864, experiencing a feeling that he needed to be more in touch with the natural world, Muir followed the example of William Wordsworth (*The Prelude*) and Lord Byron (*Childe Harold*) and went into the wilderness in search of solitary peace of soul. His first experience in the American wilderness, along the Wisconsin River valley, whetted his appetite; on his next trip, Muir decided, he would walk to the Gulf of Mexico and through South America. In September 1867 he took the first step.*

He never reached South America. A year later—in 1868—Muir walked into California and saw Yosemite Valley. Fascinated by the beauty, the abundance of animals and plants, and the geological phenomena, he stayed. Within a few years, he had become the chief spokesman on Yosemite; he undertook heroic solitary explorations, led visitors to the spectacular sights, educated himself on glacier theory, and gave lectures on Yosemite to anyone who would listen. Muir was a founder of the Sierra Club, whose first mission was to preserve Yosemite Valley.

Muir would also become an inspiration—almost a legend—among American nature writers, although he did not write for publication until 1871. Gathering together some letters he had written about the area, he fashioned them into an article titled "Yosemite Glaciers." This tentative beginning led to many more articles, most of them published in the Overland Monthly. *Muir was, of course, pleased to have a means of reaching people with his preservation message, and glad to have the income, but he found that writing could be hard, frustrating, lonely work. Frederick Turner, in his biography of Muir,* Rediscovering America, *gives credit to a lady named Jeanne Carr for encouraging Muir to continue his writing and to publish his essays on nature. It was she, according to Turner, who engineered Muir's literary career.*

Muir's style echoes the nineteenth-century English romanticists' view of nature as a sublime, benevolent, divinely created grandeur; in this view, even the savage aspects become somehow attractive. Each encounter with nature is a moral lesson and an opportunity to come into unity with the Great Creation.

Muir also made use of transcendental philosophy in much of his writing. He had read Henry David Thoreau's The Maine Woods *with great interest and had studied the works of Ralph Waldo Emerson, who visited him in Yosemite. If ever there was a heroic model for Emerson's motto "Trust Thyself," it was John Muir.*

In the following selection we see Muir giving his own names to the mountains, claiming them as part of his personal myth, confidently starting out to find that "confiding communion" with nature. The naturalist trusts his instinct and his "oneness" with nature to lead him toward a total understanding of the universe and man's place in it.

Muir obviously trusted his physical capabilities, for which he was legendary. He was not a particularly large man; but in his stories of rescuing a climbing companion from the face of a glacier, or clinging to the top of a one-hundred-foot spruce tree in a near hurricane, or riding down the side of the valley atop an avalanche, he is literally following Thoreau's idea of driving life into a corner. Only there, at the very edge, is the spiritual truth within the physical fact to be found.

The following excerpts from The Yosemite *are prime examples of nineteenth-century American nature writing. Besides romantic metaphors and equally romantic anthropomorphic descriptions, Muir employs both the narrative first-person technique and the technique of scenic panorama, leading his readers on a tour of Yosemite's various vistas, stopping here and there to hold his verbal magnifying glass over a macrocosm of flora. His philosophical stance is subtle. There are times when Muir states his lesson with epigrammatic straightforwardness, but his usual method is to inspire the reader with images of nature, and let the reader divine the message.*

—

The Approach to the Valley

WHEN I set out on the long excursion that finally led to California I wandered afoot and alone, from Indiana to the Gulf of Mexico, with a plant-press on my back, holding a generally southward course, like the birds when they are going from summer to winter. From the west coast of Florida I crossed the gulf to Cuba, enjoyed the rich tropical flora there for a few months, intending to go thence to the north end of South America, make my way through the woods to the headwaters of the Amazon, and float down that grand river to the ocean. But I was unable to find a ship bound for South America—fortunately perhaps, for I had incredibly little money for so long a trip and had not yet fully recovered from a fever caught in the Florida swamps. Therefore I decided to visit California for a year or two to see its wonderful flora and the famous Yosemite Valley. All the world was before me and every day was a holiday,

From John Muir, *The Yosemite* (New York: Century, 1912), pp. 3–11, 22–23, 40–42, 53–60.

so it did not seem important to which one of the world's wildernesses I first should wander.

Arriving by the Panama steamer, I stopped one day in San Francisco and then inquired for the nearest way out of town. "But where do you want to go?" asked the man to whom I had applied for this important information. "To any place that is wild," I said. This reply startled him. He seemed to fear I might be crazy and therefore the sooner I was out of town the better, so he directed me to the Oakland ferry.

So on the first of April, 1868, I set out afoot for Yosemite. It was the bloom-time of the year over the lowlands and coast ranges; the landscapes of the Santa Clara Valley were fairly drenched with sunshine, all the air was quivering with the songs of the meadow-larks, and the hills were so covered with flowers that they seemed to be painted. Slow indeed was my progress through these glorious gardens, the first of the California flora I had seen. Cattle and cultivation were making few scars as yet, and I wandered enchanted in long wavering curves, knowing by my pocket map that Yosemite Valley lay to the east and that I should surely find it.

The Sierra from the West

LOOKING eastward from the summit of the Pacheco Pass one shining morning, a landscape was displayed that after all my wanderings still appears as the most beautiful I have ever beheld. At my feet lay the Great Central Valley of California, level and flowery, like a lake of pure sunshine, forty or fifty miles wide, five hundred miles long, one rich furred garden of yellow *Compositæ*. And from the eastern boundary of this vast golden flower-bed rose the mighty Sierra, miles in height, and so gloriously colored and so radiant, it seemed not clothed with light, but wholly composed of it, like the wall of some celestial city. Along the top and extending a good way down, was a rich pearl-gray belt of snow; below it a belt of blue and dark purple, marking the extension of the forests; and stretching along the base of the range a broad belt of rose-purple; all these colors, from the blue sky to the yellow valley smoothly blending as they do in a rainbow, making a wall of light ineffably fine. Then it seemed to me that the Sierra should be called, not the Nevada or Snowy Range, but the Range of Light. And after ten years of wandering and wondering in the heart of it, rejoicing in its glorious floods of light, the white beams of the morning streaming through the passes, the noonday radiance on the crystal rocks, the flush of the alpenglow, and the irised spray of countless waterfalls, it still seems above all others the Range of Light.

In general views no mark of man is visible upon it, nor anything to suggest the wonderful depth and grandeur of it sculpture. None of its mag-nificent forest-crowned ridges seems to rise much above the general level to publish its wealth. No great valley or river is seen, or group of well-marked features of any kind standing out as distinct pictures. Even the summit peaks, marshaled in glorious array so high in the sky, seem comparatively regular in form. Nevertheless the whole range five hundred miles long is fur-rowed with cañons 2,000 to 5,000 feet deep, in which once flowed majestic glaciers, and in which now flow and sing the bright rejoicing rivers.

Characteristics of the Cañons

THOUGH of such stupendous depth, these cañons are not gloomy gorges, savage and inaccessible. With rough passages here and there they are flowery pathways conducting to the snowy, icy fountains; mountain streets full of life and light, graded and sculptured by the ancient glaciers, and presenting throughout all their courses a rich variety of novel and attractive scenery—the most attractive that has yet been discovered in the mountain ranges of the world. In many places, especially in the middle region of the western flank, the main cañons widen into spacious valleys or parks diversified like landscape gardens with meadows and groves and thickets of blooming bushes, while the lofty walls, infinitely varied in form, are fringed with ferns, flowering plants, shrubs of many species, and tall evergreens and oaks that find footholds on small benches and tables, all enlivened and made glorious with rejoicing streams that come chanting in chorus over the cliffs and through side cañons in falls of every conceiv-able form, to join the river that flows in tranquil, shining beauty down the middle of each one of them.

The Incomparable Yosemite

THE most famous and accessible of these cañon valleys, and also the one that presents their most striking and sublime features on the grandest scale, is the Yosemite, situated in the basin of the Merced River at an elevation of 4000 feet above the level of the sea. It is about seven miles long, half a mile to a mile wide, and nearly a mile deep in the solid granite flank of the range. The walls are made up of rocks, moun-tains in size, partly separated from each other by side cañons, and they are so sheer in front, and so compactly and harmoniously arranged on a level floor, that the Valley, comprehensively seen, looks like an immense hall or temple lighted from above.

But no temple made with hands can compare with Yosemite. Every rock in its walls seems to glow with life. Some lean back in majestic repose; others, absolutely sheer or nearly so for thousands of feet, advance beyond their companions in thoughtful attitudes, giving welcome to storms and calms alike, seemingly aware, yet heedless, of everything going on about them. Awful in stern, immovable majesty, how softly these rocks are adorned, and how fine and reassuring the company they keep: their feet among beautiful groves and meadows, their brows in the sky, a thousand flowers leaning confidingly against their feet, bathed in floods of water, floods of light, while the snow and waterfalls, the winds and avalanches and clouds shine and sing and wreathe about them as the years go by, and myriads of small winged creatures—birds, bees, butterflies—give glad animation and help to make all the air into music. Down through the middle of the Valley flows the crystal Merced, River of Mercy, peacefully quiet, reflecting lilies and trees and the onlooking rocks; things frail and fleeting and types of endurance meeting here and blending in countless forms, as if into this one mountain mansion Nature had gathered her choicest treasures, to draw her lovers into close and confiding communion with her.

The Approach to the Valley

SAUNTERING up the foothills to Yosemite by any of the old trails or roads in use before the railway was built from the town of Merced up the river to the boundary of Yosemite Park, richer and wilder become the forests and streams. At an elevation of 6000 feet above the level of the sea the silver firs are 200 feet high, with branches whorled around the colossal shafts in regular order, and every branch beautifully pinnate like a fern frond. The Douglas spruce, the yellow and sugar pines and brown-barked Libocedrus here reach their finest developments of beauty and grandeur. The majestic Sequoia is here, too, the king of conifers, the noblest of all the noble race. These colossal trees are as wonderful in fineness of beauty and proportion as in stature—an assemblage of conifers surpassing all that have ever yet been discovered in the forests of the world. Here indeed is the tree-lover's paradise; the woods, dry and wholesome, letting in the light in shimmering masses of half sunshine, half shade; the night air as well as the day air indescribably spicy and exhilarating; plushy fir-boughs for campers' beds, and cascades to sing us to sleep. On the highest ridges, over which these old Yosemite ways passed, the silver fir (*Abies magnifica*) forms the bulk of the woods, pressing forward in glorious array to the very brink of the Valley walls on both sides, and beyond the Valley to a height of from 8000 to 9000 feet above the level of the sea. Thus it appears that Yosemite, presenting such stupendous faces of bare granite, is nevertheless imbedded in magnificent forests, and the main species of pine, fir, spruce and libocedrus are also found in the Valley itself, but there are no "big trees" (*Sequoia gigantea*) in the Valley or about the rim of it. The nearest are about ten and twenty miles beyond the lower end of the valley on small tributaries of the Merced and Tuolumne Rivers.

The First View: The Bridal Veil

FROM the margin of these glorious forests the first general view of the Valley used to be gained—a revelation in landscape affairs that enriches one's life forever. Entering the Valley, gazing overwhelmed with the multitude of grand objects about us, perhaps the first to fix our attention will be the Bridal Veil, a beautiful waterfall on our right. Its brow, where it first leaps free from the cliff, is about 900 feet above us; and as it sways and sings in the wind, clad in gauzy, sun-sifted spray, half falling, half floating, it seems infinitely gentle and fine; but the hymns it sings tell the solemn fateful power hidden beneath its soft clothing.

The Bridal Veil shoots free from the upper edge of the cliff by the velocity the stream has acquired in descending a long slope above the head of the fall. Looking from the top of the rock-avalanche talus on the west side, about one hundred feet above the foot of the fall, the under surface of the water arch is seen to be finely grooved and striated; and the sky is seen through the arch between rock and water, making a novel and beautiful effect.

Under ordinary weather conditions the fall strikes on flat-topped slabs, forming a kind of ledge about two-thirds of the way down from the top, and as the fall sways back and forth with great variety of motions among these flat-topped pillars, kissing and plashing notes as well as thunder-like detonations are produced, like those of the Yosemite Fall, though on a smaller scale. . . .

The Yosemite Fall

LONG ago before I had traced this fine stream to its head back of Mount Hoffman, I was eager to reach the extreme verge to see how it behaved in flying so far through the air; but after enjoying this view and getting safely away I have never advised any one to follow my steps. The last incline down which the stream journeys so gracefully is so steep and smooth one must slip cautiously forward on hands and feet alongside the rushing water, which so near one's head is very exciting. But to gain a perfect view one must go yet farther, over a curving brow to a slight shelf on the extreme brink. This shelf, formed by the flaking off of a fold of granite, is about three inches wide, just wide enough for a safe rest for one's heels. To me it seemed nerve-trying to slip to this narrow foothold and poise on the edge of such a precipice so close to the confusing whirl of the waters; and after casting longing glances over the shining brow of the fall and listening to its sublime psalm, I concluded not to attempt to go nearer, but, nevertheless, against reasonable judgment, I did. Noticing some tufts of artemisia in a cleft of rock, I filled my mouth with the leaves, hoping their bitter taste might help to keep caution keen and prevent giddiness. In spite of myself I reached the little ledge, got my heels well set, and worked sidewise twenty or thirty feet to a point close to the out-plunging current. Here the view is perfectly free down into the heart of the bright irised throng of comet-like streamers into which the whole ponderous volume of the fall separates, two or three hundred feet below the brow. So glorious a display of pure wildness, acting at close range while cut off from all the world beside, is terribly impressive. A less nerve-trying view may be obtained from a fissured portion of the edge of the cliff about forty yards to the eastward of the fall. Seen from this point towards noon, in the spring, the rainbow on its brow seems to be broken up and mingled with the rushing comets until all the fall is stained with iris colors, leaving no white water visible. This is the best of the safe views from above, the huge steadfast rocks, the flying waters, and the rainbow light forming one of the most glorious pictures conceivable.

The Yosemite Fall is separated into an upper and a lower fall with a series of falls and cascades between them, but when viewed in front from the bottom of the Valley they all appear as one.

So grandly does this magnificent fall display itself from the floor of the Valley, few visitors take the trouble to climb the walls to gain nearer views, unable to realize how vastly more impressive it is near by than at a distance of one or two miles. . . .

An Unexpected Adventure

A WILD scene, but not a safe one, is made by the moon as it appears through the edge of the Yosemite Fall when one is behind it. Once, after enjoying the night-song of the waters and watching the formation of the colored bow as the moon came round the domes and sent her beams into the wild uproar, I ventured out on the narrow bench that extends back of the fall from Fern Ledge and began to admire the dim-veiled grandeur of the view. I could see the fine gauzy threads of the fall's filmy border by having the light in front; and wishing to look at the moon through the meshes of some of the denser portions of the fall, I ventured to creep farther behind it while it was gently wind-swayed, without taking sufficient thought about the consequences of its swaying back to its natural position after the wind-pressure should be removed. The effect was enchanting: fine, savage music sounding above, beneath, around me; while the moon, apparently in the very midst of the rushing waters, seemed to be struggling to keep her place, on account of the ever-varying form and density of the water masses through which she was seen, now darkly veiled or eclipsed by a rush of thick-headed comets, now flashing out through openings between their tails. I was in fairyland between the dark wall and the wild throng of illumined waters, but suffered sudden disenchantment; for, like the witch-scene in Alloway Kirk, "in an instant all was dark."[3] Down came a dash of spent comets, thin and harmless-looking in the distance, but they felt desperately solid and stony when they struck my shoulders, like a mixture of choking spray and gravel and big hailstones. Instinctively dropping on my knees, I gripped an angle of the rock, curled up like a young fern frond with my face pressed against my breast, and in this attitude submitted as best I could to my thundering bath. The heavier masses seemed to strike like cobblestones, and there was a confused noise of many waters about my ears—hissing, gurgling, clashing sounds that were not heard as music. The situation was quickly realized. How fast one's thoughts burn in such times of stress! I was weighing chances of escape. Would the column be swayed a few inches away from the wall, or would it come yet closer? The fall was in flood and not so lightly would its ponderous mass be swayed. My fate seemed to depend on a breath of the "idle wind." It was moved gently forward, the pounding ceased, and I was once more visited by glimpses of the moon. But fearing I might be caught at a disadvantage in making too hasty a retreat, I moved only a few feet along the bench to where a block of ice lay. I wedged myself between the ice and the wall, and lay face downwards, until the steadiness of light gave encouragement to rise and get away. Somewhat nerve-shaken, drenched, and benumbed, I made out to build a fire, warmed myself, ran home, reached my cabin before daylight, got an hour or two of sleep, and awoke sound and comfortable, better, not worse, for my hard midnight bath. . . .

3. The reference is to Robert Burns's poem "Tam o'Shanter."

An Extraordinary Storm and Flood

GLORIOUS as are these rocks and waters arrayed in storm robes, or chanting rejoicing in every-day dress, they are still more glorious when rare weather conditions meet to make them sing with floods. Only once during all the years I have lived in the Valley have I seen it in full flood bloom. In 1871 the early winter weather was delightful; the days all sunshine, the nights all starry and calm, calling forth fine crops of frost-crystals on the pines and withered ferns and grasses for the morning sunbeams to sift through. In the afternoon of December 16, when I was sauntering on the meadows, I noticed a massive crimson cloud growing in solitary grandeur above the Cathedral Rocks, its form scarcely less striking than its color. It had a picturesque, bulging base like an old sequoia, a smooth, tapering stem, and a bossy, down-curling crown like a mushroom; all its parts were colored alike, making one mass of translucent crimson. Wondering what the meaning of that strange, lonely red cloud might be, I was up betimes next morning looking at the weather, but all seemed tranquil as yet. Towards noon gray clouds with a close, curly grain like bird's-eye maple began to grow, and late at night rain fell, which soon changed to snow. Next morning the snow on the meadows was about ten inches deep, and it was still falling in a fine, cordial storm. During the night of the 18th heavy rain fell on the snow, but as the temperature was 34°, the snow-line was only a few hundred feet above the bottom of the Valley, and one had only to climb a little higher than the tops of the pines to get out of the rain-storm into the snow-storm. The streams, instead of being increased in volume by the storm, were diminished, because the snow sponged up part of their waters and choked the smaller tributaries. But about midnight the temperature suddenly rose to 42°, carrying the snow-line far beyond the Valley walls, and next morning Yosemite was rejoicing in a glorious flood. The comparatively warm rain falling on the snow was at first absorbed and held back, and so also was that portion of the snow that the rain melted, and all that was melted by the warm wind, until the whole mass of snow was saturated and became sludgy, and at length slipped and rushed simultaneously from a thousand slopes in wildest extravagance, heaping and swelling flood over flood, and plunging into the Valley in stupendous avalanches.

Awakened by the roar, I looked out and at once recognized the extraordinary character of the storm. The rain was still pouring in torrent abundance and the wind at gale speed was doing all it could with the flood-making rain.

The section of the north wall visible from my cabin was fairly streaked with new falls—wild roaring singers that seemed strangely out of place.

Eager to get into the midst of the show, I snatched a piece of bread for breakfast and ran out. The mountain waters, suddenly liberated, seemed to be holding a grand jubilee. The two Sentinel Cascades rivaled the great falls at ordinary stages, and across the Valley by the Three Brothers I caught glimpses of more falls than I could readily count; while the whole Valley throbbed and trembled, and was filled with an awful, massive, solemn, sea-like roar. After gazing a while enchanted with the network of new falls that were adorning and transfiguring every rock in sight, I tried to reach the upper meadows, where the Valley is widest, that I might be able to see the walls on both sides, and thus gain general views. But the river was over its banks and the meadows were flooded, forming an almost continuous lake dotted with blue sludgy islands, while innumerable streams roared like lions across my path and were sweeping forward rocks and logs with tremendous energy over ground where tiny gilias had been growing but a short time before. Climbing into the talus slopes, where these savage torrents were broken among earthquake boulders, I managed to cross them, and force my way up the Valley to Hutchings' Bridge, where I crossed the river and waded to the middle of the upper meadow. Here most of the new falls were in sight, probably the most glorious assemblage of waterfalls ever displayed from any one standpoint. On that portion of the south wall between Hutchings' and the Sentinel there were ten falls plunging and booming from a height of nearly three thousand feet, the smallest of which might have been heard miles away. In the neighborhood of Glacier Point there were six; between the Three Brothers and Yosemite Fall, nine; between Yosemite and Royal Arch Falls, ten; from Washington Column to Mount Watkins, ten; on the slopes of Half Dome and Clouds' Rest, facing Mirror Lake and Tenaya Cañon, eight; on the shoulder of Half Dome, facing the Valley, three: fifty-six new falls occupying the upper end of the Valley, besides a countless host of silvery threads gleaming everywhere. In all the Valley there must have been upwards of a hundred. As if celebrating some great event, falls and cascades in Yosemite costume were coming down everywhere from fountain basins, far and near; and, though newcomers, they behaved and sang as if they had lived here always.

All summer-visitors will remember the comet forms of the Yosemite Fall and the laces of the Bridal Veil and Nevada. In the falls of this winter jubilee the lace forms predominated, but there was no lack of thunder-toned comets. The lower portion of one of the Sentinel Cascades was composed of two main white torrents with the space between them filled in with chained and beaded gauze of intricate pattern, through the singing threads of which the purplish-gray rock could be dimly seen. The series above Glacier Point was still more complicated in structure, displaying every form that one could imagine water might be dashed and combed and woven into. Those on the north wall between Washington Column and the Royal Arch Fall were so nearly related they formed an almost continuous sheet, and these again were but slightly separated from those about Indian Cañon. The group about the Three Brothers and El Capitan, owing to the topography and cleavage of the cliffs back of them, was more broken and irregular. The Tissiack Cascades were comparatively small, yet sufficient to give that noblest of mountain rocks a glorious voice. In the midst of all this extravagant rejoicing the great Yosemite Fall was scarce heard until about three o'clock in the afternoon. Then I was startled by a sudden thundering crash as if a rock avalanche had come to the help of the roaring waters. This was the flood-wave of Yosemite Creek, which had just arrived, delayed by the distance it had to travel, and by the choking snows of its widespread fountains. Now, with volume ten-fold increased beyond its springtime fullness, it took its place as leader of the glorious choir.

And the winds, too, were singing in wild accord, playing on every tree and rock, surging against the huge brows and domes and outstanding battlements, deflected hither and thither and broken into a thousand cascading, roaring currents in the cañons, and low bass, drumming swirls in the hollows. And these again, reacting on the clouds, eroded immense cavernous spaces in their gray depths and swept forward the resulting detritus in ragged trains like the moraines of glaciers. These cloud movements in turn published the work of the winds, giving them a visible body, and enabling us to trace them. As if endowed with independent motion, a detached cloud would rise hastily to the very top of the wall as if on some important errand, examining the faces of the cliffs, and then perhaps as suddenly descend to sweep imposingly along the meadows, trailing its draggled fringes through the pines, fondling the waving spires with infinite gentleness, or, gliding behind a grove or a single tree, bringing it into striking relief, as it bowed and waved in solemn rhythm. Sometimes, as the busy clouds drooped and condensed or dissolved to misty gauze, half of the Valley would be suddenly veiled, leaving here and there some lofty headland cut off from all visible connection with the walls, looming alone, dim, spectral, as if belonging to the sky—visitors, like the new falls, come to take part in the glorious festival. Thus for two days and nights in measureless extravagance the storm went on, and mostly without spectators, at least of a terrestrial kind. I saw nobody out—bird, bear, squirrel, or man. Tourists had vanished months before, and the hotel people and laborers were out of sight, careful about getting cold, and satisfied with views from windows. The bears, I suppose, were in their cañon-boulder dens, the squirrels in their knot-hole nests, the grouse in close fir groves, and the small singers in the Indian Cañon chaparral, trying to keep warm and dry. Strange to say, I did not see even the water-ouzels, though they must have greatly enjoyed the storm.

This was the most sublime waterfall flood I ever saw—clouds, winds, rocks, waters, throbbing together as one. And then to contemplate what was going on simultaneously with all this in other mountain temples; the Big Tuolumne Cañon—how the white waters and the winds were singing there! And in Hetch Hetchy Valley and the great King's River yosemite, and in all the other Sierra cañons and valleys from Shasta to the southern-most fountains of the Kern, thousands of rejoicing flood waterfalls chanting together in jubilee dress.

Emerson Hough

1857-1923

—

1897: *The Story of the Cowboy*
1900: *The Girl at the Halfway House*
1902: *The Mississippi Bubble*
1905: *Heart's Desire*
1918: *The Passing of the Frontier*
1922: *The Covered Wagon*
1923: *North of 36*

—

SOUTH *of Albuquerque, squarely between the Rio Grande and the Pecos River, is a large county known for its rolling cattle land, for the rich mines of its forested mountains, and for the Lincoln County War. The shooting in that "war" began in 1878 when a merchant, John Tunstall, was killed. It ended in 1881, when Sheriff Pat Garrett, the hero of countless pulp and celluloid Westerns, gunned down Billy the Kid.*

Emerson Hough was attending the State University of Iowa through 1880 while all this shooting was going on in the faraway, wild territory of New Mexico. At his father's insistence, he studied for and passed his bar exams, and the next thing he knew—for reasons he later admitted were never very clear—he was on his way to White Oaks, New Mexico, in the middle of Lincoln County. He arrived in 1883 and hung his shingle, too late to witness any of the conflict but still in time to observe a genuine cow-town society. He quickly found the law to be a "disgraceful" profession and wanted no more to do with it.[1] But he was also lacking in business acumen, and so he finally took up writing as his livelihood. Between the White Oaks sojourn and his few years of journalism experience in Kansas cattle country, Hough gleaned invaluable material for his books. The Mississippi

---

1. Delbert E. Wylder, *Emerson Hough* (Boston: Twayne, 1981), p. 21.

Bubble, *published in 1902, turned out to be profitable for Hough, and he found that he could grind out magazine articles by the dozens. In 1905 or thereabouts, Emerson Hough became a self-supporting author.*

In the course of his career, Hough wrote more than a hundred articles advocating wildlife conservation and national park expansion, and these articles inspired hundreds more by other authors. His essays on western history, gathered into such books as The Story of the Cowboy *and* The Passing of the Frontier, *gave later writers of Westerns the full flavor of the cowboy days. Hough's novels pioneered the technique of blending western history with romantic sentiment: Louis L'Amour's well-known formula of authentic backgrounds and romantically heroic characters is a modern echo of Hough.*

One of Hough's novel's, The Covered Wagon, *was produced in 1923 as a silent film and broke box-office records. Instead of using standard movie sets,* The Covered Wagon *featured a long wagon train in movement. Soon other western films showed heroes, heroines, and villains traveling across vast expanses of western landscape. The "epic" idea had become a permanent part of western film and fiction.*

Cowboy fiction is not difficult to find. But finding a good, readable account of what it was really like to live in the cattle-town days is not so easy. Theodore Roosevelt admired The Story of the Cowboy; *it told the truth about ranch life and cowboy life and told it with frequent flashes of genuine good humor. "Society in the Cow Country," first published in the* Chautauquan *magazine in 1900, displays not only Hough's ability to gather details, but his understated humor as well. It is the old-fashioned kind of magazine essay, in which the writer describes an exotic culture to his sophisticated readers, gives them authentic-sounding facts to establish his reportorial credentials, and then amuses them with those sweeping generalizations—stereotypes—for which such writers as Mark Twain and Bret Harte became famous. And, like Twain, Hough is not afraid to set himself in the scene as part of an amusing spectacle. "John Jones, Attorney-at-Law. Real Estate and Insurance. Collections promptly attended to at all hours of the day and night. Good Ohio cider for sale at 5 cents a glass." Hough may often have thought of putting a similar advertisement on his own shingle, back when he was a struggling young lawyer in lawless Lincoln County.*

———

Society in the Cow Country

THE WEST in the good old times, before the influx of the so-called better classes, was a great and lovable country. We go back to it yet in search of that vigorous individuality which all men love. In the cities men are much alike, and, for the most part, built upon rather a poor pattern of a man. The polish of generations wears out fibre and cuts down grain, so that eventually we have a finished product with little left of it except the finish. In modern life the test of survival is much a question of the money a man is able to make. The successful money-maker can buy a part of the desirable things of life, and he may found a family, the latter, perhaps, not begun in love and mutual admiration of person so much as in admiration of the tangible evidences of that which is called success. Men do not love women because they are rich, nor do women admire men because they are rich; and, after all, the only problems of life are those of bread and butter and of love. All the rest is a mere juggling of these two. Such is the society of the artificial modern life of large communities. In the West the individual reigned, and there had not been established any creed of sandpaper. Should we break up the organizations of society as it is known to-day in the focal points of civilization, should we cast abroad the men of the cities and bring in the men of the old plains, what a changing about there would be then! Society and human nature and the human race might be benefited by it. But this may never be, and in this country, as in the history of all other countries, there must go on the slow story told by the ages, of more and more wealth, more and more artificiality, more and more degeneration. And yet good human nature, dragged by the hand of the spirit of complex civilization, looks back always at the past. Aside from the love of tinsel, which in time becomes a necessity for many natures, mankind has always loved the strong, because it is only the strong which is fit to be loved. So we go back continually, fascinated, and revel in the stories of strong times.

From Emerson Hough, *The Story of the Cowboy* (New York: Grosset and Dunlap, 1897), pp. 237–63.

Among the little cow towns of the frontier the searcher for vivid things might have found abundance of material. Society was certainly a mixed matter enough. It was a womanless society for the most part, hence with some added virtues and lost vices, as well as with certain inversions of that phase. The inhabitants might be cowboys, half-breeds, gamblers, teamsters, hunters, freighters, small storekeepers, petty officials, dissipated professional men. The town was simply an eddy in the troubled stream of Western immigration, and it caught the odd bits of drift wood and wreck—the flotsam and jetsam of a chaotic flood.

In the life of a modern business community a man must beware of too much wisdom. The specialist is the man who succeeds, and having once set his hand to an occupation, one dare never leave it, under penalty of failure in what he has chosen as his life work. In the city he who shifts and changes his employment loses the confidence of his fellow-mortals, who agree that he should know how to do one thing and nothing else, and should continue to do it diligently all his life. In the West all this was different. Versatility was a necessity. The successful man must know how to do many things. The gleanings of any one field of activity were too small to afford a living of themselves. This fact was accepted by the citizens of the country, sometimes with the grim humour which marked the West. A young lawyer in a Western town had out a sign which read, "John Jones, Attorney-at-Law. Real Estate and Insurance. Collections promptly attended to at all hours of the day and night. Good Ohio cider for sale at 5 cents a glass." A storekeeper had on his window the legend, "Wall Paper and Marriage Licenses," thus announcing two commodities for which there was but very small demand. One of the prominent citizens of such a town was a gambler, a farmer, a fighter, and a school teacher all in one. One of the leaders of the rustlers and cattle thieves who made a little cow town their headquarters was a Methodist minister. It was not unusual for a justice of the peace to be a barber. The leading minister of a certain thriving cow town, which experienced a "boom" in the early railroad days, eked out his scanty salary by working as a sign painter during the week. There seemed to the minds of the inhabitants of the country nothing incongruous in this mixing up of occupations, it being taken for granted that a man would endeavour to make a living in the ways for which he seemed best fitted.

In any early cow town or mining camp of the West there was sure to be a man from Leavenworth. No apparent reason for this curious fact seems ever to have been given, yet it is certainly true that no such town ever was settled without a man from Leavenworth to take part in the inauguration. He was apt afterward to be one of the town officers. He was nearly always a lawyer, or claimed to have once been one. He was sure to be the first justice of the peace, and in that capacity of high dignity presented an interesting spectacle. The early Western justice of the peace was a curious being at best. Apt to be fully alive to his own importance, he presided at his sessions with a wisdom and solemnity not to be equalled in the most august courts of the land. It was rarely that the justice knew much law, but he nearly always was acquainted with the parties to any suit and with the prisoner who happened to be at bar, and usually he had a pretty accurate idea of what he was going to do with the case before it came up for trial. It may have been such a justice as this of whom the story is told that he made the defendant's lawyer sit down when he arose to reply to the arguments of the prosecution, saying that the counsel's talk served to "confuse the mind of the court." Yet the frontier justice of the peace usually came well within the bounds of common sense in his decisions, as witness the ruling of that Texas justice who gravely declared "unconstitutional" a certain State law which restricted the sale of liquor in his town in many unwelcome ways, he holding that such a law must necessarily be contrary to public policy and against good morals. This man was later elected to the State senate.

The first female inhabitants of the town were also sure to come from Kansas. There seems to be no special reason for this curious feature of the fauna of the cow town in the early days, and it seems difficult to tell why all the men seemed to have left Leavenworth and all the women to have abandoned the State of Kansas, though the fact remained none the less apparent. The family from Kansas nearly always came in a wagon, and among the family there were usually two or three girls, sure to become objects of admiration for a large cowboy contingent in a short period of time. There never was a cow town which did not have a family including "them girls from Kansas," and their fame was sure to be known abroad all over the local range. One by one the girls from Kansas disappeared down the tortuous road of matrimony, yet still the supply seemed unexhausted, more girls coming from Kansas in some mysterious way.

There was always a Jew merchant in any cow town, who handled the bulk of the business in general supplies. The infallible instinct of his kind led him to a place so free with its money and so loose in its business ideas. The Jew did not come from Kansas, but dropped down from above, came up from below, or blew in upon the wind, no one knew how, but he was always there. He advertised in the local paper, complaining about the rates, of course. "Keep your eye on Whiteman" read his advertisement, and "Geep your eye on Viteman" was the burden of his talk to his customers. It was, indeed, a very wise thing to keep your eye on Whiteman, though perhaps the latter did not mean it in that way in his boastful advice.

There was always a sheriff in a cow town, and he was always the same sort of man—quiet, courageous, just, and much respected by his fellow-men. The public of the cow town had little real respect for the courts, and the judicial side of the law was sometimes farcical; but, by some queer inversion of the matter, all had respect for the executive side of the law, and indeed, recognised that side alone as the law itself. The sheriff was the law. He was worthy of this feeling, for nearly always he was a strong and noble nature, worthy of an unqualified admiration.

There was always a barber in a cow town, and when a town was so run down that it could not support a barber it was spoken of with contempt. There might not be any minister of the Gospel or any church, but there were two or three saloons, which served as town hall and general club-rooms, being the meeting places of the inhabitants. There was no dentist or doctor, though there might be a druggist, who kept half a dozen or so jars and bottles. If a cowpuncher wanted a little alum to cure a hide, the druggist charged him at about the rate of ten or fifteen dollars a pound for it, according to the extent of the need he had just then for the money. If the druggist was playing in fair luck at the time in the nightly poker game, alum was cheaper.

There was always a little newspaper, a whimsical, curious little affair, which lived in some strange fashion, and whose columns showed a medley of registered and published brands and marks for the members of the cattle association living in that district, this business being almost the only source of revenue for the newspaper. Of news there was none, except such as all men knew. The editor of the paper had a certain prestige in political matters, but led withal an existence properly to be termed extra hazardous. The editor always drank whisky when he could get it, just as everybody else did, it being quite too much to ask that he should depart from popular custom; but the paper was ground out from the hand press every week, or almost every week, with a regularity which under the circumstances was very commendable. Sooner or later, if one paper began to make more than a living, another paper came in, and then life assumed an added interest with the inhabitants. Both papers were then read, so that everybody might see what one editor was saying of the other. The second editor was nearly always a more vindictive man than the first one, and he drank more whisky, and wrote worse English and had a redder nose; but he added life to the town, and he was sure of a fair showing until at some unfortunate time he said the wrong thing. This wrong thing was never far away in the journalism of the range. It behooved the editor to be careful in his criticism of any one, and always to be sure to "boom the town," no matter what else might be omitted.

One of the owners of the saloons was sure to be a gambler as well as a dispenser of fluids. He had more money than anybody else, and also a surer chance of sudden death. He always killed one or two men before his own time came, but his time came some day. He was then properly mourned and buried, and the affair was discreetly mentioned in the papers. If it seemed that the gambler's partner was getting too "bad" to be needed in the economy of the town, he was asked to "move on," and this he was wise enough to do. Another gambler came in then.

The lawyer of the town was something of a personage. His library did not amount to so much, consisting probably of not more than two or three books, not very many, for one can not carry many books when on foot, and the lawyer nearly always walked into town; but the lawyer had all the authorities in his head, and so did not need a library. The lawyer was naturally a candidate for the territorial council, for county assessor, or anything else that had any pay attached to it. Of strictly legal work there was not much to do, but the lawyer always remembered his dignity, and you could always tell him in a crowd, for he was the only man in the town who did not wear "chaps" or overalls. The lawyer and the county surveyor sometimes had work to do in settling the lines of a homestead or some such thing when water rights were in dispute. He had no occasion to prosecute or defend any client for theft, for everybody in that country was afraid to steal; and burglary was a crime unknown. It was rarely that a man was prosecuted for horse stealing; never, unless the sheriff got to him first. A "killing" sometimes gave the lawyer a chance, but this was not a thing to make much stir about, and very often the killer was set free, because it was usually certain that the other man would have killed him if he could, and that is defence at law. Much more interesting was it when a man was shot and not killed, alike for the rarity of the occasion and for its probable consequences. Everybody wondered then which would be the one to get killed when he was well and around shooting again.

The cow town was very proud of any public improvements, very resentful of any attempt to cast slight upon such improvements, and very jealous of the pretensions of any other town of its neighbourhood. It being rumoured that a certain foothills city over toward the edge of the range was to have a railroad tunnel which would add to its attractions, it was gravely suggested by the citizens of a rival town located well out on the plains that the latter should also have a tunnel, and not allow itself to be surpassed in the "race of progress" by any "one-armed sheep-herding village." The county surveyor lost popularity because he tried to point out how expensive it would be to construct a tunnel out on the prairie.

The first coal-burning stove, the first piano, the first full-length mirror to come to town made each an occasion of popular rejoicing. At a time when all was progressing as usual in the leading saloon of such a town one evening, two of the players at a card table, without word of warning, arose and began shooting at each other in the celeritous yet painstaking fashion of the country. They were both caught by friends before any damage was done to either man, but the aim of one being disconcerted by the grasp upon his wrist, his bullet missed its mark and shattered the stove door, on the big new stove which was the boast of the community. For this careless shooting he received a general censure.

One time there came to a certain cow town on the range a Missouri family who brought along a few hogs, about half a dozen young porkers of very ordinary appearance, but which none the less became the objects of a popular ovation, as being the first hogs ever brought in on the range, and an attraction which it was not pretended could be duplicated by the rival town over in the foothills. These hogs were the pride of the settlement for some time, until at an evil hour they chanced to be spied by a drunken cowpuncher, who was visiting town that day and enjoying himself according to his lights. When the cowpuncher saw these new and strange creatures in the streets of the town, he at once went back to his horse, got his rifle from his saddle, and forthwith inaugurated a hunt after them, this resulting in the early and violent death of all the "shotes." No one objected in the least to his shooting in the streets, for that was the privilege of all men, but it was voted a public offence to kill those hogs. The cowpuncher was censured by some of the citizens, including the druggist, who at that time was pleasantly intoxicated himself, and he would have killed the druggist had not the latter pleaded that he was not armed. The cowpuncher, very fairly, it must be acknowledged, told the druggist to go back to his store and get his gun, and then to come on and they would have their little matter out together. With this invitation the druggist complied, and soon appeared at the corner of his cabin with a long six-shooter in hand, calling to the cowpuncher to come on down the street and be killed like a gentleman. The street was properly cleared for the accommodation of the two, a number of us stepping into the newspaper office, and standing well back inside the door, though with heads out to see what was going to happen.

At this moment there appeared on the scene the sheriff of the county, who had concluded that this was a matter of sufficient note to warrant his interference. The sheriff was a large, burly man, who spoke very little at any time and was now quite silent as he walked up the street steadily, without any hurry, into a line directly between the hostile forces. His hands, with the thumbs lightly resting in his belt, made no move toward the long guns which hung at each side. His face was quite calm and stolid, and with a certain dignity not easy to forget. As he passed the newspaper office, some one made some light remark to him—for all the time he was walking straight up to the rifle of the cowpuncher, who was warning him to step aside, so that he could kill the druggist, whom he appeared to dislike at the time. To the remark the sheriff made no answer, but turned his heavy, solemn face, with a look which said plainly that in his opinion a man ought not to be interrupted when he was in pursuit of a duty which might end in his death. The sheriff was not afraid, but he knew what was to be done. The deputy, who accompanied him, was white as paper and evidently badly scared. The two walked on up the street slowly, the sheriff never hastening a step, until finally they reached the place where the cowpuncher stood, the latter having been puzzled by the slow and quiet advance until he had forgotten to begin shooting, though the druggist continued to shout out defiance. The sheriff said nothing, and made no attempt to pull his gun, or to cover his man in the style usually mentioned in lurid Western literature. He simply reached out his hand and took the cowpuncher's rifle away from him, setting it down against the side of a near-by house. Then he said: "Now, Jack, you d——d little fool you, I don't want no more of this. You go on down to my house an' go to bed to onct, an' don't you come out till you git plum sober. Go on, now." And Jack went.

The sheriff then went on down to the druggist, who had by this time slipped into his store and hid his gun. Him the sheriff rated well as a disturber, but did not take in charge at all. The loss of the "shotes" was generally lamented, but on the following morning Jack apologized about that, paid for the "shotes," invited everybody to drink to their memory, and at the suggestion of friends both he and the druggist shook hands over the matter and forgot all about it. This affair of course never got into the courts, as indeed why should it? The settlement reached was eminently the wisest and most effectual thing that could have been done, and showed well enough the sterling common sense of the sheriff, who retained the friendship of all parties. His deputy, if left alone, would have tried to "cover his man," would very likely have been killed himself, and had he succeeded in getting his man to jail the latter would very likely have killed the druggist as a point of honour as soon as he got out. The peace and dignity of the town were far better preserved as it was.

In the communities of the frontier men were sometimes apt to be a trifle touchy and suspicious of their fellow-men, perhaps a bit ultra in their notions of personal honour and personal rights. A cowpuncher from the Two Hat outfit was once heard explaining a little instance of this. "It was this a' way," said he, speaking of the recent killing over on Crooked Creek of Bill Peterson, who had been shot by his neighbour, a man by name of Sanders. "Peterson an' Sanders had both of 'em started hen ranches, allowin' to make plenty o' money next year, when the hens had sort o' got used to the range an' begun to do well on the feed. Sanders, he come in there first, an' he 'lowed he wouldn't have no one to buck aginst in the aig business, but Peterson he moves in on the creek too, and lays out his ranch right up agin Sanders, an' that makes Sanders plenty mad. Them two fellers, they got so blame jealous of each other they used to be afraid to go to sleep, for fear the other feller would think up some scheme or other. The wild cats and coyotes got in among the corrals like, an' before long they mighty nigh cleaned up the whole cavvieyard[2] o' hens fer both of 'em, but they couldn't see it that way, an' each accused the other of stealin' his hens, which of course we knowed meant trouble some day.

"Fin'ly, these fellers got so jealous of each other that one feller he'd stay out in his hen pasture all day, a-herdin' back the grasshoppers to keep 'em from goin' on to the other feller's range—which them grasshoppers is shore good feed fer hens. Peterson, he consults a lawyer about this, and he comes back and tells Sanders that grasshoppers is critters *ferry natoory,*[3] or somethin' o' that sort, and so they belongs to everybody alike. Sanders he says he don't care a d——n about that, he aint goin' to have Peterson's hens a-eatin' his 'hoppers, because he saw the place first. So they at last got to sort o' havin' it in fer each other. One day Sanders he come down to me an' ast me to lend him my gun, because his was out o' order, an' he had to kill Peterson purty soon. So I let him take my gun, which is a shore daisy, an' next mornin' he laid fer Peterson when he come out the house. Peterson he saw him, an' he come out a-shootin', but Sanders he was a leetle too quick fer him. Sanders he quit the ranch then, an' now you kaint get a aig in this whole country fer a dollar a aig, not noways."

2. An American corruption of the Spanish term *caballada,* meaning a herd (usually of horses).

3. *Farae naturae*—a Latin legalism for animals existing in a wild, untamed condition (therefore not "owned").

In the rude conditions of the society of the frontier the man of "sand" was the man most respected. If one allowed himself to be "run over" by the first person, he might as well be prepared to meet the contempt of all the others. Sooner or later a man was put to the test and "sized up" for what sort of timber he contained. If he proved himself able to take care of himself, he was much less apt to meet trouble thereafter. The man who was willing to mind his own business was not apt to meet with the professional bully or bad man of the town. The latter was a person who understood the theory of killing and escaping the law. He was confident in his own ability to pull quick, and it was his plan to so irritate his antagonist that the latter would "go for his gun." After that it was a case of self-defence. In the great cities the man who draws a deadly weapon is severely handled by the law, but in the old days on the frontier the bearing of arms was a necessity, and their general use made all men familiar with them and deprived them of half their terror. The stranger in the cow town was at first much troubled when he heard of a "killing" next door to him, but soon he became accustomed to such things and came to think little of them. The fashions of a country are its own and are not easily changed by a few; the change is apt to operate in quite the opposite direction. It is not the case that all the dwellers on the frontier were brave men, but courage is much a matter of association, and comes partly from habit after long acquaintance with scenes of danger and violence. The citizens of the cow town all wore guns, and did not feel fully dressed without such appurtenances. There was but one respectable way of settling a quarrel. It was not referred to the community, but to the individual, for in that land the individual was the supreme arbiter. None the less, many a coward's heart has beaten above a pistol belt, and nowhere in the world was such a fact more swiftly and unerringly determined than in a primitive community such as that in question. Upon the other hand, the rudest of the inhabitants of that community would recognise the quality of actual courage very quickly, and the man who stood highest in the esteem of his fellow-men was he who had the reputation of being a "square man," not "looking for trouble," but always ready to meet it if it came.

A wealthy and respected cattleman of a certain part of the cow range had a niece who ran away and married a renegade ranch foreman against whom she had been warned. This man soon began to abuse her, and she returned to her former home. The quarrel was patched up, but the girl's uncle sent word to the husband that if she ever was obliged to come back home again, she should never again go away to live with him. The husband sent back word that he would kill the uncle on sight. To this the cowman made no reply, but he always rode abroad with a rifle across his lap. One day he had word that his enemy was about to waylay him, and accordingly he was upon the lookout for him. As he entered the edge of a bit of wood, he saw the dutiful relative waiting for him, but luckily looking in the wrong direction. The wind being in his favour, the cowman drove up within a short distance of the man who was seeking to kill him, and then calling to him, killed him in his tracks when he turned. In this act he was upheld by all the society of the range, and was never in the least called to account for it, as it was thought he had done quite what was right and needful. He was never molested by any more relatives after that. This incident was long ago forgotten in his history, and a quieter, more respected, or more useful citizen does not live than he is to-day, nor one more marked for his mildness and even-tempered disposition. He did only what in his time and under his surroundings was the fit and needful thing to do.

Such a man as this was the cowman who happened to be standing in a saloon one day, talking with some friends as he rested his elbows back of him on the bar against which he was leaning. The conversation was interrupted by a cowpuncher of the frisky sort, such as in those days occasionally materialized in the cow town for a little lark. This cowpuncher rode his horse into the saloon and up to the bar, declaring that both he and the horse had come a long way and were thirsty, and must both have a drink. His requests having been complied with, he began to shoot around a little, and drove everybody out of the saloon except this one cattleman, who still stood quietly with his back against the bar, leaning back upon his elbows, this directly in the middle of the room, which was only about twenty feet square. The cattleman stood there saying nothing, and finally the cowpuncher rode on out. When asked why he had not driven out the "old man" too, he replied that he had not seen him.

"You could shore of seen him if you looked hard," said one of his friends, "fer he was right at you there in the middle of the room."

"Well, I never did see him," said the cowpuncher gravely. "My eyes ain't allus as good as they ought to be, sometimes." As a matter of fact the reputation of the "old man" was such that the cowboy was very wise in not seeing him and undertaking to run him out.

Sometimes in the winter season society in the cow town would be enlivened by a ball. Such a ball was a singular and somewhat austere event, and one which it would be difficult to match to-day in all the land. The news of the coming ball spread after the mysterious fashion of the plains, so that in some way it became known in a short time far and wide across the range. The cowboys fifty miles away were sure to hear of it and to be on hand, coming horseback from their ranches, each man clad in what he thought was his best. The entire populace of the cow town was there, the ballroom being the largest room to be found in the town, wherever that might chance to be. Refreshments were on hand, sometimes actually cake, made by the fair hands of the girls from Kansas. A fiddler was obtained from some place, for where a few men are gathered together there is always sure to be a fiddler; and this well meaning, if not always melodious, individual was certain to have a hard night's work ahead of him.

Of course there was a great scarcity of lady partners, for the men outnumbered the women a dozen to one. No woman, whatever her personal description, needed to fear being slighted at such a ball. There were no wall flowers on the range. The Mexican wash-woman was sure of a partner for every dance, and the big girl from Kansas, the little girl from Kansas, the wife of the man from Missouri, and all the other ladies of the country there assembled, were fairly in danger of having their heads turned at the praise of their own loveliness. In the Southwest such a dance was called a *baille*, and among the women attending it were sure to be some dark-eyed *señoritas* with *mantilla* and *reboso*, whose costume made contrast with the calico and gingham of the "American" ladies. The dancing costume of the men was various, but it was held matter of course if a cowboy chose to dance in his regulation garb, "chaps," spurs and all. In the more advanced stages of society it became etiquette for a gentleman to lay aside his gun when engaging in the dance, but he nearly always retained a pistol or knife somewhere about him, for he knew there might be occasion to use it. Sometimes the cowpuncher danced with his hat on, but this later became improper. There are few more startling spectacles, when one pauses to think of it from a distance, than a cowboy quadrille in which there was a Mexican woman with only one leg, a girl from Kansas who had red hair, and two cowboys who wore full range costume.

Between dances the cowpuncher entertained his fair one with the polite small talk of the place; surmises that the weekly mail had been delayed by some mule getting "alkalied over on the flats"; talk of the last hold-up of the mail; statistics of the number of cattle shipped last year, and the probable number to be shipped this; details of the last "killing" in the part of the country from which the cowpuncher came, etc. Meantime the lady was complimented openly upon her good points and those of her costume, not to her personal displeasure, for human nature is much the same no matter where the ball is held. It sometimes happened that the lady was not averse to sharing with her escort of a bit of the liquid refreshments that were provided. The effects of this, the stir of the dancing, the music, the whirl and go of it all, so unusual in the experiences of most of the attendants, kept things moving in a fashion that became more and more lively as the hours passed by. The belated range man, riding full gallop to town, could see from a distance the red lights of the windows at the hall, and could hear afar the sound of revelry by night. Excited by this, he spurred on his horse the faster, answering to the dancers with the shrill yell of the plains, so that all might know another man was coming to join in the frolic. He cast his bridle rein over the nearest corral post, and forthwith rushed in to mingle with the others in a merriment that was sure to last to daybreak. Out of this ball, as out of other balls, were sure to arise happiness, heartburnings, jealousies, and some marriages. An engagement on the plains was usually soon followed by a marriage, and such an engagement was not made to be broken; or if it was broken to the advantage of another man, there was apt to be trouble over it between the men. Sometimes the night of the ball did not pass without such trouble. Any such affair was apt to be handled most delicately in the next issue of the paper; although funeral notices were not customary there, the papers being printed only each week or so.

The cow town was sure to have among its dwellers some of the odd characters which drifted about the West in the old times, men who had somehow gotten a warp into their natures, and had ceased to fit in with the specifications of civilization. Such men might be teamsters, cowboys, or those mysterious beings who in some way manage always to live without doing any work—these not to be called tramps, for the tramp was something unknown in the cow town. Such a man might have a little cabin of his own, with a fireplace and a bed of blankets. Nearly all the male population of the town was made up of single men, and of these nearly all did their own cooking, living in a desultory, happy-go-lucky sort of fashion, with no regularity in any habits. Some of these men were educated, and had known other conditions of life. Bitterer cynics never lived than some of these wrecks of the range. There was Tom O——, a cowpuncher, apparently as ignorant and illiterate as any man that ever walked, but who had his Shakespeare at his tongue's end, and could quote Byron by the yard. Tom's only song was—

"I never loved a fond gazel-l-e!"

The song rarely got further along than that. A cheerful fatalist, Tom accepted the fact that luck was against him, and looked upon life as the grimmest of jokes, prepared for his edification. No matter how ill his fortune, Tom never complained, even as he never hoped. He had, too, a certain amount of enterprise in his character. At last accounts he was headed for the Indian Nations, it being his expressed intention to marry an Indian woman and so become a member of the tribe, this being the easiest way open to fortune which offered to his mind. He had several wives scattered over the range at different points, and at times he was wont to discuss the good and bad points of these with the utmost candour and impartiality, thus showing himself a liberal and philosophical man.

The foreman of the O T ranch was a good cowman, who stood well with the men of his own outfit and of the neighbouring ranches. This man never at any time, either upon his own ranch or in town, was known by any other name but that of "Springtime." His accounts at the stores were run under the name of "Springtime" and in no other way. His real name one can not give, for it seems that no one ever thought of asking him what it was. "Springtime" was a quiet man, although, like Tom at times, given to meditative song. As in the case of Tom, his song never got beyond the first line, which ran—

"Whe-e-en the springtime cometh, ge-e-ntle Annie-e-e-e!"

It never seemed to trouble him what had happened or might happen in the springtime, and for him the springtime never seemed to get any closer. Nor did this fact give concern to his neighbours, who gave him the name "Springtime" in all gravity, as being the title by which he would be most readily and generally known.

Other citizens of the cow town were One-eyed Davis, and Hard-winter Johnson, and Cut-bank Bill, and Two-finger Haines, and Straight-goods Allen, and, of course, Tex and Shorty and Red, and all sorts of citizens whose names never got further along than that, unless in connection with their respective ranch brands. Thus, in speaking of an event of interest, down at the saloon or store, the proprietor would say, "Yesterday, that feller Charlie, from down on the Hashknife, he comes in here an' he says," etc. And in course of reply some one else might cite what Pinto, of the Hat brand, had said upon the subject, all men knowing by those presents that there was meant a certain individual whose vast extent of freckles had by common consent earned for him the name of "Pinto." No one seemed to take amiss these clinging nicknames, and indeed it was as well to accept them without protest. A singular incident in a man's life, or a distinguishing personal peculiarity, was usually the origin of the name. In the simple and direct methods of thought which obtained it was considered wise to give a man a name by which he would be known easily and precisely. There might be many men by the name of John Jones, but there would be only one Overcoat Jones—a man who had the odd habit of wearing an overcoat all summer, for reasons which seemed to suit himself, and which therefore suited his acquaintances. There might be many Wallaces, but Big Foot Wallace was known from one end of the range to the other. There might, indeed, have been a certain courtesy in this plains nomenclature. It was one of the jests of the later West to ask a man, "What was your name back in the States?" but this was never seriously done in the cow country of the early times, because it might have been one of the things one would rather have left unsaid. Too much personal curiosity was not good form, and met with many discouragements. Under the system of the society of the cow town, it was quite enough to know a man by his local and accepted name, which should distinguish him easily; and the man was valued for what he was, not for what his name was, or for what that of his father had been. Some cheap persons of the later West bestowed upon themselves nicknames of rather ferocious sort for the purpose of impressing upon dwellers of the East a sense of their wild Western character; but the man who had his card engraved as Dead Shot Dick, or Charlie the Killer, or that sort of thing, did not make a practice of claiming his title when he was away from the new settlements and back in the society of the old cow country, where life was real and earnest in its lines, and assertions of a personal sort apt to be taken up for serious investigation.

In short, the cow town of the good old times was a gathering of men of most heterogeneous sorts, a mass of particles which could not mix or blend. Of types there was abundance, for each man was a study of himself. He had lived alone, forced to defend himself and to support himself under the most varying and trying circumstances, very often cut off from all manner of human aid or companionship for months at a time. Needing his self-reliance, his self-reliance grew. Forced to be independent, his independence grew. Many of these men had been crowded out of the herd in the States, and had so wandered far away from the original pastures of their fellows. They met in the great and kindly country of the old West, a number of these rogues of the herd, and it was a rough sort of herd they made up among themselves. They could not blend; not until again the sweep of the original herd had caught up with them, and perforce taken them in again among its numbers. Then, as they saw the inevitable, as they saw the old West gone forever, leaving no place whither they might wander farther, they turned their hands to the ways of civilization, and did as best they could. In many cases they became quiet and useful and diligent citizens, who to-day resent the raking up of the grotesque features of their past, and have a contempt for the men who try to write about that past with feigned wisdom and unfeigned sensationalism. Among those citizens of the old cow town were many strange characters, but also many noble ones, many lovable ones. A friend in that society was really a friend. Alike the basest and the grandest traits of human nature were shown in the daily life of the place. Honour was something more than a name, and truth something less than a jest. The cynicisms were large, they were never petty. The surroundings were large, the men were large, their character was large. Good manhood was something respected, and true womanhood something revered. We do very ill if we find only grotesque and ludicrous things in such a society as this. We might do well if we went to it for some of its essential traits—traits now so uncommon among us that we call them peculiarities.

A more curiously democratic form of society never existed upon earth than that of the old cow town. Each man knew his own place, but felt that that place was as good as any other man's. In the cow town, if anywhere, all men were free and equal. Perhaps no better instance of this curious independence in the genuine cowpuncher could well be found than in the story of a certain ranch foreman, whom we may as well call Jim, and his relations with his employer, who, according to the story, was a foreigner, an Earl of something or other, who had come to America to engage in the cow business. It seems that upon the first day they spent upon the ranch together Jim appeared at the dinner table without any invitation, and moreover without removing his hat. The earl objected not only to Jim's hat but to his presence, saying that he was not accustomed to dining with his servants. This was an error on the part of the earl, really a most unfortunate remark to make, but in extenuation it should be added that he was not to be blamed so much for it, for he was a newcomer in the cow country and had had very little time to become acquainted with its ways. But this fact Jim did not pause to consider. Without protest or parley, he drew his revolver, and so beat the earl about the head with it as nearly to kill him, though not so nearly, so says the story, as to prevent his apologizing freely.

"Why, that feller," said Jim, in a surprised and injured manner, when later speaking of the occurrence, "he put on more airs than a cook! . . . But," he added later, "he was all right after that, an' after a while he got to be a pretty good sort o' feller, fer a Englishman."

Over this vast, unsettled region of the old West the cattle of the cowman roamed, and this wild grazing was almost the only possible industry of the country. Therefore the employments of the cowman's occupation were practically the only ones open to a man in search of a means of making a living. Almost everybody had at one time or another tried his hand at "punching cows," and therefore the little town which made the headquarters of the surrounding country was sure to have all the flavour of the range.

Its existence, of course, depended upon the trade of the great ranches which lay about it, at distances perhaps of forty, fifty, or even nearly a hundred miles. Distances had not the same values in that country that they have in the older States. A neighbour who was only fifty miles away was comparatively near. All the supplies of the town were freighted in perhaps a hundred and fifty miles from the railroad. The rancher thought nothing of driving sixty or seventy-five miles in to town to get his groceries. The cowboy would ride thirty or forty miles after the ranch mail, and think no more of it than one does of going down town on the street car. The roads were usually hard and good, and the air pure and stimulating. Either man or horse can endure very much more physical exercise in the country than in the city, because the air is better. The atmosphere of the plains was very fresh and pure.

Now and then, therefore, the residents of the town, who perhaps themselves had ranch interests or "claims" somewhere out in the country, would have the quiet of their daily lives broken by the visits of the men from the cow ranches, near or far. Then the merchant sold his goods, the saloon keeper smiled with pleasure, the editor had use for his pencil, the lawyer stood in readiness, the justice of the peace pricked up his ears, and the coroner idly sauntered forth. The cowman was great. He was the baron of the range. Cheap cattle and still cheaper Mavericks, free grass and free water, with prices always rising in the markets at the end of the drive—no wonder that the cowman was king and that money was free upon the range. No wonder that things were lively when the cow outfit rolled into town, and that the pleasantries of the men were tolerated. It was known that if they shot holes in the saloon looking-glasses, they would come in the next day and settle for the damage, and beside throw the saloon open to the public. Those were the good old days—the days when one cowman rode into a restaurant and ordered "a hundred dollars worth of ham and eggs" for his supper; or when a certain cowman who had just sold his beef drive to good advantage came home and "opened the town," ending his protracted season of festivities by ordering for himself at the little tumble-down hotel a bath of champagne, filled with the wine at five dollars a bottle. He said he wanted a bath, and that nothing was too good for him at the time; and his wishes were complied with cheerfully, though the last champagne of the cow town went into the bath.

One can see it now, the little cow town of the far-away country, a speck on the great gray plain, the mountains lying beyond it, blue and calm, all about the face of Nature looking on at it sleepily, through eyes half shut and amused, everywhere a strange, moving, thrilling silence, that mysterious, awful, fascinating silence of the plains, whose charm steals into the blood, never thereafter to be eliminated.

The cark of care, the grind of grief, the racking of regret—

all these things are gone, vanished from the face of this silent, smiling, resting land.

> A dark-hued lizard on the dark-hued sand;
> A rock; a short gray tree; an earth-built hut.
> Around, an edgeless plain; above, an equal sky.
> She sits and dreams. The whiteless blue of heaven
> Comes down to meet the greenless gray of earth—
> And compasses her dream.

It is high and glaring noon in the little town, but it still sleeps. In their cabins some of the men have not yet thrown off their blankets. Along the one long, straggling street there are few persons moving, and those not hastily. Far out on the plain is a trail of dust winding along, where a big ranch wagon is coming in. Upon the opposite side of the town a second and more rapid trail tells where a buckboard is coming, drawn by a pair of trotting ponies. At the end of the street, just coming up from the *arroyo,* is the figure of a horseman—a tall, slim, young man—who sits straight up on his trotting pony, his gloved hand held high and daintily, his bright kerchief just lopping up and down a bit at his neck as he sits the jogging horse, his big hat pushed back a little over his forehead. All these low buildings, not one of them above a single story, are the colour of the earth. They hold to the earth therefore as though they belonged there. This rider is also in his garb the colour of the earth, and he fits into this scene with perfect right. He also belongs there, this strong, erect, and self-sufficient figure. The environment has produced its man.

Andy Adams
1859-1935

—

1903: *The Log of a Cowboy*
1904: *A Texas Matchmaker*
1905: *The Outlet*
1906: *Cattle Brands*

—

ANDY ADAMS *left his Indiana birthplace and went west at the age of fifteen, heading for southern Texas. There the end of the Civil War in 1865 and the completion of the transcontinental railroad in 1869 had indirectly created the American cattle industry. The war had interrupted cattle shipments and had produced a manpower shortage, leaving a large surplus of beef on the rich grasslands of Texas; when the war ended, that surplus was needed in the East. With veterans drifting into Texas looking for work, the Texas livestock owners soon had enough manpower as well as plenty of cattle. The railroad waited to take those cattle to eastern and California markets, and the government wanted to buy Texas beef for the reservation Indians in Wyoming and Montana.*

Thus began the great era of the trail-drive cowboy. It lasted just long enough for Andy Adams to experience it; then the same railroad that came to pick up the Texas cattle—in Omaha, Abilene, Denver, and Dodge City—started to bring in the American Farmer. It was time for the saddle tramps to leave the stage and ride into legend as heroes on horseback, forced to make room for the new sodbusters and their sagas. These aspiring agriculturalists brought law and order along with the plow, and they also brought a hated symbol of the grassland farmer, an invention patented by Joseph Glidden in 1873: barbed wire.

The "devil's hatband" quickly strangled the "long drive," but Andy Adams did not wait around to see the end. In 1893 he chased a gold rush rumor all the way to Colorado. There he realized that he would never get rich in the creeks; however, he discovered that people were interested in hearing his stories of the trail drive and that if he wrote the stories down, he could make a living by selling them. Moving to Colorado Springs in 1894, Adams became known as a writer, lecturer, and professional "local character," remaining a resident there until his death.

The Log of a Cowboy, Adams's best-known book, is a novel but reads like a detailed autobiography. To create the illusion that this narrative of a single trail drive was factual recollection, Adams drew from his own experiences on many trail drives, gathered anecdotes from other trail hands, and researched what literature on the cattle industry he could find. It can be fairly argued that Adams makes stereotypes out of his cowboys and that he gives them overly contrived names (such as "Moss Strayhorn" and "Fox Quarternight"), and it is frequently suggested that his "actual" episodes are a little too neatly arranged. But The Log of a Cowboy *is still a dependable picture of a uniquely American institution—the cattle drive.*

"The Double Trail" is a good demonstration of Adams's talent for observation and of his knack for making a piece of fiction sound like an actual incident. His characters seem familiar to us . . . the boss-man with the almost invisible sense of humor, the greenhorn who is green enough to give his correct name (and who asks far too many questions for his own good), and the hard-drinking drover who is a renowned liar (famous even among men who had raised the "big fib" to artistic status). "The Double Trail" is also full of cowboy slang: those who read the story closely will chuckle over Stubb's "bar-room astronomy" (meaning, presumably, that Stubb spent much of his saloon time looking at the ceiling through a glass) and the phrase coffin varnish *(a comment on the taste, appearance, and possible aftereffect of bootleg alcohol). The story includes not only common cowboy and cattle-drive terms, such as* mill *and* balk *and* swing, *but idioms from other occupations as well.* Black jack, *for example, refers to barren, useless outcroppings of dark gray rock; a silver miner would recognize it as a term for worthless zinc ore. A man who had failed at mining and had turned to fiction could see it as a nugget of authentic detail.*

The Double Trail

EARLY in the summer of '78 we were rocking along with a herd of Laurel Leaf cattle, going up the old Chisholm trail in the Indian Territory. The cattle were in charge of Ike Inks as foreman, and had been sold for delivery somewhere in the Strip.[1]

From Andy Adams, *Cattle Brands* (Boston: Houghton Mifflin, 1906), pp. 107–30.

1. The Oklahoma Strip. Between 1834 and the first of a series of homestead "runs" in 1889, approximately fifty Indian tribes were relocated into present Oklahoma. For this reason, it was known as the "Indian Territory," or "the Nations," or "the Indian Nation."

There were thirty-one hundred head, straight "twos," and in the single ranch brand. We had been out about four months on the trail, and all felt that a few weeks at the farthest would let us out, for the day before we had crossed the Cimarron River, ninety miles south of the state line of Kansas.

The foreman was simply killing time, waiting for orders concerning the delivery of the cattle. All kinds of jokes were in order, for we all felt that we would soon be set free. One of our men had been taken sick, as we crossed Red River into the Nations, and not wanting to cross this Indian country short-handed, Inks had picked up a young fellow who evidently had never been over the trail before. He gave the outfit his correct name, on joining us, but it proved unpronounceable, and for convenience some one rechristened him Lucy, as he had quite a feminine appearance. He was anxious to learn, and was in evidence in everything that went on.

The trail from the Cimarron to Little Turkey Creek, where we were now camped, had originally been to the east of the present one, skirting a black-jack country. After being used several years it had been abandoned, being sandy, and the new route followed up the bottoms of Big Turkey, since it was firmer soil, affording better footing to cattle. These two trails came together again at Little Turkey. At no place were they over two or three miles apart, and from where they separated to where they came together again was about seven miles.

It troubled Lucy not to know why this was thus. Why did these routes separate and come together again? He was fruitful with inquiries as to where this trail or that road led. The boss-man had a vein of humor in his make-up, though it was not visible; so he told the young man that he did not know, as he had been over this route but once before, but he thought that Stubb, who was then on herd, could tell him how it was; he had been over the trail every year since it was laid out. This was sufficient to secure Stubb an interview, as soon as he was relieved from duty and had returned to the wagon. So Ike posted one of the men who was next on guard to tell Stubb what to expect, and to be sure to tell it to him scary.

A brief description of Stubb necessarily intrudes, though this nickname describes the man. Extremely short in stature, he was inclined to be fleshy. In fact, a rear view of Stubb looked as though some one had hollowed out a place to set his head between his ample shoulders. But a front view revealed a face like a full moon. In disposition he was very amiable. His laugh was enough to drive away the worst case of the blues. It bubbled up from some inward source and seemed perennial. His worst fault was his bar-room astronomy. If there was any one thing that he shone in, it was rustling coffin varnish during the early prohibition days along the Kansas border. His patronage was limited only by his income, coupled with what credit he enjoyed.

Once, about midnight, he tried to arouse a drug clerk who slept in the store, and as he had worked this racket before, he coppered the play to repeat.[2] So he tapped gently on the window at the rear where the clerk slept, calling him by name. This he repeated any number of times. Finally, he threatened to have a fit; even this did not work to his advantage. Then he pretended to be very angry, but there was no response. After fifteen minutes had been fruitlessly spent, he went back to the window, tapped on it once more, saying, "Lon, lie still, you little son-of-a-sheep-thief," which may not be what he said, and walked away. A party who had forgotten his name was once inquiring for him, describing him thus, "He's a little short, fat fellow, sits around the Maverick Hotel, talks cattle talk, and punishes a power of whiskey."[3]

So before Stubb had even time to unsaddle his horse, he was approached to know the history of these two trails.

"Well," said Stubb somewhat hesitatingly, "I never like to refer to it. You see, I killed a man the day that right-hand trail was made: I'll tell you about it some other time."

"But why not now?" said Lucy, his curiosity aroused, as keen as a woman's.

"Some other day," said Stubb. "But did you notice those three graves on the last ridge of sand-hills to the right as we came out of the Cimarron bottoms yesterday? You did? Their tenants were killed over that trail; you see now why I hate to refer to it, don't you? I was afraid to go back to Texas for three years afterward."

"But why not tell me?" said the young man.

"Oh," said Stubb, as he knelt down to put a hobble on his horse, "it would injure my reputation as a peaceable citizen, and I don't mind telling you that I expect to marry soon."

Having worked up the proper interest in his listener, besides exacting a promise that he would not repeat the story where it might do injury to him, he dragged his saddle up to the camp-fire. Making a comfortable seat with it, he riveted his gaze on the fire, and with a splendid sang-froid reluctantly told the history of the double trail.

"You see," began Stubb, "the Chisholm route had been used more or less for ten years. This right-hand trail was made in '73. I bossed that year

---

2. "Coppered the play to repeat"—bet that it would happen again. *Copper* is a slang term for a coin.

3. "Punishes a power"—drinks a large quantity of.

from Van Zandt County, for old Andy Erath, who, by the way, was a dead square cowman with not a hide-bound idea in his make-up. Son, it was a pleasure to know old Andy. You can tell he was a good man, for if he ever got a drink too much, though he would never mention her otherwise, he always praised his wife. I've been with him up beyond the Yellowstone, two thousand miles from home, and you always knew when the old man was primed. He would praise his wife, and would call on us boys to confirm the fact that Mary, his wife, was a good woman.

"That year we had the better of twenty-nine hundred head, all steer cattle, threes and up, a likely bunch, better than these we are shadowing now. You see, my people are not driving this year, which is the reason that I am making a common hand with Inks. If I was to lay off a season, or go to the seacoast, I might forget the way. In those days I always hired my own men. The year that this right-hand trail was made, I had an outfit of men who would rather fight than eat; in fact, I selected them on account of their special fitness in the use of firearms. Why, Inks here couldn't have cooked for my outfit that season, let alone rode. There was no particular incident worth mentioning till we struck Red River, where we overtook five or six herds that were laying over on account of a freshet in the river. I wouldn't have a man those days who was not as good in the water as out. When I rode up to the river, one or two of my men were with me. It looked red and muddy and rolled just a trifle, but I ordered one of the boys to hit it on his horse, to see what it was like. Well, he never wet the seat of his saddle going or coming, though his horse was in swimming water good sixty yards. All the other bosses rode up, and each one examined his peg to see if the rise was falling. One fellow named Bob Brown, boss-man for John Blocker, asked me what I thought about the crossing. I said to him, 'If this ferryman can cross our wagon for me, and you fellows will open out a little and let me in, I'll show you all a crossing, and it'll be no miracle either.'

"Well, the ferryman said he'd set the wagon over, so the men went back to bring up the herd. They were delayed some little time, changing to their swimming horses. It was nearly an hour before the herd came up, the others opening out, so as to give us a clear field, in case of a mill or balk. I never had to give an order; my boys knew just what to do. Why, there's men in this outfit right now that couldn't have greased my wagon that year.

"Well, the men on the points[4] brought the herd to the water with a

___

4. "Points"—the riders who stayed in front of a trail herd. On each side of the herd rode the "swing" riders, whose job was to prevent cattle from straying. Bringing up the rear, in the dust, were the "drag" riders.

good head on, and before the leaders knew it, they were halfway across the channel, swimming like fish. The swing-men fed them in, free and plenty. Most of my outfit took to the water, and kept the cattle from drifting downstream. The boys from the other herds—good men, too—kept shooting them into the water, and inside fifteen minutes' time we were in the big Injun Territory. After crossing the saddle stock and the wagon, I swam my horse back to the Texas side. I wanted to eat dinner with Blocker's man, just to see how they fed. Might want to work for him some time, you see. I pretended that I'd help him over if he wanted to cross, but he said his dogies could never breast that water. I remarked to him at dinner, 'You're feeding a mite better this year, ain't you?' 'Not that I can notice,' he replied, as the cook handed him a tin plate heaping with navy beans, 'and I'm eating rather regular with the wagon, too.' I killed time around for a while, and then we rode down to the river together. The cattle had tramped out his peg, so after setting a new one, and pow-wowing around, I told him goodby and said to him, 'Bob, old man, when I hit Dodge, I'll take a drink and think of you back here on the trail, and regret that you are not with me, so as to make it two-handed.' We said our 'so-longs' to each other, and I gave the gray his head and he took the water like a duck. He could outswim any horse I ever saw, but I drowned him in the Washita two weeks later. Yes, tangled his feet in some vines in a sunken treetop, and the poor fellow's light went out. My own candle came near being snuffed. I never felt so bad over a little thing since I burned my new red topboots when I was a kid, as in drownding that horse.

"There was nothing else worth mentioning until we struck the Cimarron back here, where we overtook a herd of Chisholm's that had come in from the east. They had crossed through the Arbuckle Mountains—came in over the old Whiskey Trail. Here was another herd waterbound, and the boss-man was as important as a hen with one chicken. He told me that the river would n't be fordable for a week; wanted me to fall back at least five miles; wanted all this river bottom for his cattle; said he didn't need any help to cross his herd, though he thanked me for the offer with an air of contempt. I informed him that our cattle were sold for delivery on the North Platte, and that we wanted to go through on time. I assured him if he would drop his cattle a mile down the river, it would give us plenty of room. I told him plainly that our cattle, horses, and men could all swim, and that we never let a little thing like swimming water stop us.

"No! No! he couldn't do that; we might as well fall back and take our turn. 'Oh, well,' said I, 'if you want to act contrary about it, I'll go up to the King-Fisher crossing, only three miles above here. I've almost got time to cross yet this evening.'

"Then he wilted and inquired, 'Do you think I can cross if it swims them any?'

"'I'm not doing your thinking, sir,' I answered, 'but I'll bring up eight or nine good men and help you rather than make a six-mile elbow.' I said this with some spirit and gave him a mean look.

"'All right,' said he, 'bring up your boys, say eight o'clock, and we will try the ford. Let me add right here,' he continued, 'and I'm a stranger to you, young man, but my outfit don't take anybody's slack, and as I am older than you, let me give you this little bit of advice: when you bring your men here in the morning, don't let them whirl too big a loop, or drag their ropes looking for trouble,[5] for I've got fellows with me that don't turn out of the trail for anybody.'

"'All right, sir,' I said. 'Really, I'm glad to hear that you have some good men, still I'm pained to find them on the wrong side of the river for travelers. But I'll be here in the morning,' I called back as I rode away. So telling my boys that we were likely to have some fun in the morning, and what to expect, I gave it no further attention. When we were catching up our horses next morning for the day, I ordered two of my lads on herd, which was a surprise to them, as they were both handy with a gun. I explained it to them all,—that we wished to avoid trouble, but if it came up unavoidable, to overlook no bets—to copper every play as it fell.

"We got to the river too early to suit Chisholm's boss-man. He seemed to think that his cattle would take the water better about ten o'clock. To kill time my boys rode across and back several times to see what the water was like. 'Well, any one that would let as little swimming water as that stop them must be a heap sight sorry outfit,' remarked one-eyed Jim Reed, as he rode out of the river, dismounting to set his saddle forward and tighten his cinches, not noticing that this foreman heard him. I rode around and gave him a look, and he looked up at me and muttered, 'Scuse me, boss, I plumb forgot!' Then I rode back and apologized to this boss-man: 'Don't pay any attention to my boys; they are just showing off, and are a trifle windy this morning.'

"'That's all right,' he retorted, 'but don't forget what I told you yesterday, and let it be enough said.'

"'Well, let's put the cattle in,' I urged, seeing that he was getting hot under the collar. 'We're burning daylight, pardner.'

"'Well, I'm going to cross my wagon first,' said he.

---

5. "Whirl too big a loop"—attempt more than you can handle (also refers, sometimes, to rustling). A cowboy who is "dragging a rope" or "shaking out a loop" is one who is ready for a fight.

" 'That's a good idea,' I answered. 'Bring her up.' Their cook seemed to have a little sense, for he brought up his wagon in good shape. We tied some guy ropes to the upper side, and taking long ropes from the end of the tongue to the pommels of our saddles, the ease with which we set that commissary over didn't trouble any one but the boss-man, whose orders were not very distinct from the distance between banks. It was a good hour then before he would bring up his cattle. The main trouble seemed to be to devise means to keep their guns and cartridges dry, as though that was more important than getting the whole herd of nearly thirty-five hundred cattle over. We gave them a clean cloth[6] until they needed us, but as they came up we divided out and were ready to give the lead a good push. If a cow changed his mind about taking a swim that morning, he changed it right back and took it. For in less than twenty minutes' time they were all over, much to the surprise of the boss and his men; besides, their weapons were quite dry; just the splash had wet them.

"I told the boss that we would not need any help to cross ours, but to keep well out of our way, as we would try and cross by noon, which ought to give him a good five-mile start. Well, we crossed and nooned,[7] lying around on purpose to give them a good lead, and when we hit the trail back in these sand-hills, there he was, not a mile ahead, and you can see there was no chance to get around. I intended to take the Dodge trail, from this creek where we are now, but there we were, blocked in! I was getting a trifle wolfish over the way they were acting, so I rode forward to see what the trouble was.[8]

" 'Oh, I'm in no hurry. You're driving too fast. This is your first trip is n't it?' he inquired, as he felt of a pair of checked pants drying on the wagon wheel.

" 'Don't you let any idea like that disturb your Christian spirit, old man,' I replied with some resentment. 'But if you think I am driving too fast, you might suggest some creek where I could delude myself with the idea, for a week or so, that it was not fordable.'

6. "Gave them a clean cloth"—probably a poker term, meaning that the other player was being allowed to make the first bet, or make the first move ("cloth" referring to the felt covering on a poker table).

7. "Nooning" was the practice of halting the herd during the middle of the day to give the animals and men a rest.

8. The narrator is getting "wolfish," or angry, because it was considered to be an un-written rule that a slow-moving or stalled herd be "thrown off the trail" to let a faster herd go by. This meant moving the slow herd several miles out of the way: if the two herds got mixed up together, or went on a "run" (stampede) into each other, separating them would mean an expensive delay.

"Assuming an air of superiority he observed, 'You seem to have forgot what I said to you yesterday.'

"'No, I have n't,' I answered, 'but are you going to stay all night here?'

"'I certainly am, if that's any satisfaction to you,' he answered.

"I got off my horse and asked him for a match, though I had plenty in my pocket, to light a cigarette which I had rolled during the conversation. I had no gun on, having left mine in our wagon, but fancied I'd stir him up and see how bad he really was. I thought it best to stroke him with and against the fur, try and keep on neutral ground, so I said,—

"'You ain't figuring none that in case of a run to-night we're a trifle close together for cow-herds. Besides, my men on a guard last night heard gray wolves in these sand-hills. They are liable to show up to-night. Didn't I notice some young calves among your cattle this morning? Young calves, you know, make larruping⁹ fine eating for grays.'

"'Now, look here, Shorty,' he said in a patronizing tone, as though he might let a little of his superior cow-sense shine in on my darkened intellect, 'I haven't asked you to crowd up here on me. You are perfectly at liberty to drop back to your heart's content. If wolves bother us to-night, you stay in your blankets snug and warm, and pleasant dreams of old sweethearts on the Trinity to you. We won't need you. We'll try and worry along without you.'

"Two or three of his men laughed gruffly at these remarks, and threw leer-eyed looks at me. I asked one who seemed bad, what calibre his gun was. 'Forty-five ha'r trigger,' he answered. I nosed around over their plunder purpose.¹⁰ They had things drying around like Bannock squaws jerking venison.

"When I got on my horse, I said to the boss, 'I want to pass your outfit in the morning, as you are in no hurry and I am.'

"'That will depend,' said he.

"'Depend on what?' I asked.

"'Depend on whether we are willing to let you,' he snarled.

"I gave him as mean a look as I could command and said tauntingly, 'Now, look here, old girl: there's no occasion for you to tear your clothes with me this way.¹¹ Besides, I sometimes get on the prod myself, and when I do, I don't bar no man, Jew nor Gentile, horse, mare or gelding. You may

9. "Larruping"—delicious.

10. "Plunder purpose"—equipment situation. Their "plunder" (or "stuff") is hanging up to dry all over camp, indicating that they intend to stay there until everything is dry again.

11. "Tear your clothes with me"—to swell up with self-importance.

think different, but I'm not afraid of any man in your outfit, from the gimlet to the big auger.[12] I've tried to treat you white, but I see I've failed. Now I want to give it out to you straight and cold, that I'll pass you to-morrow, or mix two herds trying. Think it over to-night and nominate your choice— be a gentleman or a hog. Let your own sweet will determine which.'

"I rode away in a walk, to give them a chance to say anything they wanted to, but there were no further remarks. My men were all hopping mad when I told them, but I promised them that to-morrow we would fix them plenty or use up our supply of cartridges if necessary. We dropped back a mile off the trail and camped for the night. Early the next morning I sent one of my boys out on the highest sand dune to Injun around and see what they were doing. After being gone for an hour he came back and said they had thrown their cattle off the bed-ground up the trail, and were pottering around like as they aimed to move. Breakfast over, I sent him back again to make sure, for I wanted yet to avoid trouble if they didn't draw it on. It was another hour before he gave us the signal to come on. We were nicely strung out where you saw those graves on that last ridge of sand-hills, when there they were about a mile ahead of us, moseying along. This side of Chapman's, the Indian trader's store, the old route turns to the right and follows up this black-jack ridge. We kept up close, and just as soon as they turned in to the right,—the only trail there was then,—we threw off the course and came straight ahead, cross-country style, same route we came over today, except there was no trail there; we had to make a new one.

"Now they watched us a plenty, but it seemed they couldn't make out our game. When we pulled up even with them, half a mile apart, they tumbled that my bluff of the day before was due to take effect without further notice. Then they began to circle and ride around, and one fellow went back, only hitting the high places,[13] to their wagon and saddle horses, and they were brought up on a trot. We were by this time three quarters of a mile apart, when the boss of their outfit was noticed riding out toward us. Calling one of my men, we rode out and met him halfway. 'Young man, do you know just what you are trying to do?' he asked.

"'I think I do. You and myself as cowmen don't pace in the same class, as you will see, if you will only watch the smoke of our tepee. Watch us close, and I'll pass you between here and the next water.'

12. A "gimlet" is a very small leather punch, not much larger than a stout needle. An "auger" is a large, heavy-duty drill for wood.

13. "Only hitting the high places"—going so fast that the horse hits only the high spots on the ground, possibly an exaggeration.

"'We will see you in hell first!' he said, as he whirled his horse and galloped back to his men. The race was on in a brisk walk. His wagon, we noticed, cut in between the herds, until it reached the lead of his cattle, when it halted suddenly, and we noticed that they were cutting off a dry cowskin that swung under the wagon. At the same time two of his men cut out a wild steer, and as he ran near their wagon one of them roped and the other heeled him. It was neatly done. I called Big Dick, my boss roper, and told him what I suspected,—that they were going to try and stampede us with a dry cowskin tied to that steer's tail they had down. As they let him up, it was clear I had called the turn, as they headed him for our herd, the flint thumping at his heels. Dick rode out in a lope, and I signaled for my crowd to come on and we would back Dick's play. As we rode out together, I said to my boys, 'The stuff's off, fellows! Shoot, and shoot to hurt!'

"It seemed their whole outfit was driving that one steer, and turning the others loose to graze. Dick never changed the course of that steer, but let him head for ours, and as they met and passed, he turned his horse and rode onto him as though he was a post driven in the ground. Whirling a loop big enough to take in a yoke of oxen, he dropped it over his off fore shoulder, took up his slack rope, and when that steer went to the end of the rope, he was thrown in the air and came down on his head with a broken neck. Dick shook the rope off the dead steer's forelegs without dismounting, and was just beginning to coil his rope when those varmints made a dash at him, shooting and yelling.

"That called for a counter play on our part, except our aim was low, for if we didn't get a man, we were sure to leave one afoot. Just for a minute the air was full of smoke. Two horses on our side went down before you could say 'Jack Robinson,' but the men were unhurt, and soon flattened themselves on the ground Indian fashion, and burnt the grass in a half-circle in front of them. When everybody had emptied his gun, each outfit broke back to its wagon to reload. Two of my men came back afoot, each claiming that he had got his man all right, all right. We were no men shy, which was lucky. Filling our guns with cartridges out of our belts, we rode out to reconnoitre and try and get the boys' saddles.

"The first swell of the ground showed us the field. There were the dead steer, and five or six horses scattered around likewise, but the grass was too high to show the men that we felt were there. As the opposition was keeping close to their wagon, we rode up to the scene of carnage. While some of the boys were getting the saddles off the dead horses, we found three men taking their last nap in the grass. I recognized them as the boss-man, the fellow with the ha'r-trigger gun, and a fool kid that had two guns on him when we were crossing their cattle the day before. One gun was n't plenty to do the fighting he was hankering for; he had about as much use for two guns as a toad has for a stinger.

"The boys got the saddles off the dead horses, and went flying back to our men afoot, and then rejoined us. The fight seemed over, or there was some hitch in the programme, for we could see them hovering near their wagon, tearing up white biled shirts out of a trunk and bandaging up arms and legs, that they hadn't figured on any. Our herd had been overlooked during the scrimmage, and had scattered so that I had to send one man and the horse wrangler to round them in. We had ten men left, and it was beginning to look as though hostilities had ceased by mutual consent. You can see, son, we didn't bring it on. We turned over the dead steer, and he proved to be a stray; at least he hadn't their road brand on. One-eyed Jim said the ranch brand belonged in San Saba County; he knew it well, the X—2. Well, it wasn't long until our men afoot got a remount and only two horses shy on the first round. We could stand another on the same terms in case they attacked us. We rode out on a little hill about a quarter-mile from their wagon, scattering out so as not to give them a pot shot, in case they wanted to renew the unpleasantness.

"When they saw us there, one fellow started toward us, waving his handkerchief. We began speculating which one it was, but soon made him out to be the cook; his occupation kept him out of the first round. When he came within a hundred yards, I rode out and met him. He offered me his hand and said, 'We are in a bad fix. Two of our crowd have bad flesh wounds. Do you suppose we could get any whiskey back at this Indian trader's store?'

" 'If there is any man in this territory can get any I can if they have it,' I told him. 'Besides, if your lay-out has had all the satisfaction fighting they want, we'll turn to and give you a lift. It seems like you all have some dead men over back here. They will have to be planted. So if your outfit feel as though you had your belly-full of fighting for the present, consider us at your service. You're the cook, ain't you?'

" 'Yes, sir,' he answered. 'Are all three dead?' he then inquired.

" 'Dead as heck,' I told him.

" 'Well, we are certainly in a bad box,' said he meditatingly. 'But won't you all ride over to our wagon with me? I think our fellows are pacified for the present.'

"I motioned to our crowd, and we all rode over to their wagon with him. There wasn't a gun in sight. The ragged edge of despair don't describe them. I made them a little talk; told them that their boss had cashed in, back over the hill; also if there was any segundo[14] in their outfit, the position of big augur was open to him, and we were at his service.

"There wasn't a man among them that had any sense left but the cook. He told me to take charge of the killed, and if I could rustle a little whiskey to do so. So I told the cook to empty out his wagon, and we would take the dead ones back, make boxes for them, and bury them at the store. Then I sent three of my men back to the store to have the boxes ready and dig the graves. Before these three rode away, I said, aside to Jim, who was one of them, 'Don't bother about any whiskey; branch water is plenty nourishing for the wounded. It would be a sin and shame to waste good liquor on plafry[15] like them.'

"The balance of us went over to the field of carnage and stripped the saddles off their dead horses, and arranged the departed in a row, covering them with saddle blankets, pending the planting act. I sent part of my boys with our wagon to look after our own cattle for the day. It took us all the afternoon to clean up a minute's work in the morning.

"I never like to refer to it. Fact was, all the boys felt gloomy for weeks, but there was no avoiding it. Two months later, we met old man Andy, way up at Fort Laramie on the North Platte. He was tickled to death to meet us all. The herd had come through in fine condition. We never told him anything about this until the cattle were delivered, and we were celebrating the success of that drive at a near-by town.

"Big Dick told him about this incident, and the old man feeling his oats, as he leaned with his back against the bar, said to us with a noticeable degree of pride, 'Lads, I'm proud of every one of you. Men who will fight to protect my interests has my purse at their command. This year's drive has been a success. Next year we will drive twice as many. I want every rascal of you to work for me. You all know how I mount, feed, and pay my men, and as long as my name is Erath and I own a cow, you can count on a job with me.'"

"But why did you take them back to the sand-hills to bury them?" cut in Lucy.

"Oh, that was Big Dick's idea. He thought the sand would dig easier, and laziness guided every act of his life. That was five years ago, son, that this lower trail was made, and for the reasons I have just given you. No, I can't tell you any more personal experiences tonight; I'm too sleepy."

14. "Segundo"—Spanish for second-in-command; an assistant foreman.
15. "Plafry"—probably a corruption of *pilfery*, items of little value.

Owen Wister
1860-1938

—

—

THE VIRGINIAN *is the prototypical hero of cowboy fiction, and his shoot-out with Trampas is the beginning of the gunfight tradition. That cowboy hero was created by Owen Wister, who was born into a Philadelphia family of comfortable wealth and who grew up in an atmosphere of culture and gentility. In 1882 Wister graduated with honors from Harvard, where he had become friends with Theodore Roosevelt, and went to Europe to study music. He soon returned home, however, and worked in a brokerage firm. Then health problems caused him to seek a change of climate. The pure, dry air of the West was considered to be good for the health, so in 1885 Wister followed Roosevelt's example and spent a summer in Wyoming. That fall he was well enough to enter Harvard's law school, and he graduated from there in 1888.*

But literature, not law, became Wister's calling. Like Roosevelt, he had an intellectual's enthusiastic fascination with the West; and like the tenderfoot in The Virginian, *he was "green" but willing to watch and listen and learn. Wister made fifteen visits to the West, and each time he went, he kept careful notes on the slang and the occupations of the men he met. He wrote down their tales, he recorded the details of their environment, and when he thought of a good story, he would tell it to the cowboys to make sure that it sounded authentic. Thus it was no accident that* The Virginian *became a popular sensation when the book came out in 1902, and no surprise that dozens of writers of pulp Westerns have since used the Virginian as a model for their own protagonists. Among Wister's famous characterizations are the strong silent cowboy, the villainous backshooter, the comic sidekick, and the supercilious schoolmarm. Wister's showdown at sunrise is widely imitated. Harvard had given Wister an education in classic drama and literature; out West he saw the living and vital dramatic potential in the people he encountered.*

Wister's liberal education afforded him a clear understanding of his own potential contribution to American literature. The evidence of this is found in his letters, in the prefaces to his works, and in his biographical writing. In Roosevelt: The Story of a Friendship, *Wister relates a conversation he had with a fellow western enthusiast, at a place he refers to as "the club."*

Why wasn't some Kipling saving the sage-brush for American literature, before the sagebrush and all that it signified went the way of the California forty-niner, went the way of the Mississippi steam-boat, went the way of everything? . . . But what was fiction doing, fiction the only thing that has always outlived fact? Must it be perpetual tea-cups?[1]

In the preface to The Virginian, *Wister appropriately called his novel a "colonial romance." He also called it a "historical novel" and carefully defined what he meant by that term. "Any narrative which presents faithfully a day and a generation is of necessity historical; and this one presents Wyoming between 1874 and 1890." Wister admitted that the hero in this historical context was romantic, a "hero without wings," similar to the romantic heroes of Rudyard Kipling or Sir Walter Scott.*[2]

A romance is characterized by an emphasis on action and adventure, usually uncommon adventure; overt conflict and movement take precedence over description and meditation; and a fast sequence of incidents is preferable to a carefully crafted plot. But Wister was aware of plot and knew how to use it. In the preface to Lin McLean *(a book some prefer to* The Virginian*), he described his plan to write a "chain of short stories" that would all contribute to an "underlying drama" and would proceed "through climax and catastrophe to solution."*[3] *What he had in mind was the kind of structure that readers could find in most European-style fiction. By the second edition, however, he realized that his American audience would rather see a well-told adventure than a clever framework.*

1. Owen Wister, *Roosevelt: The Story of a Friendship, 1880–1919* (New York: Macmillan, 1930), p. 29.

2. Owen Wister, *The Virginian* (New York: Macmillan, 1902), p. ix.

3. Owen Wister, *Lin McLean* (New York: Harper and Brothers, 1907), p. vii.

In "The Jimmyjohn Boss," a well-told story is just what we have. Wister displays his skill in manipulating the narrative in the same way that the young "boss" shows his skill in dealing with the rebellious "buccaroos." Both the writer and his protagonist illustrate the truth of the remark that the Virginian made when he and the narrator found Shorty murdered. Shorty had been a poor judge of character and had not been vigilant enough. "There was no natural harm in him," said the Virginian. "But you must do a thing well in this country." [4]

—

The Jimmyjohn Boss

I

ONE day at Nampa, which is in Idaho, a ruddy old massive jovial man stood by the Silver City stage, patting his beard with his left hand, and with his right the shoulder of a boy who stood beside him. He had come with the boy on the branch train from Boisé, because he was a careful German and liked to say everything twice—twice at least when it was a matter of business. This was a matter of very particular business, and the German had repeated himself for nineteen miles. Presently the east-bound on the main line would arrive from Portland; then the Silver City stage would take the boy south on his new mission, and the man would journey by the branch train back to Boisé. From Boisé no one could say where he might not go, west or east. He was a great and pervasive cattle man in Oregon, California, and other places. Vogel and Lex—even to-day you may hear the two ranch partners spoken of. So the veteran Vogel was now once more going over his notions and commands to his youthful deputy during the last precious minutes until the east-bound should arrive.

"Und if only you haf someding like dis," said the old man, as he tapped his beard and patted the boy, "it would be five hoondert more dollars salary in your liddle pants."

The boy winked up at his employer. He had a gray, humorous eye; he was slim and alert, like a sparrow-hawk—the sort of boy his father openly rejoices in and his mother is secretly in prayer over. Only, this boy had neither father nor mother. Since the age of twelve he had looked out for

From Owen Wister, *The Jimmyjohn Boss and Other Stories* (New York: Harper and Brothers, 1900), pp. 3–63.

4. Wister, *The Virginian*, p. 420.

himself, never quite without bread, sometimes attaining champagne, getting along in his American way variously, on horse or afoot, across regions of wide plains and mountains, through towns where not a soul knew his name. He closed one of his gray eyes at his employer, and beyond this made no remark.

"Vat you mean by dat vink, anyhow?" demanded the elder.

"Say," said the boy, confidentially—"honest now. How about you and me? Five hundred dollars if I had your beard. You've got a record and I've got a future. And my bloom's on me rich, without a scratch. How many dollars you gif me for dat bloom?" The sparrow-hawk sailed into a freakish imitation of his master.

"You are a liddle rascal!" cried the master, shaking with entertainment. "Und if der peoples vas to hear you sass old Max Vogel in dis style they would say, 'Poor old Max, he lose his gr-rip.' But I don't lose it." His great hand closed suddenly on the boy's shoulder, his voice cut clean and heavy as an axe, and then no more joking about him. "Haf you understand that?" he said.

"Yes, sir."

"How old are you, son?"

"Nineteen, sir."

"Oh my, that is offle young for the job I gif you. Some of dose man you go to boss might be your father. Und how much do you weigh?"

"About a hundred and thirty."

"Too light, too light. Und I haf keep my eye on you in Boisé. You are not so goot a boy as you might be."

"Well, sir, I guess not."

"But you was not so bad a boy as you might be, neider. You don't lie about it. Now it must be farewell to all that foolishness. Haf you understand? You go to set an example where one is needed very bad. If those men see you drink a liddle, they drink a big lot. You forbid them, they laugh at you. You must not allow one drop of whiskey at the whole place. Haf you well understand?"

"Yes, sir. Me and whiskey are not necessary to each other's happiness."

"It is not you, it is them. How are you mit your gun?"

Vogel took the boy's pistol from its holster and aimed at an empty bottle which was sticking in the thin December snow. "Can you do this?" he said, carelessly, and fired. The snow struck the bottle, but the unharming bullet was buried half an inch to the left.

The boy took his pistol with solemnity. "No," he said. "Guess I can't do that." He fired, and the glass splintered into shapelessness. "Told you I couldn't miss as close as you did," said he.

"You are a darling," said Mr. Vogel. "Gif me dat lofely weapon."

A fortunate store of bottles lay, leaned, or stood about in the white snow of Nampa, and Mr. Vogel began at them.

"May I ask if anything is the matter?" inquired a mild voice from the stage.

"Stick that lily head in-doors," shouted Vogel; and the face and eye-glasses withdrew again into the stage. "The school-teacher he will be beautifool virtuous company for you at Malheur Agency," continued Vogel, shooting again; and presently the large old German destroyed a bottle with a crashing smack. "Ah!" said he, in unison with the smack. "Ah-ha! No von shall say der old Max lose his gr-rip. I shoot it efry time now, but the train she whistle. I hear her."

The boy affected to listen earnestly.

"Bah! I tell you I hear de whistle coming."

"Did you say there was a whistle?" ventured the occupant of the stage. The snow shone white on his glasses as he peered out.

"Nobody whistle for you," returned the robust Vogel. "You listen to me," he continued to the boy. "You are offle yoong. But I watch you plenty this long time. I see you work mit my stock on the Owyhee and the Malheur; I see you mit my oder men. My men they say always more and more, 'Yoong Drake he is a goot one,' und I think you are a goot one mine own self. I am the biggest cattle man on the Pacific slope, und I am also an old devil. I have think a lot, und I like you."

"I'm obliged to you, sir."

"Shut oop. I like you, und therefore I make you my new sooperinten-dent at my Malheur Agency r-ranch, mit a bigger salary as you don't get before. If you are a sookcess, I r-raise you some more."

"I am satisfied now, sir."

"Bah! Never do you tell any goot business man you are satisfied mit vat he gif you, for eider he don't believe you or else he think you are a fool. Und eider ways you go down in his estimation. You make those men at Malheur Agency behave themselves und I r-raise you. Only I do vish, I do certainly vish you had some beard on that yoong chin."

The boy glanced at his pistol.

"No, no, no, my son," said the sharp old German. "I don't want gun-powder in dis affair. You must act kviet und decisif und keep your liddle shirt on. What you accomplish shootin'? You kill somebody, und then, pop! somebody kills you. What goot is all that nonsense to me?"

"It would annoy me some, too," retorted the boy, eying the capitalist. "Don't leave me out of the proposition."

"Broposition! Broposition! Now you get hot mit old Max for nothing."

"If you didn't contemplate trouble," pursued the boy, "what was your point just now in sampling my marksmanship?" He kicked some snow in the direction of the shattered bottle. "It's understood no whiskey comes on that ranch. But if no gunpowder goes along with me, either, let's call the deal off. Buy some other fool."

"You haf not understand, my boy. Und you get very hot because I happen to make that liddle joke about somebody killing you. Was you thinking maybe old Max not care what happen to you?"

A moment of silence passed before the answer came: "Suppose we talk business?"

"Very well, very well. Only notice this thing. When oder peoples talk oop to me like you haf done many times, it is not they who does the getting hot. It is me—old Max. Und when old Max gets hot he slings them out of his road anywheres. Some haf been very sorry they get so slung. You invite me to buy some oder fool? Oh, my boy, I will buy no oder fool except you, for that was just like me when I was yoong Max!" Again the ruddy and grizzled magnate put his hand on the shoulder of the boy, who stood looking away at the bottles, at the railroad track, at anything save his employer.

The employer proceeded: "I was afraid of nobody und noding in those days. You are afraid of nobody and noding. But those days was different. No Pullman sleepers, no railroad at all. We come oop the Columbia in the steamboat, we travel hoonderts of miles by team, we sleep, we eat nowheres in particular mit many unexpected interooptions. There was Indians, there was offle bad white men, und if you was not offle yourself you vanished quickly. Therefore in those days was Max Vogel hell und repeat."

The magnate smiled a broad fond smile over the past which he had kicked, driven, shot, bled, and battled through to present power; and the boy winked up at him again now.

"I don't propose to vanish, myself," said he.

"Ah-ha! you was no longer mad mit der old Max! Of coorse I care what happens to you. I was alone in the world myself in those lofely wicked days."

Reserve again made flinty the boy's face.

"Neider did I talk about my feelings," continued Max Vogel, "but I nefer show them too quick. If I was injured I wait, and I strike to kill. We all paddles our own dugout, eh? We ask no favors from nobody; we must win our spurs! Not so? Now I talk business with you where you interroopt me. If cow-boys was not so offle scarce in the country, I would long ago haf bounce the lot of those drunken fellows. But they cannot be spared; we must get along so. I cannot send Brock, he is needed at Harper's. The dumb fellow at Alvord Lake is too dumb; he is not quickly coorageous. They would play high jinks mit him. Therefore I send you. Brock he say to me you haf joodgement. I watch, und I say to myself also, this boy haf goot joodgement. Und when you look at your pistol so quick, I tell you quick I don't send you to kill men when they are so scarce already! My boy, it is ever the moral, the say-noding strength what gets there—mit always the liddle pistol behind, in case—joost in case. Haf you understand? I ask you to shoot. I see you know how, as Brock told me. I recommend you to let them see that aggomplishment in a friendly way. Maybe a shooting-match mit prizes—I pay for them—pretty soon after you come. Und joodgement— und joodgement. Here comes that train. Haf you well understand?"

Upon this the two shook hands, looking square friendship in each other's eyes. The east-bound, long quiet and dark beneath its flowing clots of smoke, slowed to a halt. A few valises and legs descended, ascended, herding and hurrying; a few trunks were thrown resoundingly in and out of the train; a woolly, crooked old man came with a box and a bandanna bundle from the second-class car; the travellers of a thousand miles looked torpidly at him through the dim, dusty windows of their Pullman, and settled again for a thousand miles more. Then the east-bound, shooting heavier clots of smoke laboriously into the air, drew its slow length out of Nampa, and away.

"Where's that stage?" shrilled the woolly old man. "That's what I'm after."

"Why, hello!" shouted Vogel. "Hello, Uncle Pasco! I heard you was dead."

Uncle Pasco blinked his small eyes to see who hailed him. "Oh!" said he, in his light, crusty voice. "Dutchy Vogel. No, I ain't dead. You guessed wrong. Not dead. Help me up, Dutchy."

A tolerant smile broadened Vogel's face. "It was ten years since I see you," said he, carrying the old man's box.

"Shouldn't wonder. Maybe it'll be another ten till you see me next." He stopped by the stage step, and wheeling nimbly, surveyed his old-time acquaintance, noting the good hat, the prosperous watch-chain, the big, well-blacked boots. "Not seen me for ten years. Hee-hee! No. Usen't to have a cent more than me. Twins in poverty. That's how Dutchy and me started. If we was buried to-morrow they'd mark him 'Pecunious' and me 'Impecunious.' That's what. Twins in poverty."

"I stick to von business at a time, Uncle," said good-natured, success-ful Max.

A flicker of aberration lighted in the old man's eye. "H'm, yes," said he, pondering. "Stuck to one business. So you did. H'm." Then, suddenly sly, he chirped: "But I've struck it rich now." He tapped his box. "Jewelry," he half-whispered. "Miners and cow-boys."

"Yes," said Vogel. "Those poor, deluded fellows, they buy such stuff." And he laughed at the seedy visionary who had begun frontier life with him on the bottom rung and would end it there. "Do you play that concertina yet, Uncle?" he inquired.

"Yes, yes. I always play. It's in here with my tooth-brush and socks." Uncle Pasco held up the bandanna. "Well, he's getting ready to start. I guess I'll be climbing inside. Holy Gertrude!"

This shrill comment was at sight of the school-master, patient within the stage. "What business are you in?" demanded Uncle Pasco.

"I am in the spelling business," replied the teacher, and smiled, faintly.

"Hell!" piped Uncle Pasco. "Take this."

He handed in his bandanna to the traveller, who received it politely. Max Vogel lifted the box of cheap jewelry; and both he and the boy came behind to boost the old man up on the stage step. But with a nettled look he leaped up to evade them, tottered half-way, and then, light as a husk of grain, got himself to his seat and scowled at the schoolmaster.

After a brief inspection of that pale, spectacled face, "Dutchy," he called out of the door, "this country is not what it was."

But old Max Vogel was inattentive. He was speaking to the boy, Dean Drake, and held a flask in his hand. He reached the flask to his new superin-tendent. "Drink hearty," said he. "There, son! Don't be shy. Haf you forgot it is forbidden fruit after now?"

"Kid sworn off?" inquired Uncle Pasco of the school-master.

"I understand," replied this person, "that Mr. Vogel will not allow his cow-boys at the Malheur Agency to have any whiskey brought there. Per-sonally, I feel gratified." And Mr. Bolles, the new school-master, gave his faint smile.

"Oh," muttered Uncle Pasco. "Forbidden to bring whiskey on the ranch? H'm." His eyes wandered to the jewelry-box. "H'm," said he again; and becoming thoughtful, he laid back his moth-eaten sly head, and spoke no further with Mr. Bolles.

Dean Drake climbed into the stage and the vehicle started.

"Goot luck, goot luck, my son!" shouted the hearty Max, and opened and waved both his big arms at the departing boy. He stood looking after the stage. "I hope he come back," said he. "I think he come back. If he come I r-raise him fifty dollars without any beard."

II

The stage had not trundled so far on its Silver City road but that a whistle from Nampa station reached its three occupants. This was the branch train starting back to Boisé with Max Vogel aboard; and the boy looked out at the locomotive with a sigh.

"Only five days of town," he murmured. "Six months more wilderness now."

"My life has been too much town," said the new school-master. "I am looking forward to a little wilderness for a change."

Old Uncle Pasco, leaning back, said nothing; he kept his eyes shut and his ears open.

"Change is what I don't get," sighed Dean Drake. In a few miles, however, before they had come to the ferry over Snake River, the recent leave-taking and his employer's kind but dominating repression lifted from the boy's spirit. His gray eye wakened keen again, and he began to whistle light opera tunes, looking about him alertly, like the sparrow-hawk that he was. "Ever see Jeannie Winston in 'Fatinitza'?" he inquired of Mr. Bolles.

The school-master, with a startled, thankful countenance, stated that he had never.

"Ought to," said Drake.

> " 'You a man? that can't be true!
> Men have never eyes like you.'

That's what the girls in the harem sing in the second act. Golly whiz!" The boy gleamed over the memory of that evening.

"You have a hard job before you," said the school-master, changing the subject.

"Yep. Hard." The wary Drake shook his head warningly at Mr. Bolles to keep off that subject, and he glanced in the direction of slumbering Uncle Pasco. Uncle Pasco was quite aware of all this. "I wouldn't take another lonesome job so soon," pursued Drake, "but I want the money. I've been working eleven months along the Owyhee as a sort of junior boss, and I'd earned my vacation. Just got it started hot in Portland, when biff! old Vogel telegraphs me. Well, I'll be saving instead of squandering. But it feels so good to squander!"

"I have never had anything to squander," said Bolles, rather sadly.

"You don't say! Well, old man, I hope you will. It gives a man a lot he'll never get out of spelling-books. Are you cold? Here." And despite the school-master's protest, Dean Drake tucked his buffalo coat round and over him. "Some day, when I'm old," he went on, "I mean to live respectable under my own cabin and vine. Wife and everything. But not, anyway, till I'm thirty-five."

He dropped into his opera tunes for a while; but evidently it was not "Fatinitza" and his vanished holiday over which he was chiefly meditating, for presently he exclaimed: "I'll give them a shooting-match in the morning. You shoot?"

Bolles hoped he was going to learn in this country, and exhibited a .22 Smith & Wesson revolver.

Drake grieved over it. "Wrap it up warm," said he. "I'll lend you a real one when we get to the Malheur Agency. But you can eat, anyhow. Christmas being next week, you see, my programme is, shoot all A.M. and eat all P.M. I wish you could light on a notion what prizes to give my buccaroos."

"Buccaroos?" said Bolles.

"Yep. Cow-punchers. Vaqueros. Buccaroos in Oregon. Bastard Spanish word, you see, drifted up from Mexico. Vogel would not care to have me give 'em money as prizes."

At this Uncle Pasco opened an eye.

"How many buccaroos will there be?" Bolles inquired.

"At the Malheur Agency? It's the headquarters of five of our ranches. There ought to be quite a crowd. A dozen, probably, at this time of year."

Uncle Pasco opened his other eye. "Here, you!" he said, dragging at his box under the seat. "Pull it, can't you? There. Just what you're after. There's your prizes." Querulous and watchful, like some aged, rickety ape, the old man drew out his trinkets in shallow shelves.

"Sooner give 'em nothing," said Dean Drake.

"What's that? What's the matter with them?"

"Guess the boys have had all the brass rings and glass diamonds they want."

"That's all you know, then. I sold that box clean empty through the Palouse country last week, 'cept the bottom drawer, and an outfit on Meacham's hill took that. Shows all you know. I'm going clean through your country after I've quit Silver City. I'll start in by Baker City again, and I'll strike Harney, and maybe I'll go to Linkville. I know what buccaroos want. I'll go to Fort Rinehart, and I'll go to the Island Ranch, and first thing you'll be seeing your boys wearing my stuff all over their fingers and Sunday shirts, and giving their girls my stuff right in Harney City. That's what."

"All right, Uncle. It's a free country."

"Shaw! Guess it is. I was in it before you was, too. You were wet behind the ears when I was jammin' all around here. How many are they up at your place, did you say?"

"I said about twelve. If you're coming our way, stop and eat with us."

"Maybe I will and maybe I won't." Uncle Pasco crossly shoved his box back.

"All right, Uncle. It's a free country," repeated Drake.

Not much was said after this. Uncle Pasco unwrapped his concertina from the red handkerchief and played nimbly for his own benefit. At Silver City he disappeared, and, finding he had stolen nothing from them, they did not regret him. Dean Drake had some affairs to see to here before starting for Harper's ranch, and it was pleasant to Bolles to find how Drake was esteemed through this country. The school-master was to board at the Malheur Agency, and had come this way round because the new superintendent must so travel. They were scarcely birds of a feather, Drake and Bolles, yet since one remote roof was to cover them, the in-door man was glad this boy-host had won so much good-will from high and low. That the shrewd old Vogel should trust so much in a nineteen-year-old was proof enough at least of his character; but when Brock, the foreman from Harper's, came for them at Silver City, Bolles witnessed the affection that the rougher man held for Drake. Brock shook the boy's hand with that serious quietness and absence of words which shows the Western heart is speaking. After a look at Bolles and a silent bestowing of the baggage aboard the team, he cracked his long whip and the three rattled happily away through the dips of an open country where clear streams ran blue beneath the winter air. They followed the Jordan (that Idaho Jordan) west towards Oregon and the Owyhee, Brock often turning in his driver's seat so as to speak with Drake. He had a long, gradual chapter of confidences and events; through miles he unburdened these to his favorite:

The California mare was doing well in harness. The eagle over at White-horse ranch had fought the cat most terrible. Gilbert had got a mule-kick in the stomach, but was eating his three meals. They had a new boy who played the guitar. He used maple-syrup on his meat, and claimed he was from Alabama. Brock guessed things were about as usual in most ways. The new well had caved in again. Then, in the midst of his gossip, the thing he had wanted to say all along came out: "We're pleased about your promotion," said he; and, blushing, shook Drake's hand again.

Warmth kindled the boy's face, and next, with a sudden severity, he said: "You're keeping back something."

The honest Brock looked blank, then labored in his memory.

"Has the sorrel girl in Harney married you yet?" said Drake.

Brock slapped his leg, and the horses jumped at his mirth. He was mostly grave-mannered, but when his boy superintendent joked, he rejoiced with the same pride that he took in all of Drake's excellences.

"The boys in this country will back you up," said he, next day; and Drake inquired: "What news from the Malheur Agency?"

"Since the new Chinaman has been cooking for them," said Brock, "they have been peaceful as a man could wish."

"They'll approve of me, then," Drake answered. "I'm feeding 'em hyas Christmas muck-a-muck."

"And what may that be?" asked the schoolmaster.

"You no kumtux Chinook?" inquired Drake. "Travel with me and you'll learn all sorts of languages. It means just a big feed. All whiskey is barred," he added to Brock.

"It's the only way," said the foreman. "They've got those Pennsylvania men up there."

Drake had not encountered these.

"The three brothers Drinker," said Brock. "Full, Half-past Full, and Drunk are what they call them. Them's the names; they've brought them from Klamath and Rogue River."

"I should not think a Chinaman would enjoy such comrades," ventured Mr. Bolles.

"Chinamen don't have comrades in this country," said Brock, briefly. "They like his cooking. It's a lonesome section up there, and a Chinaman could hardly quit it, not if he was expected to stay. Suppose they kick about the whiskey rule?" he suggested to Drake.

"Can't help what they do. Oh, I'll give each boy his turn in Harney City when he gets anxious. It's the whole united lot I don't propose to have cut up on me."

A look of concern for the boy came over the face of foreman Brock. Several times again before their parting did he thus look at his favorite. They paused at Harper's for a day to attend to some matters, and when Drake was leaving this place one of the men said to him: "We'll stand by you." But from his blithe appearance and talk as the slim boy journeyed to the Malheur

River and Headquarter ranch, nothing seemed to be on his mind. Oregon twinkled with sun and fine white snow. They crossed through a world of pines and creviced streams and exhilarating silence. The little waters fell tinkling through icicles in the loneliness of the woods, and snowshoe rabbits dived into the brush. East Oregon, the Owyhee and the Malheur country, the old trails of General Crook, the willows by the streams, the open swales, the high woods where once Buffalo Horn and Chief E-egante and O-its the medicine-man prospered, through this domain of war and memories went Bolles the school-master with Dean Drake and Brock. The third noon from Harper's they came leisurely down to the old Malheur Agency, where once the hostile Indians had drawn pictures on the door, and where Castle Rock frowned down unchanged.

"I wish I was going to stay here with you," said Brock to Drake. "By Indian Creek you can send word to me quicker than we've come."

"Why, you're an old bat!" said the boy to his foreman, and clapped him farewell on the shoulder.

Brock drove away, thoughtful. He was not a large man. His face was clean-cut, almost delicate. He had a well-trimmed, yellow mustache, and it was chiefly in his blue eye and lean cheek-bone that the frontiersman showed. He loved Dean Drake more than he would ever tell, even to himself.

The young superintendent set at work to ranch-work this afternoon of Brock's leaving, and the buccaroos made his acquaintance one by one and stared at him. Villany did not sit outwardly upon their faces; they were not villains; but they stared at the boy sent to control them, and they spoke together, laughing. Drake took the head of the table at supper, with Bolles on his right. Down the table some silence, some staring, much laughing went on—the rich brute laugh of the belly untroubled by the brain. Sam, the Chinaman, rapid and noiseless, served the dishes.

"What is it?" said a buccaroo.

"Can it bite?" said another.

"If you guess what it is, you can have it," said a third.

"It's meat," remarked Drake, incisively, helping himself; "and tougher than it looks."

The brute laugh rose from the crowd and fell into surprised silence; but no rejoinder came, and they ate their supper somewhat thoughtfully. The Chinaman's quick, soft eye had glanced at Dean Drake when they laughed. He served his dinner solicitously. In his kitchen that evening he and Bolles unpacked the good things—the olives, the dried fruits, the cigars—brought by the new superintendent for Christmas; and finding Bolles harmless, like his gentle Asiatic self, Sam looked cautiously about and spoke:

"You not know why they laugh," said he. "They not talk about my meat then. They mean new boss, Misser Dlake. He velly young boss."

"I think," said Bolles, "Mr. Drake understood their meaning, Sam. I have noticed that at times he expresses himself peculiarly. I also think they understood his meaning."

The Oriental pondered. "Me like Misser Dlake," said he. And drawing quite close, he observed, "They not nice man velly much."

Next day and every day "Misser Dlake" went gayly about his business, at his desk or on his horse, vigilant, near and far, with no sign save a steadier keenness in his eye. For the Christmas dinner he provided still further, sending to the Grande Ronde country for turkeys and other things. He won the heart of Bolles by lending him a good horse; but the buccaroos, though they were boisterous over the coming Christmas joy, did not seem especially grateful. Drake, however, kept his worries to himself.

"This thing happens anywhere," he said one night in the office to Bolles, puffing a cigar. "I've seen a troop of cavalry demoralize itself by a sort of contagion from two or three men."

"I think it was wicked to send you here by yourself," blurted Bolles.

"Poppycock! It's the chance of my life, and I'll jam her through or bust."

"I think they have decided you are getting turkeys because you are afraid of them," said Bolles.

"Why, of course! But d' you figure I'm the man to abandon my Christmas turkey because my motives for eating it are misconstrued?"

Dean Drake smoked for a while; then a knock came at the door. Five buccaroos entered and stood close, as is the way with the guilty who feel uncertain.

"We were thinking as maybe you'd let us go over to town," said Half-past Full, the spokesman.

"When?"

"Oh, any day along this week."

"Can't spare you till after Christmas."

"Maybe you'll not object to one of us goin'?"

"You'll each have your turn after this week."

A slight pause followed. Then Half-past Full said: "What would you do if I went, anyway?"

"Can't imagine," Drake answered, easily. "Go, and I'll be in a position to inform you."

The buccaroo dropped his stolid bull eyes, but raised them again and grinned. "Well, I'm not particular about goin' this week, boss."

"That's not my name," said Drake, "but it's what I am."

They stood a moment. Then they shuffled out. It was an orderly retreat—almost.

Drake winked over to Bolles. "That was a graze," said he, and smoked for a while. "They'll not go this time. Question is, will they go next?"

III

Drake took a fresh cigar, and threw his legs over the chair arm.

"I think you smoke too much," said Bolles, whom three days had made familiar and friendly.

"Yep. Have to just now. That's what! as Uncle Pasco would say. They are a half-breed lot, though," the boy continued, returning to the buccaroos and their recent visit. "Weaken in the face of a straight bluff, you see, unless they get whiskey-courageous. And I've called 'em down on that."

"Oh!" said Bolles, comprehending.

"Didn't you see that was their game? But he will not go after it."

"The flesh is all they seem to understand," murmured Bolles.

Half-past Full did not go to Harney City for the tabooed whiskey, nor did any one. Drake read his buccaroos like the children that they were. After the late encounter of grit, the atmosphere was relieved of storm. The children, the primitive, pagan, dangerous children, forgot all about whiskey, and lusted joyously for Christmas. Christmas was coming! No work! A shooting-match! A big feed! Cheerfulness bubbled at the Malheur Agency. The weather itself was in tune. Castle Rock seemed no longer to frown, but rose into the shining air, a mass of friendly strength. Except when a rare sledge or horseman passed, Mr. Bolles's journeys to the school were all to show it was not some pioneer colony in a new, white, silent world that heard only the playful shouts and songs of the buccaroos. The sun overhead and the hard-crushing snow underfoot filled every one with a crisp, tingling hilarity.

Before the sun first touched Castle Rock on the morning of the feast they were up and in high feather over at the bunk-house. They raced across to see what Sam was cooking; they begged and joyfully swallowed lumps of his raw plum-pudding. "Merry Christmas!" they wished him, and "Melly Clismas!" said he to them. They played leap-frog over by the stable, they put snow down each other's backs. Their shouts rang round corners; it was like boys let out of school. When Drake gathered them for the shooting-match, they cheered him; when he told them there were no prizes, what did they care for prizes? When he beat them all the first round, they cheered him again. Pity he hadn't offered prizes! He wasn't a good business man, after all!

The rounds at the target proceeded through the forenoon, Drake the acclaimed leader; and the Christmas sun drew to mid-sky. But as its splendor in the heavens increased, the happy shoutings on earth began to wane. The body was all that the buccaroos knew; well, the flesh comes pretty natural to all of us—and who had ever taught these men about the spirit? The further they were from breakfast the nearer they were to dinner; yet the happy shoutings waned! The spirit is a strange thing. Often it dwells dumb in human clay, then unexpectedly speaks out of the clay's darkness.

It was no longer a crowd Drake had at the target. He became aware that quietness had been gradually coming over the buccaroos. He looked, and saw a man wandering by himself in the lane. Another leaned by the stable corner, with a vacant face. Through the windows of the bunk-house he could see two or three on their beds. The children were tired of shouting. Drake went in-doors and threw a great log on the fire. It blazed up high with sparks, and he watched it, although the sun shown bright on the window-sill. Presently he noticed that a man had come in and taken a chair. It was Half-past Full, and with his boots stretched to the warmth, he sat gazing into the fire. The door opened and another buccaroo entered and sat off in a corner. He had a bundle of old letters, smeared sheets tied with a twisted old ribbon. While his large, rope-toughened fingers softly loosened the ribbon, he sat with his back to the room and presently began to read the letters over, one by one. Most of the men came in before long, and silently joined the watchers round the great fireplace. Drake threw another log on, and in a short time this, too, broke into ample flame. The silence was long; a slice of shadow had fallen across the window-sill, when a young man spoke, addressing the logs:

"I skinned a coon in San Saba, Texas, this day a year."

At the sound of a voice, some of their eyes turned on the speaker, but turned back to the fire again. The spirit had spoken from the clay, aloud; and the clay was uncomfortable at hearing it.

After some more minutes a neighbor whispered to a neighbor, "Play you a game of crib."

The man nodded, stole over to where the board was, and brought it across the floor on creaking tip-toe. They set it between them, and now and then the cards made a light sound in the room.

"I treed that coon on Honey," said the young man, after a while—

"Honey Creek, San Saba. Kind o' dry creek. Used to flow into Big Brady when it rained."

The flames crackled on, the neighbors still played their cribbage. Still was the day bright, but the shrinking wedge of sun had gone entirely from the window-sill. Half-past Full had drawn from his pocket a mouth-organ, breathing half-tunes upon it; in the middle of "Suwanee River" the man who sat in the corner laid the letter he was beginning upon the heap on his knees and read no more. The great genial logs lay glowing, burning; from the fresher one the flames flowed and forked; along the embered surface of the others ran red and blue shivers of iridescence. With legs and arms crooked and sprawled, the buccaroos brooded, staring into the glow with seldom-winking eyes, while deep inside the clay the spirit spoke quietly. Christmas Day was passing, but the sun shone still two good hours high. Outside, over the snow and pines, it was only in the deeper folds of the hills that the blue shadows had come; the rest of the world was gold and silver; and from far across that silence into this silence by the fire came a tinkling stir of sound. Sleigh-bells it was, steadily coming, too early for Bolles to be back from his school festival. The toy-thrill of the jingling grew clear and sweet, a spirit of enchantment that did not wake the stillness, but cast it into a deeper dream. The bells came near the door and stopped, and then Drake opened it.

"Hello, Uncle Pasco!" said he. "Thought you were Santa Claus."

"Santa Claus! H'm. Yes. That's what. Told you maybe I'd come."

"So you did. Turkey is due in—let's see—ninety minutes. Here, boys! some of you take Uncle Pasco's horse."

"No, no, I won't. You leave me alone. I ain't stoppin' here. I ain't hungry. I just grubbed at the school. Sleepin' at Missouri Pete's to-night. Got to make the railroad tomorrow." The old man stopped his precipitate statements. He sat in his sledge deeply muffled, blinking at Drake and the buccaroos, who had strolled out to look at him, "Done a big business this trip," said he. "Told you I would. Now if you was only givin' your children a Christmas-tree like that I seen that feller yer school-marm doin' just now— hee-hee!" From his blankets he revealed the well-known case. "Them things would shine on a tree," concluded Uncle Pasco.

"Hang 'em in the woods, then," said Drake.

"Jewelry, is it?" inquired the young Texas man.

Uncle Pasco whipped open his case. "There you are," said he. "All what's left. That ring 'll cost you a dollar."

"I've a dollar somewheres," said the young man, fumbling.

Half-past Full, on the other side of the sleigh, stood visibly fascinated by the wares he was given a skilful glimpse of down among the blankets.

He peered and he pondered while Uncle Pasco glibly spoke to him.

"Scatter your truck out plain!" the buccaroo exclaimed, suddenly. "I'm not buying in the dark. Come over to the bunk-house and scatter."

"Brass will look just the same anywhere," said Drake.

"Brass!" screamed Uncle. "Brass your eye!"

But the buccaroos, plainly glad for distraction, took the woolly old scolding man with them. Drake shouted that if getting cheated cheered them, by all means to invest heavily, and he returned alone to his fire, where Bolles soon joined him. They waited, accordingly, and by-and-by the sleigh-bells jingled again. As they had come out of the silence, so did they go into it, their little silvery tinkle dancing away in the distance, faint and fainter, then, like a breath, gone.

Uncle Pasco's trinkets had audibly raised the men's spirits. They remained in the bunk-house, their laughter reaching Drake and Bolles more and more. Sometimes they would scuffle and laugh loudly.

"Do you imagine it's more leap-frog?" inquired the school-master.

"Gambling," said Drake. "They'll keep at it now till one of them wins everything the rest have bought."

"Have they been lively ever since morning?"

"Had a reaction about noon," said Drake. "Regular home-sick spell. I felt sorry for 'em."

"They seem full of reaction," said Bolles. "Listen to that!"

It was now near four o'clock, and Sam came in, announcing dinner.

"All leady," said the smiling Chinaman.

"Pass the good word to the bunk-house," said Drake, "if they can hear you."

Sam went across, and the shouting stopped. Then arose a thick volley of screams and cheers.

"That don't sound right," said Drake, leaping to his feet. In the next instant the Chinaman, terrified, returned through the open door. Behind him lurched Half-past Full, and stumbled into the room. His boot caught, and he pitched, but saved himself and stood swaying, heavily looking at Drake. The hair curled dense over his bull head, his mustache was spread with his grin, the light of cloddish humor and destruction burned in his big eye. The clay had buried the spirit like a caving pit.

" 'Twas false jewelry all right!" he roared, at the top of his voice. "A good old jimmyjohn full, boss.[5] Say, boss, goin' to run our jimmyjohn off the ranch? Try it on, kid. Come over and try it on!" The bull beat on the table.

---

5. "Jimmyjohn"—a demijohn, or large jug-like bottle. A modern demijohn holds 4.9 gallons.

Dean Drake had sat quickly down in his chair, his gray eye upon the hulking buccaroo. Small and dauntless he sat, a sparrow-hawk caught in a trap, and game to the end—whatever end.

"It's a trifle tardy to outline any policy about your demijohn," said he, seriously. "You folks had better come in and eat before you're beyond appreciating."

"Ho, we'll eat your grub, boss. Sam's cooking goes." The buccaroo lurched out and away to the bunk-house, where new bellowing was set up.

"I've got to carve this turkey, friend," said the boy to Bolles.

"I'll do my best to help eat it," returned the school-master, smiling.

"Misser Dlake," said poor Sam, "I solly you. I velly solly you."

IV

"Reserve your sorrow, Sam," said Dean Drake. "Give us your soup for a starter. Come," he said to Bolles. "Quick."

He went into the dining-room, prompt in his seat at the head of the table, with the school-master next to him.

"Nice man, Uncle Pasco," he continued. "But his time is not now. We have nothing to do for the present but sit like every day and act perfectly natural."

"I have known simpler tasks," said Mr. Bolles, "but I'll begin by spreading this excellently clean napkin."

"You're no school-marm!" exclaimed Drake; "you please me."

"The worst of a bad thing," said the mild Bolles, "is having time to think about it, and we have been spared that."

"Here they come," said Drake.

They did come. But Drake's alert strategy served the end he had tried for. The drunken buccaroos swarmed disorderly to the door and halted. Once more the new superintendent's ways took them aback. Here was the decent table with lights serenely burning, with unwonted good things arranged upon it—the olives, the oranges, the preserves. Neat as parade drill were the men's places, all the cups and forks symmetrical along the white cloth. There, waiting his guests at the far end, sat the slim young boss talking with his boarder, Mr. Bolles, the parts in their smooth hair going with all the rest of this propriety. Even the daily tin dishes were banished in favor of crockery.

"Bashful of Sam's napkins, boys?" said the boss. "Or is it the bald-headed china?"

At this bidding they came in uncertainly. Their whiskey was ashamed inside. They took their seats, glancing across at each other in a transient silence, drawing their chairs gingerly beneath them. Thus ceremony fell unexpected upon the gathering, and for a while they swallowed in awkwardness what the swift, noiseless Sam brought them. He in a long white apron passed and repassed with his things from his kitchen, doubly efficient and civil under stress of anxiety for his young master. In the pauses of his serving he watched from the background, with a face that presently caught the notice of one of them.

"Smile, you almond-eyed highbinder," said the buccaroo. And the Chinaman smiled his best.

"I've forgot something," said Half-past Full, rising. "Don't let 'em skip a course on me." Half-past left the room.

"That's what I have been hoping for," said Drake to Bolles.

Half-past returned presently and caught Drake's look of expectancy. "Oh no, boss," said the buccaroo, instantly, from the door. "You're on to me, but I'm on to you." He slammed the door with ostentation and dropped with a loud laugh into his seat.

"First smart thing I've known him do," said Drake to Bolles. "I am disappointed."

Two buccaroos next left the room together.

"They may get lost in the snow," said the humorous Half-past. "I'll just show 'em the trail." Once more he rose from the dinner and went out.

"Yes, he knew too much to bring it in here," said Drake to Bolles. "He knew none but two or three would dare drink, with me looking on."

"Don't you think he is afraid to bring it in the same room with you at all?" Bolles suggested.

"And me temperance this season? Now, Bolles, that's unkind."

"Oh, dear, that is not at all what—"

"I know what you meant, Bolles. I was only just making a little merry over this casualty. No, he don't mind me to that extent, except when he's sober. Look at him!"

Half-past was returning with his friends. Quite evidently they had all found the trail.

"Uncle Pasco is a nice old man!" pursued Drake. "I haven't got my gun on. Have you?"

"Yes," said Bolles, but with a sheepish swerve of the eye.

Drake guessed at once. "Not Baby Bunting? Oh, Lord! and I promised to give you an adult weapon!—the kind they're wearing now by way of full-dress."

"Talkin' secrets, boss?" said Half-past Full.

The well-meaning Sam filled his cup, and this proceeding shifted the buccaroo's truculent attention.

"What's that mud?" he demanded.

"Coffee," said Sam, politely.

The buccaroo swept his cup to the ground, and the next man howled dismay.

"Burn your poor legs?" said Half-past. He poured his glass over the victim. They wrestled, the company pounded the table, betting hoarsely, until Half-past went to the floor, and his plate with him.

"Go easy," said Drake. "You're smashing the company's property."

"Bald-headed china for sure, boss!" said a second of the brothers Drinker, and dropped a dish.

"I'll merely tell you," said Drake, "that the company don't pay for this china twice."

"Not twice?" said Half-past Full, smashing some more. "How about thrice?"

"Want your money now?" another inquired.

A riot of banter seized upon all of them, and they began to laugh and destroy.

"How much did this cost?" said one, prying askew his three-tined fork.

"How much did you cost yourself?" said another to Drake.

"What, our kid boss? Two bits, I guess."

"Hyas markook. Too dear!"

They bawled at their own jokes, loud and ominous; threat sounded beneath their lightest word, the new crashes of china that they threw on the floor struck sharply through the foreboding din of their mirth. The spirit that Drake since his arrival had kept under in them day by day, but not quelled, rose visibly each few succeeding minutes, swelling upward as the tide does. Buoyed up on the whiskey, it glittered in their eyes and yelled mutinously in their voices.

"I'm waiting all orders," said Bolles to Drake.

"I haven't any," said Drake. "New ones, that is. We've sat down to see this meal out. Got to keep sitting."

He leaned back, eating deliberately, saying no more to the buccaroos; thus they saw he would never leave the room till they did. As he had taken his chair the first, so was the boy bound to quit it the last. The game of prying fork-tines staled on them one by one, and they took to songs, mostly of love and parting. With the red whiskey in their eyes they shouted plaintively of sweethearts, and vows, and lips, and meeting in the wild wood. From these they went to ballads of the cattle-trail and the Yuba River, and so inevitably worked to the old coast song, made of three languages, with its verses rhymed on each year since the first beginning. Tradition laid it heavy upon each singer in his turn to keep the pot a-boiling by memory or by new invention, and the chant went forward with hypnotic cadence to a tune of larkish, ripping gayety. He who had read over his old stained letters in the homesick afternoon had waked from such dreaming and now sang:

> "Once, jes' onced in the year o' '49,
> I met a fancy thing by the name o' Keroline;
> I never could persuade her for to leave me be;
> She went and she took and she married me."

His neighbor was ready with an original contribution:

> "Once, once again in the year o' '64,
> By the city of Whatcom down along the shore—
> I never could persuade them for to leave me be—
> A Siwash squaw went and took and married me."

"What was you doin' between all them years?" called Half-past Full.
"Shut yer mouth," said the next singer:

> "Once, once again in the year o' '71
> ('Twas the suddenest deed that I ever done)—
> I never could persuade them for to leave me be—
> A rich banker's daughter she took and married me."

"This is looking better," said Bolles to Drake.
"Don't you believe it," said the boy.
Ten or a dozen years were thus sung.
"I never could persuade them for to leave me be" tempestuously brought down the chorus and the fists, until the drunkards could sit no more, but stood up to sing, tramping the tune heavily together. Then, just as the turn came round to Drake himself, they dashed their chairs down and herded out of the room behind Half-past Full, slamming the door.

Drake sat a moment at the head of his Christmas dinner, the fallen chairs, the lumpy wreck. Blood charged his face from his hair to his collar. "Let's smoke," said he. They went from the dinner through the room of the great fireplace to his office beyond.

"Have a mild one?" he said to the school-master.

"No, a strong one to-night, if you please." And Bolles gave his mild smile.

"You do me good now and then," said Drake.

"Dear me," said the teacher, "I have found it the other way."

All the rooms fronted on the road with doors—the old-time agency doors, where the hostiles had drawn their pictures in the days before peace had come to reign over this country. Drake looked out, because the singing had stopped and they were very quiet in the bunk-house. He saw the Chinaman steal from his kitchen.

"Sam is tired of us," he said to Bolles.

"Tired?"

"Running away, I guess. I'd prefer a new situation myself. That's where you're deficient, Bolles. Only got sense enough to stay where you happen to be. Hello. What is he up to?"

Sam had gone beside a window of the bunk-house and was listening there, flat like a shadow. Suddenly he crouched, and was gone among the sheds. Out of the bunk-house immediately came a procession, the buccaroos still quiet, a careful, gradual body.

Drake closed his door and sat in the chair again. "They're escorting that jug over here," said he. "A new move, and a big one."

He and Bolles heard them enter the next room, always without much noise or talk—the loudest sound was the jug when they set it on the floor. Then they seemed to sit, talking little.

"Bolles," said Drake, "the sun has set. If you want to take after Sam—"

But the door of the sitting-room opened and the Chinaman himself came in. He left the door a-swing and spoke clearly. "Misser Dlake," said he, "slove bloke" (stove broke).

The superintendent came out of his office, following Sam to the kitchen. He gave no look or word to the buccaroos with their demijohn; he merely held his cigar sidewise in his teeth and walked with no hurry through the sitting-room. Sam took him through to the kitchen and round to a hind corner of the stove, pointing.

"Misser Dlake," said he, "slove no bloke. I hear them inside. They going kill you."

"That's about the way I was figuring it," mused Dean Drake.

"Misser Dlake," said the Chinaman, with appealing eyes, "I velly solly you. They no hurtee me. Me cook."

"Sam, there is much meat in your words. Condensed beef don't class with you. But reserve your sorrows yet a while. Now what's my policy?" he debated, tapping the stove here and there for appearances; somebody might look in. "Shall I go back to my office and get my guns?"

"You not goin' run now?" said the Chinaman, anxiously.

"Oh yes, Sam. But I like my gun travelling. Keeps me kind of warm.

Now if they should get a sight of me arming—no, she's got to stay here till I come back for her. So long, Sam! See you later. And I'll have time to thank you then."

Drake went to the corral in a strolling manner. There he roped the strongest of the horses, and also the school-master's. In the midst of his saddling, Bolles came down.

"Can I help you in any way?" said Bolles.

"You've done it. Saved me a bothering touch-and-go play to get you out here and seem innocent. I'm going to drift."

"Drift?"

"There are times to stay and times to leave, Bolles; and this is a case of the latter. Have you a real gun on now?"

Poor Bolles brought out guiltily his .22 Smith & Wesson. "I don't seem to think of things," said he.

"Cheer up," said Drake. "How could you thought-read me? Hide Baby Bunting, though. Now we're off. Quietly, at the start. As if we were merely jogging to pasture."

Sam stood at his kitchen door, mutely wishing them well. The horses were walking without noise, but Half-past Full looked out of the window.

"We're by, anyhow," said Drake. "Quick now. Burn the earth." The horse sprang at his spurs. "Dust, you son of a gun! Rattle your hocks! Brindle! Vamoose!" Each shouted word was a lash with his quirt. "Duck!" he called to Bolles.

Bolles ducked, and bullets grooved the spraying snow. They rounded a corner and saw the crowd jumping into the corral, and Sam's door empty of that prudent Celestial.

"He's a very wise Chinaman!" shouted Drake, as they rushed.

"What?" screamed Bolles.

"Very wise Chinaman. He'll break that stove now to prove his innocence."

"Who did you say was innocent?" screamed Bolles.

"Oh, I said you were," yelled Drake, disgusted; and he gave over this effort at conversation as their horses rushed along.

V

It was a dim, wide stretch of winter into which Drake and Bolles galloped from the howling pursuit. Twilight already veiled the base of Castle Rock, and as they forged heavily up a ridge through the caking snow, and the yells came after them, Bolles looked seriously at Dean Drake; but that youth wore an expression of rising merriment. Bolles looked back at the dusk from which the yells were sounding, then forward to the spreading skein of night where the trail was taking him and the boy, and in neither direction could he discern cause for gayety.

"May I ask where we are going?" said he.

"Away," Drake answered. "Just away, Bolles. It's a healthy resort."

Ten miles were travelled before either spoke again. The drunken bucca-roos yelled hot on their heels at first, holding more obstinately to this chase than sober ruffians would have attempted. Ten cold, dark miles across the hills it took to cure them; but when their shoutings, that had followed over heights where the pines grew and down through the open swales between, dropped off, and died finally away among the willows along the south fork of the Malheur, Drake reined in his horse with a jerk.

"Now isn't that too bad!" he exclaimed.

"It is all very bad," said Bolles, sorry to hear the boy's tone of disap-pointment.

"I didn't think they'd fool me again," continued Drake, jumping down.

"Again?" inquired the interested Bolles.

"Why, they've gone home!" said the boy, in disgust.

"I was hoping so," said the school-master.

"Hoping? Why, it's sad, Bolles. Four miles farther and I'd have had them lost."

"Oh!" said Bolles.

"I wanted them to keep after us," complained Drake. "Soon as we had a good lead I coaxed them. Coaxed them along on purpose by a trail they knew, and four miles from here I'd have swung south into the mountains they don't know. There they'd have been good and far from home in the snow without supper, like you and me, Bolles. But after all my trouble they've gone back snug to that fireside. Well, let us be as cosey as we can."

He built a bright fire, and he whistled as he kicked the snow from his boots, busying over the horses and the blankets. "Take a rest," he said to Bolles. "One man's enough to do the work. Be with you soon to share our little cottage." Presently Bolles heard him reciting confidentially to his horse, " 'Twas the night after Christmas, and all in the house—only we are not all in the house!" He slapped the belly of his horse Tyee, who gambolled away to the limit of his picket-rope.

"Appreciating the moon, Bolles?" said he, returning at length to the fire. "What are you so gazeful about, father?"

"This is all my own doing," lamented the school-master.

"What, the moon is?"

"It has just come over me," Bolles continued. "It was before you got in the stage at Nampa. I was talking. I told Uncle Pasco that I was glad no whiskey was to be allowed on the ranch. It all comes from my folly!"

"Why, you hungry old New England conscience!" cried the boy, clapping him on the shoulder. "How in the world could you foresee the crookedness of that hoary Beelzebub?"

"That's all very well," said Bolles, miserably. "You would never have mentioned it yourself to him."

"You and I, Bolles, are different. I was raised on miscellaneous wickedness. A look at my insides would be liable to make you say your prayers."

The school-master smiled. "If I said any prayers," he replied, "you would be in them."

Drake looked moodily at the fire. "The Lord helps those who help themselves," said he. "I've prospered. For a nineteen-year-old I've hooked my claw fairly deep here and there. As for to-day—why, that's in the game too. It was their deal. Could they have won it on their own play? A joker dropped into their hand. It's my deal now, and I have some jokers myself. Go to sleep, Bolles. We've a ride ahead of us."

The boy rolled himself in his blanket skilfully. Bolles heard him say once or twice in a sort of judicial conversation with the blanket—"and all in the house—but we were not all in the house. Not all. Not a full house—" His tones drowsed comfortably into murmur, and then to quiet breathing. Bolles fed the fire, thatched the unneeded wind-break (for the calm, dry night was breathless), and for a long while watched the moon and a tuft of the sleeping boy's hair.

"If he is blamed," said the school-master, "I'll never forgive myself. I'll never forgive myself anyhow."

A paternal, or rather maternal, expression came over Bolles's face, and he removed his large, serious glasses. He did not sleep very well.

The boy did. "I'm feeling like a bird," said he, as they crossed through the mountains next morning on a short cut to the Owyhee. "Breakfast will brace you up, Bolles. There'll be a cabin pretty soon after we strike the other road. Keep thinking hard about coffee."

"I wish I could," said poor Bolles. He was forgiving himself less and less.

Their start had been very early; as Drake bid the school-master observe, to have nothing to detain you, nothing to eat and nothing to pack, is a great help in journeys of haste. The warming day, and Indian Creek well behind them, brought Drake to whistling again, but depression sat upon the self-accusing Bolles. Even when they sighted the Owyhee road below them, no cheerfulness waked in him; not at the nearing coffee, nor yet at the companionable tinkle of sleigh-bells dancing faintly upward through the bright, silent air.

"Why, if it ain't Uncle Pasco!" said Drake, peering down through a gap in the foot-hill. "We'll get breakfast sooner than I expected. Quick! Give me Baby Bunting!"

"Are you going to kill him?" whispered the school-master, with a beaming countenance. And he scuffled with his pocket to hand over his hitherto belittled weapon.

Drake considered him. "Bolles, Bolles," said he, "you have got the New England conscience rank. Plymouth Rock is a pudding to your heart. Remind me to pray for you first spare minute I get. Now follow me close. He'll be much more useful to us alive."

They slipped from their horses, stole swiftly down a shoulder of the hill, and waited among some brush. The bells jingled unsuspectingly onward to this ambush.

"Only hear 'em!" said Drake. "All full of silver and Merry Christmas. Don't gaze at me like that, Bolles, or I'll laugh and give the whole snap away. See him come! The old man's breath streams out so calm. He's not worried with New England conscience. One, two, three—" Just before the sleigh came opposite, Dean Drake stepped out. "Morning, Uncle!" said he. "Throw up your hands!"

Uncle Pasco stopped dead, his eyes blinking. Then he stood up in the sleigh among his blankets. "H'm," said he. "The Kid."

"Throw up your hands! Quit fooling with that blanket!" Drake spoke dangerously now. "Bolles," he continued, "pitch everything out of the sleigh while I cover him. He's got a shot-gun under that blanket. Sling it out."

It was slung. The wraps followed. Uncle Pasco stepped obediently down, and soon the chattels of the emptied sleigh littered the snow. The old gentleman was invited to undress until they reached the six-shooter that Drake suspected. Then they eat his lunch, drank some whiskey that he had not sold to the buccaroos, told him to repack the sleigh, allowed him to wrap up again, bade him take the reins, and they would use his six-shooter and shot-gun to point out the road to him.

He had said very little, had Uncle Pasco, but stood blinking, obedient and malignant. "H'm," said he now, "goin' to ride with me, are you?"

He was told yes, that for the present he was their coachman. Their horses were tired and would follow, tied behind. "We're weary, too," said Drake, getting in. "Take your legs out of my way or I'll kick off your shins. Bolles, are you fixed warm and comfortable? Now start her up for Harper ranch, Uncle."

"What are you proposing to do with me?" inquired Uncle Pasco.

"Not going to wring your neck, and that's enough for the present. Faster, Uncle. Get a gait on. Bolles, here's Baby Bunting. Much obliged to you for the loan of it, old man."

Uncle Pasco's eye fell on the .22-caliber pistol. "Did you hold me up with that lemonade straw?" he asked, huskily.

"Yep," said Drake. "That's what."

"Oh, hell!" murmured Uncle Pasco. And for the first time he seemed dispirited.

"Uncle, you're not making time," said Drake after a few miles. "I'll thank you for the reins. Open your bandanna and get your concertina. Jerk the bellows for us."

"That I'll not!" screamed Uncle Pasco.

"It's music or walk home," said the boy. "Take your choice."

Uncle Pasco took his choice, opening with the melody of "The Last Rose of Summer." The sleigh whirled up the Owyhee by the winter willows, and the levels, and the meadow pools, bright frozen under the blue sky. Late in this day the amazed Brock by his corrals at Harper's beheld arrive his favorite, his boy superintendent, driving in with the school-master staring through his glasses, and Uncle Pasco throwing out active strains upon his concertina. The old man had been bidden to bellows away for his neck.

Drake was not long in explaining his need to the men. "This thing must be worked quick," said he. "Who'll stand by me?"

All of them would, and he took ten, with the faithful Brock. Brock would not allow Gilbert to go, because he had received another mule-kick in the stomach. Nor was Bolles permitted to be of the expedition. To all his protests, Drake had but the single word: "This is not your fight, old man. You've done your share with Baby Bunting."

Thus was the school-master in sorrow compelled to see them start back to Indian Creek and the Malheur without him. With him Uncle Pasco would have joyfully exchanged. He was taken along with the avengers. They would not wring his neck, but they would play cat and mouse with him and his concertina; and they did. But the conscience of Bolles still toiled. When Drake and the men were safe away, he got on the wagon going for the mail, thus making his way next morning to the railroad and Boisé, where Max Vogel listened to him; and together this couple hastily took train and team for the Malheur Agency.

The avengers reached Indian Creek duly, and the fourth day after his Christmas dinner Drake came once more in sight of Castle Rock.

"I am doing this thing myself, understand," he said to Brock. "I am responsible."

"We're here to take your orders," returned the foreman. But as the agency buildings grew plain and the time for action was coming, Brock's anxious heart spoke out of its fulness. "If they start in to—to—they might—I wish you'd let me get in front," he begged, all at once.

"I thought you thought better of me," said Drake.

"Excuse me," said the man. Then presently: "I don't see how anybody could 'a' told he'd smuggle whiskey that way. If the old man [Brock meant Max Vogel] goes to blame you, I'll give him my opinion straight."

"The old man's got no use for opinions," said Drake. "He goes on results. He trusted me with this job, and we're going to have results now."

The drunkards were sitting round outside the ranch house. It was evening. They cast a sullen inspection on the new-comers, who returned them no inspection whatever. Drake had his men together and took them to the stable first, a shed with mangers. Here he had them unsaddle. "Because," he mentioned to Brock, "in case of trouble we'll be sure of their all staying. I'm taking no chances now."

Soon the drunkards strolled over, saying good-day, hazarding a few comments on the weather and like topics, and meeting sufficient answers.

"Goin' to stay?"

"Don't know."

"That's a good horse you've got."

"Fair."

But Sam was the blithest spirit at the Malheur Agency. "Hiyah!" he exclaimed. "Misser Dlake! How fashion you come quick so?" And the excellent Chinaman took pride in the meal of welcome that he prepared.

"Supper's now," said Drake to his men. "Sit anywhere you feel like. Don't mind whose chair you're taking—and we'll keep our guns on."

Thus they followed him, and sat. The boy took his customary perch at the head of the table, with Brock at his right. "I miss old Bolles," he told his foreman. "You don't appreciate Bolles."

"From what you tell of him," said Brock, "I'll examine him more careful."

Seeing their boss, the sparrow-hawk, back in his place, flanked with supporters, and his gray eye indifferently upon them, the buccaroos grew polite to oppressiveness. While Sam handed his dishes to Drake and the new-comers, and the new-comers eat what was good before the old inhabitants got a taste, these latter grew more and more solicitous. They offered sugar to the strangers, they offered their beds; Half-past Full urged them to sit companionably in the room where the fire was burning. But when the meal was over, the visitors went to another room with their arms, and lighted their own fire. They brought blankets from their saddles, and after a little concertina they permitted the nearly perished Uncle Pasco to slumber. Soon they slumbered themselves, with the door left open, and Drake watching. He would not even share vigil with Brock, and all night he heard the voices of the buccaroos, holding grand, unending council.

When the relentless morning came, and breakfast with the visitors again in their seats, unapproachable, the drunkards felt the crisis to be a strain upon their sobered nerves. They glanced up from their plates, and down; along to Dean Drake eating his hearty porridge, and back at one another, and at the hungry, well-occupied strangers.

"Say, we don't want trouble," they began to the strangers.

"Course you don't. Breakfast's what you're after."

"Oh, well, you'd have got gay. A man gets gay."

"Sure."

"Mr. Drake," said Half-past Full, sweating with his effort, "we were sorry while we was a-fogging you up."

"Yes," said Drake. "You must have been just overcome by contrition."

A large laugh went up from the visitors, and the meal was finished without further diplomacy.

"One matter, Mr. Drake," stammered Half-past Full, as the party rose. "Our jobs. We're glad to pay for any things what got sort of broke."

"Sort of broke," repeated the boy, eying him. "So you want to hold your jobs?"

"If—" began the buccaroo, and halted.

"Fact is, you're a set of cowards," said Drake, briefly. "I notice you've forgot to remove that whiskey jug."

The demijohn still stood by the great fireplace. Drake entered and laid hold of it, the crowd standing back and watching. He took it out, with what remained in its capacious bottom, set it on a stump, stepped back, levelled his gun, and shattered the vessel to pieces. The whiskey drained down, wetting the stump, creeping to the ground.

Much potency lies in the object-lesson, and a grin was on the faces of all present, save Uncle Pasco's. It had been his demijohn, and when the shot struck it he blinked nervously.

"You ornery old mink!" said Drake, looking at him. "You keep to the jewelry business hereafter."

The buccaroos grinned again. It was reassuring to witness wrath turn upon another.

"You want to hold your jobs?" Drake resumed to them. "You can trust yourselves?"

"Yes, sir," said Half-past Full.

"But I don't trust you," stated Drake, genially; and the buccaroos' hopeful eyes dropped. "I'm going to divide you," pursued the new superintendent. "Split you far and wide among the company's ranches. Stir you in with decenter blood. You'll go to White-horse ranch, just across the line of Nevada," he said to Half-past Full. "I'm tired of the brothers Drinker. You'll go—let's see—"

Drake paused in his apportionment, and a sleigh came swiftly round the turn, the horse loping and lathery.

"What vas dat shooting I hear joost now?" shouted Max Vogel, before he could arrive. He did not wait for any answer. "Thank the good God!" he exclaimed, at seeing the boy Dean Drake unharmed, standing with a gun. And to their amazement he sped past them, never slacking his horse's lope until he reached the corral. There he tossed the reins to the placid Bolles, and springing out like a sure-footed elephant, counted his saddle-horses; for he was a general. Satisfied, he strode back to the crowd by the demijohn. "When dem men get restless," he explained to Drake at once, "always look out. Somebody might steal a horse."

The boy closed one gray, confidential eye at his employer. "Just my idea," said he, "when I counted 'em before breakfast."

"You liddle r-rascal," said Max, fondly. "What you shoot at?"

Drake pointed at the demijohn. "It was bigger than those bottles at Nampa," said he. "Guess you could have hit it yourself."

Max's great belly shook. He took in the situation. It had a flavor that he liked. He paused to relish it a little more in silence.

"Und you have killed noding else?" said he, looking at Uncle Pasco, who blinked copiously. "Mine old friend, you never get rich if you change your business so frequent. I tell you that thirty years now." Max's hand found Drake's shoulder, but he addressed Brock. "He is all what you tell me," said he to the foreman. "He have joodgement."

Thus the huge, jovial Teuton took command, but found Drake had left little for him to do. The buccaroos were dispersed at Harper's, at Fort Rinehart, at Alvord Lake, towards Stein's peak, and at the Island Ranch by Harney Lake. And if you know east Oregon, or the land where Chief E-egante helped out Specimen Jones, his white soldier friend, when the hostile Bannocks were planning his immediate death as a spy, you will know what wide regions separated the buccaroos. Bolles was taken into Max Vogel's esteem; also was Chinese Sam. But Max sat smoking in the office with his boy superintendent, in particular satisfaction.

"You are a liddle r-rascal," said he. "Und I r-raise you fifty dollars."

Frederick Jackson Turner
1861-1932

■

1893: "The Significance of the Frontier
in American History"
1906: *The Rise of the New West, 1819–1829*
1920: *The Frontier in American History*
1932: *The Significance of Sections in American History*
1935: *The United States, 1830–1850*

■

A S EARLY *as 1776, European historians and social essayists were noting that the "Americans" were different, in important ways, from their continental forebears. What had happened to cause such a rapid and radical change in societal personality? The question intrigued many social theorists, who offered a number of hypothetical explanations. The melting pot theory was popular; advocates of this idea believed that Americans did not act like any specific European race because they were a mixture of many races. The germ theory held that certain dormant traits had suddenly flourished, like seeds, in the new ground. Other authorities speculated that the peculiarities of the American character grew out of the tension between the industrial North and the agrarian South. Then, in 1893, a young historian stood up before the annual meeting of the American Historical Association and read an essay that was to become widely known as the "Turner thesis" or "frontier thesis."*

Turner's theory dismissed the ideas of the melting pot, of cultural "germination" in new soil, and of the North/South tension as insignificant factors. No, Turner said, it is the frontier's presence that forms American character—even those who do not actually set foot on the frontier are changed by its presence. The frontier furnishes "the forces dominating American character."

Henry Nash Smith has pointed out that the general idea of the frontier thesis was recognized earlier by many people, including J. Hector St. John de Crève-

coeur, Benjamin Franklin, Ralph Waldo Emerson, Abraham Lincoln, and Walt Whitman; but it was Turner who formalized it. And soon, "a whole generation of historians took over his hypothesis and rewrote American history in terms of it. . . . it is still by far the most familiar interpretation of the American past." [1]

Each of the three main premises in Turner's thesis enhances our understanding of the literature of the American West. First, there is the nature of the frontier itself. The frontier was not just Daniel Boone alone in the wilderness, nor a long train of Conestogas crossing the prairie. It was a series of encounters, most of them unrelated to each other, between primitive and civilized forces. Turner pointed out that there was a military frontier, an agricultural frontier, a trapper's frontier, a salt frontier, etc. In each case, a civilized force encountered primitive conditions, succumbed temporarily to those conditions, and finally reemerged as a new and unique society.

This "perennial rebirth" of American character is Turner's second clarification of western literature's context. As the protagonists in western fiction come into conflict with their surroundings, they are not merely developing in the sense that figures in European novels develop but instead are undergoing the rebirth process, and so seem to support Turner's theory. In that process they acquire, or at least exercise, certain unique "intellectual traits of profound importance"—Turner's third point. Through Turner, we see more significance in the fact that so many characters in western fiction are restless, coarse, strong, and practical.

Critics have pointed out that Turner's thesis relies heavily on grandiose, over-generalized conclusions and is based on questionable methodology; they also call attention to the way Turner used metaphors in place of concrete statements (such as his "moraines" of social evolution and "waves" of settlement). But disturbing questions remain: is the frontier gone, and as a consequence, will those American traits eventually vanish as well?

Turner's thesis remains one of the most important statements in American thought. Henry Nash Smith has called it not only important, but essential. "A new intellectual system was requisite before the West could be adequately dealt with in literature or its social development fully understood." [2]

———

1. Henry Nash Smith, *Virgin Land: The American West as Symbol and Myth* (Cambridge, Mass.: Harvard University Press, 1950), pp. 3–4.
2. Ibid., p. 260.

The American Personality

I N A RECENT bulletin of the Superintendent of the Census for 1890 appear these significant words: "Up to and including 1880 the country had a frontier of settlement, but at present the unsettled area has been so broken into by isolated bodies of settlement that there can hardly be said to be a frontier line. In the discussion of its extent, its westward movement, etc., it can not, therefore, any longer have a place in the census reports." This brief official statement marks the closing of a great historic movement. Up to our own day American history has been in a large degree the history of the colonization of the Great West. The existence of an area of free land, its continuous recession, and the advance of American settlement westward, explain American development.

Behind institutions, behind constitutional forms and modifications, lie the vital forces that call these organs into life and shape them to meet changing conditions. The peculiarity of American institutions is, the fact that they have been compelled to adapt themselves to the changes of an expanding people—to the changes involved in crossing a continent, in winning a wilderness, and in developing at each area of this progress out of the primitive economic and political conditions of the frontier into the complexity of city life. Said Calhoun in 1817, "We are great, and rapidly—I was about to say fearfully—growing!" So saying, he touched the distinguishing feature of American life. All peoples show development; the germ theory of politics has been sufficiently emphasized. In the case of most nations, however, the development has occurred in a limited area; and if the nation has expanded, it has met other growing peoples whom it has conquered. But in the case of the United States we have a different phenomenon. Limiting our attention to the Atlantic coast, we have the familiar phenomenon of the evolution of institutions in a limited area, such as the rise of representative government; the differentiation of simple colonial governments into com-

From Frederick J. Turner, "The Significance of the Frontier in American History," *Annual Report of the American Historical Association for 1893* (Washington, D.C.: GPO, 1894), pp. 199–201, 213–15, 226–27.

plex organs; the progress from primitive industrial society, without division of labor, up to manufacturing civilization. But we have in addition to this a recurrence of the process of evolution in each western area reached in the process of expansion. Thus American development has exhibited not merely advance along a single line, but a return to primitive conditions on a continually advancing frontier line, and a new development for that area. American social development has been continually beginning over again on the frontier. This perennial rebirth, this fluidity of American life, this expansion westward with its new opportunities, its continuous touch with the simplicity of primitive society, furnish the forces dominating American character. The true point of view in the history of this nation is not the Atlantic coast, it is the great West. Even the slavery struggle, which is made so exclusive an object of attention by writers like Prof. von Holst, occupies its important place in American history because of its relation to westward expansion.

In this advance, the frontier is the outer edge of the wave—the meeting point between savagery and civilization. Much has been written about the frontier from the point of view of border warfare and the chase, but as a field for the serious study of the economist and the historian it has been neglected.

The American frontier is sharply distinguished from the European frontier—a fortified boundary line running through dense populations. The most significant thing about the American frontier is, that it lies at the hither edge of free land. In the census reports it is treated as the margin of that settlement which has a density of two or more to the square mile. The term is an elastic one, and for our purposes does not need sharp definition. We shall consider the whole frontier belt, including the Indian country and the outer margin of the "settled area" of the census reports. This paper will make no attempt to treat the subject exhaustively; its aim is simply to call attention to the frontier as a fertile field for investigation, and to suggest some of the problems which arise in connection with it.

In the settlement of America we have to observe how European life entered the continent, and how America modified and developed that life and reacted on Europe. Our early history is the study of European germs developing in an American environment. Too exclusive attention has been paid by institutional students to the Germanic origins, too little to the American factors. The frontier is the line of most rapid and effective Americanization. The wilderness masters the colonist. It finds him a European in dress, industries, tools, modes of travel, and thought. It takes him from the railroad car and puts him in the birch canoe. It strips off the garments of civilization and arrays him in the hunting shirt and the moccasin. It puts him in the log cabin of the Cherokee and Iroquois and runs an Indian palisade around him. Before long he has gone to planting Indian corn and plowing with a sharp stick; he shouts the war cry and takes the scalp in orthodox Indian fashion. In short, at the frontier the environment is at first too strong for the man. He must accept the conditions which it furnishes, or perish, and so he fits himself into the Indian clearings and follows the Indian trails. Little by little he transforms the wilderness, but the outcome is not the old Europe, not simply the development of Germanic germs, any more than the first phenomenon was a case of reversion to the Germanic mark. The fact is, that here is a new product that is American. At first, the frontier was the Atlantic coast. It was the frontier of Europe in a very real sense. Moving westward, the frontier became more and more American. As successive terminal moraines result from successive glaciations, so each frontier leaves its traces behind it, and when it becomes a settled area the region still partakes of the frontier characteristics. Thus the advance of the frontier has meant a steady movement away from the influence of Europe, a steady growth of independence on American lines. And to study this advance, the men who grew up under these conditions, and the political, economic, and social results of it, is to study the really American part of our history. . . .

Land

The exploitation of the beasts took hunter and trader to the west, the exploitation of the grasses took the rancher west, and the exploitation of the virgin soil of the river valleys and prairies attracted the farmer. Good soils have been the most continuous attraction to the farmer's frontier. The land hunger of the Virginians drew them down the rivers into Carolina, in early colonial days; the search for soils took the Massachusetts men to Pennsylvania and to New York. As the eastern lands were taken up migration flowed across them to the west. Daniel Boone, the great backwoodsman, who combined the occupations of hunter, trader, cattle-raiser, farmer, and surveyor—learning, probably from the traders, of the fertility of the lands on the upper Yadkin, where the traders were wont to rest as they took their way to the Indians, left his Pennsylvania home with his father, and passed down the Great Valley road to that stream. Learning from a trader whose posts were on the Red River in Kentucky of its game and rich pastures, he pioneered the way for the farmers to that region. Thence he passed to the frontier of Missouri, where his settlement was long a landmark on the frontier. Here again he helped to open the way for civilization, finding salt licks, and trails, and land. His son was among the earliest trappers in the passes of the Rocky Mountains, and his party are said to have been the first to camp on the present site of Denver. His grandson, Col. A. J. Boone, of Colorado, was a power among the Indians of the Rocky Mountains, and was appointed an agent by the Government. Kit Carson's mother was a Boone. Thus this family epitomizes the backwoodsman's advance across the continent.

The farmer's advance came in a distinct series of waves. In Peck's New Guide to the West, published in Boston in 1837, occurs this suggestive passage:

> Generally, in all the western settlements, three classes, like the waves of the ocean, have rolled one after the other. First comes the pioneer, who depends for the subsistence of his family chiefly upon the natural growth of vegetation, called the "range," and the proceeds of hunting. His implements of agriculture are rude, chiefly of his own make, and his efforts directed mainly to a crop of corn and a "truck patch." The last is a rude garden for growing cabbage, beans, corn for roasting ears, cucumbers, and potatoes. A log cabin, and, occasionally, a stable and corn-crib, and a field of a dozen acres, the timber girdled or "deadened," and fenced, are enough for his occupancy. It is quite immaterial whether he ever becomes the owner of the soil. He is the occupant for the time being, pays no rent, and feels as independent as the "lord of the manor." With a horse, cow, and one or two breeders of swine, he strikes into the woods with his family, and becomes the founder of a new county, or perhaps state. He builds his cabin, gathers around him a few other families of similar tastes and habits, and occupies till the range is somewhat subdued, and hunting a little precarious, or, which is more frequently the case, till the neighbors crowd around, roads, bridges, and fields annoy him, and he lacks elbow room. The preemption law enables him to dispose of his cabin and cornfield to the next class of emigrants; and, to employ his own figures, he "breaks for the high timber," "clears out for the New Purchase," or migrates to Arkansas or Texas, to work the same process over.

> The next class of emigrants purchase the lands, add field to field, clear out the roads, throw rough bridges over the streams, put up hewn log houses with glass windows and brick or stone chimneys, occasionally plant orchards, build mills, schoolhouses, court-houses, etc., and exhibit the picture and forms of plain, frugal, civilized life.

> Another wave rolls on. The men of capital and enterprise come.

The settler is ready to sell out and take the advantage of the rise in property, push farther into the interior and become, himself, a man of capital and enterprise in turn. The small village rises to a spacious town or city; substantial edifices of brick, extensive fields, orchards, gardens, colleges, and churches are seen. Broadcloths, silks, leghorns, crapes, and all the refinements, luxuries, elegancies, frivolities, and fashions are in vogue. Thus wave after wave is rolling westward; the real Eldorado is still farther on.

A portion of the two first classes remain stationary amidst the general movement, improve their habits and condition, and rise in the scale of society.

The writer has traveled much amongst the first class, the real pioneers. He has lived many years in connection with the second grade; and now the third wave is sweeping over large districts of Indiana, Illinois, and Missouri. Migration has become almost a habit in the West. Hundreds of men can be found, not over 50 years of age, who have settled for the fourth, fifth, or sixth time on a new spot. To sell out and remove only a few hundred miles makes up a portion of the variety of backwoods life and manners.

Omitting those of the pioneer farmers who move from the love of adventure, the advance of the more steady farmer is easy to understand. Obviously the immigrant was attracted by the cheap lands of the frontier, and even the native farmer felt their influence strongly. Year by year the farmers who lived on soil whose returns were diminished by unrotated crops were offered the virgin soil of the frontier at nominal prices. Their growing families demanded more lands, and these were dear. The competition of the unexhausted, cheap, and easily tilled prairie lands compelled the farmer either to go west and continue the exhaustion of the soil on a new frontier, or to adopt intensive culture. Thus the census of 1890 shows, in the Northwest, many counties in which there is an absolute or a relative decrease of population. These States have been sending farmers to advance the frontier on the plains, and have themselves begun to turn to intensive farming and to manufacture. A decade before this, Ohio had shown the same transition stage. Thus the demand for land and the love of wilderness freedom drew the frontier ever onward. . . .

Intellectual Traits

From the conditions of frontier life came intellectual traits of profound importance. The works of travelers along each frontier from colonial days

onward describe certain common traits, and these traits have, while softening down, still persisted as survivals in the place of their origin, even when
a higher social organization succeeded. The result is that to the frontier
the American intellect owes its striking characteristics. That coarseness and
strength combined with acuteness and inquisitiveness; that practical, inven-
tive turn of mind, quick to find expedients; that masterful grasp of material
things, lacking in the artistic but powerful to effect great ends; that restless, nervous energy; that dominant individualism, working for good and
for evil, and withal that buoyancy and exuberance which comes with freedom—these are traits of the frontier, or traits called out elsewhere because
of the existence of the frontier. Since the days when the fleet of Columbus
sailed into the waters of the New World, America has been another name
for opportunity, and the people of the United States have taken their tone
from the incessant expansion which has not only been open but has even
been forced upon them. He would be a rash prophet who should assert that
the expansive character of American life has now entirely ceased. Movement
has been its dominant fact, and, unless this training has no effect upon a
people, the American energy will continually demand a wider field for its
exercise. But never again will such gifts of free land offer themselves. For a
moment, at the frontier, the bonds of custom are broken and unrestraint is
triumphant. There is not *tabula rasa*.[3] The stubborn American environment
is there with its imperious summons to accept its conditions; the inherited
ways of doing things are also there; and yet, in spite of environment, and
in spite of custom, each frontier did indeed furnish a new field of opportunity, a gate of escape from the bondage of the past; and freshness, and
confidence, and scorn of older society, impatience of its restraints and its
ideas, and indifference to its lessons, have accompanied the frontier. What
the Mediterranean Sea was to the Greeks, breaking the bond of custom,
offering new experiences, calling out new institutions and activities, that,
and more, the ever retreating frontier has been to the United States directly,
and to the nations of Europe more remotely. And now, four centuries from
the discovery of America, at the end of a hundred years of life under the
Constitution, the frontier has gone, and with its going has closed the first
period of American history.

---

3. *Tabula rasa*—a blank slate. Turner is suggesting that in spite of the absence of law
and order, the frontier still imposes certain kinds of restrictions.

Mary Hunter Austin
1868-1934

▬

1903: *The Land of Little Rain*
1909: *Lost Borders*
1917: *The Ford*
1920: *26 Jayne Street*
1924: *The Land of Journey's Ending*

▬

N O L I S T *of titles can adequately represent the span of Austin's literary accomplishments. Berten W. Allred credits her with twenty-seven
books and eighty-five articles, stories, and poems (appearing in fifty-
seven magazines).*[1] *From her quiet poems to her feminist tracts, from her plays
and novels to her personal reminiscences and accounts of Indian myths, Austin's
work is as rich as it is various. She is best known for her nature essays, which
are accounts of her frequent and extensive explorations—usually alone—in the
deserts of California and the Southwest.*

*The Hunter family homesteaded in California's southern San Joaquin Valley
in 1888, the year of Mary's graduation from Blackburn College in Illinois. In
1891, she and Stafford Wallace Austin were married and soon moved to the desert
region between the Sierra Nevada range and Death Valley. Mary taught school,
published stories, and explored the deserts. She became a principal figure in a circle
of writers that included Jack London, Ambrose Bierce, and Lincoln Steffens. In
1925, Mary Austin went to Santa Fe and became part of the famous literary
circle flourishing there.*

*Austin seems to have spent as much time conversing with well-known authors
as she did writing. She knew dozens of major literary figures, among them John*

---

1. Berten W. Allred, "Mary Hunter Austin," in *The Reader's Encyclopedia of the American West*, ed. Howard R. Lamar (New York: Harper and Row, 1977), p. 65.

*Muir, H. G. Wells, Henry James, W. B. Yeats, and Joseph Conrad. And although Austin had high regard for many of these writers, her work is free of their influence. One typical example is "The Walking Woman," an essay that is highly original in structure, style, and theme. "The Walking Woman" is nature writing based on personal experience, like Muir's writing, but it contains none of the romantic or transcendental traits that are found in Muir's works. It is also a western character sketch but avoids the sentimental tone typical of sketches by Jack London or Bret Harte. There is even an elusive tone of philosophical message in "The Walking Woman," but it is too subtle for any comparisons. Mary Austin's principal books—*The Land of Little Rain, Lost Borders, *and *The Land of Journey's Ending—express her belief in a unity between humankind and nature, a relationship in which the human is merely another animal species. She does not shrink from nature's cruel realities, nor does she let those realities upset her evenly balanced outlook. Her prose style, like her philosophy, is subtle, simple, and unembellished; however, that unadorned style conveys an unusually clear-eyed, sophisticated perspective on life.*

—

The Walking Woman

THE FIRST time of my hearing of her was at Temblor. We had come all one day between blunt, whitish bluffs rising from mirage water, with a thick, pale wake of dust billowing from the wheels, all the dead wall of the foothills sliding and shimmering with heat, to learn that the Walking Woman had passed us somewhere in the dizzying dimness, going down to the Tulares on her own feet. We heard of her again in the Carrisal, and again at Adobe Station, where she had passed a week before the shearing, and at last I had a glimpse of her at the Eighteen-Mile House[2] as I went hurriedly northward on the Mojave stage; and afterward sheepherders at whose camps she slept, and cowboys at rodeos, told me as much of her way of life as they could understand. Like enough they told her as much of mine. That was very little. She was the Walking Woman, and no one knew her name, but because she was a sort of whom men speak respectfully, they called her to her face Mrs. Walker, and she answered to it if she was so inclined. She came and went about our western world on

From Mary Hunter Austin, *Lost Borders* (New York: Harper and Brothers, 1909), pp. 195–209.

2. The places Austin names are many miles apart, but all are in the area southwest of Death Valley in Southern California.

no discoverable errand, and whether she had some place of refuge where she lay by in the interim, or whether between her seldom, unaccountable appearances in our quarter she went on steadily walking, we never learned. She came and went, oftenest in a kind of muse of travel which the untrammelled space begets, or at rare intervals flooding wondrously with talk, never of herself, but of things she had known and seen. She must have seen some rare happenings, too—by report. She was at Maverick the time of the Big Snow, and at Tres Piños when they brought home the body of Morena; and if anybody could have told whether De Borba killed Mariana for spite or defence, it would have been she, only she could not be found when most wanted. She was at Tunawai at the time of the cloud-burst, and if she had cared for it could have known most desirable things of the ways of trail-making, burrow-habiting small things.

All of which should have made her worth meeting, though it was not, in fact, for such things I was wishful to meet her; and as it turned out, it was not of these things we talked when at last we came together. For one thing, she was a woman, not old, who had gone about alone in a country where the number of women is as one in fifteen. She had eaten and slept at the herder's camps, and laid by for days at one-man stations whose masters had no other touch of human kind than the passing of chance prospectors, or the halting of the tri-weekly stage. She had been set on her way by teamsters who lifted her out of white, hot desertness and put her down at the crossing of unnamed ways, days distant from anywhere. And through all this she passed unarmed and unoffended. I had the best testimony to this, the witness of the men themselves. I think they talked of it because they were so much surprised at it. It was not, on the whole, what they expected of themselves.

Well I understand that nature which wastes its borders with too eager burning, beyond which rim of desolation it flares forever quick and white, and have had some inkling of the isolating calm of a desire too high to stoop to satisfaction. But you could not think of these things pertaining to the Walking Woman; and if there were ever any truth in the exemption from offence residing in a frame of behavior called ladylike, it should have been inoperative here. What this really means is that you get no affront so long as your behavior in the estimate of the particular audience invites none. In the estimate of the immediate audience—conduct which affords protection in Mayfair gets you no consideration in Maverick. And by no canon could it be considered ladylike to go about on your own feet, with a blanket and a black bag and almost no money in your purse, in and about the haunts of rude and solitary men.

There were other things that pointed the wish for a personal encounter with the Walking Woman. One of them was the contradiction of reports of her—as to whether she was comely, for example. Report said yes, and again, plain to the point of deformity. She had a twist to her face, some said; a hitch to one shoulder; they averred she limped as she walked. But by the distance she covered she should have been straight and young. As to sanity, equal incertitude. On the mere evidence of her way of life she was cracked; not quite broken, but unserviceable. Yet in her talk there was both wisdom and information, and the word she brought about trails and water-holes was as reliable as an Indian's.

By her own account she had begun by walking off an illness. There had been an invalid to be taken care of for years, leaving her at last broken in body, and with no recourse but her own feet to carry her out of that predicament. It seemed there had been, besides the death of her invalid, some other worrying affairs, upon which, and the nature of her illness, she was never quite clear, so that it might very well have been an unsoundness of mind which drove her to the open, sobered and healed at last by the large soundness of nature. It must have been about that time that she lost her name. I am convinced that she never told it because she did not know it herself. She was the Walking Woman, and the country people called her Mrs. Walker. At the time I knew her, though she wore short hair and a man's boots, and had a fine down over all her face from exposure to the weather, she was perfectly sweet and sane.

I had met her occasionally at ranch-houses and road-stations, and had got as much acquaintance as the place allowed; but for the things I wished to know there wanted a time of leisure and isolation. And when the occasion came we talked altogether of other things.

It was at Warm Spring in the Little Antelope I came upon her in the heart of a clear forenoon. The spring lies off a mile from the main trail, and has the only trees about it known in that country. First you come upon a pool of waste full of weeds of a poisonous dark green, every reed ringed about the water-level with a muddy white incrustation. Then the three oaks appear staggering on the slope, and the spring sobs and blubbers below them in ashy-colored mud. All the hills of that country have the down plunge toward the desert and back abruptly toward the Sierra. The grass is thick and brittle and bleached straw-color toward the end of the season. As I rode up the swale of the spring I saw the Walking Woman sitting where the grass was deepest, with her black bag and blanket, which she carried on a stick, beside her. It was one of those days when the genius of talk flows as smoothly as the rivers of mirage through the blue hot desert morning.

You are not to suppose that in my report of a Borderer I give you the words only, but the full meaning of the speech. Very often the words are merely the punctuation of thought; rather, the crests of the long waves of intercommunicative silences. Yet the speech of the Walking Woman was fuller than most.

The best of our talk that day began in some dropped word of hers from which I inferred that she had had a child. I was surprised at that, and then wondered why I should have been surprised, for it is the most natural of all experiences to have children. I said something of that purport, and also that it was one of the perquisites of living I should be least willing to do without. And that led to the Walking Woman saying that there were three things which if you had known you could cut out all the rest, and they were good any way you got them, but best if, as in her case, they were related to and grew each one out of the others. It was while she talked that I decided that she really did have a twist to her face, a sort of natural warp or skew into which it fell when it was worn merely as a countenance, but which disappeared the moment it became the vehicle of thought or feeling.

The first of the experiences the Walking Woman had found most worth while had come to her in a sand-storm on the south slope of Tehachapi in a dateless spring. I judged it should have been about the time she began to find herself, after the period of worry and loss in which her wandering began. She had come, in a day pricked full of intimations of a storm, to the camp of Filon Geraud, whose companion shepherd had gone a three days' *pasear*[3] to Mojave for supplies. Geraud was of great hardihood, red-blooded, of a full laughing eye, and an indubitable spark for women. It was the season of the year when there is a soft bloom on the days, but the nights are cowering cold and the lambs tender, not yet flockwise. At such times a sand-storm works incalculable disaster. The lift of the wind is so great that the whole surface of the ground appears to travel upon it slantwise, thinning out miles high in air. In the intolerable smother the lambs are lost from the ewes; neither dogs nor man make headway against it.

The morning flared through a horizon of yellow smudge, and by mid-forenoon the flock broke.

"There were but the two of us to deal with the trouble," said the Walking Woman. "Until that time I had not known how strong I was, nor how good it is to run when running is worth while. The flock travelled down the wind, the sand bit our faces; we called, and after a time heard the words broken and beaten small by the wind. But after a little we had not to call.

---

3. "*Pasear*"—a trip, often a slow and leisurely one.

All the time of our running in the yellow dusk of day and the black dark of night, I knew where Filon was. A flock-length away, I knew him. Feel? What should I feel? I knew. I ran with the flock and turned it this way and that as Filon would have.

"Such was the force of the wind that when we came together we held by one another and talked a little between pantings. We snatched and ate what we could as we ran. All that day and night until the next afternoon the camp kit was not out of the cayaques.[4] But we held the flock. We herded them under a butte when the wind fell off a little, and the lambs sucked; when the storm rose they broke, but we kept upon their track and brought them together again. At night the wind quieted, and we slept by turns; at least Filon slept. I lay on the ground when my turn was and beat with the storm. I was no more tired than the earth was. The sand filled in the creases of the blanket, and where I turned, dripped back upon the ground. But we saved the sheep. Some ewes there were that would not give down their milk because of the worry of the storm, and the lambs died. But we kept the flock together. And I was not tired."

The Walking Woman stretched out her arms and clasped herself, rocking in them as if she would have hugged the recollection to her breast.

"For you see," said she, "I worked with a man, without excusing, without any burden on me of looking or seeming. Not fiddling or fumbling as women work, and hoping it will all turn out for the best. It was not for Filon to ask, Can you, or Will you. He said, Do, and I did. And my work was good. We held the flock. And that," said the Walking Woman, the twist coming in her face again, "is one of the things that make you able to do without the others."

"Yes," I said; and then, "What others?"

"Oh," she said, as if it pricked her, "the looking and the seeming."

And I had not thought until that time that one who had the courage to be the Walking Woman would have cared! We sat and looked at the pattern of the thick crushed grass on the slope, wavering in the fierce noon like the waterings in the coat of a tranquil beast; the ache of a world-old bitterness sobbed and whispered in the spring. At last—

"It is by the looking and the seeming," said I, "that the opportunity finds you out."

"Filon found out," said the Walking Woman. She smiled; and went on from that to tell me how, when the wind went down about four o'clock

---

4. "Cayaques"—origin of the term is not certain, but it probably refers to camp boxes in which equipment (such as the cooking, or "camp," kit) and food were kept.

and left the afternoon clear and tender, the flock began to feed, and they had out the kit from the cayaques, and cooked a meal. When it was over, and Filon had his pipe between his teeth, he came over from his side of the fire, of his own notion, and stretched himself on the ground beside her. Of his own notion. There was that in the way she said it that made it seem as if nothing of the sort had happened before to the Walking Woman, and for a moment I thought she was about to tell me one of the things I wished to know; but she went on to say what Filon had said to her of her work with the flock. Obvious, kindly things, such as any man in sheer decency would have said, so that there must have something more gone with the words to make them so treasured of the Walking Woman.

"We were very comfortable," said she, "and not so tired as we expected to be. Filon leaned up on his elbow. I had not noticed until then how broad he was in the shoulders, and how strong in the arms. And we had saved the flock together. We felt that. There was something that said together, in the slope of his shoulders toward me. It was around his mouth and on the cheek high up under the shine of his eyes. And under the shine the look— the look that said, 'We are of one sort and one mind'—his eyes that were the color of the flat water in the toulares—do you know the look?"

"I know it."

"The wind was stopped and all the earth smelled of dust, and Filon understood very well that what I had done with him I could not have done so well with another. And the look—the look in the eyes—"

"Ah-ah—!"

I have always said, I will say again, I do not know why at this point the Walking Woman touched me. If it were merely a response to my unconscious throb of sympathy, or the unpremeditated way of her heart to declare that this, after all, was the best of all indispensable experiences; or if in some flash of forward vision, encompassing the unimpassioned years, the stir, the movement of tenderness were for *me*—but no; as often as I have thought of it, I have thought of a different reason, but no conclusive one, why the Walking Woman should have put out her hand and laid it on my arm.

"To work together, to love together," said the Walking Woman, withdrawing her hand again; "there you have two of the things; the other you know."

"The mouth at the breast," said I.

"The lips and the hands," said the Walking Woman. "The little, pushing hands and the small cry." There ensued a pause of fullest understanding, while the land before us swam in the noon, and a dove in the oaks behind the spring began to call. A little red fox came out of the hills and lapped delicately at the pool.

"I stayed with Filon until the fall," said she. "All that summer in the Sierras, until it was time to turn south on the trail. It was a good time, and longer than he could be expected to have loved one like me. And besides, I was no longer able to keep the trail. My baby was born in October."

Whatever more there was to say to this, the Walking Woman's hand said it, straying with remembering gesture to her breast. There are so many ways of loving and working, but only one way of the first-born. She added after an interval, that she did not know if she would have given up her walking to keep at home and tend him, or whether the thought of her son's small feet running beside her in the trails would have driven her to the open again. The baby had not stayed long enough for that. "And whenever the wind blows in the night," said the Walking Woman, "I wake and wonder if he is well covered."

She took up her black bag and her blanket; there was the ranch-house of Dos Palos to be made before night, and she went as outliers do, without a hope expressed of another meeting and no word of good-bye. She was the Walking Woman. That was it. She had walked off all sense of society-made values, and, knowing the best when the best came to her, was able to take it. Work—as I believed; love—as the Walking Woman had proved it; a child—as you subscribe to it. But look you: it was the naked thing the Walking Woman grasped, not dressed and tricked out, for instance, by prejudices in favor of certain occupations; and love, man love, taken as it came, not picked over and rejected if it carried no obligation of permanency; and a child; *any* way you get it, a child is good to have, say nature and the Walking Woman; to have it and not to wait upon a proper concurrence of so many decorations that the event may not come at all.

At least one of us is wrong. To work and to love and to bear children. *That* sounds easy enough. But the way we live establishes so many things of much more importance.

Far down the dim, hot valley I could see the Walking Woman with her blanket and black bag over her shoulder. She had a queer, sidelong gait, as if in fact she had a twist all through her.

Recollecting suddenly that people called her lame, I ran down to the open place below the spring where she had passed. There in the bare, hot sand the track of her two feet bore evenly and white.

Luther Standing Bear
[Plenty-Kill]
c. 1868-1939

———

1928: *My People the Sioux*
1931: *My Indian Boyhood*
1933: *Land of the Spotted Eagle*
1934: *Stories of the Sioux*

———

IN THE SPRING *of 1869 friends and relatives gathered to celebrate the ear piercing of a male infant. He was a strong, straight baby and had been given a strong name, and all of his parents' friends agreed that he would become a proficient hunter, a brave soldier, and a man of good character. As he grew, he learned the history and the religion of his society, played its games, and obeyed its laws. By the time he was nine years old, old enough to go with his father on a buffalo hunt, events were taking place that would forever change the course of Sioux history.*

Plenty-Kill and his young companions would be the last members of the tribe to be raised and educated in the traditional way. General George A. Custer met his end at the Little Big Horn in 1876, and a year later the war chief Crazy Horse, a friend of Plenty-Kill's father, was murdered. The Sioux Wars were virtually over, and the idea of acculturation and assimilation of the Indians was in favor in the government. So, in 1879, Plenty Kill traveled to Carlisle, Pennsylvania, as part of the first group of students to enter the Carlisle Indian Industrial School, which had been established to give Indian youth an Anglo-American education.

Plenty Kill's name had been ceremonially given to him according to the way of the Sioux; at Carlisle, there was a different way of giving names. The boy, who could not read a word of English, was told to point to one of the names listed on the blackboard. He pointed to "Luther." His father's name was Standing Bear. Now the boy had proper first and last names.

Luther Standing Bear was a model of successful adaptation to white culture. He learned to speak, read, and write English, did well at various jobs after returning to the Rosebud Indian Reservation, owned a small ranch, accompanied Buffalo Bill's Wild West show to Europe, and finally traveled to California, where he acted in several movies. At the time of his death in 1939, he was working on the film Union Pacific, *a Western about the building of the railroad that had been instrumental in the destruction of the buffalo herds, sealing the fate of the Sioux.*

In California, Luther Standing Bear gave public lectures on Sioux traditions, and wrote his books. My People the Sioux, My Indian Boyhood, *and* Land of the Spotted Eagle *are invaluable firsthand accounts of Sioux life and are also powerful arguments for better education about Indians. "No longer should the Indian be dehumanized in order to make material for lurid and cheap fiction to embellish street-stands," he wrote in* Land of the Spotted Eagle. *"Rather, a fair and correct history of the native American should be incorporated in the curriculum of the public school." Luther Standing Bear observed: "In denying the Indian his ancestral rights and heritages, the white race is but robbing itself. But America can be revived, rejuvenated, by recognizing a native school of thought. The Indian can save America."* [1]

—

Indian Wisdom

Nature

THE LAKOTA was a true naturist—a lover of Nature. He loved the earth and all things of the earth, the attachment growing with age. The old people came literally to love the soil and they sat or reclined on the ground with a feeling of being close to a mothering power. It was good for the skin to touch the earth and the old people liked to remove their moccasins and walk with bare feet on the sacred earth. Their tipis were built upon the earth and their altars were made of earth. The birds that flew in the air came to rest upon the earth and it was the final abiding place of all

From Luther Standing Bear, *Land of the Spotted Eagle* (1933; reprint, Lincoln: University of Nebraska Press, 1978), pp. 192–97, 202–7. Copyright © 1933 by Luther Standing Bear; renewal copyright © 1960 by May Jones.

1. Luther Standing Bear, *Land of the Spotted Eagle* (Boston: Houghton Mifflin, 1933), pp. 254, 255.

things that lived and grew. The soil was soothing, strengthening, cleansing, and healing.

This is why the old Indian still sits upon the earth instead of propping himself up and away from its life-giving forces. For him, to sit or lie upon the ground is to be able to think more deeply and to feel more keenly; he can see more clearly into the mysteries of life and come closer in kinship to other lives about him.

The earth was full of sounds which the old-time Indian could hear, sometimes putting his ear to it so as to hear more clearly. The forefathers of the Lakotas had done this for long ages until there had come to them real understanding of earth ways. It was almost as if the man were still a part of the earth as he was in the beginning, according to the legend of the tribe. This beautiful story of the genesis of the Lakota people furnished the foundation for the love they bore for earth and all things of the earth. Wherever the Lakota went, he was with Mother Earth. No matter where he roamed by day or slept by night, he was safe with her. This thought comforted and sustained the Lakota and he was eternally filled with gratitude.

From Wakan Tanka there came a great unifying life force that flowed in and through all things—the flowers of the plains, blowing winds, rocks, trees, birds, animals—and was the same force that had been breathed into the first man. Thus all things were kindred and brought together by the same Great Mystery.

Kinship with all creatures of the earth, sky, and water was a real and active principle. For the animal and bird world there existed a brotherly feeling that kept the Lakota safe among them. And so close did some of the Lakotas come to their feathered and furred friends that in true brotherhood they spoke a common tongue.

The animal had rights—the right of man's protection, the right to live, the right to multiply, the right to freedom, and the right to man's indebtedness—and in recognition of these rights the Lakota never enslaved the animal, and spared all life that was not needed for food and clothing.

This concept of life and its relations was humanizing and gave to the Lakota an abiding love. It filled his being with the joy and mystery of living; it gave him reverence for all life; it made a place for all things in the scheme of existence with equal importance to all. The Lakota could despise no creature, for all were of one blood, made by the same hand, and filled with the essence of the Great Mystery. In spirit the Lakota was humble and meek. 'Blessed are the meek: for they shall inherit the earth,' was true for the Lakota, and from the earth he inherited secrets long since forgotten. His religion was sane, normal, and human.

Reflection upon life and its meaning, consideration of its wonders, and observation of the world of creatures, began with childhood. The earth, which was called *Maka,* and the sun, called *Anpetuwi,* represented two functions somewhat analogous to those of male and female. The earth brought forth life, but the warming, enticing rays of the sun coaxed it into being. The earth yielded, the sun engendered.

In talking to children, the old Lakota would place a hand on the ground and explain: 'We sit in the lap of our Mother. From her we, and all other living things, come. We shall soon pass, but the place where we now rest will last forever.' So we, too, learned to sit or lie on the ground and become conscious of life about us in its multitude of forms. Sometimes we boys would sit motionless and watch the swallow, the tiny ants, or perhaps some small animal at its work and ponder on its industry and ingenuity; or we lay on our backs and looked long at the sky and when the stars came out made shapes from the various groups. The morning and evening star always attracted attention, and the Milky Way was a path which was traveled by the ghosts. The old people told us to heed *wa maka skan,* which were the 'moving things of earth.' This meant, of course, the animals that lived and moved about, and the stories they told of *wa maka skan* increased our interest and delight. The wolf, duck, eagle, hawk, spider, bear, and other creatures, had marvelous powers, and each one was useful and helpful to us. Then there were the warriors who lived in the sky and dashed about on their spirited horses during a thunder storm, their lances clashing with the thunder and glittering with the lightning. There was *wiwila,* the living spirit of the spring, and the stones that flew like a bird and talked like a man. Everything was possessed of personality, only differing with us in form. Knowledge was inherent in all things. The world was a library and its books were the stones, leaves, grass, brooks, and the birds and animals that shared, alike with us, the storms and blessings of earth. We learned to do what only the student of nature ever learns, and that was to feel beauty. We never railed at the storms, the furious winds, and the biting frosts and snows. To do so intensified human futility, so whatever came we adjusted ourselves, by more effort and energy if necessary, but without complaint. Even the lightning did us no harm, for whenever it came too close, mothers and grandmothers in every tipi put cedar leaves on the coals and their magic kept danger away. Bright days and dark days were both expressions of the Great Mystery, and the Indian reveled in being close to the Big Holy. His worship was unalloyed, free from the fears of civilization.

I have come to know that the white mind does not feel toward nature as does the Indian mind, and it is because, I believe, of the difference in childhood instruction. I have often noticed white boys gathered in a city by-street or alley jostling and pushing one another in a foolish manner. They spend much time in this aimless fashion, their natural faculties neither seeing, hearing, nor feeling the varied life that surrounds them. There is about them no awareness, no acuteness, and it is this dullness that gives ugly mannerisms full play; it takes from them natural poise and stimulation. In contrast, Indian boys, who are naturally reared, are alert to their surroundings; their senses are not narrowed to observing only one another, and they cannot spend hours seeing nothing, hearing nothing, and thinking nothing in particular. Observation was certain in its rewards; interest, wonder, admiration grew, and the fact was appreciated that life was more than mere human manifestation; that it was expressed in a multitude of forms. This appreciation enriched Lakota existence. Life was vivid and pulsing; nothing was casual and commonplace. The Indian lived—lived in every sense of the word—from his first to his last breath.

The character of the Indian's emotion left little room in his heart for antagonism toward his fellow creatures, this attitude giving him what is sometimes referred to as 'the Indian point of view.' Every true student, every lover of nature has 'the Indian point of view,' but there are few such students, for few white men approach nature in the Indian manner. The Indian and the white man sense things differently because the white man has put distance between himself and nature; and assuming a lofty place in the scheme of order of things has lost for him both reverence and understanding. Consequently the white man finds Indian philosophy obscure—wrapped, as he says, in a maze of ideas and symbols which he does not understand. A writer friend, a white man whose knowledge of 'Injuns' is far more profound and sympathetic than the average, once said that he had been privileged, on two occasions, to see the contents of an Indian medicine-man's bag in which were bits of earth, feathers, stones, and various other articles of symbolic nature; that a 'collector' showed him one and laughed, but a great and world-famous archeologist showed him the other with admiration and wonder. Many times the Indian is embarrassed and baffled by the white man's allusions to nature in such terms as crude, primitive, wild, rude, untamed, and savage. For the Lakota, mountains, lakes, rivers, springs, valleys, and woods were all finished beauty; winds, rain, snow, sunshine, day, night, and change of seasons brought interest; birds, insects, and animals filled the world with knowledge that defied the discernment of man.

But nothing the Great Mystery placed in the land of the Indian pleased the white man, and nothing escaped his transforming hand. Wherever forests have not been mowed down; wherever the animal is recessed in their quiet protection; wherever the earth is not bereft of four-footed life—that to him is an 'unbroken wilderness.' But since for the Lakota there was no wilderness; since nature was not dangerous but hospitable; not forbidding but friendly, Lakota philosophy was healthy—free from fear and dogmatism. And here I find the great distinction between the faith of the Indian and the white man. Indian faith sought the harmony of man with his surroundings; the other sought the dominance of surroundings. In sharing, in loving all and everything, one people naturally found a measure of the thing they sought; while, in fearing, the other found need of conquest. For one man the world was full of beauty; for the other it was a place of sin and ugliness to be endured until he went to another world, there to become a creature of wings, half-man and half-bird. Forever one man directed his Mystery to change the world He had made; forever this man pleaded with Him to chastise His wicked ones; and forever he implored his Wakan Tanka to send His light to earth. Small wonder this man could not understand the other.

But the old Lakota was wise. He knew that man's heart, away from nature, becomes hard; he knew that lack of respect for growing, living things soon led to lack of respect for humans too. So he kept his youth close to its softening influence.

Religion

The Lakota loved the sun and earth, but he worshiped only Wakan Tanka, or Big Holy, who was the Maker of all things of earth, sky, and water. Wakan Tanka breathed life and motion into all things, both visible and invisible. He was over all, through all, and in all, and great as was the sun, and good as was the earth, the greatness and goodness of the Big Holy were not surpassed. The Lakota could look at nothing without at the same time looking at Wakan Tanka, and he could not, if he wished, evade His presence, for it pervaded all things and filled all space. All the mysteries of birth, life, and death; all the wonders of lightning, thunder, wind, and rain were but the evidence of His everlasting and encompassing power.

Wakan Tanka prepared the earth and put upon it both man and animal. He dispensed earthly blessings, and when life on earth was finished provided a home, *Wanagi yata,* the place where the souls gather. To this home all souls went after death, for there were no wicked to be excluded. . . .

[*The Pipe of Peace*]

. . . Peace was the pipe's greatest significance—a peace never more deeply and thoughtfully conceived by any man or society of men. Of all symbols that ever inspired men the Pipe of Peace was the strongest. Standards, typifying the ideals of societies, have been worshiped and followed, but none have exerted so great an influence toward peace and brotherhood as this symbol. Its motto was *Wolakota wa yaka cola*, 'Peace without slavery!' Not another standard but has been desecrated by war; not another but has led men into unholy conflict and there *are none to keep them from war except the Pipe of Peace*. If this sacred symbol was taken to Lakota warriors in the thickest of battle, they would at once obey its mandate and retire. To disobey was to suffer personal disaster and it is Lakota history that no warrior ever disobeyed without at last dying an ignominious death.

Peace—that ideal which man may sometime reach—was symbolized in the Pipe of Peace and, under the society of the pipe, or codes symbolized by the pipe, native man made the most effectual effort at arriving at peace ever made on this continent. It was but a start, perhaps, but its strength lay in the fact that under the Great Peace, women had begun the necessary foundational work for the elimination of war by raising sons who could participate only in pursuits of peace. War was excluded from the existence of a certain portion of the male population and in this move the Indian mother pointed the way and the only road to the realization of peace between all men. The acceptance of a kinship with other orders of life was the first step toward humanization and the second step was the dedication of sons to peace, the spiritual value of which is incalculable; and not until the women of the land come back to the forsaken road, emulate the Indian mother, and again raise sons for peace will there be any substantial move toward 'peace on earth and good-will toward men.'

Perhaps more nonsense has been written about the medicine-men than about other persons of the tribe, for their rights and powers, like those of the chiefs, have been overestimated, misunderstood, and misinterpreted. A medicine-man was simply a healer—curing, or trying to cure, such few diseases and ailments as beset his people in the body, having nothing to do with their spiritual suffering. A medicine-man was no holier than other men, no closer to Wakan Tanka and no more honored than a brave or a scout. He lived the same life in the band that other men did, wore the same kind of clothes, ate the same variety of food, lived in the same sort of tipi, and took care of his wife and family, becoming a fair hunter and sometimes a very good one. More often he was an excellent scout, but seldom a great warrior. But as a member of his band he occupied no superior position, and simply filled his calling with as much skill as he could command, just as any physician, lawyer, or baker does today.

The medicine-man was a true benefactor of his people in that his work was founded upon and promoted the Indian ideal of brotherhood, and all service rendered to fellow beings was for the good of the tribe. Such wisdom and 'magic power' as he had achieved must be shared, as were food and clothing, with his fellow man. He made no charge for his helpfulness in ministering to the sick, for the comforting songs he sang, nor the strength he gave them; and when a medicine-man was called, he never was known to refuse the summons.

Now the medicine-man derived his knowledge from the infinite source— Wakan Tanka. For him knowledge was not in books, nor in the heads of professors, but in the works of Wakan Tanka as manifested in the creatures and beings of nature. This association of knowledge with all the creatures of earth caused him to look to them for his knowledge, and assuming their spiritual fineness to be of the quality of his own, he sought with them a true rapport. If the man could prove to some bird or animal that he was a worthy friend, it would share with him precious secrets and there would be formed bonds of loyalty never to be broken; the man would protect the rights and life of the animal, and the animal would share with the man his power, skill, and wisdom. In this manner was the great brotherhood of mutual helpfulness formed, adding to the reverence for life orders other than man. The taking of animal life for food and clothing only became established, and frugality became regarded as a virtue. Animal life took its place in the scheme of things, and there was no slavery and no torture of four-footed and winged things. By acknowledging the virtues of other beings the Lakota came to possess them for himself, and for his wonder and reverence and for his unsurpassed humbleness and meekness Wakan Tanka revealed himself to the medicine-man.

In order to place himself in communication with the other earth entities the Lakota submitted to the purification ceremony, the fast and vigil in solitude, for only in so doing could he experience the vision or dream during which the dumb creatures could converse with him. But not every man who tried was fortunate enough to receive the vision. It was a test which required fortitude and strength, and though most young men tried, few were successful. Nevertheless, every boy longed for the vision, and even as children we tried to hear and see things that would add to our knowledge and power. We watched the medicine-men and repeated their acts in our play until the time came to try to be a dreamer. If the young man in solitude was unable to meet and talk with some spirit entity he could never share its powers, and even though he met every sacrifice the communion might not come about; and if it did not he would never be a medicine-man.

To go into the vision was, of course, to go into the presence of the Great Mystery, and this no Lakota man would attempt to do without first cleansing himself physically and spiritually. Accordingly he began the task of purification; he purged himself of material things, putting aside the thought of food, the chase, fine clothes, the ceremony, and dance. In the solitudes the dream-seeker felt that he would come into the precinct of spiritual power; would speak to beings with whom he could not speak in life's daily existence, and in recognition of his high resolve they might offer to him the gift of their powers and for this exalted contact he wished in every way to be worthy. Earnestly a young man endeavored to cast fear from his mind. The danger from prowling enemies was ever constant and he would be defenseless and, perhaps, weak in body from the fast; so, however devout in his purpose a youth might be, he did not always go through with his self-imposed task. Sometimes a young man stayed his allotted time only to be unrewarded for his vigil, while another's youthful fears brought him home without accomplishing his dream.

A young man having decided to begin purification, asked the assistance of the medicine-man, for only occasionally did a man get a dream without taking the purification ritual, and still less occasionally did a woman receive a dream and become a medicine-woman, for they never took the fast and the lonesome vigil. Upon request, the medicine-man arranged the sweat-lodge, carpeted it with wild-sage, and built an altar in front of its door. He, and perhaps some friends of the dream-seeker, went into the lodge and the purification ceremony began with the smoking of the pipe. All in the group took the sweat while the medicine-man sang, and when the ceremony was over each one rubbed his body with the leaves and branches of sage. This ceremony might be repeated for several days, or until the young man felt that he was thoroughly pure in body, and by that time the songs would have strengthened and fortified him in mind and spirit also.

The youth then started on his journey to the place of his vigil, wrapped only in his robe. The friends who accompanied him, usually two in number, carried for him the four staffs to mark the four corners of his resting place, and when they arrived there, they planted the staffs in the earth and tied to the top of each a flag of red or blue cloth or buckskin. Sometimes ten small sticks, each topped with a small bundle of tobacco, were placed at the foot of each large staff. A buffalo robe was spread in the center of the square marked by the four staffs and on the robe the young brave lay or sat, the pipe clasped in his hands. His friends then left and he was alone. Were he fortunate and received a dream, he was thereafter known as a dreamer or medicine-man.

The Lakotas had some wonderful medicine-men who not only cured the sick, but they looked into the future and prophesied events, located lost or hidden articles, assisted the hunters by coaxing the buffalo near, made themselves invisible when near the enemy, and performed wonderful and magic things. Last Horse was one of our famous medicine-men and was an exception in that he was a splendid warrior as well. When I was a boy I noticed that Last Horse at the ceremonies always came out and performed a dance around the fire by himself before the other dancers came in. When I became older I came to know that Last Horse was a Thunder Dreamer and that it was his place to bless the dog feast, always served for Thunder Dreamers, before the others partook of the food. The powers that helped Last Horse were the Thunder Warriors of the sky, and oftentimes he, and other Thunder Dreamers also, combed their hair in a peculiar way, as they imagined the warriors of the sky did. Their long hair was brought forward and tied in the middle of the forehead, and into the knot a feather, which pointed back, was fastened. This made them look fierce and warlike, as they supposed the thunderous sky warriors must look.

In 1878 I saw Last Horse perform one of his miracles. Some of my band, the Oglalas, went to visit the Brule band and by way of entertainment preparations were made for a dance and feast. The day was bright and beautiful, and everyone was dressed in feathers and painted buckskin. But a storm came up suddenly, threatening to disrupt the gathering, so of course there was much unhappiness as the wind began to blow harder and rain began to fall. Last Horse walked into his tipi and disrobed, coming out wearing only breechclout and moccasins. His hair streamed down his back and in his hand he carried his rattle. Walking slowly to the center of the village he raised his face to the sky and sang his Thunder songs, which commanded the clouds to part. Slowly but surely, under the magic of the song, the clouds parted and the sky was clear once more.

Sharlot Hall
1870-1943

—

1911: *Cactus and Pine* (revised edition, 1924)
1953: *Poems of a Ranch Woman,*
comp. Josephine Mackenzie
1975: *Sharlot Hall on the Arizona Strip,*
comp. C. Gregory Crampton

—

S HARLOT HALL *participated in the western myth as it was being created. Her father was a trapper and buffalo hunter in Kansas before he left
the dust of one dream in 1881 and took his family in search of another
dream in Arizona. Sharlot was only eleven that year, but she rode horseback the
whole length of the Santa Fe Trail and on into Arizona Territory.*

*Hall was one of those industrious, durable women that storywriters make hero-
ines of. She fought droughts and blizzards as she struggled to make her parents'
mine and ranch produce a living. Death and violence were frequent experiences. But mere survival was not her only accomplishment. Her poetry caught
the attention of Charles Lummis, the influential editor of* Out West *magazine,
and Lummis's friendship was instrumental in establishing her as a poet and historian. Another of Hall's accomplishments was to write firsthand descriptions of
the Arizona Strip, a dangerous and little-known part of the state. With only one
companion and the few supplies that her light wagon could carry, she made an
exploratory survey of the wild and isolated region north of the Grand Canyon.*

*Hall's writings do not fill many volumes, but they are representative of the lyric
voice of the myth-making period, the voice of even-tempered sensitivity. Hall also
epitomizes a certain tough-minded new breed of western poet, one who is not to
be deterred from seeing the beauty beneath the harshness—and one who views the
western male, sometimes, with bemused understanding.*

In her later life, Hall contributed to the preservation of the arts and humani-

ties in the Southwest by campaigning to have the territorial governor's mansion restored as a museum. She contributed an extensive personal collection of historical documents and artifacts to this same institution, now known as the Sharlot Hall Museum of Arizona, in Prescott. Finally, Hall is somewhat of a historical phenomenon in her own right; she was probably the first white person born in Lincoln County, Kansas, and was definitely the first woman to hold a public office in Arizona.

During World War I, an ammunition maker buying scrap metal to melt down for artillery shells found the printing plates of Sharlot Hall's first book of poetry and added them to the vat. When asked for her reaction to the idea of her poems being melted down for ammunition, Hall commented that her verses had "done their part in winning the war in a decidedly original way."[1] Few poets can say that their poems have literally been aimed at the enemies of culture.

Wild Morning Glories

Once in a wind-swept, sunburned land
Where long, rough hills come crawling down,
Crowding the little valley hard
With buttes like paws, rock-clawed and brown,
One great split boulder in the sand
Made spots of shade where wild vines grew,
All hung with swinging bells of bloom—
In sunset colors pink and blue.
Small morning glory vines that clung
Back in the rock rifts dim and cool—
And two ranch children all through May
Were tardy every day at school.

The first four selections of Sharlot Hall's verse included here are from *Poems of a Ranch Woman*, comp. Josephine Mackenzie (Prescott, Ariz.: Sharlot Hall Historical Society, 1953), pp. 42, 55–56, 57, 61. The last two selections are from *Cactus and Pine*, rev. ed. (Phoenix: Arizona Republican Print Shop, 1924), pp. 26–27, 75–76. Reprinted by permission of the Sharlot Hall Historical Society.

1. Sharlot M. Hall, *Cactus and Pine: Songs of the Southwest* (Phoenix: Arizona Republican Print Shop, 1924), p. 2.

Dry Bones

The fence posts blister in the burning sun,
And wisps of wind like hungry hunting dogs
Sniff dry bones gnawed and left to crack and bleach.
Dry bones are plenty on the water trails
Where long before the sun comes up the dust
Swings in the air like low-hung graying haze
Where staggering cows creep slowly in to drink—
Hides taut and hard, and hair like sun-dried grass.

The thin warm mud is nectar to their tongues,
And water green with moss is wine of life.
They gulp and gulp and grow big-barreled like drums
And stagger out and fall, and never rise.
Or, sway-backed and wobbly-legged
Feel with their hoofs to find the deep-worn trail
And reach the mesa. And lie down all water-logged
With weight they have not strength to bear—
                              And so they die.

All but a few, who rest, and rise and struggle on
To reach some spot of sere and burned-out grass
That breaks and crackles underneath their tongues.
The dry wind breaks the rattling stalks of corn.
Around the shrinking pools the buzzards wheel
Full-fed and fat, and shining glossy black;
And sleek coyotes hardly wait for death
Until they feast; and russet foxes sniff
The last faint breath that will not come again.

When all the range is green with grass again
And clean, cool water ripples in the pools

The great bone-wagons will follow all the trails[2]
And camp beside the springs that have come back.
The sun-bleached bones are piled and heaped up high
Above the wagon beds, like evil wood
With branches hoofed and horned,
                                        And bent in pain.

———

Smell of Rain

Smell of drought on every side;
Every whirlwind flings aside
Acrid, evil-smelling dust
Like some burning mold or musk.
Wind across the garden brings
Scent of blistered, dying things.
Deep corral dust trampled fine
Stings the lips like bitter wine.
Warping boards ooze drops of pitch
Scented with a memory rich
Of cool forests far away.
In the sunbaked fields the hay
Yields a piteous, panting breath
As it slowly burns to death.
Roses in the ranch-house yard
Turn to mummies dry and hard.
Out of dusk and out of dawn
Every fragrance is withdrawn.
Hot, hot winds, and clear, hot sky
Burn the throat and sear the eye.
Then, at last, a cool dawn wind
Pitying and deeply kind,
Brings a far-off scent of rain.
Ah, the sick earth lives again!
Herds that straggle dusty-pale
Down the deep-worn water trail,

2. A common sight on the prairies in the late 1800s, the "bonepickers" traveled around
in large wagons, collecting the bones of bison and livestock to be ground up for fertilizer.

Lift their sunken eyes with hope
To the distant mountain slope.
Lean work horses shy and snort
In an awkward, eager sport;
And the ranch dogs, baying, run
Out to meet the rising sun.
In the yard a woman stands,
Touching with bewildered hands
Wan buds trying to unclose
On a parched and dying rose.

——

Man-Sized Job

"Wimmin's bizness, it's to cook,
Keep th' house a-goin',
See th' pigs an' chickens fed,
Do a little hoein'
In th' garden summer times,
Jist to keep things growin'!
Cow-men don't like garden dirt
On their han's an' faces.
You won't find no garden truck
'Round real cow-men's places.
That's a job fer wimmin folks,
Like milkin', churnin' butter.
Cow-men never milks no cows.
Hain't no time ter putter.
Keeps me humpin' ridin' range,
Brandin', ropin', tyin';
Runnin' the whole outfit right—
Wimmins got no use tryin'.
Couldn't run this ranch like me—
Sure, ye couldn't, Maw.
This job calls fer intellec' . . ."
          (Chaw—spit—chaw).

——

Spring in the Desert

Silence, and the heat lights shimmer like a mist of sifted silver
Down across the wide, low washes where the strange sand rivers
    flow;
Brown and sun-baked, quiet, waveless—trailed with bleaching,
    flood-swept boulders;
Rippled into mimic water where the restless whirlwinds go.

On the banks the gray mesquite trees droop their slender,
    lace-leafed branches;
Fill the lonely air with fragrance, as a beauty unconfessed;
Till the wild quail comes at sunset with her timorous, plumed
    covey,
And the iris-throated pigeon coos above her hidden nest.

Every shrub distills vague sweetness; every poorest leaf has
    gathered
Some rare breath to tell its gladness in a fitter way than speech;
Here the silken cactus blossoms flaunt their rose and gold and
    crimson,
And the proud zahuaro lifts its pearl-carved crown from careless
    reach.

Like to Lilith's[3] hair down-streaming, soft and shining, glorious,
    golden,
Sways the queenly palo verde,[4] robed and wreathed in golden
    flowers;

---

3. Lilith, according to Talmudists, was Adam's first wife. She was forced to leave Eden and go into the desert because she refused to accept Adam as her superior; there, she became a demon spirit who haunts wilderness places. See Isaiah 34:14, where she is referred to as the "screech owl," or the "night hag," or the "night monster."

4. "Palo verde"—green tree (Spanish). A nearly leafless bush that blossoms with bright yellow flowers.

And the spirits of dead lovers might have joy again together
Where the honey-sweet acacia weaves its shadow-fretted bowers.

Velvet-soft and glad and tender goes the night wind down the
cañons,
Touching lightly every petal, rocking leaf and bud and nest;
Whispering secrets to the black bees dozing in the tall wild lilies,
Till it hails the sudden sunrise trailing down the mountain's crest.

Silence, sunshine, heat lights painting opal-tinted dream and
vision
Down across the wide, low washes where the whirlwinds wheel
and swing;—
What of dead hands, sun-dried, bleaching? What of heat and
thirst and madness?
Death and life are lost, forgotten, in the wonder of the spring.

———

The Water Tank at Dusk [5]

The wild, bare, rock-fanged hills that all day long
Shut in the hand-width valley from the world,
Like wolfish outposts which no foot might pass,
Creep closely as friendly dogs with head on paws,
And drowsy eyes that watch the evening fire.
Their tawny brown melts into mist
Of rose and violet and translucent blue,
With gold dust powdered softly through the air
That swims and shimmers as if all the earth
Were carven jewels bathed in golden light.
In the soft dusk the desert seems to pant,
Only half-rested from the burning day—
Yet stirs a little happily to feel

5. This poem was written during a summer visit to Reed's Ranch, just below the old-
time mining camp of Harrisburg in the Harqua Hala desert, one of the loveliest spots in
all the desert region of Arizona. The water tank, a little lake, had been dug out of the
adobe earth, with softly-rounded earth banks along which the Yerba Mansa, the beloved
and beautiful healing water plant brought by Spanish Fathers from South America, grew
tall and rank. [Hall's note]

The night wind, cool and gentle, whispering
In the white-flowered mesquite where wild bees hum
Delirious with honey sweets and fragrances;—
And through the leafless thorn whose tortured boughs
Were wreathed, men say, to crown the suffering Christ
On his high cross—(And still each Passion Week
The sorrowing tree wears buds like drops of blood
In memory.) With swift, soft whirr of wings
The gray doves flutter down beside the pool,
Cooing their love notes sweet as fairy flutes;
And in the grass the fiddler-crickets chirp.

The spotted night hawk saws his raucous note
Like some harsh rasp upon an o'er-drawn string;
The squeaking bats drop from the cottonwood trees,
Dipping and diving round the shining pool
Where night moths hover like moon-elves astray.
It seems the deep blue sky has fallen there
In the blue, star-set water, where the wind
Makes mimic waves that hardly over-toss
The peach-leaf boat on which the dragon-fly
Rides sailor-wise to rest his gorgeous wings.
The hot, dry, day-time scent of sun-burned sand
Is drowned in sweetness of the blossoming grape,
And pungent odor of the wax-white cups
Of yerba mansa, hedging the blue pool
With a green wall whose every flower
Blooms twice—once on its tall-leafed stalk, and once
Down where the waves like silver mirrors mix
Its whiteness with the red pomegranate stars.
In the shadow of the plume-branched tamarask
There is a half-hushed, honey-throated call,
And from the cottonwood's topmost moonlit bough
Music's enraptured soul seems waked to answer,
So sweet, so low, so pure, so tender-clear;
So brimmed with joy; so wistful, plaintive-sad;
As if all love o' the world pulsed in that throat—
As if all pain o' life beat in the heart below.
It is the mocking bird to his brown mate—
The desert's vesper song of rest and peace.

Stephen Crane

1871-1900

▬

1893: *Maggie: A Girl of the Streets*
1895: *The Red Badge of Courage*
1897: "The Open Boat"
1898: "The Bride Comes to Yellow Sky"
1899: "The Blue Hotel"

▬

T O HAMLIN GARLAND of the great honest West, from Stephen Crane of the false East.[1] *So reads Crane's inscription in a book he sent to Garland. Although Crane was an easterner—born in New Jersey and educated in New York—and although his visit to the American West was less than half a year in duration, his western stories must be included among the best literature of the region. "The Blue Hotel" and "The Bride Comes to Yellow Sky" are only two of the fourteen stories and ten essays collected in Frank Bergon's edition of* The Western Writings of Stephen Crane.[2] *They are stories of such literary merit that they are regularly included in collections of American fiction.*

"The Bride Comes to Yellow Sky" offers an unusual perspective of a familiar theme: the final taming of the wild West. With the frontier declared "closed" in 1890, and with the introduction of such civilized luxuries as the Pullman railway car as early as 1865, western society was becoming increasingly law-abiding and respectable.

Crane's short story is interesting for several reasons. As a showdown story, for instance, it predates Owen Wister's The Virginian, *which is usually thought of as the first novel to feature a gunfight. Crane's narrative in some respects is an anti-*

---

1. John Berryman, *Stephen Crane* (New York: William Sloane Associates, 1950), p. 97.
2. *The Western Writings of Stephen Crane*, ed. Frank Bergon (New York: New American Library, 1979).

formula story or an "anti-Western," a parody of the western dime-novel formula. Finally, it is an example of literary realism or literary naturalism, a sharply focused portrait of the forces that act upon human lives. The forces are biological (the marshal's sudden and unexpected marriage), economic (the drummer's job necessarily bringing him into the line of fire of an unemployed cowboy), and social (the marshal's fear of a "showdown" with the unprepared town folk, and Scratchy's confusion in the face of the "foreign condition"). To end the story with a shoot-out, so that the representative of Good might destroy the agent of Primitive Evil, might have been more satisfying to some readers. Crane, however, would see this as artificial: in reality, the wild West towns like Yellow Sky were finally civilized and tamed not by the six-gun but by the arrival of women.

▬

The Bride Comes to Yellow Sky

I

THE GREAT Pullman was whirling onward with such dignity of motion that a glance from the window seemed simply to prove that the plains of Texas were pouring eastward. Vast flats of green grass, dull-hued spaces of mesquite and cactus, little groups of frame houses, woods of light and tender trees, all were sweeping into the east, sweeping over the horizon, a precipice.

A newly married pair had boarded this coach at San Antonio. The man's face was reddened from many days in the wind and sun, and a direct result of his new black clothes was that his brick-colored hands were constantly performing in a most conscious fashion. From time to time he looked down respectfully at his attire. He sat with a hand on each knee, like a man waiting in a barber's shop. The glances he devoted to other passengers were furtive and shy.

The bride was not pretty, nor was she very young. She wore a dress of blue cashmere, with small reservations of velvet here and there and with steel buttons abounding. She continually twisted her head to regard her puff sleeves, very stiff, straight, and high. They embarrassed her. It was quite apparent that she had cooked, and that she expected to cook, dutifully. The blushes caused by the careless scrutiny of some passengers as

From *McClure's Magazine* 10 (February 1898): 377–84.

she had entered the car were strange to see upon this plain, under-class countenance, which was drawn in placid, almost emotionless lines.

They were evidently very happy. "Ever been in a parlor-car before?" he asked, smiling with delight.

"No," she answered. "I never was. It's fine, ain't it?"

"Great! And then after a while we'll go forward to the diner and get a big layout. Finest meal in the world. Charge a dollar."

"Oh, do they?" cried the bride. "Charge a dollar? Why, that's too much—for us—ain't it, Jack?"

"Not this trip, anyhow," he answered bravely. "We're going to go the whole thing."

Later, he explained to her about the trains. "You see, it's a thousand miles from one end of Texas to the other, and this train runs right across it and never stops but four times." He had the pride of an owner. He pointed out to her the dazzling fittings of the coach, and in truth her eyes opened wider as she contemplated the sea-green figured velvet, the shining brass, silver, and glass, the wood that gleamed as darkly brilliant as the surface of a pool of oil. At one end a bronze figure sturdily held a support for a separated chamber, and at convenient places on the ceiling were frescoes in olive and silver.

To the minds of the pair, their surroundings reflected the glory of their marriage that morning in San Antonio. This was the environment of their new estate, and the man's face in particular beamed with an elation that made him appear ridiculous to the negro porter. This individual at times surveyed them from afar with an amused and superior grin. On other occasions he bullied them with skill in ways that did not make it exactly plain to them that they were being bullied. He subtly used all the manners of the most unconquerable kind of snobbery. He oppressed them, but of this oppression they had small knowledge, and they speedily forgot that infrequently a number of travelers covered them with stares of derisive enjoyment. Historically there was supposed to be something infinitely humorous in their situation.

"We are due in Yellow Sky at 3.42," he said, looking tenderly into her eyes.

"Oh, are we?" she said, as if she had not been aware of it. To evince surprise at her husband's statement was part of her wifely amiability. She took from a pocket a little silver watch, and as she held it before her and stared at it with a frown of attention, the new husband's face shone.

"I bought it in San Anton' from a friend of mine," he told her gleefully.

"It's seventeen minutes past twelve," she said, looking up at him with a kind of shy and clumsy coquetry. A passenger, noting this play, grew excessively sardonic, and winked at himself in one of the numerous mirrors.

At last they went to the dining-car. Two rows of negro waiters, in glowing white suits, surveyed their entrance with the interest and also the equanimity of men who had been forewarned. The pair fell to the lot of a waiter who happened to feel pleasure in steering them through their meal. He viewed them with the manner of a fatherly pilot, his countenance radiant with benevolence. The patronage, entwined with the ordinary deference, was not plain to them. And yet, as they returned to their coach, they showed in their faces a sense of escape.

To the left, miles down a long purple slope, was a little ribbon of mist where moved the keening Rio Grande. The train was approaching it at an angle, and the apex was Yellow Sky. Presently it was apparent that, as the distance from Yellow Sky grew shorter, the husband became commensurately restless. His brick-red hands were more insistent in their prominence. Occasionally he was even rather absent-minded and far-away when the bride leaned forward and addressed him.

As a matter of truth, Jack Potter was beginning to find the shadow of a deed weigh upon him like a leaden slab. He, the town marshal of Yellow Sky, a man known, liked, and feared in his corner, a prominent person, had gone to San Antonio to meet a girl he believed he loved, and there, after the usual prayers, had actually induced her to marry him, without consulting Yellow Sky for any part of the transaction. He was now bringing his bride before an innocent and unsuspecting community.

Of course, people in Yellow Sky married as it pleased them, in accordance with a general custom; but such was Potter's thought of his duty to his friends, or of their idea of his duty, or of an unspoken form which does not control men in these matters, that he felt he was heinous. He had committed an extraordinary crime. Face to face with this girl in San Antonio, and spurred by his sharp impulse, he had gone headlong over all the social hedges. At San Antonio he was like a man hidden in the dark. A knife to sever any friendly duty, any form, was easy to his hand in that remote city. But the hour of Yellow Sky, the hour of daylight, was approaching.

He knew full well that his marriage was an important thing to his town. It could only be exceeded by the burning of the new hotel. His friends could not forgive him. Frequently he had reflected on the advisability of telling them by telegraph, but a new cowardice had been upon him. He feared to do it. And now the train was hurrying him toward a scene of amazement, glee, and reproach. He glanced out of the window at the line of haze swinging slowly in towards the train.

Yellow Sky had a kind of brass band, which played painfully, to the delight of the populace. He laughed without heart as he thought of it. If the citizens could dream of his prospective arrival with his bride, they would parade the band at the station and escort them, amid cheers and laughing congratulations, to his adobe home.

He resolved that he would use all the devices of speed and plains-craft in making the journey from the station to his house. Once within that safe citadel, he could issue some sort of a vocal bulletin, and then not go among the citizens until they had time to wear off a little of their enthusiasm.

The bride looked anxiously at him. "What's worrying you, Jack?"

He laughed again. "I'm not worrying, girl. I'm only thinking of Yellow Sky."

She flushed in comprehension.

A sense of mutual guilt invaded their minds and developed a finer tenderness. They looked at each other with eyes softly aglow. But Potter often laughed the same nervous laugh. The flush upon the bride's face seemed quite permanent.

The traitor to the feelings of Yellow Sky narrowly watched the speeding landscape. "We're nearly there," he said.

Presently the porter came and announced the proximity of Potter's home. He held a brush in his hand and, with all his airy superiority gone, he brushed Potter's new clothes as the latter slowly turned this way and that way. Potter fumbled out a coin and gave it to the porter, as he had seen others do. It was a heavy and musclebound business, as that of a man shoeing his first horse.

The porter took their bag, and as the train began to slow they moved forward to the hooded platform of the car. Presently the two engines and their long string of coaches rushed into the station of Yellow Sky.

"They have to take water here," said Potter, from a constricted throat and in mournful cadence, as one announcing death. Before the train stopped, his eye had swept the length of the platform, and he was glad and astonished to see there was none upon it but the station-agent, who, with a slightly hurried and anxious air, was walking toward the water-tanks. When the train had halted, the porter alighted first and placed in position a little temporary step.

"Come on, girl," said Potter hoarsely. As he helped her down they each laughed on a false note. He took the bag from the negro, and bade his wife cling to his arm. As they slunk rapidly away, his hang-dog glance perceived that they were unloading the two trunks, and also that the station-agent far ahead near the baggage-car had turned and was running toward him, making gestures. He laughed, and groaned as he laughed, when he noted the first effect of his marital bliss upon Yellow Sky. He gripped his wife's arm firmly to his side, and they fled. Behind them the porter stood chuckling fatuously.

II

The California Express on the Southern Railway was due at Yellow Sky in twenty-one minutes. There were six men at the bar of the "Weary Gentleman" saloon. One was a drummer[3] who talked a great deal and rapidly; three were Texans who did not care to talk at that time; and two were Mexican sheep-herders who did not talk as a general practice in the "Weary Gentleman" saloon. The barkeeper's dog lay on the board walk that crossed in front of the door. His head was on his paws, and he glanced drowsily here and there with the constant vigilance of a dog that is kicked on occasion. Across the sandy street were some vivid green grass plots, so wonderful in appearance amid the sands that burned near them in a blazing sun that they caused a doubt in the mind. They exactly resembled the grass mats used to represent lawns on the stage. At the cooler end of the railway station a man without a coat sat in a tilted chair and smoked his pipe. The fresh-cut bank of the Rio Grande circled near the town, and there could be seen beyond it a great, plum-colored plain of mesquite.

Save for the busy drummer and his companions in the saloon, Yellow Sky was dozing. The new-comer leaned gracefully upon the bar, and recited many tales with the confidence of a bard who has come upon a new field.

"—and at the moment that the old man fell down stairs with the bureau in his arms, the old woman was coming up with two scuttles of coal, and, of course—"

The drummer's tale was interrupted by a young man who suddenly appeared in the open door. He cried: "Scratchy Wilson's drunk, and has turned loose with both hands." The two Mexicans at once set down their glasses and faded out of the rear entrance of the saloon.

The drummer, innocent and jocular, answered: "All right, old man. S'pose he has. Come in and have a drink, anyhow."

But the information had made such an obvious cleft in every skull in the room that the drummer was obliged to see its importance. All had become

3. "Drummer"—a traveling salesman.

instantly solemn. "Say," said he, mystified, "what is this?" His three companions made the introductory gesture of eloquent speech, but the young man at the door forestalled them.

"It means, my friend," he answered, as he came into the saloon, "that for the next two hours this town won't be a health resort."

The barkeeper went to the door and locked and barred it. Reaching out of the window, he pulled in heavy wooden shutters and barred them. Immediately a solemn, chapel-like gloom was upon the place. The drummer was looking from one to another.

"But, say," he cried, "what is this, anyhow? You don't mean there is going to be a gun-fight?"

"Don't know whether there'll be a fight or not," answered one man grimly. "But there'll be some shootin'—some good shootin'."

The young man who had warned them waved his hand. "Oh, there'll be a fight fast enough, if anyone wants it. Anybody can get a fight out there in the street. There's a fight just waiting."

The drummer seemed to be swayed between the interest of a foreigner and a perception of personal danger.

"What did you say his name was?" he asked.

"Scratchy Wilson," they answered in chorus.

"And will he kill anybody? What are you going to do? Does this happen often? Does he rampage around like this once a week or so? Can he break in that door?"

"No, he can't break down that door," replied the barkeeper. "He's tried it three times. But when he comes you'd better lay down on the floor, stranger. He's dead sure to shoot at it, and a bullet may come through."

Thereafter the drummer kept a strict eye upon the door. The time had not yet been called for him to hug the floor, but, as a minor precaution, he sidled near to the wall. "Will he kill anybody?" he said again.

The men laughed low and scornfully at the question.

"He's out to shoot, and he's out for trouble. Don't see any good in experimentin' with him."

"But what do you do in a case like this? What do you do?"

A man responded: "Why, he and Jack Potter—"

"But," in chorus, the other men interrupted, "Jack Potter's in San Anton'."

"Well, who is he? What's he got to do with it?"

"Oh, he's the town marshal. He goes out and fights Scratchy when he gets on one of these tears."

"Wow," said the drummer, mopping his brow. "Nice job he's got."

The voices had toned away to mere whisperings. The drummer wished to ask further questions which were born of an increasing anxiety and bewilderment; but when he attempted them, the men merely looked at him in irritation and motioned him to remain silent. A tense waiting hush was upon them. In the deep shadows of the room their eyes shone as they listened for sounds from the street. One man made three gestures at the barkeeper, and the latter, moving like a ghost, handed him a glass and a bottle. The man poured a full glass of whisky, and set down the bottle noiselessly. He gulped the whisky in a swallow, and turned again toward the door in immovable silence. The drummer saw that the barkeeper, without a sound, had taken a Winchester from beneath the bar. Later he saw this individual beckoning to him, so he tiptoed across the room.

"You better come with me back of the bar."

"No, thanks," said the drummer, perspiring. "I'd rather be where I can make a break for the back door."

Whereupon the man of bottles made a kindly but peremptory gesture. The drummer obeyed it, and finding himself seated on a box with his head below the level of the bar, balm was laid upon his soul at sight of various zinc and copper fittings that bore a resemblance to armor-plate. The barkeeper took a seat comfortably upon an adjacent box.

"You see," he whispered, "this here Scratchy Wilson is a wonder with a gun—a perfect wonder—and when he goes on the war trail, we hunt our holes—naturally. He's about the last one of the old gang that used to hang out along the river here. He's a terror when he's drunk. When he's sober he's all right—kind of simple—wouldn't hurt a fly—nicest fellow in town. But when he's drunk—whoo!"

There were periods of stillness. "I wish Jack Potter was back from San Anton'," said the barkeeper. "He shot Wilson up once—in the leg—and he would sail in and pull out the kinks in this thing."

Presently they heard from a distance the sound of a shot, followed by three wild yowls. It instantly removed a bond from the men in the darkened saloon. There was a shuffling of feet. They looked at each other. "Here he comes," they said.

III

A man in a maroon-colored flannel shirt, which had been purchased for purposes of decoration and made, principally, by some Jewish women on the east side of New York, rounded a corner and walked into the middle of the main street of Yellow Sky. In either hand the man held a long, heavy, blue-black revolver. Often he yelled, and these cries rang through a semblance of a deserted village, shrilly flying over the roofs in a volume that seemed to have no relation to the ordinary vocal strength of a man. It was as if the surrounding stillness formed the arch of a tomb over him. These cries of ferocious challenge rang against walls of silence. And his boots had red tops with gilded imprints, of the kind beloved in winter by little sledding boys on the hillsides of New England.

The man's face flamed in a rage begot of whisky. His eyes, rolling and yet keen for ambush, hunted the still doorways and windows. He walked with the creeping movement of the midnight cat. As it occurred to him, he roared menacing information. The long revolvers in his hands were as easy as straws; they were moved with an electric swiftness. The little fingers of each hand played sometimes in a musician's way. Plain from the low collar of the shirt, the cords of his neck straightened and sank, straightened and sank, as passion moved him. The only sounds were his terrible invitations. The calm adobes preserved their demeanor at the passing of this small thing in the middle of the street.

There was no offer of fight; no offer of fight. The man called to the sky. There were no attractions. He bellowed and fumed and swayed his revolvers here and everywhere.

The dog of the barkeeper of the "Weary Gentleman" saloon had not appreciated the advance of events. He yet lay dozing in front of his master's door. At sight of the dog, the man paused and raised his revolver humorously. At sight of the man, the dog sprang up and walked diagonally away, with a sullen head, and growling. The man yelled, and the dog broke into a gallop. As it was about to enter an alley, there was a loud noise, a whistling, and something spat the ground directly before it. The dog screamed, and, wheeling in terror, galloped headlong in a new direction. Again there was a noise, a whistling, and sand was kicked viciously before it. Fear-stricken, the dog turned and flurried like an animal in a pen. The man stood laughing, his weapons at his hips.

Ultimately the man was attracted by the closed door of the "Weary Gentleman" saloon. He went to it, and hammering with a revolver, demanded drink.

The door remaining imperturbable, he picked a bit of paper from the walk and nailed it to the framework with a knife. He then turned his back contemptuously upon this popular resort, and walking to the opposite side of the street, and spinning there on his heel quickly and lithely, fired at the bit of paper. He missed it by a half inch. He swore at himself, and went away. Later, he comfortably fusilladed the windows of his most intimate friend. The man was playing with this town. It was a toy for him.

But still there was no offer of fight. The name of Jack Potter, his ancient antagonist, entered his mind, and he concluded that it would be a glad thing if he should go to Potter's house and by bombardment induce him to come out and fight. He moved in the direction of his desire, chanting Apache scalp-music.

When he arrived at it, Potter's house presented the same still front as had the other adobes. Taking up a strategic position, the man howled a challenge. But this house regarded him as might a great stone god. It gave no sign. After a decent wait, the man howled further challenges, mingling with them wonderful epithets.

Presently there came the spectacle of a man churning himself into deepest rage over the immobility of a house. He fumed at it as the winter wind attacks a prairie cabin in the North. To the distance there should have gone the sound of a tumult like the fighting of 200 Mexicans. As necessity bade him, he paused for breath or to reload his revolvers.

IV

Potter and his bride walked sheepishly and with speed. Sometimes they laughed together shamefacedly and low.

"Next corner, dear," he said finally.

They put forth the efforts of a pair walking bowed against a strong wind. Potter was about to raise a finger to point the first appearance of the new home when, as they circled the corner, they came face to face with a man in a maroon-colored shirt who was feverishly pushing cartridges into a large revolver. Upon the instant the man dropped his revolver to the ground, and, like lightning, whipped another from its holster. The second weapon was aimed at the bridegroom's chest.

There was a silence. Potter's mouth seemed to be merely a grave for his tongue. He exhibited an instinct to at once loosen his arm from the woman's grip, and he dropped the bag to the sand. As for the bride, her face had gone as yellow as old cloth. She was a slave to hideous rites gazing at the apparitional snake.

The two men faced each other at a distance of three paces. He of the revolver smiled with a new and quiet ferocity.

"Tried to sneak up on me," he said. "Tried to sneak up on me!" His eyes grew more baleful. As Potter made a slight movement, the man thrust his revolver venomously forward. "No, don't you do it, Jack Potter. Don't you move a finger toward a gun just yet. Don't you move an eyelash. The time has come for me to settle with you, and I'm goin' to do it my own way and loaf along with no interferin'. So if you don't want a gun bent on you, just mind what I tell you."

Potter looked at his enemy. "I ain't got a gun on me, Scratchy," he said. "Honest, I ain't." He was stiffening and steadying, but yet somewhere at the back of his mind a vision of the Pullman floated, the sea-green figured velvet, the shining brass, silver, and glass, the wood that gleamed as darkly brilliant as the surface of a pool of oil—all the glory of the marriage, the environment of the new estate. "You know I fight when it comes to fighting, Scratchy Wilson, but I ain't got a gun on me. You'll have to do all the shootin' yourself."

His enemy's face went livid. He stepped forward and lashed his weapon to and fro before Potter's chest. "Don't you tell me you ain't got no gun on you, you whelp. Don't tell me no lie like that. There ain't a man in Texas ever seen you without no gun. Don't take me for no kid." His eyes blazed with light, and his throat worked like a pump.

"I ain't takin' you for no kid," answered Potter. His heels had not moved an inch backward. "I'm takin' you for a —— fool. I tell you I ain't got a gun, and I ain't. If you're goin' to shoot me up, you better begin now. You'll never get a chance like this again."

So much enforced reasoning had told on Wilson's rage. He was calmer. "If you ain't got a gun, why ain't you got a gun?" he sneered. "Been to Sunday-school?"

"I ain't got a gun because I've just come from San Anton' with my wife. I'm married," said Potter. "And if I'd thought there was going to be any galoots like you prowling around when I brought my wife home, I'd had a gun, and don't you forget it."

"Married!" said Scratchy, not at all comprehending.

"Yes, married. I'm married," said Potter distinctly.

"Married?" said Scratchy. Seemingly for the first time he saw the drooping, drowning woman at the other man's side. "No!" he said. He was like a creature allowed a glimpse of another world. He moved a pace backward, and his arm with the revolver dropped to his side. "Is this the lady?" he asked.

"Yes, this is the lady," answered Potter.

There was another period of silence.

"Well," said Wilson at last, slowly, "I s'pose it's all off now."

"It's all off if you say so, Scratchy. You know I didn't make the trouble." Potter lifted his valise.

"Well, I 'low it's off, Jack," said Wilson. He was looking at the ground. "Married!" He was not a student of chivalry; it was merely that in the presence of this foreign condition he was a simple child of the earlier plains. He picked up his starboard revolver, and placing both weapons in their holsters, he went away. His feet made funnel-shaped tracks in the heavy sand.

Willa Cather
1873-1947

1905: *The Troll Garden*
1913: *O Pioneers!*
1915: *Song of the Lark*
1918: *My Ántonia*
1925: *The Professor's House*
1927: *Death Comes for the Archbishop*

R ED CLOUD, *Nebraska, where Willa Cather grew up, consisted of more than just four blocks of brick and frame storefronts facing each other across a dusty street. It was a spread-out society of farms and ranches, of wide-open prairie and wooded river bottom. It was a community of immigrants, or children of immigrants. Some, like Cather's father, were second- or third-generation Americans who had come from the eastern states. Others still spoke German, Russian, Czech, or Scandinavian. Most of them were, by necessity as well as by heritage, intensely materialistic people.*

Until she entered Red Cloud's high school, Cather had received all her education at home. By the time she entered the University of Nebraska she was already an accomplished student in several languages, Greek and Latin classics, literature, and music. She graduated from the university in 1895 and went to Pittsburgh as a journalist. Then after a brief trip to France she went to work in 1906 as an editor for McClure's Magazine *in New York. She remained with* McClure's *until 1912.*

Cather developed a very wide range of knowledge, traveling in Europe and the Southwest and making friends with other intellectuals and writers, of whom one of the most influential was the New England author Sarah Orne Jewett. Eventually—at thirty-nine—Cather felt she was ready to become a full-time novelist.

*Although she wrote about places other than the American West, Cather is best known for two Nebraska novels—*O Pioneers! *and* My Ántonia—*and for two Southwest novels,* The Professor's House *and* Death Comes for the Archbishop. *Her western fiction is difficult to categorize or to give a literary label to. At times it is romantic; at other times it is very realistic, almost harsh. The two stories presented here are examples of Cather's ability to combine romance and naturalism, abstract ideals and realism. "The Sculptor's Funeral," for instance, is romantic in that the sculptor's students and followers place a palm of victory on his casket. Yet the cold parlor in which the sculptor's townsmen hold their vigil is as real and disturbing as the narrow minds of the mourners. Likewise, "The Enchanted Bluff" legend is tragic and romantic, but the detailed description of the river and the sandbar is very precise, and Cather's account of the boys and their conversations has a realistic tone.*

Beyond her artistry in prose, which is impressive, Cather deserves credit for having a personal artistic vision that transcends such considerations as authenticity and romanticism. As we see in the story of the boys who want to explore that Enchanted Bluff, Cather believes in having faith in one's dreams; one such dream, strong among Nebraska pioneers, was that America would always have a future as long as its youth had imagination and vision. Second, Cather believes there is a beauty to be found in certain human spirits, a beauty that, like the sculptor's, can persist even in the face of the most discouraging coarseness. Finally, she sees a real heroism in people who persevere to rise above their apparent limits. Faith in a dream, beauty of spirit, heroic tenacity: these traits are seen in Thea Kronborg of Song of the Lark, *in Tom Outland of* The Professor's House, *and in Archbishop Jean Marie Latour and his vicar of* Death Comes for the Archbishop—*are seen over and over in the characters who make Cather's fiction memorable.*

—

The Sculptor's Funeral

A GROUP of the townspeople stood on the station siding of a little Kansas town, awaiting the coming of the night train, which was already twenty minutes overdue. The snow had fallen thick over everything; in the pale starlight the line of bluffs across the wide, white meadows south of the town made soft, smoke-coloured curves against the

First published in *McClure's Magazine* 24 (January 1905): 329–36. Reprinted from Willa Cather, *Collected Short Fiction, 1892–1912* (Lincoln: University of Nebraska Press, 1965), pp. 173–85. Copyright © 1965, 1970 by the University of Nebraska Press.

clear sky. The men on the siding stood first on one foot and then on the other, their hands thrust deep into their trousers pockets, their overcoats open, their shoulders screwed up with the cold; and they glanced from time to time toward the southeast, where the railroad track wound along the river shore. They conversed in low tones and moved about restlessly, seeming uncertain as to what was expected of them. There was but one of the company who looked as though he knew exactly why he was there; and he kept conspicuously apart; walking to the far end of the platform, returning to the station door, then pacing up the track again, his chin sunk in the high collar of his overcoat, his burly shoulders drooping forward, his gait heavy and dogged. Presently he was approached by a tall, spare, grizzled man clad in a faded Grand Army suit,[1] who shuffled out from the group and advanced with a certain deference, craning his neck forward until his back made the angle of a jack-knife three-quarters open.

"I reckon she's a-goin' to be pretty late agin to-night, Jim," he remarked in a squeaky falsetto. "S'pose it's the snow?"

"I don't know," responded the other man with a shade of annoyance, speaking from out an astonishing cataract of red beard that grew fiercely and thickly in all directions.

The spare man shifted the quill toothpick he was chewing to the other side of his mouth. "It ain't likely that anybody from the East will come with the corpse, I s'pose," he went on reflectively.

"I don't know," responded the other, more curtly than before.

"It's too bad he didn't belong to some lodge or other. I like an order funeral myself. They seem more appropriate for people of some repytation," the spare man continued, with an ingratiating concession in his shrill voice, as he carefully placed his toothpick in his vest pocket. He always carried the flag at the G.A.R. funerals in the town.

The heavy man turned on his heel, without replying, and walked up the siding. The spare man shuffled back to the uneasy group. "Jim's ez full ez a tick, ez ushel," he commented commiseratingly.

Just then a distant whistle sounded, and there was a shuffling of feet on the platform. A number of lanky boys of all ages appeared as suddenly and slimily as eels wakened by the crack of thunder; some came from the waiting-room, where they had been warming themselves by the red stove, or half asleep on the slat benches; others uncoiled themselves from baggage

1. The Grand Army of the Republic, or G. A. R., was founded in 1866 as a fraternal organization for Union veterans of the Civil War. Its objectives included giving aid to needy families, performing community service, and promoting patriotism.

trucks or slid out of express wagons. Two clambered down from the driver's seat of a hearse that stood backed up against the siding. They straightened their stooping shoulders and lifted their heads, and a flash of momentary animation kindled their dull eyes at that cold, vibrant scream, the world-wide call for men. It stirred them like the note of a trumpet; just as it had often stirred the man who was coming home to-night, in his boyhood.

The night express shot, red as a rocket, from out the eastward marsh lands and wound along the river shore under the long lines of shivering poplars that sentinelled the meadows, the escaping steam hanging in grey masses against the pale sky and blotting out the Milky Way. In a moment the red glare from the headlight streamed up the snow-covered track before the siding and glittered on the wet, black rails. The burly man with the dishevelled red beard walked swiftly up the platform toward the approaching train, uncovering his head as he went. The group of men behind him hesitated, glanced questioningly at one another, and awkwardly followed his example. The train stopped, and the crowd shuffled up to the express car just as the door was thrown open, the spare man in the G.A.R. suit thrusting his head forward with curiosity. The express messenger appeared in the doorway, accompanied by a young man in a long ulster and travelling cap.

"Are Mr. Merrick's friends here?" inquired the young man.

The group on the platform swayed and shuffled uneasily. Philip Phelps, the banker, responded with dignity: "We have come to take charge of the body. Mr. Merrick's father is very feeble and can't be about."

"Send the agent out here," growled the express messenger, "and tell the operator to lend a hand."

The coffin was got out of its rough box and down on the snowy platform. The townspeople drew back enough to make room for it and then formed a close semicircle about it, looking curiously at the palm leaf which lay across the black cover. No one said anything. The baggage man stood by his truck, waiting to get at the trunks. The engine panted heavily, and the fireman dodged in and out among the wheels with his yellow torch and long oil-can, snapping the spindle boxes. The young Bostonian, one of the dead sculptor's pupils who had come with the body, looked about him helplessly. He turned to the banker, the only one of that black, uneasy, stoop-shouldered group who seemed enough of an individual to be addressed.

"None of Mr. Merrick's brothers are here?" he asked uncertainly.

The man with the red beard for the first time stepped up and joined the group. "No, they have not come yet; the family is scattered. The body will be taken directly to the house." He stooped and took hold of one of the handles of the coffin.

"Take the long hill road up, Thompson, it will be easier on the horses," called the liveryman as the undertaker snapped the door of the hearse and prepared to mount to the driver's seat.

Laird, the red-bearded lawyer, turned again to the stranger: "We didn't know whether there would be any one with him or not," he explained. "It's a long walk, so you'd better go up in the hack." He pointed to a single battered conveyance, but the young man replied stiffly: "Thank you, but I think I will go up with the hearse. If you don't object," turning to the undertaker, "I'll ride with you."

They clambered up over the wheels and drove off in the starlight up the long, white hill toward the town. The lamps in the still village were shining from under the low, snow-burdened roofs; and beyond, on every side, the plains reached out into emptiness, peaceful and wide as the soft sky itself, and wrapped in a tangible, white silence.

When the hearse backed up to a wooden sidewalk before a naked, weather-beaten frame house, the same composite, ill-defined group that had stood upon the station siding was huddled about the gate. The front yard was an icy swamp, and a couple of warped planks, extending from the sidewalk to the door, made a sort of rickety footbridge. The gate hung on one hinge, and was opened wide with difficulty. Steavens, the young stranger, noticed that something black was tied to the knob of the front door.

The grating sound made by the casket, at it was drawn from the hearse, was answered by a scream from the house; the front door was wrenched open, and a tall, corpulent woman rushed out bareheaded into the snow and flung herself upon the coffin, shrieking: "My boy, my boy! And this is how you've come home to me!"

As Steavens turned away and closed his eyes with a shudder of unutterable repulsion, another woman, also tall, but flat and angular, dressed entirely in black, darted out of the house and caught Mrs. Merrick by the shoulders, crying sharply: "Come, come, mother; you musn't go on like this!" Her tone changed to one of obsequious solemnity as she turned to the banker: "The parlour is ready, Mr. Phelps."

The bearers carried the coffin along the narrow boards, while the undertaker ran ahead with the coffin-rests. They bore it into a large, unheated room that smelled of dampness and disuse and furniture polish, and set it down under a hanging lamp ornamented with jingling glass prisms and before a "Rogers group" of John Alden and Priscilla, wreathed with smilax.[2]

2. Smilax is a climbing vine with glossy leaves. Like the bric-a-brac, lamp, and green Brussels carpet, it represents Mrs. Merrick's idea of tasteful decor. John Rogers (1829–1904) was an American sculptor who specialized in statuette groups.

Henry Steavens stared about him with the sickening conviction that there had been some horrible mistake, and that he had somehow arrived at the wrong destination. He looked painfully about over the clover-green Brussels, the fat plush upholstery; among the hand-painted china plaques and panels, and vases, for some mark of identification, for something that might once conceivably have belonged to Harvey Merrick. It was not until he recognized his friend in the crayon portrait of a little boy in kilts and curls hanging above the piano, that he felt willing to let any of these people approach the coffin.

"Take the lid off, Mr. Thompson; let me see my boy's face," wailed the elder woman between her sobs. This time Steavens looked fearfully, almost beseechingly into her face, red and swollen under its masses of strong, black, shiny hair. He flushed, dropped his eyes, and then, almost incredulously, looked again. There was a kind of power about her face—a kind of brutal handsomeness, even, but it was scarred and furrowed by violence, and so coloured and coarsened by fiercer passions that grief seemed never to have laid a gentle finger there. The long nose was distended and knobbed at the end, and there were deep lines on either side of it; her heavy, black brows almost met across her forehead, her teeth were large and square, and set far apart—teeth that could tear. She filled the room; the men were obliterated, seemed tossed about like twigs in an angry water, and even Steavens felt himself being drawn into the whirlpool.

The daughter—the tall, raw-boned woman in crêpe, with a mourning comb in her hair which curiously lengthened her long face—sat stiffly upon the sofa, her hands, conspicuous for their large knuckles, folded in her lap, her mouth and eyes drawn down, solemnly awaiting the opening of the coffin. Near the door stood a mulatto woman, evidently a servant in the house, with a timid bearing and an emaciated face pitifully sad and gentle. She was weeping silently, the corner of her calico apron lifted to her eyes, occasionally suppressing a long, quivering sob. Steavens walked over and stood beside her.

Feeble steps were heard on the stairs, and an old man, tall and frail, odorous of pipe smoke, with shaggy, unkept grey hair and a dingy beard, tobacco stained about the mouth, entered uncertainly. He went slowly up to the coffin and stood rolling a blue cotton handkerchief between his hands, seeming so pained and embarrassed by his wife's orgy of grief that he had no consciousness of anything else.

"There, there, Annie, dear, don't take on so," he quavered timidly, putting out a shaking hand and awkwardly patting her elbow. She turned with a cry, and sank upon his shoulder with such violence that he tottered a little. He did not even glance toward the coffin, but continued to look at her with a dull, frightened, appealing expression, as a spaniel looks at the whip. His sunken cheeks slowly reddened and burned with miserable shame. When his wife rushed from the room, her daughter strode after her with set lips. The servant stole up to the coffin, bent over it for a moment, and then slipped away to the kitchen, leaving Steavens, the lawyer and the father to themselves. The old man stood trembling and looking down at his dead son's face. The sculptor's splendid head seemed even more noble in its rigid stillness than in life. The dark hair had crept down upon the wide forehead; the face seemed strangely long, but in it there was not that beautiful and chaste repose which we expect to find in the faces of the dead. The brows were so drawn that there were two deep lines above the beaked nose, and the chin was thrust forward defiantly. It was as though the strain of life had been so sharp and bitter that death could not at once wholly relax the tension and smooth the countenance into perfect peace—as though he were still guarding something precious and holy, which might even yet be wrested from him.

The old man's lips were working under his stained beard. He turned to the lawyer with timid deference: "Phelps and the rest are comin' back to set up with Harve, ain't they?" he asked. "Thank 'ee, Jim, thank 'ee." He brushed the hair back gently from his son's forehead. "He was a good boy, Jim; always a good boy. He was ez gentle ez a child and the kindest of 'em all—only we didn't none of us ever onderstand him." The tears trickled slowly down his beard and dropped upon the sculptor's coat.

"Martin, Martin. Oh, Martin! come here," his wife wailed from the top of the stairs. The old man started timorously: "Yes, Annie, I'm coming." He turned away, hesitated, stood for a moment in miserable indecision; then reached back and patted the dead man's hair softly, and stumbled from the room.

"Poor old man, I didn't think he had any tears left. Seems as if his eyes would have gone dry long ago. At his age nothing cuts very deep," remarked the lawyer.

Something in his tone made Steavens glance up. While the mother had been in the room, the young man had scarcely seen anyone else; but now, from the moment he first glanced into Jim Laird's florid face and blood-shot eyes, he knew that he had found what he had been heartsick at not finding before—the feeling, the understanding, that must exist in some one, even here.

The man was red as his beard, with features swollen and blurred by dissipation, and a hot, blazing blue eye. His face was strained—that of a man who is controlling himself with difficulty—and he kept plucking at his beard with a sort of fierce resentment. Steavens, sitting by the window, watched him turn down the glaring lamp, still its jangling pendants with an angry gesture, and then stand with his hands locked behind him, staring down into the master's face. He could not help wondering what link there could have been between the porcelain vessel and so sooty a lump of potter's clay.

From the kitchen an uproar was sounding; when the dining-room door opened, the import of it was clear. The mother was abusing the maid for having forgotten to make the dressing for the chicken salad which had been prepared for the watchers. Steavens had never heard anything in the least like it; it was injured, emotional, dramatic abuse, unique and masterly in its excruciating cruelty, as violent and unrestrained as had been her grief of twenty minutes before. With a shudder of disgust the lawyer went into the dining-room and closed the door into the kitchen.

"Poor Roxy's getting it now," he remarked when he came back. "The Merricks took her out of the poor-house years ago; and if her loyalty would let her, I guess the poor old thing could tell tales that would curdle your blood. She's the mulatto woman who was standing in here a while ago, with her apron to her eyes. The old woman is a fury; there never was anybody like her for demonstrative piety and ingenious cruelty. She made Harvey's life a hell for him when he lived at home; he was so sick ashamed of it. I never could see how he kept himself so sweet."

"He was wonderful," said Steavens slowly, "wonderful; but until to-night I have never known how wonderful."

"That is the true and eternal wonder of it, anyway; that it can come even from such a dung heap as this," the lawyer cried, with a sweeping gesture which seemed to indicate much more than the four walls within which they stood.

"I think I'll see whether I can get a little air. The room is so close I am beginning to feel rather faint," murmured Steavens, struggling with one of the windows. The sash was stuck, however, and would not yield, so he sat down dejectedly and began pulling at his collar. The lawyer came over, loosened the sash with one blow of his red fist and sent the window up a few inches. Steavens thanked him, but the nausea which had been gradually climbing into his throat for the last half hour left him with but one desire— a desperate feeling that he must get away from this place with what was left of Harvey Merrick. Oh, he comprehended well enough now the quiet bitterness of the smile that he had seen so often on his master's lips!

He remembered that once, when Merrick returned from a visit home, he brought with him a singularly feeling and suggestive bas-relief of a thin, faded old woman, sitting and sewing something pinned to her knee; while a full-lipped, full-blooded little urchin, his trousers held up by a single gallus, stood beside her, impatiently twitching her gown to call her attention to a butterfly he had caught. Steavens, impressed by the tender and delicate modelling of the thin, tired face, had asked him if it were his mother. He remembered the dull flush that had burned up in the sculptor's face.

The lawyer was sitting in a rocking-chair beside the coffin, his head thrown back and his eyes closed. Steavens looked at him earnestly, puzzled at the line of the chin, and wondering why a man should conceal a feature of such distinction under that disfiguring shock of beard. Suddenly, as though he felt the young sculptor's keen glance, he opened his eyes.

"Was he always a good deal of an oyster?" he asked abruptly. "He was terribly shy as a boy."

"Yes, he was an oyster, since you put it so," rejoined Steavens. "Although he could be very fond of people, he always gave one the impression of being detached. He disliked violent emotion; he was reflective, and rather distrustful of himself—except, of course, as regarded his work. He was sure-footed enough there. He distrusted men pretty thoroughly and women even more, yet somehow without believing ill of them. He was determined, indeed, to believe the best, but he seemed afraid to investigate."

"A burnt dog dreads the fire," said the lawyer grimly, and closed his eyes.

Steavens went on and on, reconstructing that whole miserable boyhood. All this raw, biting ugliness had been the portion of the man whose tastes were refined beyond the limits of the reasonable—whose mind was an exhaustless gallery of beautiful impressions, and so sensitive that the mere shadow of a poplar leaf flickering against a sunny wall would be etched and held there forever. Surely, if ever a man had the magic word in his finger tips, it was Merrick. Whatever he touched, he revealed its holiest secret; liberated it from enchantment and restored it to its pristine loveliness, like the Arabian prince who fought the enchantress spell for spell. Upon whatever he had come in contact with, he had left a beautiful record of the experience—a sort of ethereal signature; a scent, a sound, a colour that was his own.

Steavens understood now the real tragedy of his master's life; neither love nor wine, as many had conjectured; but a blow which had fallen earlier and cut deeper than these could have done—a shame not his, and yet so unescapably his, to hide in his heart from his very boyhood. And without—

the frontier warfare; the yearning of a boy, cast ashore upon a desert of newness and ugliness and sordidness, for all that is chastened and old, and noble with traditions.

At eleven o'clock the tall, flat woman in black crêpe entered and announced that the watchers were arriving, and asked them "to step into the dining-room." As Steavens rose, the lawyer said dryly: "You go on—it'll be a good experience for you, doubtless; as for me, I'm not equal to that crowd to-night; I've had twenty years of them."

As Steavens closed the door after him he glanced back at the lawyer, sitting by the coffin in the dim light, with his chin resting on his hand.

The same misty group that had stood before the door of the express car shuffled into the dining-room. In the light of the kerosene lamp they separated and became individuals. The minister, a pale, feeble-looking man with white hair and blond chin-whiskers, took his seat beside a small side table and placed his Bible upon it. The Grand Army man sat down behind the stove and tilted his chair back comfortably against the wall, fishing his quill toothpick from his waistcoat pocket. The two bankers, Phelps and Elder, sat off in a corner behind the dinner-table, where they could finish their discussion of the new usury law and its effect on chattel security loans. The real estate agent, an old man with a smiling, hypocritical face, soon joined them. The coal and lumber dealer and the cattle shipper sat on opposite sides of the hard coal-burner, their feet on the nickel-work. Steavens took a book from his pocket and began to read. The talk around him ranged through various topics of local interest while the house was quieting down. When it was clear that the members of the family were in bed, the Grand Army man hitched his shoulders and, untangling his long legs, caught his heels on the rounds of his chair.

"S'pose there'll be a will, Phelps?" he queried in his weak falsetto.

The banker laughed disagreeably and began trimming his nails with a pearl-handled pocket-knife.

"There'll scarcely be any need for one, will there?" he queried in his turn.

The restless Grand Army man shifted his position again, getting his knees still nearer his chin. "Why, the ole man says Harve's done right well lately," he chirped.

The other banker spoke up. "I reckon he means by that Harve ain't asked him to mortgage any more farms lately, so as he could go on with his education."

"Seems like my mind don't reach back to a time when Harve wasn't bein' edycated," tittered the Grand Army man.

There was a general chuckle. The minister took out his handkerchief and blew his nose sonorously. Banker Phelps closed his knife with a snap. "It's too bad the old man's sons didn't turn out better," he remarked with reflective authority. "They never hung together. He spent money enough on Harve to stock a dozen cattle-farms and he might as well have poured it into Sand Creek. If Harve had stayed at home and helped nurse what little they had, and gone into stock on the old man's bottom farm, they might all have been well fixed. But the old man had to trust everything to tenants and was cheated right and left."

"Harve never could have handled stock none," interposed the cattle-man. "He hadn't it in him to be sharp. Do you remember when he bought Sander's mules for eight-year-olds, when everybody in town knew that Sander's father-in-law give 'em to his wife for a wedding present eighteen years before, an' they was full-grown mules then."

Everyone chuckled, and the Grand Army man rubbed his knees with a spasm of childish delight.

"Harve never was much account for anything practical, and he shore was never fond of work," began the coal and lumber dealer. "I mind the last time he was home; the day he left, when the old man was out to the barn helpin' his hand hitch up to take Harve to the train, and Cal Moots was patchin' up the fence, Harve, he come out on the step and sings out, in his lady-like voice: 'Cal Moots, Cal Moots! please come cord my trunk.'"

"That's Harve for you," approved the Grand Army man gleefully. "I kin hear him howlin' yet when he was a big feller in long pants and his mother used to whale him with a rawhide in the barn for lettin' the cows git foun-dered in the cornfield when he was drivin' 'em home from pasture. He killed a cow of mine that-a-way onct—a pure Jersey and the best milker I had, an' the ole man had to put up for her. Harve, he was watchin' the sun set acrost the marshes when the anamile got away; he argued that sunset was oncommon fine."

"Where the old man made his mistake was in sending the boy East to school," said Phelps, stroking his goatee and speaking in a deliberate, judi-cial tone. "There was where he got his head full of trapesing to Paris and all such folly. What Harve needed, of all people, was a course in some first-class Kansas City business college."

The letters were swimming before Steavens's eyes. Was it possible that these men did not understand, that the palm on the coffin meant nothing to them? The very name of their town would have remained forever buried in the postal guide had it not been now and again mentioned in the world in connection with Harvey Merrick's. He remembered what his master had said to him on the day of his death, after the congestion of both lungs had shut off any probability of recovery, and the sculptor had asked his pupil to send his body home. "It's not a pleasant place to be lying while the world is moving and doing and bettering," he had said with a feeble smile, "but it rather seems as though we ought to go back to the place we came from in the end. The townspeople will come in for a look at me; and after they have had their say I shan't have much to fear from the judgment of God. The wings of the Victory, in there"—with a weak gesture toward his studio— "will not shelter me."

The cattleman took up the comment. "Forty's young for a Merrick to cash in; they usually hang on pretty well. Probably he helped it along with whisky."

"His mother's people were not long lived, and Harvey never had a robust constitution," said the minister mildly. He would have liked to say more. He had been the boy's Sunday-school teacher, and had been fond of him; but he felt that he was not in a position to speak. His own sons had turned out badly, and it was not a year since one of them had made his last trip home in the express car, shot in a gambling-house in the Black Hills.

"Nevertheless, there is no disputin' that Harve frequently looked upon the wine when it was red, also variegated, and it shore made an oncommon fool of him," moralized the cattleman.

Just then the door leading into the parlour rattled loudly, and everyone started involuntarily, looking relieved when only Jim Laird came out. His red face was convulsed with anger, and the Grand Army man ducked his head when he saw the spark in his blue, blood-shot eye. They were all afraid of Jim; he was a drunkard, but he could twist the law to suit his client's needs as no other man in all western Kansas could do; and there were many who tried. The lawyer closed the door gently behind him, leaned back against it and folded his arms, cocking his head a little to one side. When he assumed this attitude in the court-room, ears were always pricked up, as it usually foretold a flood of withering sarcasm.

"I've been with you gentlemen before," he began in a dry, even tone, "when you've sat by the coffins of boys born and raised in this town; and, if I remember rightly, you were never any too well satisfied when you checked them up. What's the matter, anyhow? Why is it that reputable young men are as scarce as millionaires in Sand City? It might almost seem to a stranger that there was some way something the matter with your progressive town. Why did Ruben Sayer, the brightest young lawyer you ever turned out, after he had come home from the university as straight as a die, take to drinking and forge a check and shoot himself? Why did Bill Merrit's son die of the shakes in a saloon in Omaha? Why was Mr. Thomas's son, here, shot in a gambling-house? Why did young Adams burn his mill to beat the insurance companies and go to the pen?"

The lawyer paused and unfolded his arms, laying one clenched fist quietly on the table. "I'll tell you why. Because you drummed nothing but money and knavery into their ears from the time they wore knickerbockers; because you carped away at them as you've been carping here to-night, holding our friends Phelps and Elder up to them for their models, as our grandfathers held up George Washington and John Adams. But the boys, worse luck, were young, and raw at the business you put them to; and how could they match coppers with such artists as Phelps and Elder? You wanted them to be successful rascals; they were only unsuccessful ones—that's all the difference. There was only one boy ever raised in this borderland between ruffianism and civilization, who didn't come to grief, and you hated Harvey Merrick more for winning out than you hated all the other boys who got under the wheels. Lord, Lord, how you did hate him! Phelps, here, is fond of saying that he could buy and sell us all out any time he's a mind to; but he knew Harve wouldn't have given a tinker's damn for his bank and all his cattle-farms put together; and a lack of appreciation, that way, goes hard with Phelps.

"Old Nimrod, here, thinks Harve drank too much; and this from such as Nimrod and me!

"Brother Elder says Harve was too free with the old man's money— fell short in filial consideration, maybe. Well, we can all remember the very tone in which brother Elder swore his own father was a liar, in the county court; and we all know that the old man came out of that partnership with his son as bare as a sheared lamb. But maybe I'm getting personal, and I'd better be driving ahead at what I want to say."

The lawyer paused a moment, squared his heavy shoulders, and went on: "Harvey Merrick and I went to school together, back East. We were dead in earnest, and we wanted you all to be proud of us some day. We meant to be great men. Even I, and I haven't lost my sense of humour, gentlemen, I meant to be a great man. I came back here to practise, and I found you didn't in the least want me to be a great man. You wanted me to be a shrewd lawyer—oh, yes! Our veteran here wanted me to get him an increase of pension, because he had dyspepsia; Phelps wanted a new county survey that would put the widow Wilson's little bottom farm inside his south line; Elder wanted to lend money at 5 per cent a month, and get it collected; old Stark here wanted to wheedle old women up in Vermont into investing their annuities in real estate mortgages that are not worth the paper they are written on. Oh, you needed me hard enough, and you'll go on needing me; and that's why I'm not afraid to plug the truth home to you this once.

"Well, I came back here and became the damned shyster you wanted me to be. You pretend to have some sort of respect for me; and yet you'll stand up and throw mud at Harvey Merrick, whose soul you couldn't dirty and whose hands you couldn't tie. Oh, you're a discriminating lot of Christians! There have been times when the sight of Harvey's name in some Eastern paper has made me hang my head like a whipped dog; and, again, times when I liked to think of him off there in the world, away from all this hog-wallow, doing his great work and climbing the big, clean up-grade he'd set for himself.

"And we? Now that we've fought and lied and sweated and stolen, and hated as only the disappointed strugglers in a bitter, dead little Western town know how to do, what have we got to show for it? Harvey Merrick wouldn't have given one sunset over your marshes for all you've got put together, and you know it. It's not for me to say why, in the inscrutable wisdom of God, a genius should ever have been called from this place of hatred and bitter waters; but I want this Boston man to know that the drivel he's been hearing here to-night is the only tribute any truly great man could ever have from such a lot of sick, side-tracked, burnt-dog, land-poor sharks as the here-present financiers of Sand City—upon which town may God have mercy!"

The lawyer thrust out his hand to Steavens as he passed him, caught up his overcoat in the hall, and had left the house before the Grand Army man had had time to lift his ducked head and crane his long neck about at his fellows.

Next day Jim Laird was drunk and unable to attend the funeral services. Steavens called twice at his office, but was compelled to start East without seeing him. He had a presentiment that he would hear from him again, and left his address on the lawyer's table; but if Laird found it, he never acknowledged it. The thing in him that Harvey Merrick had loved must have gone underground with Harvey Merrick's coffin; for it never spoke again, and Jim got the cold he died of driving across the Colorado mountains to defend one of Phelps's sons who had got into trouble out there by cutting government timber.

——

The Enchanted Bluff

W E HAD our swim before sundown, and while we were cooking our supper the oblique rays of light made a dazzling glare
on the white sand about us. The translucent red ball itself sank
behind the brown stretches of corn field as we sat down to eat, and the
warm layer of air that had rested over the water and our clean sand bar grew
fresher and smelled of the rank ironweed and sunflowers growing on the
flatter shore. The river was brown and sluggish, like any other of the half-
dozen streams that water the Nebraska corn lands. On one shore was an
irregular line of bald clay bluffs where a few scrub oaks with thick trunks
and flat, twisted tops threw light shadows on the long grass. The western
shore was low and level, with corn fields that stretched to the skyline, and
all along the water's edge were little sandy coves and beaches where slim
cottonwoods and willow saplings flickered.

The turbulence of the river in springtime discouraged milling, and, beyond keeping the old red bridge in repair, the busy farmers did not concern
themselves with the stream; so the Sandtown boys were left in undisputed
possession. In the autumn we hunted quail through the miles of stubble
and fodder land along the flat shore, and, after the winter skating season
was over and the ice had gone out, the spring freshets and flooded bottoms
gave us our great excitement of the year. The channel was never the same
for two successive seasons. Every spring the swollen stream undermined a
bluff to the east, or bit out a few acres of corn field to the west and whirled
the soil away to deposit it in spumy mud banks somewhere else. When the
water fell low in midsummer, new sand bars were thus exposed to dry and
whiten in the August sun. Sometimes these were banked so firmly that the
fury of the next freshet failed to unseat them; the little willow seedlings
emerged triumphantly from the yellow froth, broke into spring leaf, shot
up into summer growth, and with their mesh of roots bound together the

First published in *Harper's* 118 (April 1909): 774–78, 780–81. Reprinted from Willa
Cather, *Collected Short Fiction, 1892–1912* (Lincoln: University of Nebraska Press, 1965),
pp. 69–77. Copyright © 1965, 1970 by the University of Nebraska Press.

moist sand beneath them against the batterings of another April. Here and there a cottonwood soon glittered among them, quivering in the low current of air that, even on breathless days when the dust hung like smoke above the wagon road, trembled along the face of the water.

It was on such an island, in the third summer of its yellow green, that we built our watch fire; not in the thicket of dancing willow wands, but on the level terrace of fine sand which had been added that spring; a little new bit of world, beautifully ridged with ripple marks, and strewn with the tiny skeletons of turtles and fish, all as white and dry as if they had been expertly cured. We had been careful not to mar the freshness of the place, although we often swam to it on summer evenings and lay on the sand to rest.

This was our last watch fire of the year, and there were reasons why I should remember it better than any of the others. Next week the other boys were to file back to their old places in the Sandtown High School, but I was to go up to the Divide to teach my first country school in the Norwegian district. I was already homesick at the thought of quitting the boys with whom I had always played; of leaving the river, and going up into a windy plain that was all windmills and corn fields and big pastures; where there was nothing wilful or unmanageable in the landscape, no new islands, and no chance of unfamiliar birds—such as often followed the watercourses.

Other boys came and went and used the river for fishing or skating, but we six were sworn to the spirit of the stream, and we were friends mainly because of the river. There were the two Hassler boys, Fritz and Otto, sons of the little German tailor. They were the youngest of us; ragged boys of ten and twelve, with sunburned hair, weather-stained faces, and pale blue eyes. Otto, the elder, was the best mathematician in school, and clever at his books, but he always dropped out in the spring term as if the river could not get on without him. He and Fritz caught the fat, horned catfish and sold them about the town, and they lived so much in the water that they were as brown and sandy as the river itself.

There was Percy Pound, a fat, freckled boy with chubby cheeks, who took half a dozen boys' story-papers and was always being kept in for reading detective stories behind his desk. There was Tip Smith, destined by his freckles and red hair to be the buffoon in all our games, though he walked like a timid little old man and had a funny, cracked laugh. Tip worked hard in his father's grocery store every afternoon, and swept it out before school in the morning. Even his recreations were laborious. He collected cigarette cards and tin tobacco-tags indefatigably, and would sit for hours humped up over a snarling little scroll-saw which he kept in his attic. His dearest possessions were some little pill bottles that purported to contain grains of wheat from the Holy Land, water from the Jordan and the Dead Sea, and earth from the Mount of Olives. His father had brought these dull things from a Baptist missionary who peddled them, and Tip seemed to derive great satisfaction from their remote origin.

The tall boy was Arthur Adams. He had fine hazel eyes that were almost too reflective and sympathetic for a boy, and such a pleasant voice that we all loved to hear him read aloud. Even when he had to read poetry aloud at school, no one ever thought of laughing. To be sure, he was not at school very much of the time. He was seventeen and should have finished the High School the year before, but he was always off somewhere with his gun. Arthur's mother was dead, and his father, who was feverishly absorbed in promoting schemes, wanted to send the boy away to school and get him off his hands; but Arthur always begged off for another year and promised to study. I remember him as a tall, brown boy with an intelligent face, always lounging among a lot of us little fellows, laughing at us oftener than with us, but such a soft, satisfied laugh that we felt rather flattered when we provoked it. In after-years people said that Arthur had been given to evil ways even as a lad, and it is true that we often saw him with the gambler's sons and with old Spanish Fanny's boy, but if he learned anything ugly in their company he never betrayed it to us. We would have followed Arthur anywhere, and I am bound to say that he led us into no worse places than the cattail marshes and the stubble fields. These, then, were the boys who camped with me that summer night upon the sand bar.

After we finished our supper we beat the willow thicket for driftwood. By the time we had collected enough, night had fallen, and the pungent, weedy smell from the shore increased with the coolness. We threw ourselves down about the fire and made another futile effort to show Percy Pound the Little Dipper. We had tried it often before, but he could never be got past the big one.

"You see those three big stars just below the handle, with the bright one in the middle?" said Otto Hassler; "that's Orion's belt, and the bright one is the clasp." I crawled behind Otto's shoulder and sighted up his arm to the star that seemed perched upon the tip of his steady forefinger. The Hassler boys did seine-fishing at night, and they knew a good many stars.

Percy gave up the Little Dipper and lay back on the sand, his hands clasped under his head. "I can see the North Star," he announced, contentedly, pointing toward it with his big toe. "Anyone might get lost and need to know that."

We all looked up at it.

"How do you suppose Columbus felt when his compass didn't point north any more?" Tip asked.

Otto shook his head. "My father says that there was another North Star once, and that maybe this one won't last always. I wonder what would happen to us down here if anything went wrong with it?"

Arthur chuckled. "I wouldn't worry, Ott. Nothing's apt to happen to it in your time. Look at the Milky Way! There must be lots of good dead Indians."

We lay back and looked, meditating, at the dark cover of the world. The gurgle of the water had become heavier. We had often noticed a mutinous, complaining note in it at night, quite different from its cheerful daytime chuckle, and seeming like the voice of a much deeper and more powerful stream. Our water had always these two moods: the one of sunny complaisance, the other of inconsolable, passionate regret.

"Queer how the stars are all in sort of diagrams," remarked Otto. "You could do most any proposition in geometry with 'em. They always look as if they meant something. Some folks say everybody's fortune is all written out in the stars, don't they?"

"They believe so in the old country," Fritz affirmed.

But Arthur only laughed at him. "You're thinking of Napoleon, Fritzey. He had a star that went out when he began to lose battles. I guess the stars don't keep any close tally on Sandtown folks."

We were speculating on how many times we could count a hundred before the evening star went down behind the corn fields, when someone cried, "There comes the moon, and it's as big as a cart wheel!"

We all jumped up to greet it as it swam over the bluffs behind us. It came up like a galleon in full sail; an enormous, barbaric thing, red as an angry heathen god.

"When the moon came up red like that, the Aztecs used to sacrifice their prisoners on the temple top," Percy announced.

"Go on, Perce. You got that out of *Golden Days*. Do you believe that, Arthur?" I appealed.

Arthur answered, quite seriously: "Like as not. The moon was one of their gods. When my father was in Mexico City he saw the stone where they used to sacrifice their prisoners."

As we dropped down by the fire again some one asked whether the Mound-Builders were older than the Aztecs. When we once got upon the Mound-Builders we never willingly got away from them, and we were still conjecturing when we heard a loud splash in the water.

"Must have been a big cat jumping," said Fritz. "They do sometimes. They must see bugs in the dark. Look what a track the moon makes!"

There was a long, silvery streak on the water, and where the current fretted over a big log it boiled up like gold pieces.

"Suppose there ever *was* any gold hid away in this old river?" Fritz asked. He lay like a little brown Indian, close to the fire, his chin on his hand and his bare feet in the air. His brother laughed at him, but Arthur took his suggestion seriously.

"Some of the Spaniards thought there was gold up here somewhere. Seven cities chuck full of gold, they had it, and Coronado and his men came up to hunt it. The Spaniards were all over this country once."

Percy looked interested. "Was that before the Mormons went through?" We all laughed at this.

"Long enough before. Before the Pilgrim Fathers, Perce. Maybe they came along this very river. They always followed the watercourses."

"I wonder where this river really does begin?" Tip mused. That was an old and a favorite mystery which the map did not clearly explain. On the map the little black line stopped somewhere in western Kansas; but since rivers generally rose in mountains, it was only reasonable to suppose that ours came from the Rockies. Its destination, we knew, was the Missouri, and the Hassler boys always maintained that we could embark at Sandtown in floodtime, follow our noses, and eventually arrive at New Orleans. Now they took up their old argument. "If us boys had grit enough to try it, it wouldn't take no time to get to Kansas City and St. Joe."

We began to talk about the places we wanted to go to. The Hassler boys wanted to see the stockyards in Kansas City, and Percy wanted to see a big store in Chicago. Arthur was interlocutor and did not betray himself.

"Now it's your turn, Tip."

Tip rolled over on his elbow and poked the fire, and his eyes looked shyly out of his queer, tight little face. "My place is awful far away. My Uncle Bill told me about it."

Tip's Uncle Bill was a wanderer, bitten with mining fever, who had drifted into Sandtown with a broken arm, and when it was well had drifted out again.

"Where is it?"

"Aw, it's down in New Mexico somewheres. There aren't no railroads or anything. You have to go on mules, and you run out of water before you get there and have to drink canned tomatoes."

"Well, go on, kid. What's it like when you do get there?"

Tip sat up and excitedly began his story.

"There's a big red rock there that goes right up out of the sand for about nine hundred feet. The country's flat all around it, and this here rock goes up all by itself, like a monument. They call it the Enchanted Bluff down there, because no white man has ever been on top of it.[3] The sides are smooth rock, and straight up, like a wall. The Indians say that hundreds of years ago, before the Spaniards came, there was a village away up there in the air. The tribe that lived there had some sort of steps, made out of wood and bark, hung down over the face of the bluff, and the braves went down to hunt and carried water up in big jars swung on their backs. They kept a big supply of water and dried meat up there, and never went down except to hunt. They were a peaceful tribe that made cloth and pottery, and they went up there to get out of the wars. You see, they could pick off any war party that tried to get up their little steps. The Indians say they were a handsome people, and they had some sort of queer religion. Uncle Bill thinks they were Cliff-Dwellers who had got into trouble and left home. They weren't fighters, anyhow.

"One time the braves were down hunting and an awful storm came up— a kind of waterspout—and when they got back to their rock they found their little staircase had been all broken to pieces, and only a few steps were left hanging away up in the air. While they were camped at the foot of the rock, wondering what to do, a war party from the north came along and massacred 'em to a man, with all the old folks and women looking on from the rock. Then the war party went on south and left the village to get down the best way they could. Of course they never got down. They starved to death up there, and when the war party came back on their way north, they could hear the children crying from the edge of the bluff where they had crawled out, but they didn't see a sign of a grown Indian, and nobody has ever been up there since."

We exclaimed at this dolorous legend and sat up.

"There couldn't have been many people up there," Percy demurred. "How big is the top, Tip?"

"Oh, pretty big. Big enough so that the rock doesn't look nearly as tall as it is. The top's bigger than the base. The bluff is sort of worn away for several hundred feet up. That's one reason it's so hard to climb."

I asked how the Indians got up, in the first place.

---

3. Fifty miles west of Albuquerque is the unique mesa-top pueblo of Ácoma, the Sky City. According to the legend, the ancient people had lived on the Enchanted Mesa, three miles away, until the tragedy that Cather recounts here. In the legend, there were survivors who reestablished themselves at Sky City.

"Nobody knows how they got up or when. A hunting party came along once and saw that there was a town up there, and that was all."

Otto rubbed his chin and looked thoughtful. "Of course there must be some way to get up there. Couldn't people get a rope over someway and pull a ladder up?"

Tip's little eyes were shining with excitement. "I know a way. Me and Uncle Bill talked it all over. There's a kind of rocket that would take a rope over—life-savers use 'em—and then you could hoist a rope ladder and peg it down at the bottom and make it tight with guy ropes on the other side. I'm going to climb that there bluff, and I've got it all planned out."

Fritz asked what he expected to find when he got up there.

"Bones, maybe, or the ruins of their town, or pottery, or some of their idols. There might be 'most anything up there. Anyhow, I want to see."

"Sure nobody else has been up there, Tip?" Arthur asked.

"Dead sure. Hardly anybody ever goes down there. Some hunters tried to cut steps in the rock once, but they didn't get higher than a man can reach. The Bluff's all red granite, and Uncle Bill thinks it's a boulder the glaciers left. It's a queer place, anyhow. Nothing but cactus and desert for hundreds of miles, and yet right under the Bluff there's good water and plenty of grass. That's why the bison used to go down there."

Suddenly we heard a scream above our fire, and jumped up to see a dark, slim bird floating southward far above us—a whooping crane, we knew by her cry and her long neck. We ran to the edge of the island, hoping we might see her alight, but she wavered southward along the rivercourse until we lost her. The Hassler boys declared that by the look of the heavens it must be after midnight, so we threw more wood on our fire, put on our jackets, and curled down in the warm sand. Several of us pretended to doze, but I fancy we were really thinking about Tip's Bluff and the extinct people. Over in the wood the ring doves were calling mournfully to one another, and once we heard a dog bark, far away. "Somebody getting into old Tommy's melon patch," Fritz murmured sleepily, but nobody answered him. By and by Percy spoke out of the shadows.

"Say, Tip, when you go down there will you take me with you?"

"Maybe."

"Suppose one of us beats you down there, Tip?"

"Whoever gets to the Bluff first has got to promise to tell the rest of us exactly what he finds," remarked one of the Hassler boys, and to this we all readily assented.

Somewhat reassured, I dropped to sleep. I must have dreamed about a race for the Bluff, for I awoke in a kind of fear that other people were getting ahead of me and that I was losing my chance. I sat up in my damp clothes and looked at the other boys, who lay tumbled in uneasy attitudes about the dead fire. It was still dark, but the sky was blue with the last wonderful azure of night. The stars glistened like crystal globes, and trembled as if they shone through a depth of clear water. Even as I watched, they began to pale and the sky brightened. Day came suddenly, almost instantaneously. I turned for another look at the blue night, and it was gone. Everywhere the birds began to call, and all manner of little insects began to chirp and hop about in the willows. A breeze sprang up from the west and brought the heavy smell of ripened corn. The boys rolled over and shook themselves. We stripped and plunged into the river just as the sun came up over the windy bluffs.

When I came home to Sandtown at Christmas time, we skated out to our island and talked over the whole project of the Enchanted Bluff, renewing our resolution to find it.

* * *

Although that was twenty years ago, none of us have ever climbed the Enchanted Bluff. Percy Pound is a stockbroker in Kansas City and will go nowhere that his red touring car cannot carry him. Otto Hassler went on the railroad and lost his foot braking; after which he and Fritz succeeded their father as the town tailors.

Arthur sat about the sleepy little town all his life—he died before he was twenty-five. The last time I saw him, when I was home on one of my college vacations, he was sitting in a steamer chair under a cottonwood tree in the little yard behind one of the two Sandtown saloons. He was very untidy and his hand was not steady, but when he rose, unabashed, to greet me, his eyes were as clear and warm as ever. When I had talked with him for an hour and heard him laugh again, I wondered how it was that when Nature had taken such pains with a man, from his hands to the arch of his long foot, she had ever lost him in Sandtown. He joked about Tip Smith's Bluff, and declared he was going down there just as soon as the weather got cooler; he thought the Grand Canyon might be worth while, too.

I was perfectly sure when I left him that he would never get beyond the high plank fence and the comfortable shade of the cottonwood. And, indeed, it was under that very tree that he died one summer morning.

Tip Smith still talks about going to New Mexico. He married a slatternly, unthrifty country girl, has been much tied to a perambulator, and has grown stooped and gray from irregular meals and broken sleep. But the worst of his difficulties are now over, and he has, as he says, come into easy water. When I was last in Sandtown I walked home with him late one moonlight night, after he had balanced his cash and shut up his store. We took the long way around and sat down on the schoolhouse steps, and between us we quite revived the romance of the lone red rock and the extinct people. Tip insists that he still means to go down there, but he thinks now he will wait until his boy Bert is old enough to go with him. Bert has been let into the story, and thinks of nothing but the Enchanted Bluff.

Stewart Edward White
1873-1946

▬

1901: *The Westerners*
1907: *Arizona Nights*
1932: *The Long Rifle*
1933: *Ranchero*
1934: *Folded Hills*
1942: *Stampede*
1947: *The Saga of Andy Burnett*

▬

S TEWART EDWARD WHITE *wrote more than sixty works in a half-dozen genres. He preferred writing history and historical fiction, but he also published nature writing, personal essays, romantic fiction, and philosophy. Probably his best-known work is* The Blazed Trail *(1902), an adventure novel dramatizing corruption and graft in the logging industry.*

White is an example of Theodore Roosevelt's "new breed" of American writers. Roosevelt encouraged White, as he had encouraged Owen Wister and Emerson Hough, to record the stories of the American Heroes, men of high ideals and physical courage. He felt that such heroic tales should be written by men who had led admirable and adventurous lives themselves.

White graduated from the University of Michigan and was admitted to the Columbia University law school, where his writing professor encouraged him to submit a story for publication. When it was accepted, White was launched on the career he had always wanted to follow. He knew the meaning of hard manual labor too, having worked as a lumberjack, a forester, and a cowboy. Above all, White was adventurous; from boyhood he was an avid explorer of new places, and he was an accomplished outdoorsman. His long sojourns took him from Michigan's northern woods to Arizona and from the California Sierra Nevada to Kenya. As a writer, White was always dedicated to authenticity. At the age of eleven he began the lifelong habit of keeping a daily journal in which he wrote down details of places he saw, historical information, descriptions of characters, local anecdotes, and notes on dialect. Later on, he supplemented these careful journals with extensive research.

The Saga of Andy Burnett is a series of historical novels that trace Burnett's heritage, his initiation into the West, and finally his development as a settler in California. First in the series is a romanticized adventure biography for boys, Daniel Boone, Wilderness Scout *(1922). In White's sequel,* The Long Rifle, *Boone gives his famed rifle to one of his scouts; in time, the weapon is handed down to the scout's grandson, Andy Burnett.*

Andy travels into the West with the mountain men, who teach him how to be an accomplished backwoodsman. But after witnessing the death of a mountain man and some friendly Blackfeet at the 1832 rendezvous, Andy realizes that the trappers' way of life is coming to an end, and he leaves the Rocky Mountains. The next novel, Ranchero, *presents Burnett as a "Californio" who marries into a wealthy ranching family. As Don Andres in the next novel,* Folded Hills, *Burnett sees his son growing up in the middle of California's turbulent prestatehood era. This leads into yet another sequel,* Stampede. *Here the son is the central figure, but it is Don Andres's ingenuity that saves the historic ranch from squatters.*

Throughout this long series, Andy Burnett is a consistent and plausible character; he also clearly represents the western heritage. Just as he had once put his faith in Boone's long rifle, he learns to trust his own courage, honesty, sensitivity, and resourcefulness, traits that he passes on to his son. It was the mountain men who first recognized those characteristics in him, frontier traits that were being "lifted by the sweep of greater destinies."

—

The Mountain Man

ANDY traveled the back roads through the forests and by the little backwoods farms. He did so partly to avoid possible inquiry and pursuit; partly because he was only nineteen. With the long Kentucky rifle across his shoulder, his bundle at his back, the powder horn just nudging his elbow, the tomahawk and knife touching his hip, he felt somehow romantic as though he had set the clock back fifty years. The spring was swelling to maturity and the tonic of her intoxication was strong. Andy

From Stewart Edward White, *The Long Rifle* (Garden City, N.Y.: Doubleday, 1932), 73–92.

stopped of nights at one or another of the rare farmhouses. He started out afoot betimes of each morning. On most days he managed to hitch-hike a good proportion of the way on farm wagons or slower-moving ox carts. At noons he stopped to eat his lunch, furnished him by his last night's hostess. Before resuming his journey after the meal, he drew the knife from its sheath at his belt and practised throwing it at a selected mark on a tree. He cast it with a full round sweep of the arm. The long blade, turning slowly, nevertheless invariably struck point-in. Andrew did this practice studiously, pacing off odd distances, considering thoughtfully the result of each throw. The same care he bestowed on his rifle practice, for invariably each day he fired five shots. Then, having cleaned the piece, he resumed his journey. All this he performed with an intense gravity of purpose, a gravity underscored, as it were, to the beholder, by the cast of his dark complexion and the straight heavy line of his eyebrows. His earnestness managed to impart indeed quite an Indian-behind-every-tree illusion to the woods, an illusion only partly dissipated by the tootling of the stagecoach horn on the great highway a half-mile distant, or the peaceful blatting of the sheep in pasture just beyond the forest's screen. Certainly Andy himself, running away to the wild West, entered whole-heartedly into his game.

Therefore it was that, turning at the sound of a chuckle behind him, he experienced no immediate shock of surprise at the figure he beheld. Only after a moment or so did he come to a realization of its extreme and theatrical incongruity in this peaceful and ordered land.

He saw a tall, slender, and wiry man of uncertain age. His face was clean-shaven, lean, leathery, and brown; his deep-set eyes were blue and twinkling with humor. His head, innocent of hat, was bound about by a blue kerchief from beneath which escaped long hair. A plain cotton shirt was confined at the waist by a buckskin girdle from which depended a variety of little bags. Another belt, crossing his left shoulder supported, under his right arm, a powder horn and shot pouch. He wore no breeches. In their stead his legs were covered by leggings cut away at the seat, so that as he moved Andy saw the breech clout and the leathery, chapped, browned hard skin of the man's buttocks. The leggings themselves were tied at the knee, and were ornamented by many fringes, embroideries in beads, tufts of hair and feathers dyed in brilliant colors. His feet were encased in decorated moccasins. He carried across the crook of his left arm a rifle not unlike Andy's own except that it was somewhat shorter and heavier.

Andrew stared at this strange figure, taking in these many details, his mind separating it slowly from the congruity of his play-acting, where it belonged, to the unbelievable actuality of the tamed countryside from which it should have vanished generations agone.

The man chuckled again, evidently relishing Andy's bewilderment.

"Look yore fill, lad, I'm used to it," said he. "Lord love you, an you keep on far enough on the road you travel you'll see many a more of mountain men besides Joe Crane."

He seated himself on a fallen tree, laid aside his rifle, slipped from beneath his belt a pipe of stone with a long reed stem, which he proceeded leisurely to stuff with tobacco. His form was relaxed in every muscle; but his blue eyes were never still. Even as he drawled on they flitted here and there about him. Not for an instant did they seem to rest, yet somehow Andy felt that their sharp scrutiny was seizing upon every item of his own appearance and equipment; and that behind them a shrewd brain was estimating him.

"Come, lad, sit down," advised the stranger, puffing forth a cloud of smoke. He reached out a long arm to pluck Andy's knife from the tree into which the last cast had buried its point.

"That is a proper blade." He balanced it appraisingly. "And you cast it not badly. But you lose yore force."

He flickered his arm. The knife flashed through the air, to bury itself half-hilt deep in the soft pine.

"See!" commented the stranger. " 'Tis a trick; I'll larn ye."

He reached for Andy's rifle, which he examined as critically.

"A proper piece too," he said, "properly made and kept. Though a leetle on the light side for buffalo. Still, it's said its say in its day, I'll warrant, and will say it again. Give me a good flint gun. Your percussion arms are all right,"—he held up a didactic forefinger—"and you'll find a-many to urge you to a change. They'll tell you that in wet weather they are more sartin, and that the high wind of the prairies will blow away your flint gun's priming. That may be so for a *mangeur de lard* but not for one who looks to his priming as an old *hivernant* [1] should. And mark you this, lad; with these newfangled cap guns, when you run out of caps you're done. You ain't got no gun. She ain't even a good club. But with a flint gun, as long as they's rocks, you can chip you off a new flint. And thar you be!" he ended triumphantly. His scrutiny fell upon the patch box plate and its inscription. His eye narrowed, and he looked up suddenly at Andy, but he said nothing.

---

1. A "*hivernant*" (from the French *hiver,* meaning winter) is a mountain man who spends the winter in the mountains. A "*mangeur de lard*" (literally "bacon-eater") is a man who is accustomed to "soft" living.

Andy's scattered wits focused at last.

"Who are you?" he blurted out. "What are you doing here?"

The stranger's face darkened momentarily; then cleared. He threw back his head and laughed.

"I nearly forgot," said he, "and came nigh to anger. You are a likely lad, but you have much to larn. When you come to the prairie do not ask a man his name or his business. That is not taken kindly."

"I'm sorry," stammered Andy. "I meant no harm."

"No harm is done," conceded the stranger handsomely, "and mebbe you are not to blame. 'Tis a matter of upbringing mebbe. But look yere, I didn't ask yo' nothin' about yoreself, though you carry here Boone's rifle, as the mark on it states; and that is sure enough to make a man curious!" He glanced down at himself humorously. "I'd as soon tell you of myself, lad. I am from Washington, jist now, whar I've been to speak to the President of sartin things which have to do with the fur. It was decided that someone must speak. So I have been; and now I return."

"You have been to Washington—you have seen Mr. Monroe—" Andy broke off, embarrassed that his bewilderment had carried him so far.

But the mountain man read him perfectly.

"In this guise?" He chuckled again. "Even so. I might well, thinks you, put on the foofaraw of proper dress, but, thinks I: Joe Crane, never in all your life have you acted like anybody but yoreself. Do not make yoreself out a fool by trying to ape other folks now. Joe Crane you have always been, and Joe Crane you still remain. Go ahead, Joe Crane!"

"I see," murmured Andy. "And was your—did you succeed in your mission, Mr. Crane?"

"I know now what I only suspicioned afore," replied the mountain man cryptically. "And now that you have shown me the way to the manners of this country, I'll make bold myself. How came ye by Dan'l Boone's rifle, and whither go ye with it?"

"It was my grandfather's, given him by Colonel Boone himself."

"Your name?" enquired Crane quickly.

"Andrew Burnett."

"Wagh! Then you're Gail Burnett's son—no, his grandson?"

"Yes. Did you know him?"

"I hear'n tell of him. Old Dan'l set store by him."

"You knew Boone?"

"Not to say knew him. No. He was afore my time. But I met up with him one time on the Platte." Under Andy's breathless urging he elaborated. it was at the time of Boone's great age, when he was living on the farm of

Nathan, his son. He had heard trappers' tales of the salt mountains, lakes, and ponds, and he had made up his mind to see them. So, disregarding the family's protests, he set out.

"I was comin' in to St. Louey with my furs and 'possibles,'" said Crane, "and I run across him on the Platte. He had jist one Injin with him. He was a good Injin, an Osage. I talked with him. He told me he had orders to bring Dan'l back dead or alive before snowfall, and he was a-goin' to do it. The old Colonel was risin' on eighty-four years but he was as straight as an arrow. His eyes wasn't good. He had little pieces of white paper on his sights so he could see 'em; but his hand was as steady as mine is to-day, and he was eatin' his own meat. We come back together to Missouri. He shore hated to quit without seein' them salt lakes; but winter was comin' and his Injin headed him back. He allowed he'd make it next spring. We made heap many smokes together. He was worse'n you for makin' me palaver. Nothin' must do but I had to tell him all about the Mountains. Allowed mebbe he'd git him two-three Osages, and mebbe a white man or two and go see. So you're Gail Burnett's kin! Well, from what old Dan'l told me, you come of good stock."

The mountain man glanced at the position of the sun and arose from the log.

"You live yereabouts?" he asked Andy.

"No: I'm traveling too." Andy hesitated. "I'm going west."

Crane dropped the butt of his rifle to earth with emphatic delight.

"Wagh!" he cried. "So that's the way yore stick floats![2] We will e'en travel together!"

2

For the first time in his life Andrew slept out in bivouac, for Crane declined flatly to stop at a farmhouse or an inn. All the days through he strode behind the untiring figure of the mountain man; for he soon found by experiment that Crane was impatient of conversation while journeying, and favored single file. Andy was willing to trail along behind. The strange barbaric figure of the mountain man, his head turning constantly in a habit of watchfulness, was very satisfying to the romanticism of his years. And, truth to tell, Andy found that after the first hour of the morning, he had scant breath wherewith to talk if he would. The frontiersman did not appear to

---

2. To locate sprung beaver traps, the trappers attached a stick of wood to the trap, on the end of a chain. The expression "the way your stick floats" means "so that is your business," or "that is what you are up to," or "that is the way you have to go."

hurry, but the swing of his stride was such that Andy was well put to it to keep pace.

But in the evening when the campfire had been lighted and the simple evening meal disposed, Crane became as conversational as one could desire. Before Andy realized that he was being drawn out, he found himself confiding in his new acquaintance. The latter listened attentively, without other comment than the strange, throat-scraping *wagh*! That Andy should run away from a harsh and fanatical stepfather seemed to him a matter of course. That he should travel west only natural to a grandson of Gail Burnett. But that he should be going to Missouri with the idea of taking up a farm was too fantastic to rate consideration. Crane brushed that notion aside as though it were a mosquito.

"I don't deny you're green for the prairies," said he. "You can shoot, purty fair; and you can throw a knife, a little. Beyond that you're mostly a total loss. You'd lose yore ha'r in two days. But yo're likely in larnin'. You've the makin's in you. *Farm!* Wagh! That don't shine with me! Leave them things to farmers. They don't fit with Burnett."

Immediately after this talk he took charge of Andy's schooling. He found the young man's ignorance appalling.

"Why, you ain't had any eddication at all!" he protested.

The curriculum was quite haphazard.

"If you see buffalo runnin' around in leetle small groups," Crane would observe suddenly, "you'll know they's been chased by Injins not long ago." . . .

. . . "If you're looking a way through strange mountains, remember to look for black rock, for when rocks is black snow has not stuck—and this: where snow don't stick a man can't climb." . . .

. . . "In Injin country quakin' asp's yore best fire. It ain't got no smoke nor smell." . . .

. . . "If you git caught in the fog in strange mountains, throw rocks ahead. If no sound comes back, set still." . . .

These and many other brief and pithy but unrelated bits of wisdom Crane threw back over his shoulder as he strode along. Later, perhaps at a resting period, perhaps at the evening fire, he would test Andy's memory, proposing imaginary emergencies to which the lad must state his remedy. And each evening Crane catechized him strictly as to what he had observed along the road. Andy found that to notice a chipmunk trail counted more with the mountain man than any number of red-painted barns!

At every opportunity Crane drilled him in the handling of his weapons. Mere marksmanship with the rifle received little of his attention.

"You hold well enough," said he indifferently, "and you'll hold better. Burn powder, lad; that is all. But you must learn to load, for an empty piece helps no man but yore enemy."

It was not sufficient, it seemed, merely to understand the proper charging of the rifle. One must be able to accomplish that necessary act in all varieties of circumstances, lying down, in cramped space, even running at full speed, on horseback. Crane practised him at estimating his powder charge poured direct from the horn. He showed him how a supply of bullets carried in the mouth could be flipped skillfully into the barrel by the tongue, and driven home by a smart smack of the butt of the weapon against a stone or a tree or even hard earth; or the pommel of the saddle if one were ahorseback.

"The spit'll hold her," explained Crane. "Don't need no patch for that." He removed from his mouth the long-stemmed stone pipe and pointed it didactically. "It's all right to measure yore powder to the last grain when you got time. But if you have to load quick, yo're so close that you'll hit anyways. If yo're fur away, you got time to load with a proper charge and a proper patch fur fine shootin'."

He made Andy perform the maneuver over and over. At first Andy was clumsy. He was appalled at the amount of powder he spilled and wasted.

"Never mind spilled powder. Powder's cheaper'n ha'r," said Crane grimly.

He himself, in demonstration, spilled no powder. He was extraordinarily deft and could charge, prime, and discharge his rifle in an incredibly brief period, whether running, lying, or huddled behind shelter.

Likewise he kept Andy almost tiresomely at his knife-throwing. In this the boy made faster progress. He learned the knack that drove the point deep. And now he discovered that he should also be able to cast the weapon, not only straight ahead, but to right or left, and even over his shoulder; and that without turning his body. Crane possessed uncanny skill with his own knife. He insisted on Andy's practising with that weapon also.

"She's a standard blade," Crane explained, "such as you will find in the sheath of every *hivernant,* and once you have the feel of one of them, you know them all."

The balance differed only slightly from that with which Andy was familiar, and his progress was so rapid that Crane expressed approval.

"That shines!" he cried; and patted Andy on the shoulder.

The schooling for the evening finished, the mountain man smoked and talked. Andy drank it in. The talk was of the sweep of plains, and the buffalo, and the rise of foothills, and the snowy peaks of great ranges, and the fall of beaver waters, and strange wild people, and hidden parks. And above all space and size and the fling of distances. Crane somehow made this country in which they journeyed seem very small and tame.

"Ain't hardly room to take exercise," said he contemptuously. He dismissed the surrounding forest with a lift of scorn. "Call them trees! Wagh! Why, out in the Mountains, lad, there's trees so stout it would tire a rat to run clean around them!"

3

Thus by slow stages they gained to Pittsburgh, which was at that time the point of embarkation for the West. It seemed to both the trapper and the country boy a busy and bewildering place. They made their way promptly to the river, stared at curiously; found by inquiry that a steamer was due to leave in two days, and betook themselves to camp in a hardwood grove outside the city. By now Andy, with the quick adaptability of youth, believed himself to look upon houses with a scorn equal to Crane's own. He had been accustomed to sleeping out, by a fire; and since he had had no blanket, he considered himself as a tough, hardy citizen, and was inclined to look down scornfully on such lads as passed. Indeed Andy may have strutted just a little; there is no question that he hung close to Crane and tried to look as though he had always belonged with the mountain man. Venturing, boy-like, to hint at this enormous superiority over the commonplace slaves to comfort who stared at them, he was chastened by Joe's sardonic reminder that they had up to now enjoyed perfect picnic weather. He made Andy buy himself a blanket. The boy did so, rather under protest.

"But you have no blanket," he pointed out. He did not quite dare to claim, in so many words, an equal hardihood with his hero. Crane returned an evasive reply. "We better see about gittin' on this steamboat," he turned the subject.

The river boat lay alongside a wharf. She was flat, broad, and built high in stories, with the pilot house grandly atop of all, and two tall slim smokestacks bound together with a crisscross of stays, and a diamond-shaped walking beam having a gilded Indian with drawn bow. Dozens of Negro laborers swarmed back and forth across her broad gangplanks carrying or pushing or rolling all sorts of freight. This was checked and disposed by clerks and mates, their sleeves rolled up, their shirts open, their caps thrust back, their voices hoarse, the sweat of honest exasperation on their brows. In contrast to the inferno of bustle and noise below, the upper deck dozed in a celestial calm. It was empty of life except for the figure of the captain, leaning, arms folded, over the rail. He looked cool and fresh and neat in his trim buttoned uniform: and he smoked a contemplative cheroot; and gazed down at the insane hurly-burly with the reposeful eye of complete detachment.

Joe Crane approached one of the busy checkers at the gangplank. The latter paid him no attention. After waiting uneasily for a few moments the mountain man ventured to address him. Gone was his swaggering air of self-confidence. In this alien environment of bustle and noise he was as ill-at-ease as a schoolboy.

"How much to St. Louey?" he asked in a small voice.

The checker did not even look up from his list.

"Sanborn!" he howled above the din. "Oh, you, Sanborn!"

At the summons a small, pale, fishy-eyed man popped out from a cubby hole on the lower deck. He too was in his shirt sleeves and carried a list in his hands.

"Well?" he demanded impatiently.

The checker did not reply in words, but jerked his head toward Crane and Andy. The mountain man repeated his question. The small man looked him over disparagingly.

"Hundred dollars, deck passage, find yourself," he vouchsafed at last.

"That the cheapest?" enquired Crane.

The purser half turned away.

"Fifty if you wood up," he flung scornfully over his shoulder; then vouchsafed to explain, "We'll take you for fifty dollars if you help carry wood aboard whenever we stop for fuel."

"I'm Joe Crane," said the mountain man, "I'm just back from—"

"I don't care who you are," interrupted the purser. "Do you want a ticket, or don't you?"

"Can't I work my passage?"

"We got plenty niggers already," sneered the little man.

Crane did not appear to resent this. He pondered helplessly.

"How much for a hundred and eighty pounds of freight?" he enquired at last.

"Eighteen dollars."

"That shines," replied Crane with a grin. "I'll go as freight."

The little man spun on his heel and stared malevolently at the mountain man, his eyes blazing.

"Say, you!" he snarled. "Do you think I've got nothing to do but listen to you trying to be funny? Get out of here before I have you thrown off the dock."

He turned away.

"Mr. Sanborn." The captain's cool remote voice from above arrested his steps.

"Sir?" the purser craned his neck upward.

"Book the gentleman."

"Sir?"

"I say book the gentleman. Take him as freight. And, Sanborn, stow him in the hold—under the flour barrels."

He had not raised his voice, but it had somehow carried above all the din of loading. Those within its immediate hearing burst into a roar of laughter. The Negro stevedores cackled, dropped their loads to double up in merriment unrebuked. They passed back the word to others who had not heard, and they too slapped one another in delayed appreciation. On his Olympian height the captain smoked meditative, indifferent, remote, staring across the reposeful calm he alone inhabited. Joe Crane, followed by the bewildered Andy, fell back abashed behind the warehouse shelter. He looked at his young companion, humorously shamefaced.

"*Well!*" he said comically. "Here's damp powder and no fire to dry it!"

"Haven't you any money?" asked Andy.

"My 'possible' sack is mighty nigh as clean as a hound's tooth."

"But—" Andy was nonplussed. "How did you expect—How did you—"

"I didn't need none goin' east, so I spent what I had. But it seems like Joe Crane goin' to Washington to see the President and Joe Crane goin' home again is two different beaver," confessed that individual. "Looks to me like a man ought to be allowed to work his passage, anyway."

Andrew was fumbling with the cord about his neck.

"You got money?" cried Crane interestedly. He snatched the bills from Andy's hands, stared at them a moment, then leaped into the air and uttered a wild war whoop that brought several men running around the corner of the building to see what it was all about. He paid them no attention but marched swaggering across the decks and up the broad gangplank to the purser's office, thrusting aside without ceremony the laden stevedores, glaring down the first impulse of the officer who moved to stop him.

"Here, little man," he commanded, slapping down the roll of bills. "Two tickets to St. Louey—and carry your own wood and be damned to you!"

Andy, trailing helplessly behind his triumphal progress, looked up to meet the captain's calmly amused eye.

4

Joe Crane and Andy lived during that voyage on the flat lower deck, next the water. Their sleeping accommodations were where they chose to spread their blankets—for Joe now possessed such a luxury, thanks to his discovery of Andrew's affluence. At the sound of a gong they rushed into line to receive food dished out at a galley door. The rest of the time they could do what they pleased—on the lower deck. Above—the second story—it could hardly be called a deck—was reserved for slow-moving, low-voiced, well-dressed people. The men wore tall beaver hats and ruffled shirts and blue coats and light pantaloons: the women floated wide in crinolines. They leaned on the rail occasionally to look down with faint supercilious curiosity on the lower deck. And above them again were the pilot deck and the captain and the pilots and other ship's officers remote as gods.

With these inhabitants of the upper worlds Andy was little concerned. But the lower deck was occupied by as weird a hodgepodge as one could imagine—wood choppers, backwoods settlers, peddlers, raft men, boatmen, bullwhackers, a rough, tough lot. They nearly all chewed tobacco; they all swore, and most of them quarreled gustily over the slightest difference of opinion. Nobody interfered with them save when, on rare occasions, the customary turbulence threatened to develop into a riot. Then from the engine room emerged a colossal Swede armed with an iron bar who restored order in a most businesslike and impersonal fashion, and at once disappeared.

Joe Crane fitted at once into this motley disorder. He was, when he so chose, the center of a group. The rough men listened to his tall stories of the prairie and the mountains; they listened, though many of the hat-tilted tough boys, by their attitude of having paused in the group for but a moment, and by an expression of half-sneering amusement, tried to convey their general skepticism of Crane's validity. But it was to be noted that nobody opposed or quarreled with the mountain man. The latter thought nothing of them. He laughed at Andy's first awe of them as frontiersmen.

Some of the time Andy listened, or stood by watching the interminable card games on a spread blanket; but what he liked best of all was to huddle in a place he had discovered behind two bitts[3] near the bow. He watched the river glide by.

Separated thus from the human microcosmos of the ship, Andy seemed to enter an aloof and hovering detachment. In after life, though his memory for event was always remarkably clear and detailed, this interlude of voyage never defined itself as something in which he had actually taken part. It was like a dream, having neither the dimensions of space nor time. The water swished from the blunt bow; the walking beam swung up and down, up and down, its gilded Indian pointing his arrow now low, now high; the

3. "Bitts"—thick, short posts on the deck. They are used for tying the boat to a dock.

banks glided by. Against this monochrome things appeared as shadows on a screen; and vanished again.

They stopped at Cincinnati, and went on. The hills became lower, the houses and the settlements farther apart. Occasionally they drew up at a wharf, and freight or passengers debarked or were taken on. More often they merely shoved the blunt bow against the bank and held it there until necessary business was transacted. At such times, often, the gangplanks were thrown out, and long lines of passengers working out their part fare carried aboard the long sticks of cordwood from the piles maintained by the steamboat company's wood choppers. Now Ohio lay astarboard and Kentucky aport. They differed completely in character. On the Ohio side were cleared farms and farmhouses, neatly painted, and in the New England style; on the Kentucky side were ragged fields and the large log cabins of planters and the smaller log huts of the slaves. Between them and back of them gathered close the green forest down to the water's edge. Cool and dark and mysterious it lay; and Andy saw flashes of red as the tanagers and cardinals took wing. And the rolling clouds of wood smoke from the twin stacks broke against it and eddied between the trees.

They passed the rapids at Louisville on the flood; and stopped; and many of the ship's company ended their journey there; and the most of the rest came back only at the urgent and repeated summons of the whistle, and some few were left behind, for the rougher element became unanimously drunk, and there was considerable quarrelsome disorder. Crane was drunk with the rest, and came back alone in a very disdainful mood that even included Andy.

"If yo're goin' to be a mountain man you got to learn to liquorize," was the grieved burden of his plaint.

A raftsman agreed with him profanely, adding embellishments. Crane instantly veered. Since when had a mere alligator horse acquired the right to criticize a friend of Joe Crane's? Joe offered to cut his liver out to see if it was white. Offer declined; but if Joe would lay aside his knife the raftsman would . . . They drifted away, squabbling. Andy leaned his back against the bitts. All this seemed to pass him by, could not touch the waiting suspension of his westering spirit. The journey seemed to march by him as a pageant. The stream broadened; the bluffs fell away; the country spaced to broad undulations clothed always in the now almost unbroken forest. Next the river were low, alluvial flats, with marshes and swamps and the wild cryings and uptiltings of innumerable water fowl. The farms had been left behind. The wilderness was broken only by the rare huts of the wood choppers set on blocks or piles against high water, and the stacked cordwood.

The bosom of the river was wide and glassy. One would have said it was as still as a lake were it not that here and there the slow powerful turning of oily eddies, the veer of the ship against its rudder, the hastening of the shore, betrayed its strength. As afternoons drew to a close the sun turned it to the red of dark wine and the air filled with gold, into which the steamer glided as into a mist.

And at night was the suspension of quiet. The blackness of the forest met the blackness of the river; and the dark blue-spangled sky overhead; and the rare twinkle of lights ashore, repeated waveringly in the water; and the refraction against the stillness of the blatant lights and sounds of the steamer; and the unintermitting pouring of bright sparks from the funnels that rushed up so powerfully as though with purpose, and eddied, and wavered uncertainly, and died against the evening as though rebuked.

At this time the mountain man took to deserting his other companions to stand silent near Andy, his elbows leaning on the muzzle of his long rifle, his eyes, unblinking, staring straight ahead, his head raised, as though he snuffed for something in the breeze. He seemed at last caught in the younger man's hypnotic suspense of waiting. They exchanged no words.

The river widened. The banks fell away. To the right a point defined itself, against which lay moored a strange structure. As the steamer swung in it became clear that this was a huge flatboat, a hundred feet or more in length, supporting several log houses—a store, a saloon, a gambling house: Cairo, the delta of the Mississippi. Almost as far as the eye could see rolled the breadth of the Father of Waters, the farther shore line dim and low in the distance.

"We're gittin' thar! Wagh!" cried Crane.

5

They plowed upstream against two hundred miles of heavy current. Crane, realizing that the journey was nearing its end, abandoned his careless companionships and gave his whole attention to Andy. He considered it nothing short of a crime that so likely a young man, the grandson of Gail Burnett, should become a farmer. He said so, very bluntly, and incidental to his protest sketched appealing glimpses of the wild life beyond the Missouri and the Platte. Andrew's spirit yearned toward the adventure; but he continued to shake his head.

"I promised Grandmother," he persisted steadily, "that I'd send for her when I'd made a place for her to live. This money here," he tapped his chest, "is hers. She gave it to me to pay the journey and buy land."

"You'll make more in a season with the free trappers than you'll make in ten year on a farm. And it's a man's life."

"I know," agreed Andy sighing.

"There's a country nor'west," urged Crane, "it ain't never been trapped. It's Blackfoot country. Blackfeet is bad Injins; but with a good man and a bright lad—like yourself . . . I know a park back in them mountains called the Tetons whar I g'arantee no Injins will . . . Why, lad, there's never a trap been set in them waters. We'll have it all to ourselves. If we save our ha'r we'll come out to the rendezvous with a thousand plew![4] Think of that, lad! a thousand plew; or more! That'll buy ye a dozen farms—if you still want the things. Yo'll git Missus Burnett out jist as quick; and you'll have money to make her comfortable," said Crane cunningly.

"I can't! I can't!" cried Andy with a desperation that indicated his temptation. "I promised; and I took the money; and I've no right—Besides," the words were dragged from his reluctance, "I'd be no good to you in that country. I'm such a greenhorn. I know nothing."

"Of course, if yo're afeard—" said Crane deliberately.

Andy's head jerked up. A dull red suffused his face. His hand dropped to the pan of the weapon in his lap.

"I'm not afeard," he said quietly.

Crane looked at him; sighed.

"I know ye're not, lad. I take that back. Shore yo're a greenhorn; but you got good makin's and you come of good stock. And you larn quick. Look a yere, lad." He thrust his hand forward earnestly. "We need ye. The big companies is comin' in. They're sendin' out their burgeways to build forts and liquorize the Injins. The mountain men must make a stand or the beaver streams will be tromped and the Injins hostile. The mountains won't be no place for a white man." He brooded. "What you think yore grandpop—and Dan'l Boone—would say if they knew that this,"—he reached forward and laid his hand too on the long rifle—"was a-poppin' black squirrels in a Missouri bottom, and buffalo and Injins and grizzly b'ar and antelope and sich just over the skyline?"

"I can't! I can't! I can't!" cried Andy. "And," he repeated bitterly, "I wish you'd let me be! I promised, I tell you! I don't see why you want me, anyway. I'd probably just do some fool thing."

"That's why I want you," replied Crane.

---

4. "Plew"—beaver pelts. This term, and the term *beaver*, are sometimes used to mean "money."

"What?"

"You stick," said Crane simply. "Well, if that's the way yore stick floats . . ." He spat disgustedly. "It's always a woman; young or old, it's always a woman spiles a good man."

"My grandmother—" Andy fired up at this.

"Shore! She's all right," Crane placated him. "I ain't sayin' a word agin her. But that's the way it works. The good ones is wuss'n the bad ones." He apparently gave it up. "I know. Nigh got me one time. Might have been on a farm myself if a good friend hadn't stepped in and saved my ha'r for me jist in the nick o' time. She was a good gal, too. Run plumb onto her in St. Louey when I come in with my fur, spring of '15. Hit me like a dose of alkali water. Felt queer all over like a buffalo shot in the lights.[5] Had no taste for mush and molasses, no interest in hominy and johnnycakes. I didn't care whether my rifle had hind sights or not. Couldn't help myself no more than a man who's kicked a yaller-jacket log. If it hadn't a-been for that friend I'd have been a gone beaver."

"What did he do?" asked Andy.

"He married her," said Crane.

Andy laughed. Crane grinned reluctantly.

"Don't suppose nobody'd marry yore grandmother," he admitted.

6

The steamboat curved grandly and ceremoniously to the docks at St. Louis. The ship's company had shaken off its monotony of routine and crowded the rails. Andy, clinging with difficulty in the jostling of the crowd to his place by the bitts, looked with all his eyes.

St. Louis of that day lay on a terrace below abrupt limestone bluffs, long since graded away, atop which defensive works stood like sentinels. A row of warehouses faced the docks, and behind them straggled streets parallel with the stream. The docks themselves were wide and long. At this moment they were crowded with a mixed and miscellaneous throng. Andy filled his eyes with their picturesque incongruity. There were gentlemen in the height of fashion, French *engagés* dark and vivacious; rivermen in high leather boots; absorbed and businesslike clerks in sober garb; ragged stevedores; bullwhackers swaggering bare-chested and hat-tilted; plainsmen leaning on their long rifles, eyeing the hubbub sober and aloof. And

5. "Lights"—vital organs, intestines.

here and there Andy's first plains Indians, gaudy and painted. The din was tremendous. Men shouted; the paddle wheels beat; and the safety valve took this occasion to cut loose with a devastating roar.

Joe Crane thrust himself through the crowding passengers to Andy's side. He had become abrupt; businesslike; remote.

"You can get track of me at the Rocky Mountain House, if you change your mind," said he briefly; and was gone. A moment later Andy saw the mountain man gain the wharf by a flying leap; and, indifferent to the protests and invectives hurled after him by the outraged crew, disappear in the throng.

A lump of hurt and resentment arose in Andy's throat at this abrupt and indifferent farewell. But now the gangplank was lowered, and he was swept away by the rush toward shore, carried helplessly forward, his arms jammed to his sides, crowded and jostled. It was a human stampede, each regardless of anyone but himself. Buffeted, his nostrils filled with the reek, Andy was swept forth at last to the wharf. As soon as he could do so he stepped aside, drawing a deep breath of relief, his hand seeking the little sack of money suspended about his neck beneath his shirt. The long breath strangled in his throat. The bag was gone.

The shock of the loss turned Andy physically sick for a moment. He groped for a pile head and supported himself against it. The noisy wharf had gone black in a reeling world. Gone! When? How?

Dimly he became aware that somebody was speaking his name. With difficulty he brought his mind to a focus. The captain of the steamboat stood before him. He was made to understand that the captain had a letter for him. How could a letter reach him in this crowd? More trouble, probably. He wanted to get away as quickly as possible. He took the letter mechanically.

"You sure this is mine?" he asked wondering. "How did you know—"

The captain grinned in his beard.

"There are not many boys of just your description carrying one of those things." He indicated the long rifle. "The letter was sent to the company's office at Pittsburgh, and as soon as you took passage with my ship, it was handed to me."

"Why did you not give it to me before, then?"

"Instructions. It was to be given only when you debarked." Nodding acknowledgment to Andy's thanks, he strolled away.

Andy stared at his grandmother's fine angular handwriting, and thrust the letter unopened into his pocket. In this crash of all the plans they had made together he could not bear to read it. He shouldered his entire earthly possessions and left the wharves.

For an hour or more he walked about, dark in the misery of his loss. Up the Rue Royale—business places, board sidewalk, mud; back down the Rue de l'Eglise, ditto ditto without the sidewalk; double again, one block nearer the limestone bluffs; on the Rue des Granges to the French quarter, derisively called Vide Poche. The Rue Royale was crowded; the others nearly empty. He was as though living a double exposure on a negative. His impressions were fragmentary, snatched in his brief emergences from his inner trouble: the mud; the numbers of creoles speaking French; an occasional strikingly picturesque figure of trapper, trader, or boatman; the wild rolling eyes of the otherwise stolid Indians: an overnote of truculent rowdyism; the prevalence of arms; Negroes. He was only partially aware of them. He found himself gazing fixedly at things which he did not see until slowly they seeped down to his attention. Thus the feet of a barefoot Negro in profile, grotesque, and the gradual clarifying of the picture in Andy's attention until he realized that never before had he seen heels extending back so curiously in excrescence. And with this realization a long rifle barrel thrust past Andy's shoulder; and a shattering discharge and cloud of powder smoke; and a wild yell from the Negro as he rolled about clasping his heel creased by the bullet. Shaken completely from the somnolence of his misery Andy found himself in the center of a whooping instantly gathered crowd. A tall quiet man in black thrust through and laid his hand on the shoulder of the drunken trapper with the smoking rifle. The latter protested, aggrieved.

"God a'mighty, man," explained he, "I jist aimed to trim him up so he could wear a genteel boot!"

"Kyant do no shootin' in the streets," said the tall man firmly.

He shook the drunken man, faced him about, gave him a shove in the broad of the back. He staggered away. The crowd howled with laughter. Several clapped him on the shoulder, admiring his accuracy, inviting him to "liquorize." They scattered slowly. Andy was alone again. Nobody paid any attention to the Negro, hippity-hopping away as fast as he could go.

But Andy was now shaken awake. The thing was done and over, and to be faced. Andy faced it squarely. The money entrusted to him to buy the farm was gone. He must get some more money. The only way he could think of to do that was to take up the mountain man's offer. What was it Crane had said? A thousand plew. What was a plew? He must find out. Having made this decision Andy instantly set about acting on it. Thus already he displayed two of the qualities that later were often to stand him in stead. And having come to his resolution Andy was ashamed to find, beneath the chagrin suitable to the occasion, a sudden leap of exultation. It was positively indecent! He sternly made it down-charge, turned his inner eye away from it. Nevertheless it glowed away down inside, awaiting its chance to burst out. But he *was* going west! Couldn't take that away, whatever the austere reasons!

He enquired the way to the Rocky Mountain House, and had turned in that direction when he remembered the letter in his pocket. He could read it now; albeit with still a bit of dread and shrinking. He drew to one side for the purpose.

"DEAR BOY:" it began, "You will wish the news of the farm, and the situation here; so I will say at once that your stepfather has instigated no pursuit, as I suspected, due to his great stinginess. Nor has he been disagreeable to myself, due I think to his idea that I have money to dispose, not knowing that it is already disposed. So your mind may be easy on these accounts, and you may think of me as quite happy with my Book and my memories and my thoughts of you at last doing what your blood calls you to do and which I had planned for you.

"You will be wondering why you get this letter only now and not at Pitt's town whither it was sent. I arranged that in order that you might not be tempted to turn back. By now, I think, you must know that you are not meant to be a farmer. I have known that for a long time. The knowledge of it has been the joy of my old age. I never intended you to make a place for me out there, but otherwise you might not have gone. I would be very unhappy watching you grubbing at a farm. I could never stand half that journey, now. But don't you worry about that. You'll write me of your great doings, and I'll be very happy here in my old rocking chair, for remember this, it is only through you that all that I have loved and cherish lives on. So do your part, boy, like a man. Make your mark on your time, like your grandfather before you. Let others make the farms—after you have found the country and made it safe for them." She signed her full name with the painstaking flourish of the period. But there was more. "I had not thought to touch upon it," she had added, "but the thought must occur to you, and I would not have it weaken your resolution. We may not see one another again. I am eighty-seven years old, and I know too well the dangers of the life you must lead. But we shall not be snuffed out when our bodies go. Our sort goes marching on."

7

The Rocky Mountain House proved to be a small two-storied rude structure on one of the streets back of the Rue des Granges. Nearly the whole lower story was taken up by a single large room, crowded with men. Some of them stood at a bar; a few occupied chairs; the most sat crosslegged on the floor. They were a wildly picturesque lot. Heads were covered with handkerchiefs, wide felt hats, caps of fur: bodies with cotton; with fringed and beaded buckskin yellow in newness; with buckskin black and shiny from wear. Legs also with buckskin, or with stout stroud; feet with moccasins plain and fancy. A few were dressed decently and quietly in the fashion of the cities. Smoke hazed the air.

Andy stood in the doorway accustoming his eyes to the dimness. Nobody paid him the least attention.

He was thrust aside by a man entering. The newcomer strode to the center of the room. Over his shoulder he carried a buffalo robe which he spread tanned side up. At one end he seated himself crosslegged; crashed down a hatful of silver dollars and with a sweeping motion spread a pack of cards.

"Yere's the deck and yere's the beaver!" he challenged. "Who dares set his hoss? Wagh!"

They gathered close, squatting crosslegged and on their heels. Only the man back of the bar remained standing; and two others near a farther door. Andy felt himself keenly scrutinized by them, and after a moment he recognized one of them as Crane.

He picked his way across to them.

"Well, here I am!" he announced.

Neither man replied for a moment.

"I'm going with you, after all," Andy supplemented; "that is, if you still want me," he added, the chill of the possibility rendering his voice uncertain.

Crane glanced toward his companion.

The latter was a tall man and muscular, clad from head to foot in fresh buckskin. His hair hung to hide the broad of his shoulders; but he was clean-shaven. His eyes were hard and direct, puckered into cold scrutiny.

The lines of his brown face were keen-cut and fine. His expression was of deep gravity. The general impression of the man was of power and alertness held in the reserve of repose.

"This is Jack Kelly, my pardner," said Crane, and to Kelly: "This is the lad I was tellin' you about. If he sez so," he told Andy.

Andy was conscious of the plainsman's slow appraisal, sweeping him from head to toe like a cold flame. Abruptly he spoke. His voice was low and, surprisingly, inflected with that peculiar quality we call cultivation.

"You've changed your mind—why?" he asked.

"I told you he was no farmer!" interpolated Crane confidently, "He—"

Kelly silenced him with a gesture.

"Why?" he repeated.

"Well, for one thing, somebody stole my money off me," admitted Andy, and laughed. "The money your grandmother gave you to buy a home," Kelly said bitingly. Andy flushed, but his eyes did not waver. "So you've lost it; and now you're running away."

Andy's head jerked.

"I'm not running away!" he denied hotly.

The stranger's eyes bored into his.

"Money's not hard to get," he said, "nor farms, in this country. Suppose I put you in the way of one."

"The boy's no farmer!" cried Crane.

"Shut up, Joe. Well?" Kelly challenged Andy.

Andy hesitated, then thrust his letter into the plainsman's hands. The latter read it slowly, passed it to Crane. He in turn spelled it out, his lips moving.

"Wagh!" he ejaculated when he had finished, "That old woman shines!" He turned on Kelly indignantly. "What I tell you?" he demanded. "Whar floats his stick?" He seized Andy by the shoulders. "We'll make a mountain man of you, never fear! And," he returned to Kelly, "you mark my words, he'll shore make them *come*!"[6] A sudden recollection caused the expression of his face to change ludicrously. He hesitated a moment in indecision, caught Kelly's eye fixed upon him, grinned shamefacedly. He fumbled in one of the pouches suspended from his belt; thrust something into Andy's hand.

"Reckon I might as well give you this back," he mumbled. "You ain't no

---

6. "Make them come"—succeed. The phrase probably refers to making beaver come to the trap; it can also refer to killing men or animals, as in "he made them come that day." To "shine" is also to succeed, or to excel.

farmer," he alleged defensively. "I allus said so. But somebody had to keep you from bein' one. Wagh!"

Andy looked down at the stolen sack of money. For a brief instant he felt himself as though lifted by the sweep of greater destinies than those within his command.

John G. Neihardt
1881-1973

1910: *The River and I*
1915: *The Song of Hugh Glass* *
1919: *The Song of Three Friends* *
1920: *The Splendid Wayfaring*
1925: *The Song of the Indian Wars* *
1932: *Black Elk Speaks*
1935: *The Song of the Messiah* *
1941: *The Song of Jed Smith* *
1952: *When the Tree Flowered*
Cycle of the West

JOHN NEIHARDT *wrote that he "grew up at the edge of the retreating frontier," nurtured by his dream of becoming a poet and inspired by a powerful sense of the frontier's epic dimensions. The land was timeless, mystic, and vast; its people were of heroic stature, and their conflicts with the land and with each other were epic. "Richly human saga-stuff," Neihardt called it. "The history of the American fur trade alone makes the Trojan War look like a Punch and Judy show! And the Missouri River was the path of the conquerors." He wrote, "We have the facts—but we have not Homer."* [1]

As a child, in 1892, Neihardt had a vision that convinced him it was his destiny to become a poet. As though to prepare him to meet that destiny, his college education included personal tutoring and encouragement from the faculty at Nebraska Normal College, where he immersed himself in classical studies. Despite

---

1. John G. Neihardt, *The River and I* (1910; reprint, Lincoln: University of Nebraska Press, 1968), p. 23.

his lack of a high school education, he graduated from the college in 1897 as a Bachelor of Science.

Neihardt's belief that a poet must labor, as must any man, led him to take a series of different jobs before becoming an assistant to an Indian trader to the Omahas. This position meant that he was in close daily contact with the Omaha Indians from 1900 until 1905, during which time he formed the interest that would later lead to his renowned work Black Elk Speaks. *By 1908, when Neihardt determined to earn his living by writing, he had already published poems and short stories. Soon after founding* Poetry *magazine in 1912, the critic and poet Harriet Monroe declared that "the new poetry" would be led by Neihardt and Ezra Pound.* The Song of Hugh Glass *initiated what Neihardt would call his* Cycle of the West. *In 1921, two years after he published the second of the five "songs" that would constitute the* Cycle, *Neihardt was named poet laureate of Nebraska in recognition of his having written a "national epic" contributing to the creation of "great national traditions."*[2]

In 1941 Neihardt completed The Song of Jed Smith, *the fifth and final "song" of the* Cycle of the West *(all five were collected in one volume in 1949), the epic that had absorbed much of his life. More than sixteen thousand lines long, the* Cycle *is epic in every sense. It tells of men "in struggle, triumph and defeat," it echoes and alludes to prior epics, it commemorates national history, and it proceeds with an unwavering, elevated diction.*[3] *The meter is strong and bold. The heroes suffer, bleed, and celebrate as vividly as in any novel. In size and force it is a monumental work.*

━━━

Ashley's Hundred

Who now reads clear the roster of that band?
Alas, Time scribbles with a careless hand
And often pinchbeck[4] doings from that pen
Bite deep, where deeds and dooms of mighty men
Are blotted out beneath a sordid scrawl!

Both selections from John G. Neihardt, *The Mountain Men*, vol. 1 of *The Cycle of the West* (1915; reprint, Lincoln: University of Nebraska Press, 1971), pp. 1–28. Reprinted by permission of the John G. Neihardt Trust.

2. Blair Whitney, *John G. Neihardt* (Boston: Twayne, 1976), p. 21.
3. Ibid.
4. "Pinchbeck"—shallow, cheap, or imitative.

One hundred strong they flocked to Ashley's call[5]
That spring of eighteen hundred twenty-two;
For tales of wealth, out-legending Peru,
Came wind-blown from Missouri's distant springs,
And that old sireny[6] of unknown things
Bewitched them, and they could not linger more.
They heard the song the sea winds sang the shore
When earth was flat, and black ships dared the steep
Where bloomed the purple perils of the deep
In dragon-haunted gardens. They were young.

Albeit some might feel the winter flung
Upon their heads, 'twas less like autumn's drift
Than backward April's unregarded sift
On stout oaks thrilling with the sap again.
And some had scarce attained the height of men,
Their lips unroughed, and gleaming in their eyes
The light of immemorial surprise
That life still kept the spaciousness of old
And, like the hoarded tales their grandsires told,
Might still run bravely.

                    For a little span
Their life-fires flared like torches in the van
Of westward progress, ere the great wind 'woke
To snuff them. Many vanished like a smoke
The blue air drinks; and e'en of those who burned
Down to the socket, scarce a tithe returned
To share at last the ways of quiet men,
Or see the hearth-reek drifting once again
Across the roofs of old St. Louis town.

---

5. In 1822, William Henry Ashley and Andrew Henry advertised for "enterprising young men" to go on a trapping and trading venture to the upper Missouri River. Against great odds, Ashley's men eventually opened the Rocky Mountains to the fur trade, rediscovered South Pass, established the rendezvous system, navigated parts of the Green River, and pioneered the Platte River portion of the Overland Trail.

6. The song of the Sirens lures sailors to destruction. Odysseus hears it from his "black ship" in the *Odyssey*.

And now no more the mackinaws[7] come down,
Their gunwales low with costly packs and bales,
A wind of wonder in their shabby sails,
Their homing oars flung rhythmic to the tide;
And nevermore the masted keelboats ride
Missouri's stubborn waters on the lone
Long zigzag journey to the Yellowstone.

Their hulks have found the harbor ways that know
The ships of all the Sagas, long ago—
A moony haven where no loud gale stirs.
The trappers and the singing *voyageurs*
Are comrades now of Jason and his crew,
Foregathered in that timeless rendezvous
Where come at last all seekers of the Fleece.[8]

Not now of those who, dying, dropped in peace
A brimming cup of years the song shall be:
From Mississippi to the Western Sea,
From Britain's country to the Rio Grande
Their names are written deep across the land
In pass and trail and river, like a rune.[9]

Pore long upon that roster by the moon
Of things remembered dimly. Tangled, blear
The writing runs; yet presently appear
Three names[10] of men that, spoken, somehow seem
Incantatory trumpets of a dream
Obscurely blowing from the hinter-gloom.
Of these and that inexorable doom
That followed like a hound upon the scent,
Here runs the tale.

---

7. A "mackinaw" was a large, flat-bottomed rowboat used in the Missouri fur trade.

8. This is a reference to the Greek legend of Jason, who led his Argonauts in quest of the Golden Fleece.

9. "Rune"—ancient lettering.

10. Will Carpenter, Mike Fink, and Frank Tableau, members of "Ashley's Hundred."

The Up-Stream Men

When Major Henry went
Up river at the head of Ashley's band,
Already there were robins in the land.
Home-keeping men were following the plows
And through the smoke-thin greenery of boughs
The scattering wild-fire of the fruit bloom ran.

Behold them starting northward, if you can.
Dawn flares across the Mississippi's tide;
A tumult runs along the waterside
Where, scenting an event, St. Louis throngs.
Above the buzzling voices soar the songs
Of waiting boatmen—lilting *chansonettes* [11]
Whereof the meaning laughs, the music frets,
Nigh weeping that such gladness can not stay.
In turn, the herded horses snort and neigh
Like panic bugles. Up the gangplanks poured,
Go streams of trappers, rushing goods aboard
The snub-built keelboats, squat with seeming sloth—
Baled three-point blankets, blue and scarlet cloth,
Rum, powder, flour, guns, gauderies and lead.
And all about, goodbyes are being said.
Gauche girls with rainy April in their gaze
Cling to their beardless heroes, count the days
Between this parting and the wedding morn,
Unwitting how unhuman Fate may scorn
The youngling dream. For O how many a lad
Would see the face of Danger, and go mad
With her weird vixen beauty; aye, forget

11. *"Chansonettes"*—little songs.

This girl's face, yearning upward now and wet,
Half woman's with the first vague guess at woe!

And now commands are bellowed, boat horns blow
Haughtily in the dawn; the tumult swells.
The tow-crews, shouldering the long cordelles [12]
Slack from the mastheads, lean upon the sag.
The keelboats answer lazily and drag
Their blunt prows slowly in the gilded tide.
A steersman sings, and up the riverside
The gay contagious ditty spreads and runs
Above the shouts, the uproar of the guns,
The nickering of horses.

                              So, they say,
Went forth a hundred singing men that day;
And girlish April went ahead of them.
The music of her trailing garment's hem
Seemed scarce a league ahead. A little speed
Might yet almost surprise her in the deed
Of sorcery; for, ever as they strove,
A gray-green smudge in every poplar grove
Proclaimed the recent kindling. Aye, it seemed
That bird and bush and tree had only dreamed
Of song and leaf and blossom, till they heard
The young men's feet; when tree and bush and bird
Unleashed the whole conspiracy of awe!
Pale green was every slough about the Kaw;
About the Platte, pale green was every slough;
And still the pale green lingered at the Sioux,
So close they trailed the marching of the South.
But when they reached the Niobrara's mouth
The witchery of spring had taken flight
And, like a girl grown woman over night,
Young summer glowed.

---

12. A "cordelle" was a heavy rope, several hundred feet long, attached to the top of
the mast. The tow crew walked up the riverbank, towing the keelboat with the cordelle.

And now the river rose,
Gigantic from a feast of northern snows,
And mightily the snub prows felt the tide;
But with the loud, sail-filling South allied,
The tow-crews battled gaily day by day;
And seldom lulled the struggle on the way
But some light jest availed to fling along
The panting lines the laughter of the strong,
For joy sleeps lightly in the hero's mood.
And when the sky-wide prairie solitude
Was darkened round them, and the camp was set
Secure for well-earned sleep that came not yet,
What stories shaped for marvel or for mirth!—
Tales fit to strain the supper-tightened girth,
Looped yarns, wherein the veteran spinners vied
To color with a lie more glorified
Some thread that had veracity enough,
Spun straightway out of life's own precious stuff
That each had scutched and heckled in the raw.[13]
Then thinner grew each subsequent guffaw
While drowsily the story went the rounds
And o'er the velvet dark the summer sounds
Prevailed in weird crescendo more and more,
Until the story-teller with a snore
Gave over to a dream a tale half told.

And now the horse-guards, while the night grows old,
With intermittent singing buffet sleep
That surges subtly down the starry deep
On waves of odor from the manless miles
Of summer-haunted prairie. Now, at whiles,
The kiote's mordant clamor cleaves the drowse.
The horses stamp and blow; about the prows
Dark waters chug and gurgle; as with looms
Bugs weave a drone; a beaver's diving booms,
Whereat bluffs grumble in their sable cowls.

---

13. Before spinning flax into thread, the spinner beats, or "scutches," the flax to separate the soft, useful fibers from the woody part. Then the material is combed, or "heckled."

The devil laughter of the prairie owls
Mocks mirth anon, like unrepentant sin.
Perceptibly at last slow hours wear thin
The east, until the prairie stares with morn,
And horses nicker to the boatman's horn
That blares the music of a day begun.

So through the days of thunder and of sun
They pressed to northward. Now the river shrank,
The grass turned yellow and the men were lank
And gnarled with labor. Smooth-lipped lads matured
'Twixt moon and moon with all that they endured,
Their faces leathered by the wind and glare,
Their eyes grown ageless with the calm far stare
Of men who know the prairies or the seas.
And when they reached the village of the Rees,
One scarce might say, This man is young, this old,
Save for the beard.

                        Here loitered days of gold
And days of leisure, welcome to the crews;
For recently had come the wondrous news
Of beaver-haunts beyond the Great Divide—
So rich a tale 'twould seem the tellers lied,
Had they not much fine peltry to attest.
So now the far off River of the West
Became the goal of venture for the band;
And since the farther trail lay overland
From where the Great Falls thundered to no ear,
They paused awhile to buy more ponies here
With powder, liquor, gauds and wily words.
A horse-fond people, opulent in herds,
The Rees were; and the trade was very good.

Now camped along the river-fringing wood,
Three sullen, thunder-brewing, rainless days,
Those weathered men made merry in their ways
With tipple, euchre, story, jest and song.
The marksmen matched their cleverness; the strong
Wrestled the strong; and brawling pugilists

Displayed the boasted power of their fists
In stubborn yet half amicable fights.
And whisky went hell-roaring through the nights
Among the lodges of the fuddled Rees.
Thus merrily the trappers took their ease,
Rejoicing in the thread that Clotho spun;[14]
For it was good to feel the bright thread run,
However eager for the snipping shears.

O joy long stifled in the ruck of years!
How many came to strange and bitter ends!
And who was merrier than those three friends
Whom here a song remembers for their woe?

Will Carpenter, Mike Fink and Frank Talbeau
Were they—each gotten of a doughty breed;
For in the blood of them the ancient seed
Of Saxon, Celt and Norman grew again.
The Mississippi reared no finer men,
And rarely the Ohio knew their peers
For pluck and prowess—even in those years
When stern life yielded suck but to the strong.
Nor in the hundred Henry took along
Was found their match—and each man knew it well.
For instance, when it suited Mike to tell
A tale that called for laughter, as he thought,
The hearer laughed right heartily, or fought
And took a drubbing. Then, if more complained,
Those three lacked not for logic that explained
The situation in no doubtful way.
"Me jokes are always funny" Mike would say;
And most men freely granted that they were.

A lanky, rangy man was Carpenter,
Quite six feet two from naked heel to crown;
And, though crow-lean, he brought the steelyard down
With twice a hundred notched upon the bar.[15]

---

14. Clotho, in Greek mythology, is one of the three Fates. She spins the thread of life.
15. A "steelyard" is a type of balance scale. Carpenter, according to this, weighed two hundred pounds.

Nor was he stooped, as tall men often are;
A cedar of a man, he towered straight.
One might have judged him lumbering of gait,
When he was still; but when he walked or ran,
He stepped it lightly like a little man—
And such a one is very good to see.
Not his the tongue for quip or repartee;
His wit seemed slow; and something of the child
Came o'er his rough-hewn features, when he smiled,
To mock the porching brow and eagle nose.
'Twas when he fought the true import of those
Grew clear, though even then his mien deceived;
For less in wrath, he seemed, than mildly grieved—
Which made his blows no whit less true or hard.
His hair was flax fresh gleaming from the card;
His eyes, the flax in bloom.

                A match in might,
Fink lacked five inches of his comrade's height,
And of his weight scarce twenty pounds, they say.
His hair was black, his small eyes greenish gray
And restless as though feeling out of place
In such a jocund plenilunar[16] face
That seemed made just for laughter. Then one saw
The pert pugnacious nose, the forward jaw,
The breadth of stubborn cheekbones, and one knew
That jest and fight to him were scarcely two,
But rather shifting phases of the joy
He felt in living. Careless as a boy,
Free handed with a gift or with a blow,
And giving either unto friend or foe
With frank good will, no man disliked him long.
They say his voice could glorify a song,
However loutish might the burden be;
And all the way from Pittsburg to the sea
The Rabelaisian[17] stories of the rogue
Ran wedded to the richness of his brogue.

16. "Plenilunar"—full moon (i.e., round and large).

17. François Rabelais (c. 1494–1553) is known for his coarse, exaggerated, sometimes licentious stories. One of his characters was Pantagruel.

And wheresoever boatmen came to drink,
There someone broached some escapade of Fink
That well might fill the goat-hoofed with delight;
For Mike, the pantagruelizing wight,
Was happy in the health of bone and brawn
And had the code and conscience of the faun
To guide him blithely down the easy way.
A questionable hero, one might say:
And so indeed, by any civil law.
Moreover, at first glimpse of him one saw
A bull-necked fellow, seeming over stout;
Tremendous at a heavy lift, no doubt,
But wanting action. By the very span
Of chest and shoulders, one misjudged the man
When he was clothed. But when he stripped to swim,
Men flocked about to have a look at him,
Moved vaguely by that body's wonder-scheme
Wherein the shape of God's Adamic dream
Was victor over stubborn dust again!

O very lovely is a maiden, when
The old creative thrill is set astir
Along her blood, and all the flesh of her
Is shapen as to music! Fair indeed
A tall horse, lean of flank, clean-limbed for speed,
Deep-chested for endurance! Very fair
A soaring tree, aloof in violet air
Upon a hill! And 'tis a glorious thing
To see a bankfull river in the spring
Fight homeward! Children wonderful to see—
The Girl, the Horse, the River and the Tree—
As any suckled at the breast of sod;
Dissolving symbols leading back to God
Through vista after vista of the Plan!
But surely none is fairer than a man
In whom the lines of might and grace are one.

Bronzed with exposure to the wind and sun,
Behold the splendid creature that was Fink!
You see him strolling to the river's brink,

All ease, and yet tremendously alive.
He pauses, poised on tiptoe for the dive,
And momently it seems the mother mud,
Quick with a mystic seed whose sap is blood,
Mysteriously rears a human flower.
Clean as a windless flame the lines of power
Run rhythmic up the stout limbs, muscle-laced,
Athwart the ropy gauntness of the waist,
The huge round girth of chest, whereover spread
Enormous shoulders. Now above his head
He lifts his arms where big thews merge and flow
As in some dream of Michelangelo;
And up along the dimpling back there run,
Like lazy serpents stirring in the sun,
Slow waves that break and pile upon the slope
Of that great neck in swelling rolls, a-grope
Beneath the velvet softness of the skin.
Now suddenly the lean waist grows more thin,
The deep chest on a sudden grows more deep;
And with the swiftness of a tiger's leap,
The easy grace of hawks in swooping flight,
That terrible economy of might
And beauty plunges outward from the brink.

Thus God had made experiment with Fink,
As proving how 'twere best that men might grow.

One turned from Mike to look upon Talbeau—
A little man, scarce five feet six and slim—
And wondered what his comrades saw in him
To justify their being thus allied.
Was it a sort of planetary pride
In lunar adoration? Hark to Mike:
"Shure I declare I niver saw his like—
A skinny whiffet of a man! And yit—
Well, do ye moind the plisint way we mit
And how he interjooced hisself that day?
'Twas up at Pittsburg, liquor flowin' fray
And ivrybody happy as a fool.
I cracked me joke and thin, as is me rule,

Looked round to view the havoc of me wit;
And ivrywan was doubled up wid it,
Save only wan, and him a scrubby mite.
Says I, and shure me language was polite,
'And did ye hear me little joke?' says I.
'I did' says he. 'And can't ye laugh, me b'y?'
'I can't' says he, the sassy little chap.
Nor did I git me hand back from the slap
I give him till he landed on me glim,
And I was countin' siventeen of him
And ivry dancin' wan of him was air!
Faith, whin I hit him he was niver there;
And shure it seemed that ivry wind that blew
Was peltin' knuckles in me face. Hurroo!
That toime, fer wance, I got me fill of fun!
God bless the little whiffet! It begun
Along about the shank of afthernoon;
And whin I washed me face, I saw the moon
A-shakin' wid its laughter in the shtrame.
And whin, betoimes, he wakened from his drame,
I says to him, 'Ye needn't laugh, me b'y:
A cliver little man ye are,' says I.
And Och, the face of me! I'm tellin' fac's—
Ye'd wonder did he do it wid an ax!
'Twas foine! 'Twas art!"

> Thus, eloquent with pride,
Mike Fink, an expert witness, testified
To Talbeau's fistic prowess.

> Now they say
There lived no better boatmen in their day
Than those three comrades; and the larger twain
In that wide land three mighty rivers drain [18]
Found not their peers for skill in marksmanship.
Writes one, who made the long Ohio trip
With those boon cronies in their palmy days,
How once Mike Fink beheld a sow at graze

18. The Mississippi, the Missouri, and the Ohio.

Upon the bank amid her squealing brood;
And how Mike, being in a merry mood,
Shot off each wiggling piglet's corkscrew tail
At twenty yards, while under easy sail
The boat moved on. And Carpenter could bore
A squirrel's eye clean at thirty steps and more—
So many say. But 'twas their dual test
Of mutual love and skill they liked the best
Of all their shooting tricks—when one stood up
At sixty paces with a whisky cup
Set brimming for a target on his head,
And felt the gusty passing of the lead,
Hot from the other's rifle, lift his hair.
And ever was the tin cup smitten fair
By each, to prove the faith of each anew:
For 'twas a rite of love between the two,
And not a mere capricious feat of skill.
"Och, shure, and can ye shoot the whisky, Bill?"
So Mike would end a wrangle. "Damn it, Fink!
Let's bore a pair of cups and have a drink!"
So Carpenter would stop a row grown stale.
And neither feared that either love might fail
Or either skill might falter.

                       Thus appear
The doughty three who held each other dear
For qualities they best could comprehend.

Now came the days of leisure to an end—
The days so gaily squandered, that would seem
to men at length made laughterless, a dream
Unthinkably remote; for Ilion held
Beneath her sixfold winding sheet of Eld [19]
Seems not so hoar as bygone joy we prize
In evil days. Now vaguely pale the skies,

19. Beginning in 1871, Heinrich Schliemann's archaeological dig at Hissarlik uncovered ruins of nine or ten cities built on top of one another. The sixth or seventh layer down is believed by many to be Homer's Troy. Hence the sixfold "winding sheet" of Ilion. "Eld" is an archaic word for "old." "Hoar" here means white with age.

The glimmer neither starlight's nor the morn's.
A rude ironic merriment of horns
Startles the men yet heavy with carouse,
And sets a Ree dog mourning in the drowse,
Snout skyward from a lodge top. Sleepy birds
Chirp in the brush. A drone of sullen words
Awakes and runs increasing through the camp.
Thin smoke plumes, rising in the valley damp,
Flatten among the leathern tents and make
The whole encampment like a ghostly lake
Where bobbing heads of swimmers come and go,
As with the whimsy of an undertow
That sucks and spews them. Raising dust and din,
The horse-guards drive their shaggy rabble in
From nightlong grazing. *Voyageurs,* with packs
Of folded tents and camp gear on their backs,
Slouch boatward through the reek. But when prevails
The smell of frying pans and coffee pails,
They cease to sulk and, greatly heartened, sing
Till ponies swell the chorus, nickering,
And race-old comrades jubilate as one.

Out of a roseless dawn the heat-pale sun
Beheld them toiling northward once again—
A hundred horses and a hundred men
Hushed in a windless swelter. Day on day
The same white dawn o'ertook them on their way:
And daylong in the white glare sang no bird,
But only shrill grasshoppers clicked and whirred,
As though the heat were vocal. All the while
The dwindling current lengthened, mile on mile,
Meandrous in a labyrinth of sand.

Now e'er they left the Ree town by the Grand
The revellers had seen the spent moon roam
The morning, like a tipsy hag bound home.
A bubble-laden boat, they saw it sail
The sunset river of a fairy tale
When they were camped beside the Cannonball.
A spectral sun, it held the dusk in thrall
Nightlong about the Heart. The stars alone

Upon the cluttered Mandan lodges shone
The night they slept below the Knife. And when
Their course, long westward, shifted once again
To lead them north, the August moon was new.

The rainless Southwest wakened now and blew
A wilting, worrying, breath-sucking gale
That roared one moment in the bellied sail,
Next moment slackened to a lazy croon.
Now came the first misfortune. All forenoon
With line and pole the sweating boatmen strove
Along the east bank, while the horseguards drove
The drooping herd a little to the fore.
And then the current took the other shore.
Straight on, a maze of bar and shallow lay,
The main stream running half a mile away
To westward of a long low willow isle.
An hour they fought that stubborn half a mile
Of tumbled water. Down the running planks
The polesmen toiled in endless slanting ranks.
Now swimming, now a-flounder in the ooze
Of some blind bar, the naked cordelle crews
Sought any kind of footing for a pull;
While gust-bedevilled sails, now booming full,
Now flapping slack, gave questionable aid.

The west bank gained, along a ragged shade
Of straggling cottonwoods the boatmen sprawled
And panted. Out across the heat-enthralled,
Wind-fretted waste of shoal and bar they saw
The string of ponies ravelled up a draw
That mounted steeply eastward from the vale
Where, like a rampart flung across the trail,
A bluff rose sheer. Heads low, yet loath to graze,
They waxed and withered in the oily haze,
Now ponies, now a crawling flock of sheep.
Behind them three slack horseguards, half asleep,
Swayed limply, leaning on their saddle-bows.

The boat crews, lolling in a semi-doze,
Still watch the herd; nor do the gazers dream

What drama nears a climax over stream,
What others yonder may be watching too.
Now looming large upon the lucent blue,
The foremost ponies top the rim, and stare
High-headed down the vacancies of air
Beneath them; while the herders dawdle still
And gather wool scarce halfway up the hill—
A slumbrous sight beheld by heavy eyes.

But hark! What murmuring of far-flung cries
From yonder pocket in the folded rise
That flanks the draw? The herders also hear
And with a start glance upward to the rear.
Their spurred mounts plunge! What do they see but dust
Whipped skyward yonder in a freakish gust?
What panic overtakes them? Look again!
The rolling dust cloud vomits mounted men,
A ruck of tossing heads and gaudy gears
Beneath a bristling thicket of lean spears
Slant in a gust of onset!

                    Over stream
The boatmen stare dumfounded. Like a dream
In some vague region out of space and time
Evolves the swiftly moving pantomime
Before those loungers with ungirded loins;
Till one among them shouts *"Assiniboines!"*
And swelling to a roar, the wild word runs
Above a pellmell scramble for the guns,
Perceived as futile soon. Yet here and there
A few young hotheads fusillade the air,
And rage the more to know the deed absurd.
Some only grind their teeth without a word;
Some stand aghast, some grinningly inane,
While some, like watch-dogs rabid at the chain,
Growl curses, pacing at the river's rim.

So might unhappy spirits haunt the dim
Far shore of Styx,[20] beholding outrage done

---

20. The Styx is one of the five rivers surrounding Hades, according to Greek mythology.

To loved ones in the region of the sun—
Rage goaded by its own futility!

For one vast moment strayed from time, they see
The war band flung obliquely down the slope,
The flying herdsmen, seemingly a-grope
In sudden darkness for their saddle guns.
A murmuring shock! And now the whole scene runs
Into a dusty blur of horse and man;
And now the herd's rear surges on the van
That takes the cue of panic fear and flies
Stampeding to the margin of the skies,
Till all have vanished in the deeps of air.
Now outlined sharply on the sky-rim there
The victors pause and taunt their helpless foes
With buttocks patted and with thumbs at nose
And jeers scarce hearkened for the wind's guffaw.
They also vanish. In the sunwashed draw
Remains no sign of what has come to pass,
Save three dark splotches on the yellow grass,
Where now the drowsy horseguards have their will.

At sundown on the summit of the hill
The huddled boatmen saw the burial squad
Tuck close their comrades' coverlet of sod—
Weird silhouettes on melancholy gray.
And very few found anything to say
That night; though some spoke gently of the dead,
Remembering what that one did or said
At such and such a time. And some, more stirred
With lust of vengeance for the stolen herd,
Swore vaguely now and then beneath their breath.
Some, brooding on the imminence of death,
Grew wistful of their unreturning years;
And some who found their praying in arrears
Made shift to liquidate the debt that night.

But when once more the cheerful morning light
Came on them toiling, also came the mood
Of young adventure, and the solitude
Sang with them. For 'tis glorious to spend

One's golden days large-handed to the end—
The good broadpieces that can buy so much!
And what may hoarders purchase but a crutch
Wherewith to hobble graveward?

                          On they pressed
To where once more the river led them west;
And every day the hot wind, puff on puff,
Assailed them; every night they heard it sough
In thickets prematurely turning sere.

Then came the sudden breaking of the year.

Abruptly in a waning afternoon
The hot wind ceased, as fallen in a swoon
With its own heat. For hours the swinking crews
Had bandied scarcely credible good news
Of clouds across the dim northwestward plain;
And they who offered wagers on the rain
Found ready takers, though the gloomy rack,
With intermittent rumbling at its back,
Had mounted slowly. Now it towered high,
A blue-black wall of night across the sky
Shot through with glacial green.

                      A mystic change!
The sun was hooded and the world went strange—
A picture world! The hollow hush that fell
Made loud the creaking of the taut cordelle,
The bent spar's groan, the plunk of steering poles.
A bodeful calm lay glassy on the shoals;
The current had the look of flowing oil.
They saw the cloud's lip billow now and boil—
Black breakers gnawing at a coast of light;
They saw the stealthy wraith-arms of the night
Grope for the day to strangle it; they saw
The up-stream reaches vanish in a flaw
Of driving sand: and scarcely were the craft
Made fast to clumps of willow fore and aft,
When with a roar the blinding fury rolled

Upon them; and the breath of it was cold.
There fell no rain.

        That night was calm and clear:
Just such a night as when the waning year
Has set aflare the old Missouri wood;
When Greenings[21] are beginning to be good;
And when, so hollow is the frosty hush,
One hears the ripe persimmons falling—*plush!*—
Upon the littered leaves. The kindly time!
With cider in the vigor of its prime,
Just strong enough to edge the dullest wit
Should neighbor folk drop in awhile to sit
And gossip. O the dear flame-painted gloam,
The backlog's sputter on the hearth at home—
How far away that night! Thus many a lad,
Grown strangely old, remembered and was sad.
Wolves mourned among the bluffs. Like hanks of wool
Fog flecked the river. And the moon was full.

A week sufficed to end the trail. They came
To where the lesser river gives its name
And meed of waters to the greater stream.[22]
Here, lacking horses, they must nurse the dream
Of beaver haunts beyond the Great Divide,
Build quarters for the winter trade, and bide
The coming up of Ashley and his band.

So up and down the wooded tongue of land
That thins to where the rivers wed, awoke
The sound of many axes, stroke on stroke;
And lustily the hewers sang at whiles—
The better to forget the homeward miles
In this, the homing time. And when the geese
With cacophonic councils broke the peace

21. "Greenings"—apples that have green skin when ripe.
22. This is the junction of the Yellowstone and the Missouri, at the eastern edge of what is now Montana. Here Ashley's men built Fort Henry, later called Fort Union. From this point, Neihardt's poem goes on to tell the stories of the mountain men and the beginnings of the Rocky Mountain fur trade.

Of frosty nights before they took to wing;
When cranes went over daily, southering,
And blackbirds chattered in the painted wood,
A mile above the river junction stood
The fort, adjoining the Missouri's tide.
Foursquare and thirty paces on a side,
A wall of sharpened pickets bristled round
A group of sod-roofed cabins. Bastions frowned
From two opposing corners, set to brave
A foe on either flank; and stout gates gave
Upon the stream, where now already came
The Indian craft, lured thither by the fame
Of traders building by the mating floods.

Black Elk
1863-1950

▬

1932: John G. Neihardt, *Black Elk Speaks:*
Being the Life Story
of a Holy Man of the Ogalala Sioux
1953: Joseph Epes Brown, *The Sacred Pipe:*
Black Elk's Account of
the Seven Rites of the Ogalala Sioux

▬

THE FOLLOWING *selection is from chapter 17 of Neihardt's* Black Elk
Speaks. *In a survey of Neihardt's work, Blair Whitney calls* Black Elk
Speaks *"one of the best Westerns ever written."*[1] *But who wrote it? Black
Elk did not write or speak English. Neihardt, dedicated to writing lyric and epic
poetry, did not speak the Sioux language. Relying on interpreters, gestures, close
personal contact, flashes of insight, and an extraordinary sympathy of purpose,
Neihardt put Black Elk's story into English. Dee Brown, author of* Bury My
Heart at Wounded Knee, *calls* Black Elk Speaks *the best book ever written on
the American Indian.*

*In 1930 Neihardt drove to the Pine Ridge Reservation in South Dakota to
research the Sioux Ghost Dance for his poem* The Song of the Messiah. *There
he met Black Elk, a son and grandson of medicine men and formerly renowned as
a medicine man himself. Old and slowly growing blind, Black Elk had become a
practicing Catholic but quickly recognized that Neihardt was the person who could
"save the Great Vision." He told an interpreter: "As I sit here, I can feel in this
man beside me a strong desire to know the things of the Other World. He has been
sent to learn what I know, and I will teach him." In May 1931 the interviews
began. The result was Neihardt's "transformation" (as he called it) of Black Elk's*

1. Blair Whitney, *John G. Neihardt* (Boston: Twayne, 1976), p. 91.

life story and sacred vision into Black Elk Speaks.[2] *Neihardt's transcripts of the interviews have been edited by Raymond DeMallie in* The Sixth Grandfather: Black Elk's Teachings Given to John G. Neihardt *(1984).*

Black Elk had powerful visions as a child, visions that not only led him to perform many healings but also enabled him to warn his tribespeople away from dangerous situations. As a twelve-year-old boy, Black Elk was on the scene when Custer and his men were annihilated at the Little Big Horn in 1876. He was at Camp Robinson when Crazy Horse was killed there the next year. He followed Sitting Bull, who had fled to Canada after the Custer battle. Later, like Luther Standing Bear, he joined Buffalo Bill's Wild West and traveled with the show to England and France.

Black Elk witnessed the massacre at Wounded Knee in 1890. As a child, he had had a vision that had seemed to tell him to give his support to the Ghost Dance movement, but after the killings Black Elk declared that the dream of his people had died there in the bloody and frozen mud, that he had failed to restore the sacred hoop that meant unity and peace to the Sioux.

The hoop, or circle, is an emblem of all the life forces in harmony. It is the tension of the forces that keeps the circle true and strong. Inside the circle, a road of peace leads north and south; a road of war and trouble leads east and west. The cross inside the circle is one of humankind's most ancient symbols.

Neihardt realized that what he was writing down was not the story of an old and dying Indian but was a retelling of the ancient messages of the circle. Neihardt was a collaborator, to use his own term, in a mystical "sacred obligation."[3] Black Elk felt, at the end of his life, that he had failed his vision and had lost his power. But in the enduring and enthusiastic reception of Black Elk Speaks, *in America and across Europe in yet other languages, Neihardt saw the message still spreading.*

———

2. John G. Neihardt, *Black Elk Speaks* (1932; reprint, New York: Pocket Books, 1972), p. xi.

3. Ibid., p. xii.

The First Cure

AFTER THE HEYOKA ceremony, I came to live here where I am now between Wounded Knee Creek and Grass Creek.[4] Others came too, and we made these little gray houses of logs that you see, and they are square. It is a bad way to live, for there can be no power in a square.

You have noticed that everything an Indian does is in a circle, and that is because the Power of the World always works in circles, and everything tries to be round. In the old days when we were a strong and happy people, all our power came to us from the sacred hoop of the nation, and so long as the hoop was unbroken, the people flourished. The flowering tree was the living center of the hoop, and the circle of the four quarters nourished it. The east gave peace and light, the south gave warmth, the west gave rain, and the north with its cold and mighty wind gave strength and endurance. This knowledge came to us from the outer world with our religion. Everything the Power of the World does is done in a circle. The sky is round, and I have heard that the earth is round like a ball, and so are all the stars. The wind, in its greatest power, whirls. Birds make their nests in circles, for theirs is the same religion as ours. The sun comes forth and goes down again in a circle. The moon does the same, and both are round.

An Indian way of writing a name. it indicates Black Elk.

From John G. Neihardt, *Black Elk Speaks* (1932; reprint, Lincoln: University of Nebraska Press, 1988), pp. 198–207. Copyright © 1932, 1959 by John G. Neihardt.

4. The year is 1882. The Wounded Knee Massacre took place nearby on December 29, 1890, when the Seventh Cavalry attacked an encampment of Miniconjou Sioux, killing 146 people and wounding 51.

Even the seasons form a great circle in their changing, and always come back again to where they were. The life of a man is a circle from childhood to childhood, and so it is in everything where power moves. Our tepees were round like the nests of birds, and these were always set in a circle, the nation's hoop, a nest of many nests, where the Great Spirit meant for us to hatch our children.

But the Wasichus have put us in these square boxes. Our power is gone and we are dying, for the power is not in us any more. You can look at our boys and see how it is with us. When we were living by the power of the circle in the way we should, boys were men at twelve or thirteen years of age. But now it takes them very much longer to mature.

Well, it is as it is. We are prisoners of war while we are waiting here. But there is another world.

It was in the Moon of Shedding Ponies (May) when we had the heyoka ceremony. One day in the Moon of Fatness (June), when everything was blooming, I invited One Side to come over and eat with me. I had been thinking about the four-rayed herb that I had now seen twice—the first time in the great vision when I was nine years old, and the second time when I was lamenting on the hill. I knew that I must have this herb for curing, and I thought I could recognize the place where I had seen it growing that night when I lamented.

After One Side and I had eaten, I told him there was a herb I must find, and I wanted him to help me hunt for it. Of course I did not tell him I had seen it in a vision. He was willing to help, so we got on our horses and rode over to Grass Creek. Nobody was living over there. We came to the top of a high hill above the creek, and there we got off our horses and sat down, for I felt that we were close to where I saw the herb growing in my vision of the dog.

We sat there awhile singing together some heyoka songs. Then I began to sing alone a song I had heard in my first great vision:

> "In a sacred manner they are sending voices."

After I had sung this song, I looked down towards the west, and yonder at a certain spot beside the creek were crows and magpies, chicken hawks and spotted eagles circling around and around.

Then I knew, and I said to One Side: "Friend, right there is where the herb is growing." He said: "We will go forth and see." So we got on our horses and rode down Grass Creek until we came to a dry gulch, and this we followed up. As we neared the spot the birds all flew away, and it was a place where four or five dry gulches came together. There right on the side of the bank the herb was growing, and I knew it, although I had never seen one like it before, except in my vision.

It had a root about as long as to my elbow, and this was a little thicker than my thumb. It was flowering in four colors, blue, white, red, and yellow.

We got off our horses, and after I had offered red willow bark to the Six Powers, I made a prayer to the herb, and said to it: "Now we shall go forth to the two-leggeds, but only to the weakest ones, and there shall be happy days among the weak."

It was easy to dig the herb, because it was growing in the edge of the clay gulch. Then we started back with it. When we came to Grass Creek again, we wrapped it in some good sage that was growing there.

Something must have told me to find the herb just then, for the next evening I needed it and could have done nothing without it.

I was eating supper when a man by the name of Cuts-to-Pieces came in, and he was saying: "Hey, hey, hey!" for he was in trouble. I asked him what was the matter, and he said: "I have a boy of mine, and he is very sick and I am afraid he will die soon. He has been sick a long time. They say you have great power from the horse dance and the heyoka ceremony, so maybe you can save him for me. I think so much of him."

I told Cuts-to-Pieces that if he really wanted help, he should go home and bring me back a pipe with an eagle feather on it. While he was gone, I thought about what I had to do; and I was afraid, because I had never cured anybody yet with my power, and I was very sorry for Cuts-to-Pieces. I prayed hard for help. When Cuts-to-Pieces came back with the pipe, I told him to take it around to the left of me, leave it there, and pass out again to the right of me. When he had done this, I sent for One Side to come and help me. Then I took the pipe and went to where the sick little boy was. My father and my mother went with us, and my friend, Standing Bear, was already there.

I first offered the pipe to the Six Powers, then I passed it, and we all smoked. After that I began making a rumbling thunder sound on the drum. You know, when the power of the west comes to the two-leggeds, it comes with rumbling, and when it has passed, everything lifts up its head and is glad and there is greenness. So I made this rumbling sound. Also, the voice of the drum is an offering to the Spirit of the World. Its sound arouses the mind and makes men feel the mystery and power of things.

The sick little boy was on the northeast side of the tepee, and when we entered at the south, we went around from left to right, stopping on the west side when we had made the circle.

You want to know why we always go from left to right like that. I can tell you something of the reason, but not all. Think of this: Is not the south the source of life, and does not the flowering stick truly come from there? And does not man advance from there toward the setting sun of his life? Then does he not approach the colder north where the white hairs are? And does he not then arrive, if he lives, at the source of light and understanding, which is the east? Then does he not return to where he began, to his second childhood, there to give back his life to all life, and his flesh to the earth whence it came? The more you think about this, the more meaning you will see in it.

As I said, we went into the tepee from left to right, and sat ourselves down on the west side. The sick little boy was on the northeast side, and he looked as though he were only skin and bones. I had the pipe, the drum and the four-rayed herb already, so I asked for a wooden cup, full of water, and an eagle bone whistle, which was for the spotted eagle of my great vision. They placed the cup of water in front of me; and then I had to think awhile, because I had never done this before and I was in doubt.

I understood a little more now, so I gave the eagle bone whistle to One Side and told him how to use it in helping me. Then I filled the pipe with red willow bark, and gave it to the pretty young daughter of Cuts-to-Pieces, telling her to hold it, just as I had seen the virgin of the east holding it in my great vision.

Everything was ready now, so I made low thunder on the drum, keeping time as I sent forth a voice. Four times I cried "Hey-a-a-hey," drumming as I cried to the Spirit of the World, and while I was doing this I could feel the power coming through me from my feet up, and I knew that I could help the sick little boy.

I kept on sending a voice, while I made low thunder on the drum, saying: "My Grandfather, Great Spirit, you are the only one and to no other can any one send voices. You have made everything, they say, and you have made it good and beautiful. The four quarters and the two roads crossing each other, you have made. Also you have set a power where the sun goes down. The two-leggeds on earth are in despair. For them, my Grandfather, I send a voice to you. You have said this to me: The weak shall walk. In vision you have taken me to the center of the world and there you have shown me the power to make over. The water in the cup that you have given me, by its power shall the dying live. The herb that you have shown me, through its power shall the feeble walk upright. From where we are always facing (the south), behold, a virgin shall appear, walking the good red road, offering the pipe as she walks, and hers also is the power of the flowering tree. From where the Giant lives (the north), you have given me a sacred, cleansing wind, and where this wind passes the weak shall have strength. You have said this to me. To you and to all your powers and to Mother Earth I send a voice for help."

You see, I had never done this before, and I know now that only one power would have been enough. But I was so eager to help the sick little boy that I called on every power there is.

I had been facing the west, of course, while sending a voice. Now I walked to the north and to the east and to the south, stopping there where the source of all life is and where the good red road begins. Standing there I sang thus:

> "In a sacred manner I have made them walk.
> A sacred nation lies low.
> In a sacred manner I have made them walk.
> A sacred two-legged, he lies low.
> In a sacred manner, he shall walk."

While I was singing this I could feel something queer all through my body, something that made me want to cry for all unhappy things, and there were tears on my face.

Now I walked to the quarter of the west, where I lit the pipe, offered it to the powers, and, after I had taken a whiff of smoke, I passed it around.

When I looked at the sick little boy again, he smiled at me, and I could feel that the power was getting stronger.

I next took the cup of water, drank a little of it, and went around to where the sick little boy was. Standing before him, I stamped the earth four times. Then, putting my mouth to the pit of his stomach, I drew through him the cleansing wind of the north. I next chewed some of the herb and put it in the water, afterward blowing some of it on the boy and to the four quarters. The cup with the rest of the water I gave to the virgin, who gave it to the sick little boy to drink. Then I told the virgin to help the boy stand up and to walk around the circle with him, beginning at the south, the source of life. He was very poor and weak, but with the virgin's help he did this.

Then I went away.

Next day Cuts-to-Pieces came and told me that his little boy was feeling better and was sitting up and could eat something again. In four days he could walk around. He got well and lived to be thirty years old.

Cuts-to-Pieces gave me a good horse for doing this; but of course I would have done it for nothing.

When the people heard about how the little boy was cured, many came to me for help, and I was busy most of the time.

This was in the summer of my nineteenth year (1882), in the Moon of Making Fat.

PART 3

The Neomythic Period

1890-1914

Introduction

—

A *myth* is the organized and shaped values
of a people, a part of history and culture.
— MAX WESTBROOK

—

From the Closing of the Frontier to
the Opening of World War

ACCORDING to the superintendent of the census, America's frontier closed in 1890; coincidentally, that was the same year in which Wyoming achieved statehood. The two events are indicators of far-reaching changes in western society. The census figures, for instance, indicate that the population was moving toward the cities. By 1900, California had more people living in cities than outside of them. Dates, such as 1890, make convenient markers for literary periods; certain literary influences, however, had begun many years earlier.

For instance, Erastus Beadle began publishing his Dime Novel series in the early 1860s. During the next thirty years, his company published hundreds of titles. Dozens of imitations sprang up, all of them romanticizing the adventures of such characters as Deadwood Dick, Calamity Jane, Denver Dan, Lariat Lil, and Daisy Dare. In the pages of the pulps, the American reading public saw the West as a land of unspeakably savage redskins and unimaginably foul villains who were being fought (and vanquished, naturally) by wonderfully virile and virtuous heroes and heroines on horseback. Millions of these formula fictions were sold, painting a portrait of a Buffalo Bill West that never really existed. It became a virtually universal image, this impossible West, an image that has faded to a nostalgic shadow but that has not yet vanished. Discussing novels of the American West, John R.

Milton wrote: "Beadle retired from the Beadle and Adams publishing firm in the late 1880s also, and, as we recall that Frederick Jackson Turner set 1890 as the closing of the frontier, we might speculate that the entire western phenomenon could have—or should have—stopped right there. But the glamour and romance of the Wild West had been solidly established, and pulp magazines of the 1890s to the 1930s provided the link between the best-selling years of the dime novel and the early years of the modern western." [1]

A great many of these "penny dreadfuls" were sold to railroad passengers to amuse them while they traveled on the rails that had spread over the West like a steel spider web. And thanks to those same rails, the dime novel image of the Wild West began to weaken. The word *frontier* was seen less often in the literature, being replaced by the phrase *out West*. *Out West* began to take on negative connotations too. It seemed to stand for a place of last chances, of hard work and deprivation, a place where there was little opportunity for romance and glory. The word *pioneer* hung on in some of the few remaining remote places like Mari Sandoz's sandhills, but most writers preferred the terms *homesteader* or *farmer,* labels that lacked a feeling of heroism and nobility.

The young writer growing up in the 1890–1914 era had an ample supply of fanciful western fables. Such stories were a regular feature of pulp novels and could even be found in magazines as respectable as the *Saturday Evening Post* and *McClure's Magazine*. There were "literary" romances (Owen Wister's *The Virginian* was published in 1902), and there was that mesmerizing new media, cinema. The world's first western film, *The Great Train Robbery*, made its debut in 1903.

In the newspapers of that same period, however, we find a different version of how things were out West. Throughout the 1880s, the 1890s, and the first decade of the new century, events were signaling the end of the romantic older West. In 1886, for example, Geronimo surrendered to General Nelson Miles, putting an end to the U.S. cavalry's "Indian problem." In 1889, more than fifty thousand whites lined up in Oklahoma for the first of several "runs" to claim sections of Indian-held land. It was the last territory of any size to remain in the hands of Native Americans; the federal government declared most of it "surplus" and opened it to the last sizable influx of homesteaders the West would ever see.

Did all of those homesteaders rush out to grab their free land because

1. John R. Milton, *The Novel of the American West* (Lincoln: University of Nebraska Press, 1980), p. 11.

they saw that western farming was a booming business, an attractive lifestyle? Had the answer to that question been "yes," there would have been little need for the 1867 establishment of the National Grange of the Patrons of Husbandry—the Granger movement—or for the establishment in 1888 of the Farmer's and Laborer's Union of America. Somewhere between one million and three million people sought the benevolence and protection of these unions.

Farmers in the nineties went through season after season of poor crop yields and depressed economy. The People's party, later known as the Populist party, accumulated a large body of followers in Kansas, Nebraska, South Dakota, Minnesota, and the Northwest. The West had sufficient population to expedite political organization, and had a populace that held the federal government responsible for rural welfare. The frontier values of speculation, individualism, survival of the strong, and raw democracy were shifting; as the turn of the century approached, the idea of equal opportunity meant that the government was obligated to protect the common citizens with law, order, welfare, a regulated currency, and federally controlled systems of transportation and public utilities.

Until the 1890s, the West was the principal arena of national expansion. When the last frontier was covered by settlements, the force of manifest destiny was turned toward other territories. Aided by a growing navy and a war with Spain, the United States government occupied Hawaii, Samoa, the Philippines, and Cuba; having built railroads up and down and across North America, the United States now proposed to go south and slash a canal across Panama. Negotiations were inaugurated in 1900, digging was begun in 1904, and the Big Ditch opened for business in 1914, just in time for World War I.

New Views of a Changing West

Hamlin Garland believed that the frontier line still existed, gradually moving westward across the Midwest and the Great Plains. He called his frontier the "middle border." He was convinced, as Frederick Jackson Turner had been, that the frontier exerted a powerful shaping influence on the national character of the people. The difference, however, was that Garland believed the frontier turned people sour. In *Main-Travelled Roads* (1891), Garland dramatized how the familiar myth of hope and promise turned harsh and discordant, finally ending on a note of futility and near despair. In 1887, a writer named Joseph Kirkland published *Zury: The Meanest Man in Spring County*. Zury's frontier home is on the Illinois line of settlement, at the edge of the Great Plains. At first Zury is full of optimism about the future, but then the lonely land with its scanty opportunities gradually transforms him into a mean, miserly, ugly man. Kirkland's book illustrated Garland's thesis: the western frontier is only a disillusionment, and it makes people bad, not good. We find this theme appearing again in Mari Sandoz's story "Bone Joe and the Smokin' Woman" and in Dorothy Johnson's "The Man Who Shot Liberty Valance."

In other literature of this period, however, we do find a continuation of positive and hopeful attitudes. We even find some of the romance of the early settlement years. These were the writers who echoed Theodore Roosevelt's enthusiastic belief in the West as the cradle of Americanism, the nation's primary source of youth and exuberance and spirit. Although western literature no longer portrayed people as demigods in charge of their own destinies, it did present westerners as Americans who believed in their work. The social essayist Meridel Le Sueur wrote:

> The mechanics, lumberjacks, the lakemen, rivermen, woodcutters, plowmen, the hunkies, hanycocks, whistle-punks; the women beating the chaff, the roof-raisers, the cradle-makers, the writers of constitutions, the singers in the evening along unknown rivers; the stone masons, the quarrymen, the high slingers of words, the printers and speakers in the courthouses, the lawmakers, the carpenters, joiners, journeymen—all kept on building. Every seven years, they picked up the loans, mortgages, the grasshopper-ridden fields, the lost acres, the flat bank accounts, and went on, started over, turned a new leaf, worked harder, looked over new horizons.
>
> The heritage they give us is the belief we have in them. It is the story of their survival, the sum of adjustments, the struggle, the folk accumulation called sense and the faith we have in that collective experience. It was real and fast, and we enclose it.[2]

The shift of western attitudes becomes very obvious when we look at the changes that took place in the four most common categories of literary heroes: the mountain man, the wagon-train pioneer, the miner or prospector, and the cowboy.

The mountain man seems to have changed the least, being basically the same character he was in early accounts by such writers as Francis Parkman, Hector Lewis Garrard, and Stewart Edward White. He still leads a rigor-

---

2. Meridel Le Sueur, *Ripening: Selected Work, 1927–1980*, ed. Elaine Hedges (Old Westbury, N.Y.: Feminist Press, 1982), p. 38.

ous, dangerous existence, alone or in a brigade of his "companyeros." The problems he faces are not very complex; most of his conflicts involve man versus man or man versus nature, seldom man versus himself. He performs amazing exploits, and he measures all men—including himself—by their physical abilities and deeds. Like Homer's heroes, he is an elusive figure who appears to come from nowhere and seems to vanish again into the mountains when his era ends.

John R. Milton has called the mountain man "the epic hero of America,"[3] and as such he lives in the past, unaffected by the passage of time. His environment, his occupation, and even his hardships seem romantic. People of the 1890s, particularly farmers and ranchers, had to come to grips with complex economic and political problems. The mountain man's problems may be life threatening, but at least they are direct and simple.

The four classic novels of the mountain man are *Wolf Song*, by Harvey Fergusson; *Mountain Man*, by Vardis Fisher; *The Big Sky*, by A. B. Guthrie, Jr.; and *Lord Grizzly*, by Frederick Manfred. These novels still stress the physical conflicts and adventure, but the novelists have also emphasized the psychological aspects of motivation, fear, and doubt. Previous writers concentrated on details of fur-trade tools, language, and customs; Manfred, Guthrie, Fisher, and Fergusson show us the power of the landscape to affect men's minds and souls. Frank Waters is another writer who sees the land's effect on the human psyche as the most important phenomenon of the mountain man era. "These were the first nonindigenous men . . . to meet in mortal struggle the invisible forces of the land, and to accept its terms. . . . Not until we understand the mountain men can we understand ourselves."[4] The mountain man is larger than life, a man whose senses are in tune with nature to a degree that becomes almost mystic. He is also a tragic figure who ultimately must destroy the only world he can live in and understand.

One of the West's most familiar pictures is that of the canvas-covered prairie schooner rolling across the open prairie. The man walking beside the oxen looks resolute and capable; the woman on the seat, her child on her lap, looks strong and hopeful. But by 1890, the wagon-train pioneers of literature no longer represent the cutting edge of manifest destiny. Opening the land is no longer their story. Now, like the people in O. E. Rölvaag's *Giants in the Earth* or Mari Sandoz's *Old Jules* or in the books of Dorothy Scarborough, Hamlin Garland, Vardis Fisher, and dozens of others, the

---

3. Milton, *Novel*, p. 46.
4. Frank Waters, *The Colorado* (New York: Rinehart and Co., 1946), p. 188.

new westerners find movement to be either impossible or futile. Their problem now is not to conquer the land but to survive in it, not to discover new country but to reveal the strengths and weaknesses within themselves. The husband in the earlier wagon-train stories was a risk taker, a source of virility, an accumulator; the female was the steady, conservative, spiritual center. But these traits tend to lose their eloquence in the struggle against drought and debt. They are put aside, like the disintegrating Conestoga wagon sitting forgotten among the farm machinery.

Movement, independence, and stubborn faith in nature's bounty are the romantic values that persist in literary versions of the miner or prospector figure. Like the mountain man, the lone forty-niner with his pick and shovel seems to escape the influences of the turn of the century. From Bret Harte through Walter Van Tilburg Clark and Thomas Hornsby Ferril, the miner represents the West's persistent idea that there is a mother lode somewhere to be found and that searching for it is a perfectly valid way to spend your life. There is a great deal of sacrifice and waste, of course, as we see in Ferril's "Magenta" and Clark's "The Indian Well," and each time the prospector makes his Big Strike he becomes as tragic a figure as the mountain man. He is forced to stop his wandering life and settle down to the mundane task of removing his bonanza from the ground, usually only to waste it.

The cowboy in the literature of the neomythic period undergoes complex changes, although his basic image remains the same: he is independent, exuberant, chivalrous, resourceful, and skillful. But the free-riding buckaroo of Theodore Roosevelt's *Ranch Life and the Hunting Trail* is now fenced in by barbed wire, railroads, towns, and economics. In the romance literature, the cowboy's former world lives on, and the hero's conflicts are simple. Writers such as Clarence Mulford, Max Brand, Zane Grey, and J. Frank Dobie still show the cowboy fighting rustlers, land thieves, and murderers. At the other extreme, however, we now find cowboys grappling with heavy sociological or psychological problems.

In some stories, the cowboy is that "simple child of the earlier plains" that we meet at the end of Stephen Crane's "The Bride Comes to Yellow Sky." In other stories, he is almost the exact opposite: in Jack Schaefer's *Shane* he is a mysterious source of courage and strength, returning from the far western hills to be the champion of the settlers. In fact, Shane is such a heavily metaphoric character that most readers overlook the evidence (in chapter 5) that he was a cowboy before he was a gunfighter. And in Schaefer's *Monte Walsh* and Elmer Kelton's *The Time It Never Rained*, the cowboy is a kind of indomitable spirit that keeps on living, even though people continue to announce the disappearance of the "last cowboy." He does not disappear; he changes to survive. In the old myths, he was part of a group set apart from other men, a group that followed its own unique values and patterns of behavior. High on the list of these was independence: when a cowboy got married or took a "regular" job, he was no longer a cowboy. In the new mythology, the cowboy is largely a loner who may get married or do anything he wants for a living, as long as he exemplifies cowboy standards—independence, basic honesty, chivalry, resourcefulness, and skill.

The Land

Even using the term *environment* instead of *land* implies a whole new set of attitudes. To earlier generations, land was for conquest or was to be settled, cultivated, dominated. However, the West was too extensive, too hostile, too awesome for easy domestication. By the turn of the century, writers began to reassess the myth that the West was some sort of "promised land" for the people to put under cultivation and began to realize that the land had, in a sense, conquered the people.

> . . . the landscape remains vivid, even stark, and gains the sense of an ambient myth, a reality which imposes disciplined habits of mind and sharpens the senses to animallike alertness. Like myth, it seems to elude scientific inquiry and is richest when perceived in metaphysical communion. It functions as an extension of man's Being.[5]

Environment is used in a wide variety of ways by neomythic authors. John Steinbeck's California valley, for instance, is described as a stifling enclosure that even prevents the air from moving. In Meridel Le Sueur and A. B. Guthrie, Jr., there is a "metaphysical communion" between the humans and the land. That same theme is even stronger in Frank Waters, whose Doña Maria is an archetypal earth-mother. She and the land are one. Dorothy Johnson and Jack Schaefer, in the selections offered here, use landscape as a bleak backdrop, one so immense that it gives humans a feeling of insignificance. With such different interpretations of the environment, these six authors have something interesting in common: they all were born in the first decade of the century and went through childhood during World War I.

The literary characters, the interpretations of the western landscape, and the new value systems became just as complex as the social conditions from

5. Clinton F. Larson and William Stafford, *Modern Poetry of Western America* (Provo, Utah: Brigham Young University Press, 1975), pp. xx–xxi.

which they arose, in those few decades following the close of the frontier. And the writers were well aware that changes were taking place. In the epilogue to Harvey Fergusson's *Grant of Kingdom*, the narrator returned in 1906 to Taos, calling it "as perfect a relic of a vanished world as could be found anywhere in America." He talked with people who remembered the old pioneering days when Jean Ballard, a mountain man, had carved himself an empire out of the wilderness. "To me," wrote the narrator, "the droning tales of these old-timers had the quality of elegy. I felt as though I were witnessing the process by which the past becomes a beloved myth, simplified in memory so that one may see the meanings that are always obscured by the noise and dust of the present."[6]

6. Harvey Fergusson, *Grant of Kingdom* (Albuquerque: University of New Mexico Press, 1975), pp. 310–11.

H. L. Davis
1894-1960

—

1935: *Honey in the Horn*
1942: *Proud Riders and Other Poems*
1947: *Harp of a Thousand Strings*
1949: *Beulah Land*
1953: *Team Bells Woke Me*
and Other Stories
1978: *The Selected Poems of H. L. Davis*

—

W HEN American Mercury *published "Old Man Isbell's Wife" in the February issue of 1929, the author's biographical blurb was indifferent and brief. "H. L. Davis was born in Oregon and now lives in the State of Washington. He has worked as printer's devil, sheep-herder, harvest hand, deputy sheriff and country editor. A group of his poems was awarded the Levison Prize in 1919."[1] This scant notice is understandable, since "Old Man Isbell's Wife" was one of Davis's first publications. His literary reputation grew quickly, however, and magazines soon had more to say about him. In 1932 Davis received a Guggenheim exchange fellowship, which took him to Mexico. There he wrote his first novel,* Honey in the Horn, *the winner of the Harper Novel Prize in 1935 and the Pulitzer Prize in 1936.*

Unfortunately, the Pulitzer Prize did not elevate Davis to the ranks of major American writers. Reviewers continued to assume that Honey in the Horn *was just a lengthy pulp Western. But his next novel,* Harp of a Thousand Strings, *received some serious attention, and by the time* Winds of Morning *(1952) came*

---

1. *American Mercury* 16 (February 1929): 128. In his extensive treatment *H. L. Davis* (Boston: Twayne, 1978), Paul T. Bryant meticulously sorts out conflicting biographical information about Davis. My sketch is largely indebted to that work.

along, some critics were ready to admit that Davis's regional characters and local tales illustrated universal human conflicts and foibles. In addition to exploring significant themes, Davis often wrote in an engaging style with a dry, sometimes bitter humor that makes the reader think of Mark Twain. Davis's biographer, Paul Bryant, wrote: "As such Western writers as Wallace Stegner and Walter Van Tilburg Clark have been accepted as significant literary artists, Davis's work has been reexamined and increasingly appreciated as serious literary treatment of universal human experience. In particular, some of his best short stories, and Honey in the Horn *and* Winds of Morning *among his novels, are recognized as enduring contributions to the canon of American literature.*" [2]

—

Old Man Isbell's Wife

THE COW-TOWN started as an overnight station on the old Military Road through Eastern Oregon into Idaho. The freighters wanted a place to unhitch and get the taste of sagebrush out of their mouths. They were willing to pay for it, and one was built for them by the people who like, better than anything else, money that has been worked hard for—not to work hard for it themselves, but to take it from men who do.

The cow-town itself was a kind of accident. When they built it, they had no idea beyond fixing up a place where the freighters could buy what they wanted. They fixed it up with houses—houses to eat in, houses to get drunk in, houses to sleep in, or stay awake in, houses to stable horses in; and, as an afterthought, houses for themselves to live in while they took the freighters' and cattlemen's money. And money came—not fast, but so steadily that it got monotonous. There were no surprises, no starvation years, no fabulous winnings or profits; simply, one year with another, enough to live on and something over. They got out of the habit of thinking the place was an overnight station to make money in. They began, instead, to look at it as a place to live in. That, in Eastern Oregon, meant a change of status, a step up. The risk of the place being abandoned was over; there, straddling the

From *American Mercury* 16 (February 1929): 142–49. Copyright © 1956 by H. L. Davis. Reprinted by permission of William Morrow and Company, Inc.

2. Paul T. Bryant, "H. L. Davis," in *American Novelists, 1910–1945*, ed. James J. Martine, vol. 9, part 1 of *Dictionary of Literary Biography* (Detroit: Gale Research Co., 1981), pp. 188–92.

long road between Fort Dalles on the Columbia and Fort Boise on the Snake river, was a town.

The new status had no effect upon its appearance. Ugly and little it had begun, and ugly and little it stayed. The buildings were ramshackle and old, with the paint peeled off; and, including the stack of junk behind the blacksmith shop, the whole thing covered an area of ten blocks. Two acres of town, in the middle of a cattle range of ten thousand square miles. Yet in those ten blocks a man could live his entire lifetime, lacking nothing, and perhaps not even missing anything. Food, warmth, liquor, work, and women; love, avarice, fear, envy, anger, and, of a special kind, belonging to no other kind of life, joy.

Over the ten thousand miles of range, whole cycles of humanity—flint Indians, horse Indians, California Spaniards, emigrants, cattlemen—had passed, and each had marked it without altering its shape or color. The cow-town itself was one mark, and not the biggest, either; but that was a comparison which none of the townspeople ever made. They were too much used to it, and they had other things to think about. What interested them was their ten blocks of town, and the people who lived in it.

All country people keep track of each other's business—as a usual thing, because they haven't anything else to think about. But the cow-town people did it, not in idleness, but from actual and fundamental passion. They preferred it to anything else in the world. It was not in the least that they were fond of one another—though, of course, some of them were. That had nothing to do with their preference. It was merely that what their town did was life—clear, interesting, recognizable; and nothing else was. They stuck to what was familiar. It must be remembered that these people were not chance-takers. They were more like the peddlers who follow an army, not fighting themselves, but living on the men who do. The freighters and cattlemen, and the men from the range, were a different race; the range itself was a strange element; and they were too small to have much curiosity about either. The women were the smallest. It was they who backed the movement to ship Old Man Isbell out of town.

II

Old Man Isbell lived in the cow-town because there was no other place he could live. He had ridden the range, at one job or another, for more than fifty years, and the town would have been strange and foreign to him, even if it had made him welcome. It did not. For one thing, he was not a townsman, but a member of the race which they preyed on. For another, he was eighty-five years old, slack-witted, vacant-minded, doddering, dirty, and a bore. It took an hour to get the commonest question through his head, and another hour for him to think up an answer to it. He never tied his shoes, and he had to shuffle his feet as he walked, to keep them from falling off. Nor did he ever button his trousers, which fact was cited by the women as indicating complete moral decay. He ought to be sent away, they said, to some institution where such cases were decently taken care of.

The clerk in the general store agreed with them, and perhaps he, at least, had a right to. It was his job, every day, to sell Old Man Isbell a bill of groceries, and the old man could never remember what it was he wanted. Sometimes it took hours, and while he was there ladies couldn't come in the store, on account of his unbuttoned trousers and his pipe.

His pipe was another just ground for complaint. It was as black as tar and as soggy as a toadstool, with a smell like carrion and a rattle like a horse being choked to death. To get it lit took him hours, because his hand shook so he couldn't hold a match against the bowl. It was his palsy, no doubt, that was to blame for his unbuttoned trousers, his dangling shoestrings, and the gobs of food smeared on his clothes and through his whiskers. But that was not conclusive evidence that he was feeble-minded. Even a sane man would have trouble tying a bow-knot or hitting a buttonhole if his hands insisted on jumping two inches off the target at every heart-beat. The ladies added it to their evidence, but it should not have been allowed to count. Old Man Isbell's chief abnormality was of longer standing. He was simply, and before anything else, a natural-born bore.

The dullness of his speech was a gift of God. He had lived his eighty-five years through the most splendidly colored history that one man could ever have lived through in the world—the Civil War, the Indian campaigns in the West, the mining days, the cattle-kings, the long-line freighters, the road-agents, the stockmen's wars—the changing, with a swiftness and decision unknown to history before, of a country and its people; yes, and of a nation. Not as a spectator, either. He lived in the middle of every bit of it, and had a hand in every phase. But, for all the interest it gave to his conversation, he could just as well have spent his life at home working buttonholes.

"I remember Lincoln," he would say. "I drove him on an electioneerin' trip, back in Illinoy. Him and Stephen A. Douglas. I drove their carriage."

One would sit up and think, "Well! The old gabe does know something good, after all!" Expecting, of course, that he was about to tell some incident of the Lincoln-Douglas debates—something, maybe, that everybody else had missed. But that was all. So far as he knew, there hadn't been any incidents. They electioneered. He drove their carriage. They rode in it. That was all that had impressed him.

Or he would remember when there had been no Military Road, and no cow-town, nor even any cattle; only, instead, great herds of deer pasturing in grass belly-deep to a horse. A herd of over a hundred big mule-deer trotting close enough for a man to hang a rope on, right where the town was. But when you tried to work him for something beside the bare fact that they had been there you struck bottom. They had been there. Hundreds of them. He had seen them, that close. That ended that story. I asked him, once, if he remembered anything about Boone Helm, an early-day outlaw and all-round mean egg. He considered, sucked his pipe through a critical spell of croup, and finally said, "They used to be a road-agent by that name. He cut a feller's ears off."

It was not a prelude, but a statement of what he remembered. Some old men remember more than what actually happened; some remember things that never happened at all. Old Man Isbell remembered the exact thing, and, that being done, he stopped. He ought to have been writing military dispatches. Or had he? It never came into his head to tone up or temper down the exact and religious truth, and amplifying what he had seen simply wasn't in him.

To events that went on in the town he never appeared to pay the smallest attention. Indeed, he paid none to the people there, either, and, though they laid that to the condition of his wits, it irritated them. Yet it was no more than an old range-man's indifference to things which he considers immaterial. He was sharp enough when anything was going on that interested him—cattle-branding in the corrals below town, or the state of the water on the range. South of town was a long slope, with a big spring almost at the top, ringed with green grass except when the spring went dry. Then the grass turned brown. The old man never failed to notice that. He would stop people in the street and point it out.

They laughed at him for it, behind his back. What did it matter to him whether the cattle had a dry year or not? He had an Indian War pension to live on, and he would get it whether the cattle throve or died to the last hoof. But, of course, he remembered what cattle looked like when they died of thirst, and swelled and popped open in the unmerciful heat, their burnt tongues lolling in the dust. It excited him to think of it, and he made a nuisance of himself about it. Sometimes he would stop strangers to tell it to them, which gave the town a bad name. Beside, his critics added he smelled bad. Not being able to wait on himself, and never having been particular about washing or laundry, he did smell bad. The place for him, they agreed, was in some nice home where he could be waited on decently. He needed looking after.

In that they were right. He did need looking after. The trouble was that their plan involved sending him away from the sagebrush country, and that would have been the same thing as knocking him in the head with an ax. He was an old sagebrusher. To take him out of sight of his country—the yellow-flowered, silver-green sage, the black-foliaged greasewood, blossoming full of strong honey; the strong-scented, purple-berried junipers, and the wild cherry shrub, with its sticky, bitterish-honied flowers and dark sour fruit; the pale red-edged ridges, and the rock-breaks, blazing scarlet and orange and dead-black—to lose them would have killed him. By these things, an old sagebrusher lives. Out of reach of them, silly as it sounds to say so, he will die. I've seen them do it.

Old Man Isbell, incapable and slack-witted, helpless with age, and, so far as anybody could tell, without any suspicion of what the townspeople were thinking about him or that they were making designs against his life, did the one thing that could save him. He had nobody to take care of him. It was to see him taken care of that they wanted to send him away; and, surely without knowing it, he stumbled on the way to head them off. He got married.

The wedding threw the town into a perfect panic of delighted horror. This was one of the things that made life a fine thing to live. Other people, other communities, had diversions which the cow-town did without; this made up for them. The justice of the peace, having performed the ceremony, put out for home on a gallop to tell his wife the news. Hearing it, she came out with her hair down, and canvassed the houses on both sides of the street, knocking at every door, and yelling, without waiting for anybody to open—"Old Man Isbell's got married! You'll never guess who to!"

III

The bride alone would have made a rich story. She was about twenty-eight years old—Old Man Isbell being, as I've mentioned, eighty-five—and the rest of her was even more incongruous than her youth. She weighed close to three hundred pounds, being almost as broad as she was tall, and she had to shave her face regularly to keep down a coarse black beard, which showed in the wrinkles of fat where a razor could not reach.

As Old Man Isbell was the town nuisance, she was the town joke. Even in that scantily-womaned place, where only the dullest girls lived after they were big enough to look out for themselves, she had never had a suitor. The men were not too particular, but nobody dared pay court to her, for fear of getting laughed at. She was so fat that to walk downtown for Old Man Isbell's order of groceries took her almost an hour. It made one tired to watch her. Even the Indian squaws, riding through town, their matronly bellies overhanging the horns of their saddles, drew rein to admire Old Man Isbell's bride for an adiposity which laid theirs completely in the shade. They were fat, all right, but good heavens! They cackled and clucked to each other, pointing.

Housewives ran to peep through the curtains at the twenty-eight-year-old girl who had been hard up enough to marry an old, dirty, feeble-minded man of eighty-five. Store loafers perked up and passed remarks on her and on the match. But in spite of them all, in spite of the tittering, and the cruelty and the embarrassment, and her own exertion, she carried home the groceries every day. She cooked and cleaned house, too; and kept it clean; and one of the first things she bought after her marriage was a clothes-line. It was full every day, and the clothes on it were clean. So were Old Man Isbell's. He sat on his front porch, wobbling matches over his black gaggling pipe, without a thing in the world to bother his mind except his pipe and the spring on the slope south of town. His trousers were fully buttoned, his shoes tied, and his beard and clothing washed, brushed and straightened, without a speck upon them to show what he had eaten last, or when.

Town joke or not, the fat woman was taking care of him. She was being a housewife, attending to the duties of her station exactly as the other married women in town attended to theirs, and that was something they had not expected. There wasn't any fun for them in that. They wanted her to remain a joke; and they couldn't joke about her housework without belittling their own. They took it out on her by letting her alone. There was no woman in town for Old Man Isbell's wife to talk to, except my mother, who, being the school-teacher's wife, didn't quite belong to the towns-people, and would probably have repudiated their conventions if she had. Across the back-fence she got all of the fat woman's story—not all of it, either, but all its heroine was willing to volunteer.

The fat woman had come to the country with her father, who took up a homestead on Tub Springs Ridge. But he got himself in jail for vealing somebody else's calf, and she moved into town to live till he served out his time. For a while she lived by selling off the farm machinery he had left. But it didn't take very long to live that up—"not that I eat so much," she hastened to add, "I really don't eat as much as . . . as ordinary folks do . . ."—and, when that was gone she was broke. That was what induced her to listen, she said, to Old Man Isbell, when he first began to talk about getting married. She was desperate. It seemed the only resort, and yet it was so unheard of that she hesitated.

Finally, she borrowed a lift from a stage-driver, and went to the county jail to ask advice from her father. He knew the old man. It would be all right, he said, for her to marry him. But not unless she realized what kind of job she was taking on, and was game to live up to it. She mustn't bull into it and then try to back out. The old man would have to be tended exactly like a small infant—the work would be just as hard, and just as necessary—and, in addition, he was uglier, meaner and dirtier. If she wanted to undertake the contract, all right; but she must either stick to it or let it entirely alone. When Old Man Isbell died, she would get what money he had saved up, and his Indian War pension. Enough to keep her, probably, for life. But it was up to her to see that she earned it.

"He made me promise I would," she told my mother, "and the Lord knows I have. It's just exactly like pa said, too. He's just like a little baby. To see him set and stare at that spring for hours on end, you wouldn't believe how contrary and mean he can be around the house. All the time. He'll take a notion he wants something, and then forget the name of it and get mad because I don't guess it right. I have to pick up things and offer 'em to him, one at a time, till I manage to hit the one he's set his mind on. And him gettin' madder every time I pick up the wrong thing. Just like a baby. And his clothes—they're the same, too." She sighed into her series of stubbly chins. "It keeps me goin' every minute," she said. "It's mighty hard work."

"You do keep him clean, though," my mother said. "He was so dirty and forlorn. Everybody's talking about how clean you keep him now."

"They talk about how I married him to get his pension," the fat woman said. "How I'm just hangin' around waitin' for him to die. I know!"

"That's only some of them," my mother said. "They don't know anything about it. You work right along, and don't pay any attention to them."

"None of the ladies ever come to call on me," said the fat woman.

"I shouldn't think you'd want them to," my mother suggested. "You must be so busy, you wouldn't have time to bother with visitors. They probably think you'd sooner not be disturbed at your work."

"I do want 'em to, anyway," said the fat woman. "And they call on all the other married ladies, whether they're overworked or not. They call on Mis' Melendy, across the way, and she's got teethin' twins."

"Well, I wouldn't care whether they came to see me or not," said my mother.

"I do, though," the fat woman insisted. "I've got a house, and a husband, just the same as they have. I do my housework just the same, too. I'd like to show 'em all the work I do, and what a care it is to keep things clean, and how clean I keep 'em. If they'd come, they'd see."

My mother assented. There was no earthly chance that any of them would come, and she knew it. But the fat woman didn't know it, and it was the one thing in the world that she had her head set on. Everything else that women take pride in and nourish conceit upon she had given up; and for that very renouncement she stuck all the more fiercely to the idea of being visited by the neighbor ladies—of being received as an established house-wife, like the rest of them. There might not be any sense in the notion, but she wanted it. No matter how they came, or why, she wanted them. Even if they came prying for things to discredit her with, to trot around and gabble about, she wanted them anyway. When other women got married the neighbor ladies came to call. Now she was married, and they didn't.

The worst of it was, there was no way of breaking it to her that they weren't going to. My mother made several tries at letting her down easy, but got nowhere. She wanted it too much to give it up. Some days she would come to the fence elated and hopeful, because one of the ladies had nodded to her; sometimes she would be depressed and glum.

"I know what's keeping 'em away," she told my mother. "It's him!"

She yanked a fat arm in the direction of her husband, sitting in the sun with his mouth hanging open.

"Oh, no!" my mother protested. "Why—"

"Yes, it is!" the fat woman insisted. "And I don't blame 'em, either! Who wants to come visitin', when you've got to climb around an object like that to get into the parlor? I don't blame 'em for stayin' away. I would, my own self."

"But you've got to take care of him," my mother reminded her.

"Yes. I've got to. I promised pa I wouldn't back out on that, and I won't. But, as long as I've got him around, I won't have any visitors to entertain. I might as well quit expectin' any."

She sighed, and my mother tried to console her, knowing how deep her idiotic yearning was, and how impossible it was to gratify it. She had tried to persuade the neighbor ladies to call. There was no use wasting any more time on them. Yet, to come out bluntly with the fact that they had all refused would be silly and cruel. My mother was incapable of that. Con-cealing it, she did her best with promises and predictions, taking care to be vague, while Old Man Isbell dozed, or poked matches at his choking black pipe without any thought of human vanity or hope or disappointment, or anything but the Winter stand of grass on the range. Nobody could believe, from his looks, that he could have asked the fat woman to marry him. It was much more likely that she had hazed the notion into him. Some day, I thought, we might find out, when he could forget the range long enough.

But we never did. He died before the Winter grass got ripe enough for the cattle to sample.

IV

It was on a morning in October that my mother was awakened, about daylight, by yelling and crying from the Isbells' house. She got up and looked across, and saw, through their window, a lamp still burning, though it was already light enough to see. As she looked, the lamp went out—not from a draft, but because it had run dry. That meant that something was up which was keeping them too busy to tend to it. My mother dressed, and hurried over.

Old Man Isbell was dying. The fat woman had been up watching him all night. She sat beside the bed, while he plunged and pitched his thin hairy arms and yelled. Across her knees lay an old, heavy Sharp's plainsman's rifle.

"Watch 'em, watch 'em!" yelled Old Man Isbell. "They cut sagebrush, and push it along in front of 'em to fool you while they sneak up! If you see a bush move, shoot hell out of it! Shoot, damn it!"

The fat woman lugged the immense rifle to her shoulder and snapped the hammer. "Bang!" she yelled.

"That's you!" approved the old man, lying down again. "That's the checker! You nailed him that time, the houndish dastard! You got to watch 'em, I tell ye."

"He thinks he's standin' off Indians," the fat woman explained. "He's young again, and he thinks he's layin' out on the range with the hostiles sneakin' in on him. I've had to—All right, I'm watchin' close," she told him. "Bang!"

My mother got her something to eat, and built a fire, so that when the neighbor ladies came to help they could have a warm room to sit in. Their resolution to stay away held good only in life. When anybody was dying, social embargoes collapsed. Beside, a death was something they couldn't afford to miss. They came; all the women whom the fat woman had set her heart on being friends with; and nobody thought to remark that, instead of being responsible for their staying away, it was Old Man Isbell who had the credit of bringing them there, after all.

But the fat woman was past bothering about whether they came or stayed away. Even their remarks about the cleanness of her house went over her unnoticed. She had livelier concerns to think about. The old man was driving stage. He was going down the Clarno Grade, and a brake-rod had broken. The stage was running wild, down a twenty percent grade full of hairpin switchbacks. He was flogging his horses to keep them out from under the wheels. He yelled and swore and pitched and floundered in the bedclothes, screaming to his wife that she must climb back and try to drag the hind wheels by poking a bar between the spokes.

"And hurry, damn it!" he yelled. "Drag 'er, before that off pointer goes down!"

The neighbor women gaped and stared. This was something they had never heard of. They didn't even understand what kind of emergency the old man was yelling about. But the fat woman paid no attention to them, and did not hesitate. She climbed along the edge of the bed, reached a broom from the corner, and, poking the handle down as if into a wheel, she set back hard. Her mouth was compressed and firm, and she breathed hard with excitement. She appeared to be taking the game almost as seriously as the old man did, crying back to him that she was holding the wheel, as if it meant the saving of both their lives, though hers was in no danger, and his was burning out like a haystack flaming in a gale.

The women brought food and put it into her mouth as if she was something dangerous. They weren't used to games like this, except in children and dying men. Being neither, the fat woman had no business playing it; and they poked buttered bread into her mouth sharply, frowning as if to show her that they saw through her nonsense, and considered it uncalled for. Neither their buttered bread nor their disapproval made any impression on her. The old man was yelling that she must hold the wheel, and she, with her chins trembling with fatigue and sleeplessness, cried back that she had it where it couldn't get away.

In the afternoon he had another one going. He was in a range-camp at night, and there was a herd of wild mustangs all around his fire, trying to stampede his pack-horses. The fat woman pretended to throw rocks to scare them off.

"There's the stud!" he mumbled. "Where in hell is that gun of mine? Oh, God, if it wasn't for bringin' down them damned Siwashes, wouldn't I salivate that stud? Don't shoot! Don't you know them Injuns'll be all over us if they hear a shot? Hit him with a rock! Watch that bunch over yon! Look how their eyes shine, damn their souls! Throw! Do you want to lose all our horses, and be left out in Injun country afoot?"

All day, and till after dark, the neighbor women watching her, she threw when he ordered; and when, at dark, he switched to heading a stampede of cattle, she charged with him to turn them, swinging an imaginary rope with her fat arm, yelling and ki-yi-ing as he directed, and jouncing the bed till the whole house rocked.

About midnight he had burned his brain down to the last nub, and there the fat woman was no longer needed. He lifted himself clear of the bed, and said, "Well, hello, you damned old worthless tick-bit razor-back, you! How the hell did you get out to this country?" He sounded pleased and friendly. It had never occurred to the townspeople that he had ever had any friends. Even as it was, the fact was lost on some of them, for while he spoke he looked straight at one of the visiting women, as if he were addressing her. Somebody tittered, and she left indignantly, banging the door. Everybody jumped, and looked after her. When they looked back, Old Man Isbell was lying on his pillow, dead.

The fat woman did not want to leave him. She was dull and almost out of her head with weariness, but, when they took hold of her, gently, to put her to bed where she could rest, she fought them off.

"He might come to again," she insisted. "You can't tell, he might flash up again. And he might think of something he'd need me for. You leave me be!"

They explained to her that it wasn't possible, and that, even if it was, she must have some sleep. She mustn't kill herself to humor a man out of his mind.

"I want to!" she said. "I want to do that! All them things he's done, and been in, and seen—he never let on a word to me about 'em, and I want to hear 'em! I never knew what an adventured and high-spirited man he was. I like to do what I've been doin'!"

She fought them until they quit trying, and left her. When they came back, she had gone to sleep by herself, beside her dead husband; a fat woman, twenty-eight years old, beside the corpse of a man eighty-five.

V

She came to call on my mother after the funeral. Her mourning habit had come from a mail-order house, and, though there were yards of it, enough, I judged, to make three full-size wagon-sheets, it needed to be let out in one or two places, and she wanted advice.

"How to fix it so I can wear it, right away," she explained. "I could send it back, but I don't want to wait that long. I want to show 'em that my husband was as much loss to me as theirs would be to them. He was, too. He was a sight better man than any of theirs."

She rubbed the tears out of her eyes with the back of her wrist. My mother consoled her, and mentioned that now, at least, everybody knew what care she had taken of him.

"I don't care whether they know it or not," said the fat woman. "None of 'em come to see me, and they can all stay away for good, as far as I'm concerned. The way they acted the one time they did come settled 'em with me."

"But they helped out during your bad time," my mother said. "They meant kindly."

"Yes. Helped out. And then they come smirkin' and whisperin' around how I ought to be glad my husband was out of the way. How I must have hated takin' care of him, and what a mercy it was to be rid of him. I told 'em a few things. They'll stay away from me a spell, I can promise you that!"

She sat straight in her chair, and dropped the mourning dress on the floor.

"I was glad to take care of him," she said. "Yes, sir! I was proud of my husband. The things he'd done, and the risks he'd been through, when the men in this town was rollin' drunks and wrappin' up condensed milk. . . ."

She drew a breath, and, forgetting that my mother had been there, began to tell about the time when he had been surrounded by the Indians, creeping in on him with sagebrush tied to their heads. He fought them back and out-gamed the whole caboodle of them; and her voice rose and trembled, shrilling the scenes she had enacted with Old Man Isbell when his numb old brain was burning down through the pile of his memories, spurting a flame out of each one before they all blackened and went to nothing.

She shrilled the great scenes out defiantly, as if it were her place to defend them, as if they belonged to her, and were better, even at second hand, than anything that any of the townspeople had ever experienced. None of their common realities had ever touched her. Beauty had not; love had not, nor even friends. In place of them, she had got an eighty-five-year-old dotard and the ridicule of the townspeople. Watching over the old man when he died was the one time when she had come anywhere within reach of heroism and peril and splendor; and that one time, being worthy of it, she passed them all. And that one time was enough, because she knew it.

"The hostiles a-prowlin' around," she cried, her voice blazing. "The houndish dastards!. . . ."

Thomas Hornsby Ferril
1896-1988

1926: *High Passage*
1934: *Westering*
1944: *Trial by Time*
1946: *I Hate Thursday*
1952: *New and Selected Poems*
1966: *The Rocky Mountain
Herald Reader*
1966: *Words For Denver,
And Other Poems*
1983: *Anvil of Roses*

A S ONE *"regional poet" to another, New England's Robert Frost once wrote a poem to Colorado's Thomas Hornsby Ferril. It appeared on the cover of* New and Selected Poems *and has become a standard part of any introduction to Ferril.*

> A man is as tall as his height
> Plus the height of his home town.
> I know a Denverite
> Who, measured from sea to crown,
> Is one mile five-foot-ten,
> And he swings a commensurate pen.[1]

Unlike his forebears who had the restless American habit of "westering," Ferril took up permanent residence where he was born, the first member of his family to

---

1. Thomas Hornsby Ferril, *New and Selected Poems* (New York: Harper and Bros., 1952).

do so in five generations. His whole career was tied to Denver and the Colorado mountains. In his poetic imagination, he roamed widely through vast reaches of time, but when it came to ordinary travel, Ferril preferred just to wander around his home state. His unique reputation, however, reached out across the nation and brought other writers, such as Frost, to visit him. Many prominent literary names appeared on his "guest board," names of authors such as Carl Sandburg and Sherwood Anderson, who could say, "I know a Denverite."

Ferril's "commensurate pen" swung into prose as well as poetry, partly because of a long family association with journalism. His father bought the Rocky Mountain Herald *in 1912, when Thomas was sixteen and old enough to work at the newspaper trade. In 1939 the* Herald *was purchased by another publisher, but Thomas Hornsby Ferril and his wife continued to work for it as editors and writers. Another chapter in Ferril's journalistic experience was his weekly column, which was popular with Denver audiences for thirty-three years. The columns were eventually collected in the two volumes* I Hate Thursday *and* The Rocky Mountain Herald Reader. *Ferril's column writings are chronicles of the human circus, written with the kind of insight and wit seen in the periodical essays of Sir Richard Steele, Joseph Addison, Benjamin Franklin, Mark Twain, and another humorous western journalist, Bill Nye of the* Laramie Boomerang.

Ferril's writing is enriched with frequent allusions to world literature, modern as well as classic. Even more frequent is his use of terminology from various branches of science, especially geology and botany. Technology and science, especially mining, agriculture, ecology, and anthropology, supplied Ferril with images and metaphors, the "plausible symbols" he used for "implementing . . . ideas concretely."

To come to grips with the overwhelming, virtually unknown antiquity of the wide western landscapes, Ferril often used objective details taken from history and anthropology. In "Something Starting Over," he combined images of the Model T, prehistoric bones from eight feet down in the prairie, chariot wheels, and chips of Stone Age flint, compressing time into an image of "dance-halls and cemeteries." We cannot comprehend infinity, Ferril pointed out, but right in front of our eyes is the evidence to prove that something is always ending and something is always starting over. "You know where the hills are going," he wrote in "Time of Mountains." You can see them and feel them coming down over the fossilized vertebrate fish.

It should be pointed out, in conclusion, that Ferril's faith in hard evidence has certain drawbacks and that the knowledge of material objects does not always lead to full understanding. Science, in short, has its limits.

There's blue-stemmed grass as far as I can see,
But when I take the blue-stemmed grass in hand,

And pull the grass apart, and speak the word
For every part, I do not understand
More than I understood of grass before.[2]

—

Writing in the Rockies

ROCKY MOUNTAIN literature is devitalized by a low-grade mysticism dictated by landscape. Mysticism is a nebulous word. I use it simply as a blanket concept covering a wide field of emotional response to magnificent landscape. The imagination, transported by enormous mountains, deserts, and canyons, endeavors to answer landscape directly and tends to disregard, or curiously modify, what might otherwise be normal considerations of human experience.

Indeed Oscar Wilde may have been talking sense when he said that our West could never produce literature because, as in Switzerland, the mountains were too high. He visited the Rockies in 1882. Lloyd Lewis and Henry Justin Smith in "Oscar Wilde Discovers America" quote Wilde:

> There are subjects for the artist, but it is universally true that the only scenery which inspires utterance is that which man feels himself master of. The mountains . . . are so gigantic that they are not favorable to art or poetry. There are good poets in England and none in Switzerland.

It comes as a shock to an imaginative person to realize for the first time that landscape as such has no particular meaning and he may reject for years—costly years in the life of an artist—the human experience which gives it meaning.

But in our region poets, novelists, and—though they would be the last to have an inkling of it—writers of pulp adventure fiction are at heart rudimentary metaphysicians trying to fit some system of thought or action to the demands of pictorial nature. It is an inverted Romantic movement because no conscious philosophy accompanies it. Tom Mix in the Wild West movies is really a hangover of Rousseau.

From *Saturday Review of Literature* 15 (March 20, 1937): 3–4, 13–14. Reprinted by permission of Anne Ferril Folsom.
    2. Ferril, "Blue Stemmed Grass," *New and Selected Poems*, p. 9. For another perspective, compare Alfred, Lord Tennyson's "Flower in the Crannied Wall."

The case for landscape mysticism is clearer in poetry than in prose. Yet I believe that the same emotional influence which, in the presence of vast mountains, causes the poet to say: "This is all so big, only God could have caused it" is responsible for the notion of prose writers: "This is all so big, only super-men can cope with it." The ancestor conveniently becomes a tribal god and here, I think, in the hero convention of prose, we have a clue to the specious perpetuation of the pioneer legend as a contemporary presence.

Underlying all our imaginative writing is a religious impulse, nature worship in its simplest terms. Perhaps the Rockies are the last stronghold of animism in process, the recognition of something divine in the inanimate forms of nature. Our folk-ways are full of incipient nature myths and hero myths which have been arrested by the shift of our credulity to the myths of economics.

Let me illustrate how this religious impulse, or mysticism excited by landscape, thwarts the poet and causes him to waste time. Since the clinical evidence is clearer in poetry, I prefer to emphasize that aspect before indicating a direction for studying the problem in prose.

First: most people, beholding Nature in large and unfamiliar scale, think about what caused it and answer: God! Critically, we may have ignored a profound platitude and all that it implies, the designation of the West as *God's Country.* Discovery of God in scenery tapers off as the arroyos flatten into the Corn Belt, but in the high country the naming of a group of rocks "The Garden of the Gods" is not fortuitous; it answers a primitive impulse.

God-finding is widely distributed, in prose, poetry, postcards, advertisements. Willa Cather refers to "the Genius of the Divide, the Great Free Spirit that breathes across it." The Billings Advertising Company quotes Chief Plenty Coups: "The mountains are still as God made them," and the Colorado Association assures us that Colorado is "a land where the Creator has stamped his Eternal Monogram." Harriet Monroe, late editor of *Poetry*, told us from the rim of the Grand Canyon: "In these warm and glowing purple spaces disembodied spirits must range and soar, souls purged and purified and infinitely daring." William Winter, dramatic critic, at the Grand Canyon could only quote Coleridge on "The Invisible." "Out in Arizona where God is all the time," writes the Hon. David Kincheloe of Kentucky in the *Congressional Record*.

I might endlessly elaborate supporting data on the pandemic prevalence of God-finding and causation ideas, also simple mountain worship such as we find in the poem which Helen Hunt Jackson, author of "Ramona," wrote in the presence of Cheyenne Mountain overlooking Colorado Springs:

"Beloved Mountain, I Thy Worshipper . . ." As a rule, these poems attempt to give a verbal facsimile of the appearance of a mountain by piling up too many desperate adjectives, with hints of fear and wonder coupled with the God idea, stated as an abstraction. Stripped of applied decoration, the organic verbs and nouns say very little. The content of literally hundreds of Rocky Mountain poems is represented by Walt Whitman's "Spirit That Form'd This Scene," written in Platte Canyon, Colorado. I agree with Irene Pettit McKeehan of the University of Colorado that this poem sums up "the underlying idea" of Colorado literature, but I am disappointed in her belief that it expresses "its hope, its intention," because the Whitman who wrote this verse was moving away from the function of poetry:

> Spirit that form'd this scene,
> These tumbled rock-piles grim and red,
> These reckless heaven-ambitious peaks,
> These gorges, turbulent-clear streams, this naked freshness,
> These formless wild arrays, for reasons of their own,
> I know thee, savage spirit—we have communed together . . .

Compare Whitman's Colorado lines with a similar idea in a God-finding poem by Coleridge under the spell of Mont Blanc, "Hymn Before Sunrise in The Vale of Chamouni:"

> O dread and silent Mount! I gazed upon thee
> Till thou, still present to my bodily sense,
> Did'st vanish from my thought: entranced in prayer,
> I worshipped The Invisible alone.

Observe that Whitman is talking about an abstract spirit. Coleridge's "The Invisible" is an abstraction. Harriet Monroe gave us abstractions in the "disembodied spirits" hovering over the Grand Canyon. Willa Cather's "Genius of the Divide" is an abstraction. Unfortunately, anything which drives a poet to abstractions, drives him away from poetry. Poetry is concrete. Poetry is a passionate apprehension of experience based on the magical statement of how things sound, smell, taste, look, and feel. Poetry can work from concrete specification to abstract implication, but never, without leaning on some external context for a crutch, can it work from the abstract back to the concrete. Preponderantly is this true of religious poetry. The bewildering richness of Revelation or Genesis, or Blake, Dante, Hopkins, or Milton, leaps like flame from the concrete image.

So it appears that the mountains demand religious utterance yet deny the poet plausible symbols for implementing such ideas concretely. He may exhibit some skill in remanipulating established symbols, but somehow our mores are out of step with the revelations of Pisgah. It bores us to be asked to supply a context for these abstractions; they exert too futile a draft on our recessive faith. True, we still thirst for concrete specification in our gods, but reject it as absurd unless taken vicariously and, I think, snobbishly through what we regard as some simpler culture, Negro culture being the handiest. It answered something deep in our hearts to see God smoking a cigar in "The Green Pastures."

The Indians were the last to write successful religious poetry in this region. Had Coleridge or Whitman lived long ago in Walpi, their God need not have been "The Invisible." On the mountain top they could have described the Sun-God Ahul wearing turkey feathers, corn husks, a reddish fox skin, leggings netted with bean sprouts, and tinkling anklets terraced into rain. In this direction lies poetry.

But if mountain mysticism leads to the dilemmas of abstraction, let it not be inferred that specification is not attempted. Yet I feel that Colorado's poet laureate, Nellie Burget Miller, is using a doubtful method when she tries to make us see Galahad and Percival in mountain clouds, and Maude Freeman Osborne has not quite convinced me of the immortality of Mount Evans which has sisters and blesses lambs. In this field of specification of the supernatural, my favorite is T. O. Bigney who observed in 1875 that:

> The thorax and the pelvic space
> Of the grand old Rocky Range,
> Are the vasty, ever beauteous parks,
> Features fair and strange,
> Peculiar to this giant chain
> Which holds the continent's vast brain.

You can paste that in your memory book along with Byron's "Mont Blanc is the Monarch of Mountains."

But landscape such as ours cannot be ignored. It is an integral part of our emotional experience. A mountain range is forever a blue wall behind which something is happening. Being an emotional person, it is difficult for me to turn from those glorious ranges and say to myself: more water, better tilth, more straw needed for bedding, earlier decomposition of manure, higher yields of grain, alfalfa, sugar beets, yet this is the road to poetry: men in action, the transitoriness of life, memory, desire, agony, ecstasy.

If landscape cannot be used directly as subject matter, its beauty can be employed vividly in symbols of instrumentation. Pictorially, mountain snows are meaningless, but meaningful if the poet feels the mountain waters moving up through the grasses and the beasts into the metabolism of men with power to dream beyond the wasting of the glaciers and the granite. It is safer for the poet to be impressed by the erosion of the mountains than their enduring qualities, or any attitude which gives him the whip hand. It was good to hear Robert Frost say at George Cranmer's ranch that the mountains were pitched just right for his convenience: he could read the ferns like a book. Early in February Carl Sandburg was working in Denver on a nostalgic rough-and-tumble poem about "the God-damned Wasatch mountains" which left no doubt as to who was boss. And in lieu of the pathetic fallacy—a familiar pitfall where landscape is compelling— a disciplined poet can take the direction of empathy, projecting his own imagination into external nature as a springboard for human implication, but always keeping control.

Referring briefly to fiction, the same forces of mountain mysticism are at work. In abandoning the play for the setting, the fiction writer feels under pressure to fit his characters to the vast panorama his eyes behold. He becomes oblivious of the complexities of natural experience and naively rationalizes history to select the most active behavior appropriate to the scene. This results in a simplification of life into rather pure and tight patterns, rigidly conventionalized. He contrives heroes and heroines capable of meeting an apparent nature on its most elemental terms. I say apparent nature because actual Western experience in conflict with actual nature is as complex as elsewhere. Our economic and moral adjustment to the physical facts of climate, water, soil, mineral resources, etc., is infinitely involved and does not lend itself to the simplification the apparent landscape suggests.

It is not drawing too long a bow to regard the galloping heroes of popular fiction as vestigial tribal gods. They have emerged through about the same process which once produced centaurs and titans, but their development has been arrested at a rudimentary plane. They are supernatural in the sense that they tend toward caricature only dimly related to human life. They are clearly creatures of landscape commingled with ancestor worship, the apotheosis of the glorified pioneer. Moreover, they possess another god-attribute, timelessness; they are immune to anachronism.

Note some of the foregoing points in the ritual of the pulp paper magazines. *Thrilling Ranch Stories* wants material in which "the background of the Old West is used—no radios, automobiles, etc.,—but make the characters *modern* in spirit." Observe that satisfying landscape gives the illusion of reality: "Colorful terrain and a clear working knowledge of the vegetation and countryside bring a quality of reality," advises the editor of *Thrilling Western*, but as for life itself "we prefer the flavor of the Old West with the impression that the happenings are of today. If the setting is in the West today [again the setting dictates the play] it must be idealized. The people must be modern in spirit with boundless courage and endless endurance. Western dialect must be used and the slang of today should not be allowed to creep in." Being naive, the pulp formula may be more significant than other evidence bearing on our literary folkways.

One further observation on fiction of different quality: the case of Hamlin Garland. He wrote well on the prairie, badly in the mountains, and well on the prairie again. Possibly he illustrates my earlier point: that the inspiration of scenery works at cross-purposes with the inspiration which produces literature. If anyone ever repudiated extravagant pioneer romance, it was the Garland who wrote "Main-Travelled Roads" in 1891. This was followed by other works conceived with such savage integrity that even Howells, who admired him, felt obliged to apologize for such unconventional realism. Then Garland came to the highlands and wrote a basketful of Rocky Mountain novels in which he capitulated completely to the conventions of scenery. But back on the prairie in 1917 he gave us "A Son of the Middle Border" with the old integrity.

Carl and Mark Van Doren attribute Garland's mountain lapse to "errors of enthusiasm." This is correct. Perhaps "errors of enthusiasm" covers the field I designate "landscape mysticism." But regardless of what we call it, it is equivalent to a physical force which destroys the uncontrolled artist and delays orientation of the controlled artist. Garland, a man of considerable control, was drugged by the same lotos Whitman had tasted when Whitman wrote this nonsense:

> Talk as you like, a typical Rocky Mountain Canyon, or limitless sea-like stretch of the great Kansas or Colorado plains, under favoring circumstances, tallies, perhaps expresses, certainly awakes, those grandest and subtlest emotions of the human soul, that all marble temples and sculptures from Phideas to Thorwaldsen—all paintings, poems, reminiscences or even music—probably never can.

It isn't true, and to believe it causes the artist to waste time and effort, winding himself into cocoons of futile metaphysics. Art, as we have come to know it, does not exist in external nature, nor can external nature, powerful as it is, move us as we are moved by Shakespeare or Brahms. Landscape was irrelevant to Greek and Elizabethan dramatists. "Scenery is fine," wrote Keats, "but human nature is finer—the sward is richer for the tread of a . . . nervous English foot."

Having indicated the difficulties of poets and one novelist whose case

I believe to be representative, I might close by suggesting that our most competent writing, with richest overtones, has always come from reporters: scribes with Coronado—after 1573 all Spanish expeditions were required to keep journals;—from the scientists accompanying trappers up the Missouri and down the Columbia; the diarists of the wagon trails; the geologists; the topographers; the reporters, like Villard and Richardson who described the Pike's Peak gold rush. True, many a Parson Weems crept into the picture, but on the whole the reporting was well done and the perspectives are very deep: reporters were on the scene long before Shakespeare dipped his pen.

The dominance of the conscious literary artist characterized the last half of the nineteenth century. No sooner was the first goosequill filled with Cherry Creek gold than the artists-with-a-purpose began their spiritual exploitation. But these conscious artists, enthralled by the demands of landscape for the pure and picturesque—seeking a Western type, so to speak—rejected what was complex. Meanwhile the reporter, when he was not too busy drinking or preaching, was making a naive record of these complexities.

Take, for example, the ethnic, moral, and psychic complexities in one episode of the Meeker massacre in 1879. Here we had a full-blooded Ute chief with a British name getting drunk on Kentucky whisky and singing a Negro spiritual to a captive American girl, then asking her, like Sigmund Spaeth, if she knew what it meant, while her murdered father lay over the hill with a log chain around his neck and a barrel stave down his throat. A sound novelist, like H. L. Davis, author of "Honey in the Horn," would be interested, I believe, in developing the influences bearing on such a situation, but to the rank and file these confusing compressions of experience are outside the code. These compressions are taboo unless idealized. My father, who is considerably older than the city of Denver, spent a recent week trying to figure out how his office boy was affected by social security legislation. This was immoral: he should spend his time lamenting the passing of the bison.

It is in the summarization of reporting that the region now is becoming articulate. I refer to such books as "Here They Dug the Gold," by George Willison, whose fine work on Leadville and the Tabors was followed by a number of others; the material, if not the treatment, of "The Forty-niners" by Archer Butler Hulbert; and "Timberline," Gene Fowler's colorful but incomplete story of Bonfils and Tammen. Haniel Long's new volume, "Interlinear to Cabeza de Vaca," is a byproduct of reporting. The *Colorado Magazine*, edited by Leroy R. Hafen of the State Historical Society, is doing a competent job of revealing the past through the reporting method. The field, however, is large and I shall not attempt to give an inventory.

There has lately been an inordinate regional consciousness, tremendous eagerness to do something about the various art forms. Equipment is not lacking: The Fine Arts Center in Colorado Springs with Boardman Robinson; The Central City Play Festival directed largely by Anne Evans and Robert Edmond Jones; The Writers' Conference in The Rocky Mountains, well organized by Edward Davison, the poet. These activities have at least focused attention on our spiritual confusion by engendering marvelous cat-and-dog fights. The row over the $100,000 Speer Memorial has made every Denver ward-heeler a critic, and it is a dull barber who cannot regale you with focal points and plastic organization. Yet all this rationalization usually winds up in esthetics rather than art. None of our literary work compares in quality with what Burnham Hoyt is doing in architecture, and I prefer the workaday output of such newspaper craftsmen as Lee Taylor Casey and Larry Martin to that of the interpretive artists. Indeed few of the upland bards have as vivid a sense of poetry as appears naively in the cadenced captions, dynamic and concrete, which Martin turns out daily for *The Denver Post.*

—

Something Starting Over

You don't see buffalo skulls very much any more
On the Chugwater buttes or down the Cheyenne plains,
And when you roll at twilight over a draw,
With ages in your heart and hills in your eyes,
You can get about as much from a Model-T,
Stripped and forgotten in a sage arroyo,
As you can from asking the blue peaks over and over:
"Will something old come back again tonight?
Send something back to tell me what I want."

I do not know how long forever is,
But today is going to be long long ago,
There will be flint to find, and chariot wheels,
And silver saxophones the angels played,
So I ask myself if I can still remember
How a myth began this morning and how the people
Seemed hardly to know that something was starting over.

Oh, I get along all right with the old old times,
I've seen them sifting the ages in Nebraska

On Signal Butte at the head of Kiowa creek.
    (You can drink from the spring where old man Roubadeau
    Had his forge and anvil up in Cedar Valley,
    You can look back down the valley toward Scottsbluff
    And still see dust clouds on the Oregon trail.)
I entered the trench they cut through Signal Butte,
And I pulled a buffalo bone from the eight-foot layer,
And I watched the jasper shards and arrowheads
Bounce in the jigging screen through which fell dust
Of antelope and pieces of the world
Too small to have a meaning to the sifters.
One of them said, when I held the bone in my hand:
    "This may turn out to be the oldest bison
In North America," and I could have added:
    "How strange, for this is one of the youngest hands
That ever squeezed a rubber bulb to show
How helium particles shoot through water vapor."
And the dry wind out of Wyoming might have whispered:
    "Today is going to be long long ago."

I know how it smells and feels to sift the ages,
But something is starting over and I say
It's just as beautiful to see the yucca
And cactus blossoms rising out of a Ford
In a sage arroyo on the Chugwater flats,
And pretend you see the carbon dioxide slipping
Into the poverty weed, and pretend you see
The root hairs of the buffalo grass beginning
To suck the vanadium steel of an axle to pieces,
An axle that took somebody somewhere,
To moving picture theaters and banks,
Over the ranges, over the cattle-guards,
Took people to dance-halls and cemeteries—
I like to think of them that way together:
Dance-halls and cemeteries, bodies beginning
To come together in dance-halls where the people
Seem hardly to know that hymns are beginning too;
There's a hymn in the jerk of the sand-hill crawl of the dancers,
And all the gods are shining in their eyes;
Then bodies separating and going alone

Into the tilting uphill cemeteries,
Under the mesas, under the rimrock shadows.

I can look at an axle in a sage arroyo,
And hear them whispering, the back-seat lovers,
The old myth-makers, starting something over.

—

Bride

After the turgid incidence and when
The last mad whispering had darkly blown
Away, letting the woods be real again,
He propped his elbow on a lichened stone.
"I've climbed that mountain many times alone,"
He said at length. She stared, then asked him how
One felt at timberline. He answered "One
Feels much as we do now," remembering snow
That must have cooled whatever long ago
Had cracked the rocks with terrible ecstasy.
"It's not so wild up there, you feel as though
Something were finished. You're at peace with sky
And earth, as we are now." She pointed where
The peak seemed highest, whispering "Take me there."

—

Time of Mountains

So long ago my father led me to
The dark impounded orders of this canyon,
I have confused these rocks and waters with
My life, but not unclearly, for I know
What will be here when I am here no more.

The selections of Thomas Hornsby Ferril's verse included here are from *High Passage* (New Haven: Yale University Press, 1929), p. 50, and *Westering* (New Haven: Yale University Press, 1934), pp. 9–10, 26–30, 32–36, and 89–90, respectively. Reprinted by permission of Anne Ferril Folsom.

I've moved in the terrible cries of the prisoned water,
And prodigious stillness where the water folds
Its terrible muscles over and under each other.

When you've walked a long time on the floor of a river,
And up the steps and into the different rooms,
You know where the hills are going, you can feel them,
The far blue hills dissolving in luminous water,
The solvent mountains going home to the oceans.
Even when the river is low and clear,
And the waters are going to sleep in the upper swales,
You can feel the particles of the shining mountains
Moping against your ankles toward the sea.

Forever the mountains are coming down and I stalk
Against them, cutting the channel with my shins,
With the lurch of the stiff spray cracking over my thighs;
I feel the bones of my back bracing my body,
And I push uphill behind the vertebrate fish
That lie uphill with their bony brains uphill
Meeting and splitting the mountains coming down.

I push uphill behind the vertebrate fish
That scurry uphill, ages ahead of me.
I stop to rest but the order still keeps moving:
I mark how long it takes an aspen leaf
To float in sight, pass me, and go downstream;
I watch a willow dipping and springing back
Like something that must be a water-clock,
Measuring mine against the end of mountains.

But if I go before these mountains go,
I'm unbewildered by the time of mountains,
I, who have followed life up from the sea
Into a black incision in this planet,
Can bring an end to stone infinitives.
I have held rivers to my eyes like lenses,
And rearranged the mountains at my pleasure,
As one might change the apples in a bowl,

And I have walked a dim unearthly prairie
From which these peaks have not yet blown away.

———

Ghost Town

Here was the glint of the blossom rock,
Here Colorado dug the gold
For a sealskin vest and a rope of pearl
And a garter jewel from Amsterdam
And a house of stone with a jig-saw porch
Over the hogbacks under the moon
Out where the prairies are.

Here's where the conifers long ago
When there were conifers cried to the lovers:
        Dig in the earth for gold while you are young!
Here's where they cut the conifers and ribbed
The mines with conifers that sang no more,
And here they dug the gold and went away,
Here are the empty houses, hollow mountains,
Even the rats, the beetles and the cattle
That used these houses after they were gone
Are gone; the gold is gone,
There's nothing here,
Only the deep mines crying to be filled.

You mines, you yellow throats,
You mountainsides of yellow throats
Where all the trees are gone,
You yellow throats crying a canyon chant:
        Fill what is hollow;
Crying like thunder going home in summer:
        Fill what is hollow in the earth;
Crying deep like old trees long ago:
        Fill what is hollow now the gold is gone;
Crying deep like voices of the timbers,
Conifers blowing, feathered conifers,

Blowing the smell of resin into the rain,
Over the afternoons of timber cutters,
Over the silver axes long ago,
Over the mountains shining wet like whipsaws,
Crying like all the wind that goes away:
    Fill what is hollow,
    Send something down to fill the pits
    Now that the gold is gone;
You mines, you yellow throats,
Cry to the hills, be patient with the hills,
The hills will come, the houses do not answer.

These houses do not answer any cry.
I go from door to door, I wait an hour
Upon a ledge too high to be a street,
Saying from here a man could throw a rock
On any roof in town, but I will wait:
It's time the people came out of their houses
To show each other where the moon is rising;
Moon, do you hear the crying of the mines:
    Fill what is hollow,
    Send down the moonlight?

It's time the people kindled evening fires,
I'll watch the chimneys, then I will go down;
Steeple, why don't you ring a bell?
Why don't you ring a mad high silver bell
Against the crying of the yellow throats?
Wait for me, steeple, I will ring the bell.
    Pull the rope,
    Drift, stope,
    Pull a fathom of rock
    And a cord of ore[3]
    From the higher place to fill the lower,
    The Rocky Mountains are falling down,

---

3. A "drift" is a horizontal passage in a mine, connecting two tunnels or cutting across a vein of ore. The word here is probably being used as a verb, as is "stope," which means to cut an underground excavation in steps or levels running up an inclined vein. A "fathom" is 6 feet; a "cord" is 128 cubic feet.

Go into any house in town,
You can hear the dark in the kitchen sing,
The kitchen floor is a bubbling spring,
The mountains have sealed like the door of a tomb
The sliding doors to the dining room;
Then thump your hand on the parlor wall
And hear the Rocky Mountains fall,
Feel the plaster ribs and the paper skin
Of the Rocky Mountains caving in;
Pull the rope,
Drift, stope,
Pull down the birds out of the air,
Pull down the dust that's floating where
The conifers blew the resin rain,
Pull all the mountains down again,
Pull the steeple down
And a cord of ore
To fill the dark
On the hollow floor.

I am an animal, I enter houses.
Some of the animals have liked this house:
The first to come and go were men,
Men animals who dreamed of yellow gold,
Then small things came and the cattle came.
The cattle used this room for many years,
The floor is level with the baseboard now,
But probably the ants came first
Before the people went away;
Before the children wore the sill
With stepping in and out to die;
It may have been an afternoon
Before the conifers were dead,
An afternoon when the rain had fallen
And the children were going back to play.
You children going back to play,
Did you ask the things the animals can't ask?
Did you ask what made the mountains glisten blue?
Did you say: "The great wet mountains shine like whipsaws"?
Did you say: "We're here and there's the sun"?

Did you say: "The golden mines are playing
Yellow leapfrog down the hills"?
Did you say: "Think what it would be like
To be way up on the mountain top
And see how beautiful it is
To be where we are now"?

*The children made this doorstone look
Like a whetstone worked too hard in the center,
And the ants went out and the wall went out,
And the rats went out and the cattle came,
But they're gone now, all the animals;
If they were here, and all of us together,
What could we say about the gold we dug,
What could we say about this house we used,
What could we say that we could understand?*

*You men and women, builders of these houses,
You lovers hearing the conifers at night,
You lovers making children for the houses,
Did you say to yourselves when reckoning
The yield of gold per cord of ore,
Running drifts per cord of ore,
Stoping per fathom per cord of ore,
Filling buckets per cord of ore,
Dressing tailings per cord of ore—
You lovers making children in these mountains,
Did you say something animals can't say?
Did you say:* "We know why we built these houses"?
Did you say: "We know what the gold is for"?

*I cannot tell: you and the gold are gone,
And nearly all the animals are gone;
It seems that after animals are gone,
The green things come to houses and stay longer;
The things with blossoms take an old house down
More quietly than wind, more slow than mountains.
I say I cannot tell, I am alone,
It is too much to be the last one here,*

For now I hear only the yellow throats
Of deep mines crying to be filled again
Even with little things like bones of birds,
But I can hear some of the houses crying:

"Which of the animals did use us better?"
And I can hear the mountains falling down
Like thunder going home.

Magenta

Once, up in Gilpin County, Colorado,
When a long blue afternoon was standing on end
Like a tombstone sinking into the Rocky Mountains,
I found myself in a town where no one was,
And I noticed an empty woman lying unburied
On a pile of mining machinery over a graveyard.

She was a dressmaker's dummy called Magenta.
I named her that because, all of a sudden,
The peaks turned pink and lavender and purple,
And all the falling houses in the town
Began to smell of rats and pennyroyal.

The town was high and lonely in the mountains;
There was nothing to listen to but the wasting of
The glaciers and a wind that had no trees.
And many houses were gone, only masonry
Of stone foundations tilting over the canyon,
Like hanging gardens where successful rhubarb
Had crossed the kitchen sill and entered the parlor.

The dressmaker's dummy was meant to be like a woman:
There was no head. The breasts and belly were
A cool enamel simulating life.
The hips and thighs were made adjustable,
Encircling and equidistant from

A point within, through which, apparently,
The woman had been screwed to a pedestal,
But the threads were cut and the pedestal was broken.

I propped Magenta into an old ore-bucket,
Which gave her a skirt of iron up to her waist;
And I told a mountain at some distance to
Become her lilac hair and face and neck.
It was the fairest mountain I could find,
And then I said, "Magenta, here we are."

And Magenta said, "Why do you call me Magenta?"

The sky no longer glowed rose-aniline,
So I looked at the town and thought of a different reason.

"Magenta's a mulberry town in Italy,"
I said, and she said, "What a very excellent reason!"
(I said no more though I was prepared to make
A speech a dressmaker's dummy might have relished,
About a naked Empress of France,
And how she held her nightgown at arm's length,
And named the color of her silken nightgown
In honor of the battle of Magenta,
The very year, the very day in June,
This mining camp was started in the mountains.)[4]

The sun was low and I moved to a warmer flange
On the pile of broken mining machinery,
And Magenta said, "It's always afternoon
Up here in the hills, and I think it always was."

"Why always afternoon?" I said, and she answered:

"Mornings were crystal yellow, too hard to see through;
The realness didn't begin until afternoon;

4. "Magenta" is a village in Italy. There, in June 1859, Franco-Sardinian troops under Napoleon III defeated the Austrians and thus made the unification of Italy possible. A new dye discovered that year was named *magenta* because its color suggested the bloodiness of that battle.

We both are real, but we wouldn't have been this morning
Before the blue came up. It was always so:
Nothing real ever happened in the morning,
The men were always digging for gold in the morning;
They were dreaming deep in the earth, you never saw them,
But afternoons they'd come up to bury their wives."

Magenta stared a moment at the graveyard.

"These women wanted me to be their friend.
I spent my mornings with them making believe.
They'd sit around me talking like far-off brides
Of things beyond the mountains and the mines;
Then they would get down on their knees to me.
Praying with pins and bastings for my sanction.

"Then they would look into mirrors and come back,
They'd look out of the windows and come back,
They'd walk into the kitchen and come back,
They'd scratch the curtains with their fingernails,
As if they were trying to scratch the mountains down,
And be somewhere where there weren't any mountains.

"I wasn't what they wanted, yet I was.
Mornings were never real, but usually
By noon the women died and the men came up
From the bottom of the earth to bury them."

"Those must have been strange days," I said, and I tossed
A cog from a stamp-mill into a yawning shaft.
We listened as it clicked the sides of the mine
And we thought we heard it splash and Magenta said:

"The men would measure in cords the gold they hoped
To find, but the women reckoned by calendars
Of double chins and crows-feet at the corners
Of their eyes. When they put their china dishes on
The checkered tablecloth they'd say to themselves
'How soon can we go away?' When they made quilts
They'd say to the squares of colored cloth 'How soon?'

"They could remember coming up to the dryness
Of the mountain air in wagons, and setting the wheels
In the river overnight to tighten the spokes;
But by the time they got to the mountains the wheels
Were broken and the women wanted the wagons
To be repaired as soon as possible
For going away again, but the men would cut
The wagons into sluice boxes and stay.

"Each woman had seven children of whom two
Were living, and the two would go to church.
Sometimes the children went to the opera-house
To see the tragedies. They can still remember
The acrobats and buglers between the acts."

I spoke to Magenta of how the graves were sinking,
And Magenta said, "All this is tunneled under;
I think some of these ladies may yet find gold,
Perhaps," she sighed, "for crowns," and she continued:

"Maybe you never saw a miner dig
A grave for a woman he brought across the plains
To die at noon when she was sewing a dress
To make a mirror say she was somebody else."

"I never did," I said, and Magenta said:

"A miner would dig a grave with a pick and shovel
Often a little deeper than necessary,
And poising every shovelful of earth
An instant longer than if he were digging a grave,
And never complaining when he struck a rock;
Then he would finish, glad to have found no color."[5]

I didn't know what to say to that, so I said:

"It's getting dark at approximately the rate
Of one hundred and eighty-six thousand spruces per second,"
And Magenta smiled and said, "Oh, so it is."

5. "Color" is a miner's term for any indication of gold.

And she said, "Up here the men outnumbered women,
But there were always too many women to go around;
I should like to have known the women who did not need me."
She indicated that their skirts were shorter.

"And so should I," I said. "Are they buried here?"

Magenta said, "I think there were hardly any:
They came like far-off brides, they would appear
Each afternoon when the funerals were over.
Some disappeared, some changed into curious songs,
And some of them slowly changed into beautiful mountains."

She pointed to a peak with snowy breasts
Still tipped with fire and said, "The miners named
That mountain Silverheels after a girl
Who never was seen until along toward evening."

"This is an odd coincidence," I said,
"Because I've been using that mountain for your head."

Mari Sandoz
1896-1966

▬

1935: *Old Jules*
1937: *Slogum House*
1942: *Crazy Horse: The Strange Man
of the Oglalas*
1953: *Cheyenne Autumn*
1954: *The Buffalo Hunters: The Story of
the Hide Men*
1958: *The Cattlemen: From the Rio Grande
across the Far Marias*
1964: *The Beaver Men: Spearheads of Empire*
1966: *The Battle of the Little Bighorn*

▬

M ARI S ANDOZ *grew up in Nebraska's sandhill country west of the
hundredth meridian. Her teenage years were spent in poverty, back-
breaking work, and constant domination by her ill-tempered father.
Through harsh living, she acquired a thorough, firsthand knowledge of the land
and its pioneers, both native and newcomers. The sandhill people became her subjects as she struggled to establish herself as a writer. Her first successful book—
her best work, in the opinion of some—is the biography of a Swiss immigrant—
a cruel, egocentric, pioneering visionary known in the sandhills as Old Jules. He
was Sandoz's father.*

*Jules located his homestead on the Niobrara river in the 1880s, and there his
ambitious efforts to bring settlers into the region eventually made him a major
community figure. For many years, he surveyed farm and ranch sections in the
sandhills and helped newcomers lay claim to them. He also operated the district
post office, traded in land and livestock, and did some farming. It was young Mari
and her mother, however, who did the bulk of the heavy daily labor required on*

Jules's frontier homestead. Mari cared for five younger children in addition to baking, cleaning, washing, and sewing daily. Her father also held her responsible for the firewood, fences, water, and livestock. When a severe blizzard caught the livestock several miles from home, Jules ordered Mari to go out and find them, and as a result she suffered snow blindness and the permanent loss of sight in one eye.

Household responsibilities frequently kept Mari from going to school, but at the age of seventeen she finally finished the eighth grade and accepted a teaching position at a local rural school. Overcoming the lack of a high school diploma, she eventually gained admission to the University of Nebraska. After Old Jules, Slogum House, and Capital City made Sandoz a self-supporting author, she moved to Denver for three years and then to New York, where she resided until her death in 1966. Her research and writing, however, remained centered on the Great Plains.

As historian, biographer, and novelist, Sandoz described what happened when the immigrating races of Europe first encountered the barren, hostile, strangely captivating landscape of the dry western plains. And her versions of these events usually contradict the older myths of the pioneer era. Instead of showing the tight-knit family struggling bravely to farm the virgin soil, Old Jules depicts a family living in constant fear of a grasping, vengeful, and tyrannical father. Instead of portraying the popular image of a courageous, God-fearing race of people who sweep aside the heathen savages and march on toward manifest destiny, Cheyenne Autumn and Crazy Horse present a human drama classic in its brutality and mindlessness. The same realistic perspective also enriches Sandoz's histories of the cattlemen, the beaver men, and the cavalrymen.

Much of Sandoz's reputation rests on her nonfiction, principally the Great Plains Series, which comprises Crazy Horse, Cheyenne Autumn, The Buffalo Hunters, The Cattlemen, and The Beaver Men. But whether fiction or history, Sandoz's books take their strength from three traits. First, they stem from the author's deep love of the incomparable western landscape. Second, they accentuate the historical importance of the personal human drama. And finally, refuting popularized romantic views of the western settlers, Sandoz's books give readers both truth and realism.

Bone Joe and the Smokin' Woman

THE MORNING SUN of June lay warm and friendly over the sprawling knoll of buildings that was the home ranch of Rutherford Bills. Out on the wide sweep of meadow the shadows of a few clouds seemed to loiter before they ran toward the hills like playful colts in the wind. On the road a high-racked bone-picker's wagon was headed away from the ranch through hub-deep timothy, the little man hunched on the load prodding his four Indian ponies along as fast as he could make them go.

Although Bone Joe had been stopping at the Bills place for ten years, today was the first time he ever came with a tie around his dusty collar, and even Hippy had left his dough pans to see the sight. "Stickin' feathers on that buzzard's neck ain't gonna make no eagle outa him," the cook predicted.

"No, maybe not, Hippy," Cap Bills admitted, stuffing a long envelope away in his inside pocket. "Maybe not. But if a buzzard'd have the sense to fly high enough, few could tell the difference."

Hippy swung around on his good leg to look up at his boss, and then went limping back to his dough-punching. He had come up from Texas in the eighties with Rutherford Bills as a kid, worked with him and for him all the thirty years since. He wasn't listening to such talk. No buzzard was a-flying so high a bullet from a Bills rifle wouldn't fetch him down.

But outside, the old cowman still looked after the top-heavy bone wagon, watching it lurch slowly across the meadow toward the sand pass, the hind wheels rickety, one lower than the other, and running fast to keep up.

Until he was out of sight of the ranch, Bone Joe did his best to hustle his thin-necked ponies along with the sharp end of his willow prod. But as soon as the trail cut in between the steep hills of the pass he settled back on his

First published in *Scribner's Magazine* 105 (March 1939). Reprinted from Mari Sandoz, *Hostiles and Friendlies* (Lincoln: University of Nebraska Press, 1959), 189–222. Copyright © 1939 by Mari Sandoz. Copyright © renewed 1967 by Caroline Pifer. Reprinted by permission of McIntosh and Otis, Inc.

load of bleached bones, letting the old rope lines sag, the sore-shouldered ponies nip at the weeds alongside as they plodded the heavy sand.

As the bone wagon passed the Gaylor fork, an open roadster swept in on the trail from the town. It was Hortense Bills, old Cap's daughter, her red auto veil flying, the wheels throwing sand at every curve. When she saw the bone rack, she turned in close behind it, hit her klaxon hard, and swung out around. Barely missing the tailboard, she was gone toward the ranch without looking back, scattering dust behind her, and a scrap of bone man's song.

"Stinkin' old bone-picker, ye ha ha," she sang, for all the hills to hear.

The man knew the words well, but this time they brought no red to his wind-burned face. At the crash of the klaxon and the rush of the passing car his sleepy little ponies had shied sideways, cramping the wheels hard. The top-heavy wagon teetered a moment and went down over the small wheel, breaking the old tongue out and spilling the man in a white avalanche of bones. Caught in the stiff lines, he managed to hang on, and was dragged away on his stomach over the bunch grass and through fragrant prairie roses into a nest of bull-tongue cactus, golden-yellow with bloom.

The winded old ponies finally stopped. Slowly Bone Joe lifted his head to wipe the dust and blood from his face, moving himself cautiously, afraid the wild-eyed animals might shy again, afraid he was smashed like the old wagon rack. But he was tough as the barbed wire of a feed corral, and un-broken, though his clothes were ripped to strings from wrist to knee, his skin torn and bleeding, his tie and one shoe gone.

Carefully he went over himself, jerking the thorns away, digging with his knife blade at those broken off close, until the tears stung his raw cheeks. And long before he was done he was pulling himself up to look back toward the pass where only a thin haze of dust along the hills remained to show which way the daughter of Rutherford Bills had gone.

The dry shell of moon hung low when Bone Joe finally pulled into his own little valley. He was hungry and tired from the long job of repairing and reloading his wagon, stiff and sore from the dragging, his arms and face swollen, the cactus spines broken deep in his flesh burning like new boils. But the pale moon made a pewter saucer of the little alkali lake, and the bleaching bones scattered about the dugout looked like white chickens undisturbed by the crippled old coyote always gnawing at a dry joint or a hoof. At the first creak of the wagon, the little scavenger lifted his sharp ears and bounded off into a gully, silent as a shadow. He couldn't know that Bone Joe had no interest in him until winter primed his hide.

With the fire going in the dugout and his skinned arms and chest wrapped in flour sacking soaked in badger grease, Bone Joe stirred up a batch of flapjacks in his old syrup bucket. But long before the last one was fried he was thinking of Hortense Bills again, of her black hair, shiny as a magpie's wing, her eyes gray and straight-browed as a man's, her walk ornery as a wild colt's.

When the last of the flapjack batter was fried up, Bone Joe balanced himself precariously on the top of a nail keg to reach down the elk head over the ridgepole, a fine one he had found years ago in a grassy old blowout, the antlers wide-pronged and weathered to a dead white. With a little red velvet over the skull, stuffed out good with sawdust, it would make a mighty pretty thing, even for a high-toned young ranch lady.

II

It was a week before Bone Joe got out again. By that time he had slept the anger from his tortured muscles, soaked the last of the festering thorns from his flesh, and got into an old pair of pants some duck hunters left behind last fall. He looked better than any time since he drifted into the freeland region ten years before. Although only twenty-four then, he wasn't much on duding up for Saturday-night girling.

"That little bone-picker looks like some poor old broomtail that's been clubbed over the head and kicked away from the feed so often he can't seem to eat with any confidence," Rutherford Bills had told Hippy pityingly the first time Joe stopped at the cookhouse.

But even the cook wasted no sympathy on the bone-picker. "Them teeth a hisn bucks out so from reachin' for grub," he said in disgust after he saw Joe Leems clean up a kettle of Irish stew and all the stuff usually left on the oilcloth table, including the horse-radish and the ketchup.

Most of the other ranchers wouldn't hand out so much as a cold biscuit to the bone man, claiming he picked up stray tools, pulled their cedar posts, and left every gate or take-down open. But mostly people looked on him as a harmless runt, furnishing diversion around the post-office heater or at sales where there was always a free lunch. Not even the lone women homesteaders were afraid of him, probably because he never stopped at their doors, nor stood off looking after them as he did Hortense Bills since the first time he saw her climb up the stirrups to the back of Cap's old buckskin.

Although Bone Joe came in early enough for alfalfa land, he sneaked away into that dead little pocket, with its briny lake that smelled like a nest of old mallard eggs in August, the grass around it so gray and woody no cow would eat it—land that frosted white with alkali in the spring, especially where he broke out sod enough for his dugout.

But Joe Leems, who brought his bone wagon with him, wasn't sensitive to smells and had no farming intentions. He found that the hills hadn't been worked since the buffalo-bone men skimmed them thirty years before. By the first winter he had a long rick bleaching on the right of way at Gaylor, ready for shipment, and had heard the rollicking bone-picker's song many times as cowboys dog-loped past him out on the trails. Even the ranch children sang the one verse their mothers would countenance, shouting out the last lines good and loud and slapping their saddle leather to the chorus:

> Wagons pull in from the prairie dry
> To ricks of bleaching bones piled high.
> Four dollars a ton, but not for Sed,
> A rattler was a-watchin' that buffalo head;
> One settler less to bust up the sod
> And pray for rain from a deaf old God.
>
> Stinkin' old bone picker, ye ha ha,
> Robbin' the coyotes, eye ye ha ha.

From the first, Bone Joe got no mail and he could never be tied down to a definite statement about anything, particularly his origins. To the latecomers he was as much a part of the drab, ragged, smelly little alkali flat as though he had grown from its soil. His hair was to his neck and gray with dust, his dark and bony knees always sticking through several ragged pairs of overalls that he had picked up around some bunkhouse or livery stable where the former occupant shed them like the faded skin of a snake.

He cashed some pretty fair checks at the bank the last few years, but the money was never there long before some hard-pressed rancher slipped around to the dugout in the dark to do a little business. Once when a fresh wave of settlers came in, the new women, with ladies-aid ideas, made him a Christmas quilt. The ranch hands slapped their leather chaps hard at that one. "With you a-feedin' him, Hippy, most a the cowmen payin' him blood interest and them nester women takin' him beddin', he ought to make it to grass—"

But he really was a hustler, and so far as anybody knew Hortense Bills and her squawking klaxon were the first to interrupt his work, and then only until he could move around enough to catch up his ponies.

With his thin whiskers scraped off around the brown scabs of his healing face and the elk head in the wagon, he stopped in the Bills yard, not going in to Hippy as usual, or up to the big house as he did sometimes lately. Just waited, making no answer to the choreman's yell, "Hi, there, Joe—looks like you got you a snoot full a itch somewheres—" and pretending not to hear him whistle the bone-picker's song.

Finally Hortense came riding in from the pasture, wide-hatted, her silk shirt bright as a clump of golden sweet peas against a hill, the fringe of her gauntlets scarcely stirring, so easy was her seat on her loping pinto. At the gate she swung her arm around the stick and opened it without dismounting, closing it as handily as any cowboy, or Cap Bills himself.

While she watered her horse at the tank, Bone Joe shuffled forward, very small in his baggy clothes, holding the whitened elk head out awkwardly before him. With the pinto shying, jerking at the bit, Hortense tried to understand the man's stammerings. Suddenly she began to laugh, head thrown back, right out for all the yard and the bunkhouse to hear.

But as the man's mousy little face darkened, his knob of a chin set, she stopped. "You mean it—for me?" she asked.

"Maybe—" the man began slowly, not able to commit himself, the high apple of his neck bobbing. "Yeh—I guess maybe I could let you have the horns."

Now Hortense was laughing again, but quietly, with dimples and friendly white teeth for the man. Slyly she touched her heel to the off side of the agitated pinto and set him to an impatient crowhopping. "Oh, I couldn't let you rob yourself," she called back to the man as the horse carried her away into the yard. "But thank you for letting me see the fine horns," she added, over her shoulder.

So Bone Joe had to take the elk head back to his wagon, with the choreman and Hippy and anyone at the bunkhouse knowing, seeing it all. And when he was gone the father came out into the heat and sun of the yard, his hair blowing, shaggy as an iron-gray mustang in winter.

"You might have taken the head," he told his daughter quietly.

"From that smelly old bone-picker?"

"He picks the best bones in the country," Rutherford Bills said.

III

From his first coming, Rutherford Bills stood out tall among the cattlemen of the sandhills, his gray cowman's hat well above the rest, like a spruce rearing out of a forest of slim pines. He went at everything as he straddled a bronch, swift and confident, not sparing of bit or spur. There were some who claimed they remembered when he came in from the south like any other cowhand, with a slicker tied behind his saddle, his soogans and other traps on a pack horse. But even then his horses were good ones.

After looking around a little he settled on Fall Creek, and while the hands threw up some log buildings and pole corrals, he covered the region on Gold Dust, his buckskin. He bought up a small herd of the better Texas cattle from the later trailers, grazed them into meat on the free range, and made money selling beef to the Indians, while he built up his herd. By the time the railroad came he was ready to ship good grass-fat stock. His word was better than paper to the bank and his thick, black hair, graying early at the temples, better than gold with the ladies.

When the country tamed down some he brought in a big flat piano and a pretty little Eastern bride, with a waistline two hand-spans around, a blue chip hat with green wings pinned to her mass of light curls. He showed her off by candlelight in the ranch living room, playing sentimental little snatches at her harp or on the piano.

But soon it came out that the little bride was really as fragile as she looked and didn't like the country. The wind dried her soft, shining curls, coarsened the delicate violet-rose of her cheeks, darkened the pale shadows of her eyes and made her head ache. The people were so uncouth, the country so wide, so dreadfully empty and plain. Only one spot seemed to please her—the headwaters of the south branch of Fall Creek. The little pocket was ringed in by hills, the low marshy meadow about the palmful of lake blue with the violets of May. A few slim young cottonwoods stood shyly together at the pool springs of the upper end. Diane Bills filed on this bit of land, and her tall husband put a little doll's house for her beside the peaceful, grass-hung thread of stream, with the hills standing firm against the winds. In the fall the ailing little Diane went East and by spring there was only her portrait over the closed piano in the ranch living room and a new baby, Hortense, to remind Rutherford Bills of the few months that were like a moment of sun on a knoll ringed in by a low, gray sky.

Cap Bills was a good cowman and always made money so long as the grass was free as the wind ruffling the long timothy of his meadows. But the time came when browning fence posts marched away to all the hazes of the horizon, when the yellow streaks of new settler trails crossed the prairie in every direction, the dark blocks of their soddies cramping the sweep of the eye, their hopeful windmills joining earth and air. Neighboring ranchers hired men with six-shooters to keep the range clear, covered the land with fraudulent filings, and ate up the homesteaders' crops in the night. Cap Bills watched the covered wagons trail in, treated the newcomers like neighbors, and leased their grass, even went to the school elections to vote the maximum levy of taxes for the teacher's salary. The settlers called him damned white, but the other cattlemen stood away from him at the Stockmen's Hotel.

He didn't seem to be making much from his cattle any more, either, now that the sodbusters had so much of his hay land, and so he went in for good horses—but the swamp fever got them. Next he tried Mexican cattle, at five dollars a head. They were gaunt range stock, wild as mustangs, and tore through barbed-wire fences like so much string every time they caught sight of a woman's skirt blowing. At the first snowfall they stood in little knots out in the wind, shivering, humped up high as the back of a snaky bronch. That winter was the worst since the eighties, and when the snow broke up in April, only a handful of the new stock were still on their feet. That meant good picking for Bone Joe after two, three years of sun and rain.

All this time Hortense was in school in the East, with an aunt. But since she was eight she spent the summers loafing around the old ranch house or riding the hills with Cap. She had his dark skin that turned to a smooth, ruddy tan in the wind and sun, and two thick, dark braids with red ribbons flying out behind her as she kicked old Gold Dust into a broken-kneed little run to catch up with her father or maybe some dog-loping cowhand who had to tuck in his flapping shirttail when he saw her coming. But they liked her, teased her in a heavy way that she soon caught on to, and showed her where there might be blue Indian beads in anthills.

They taught the girl to hold a calf down with a knee on its neck, and let her roll their cigarettes that they called fish worms when she finished them. From that a story got around among the older women of the region that the Bills girl was a young cigarette fiend, a smokin' gal, as they called it.

Rutherford Bills tried to remember that his little girl was growing up, would soon be a young woman. But she seemed so natural, so free and gay with her cronies of the corrals and the cookhouse, that he couldn't bring himself to spoil her summers.

And then gradually Bone Joe noticed the Bills girl. His little eyes, like glistening brown chokecherries in the sun wrinkles of his face, began to seek her out, follow her as she rode the range alone for flowers, perhaps for little blue lizards or for sand cherries.

At a ball game the summer Hortense was twelve and growing fast, Bone Joe held out a stick of chewing gum to her, and because the ranch hands were nudging each other, she took it and was teased all the way home by the sly humming of the bone-picker's song. When Cap heard about it he told her she'd have to go back to her aunt if she couldn't learn to be a lady, saying this red-faced and angry. Hippy, with his own opinion of old maids fetching up children, got Hortense into the cookhouse. While he ironed her shirts, he told her some of the things he thought a girl ought to know with buzzards like Bone Joe, or any of the rest of the boys, for that matter, around loose.

"Life's a mighty good hoss and'll carry you a long day's travel if you learns her tricks early," he advised. "Don't never let her get her head bogged down, or clamp jaws on the bit—"

That was talk the girl could understand and with her overall pocket full of cookies she threw the reins over Gold Dust's shaggy mane and rode out into the hills to contemplate this new and appalling world that Hippy had showed her.

During the next four years Bone Joe seemed to be spreading himself pretty thin. The cattlemen had tried buying up the range, getting it safely this time. But that took money, and with a drop in beef prices and a hard winter they were borrowing running money where they could, and paying high for it. One after another, Bone Joe got to them, even risked a little on a fellow boiling potash from one of the alkali lakes down on the south road. Half-interest in the business, no matter how far it spread.

Then suddenly Germany was at war, her potash shut off to the world, and Eastern magnates came talking big production, big money to the little lake owners. But Bone Joe still scouted the range seventy, eighty miles each way for bones, except the weeks Hortense Bills was at the ranch. Then he picked the home region, his wagon crawling like a slow, awkward bug along the slopes, his little eyes always out for the darker patches of grass and for a glimpse of a girl and a horse, perhaps only for a moment against some far sky.

IV

The August after Bone Joe brought the elk head to the Bills ranch, Vangie came from school with Hortense for a visit. Before the round-cheeked, jolly blonde girl had been at the ranch a day she knew everybody's nickname and had heard about Bone Joe, especially how he trailed Hortense around at the Fourth of July picnic down at Piller's Grove. She thought it was wonderful, so romantic. Even more romantic than Nickie, the poet, who wrote sonnets to Hortense. The hands winked to each other, openly, largely, suggesting that poor Bone Joe wouldn't have a chance to slip up his gully this time.

But the girl didn't mind, went right on teasing to be taken to his dugout. So the girls got into their riding knickers and shagged over the hills toward the Leems place.

Quietly the girls circled their horses down the gully used by the old coyote to sneak up on the place. The wagon was home, standing, tongue down, among the piles of old iron and bleaching bones. And under it, his hat over his face, one foot in the air, was Bone Joe, asleep with the smell of old and stale death all around him.

At their sly giggling, the commotion of the snorting horses, the man sat up, bumping his head on the wagon bed above him. Red under his bristles, he crawled out between the wheels, rubbing his scalp and staring at Hortense in her bright silk shirt. The girl told him who Vangie was, and without waiting to be asked the two slid off their horses and tied them away from the wagon and the bone piles. Then, as though the path were made for their feet, they started toward the door of the dugout against the hill, with Bone Joe stumbling along backward before them, trying to wave them aside as a woman might, to stop a determined milk cow from a cabbage patch. Calmly Hortense walked toward the old door on leather hinges, Vangie close at her boot heels.

Inside, the dugout was a dark cave to sun-blinded eyes, the only light coming through the open, glass-paned door. Against the far wall an old cot spring hung between posts driven into the ground. Near the door a legless, two-hole stove sat in a box of ashes, with an armful of cow chips stacked on the dirt floor, and from poles of the roof dangled a low forest of dusty sacks and bundles. Even from the doorway the place smelled like the nest of an animal.

Vangie stopped, but Hortense pulled her in, to sit beside her on the cot. The girl let herself down reluctantly, touching only the barest edge of the swinging springs, and jerked at the yellow sleeve of her friend, anxious to go.

But Hortense Bills was already acting the young lady calling on a gentleman, even though it was only Bone Joe in tattered shirt and overalls standing in the doorway of a dugout, stammering. Before he could get his words made there was a scratching under the cot and a soft, furry animal looked out, sniffed the air, and started to climb up the boot nearest him.

"Shoo—git, git!" The man flapped his arms, his short upper lip jerking like a rabbit's. "Git, you—touchin' a lady—"

At that, little Vangie let one high giggle escape her and started Hortense too, laughing free, as though she were out on the open range. "A coon!" she finally cried, pretending it was the animal that was so funny.

Slowly Bone Joe began to grin, the thin skin of his mouth twitching over his buck teeth. In the meantime the young raccoon had settled himself in Hortense's lap and was pawing at the white thistle bloom in a buttonhole of her shirt, his bright little eyes on her face, his feet, like clawed hands, cautious, on the prickly flower.

Together the three watched the little fellow. He was the cutest thing, the girls said politely. Where did Mister—Mister Joe get him? And wouldn't it be nice for him here, out of the cold this winter!

No woman had ever spoken like this to Bone Joe, just as though he were anybody, and surely never Hortense Bills. So he let himself down to his nail-keg stool, dropped his hands between his knees, and began to talk a little, tasting the words cautiously. Yeh, sometimes the little bugger did seem kinda cute-like, he admitted, not committing himself completely. Guessed he just picked him up somewheres—out— Yeh, it might be nice here, round the fire, come winter. Maybe the little bugger wouldn't be here mucha the time—

Hortense understood the last. He wouldn't be here at all, not after the cold primed his hide, made it worth a dollar or so. But the young coon was sound asleep.

As their eyes accustomed themselves to the duskiness of the room, the girls looked around at the earth walls, almost covered with almanac pictures of pretty women with blue-black hair and considerable white skin showing. Half a dozen were of the same red-cheeked girl combing her loose hair beside a pool. And all the pictures had transparent clothes sketched in with pencil crosshatching.

Bone Joe noticed Vangie nudge Hortense toward the pictures and his pinched little head filled into the puffy redness of a hairy turkey gobbler. His confidence gone now, he tried once more to get the girls out. Maybe— maybe it was a-gettin' pretty late, and five, six miles to ride, with badger holes and bums loose in the country—

"It is getting late, isn't it? I guess we had better stay to supper," Hortense said, as to a heartily appreciated invitation.

"Oh," Vangie gushed, dimpling as at a beau, "it's just lovely of you to ask us, isn't it, Hortense?"

So they prodded the flustered man on between them until he lighted the smoky lantern, scooped out some of the powdery gray ashes from under the stove with an old sardine can, and stirred up such a dust that even the little coon hid his head under Hortense's arm. With the cow-chip fire roaring, Bone Joe broke off a piece of brown chicory stick for the coffee pot and got out a greasy black skillet.

"I—I guess maybe I better fix up a few flapjacks," he said apologetically as he pried at an old syrup bucket. Outside the tin was streaked and rusty and when the lid finally popped up, the inside was really lined half an inch deep with old batter, as the cowboys said, the sour smell filling the whole dugout thick.

Now it was enough for Hortense. Dumping the coon to the ground she ran for the door, and with Vangie at her heels, swung to her horse. At the first jump of her pinto she began to laugh, and all through the valley the horses ran uncurbed, the girls rocking in their saddles, laughing aloud until they had to hang to the horns, gasping.

When the girls were gone, Bone Joe let himself down on the sagging old cot. But the gloom didn't keep him from knowing what a boar's nest the dugout must have seemed to the fine young ladies. And he had hoped to walk right up to the Bills' ranch house someday, without stopping at the cookhouse for grub, without bringing money for Cap's urgent needs. Just walk up to the house like a visitor, like any man.

Several times during the winter Bone Joe stopped at the cookhouse to eat up whatever Hippy set out for him and to get a little news. Once or twice he tried to lead up to Cap's sister, living in the East someplace, and to Cap's girl, going to school there. Maybe—maybe the cook knew the town?

Yeh, Hippy admitted, Miss Hortense was a-goin' to school. But he didn't say where.

So Bone Joe finally had to watch the ranch mail sack on the route for the address. And late in February a huge valentine drifted in at the college for Hortense. It came addressed in pencil, in a box like a fiddle case, a full-sized, gilt-paper violin standing away from a lacy background, with a swirl of pink roses around it. Hidden, but readily discoverable, were the letters J. L. Only the Gaylor postmark and the soiled fingerprints made Hortense think of Bone Joe at all, or remember that his name was Joe Leems. With the valentine and the wrappings in the apron of her uplifted skirt she ran to Vangie's room. Together they laughed until they were breathless. That bum in the dugout and his flapjack bucket! "To my Beloved," it said on the white ribbon among the roses. They howled it to each other as they popped candy into their mouths, candy the poet who made sonnets for his cowgirl from the West had sent them.

Next summer—just wait until next summer. They'd think of something rare for old Bone.

V

The day Cap Bills met the two girls at the depot, the bone-picker was there in a khaki drill suit, waiting. But Hortense didn't see him. She was crying that her father looked so thin and aged; burying her face against his coat, she wiped her eyes and pretended it was joy at seeing him again.

So Bone Joe, standing off to the side, alone, stiff among the cream cans of the farmers, didn't get the greeting he hoped for—nothing at all but a hasty nod of recognition from Cap Bills.

At the ranch, while her soft little friend napped from the three-day trip, Hortense went to the cookhouse for an hour's serious talk. For the first time in his life, Hippy left the salt out of the pie crust he was mixing, and with company home, too. But it was pretty hard to admit to Hortense that every acre and hoof her father owned was mortgaged tight as a tick in a sheep's ear, and long overdue. The girl nodded slowly, her eyes still level and straight-browed, and once more she came away from the cookhouse with the world a strange, appalling place about her.

"You can't go a-lettin' on to Cap," Hippy had said.

She promised she wouldn't, and so, although the father was away on business much of the time, probably trying to raise capital or a partner, Hortense plunged into a strenuous, boisterous summer with Vangie, always on the go, mostly by saddle because the horses came free. They went to every picnic, dance, rodeo, and celebration for miles around, always with plenty of Cap Bills' old friends to ask them to dinner or to stop for the night, if it was far. Always, too, with plenty of boys, the Pillers, or other ranchers' sons, for dancing partners and to buy them pop and sandwiches at the stands, or to shoot for kewpie dolls.

"That bob-haired smokin' gal!" envious mothers told each other when they saw the arms full of silk-frilled, painted dolls the girls always had to carry around through the crowds, although none of them had ever seen Hortense take even one puff from the cigarettes she rolled so swiftly and well.

Once the girls rode clear down to Sully, the potash town where Bone Joe was said to have his investments. It was ten times noisier and dustier than the summer before, the tar-paper hulks of the refining plants spreading wider, rearing higher, pointing great chimneys into the windy sky. The thousands of workmen slept in the hot, single-board sheds, thrown together in boom-town style, or in the rows of tar-paper shacks a quarter the size of Hippy's smokehouse, each with one window and a door, set up on high blocks, only separated far enough so a horsebacker or a hurrying woman could slip between.

As the girls ate hamburgers with pop at a stand, they spied Bone Joe's old wagon in the surging alley beside the bank. Soon he himself came out of the building, and the crowd parted for him, hats and caps sliding off, men making excuses to call his name, "How'do, Mister Leems," "Nice day, Mister Leems," while farther back there were nudgings, laughings, and hurried searches for a place to spit.

As Joe Leems swung his wagon past one of the shack rows, a woman in a yellow kimono waved to him, trying to coax him in. At her first sign he prodded his ponies into a scattered, broken run, escaping with a great banging of the empty bone rack, leaving a whirl of fine, boom-town dust to settle slowly behind him.

"Must be pretty hard up for customers," a couple of old cowpunchers riding along the road shouted to each other over the racket, as they watched the bone-picker go.

When Hortense and Vangie got out on the clean, golden prairie of evening, they slowed their horses, hooked their knees around the saddle horns, and ate bananas as they considered Bone Joe's consternation at the woman's approach. It gave them an idea for the joke they planned last February, when the fancy lace valentine came for Hortense. The next morning they hunted up one of the matrimonial papers the hay waddies and ranch hands had around the bunkhouse. Between them they made up the five dollars required for the publication of a man's letter, with photograph. After reading the papers through, they described Joe Leems as the owner of "a fine cattle ranch, a large, comfortable home, well-furnished, overlooking a beautiful lake," and gave his name in care of Rutherford Bills. With a picture of Nickie's lean and beautiful face, his thick, pale hair mussed a little, to draw them, the letters began to pile in, as the mail carrier complained to the girls. "Why's your dad let that bone-picker fill his box up?"

There were packages, too, odd shapes and sizes. Debating for an hour or two the ethics of the situation in the stilted manner of their most unpopular teacher, they decided upon opening everything not strictly sealed, since, in a way, the mail was more theirs than Bone Joe's. Perhaps the purple fronds of feather sticking from a broken envelope, the crumbs of fudge leaking from a bundle really decided them. The feather was fastened to a lady's garter, a rich purple, and big enough, at least the girls decided, to go around Bone Joe's syrup bucket. There were hand-knitted socks, sleeve-holders, several ties, and in one the wedding picture of a widow, with "sod" written under the mustached man beside her.

Among the practically unsealed letters were some pretty good ones. "My beautiful curly-headed baby boy," one began, in good penmanship. Some were painstakingly done, in unaccustomed ink, with "Dear Sir" and "Yrs resp." Some of the women were kittenish and coy, pretending to have money and many admirers but romantic enough to prefer a great, strong man from the West. One came by special delivery. "Please wire Two Hundred Dollars for Fair and expenses immediately." Enclosed was the picture of a high-bosomed woman with earbobs and a commanding eye. Hortense, who had taken a minor in history, suggested that she would have made a fine general for the Prussian Army.

When the girls got tired of the mail, they rode over to the dugout in Leems' valley and emptied the grain sack full at Bone Joe's feet, the packages rolling, the cream and lavender envelopes scattering like corn leaves in the wind. The man looked at the lot and up at Hortense in confusion. There he stopped, boldly, for he saw that now the girl's dark eyes were the troubled green-black of hail clouds and not gay any more, as her mouth would make them out to be.

It was as well that the girls had their fun before, because Bone Joe didn't do anything, no stammering, no turning red, no sweating, no asking what it was about. Today he just stood there bold as a ferret, his little eyes unblinking as glass on Hortense until she hurried Vangie away to their horses. Nor was there any laughter as they rode out of the valley. Not even the daily letter from Nickie could make Hortense forget the waiting look of Bone Joe's eyes.

The next time Joe Leems shipped a car of bones and scrap iron he thumbed late through the catalogues by the light of the old lantern and finally sent for a red-satin box with sea shells all around the edges. "A gift fit for a queen," the description said, and filled with two pounds of assorted bonbons, finest quality, nineteen cents a pound, extra.

The day Joe brought the box over, Vangie and Hortense were on the top plank of the corral wall, watching the choreman provide a new mother for an orphaned white-faced calf. Hortense saw the bone wagon turn in at the yard gate, but because it was too late to get away, she waited as the man crawled down and came toward the corral, stiff in his wrinkled drill suit that was still too large, even after two hard sandhill showers on it. With his cap under his arm, he handed Hortense a package in crumpled brown paper and waited for her to open it, his short upper lip twitching in anticipation.

Once the girl started to make the bone-picker take the package back, but she remembered what Hippy had told her. "He's got both Cap and the bank where the hair's short." So she unwrapped the box, and Vangie's little squeal of delight seemed to compensate for her own silence. As she opened the lid, the choreboy came up to look over the outfit, as he called it. With much skepticism, he bit into a bonbon, nodded, and spit the candy out. "Old as them bones you pick," he grumbled.

V I

Monday, Vangie was going back to school and Hortense with her, into war work. The Saturday before there was a box social and dance at Ned Salzer's, proceeds to go to the Red Cross. Rutherford Bills was away, but Hippy chaperoned the girls, as they called it, chaperoned his own good grub, he insisted, as he sat stiffly on the outside in the roadster, his game leg cramped, holding the girls' twin box in a bleached sugar sack on his good knee. Every mile or so he pretended to steal a look inside the sack by the dim light of the dash, with Vangie grabbing at the box in mock horror that he really might see it.

"I bet you let them Piller boys get a eyeful," he protested.

Vangie shook her pale head of curls at him, but Hortense held the wheel and kept her face to the crooked trail.

"The boys are leaving for overseas tomorrow," she finally said.

At Salzer's they climbed the ladder into the long hayloft smelling clean of alfalfa, saddle leather, and kerosene from the row of lanterns hung along the gable. They were greeted noisily by the early comers, the fiddlers beginning to tune up, and the hay waddies shouting, "Let 'er go!"

With the organ unfolded, the musicians swung into "Tipperary," and the two Piller boys, tall and strange in uniform, came over. Easily they moved out upon the candle-waxed floor with the girls from the Bills ranch in ruffled voile dresses, Hortense in Alice blue, Vangie in pink; smoothly they dropped into Eastern steps the boys had picked up in college last spring. Struttin' city stuff, the home boys called it; showing off with glides, hesitations, dips, and whirling turns on the ball of the foot.

Toward midnight, the floor manager got out the broom and, pounding the bald-headed end on the floor for attention, announced the sale of the supper boxes. "One hundred per cent goes for the Red Cross an' the Yanks goin' overseas, so bid 'em up, boys, bid 'em up—"

The girls and women settled along the benches, the men gathering at the far end of the loft, for there were to be no nudgings, no signs now. And when the first box was fetched out from behind the curtain across the corner, Bone Joe came pushing forward, using his sharp elbows against the pack of men, until he was clear out in front where he could watch the faces of the girls from Bills and his signals to the auctioneer could be seen plain, for he had planned this evening a long, long time.

One box after another was held high, cried while the owner tried to look unconcerned, and sold for two, three, even eight or nine dollars.

When a red-satin box with sea shells on the edges came up, Vangie nudged Hortense and then they both pretended to look around for the blushing owner. Paying no further attention to the girls, Bone Joe began to bid. One after another the younger fellows got in against him, the older men yelling advice to their contemporary. The box went to twenty dollars. Joe hesitated, but when one of the Piller boys bid an extra quarter, he began again, slowly, thinking each bid out carefully, hanging on like a badger to a hound's throat, not saying a word, just holding up a finger or nodding woodenly for the extra quarter.

At fifty dollars he stopped again, and the other Piller boy bid a dollar raise. Once more the bone-picker started, went to sixty-three dollars, with Hortense shaking her head hard at the boys. Everybody else dropped out, and in a great rumpus of stomping and yells and calls, Bone Joe went forward to receive the box on his two open palms. Holding it like a jewel case, he slipped away to the wall through the path that opened for him. All through the rest of the bidding he stood there, straight and secure, not bothering to open the box, even to lift the lid a bit for the name inside.

When the children's boxes were gone, and $310.75 had been taken in, the crowd scattered over the loft, men with boxes finding their partners, the stags lining up to buy sandwiches and coffee, usually free at barn dances but sold by the Red Cross tonight. When everybody was settled to eat, Bone Joe once more pushed forward, this time to Hortense and Vangie sitting on a car cushion on the floor, the Piller boys before them on a dust robe, the box with the cattails between them.

"I—I guess maybe I got your box," he said to Hortense, his teeth bucking out through his little grinning mouth. He repeated the words doggedly, despite the roar of laughing that went up from the bar-wide circle watching as the girl shook her short hair.

"Isn't there a name inside?" she asked as kindly as she could, sorry that he made her do this so publicly. The bone-picker looked all around him, swiftly, as a coyote ringed in by hounds, and saw what the girl meant in their faces. Once more he plowed through the crowd, this time clear to the ladder and out to his wagon to sit on the tongue in the dim moonlight while a bunch of young squirts sneaked after him, humming the bone-picker's song from behind shadowy cars and wagons until those fathers who owed the lone man money came out angrily to send the boys flying. And inside the loft sixteen-year-old Alice Mason cried into her handkerchief. She had lost the pretty red box Hortense had given her, and the first social of her whole life was spoiled, even though her box brought the most of any.

VII

Sunday evening the girls went to Gaylor to see the Piller boys off, kissing them and wishing them great good luck with a gaiety that did not cover foreboding. By the next summer both the boys were gone, one in action, the other of gangrene; and Bone Joe had a breach-of-promise suit on his hands, one of the mail-order widows, the one Hortense said would make a good Prussian general. But she hadn't a scrap of paper to prove anything, and no jury would ever believe that she pinned Joe down to a definite promise, even though the widow was a determined woman. She walked clear out to the dugout and might have walked back for all of Joe Leems if the mail carrier hadn't felt sorry for her—thick feet stuffed into high-heeled pumps, a suitcase and something over two hundred pounds of meat to lug. Nothing came of the case because a fellow up at Gaylor who owed Joe some money and couldn't pay married the woman.

VIII

For the first time in ten years Hortense didn't come home that summer. Hippy's rare notes were full of meatless, wheatless days and bread made with black flour and potatoes, not fit for a hound dog's belly. Cap Bills, thinking of Bone Joe in a new suit, with a big car and big ways, didn't urge the girl.

The rancher had put the last cent he could raise into potash, the new wartime industry. Neglecting the interest and the taxes, he even considered mortgaging Bills Pocket, the quarter left to Hortense by her mother. But he couldn't ask the girl, and so that remained free. Everything else went into potash. Fortunes were made down at Sully. Bone Joe had sold the fifty acres of his dirty lake for ten thousand dollars, cash, it was rumored. And his interest in the potash works for a hundred thousand. That was just like a bone-picker, selling out for small potatoes, some said. Another year or two, and he'd a been a millionaire. Got scared at the talk of one side or the other in the War caving in. Germany could keep going, Cap Bills thought, now that Russia was out. Another year—that was all he needed.

Then, suddenly, the hysteria of the Armistice was upon them. Hortense's work was over and so she came home for a while. Cap met her at Gaylor, much older, but full of ideas. He was working hard for a tariff on German potash, hoping for an extension on his long overdue mortgages. Hortense tried to talk to him of these things, but he drew himself up tall as ever. "It has never been necessary for a Bills woman to worry her pretty head—" So the daughter kissed his softening cheek and saddled up her pinto for a hard ride in the hills.

IX

The next day Joe Leems came to the Bills yard, not in his bone wagon this time, but in a new yellow roadster, a long, low one he took in on a fore-closure from a potash man. He wore a new wide-striped suit—like one he saw on an actor in Sully the winter before—yellow, bumper-toe shoes and a cap. He stopped his new car alongside the house that hadn't seen paint for twelve years and went in, his bright shoes straight up on the ranch-house porch. Without knocking, he pulled the door open and walked boldly into the Bills living room.

At his step Hortense was up from the piano, to stand alone, straight and tall, against this intruder. Joe Leems tried to hold his ground, say he had a right there, but before the daughter of Rutherford Bills he was once more only a dirty bone-picker.

That night Rutherford Bills sat late before the fire in the old ranch house. Young Hortense didn't seem to have much luck with her men, he mused: her father a gut-shot old critter just hanging onto his place by his toenails, hoping; that Piller boy of hers buried in France; and then she went and fell in love with a poetry fellow. And all the time there was old Bone Joe Leems, waiting around like a bare-necked buzzard on a fence.

He had always hoped to spare the girl but now at last he saw he must tell her something of his difficulties. Of course the market would go up as soon as a tariff was put on potash. It had to come. America protected her industries. Until then he would be busy as a sheepherder in lambing time, couldn't be beauing his handsome daughter around as was proper. Now he hoped she would go to her aunt for a spell. Later, maybe, they'd take a long trip together.

And so, as though there was nothing but the thought of a holiday for the girl between them, no long knowledge of the ranch failure, no Bone Joe walking unasked into the old living room, Hortense packed. In the morn-ing, Hippy sat over a cup of coffee in the cookhouse with the girl and then hobbled to the door to watch her go. Yeh, he'd see to Cap, see to him as well as any man alive.

X

It wasn't until the second summer that Bone Joe realized that Hortense Bills wasn't coming back, even with Cap down sick. A straw boss was running the place, with Hippy living in the ranch house and the doctor coming out every week. Kidney trouble, some said. They could tell. Old Cap'd been walking stooped below the middle for months and looking the color of underdone biscuits. That cigarette-smoking girl of his belonged to home. Somebody had ought to tell her what was what. Then it got around that Bone Joe had a man look her up in New York, found her married, or that she'd better be. The next week he took over the Bills ranch.

The day Joe Leems came out, Hippy padded the back seat of the old touring car with quilts and bedding, helped Cap in and let him hold the portrait of Diane. The front seat and the running board he loaded with stovepipe and pots and pans. Behind them came one of Ned Salzer's trucks with an old stove, a few books, and the piano that hadn't been opened for two years.

By evening they were settled in Bills Pocket, with the first smoke coming from the old shack that was thrown together over twenty years ago and was now mighty leaky and airish. Cap Bills wouldn't let Hippy take out his pencil to write to the daughter. But some of the women folks saw to it that she knew, and so Hortense Bills came home. She must have brought a little money, because Hippy drove in to Gaylor, hired carpenters, and had lumber hauled out for an ell of two rooms. Saturday night, the loafers were waiting thick along the street as the carpenters drew up in the center parking. Yeh, Tensy Bills was a-comin' due, all right. They'd seen her man, too, one of them there pale potato sprouts, with hair light as a meadow full of tickle grass a-blowing, and wax-beany fingers.

The night the baby came, Cap Bills' tired old heart stopped. "The Lord giveth and the Lord taketh away," the preacher said at the funeral. Everyone in the county able to be out seemed to be there, those who had worked for Cap standing in a knot off to the side, remembering the man he was.

At the grave the old ranch cook and Nickie stood alone, the light wind lifting the thin gray hair of Hippy's bowed head, ruffling the heavy blond waves above the boyish face of the young husband. At the end, Joe Leems came edging up to stand beside them, his head sticking forward on his neck, his hat held against his stomach. As the old cook guided the sobbing Nickie away, he thought of those days when Hortense rode free over the hills. Even then the bone-picker's little eyes were after her, even before he had any paper against her father, long before he started wearing a tie to the ranch, a buzzard trying to fly as high as an eagle.

Now Rutherford Bills was gone, and his fine, wide ranch was in the hands of Bone Joe, Mr. Joseph P. Leems. By the time the potash companies were all broke, he had taken over a county-seat bank, and foreclosed the paper until he owned half a dozen of the smaller ranches that just couldn't seem to compete with South American beef. He got most of the town of Gaylor, too, including the buildings housing the post office, the city headquarters, and the fire department.

The backs of the menus at Leems Café listed the Leems hotel, pool hall, barber shop, filling station, garage, grocery and drygoods, hardware and undertaking, livery and feed, lumber and coal, insurance, loans and investments.

Although he held himself fairly straight when he remembered, inside he was still Bone Joe, even in his dark-green, belted-back suit, with a pink silk shirt, gray cowman's hat, and a bulge in the back of his pants that was said to be twenty-dollar bills, although nobody ever saw him break one.

He had a room at the hotel, offices at the bank and the city hall, and a sort of a hole in the wall with outside stairs above the feed store. Inside was an old leather davenport, a rusty two-hole stove, much like that of his old dugout, and several pictures of Theda Bara on the wall.

Women were giving him the eye now. Now and then a girl even slipped up the outside stairs to the room over the feed store, though it was generally some frightened little thing, sent because interest was due on a mortgage.

Around the livery stable there was a lot of laughing. By golly, it sure looked like old Bone Joe couldn't stand comparison, keepin' to them scared kids like he did. The story ran from the pitch players to the five-hundred club and the bridge-whist circle, growing as it went. Some thought it a mean shame, such young girls, but they weren't in a position to do much complaining, just now, owing the man money themselves. The weekly paper at the county seat, where Bone Joe was horning in, gave half a column to the story, mostly just hinting, calling it "The Shame of Our Sister City." By Thursday evening the paper was sold out. Those on the Friday mail deliveries got nothing, and the next week there was an apology, boxed in black, like an obituary, headed "UPRIGHT CITIZEN MALIGNED BY IDLE GOSSIP."

After that, Joe Leems had no more frightened night visitors in his room. Instead, he took to driving out alone in the evenings. He was walking cockier, too, as though the far pastures were pretty good. Then one night young Singer came tearing up the rickety stairs, kicked the door in, and with his fingers on Bone's scrawny throat, told him he'd cut his dirty heart out and throw it in his face if he didn't let Ellie Melkorn alone.

The next Sunday evening two cars full of white-robed figures stopped at the Melkorn place, dragged young Singer out of the kitchen where he was helping Ellie with the supper dishes, and later dumped him on his father's porch, the skin stripped from his back with a bull whip.

Hortense heard little about the excitement that swept Gaylor and the county seat. She did know that times were hard, farm produce down, war mortgages coming due, ex-servicemen out of work, and everybody looking for a whipping boy, somebody to blame. But thoughts of half-soles and sugar and flour in Bills Pocket shut out the world as surely as its ring of hills stood against the far sky. They might sell the place, have a five-hundred-dollar debt left over, no home, and no carfare to Nickie's old job in New York. And even when he could work steady, it wasn't much. If they stayed here his white skin might darken, his body grow stronger, his heart pound less. And Hippy needn't be weaned off the range.

By the time baby Diane was six months old, Hortense was back in overalls, much like all the other summers out here. But this time it wasn't play; this time she was out showing a hired man where to break up spring sod for a big garden, a plot of potatoes, sweet corn, and an acre of white beans against the doctor's bills and the undertaker's. She watched the man closely, for after this there would be no money for help.

Evenings, she worked out the plantings with Hippy, crippled up with rheumatism, not getting around much in damp weather any more, and talking as though he hadn't been limping for thirty years. But even in a wheel chair, Hippy would be handy as a silver dollar.

Sometimes, after a good day, Nickie sang a gay little song or two that his mother had taught him, his mother who died wishing for her native Pyrenees. Sometimes he played a little, too, Chopin or Debussy, reaching out suddenly to pull Hortense from her sewing to the piano bench. Her hands were clumsy now, and calloused, but she learned not to object, since the time Nickie snatched up his cap and ran out into the night.

"I can't bear to see these things happening to you," he cried out to the darkness when Hortense came to bring him in from the cold. And although he sat quietly enough the rest of the evening, his heart pounded like Hippy's hammer on the old plowshare.

He couldn't do much heavy work, but with all the new-turned breaking handy, he finally got a sod fireplace and chimney up at the far end of the living room, snaking the blocks into place with the old pinto that once carried Hortense over all the hills. Well-plastered, inside and out, with alkali mud, it was nice for the long evenings. They made a party of the first fire, and a poem.

But Nickie knew such things wouldn't buy so much as a box of matches or a pound of sugar and so he tried desperately to learn to be helpful outside. Without money for coal and with almost no trees in the country, he became the fuel provider of Bills Pocket, vice-president in charge of cow chips, as he called it. During the summer he dotted the old feed grounds west of the valley with neat little cocks to be hauled in when the team was free. The land belonged to Joe Leems now, and several times he drove around that way to see the cow-chip-picker Tensy Bills had married. But Nickie just waved his hand in greeting and dragged his old tub on.

In spite of all the care and hoeing Hortense could give to her gardening, the first years didn't yield much for sale except sweet corn and potatoes, the surer crops. One September an early frost blackened half her beans, making a long job of sorting for winter evenings. Next, the hail took all the early planting, pounding the melon vines into the ground. Then the drouth. Yet they managed, even paid a little on the debts, until the fall Nickie got sick.

One cold fall day he stayed out cow chip-picking through a slow drizzle that chilled him completely before Hortense came to the hill to call. Scolding that he hadn't hurried home to get dry, she held his hand under the warm sleeve of her jacket, his fingers ice against her side, until she couldn't stand it any longer. Yet as soon as she started to run she remembered and tried to slow down, but Nickie jogged right along to the crest of the road turning into Bills Pocket. Puffing a little, he stopped to point ahead for Hortense to see. Across from them, the smoke of Hippy's baking spread in a thin blue haze along the hills, while over it the breaking clouds of evening hung in yellow folds, burning the windows of their home to a golden light. In a flood of happiness Hortense pressed her cheek to Nickie's wet coat as he held her against him. Then she hurried him along the wet road to the house.

That night Nickie was restless and by morning he was feverish and sick. Two days later it was pneumonia, with Hortense having to admit to the doctor that he had been refused by the army—wet lungs and an unreliable heart.

It was late spring before Nickie was out again, keeping to the sunny side of the house pretty much of the time, with a knitted scarf crossed over his chest, the skin of his high, thin nose stretched tight and shiny. By this time Hortense showed the strain of the winter-long nursing, even with all the help Hippy, limping around on a cane, could give. While Nickie was still only a long skeleton under the blankets, little Diane came down with the whooping cough, and the doctor, not paid out yet for Cap Bills' illness, needed money. Hortense picked over the screenings of her beans, sold her hens and the potatoes, down to the barest necessities, even the calf she had hoped to hold for a couple of years. She looked through Nickie's writing once more, and without hope used up the last of her stamps sending the poems out. Half a dozen were accepted, bringing in fifteen dollars and a half, all in one mail. That was a grand, happy evening with a little music not too badly played.

But finally Hortense had to mortgage Bills Pocket, even though to her it meant giving the bank her home. By her twenty-seventh birthday she was looking pretty sprangly, as Hippy called it, with here and there a wiry thread of gray creeping through her dark hair.

Even now Nickie tried to write a little, a pad of paper always beside him, the desperate need of Bills Pocket a shadow about his bowing shoulder. More and more he wrote of the things he was leaving behind, soil and air and sky, a salty old friend, a daughter that he could never kiss again, a woman long and deeply loved.

And then one day Hortense ran to the old car and tried frantically to start it. Failing, she ran to the ridge road to wave down the first passer-by, send him hurrying for a telephone.

The doctor came in time to pull the sheet up over the white face of the poet, waxy as the soapweed blossoms Hortense had brought to him from the hills that morning.

And when the doctor was gone, Hortense threw an old denim jumper around the girl and, with her arm about the shaking little shoulder, went up the road to where it turned into Bills Pocket. There, off to the west, was the old feed ground where, two years before, Nickie had stayed out in the cold rain because he was so anxious to be of help. Together they had looked toward the little house, with its blue smoke clinging to the hill behind it, the clouds of evening turning the windows to gold. Once more the woman felt the rough, wet cold of Nickie's coat against her cheek, knew the loud thumping of his laboring heart.

And now she must explain death to his child.

XI

When the six months of mourning were up, Bone Joe and his driver stopped beside the garden patch where Hortense was going through the tomato vines bowed to the earth with reddening fruit. At the sound of the car the woman stopped and rose stiffly, her gunny-sack apron heavy before her as Joe Leems came uncertainly through the patch, trying to keep out of the down vines with his new shoes.

"Howdy, Tensy," he said.

"Nice day," she told him.

"Yeh—" opening his mouth several times, closing it, and finally starting, "Yeh, Tensy, I guess maybe I could let you have a house in town cheap—"

"Thank you, but we'll be all right here," she said.

The man pushed the sand around a little with a shoe and finally lifted his eyes to the strong woman figure before him, the leather brown of her face, her high, fine nose.

Once more he started. "Maybe I could let you have a little extra on the place—"

"We're better off here—"

That brought the red to his neck. "You can't go on a-living here like you been doin', with a busted-down cow cook—"

A long time the woman looked at the little man before her, once even started to lift her hand against him, knowing he was no match for her field arm. But behind the things she had suffered from him she remembered his own life-long indignities. She had upset his wagon, pushed herself into his dugout, brought him long ridicule with that matrimonial-paper advertisement. She had helped sing the bone-picker's song, make a fool of him at a box social. Anger was not her right, and so she thanked the man for his interest and turned back to her work. But when the car pulled out of the yard, Tensy Bills looked after it a long time, her hand shading her eyes uneasily.

She was right. Bone Joe had other ways of persuasion. One rainy evening there was a pounding on the door at Bills Pocket. Hortense put aside her mending and went to the door. In the rectangle of light before her stood three white-robed men, a smallish one in the middle, a wide, husky one on each side, and behind them, across the farther fringe of light, was a solid white wall.

The woman started to close the door, but one of the men poked a rifle against it. They were not here to trouble her, he said, but to protect her from a wolf, a human wolf.

"Yes, a human wolf," the other big fellow added. "We've come for him," thumbing toward the crippled man in his chair beside the lamp.

Hortense looked slowly from one masked face to another and back to the little man in the middle. So that was it. Smiling a little, with the light behind her, she reached as though for support to the door casing. Swiftly she grasped the twenty-two rifle hanging beside it, threw the gun to her shoulder, holding the barrel down upon the little man in the center, directly between the holes of his mask, her hand steady and cold.

"Now get out!" she said. "Get out, you dirty, bone-picking buzzards!"

A moment they were motionless, then there was a shift forward among those in the shadow, but the center man waved them back from him. Slowly they obeyed, until they were only a vague patch of white in the darkness, the leader scuttling into their shelter. Then, even before they were gone, Hortense set the gun down, and leaving the door wide open, she went to the table, to sit there at her work, until all the cars were gone and the last of the robed men.

It was Hippy who spoke first, from the shadows of his sunken face.

"You mighta let them bastards take these here old bones a mine," he said, in disgust at his helplessness.

Swiftly the woman was beside him. She tucked the robe in around him and slapped his arm.

"We wouldn't let those bed-sheet paraders take so much as a pants button away from a Bills. And anyway, your bones aren't bleached worth a cent—"

Somehow the story got out, was repeated around the barns, the hardware stores, and the pool halls. By golly, that Tensy Bills was the daughter of old Cap, all right, old Cap who bluffed them horse thieves out up to Wyoming and fetched back all their take. Soon after that, when the Sula girl got in trouble, the new district judge told Bone Joe right out that he was a bird of prey, and the county-seat paper came out against him and his night riders both, without apology. Times seemed to be getting pretty good.

Since Hortense laid Nickie's writing pad away in her trunk, she carried a lantern at both ends of the day. With Hippy sitting in his chair to tell her what to do, she repaired the old car, put a big box on behind, and on spring mornings she was the first at the Gaylor back doors, neat in starched calico or denim, with fresh rhubarb and asparagus, later radishes, lettuce, gooseberries, and so on, until melon and squash time.

In the afternoons Tensy worked with the ditching that brought a little water from the lake to the lower part of her cabbage patch, or hoed, weeded, and gleaned for the next morning. Gradually Bills Pocket became what the real-estate agents called a garden spot, and they began to bring their prospects around that way to show them what the country would grow. But they didn't say that Tensy Bills had learned to watch the romping of her calf and the fluttering whirl of snowbirds for storms, the first coming of the swallow to her eaves to date the season.

The first bad year in Bills Pocket, Hippy had insisted that they buy a shoat and fatten it on scraps, garden truck, and sweet-corn leavings. Cheapest meat in the world and, smoked up, was always handy for the frying pan. So Hortense consented, writing to Vangie's mother where she had tasted ham and side meat cured with the molasses and herb mixture of the old smokin' man of the community and smoked with his secret prep'ration. The recipe for the prep'ration finally came, written out with a stub pencil on a paper sack by the smokin' man himself. After that, there was always good meat, well cured, in the dry sand cave against the hill.

That summer, Ned Salzer and his young wife snapped off a car axle in a sand pass and walked to Bills Pocket to be taken home in the old topless pickup. While they rested and cooled off, Tensy set out a lunch. At first, Lillibelle just poked at the cold sliced ham, looking around at the bare little house, with nothing much but a square piano and an oil painting of a pale young woman with a harp. But when she finally tasted a bit, at the urging of old Ned, who ate zestfully with knife and fork, she found it nice, yes, quite nice. And so, finally, she suggested that, since it would soon be fall meat-making time and that what they seemed to have was just yellowing dried salt pork, suppose this—this woman came over to do the meat curing?

Ned Salzer turned red all down his bald streak behind, but without seeming to notice, Hortense refilled his coffee cup and said she would be very grateful for the opportunity.

Late that evening old Ned drove back to Bills Pocket and made his stiff, bowlegged way to Hortense watering her cabbage. He had come to say that Lillibelle didn't mean nothing today. She just didn't know. Why, Cap Bills had given him his start in stock, let him have cows on shares, and lent him haying tools, way back thirty-five years ago. And now her asking his daughter to come over like a hired woman—

But Hortense insisted that she would be glad to come. It might be a start of something, especially if they liked the meat. Might start a little business for her.

So Tensy Bills, the smokin' gal of ten years ago, became the smokin' woman, busy for weeks in the early spring and some in the fall too, swinging around the ranches and the stock farms, cutting up new pork, unjointing a ham with a twist of her knife and her strong wrist, sawing the head in two like so much wood, putting down the clean, firm meat well-rubbed with salt and the brown mixture of her jug.

By the time Diane was nine, times were getting hard again, so desperately hard that even the few ranchers left were curing their meat themselves. But Hortense and Hippy kept up the fiction of security pretty well around Diane. Not that either believed in rearing house plants, but there was no denying the girl was timid. She had even been afraid of the little brown-eyed collie Ned Salzer sent over for her sixth birthday, so afraid they gave the dog back.

Because it was eight miles to school, Tensy got a set of books from the district and a course of study, and taught the girl herself. Perhaps it was better so, better than exposing the reticent child to the taunts her made-over clothes and her isolation would bring her.

At night, when the supper dishes were done and a few sticks of choke-cherry wood or a handful of silvery sage were on the fire, Diane played over the day's lesson, played so well that Tensy Bills longed to send her away to study with her own teacher Kozal, who would bring out all the sensitiveness of the girl, her delicacy, and develop the power and strength the mother believed lay latent in the slim young body. A scholarship might be managed, but she could never hope to pay the fare and the living expenses of the girl.

These things were never spoken of before Diane, though she grew long, and skinny as a horseweed.

XII

When Diane was twelve, her mother made her a new gingham dress, pretty green and blue plaid, and took her up to Gaylor for the eighth-grade examinations. As they passed the bank, Joe Leems came out. Tensy Bills nodded and went on, but she knew that he stopped to look after them, after the straight young Diane as he had after the mother twenty-five years before. He was clean now, even in the deepest checks of his wrinkled neck, but it was still the same.

While she was trading out the last of her asparagus, Lesper Killey, Joe's bookkeeper, came whispering that Mr. Leems would see her in his bank office right away. But Tensy Bills didn't go, and so the next day the man came out to the Pocket to offer the woman a house once more. She could keep right on with her smokin' work, and the girl could go to high school. He had heard her play as he went by the place at night, sometimes. Maybe— why, maybe she could learn to play pretty good, even good enough for his moving-picture show.

Although Hortense Bills refused with friendliness enough, she leaned on her hoe until the Pocket was quiet and clean again, and all the dust had settled on the Gaylor road.

The next day a string of machinery and wagons, long as a threshing crew on the move, crept down the road into the pocket below Tensy's line. Here it broke up, and before noon a ditching machine was eating into the earth, cutting a deep trench along the fence that crossed the lower end of the little lake, piling up a high ridge along the far side. From the protection of her old shed Hortense watched, knowing that it was to draw her water away, dry out her little valley, her bit of lake and her irrigation ditches, destroy her alfalfa and her fine garden.

Then she saw Diane come in from her flower picking in the hills, running to see this new thing near her home, and so Hortense had to leave the shed, with Bone Joe there to see, and walk calmly to the house. In the doorway she stopped. Hippy had hitched his chair to the window and across his knees was the old Bills rifle.

"It ain't heavy enough to carry clear down there nohow," the man complained in disgust as Hortense took the gun from him. "But some day I'll get that buzzard from clost—"

Before the middle of August the lake was a cracking stretch of gray mud, with only a few green-scummed pools down the center. Below the fence the Leems ditch carried a steady little flow of seepage water to the winding creek bed, usually dry long before this.

Hortense considered digging a ditch across the entire lower end of the valley, deep enough to cut the seepage table and fill it with alkali mud, tamped and dried into hardpan. But that would take months, and she had to save every pound of tomatoes, every head of cabbage now, with prices down to nothing. So she carried water from the pump late into the nights, a bucket in each hand.

As the depression deepened, the best land in the region, land he had long waited for, fell into the hands of Joe Leems like wild plums, ripe and sweet. Busy with these things, he let his ditch fill with Russian thistles and mud until the water started to lay in the lower end of Tensy's lake again, and creep toward the old irrigation ditches, even with the rains slow and the winter black. In town it was said that Bone Joe was buying purple pajamas, keeping a red-headed girl up at the hotel, and walking big as when he used to lead the long, white-robed parade.

When Joe Leems took over the second county-seat bank, he began fore-closing again. Here and there an old-timer discovered that the galluses of his tattered overalls were still stout enough for a noose. But others were discovering that a common calamity becomes a common bond, and talked of organizing and rioting like in the papers, with delegations to march on the State Capitol. Lesper Killey came to tell Joe Leems that there might be rough stuff, knucks and shooting, with mobs breaking up his sheriff sales. But the foreclosure notices appeared, pages at a time, and knots of dark-faced men began to gather wherever Bone Joe was.

So Joe stayed in his hotel room and kept Lesper Killey running back and forth with a briefcase. But across the street from his window a row of men still waited, the February wind whipping their thin old overalls.

The first sale scheduled was Bills Pocket. Ned Salzer came down to see Hippy about it, the two old cowhands sitting in the window with the sand-box between them. There'd been talk of holding up Tensy's sale, Ned said, a little talk, but not enough. Too many was a-looking on it like a grudge fight between the old bone-picker and the Billses, and more had women folks who thought of Tensy as that high-flyin' smokin' gal, or that old smokin' woman.

"Yeh." Hippy shot a pale little splatter into the sandbox and wiped his mouth. "Little fellows a-fightin' amongst theirselves over matchsticks while the big fellows steals their pants—"

For the first time in her life Tensy Bills was unable to plan so much as a shelter in the wind for her two. The morning of her sale there was no gaso-line, and so she walked the two miles of gray March prairie to the grave of Rutherford Bills and was glad that he hadn't lagged too long after his time. It was at the unmarked spot beside him, where Nickie lay, that Hortense stood so still, a lone bowed figure, with no moving thing anywhere in sight.

If she hadn't come out of the West and taken Nickie from his little publishing-house job into this hard environment, he would be alive, writ-ing words that would bring to others the beautiful things his eyes saw, his heart knew. But it had seemed so right to them, their coming together, right and beautiful as the wind and the sun they found on the slopes of their little home.

Wearily the woman started back, through the winter-bleached grass, the chill gray sky low about her. Then, far out on the road, Diane came run-ning, crying, jumping up and down about her mother, whirling her in a witches' dance. Oh, no, it wasn't Hippy. It was a boy, a fine big boy who had come riding, bringing news. There was a farm-mortgage moratorium. Their place wouldn't be sold today.

Suddenly Hortense understood and dropping to the grass, dizzy, looked up at her daughter. "Child, child," she cried, only now realizing that she hadn't spared the girl anything at all.

But the moratorium was true, and so that night they used the last of the sugar to make a plate of fudge and stayed up until the lamp went dry. Early the next morning, Hortense walked across her garden ground, her plow shoes sinking into the warming earth, dark, frost-mellowed, and rich. With her fingers she cleared aside a bit of the old hay covering the rhubarb, and called aloud for Diane. Together they dug deeper into the covering, baring the first hard knuckles of the pieplant pushing through, young and pink, pink as a pretty girl's dress. Then arm in arm they went to the house to put on the coffee, to bring out all the seed catalogues Tensy had hidden from Hippy and herself as they came. Now they would look them through, every one, plan for another spring.

Joe Leems took the mortgage moratorium hard, and talked of going into politics at last. The country was run by a lot of Reds, taking a man's liberty away, cheating him out of his rightful property, out of things he'd worked years for. Yeh, that was right enough, old-timers admitted. Bone Joe'd sure been working to bust the Billses for twenty-five years.

A test case was started, but it might be years before it reached the Supreme Court. Until then, so long as the interest and taxes were paid up, Tensy's place was safe. So she dug in harder than ever, planted more sweet corn, more beans, and with the first five dollars she took Hippy to the doctor to give his joints some relief.

Farm prices went up a little, but the reluctant summer rains barely splattered the fields, and the winter earth lay bare and gray. Although the dust storms that filled the papers with alarming stories were seldom more than a red haze on the evening sun, the water table of the region was falling, the seepage springs of Bills Pocket no more than a wet spot on the outcroppings of sandstone by August. Gradually the grass moved in on the little lake until a bit of rushes in the middle was all that remained where ducks once swam over six feet of water.

When things were pretty thin, the thinnest they had ever been, because now the interest had to be paid on the dot, a woman came out and Hortense discovered that Hippy had applied for old-age pension.

At that, Hortense Bills left the house, and when she finally came back into the lamplight of the supper table, Hippy saw the first sign of tears on her face since the day, almost thirty years before, when he told her some of the things she needed to know. But the woman was calm now, listening sensibly to the practical side of the arrangement. It would be about fifteen dollars a month—the difference between enough to eat and not enough, particularly for Diane and for herself. "You got to feed a plow horse," Hippy pointed out. It would keep the interest and taxes paid, a roof against the sun.

XIII

Spring was back once more, with wind and seed catalogues and interest due. Before the heavy work was upon her, Hortense overhauled the old car, tightening the connecting rods until she couldn't turn the engine over and had to hitch up the team to start it. But today the air lay moist and still, early geese honked high overhead somewhere, and in the garden the parsnip rows were sprouting their first tips of green. Shouting a good-by to Hippy at the window, Hortense started the car off toward Gaylor and the bank. And as she drove, she hummed a little, for the motor ran sweet and in her pocket was every cent of Bone Joe's interest money.

At the hill line she waved back to Diane. The girl was fanning alfalfa seed with a screened salt-barrel hoop, tossing the sieve with slim grace, the blue of her calico skirt billowing, the pile of golden seed on the old canvas on the ground gleaming in the sun. Alfalfa prices were coming up a little. One more crop and she could send the girl away. It was time, for she was seventeen and getting valentines from Joe Leems too, just as she had at that age, when she slipped up behind his wagon, scared his horses, and upset his wagon. But Diane could never be the independent flip she had been, and besides, Joe's wheels were running pretty solid these days.

As Hortense neared Gaylor there seemed more cars on the road than usual, and in town there was a crowd, the streets parked solid, knots of men along the walks, standing thick about the bank. Hortense wondered about them, loafing in the middle of a spring week, and without the women folks, their dark faces silent, giving her no more than a nod today, even old acquaintances.

When she finally got parked, Ned Salzer separated himself from the fringe of the crowd and came over to the car. With his foot on the old running board, the sun on his bald head, he told her, keeping his eyes to the battered hat in his hand as he talked. It was the moratorium. Off, thrown out, pronounced unconstitutional by the State Supreme Court. Foreclosures were starting today where they left off five years ago. Several of the old-timers' places already gone.

So that was it. After all the years of skinning hard work, of planning and saving and fighting the man off, now it was all gone like snow before one blast of a chinook. Everything.

A long time the woman sat behind the steering wheel, gripping the bare old wood with her knotted hands, her eyes straight before her, the wind lines at her mouth deep as folds in old gray leather.

"They're a-needin' somebody educated for a few weeks, for the guide book, somebody what can wrangle a little history stuff—" Old Ned started to say. But he didn't finish, for the woman's face gave him no recognition now, drained of all life before his eyes. Touching her arm with an awkward paw, he stumbled away on his bowed old legs.

At last the woman roused to look about her. Lesper Killey was at her shoulder, jerking at the wash-faded denim of her jumper to get her attention.

"The boss'll be up there to see you after a bit," he said, nodding toward the old feed stable.

The woman only shook her head, not at him but at this moment that would be sweet as meadow honey, time-ripened and warm to the tongue of the old bone-picker.

But in the end Tensy Bills had to go, to climb the rickety old stairs to the room above the feed store, her heavy feet scarcely lifting her from step to step. Meekly, as one come new to begging, she rapped on the old door and waited, her gray hair blowing from under her hat on the platform in the rising wind, her body thin in its blue denim.

But there was no reply, and after a long time she noticed that men in the street were staring up at her, one of them saying something.

"—He's gone. I saw him drive outa town awhile ago."

So Tensy went back to the car, turned the stiff crank with dull persistence and took the road back to Bills Pocket, Leems Pocket in a day or so now. As she drove she thought once more over all the man's long wait, since she was a girl, a child, much younger than Diane—

Suddenly she pulled the gas feed down, gripping the wheel as the engine roared, hoping that the old boot in the front tire would hold. As she turned off the main road into Bills Pocket she caught the sun on a car drawn up at the shed, a new roadster, like Joe Leems'.

Even before she stopped she saw Diane, white as bone, in the corner of the ell. The girl was flattened hard to the wall, her open palms against the boards. On the ground before her lay a man in a blue-green suit, small as a boy, with one arm thrown out, crumpled and gray and old.

Jerking the car to a screeching stop, the woman ran to her daughter, held her close, and looked down upon the man. It was Bone Joe, with a dark little bullet hole in his temple, his open eyes skinning over with gray, like a dead bird's.

Inside the window Hippy sat in his chair, his slack jaw moving slowly, his fingers like claws on the old rifle across his knees.

Meridel Le Sueur
b.1900

—

1935: *Annunciation*
1940: *Salute to Spring,
and Other Stories*
1945: *North Star Country*
1970: *Corn Village*
1982: *Ripening: Selected Work,
1927–1980*

—

IN HER *early years, Meridel Le Sueur worked as a pro-labor journalist; like her politically active parents, she had wide experience with and deep empathy for the working classes. Her short stories, not unexpectedly, contained a proletarian version of the American democratic myth in which the people were heroes because of their endurance, not because of their conquests. A paragraph from Le Sueur's story "The North Star" summarizes her mythic vision of classless heroism.*

It was a new society, unique, set down green in the wilderness, adapting rapidly to climate, animals, minerals, mutually safeguarding new institutions, sharing prohibitions and extensions of freedom, rearing a new culture from the blend of diverse strands, sharing strengths, confidence, and myth, all in the bright humus of one idea: that the dignity of man is inalienable, and that by his own effort on this earth he can subjugate nature for the good of all.[1]

Le Sueur's writings include journalism, poetry, fiction, biography, history, and autobiography, but in every genre she is primarily concerned with the struggles of

---

1. Meridel Le Sueur, "The North Star," *Ripening: Selected Work, 1927–1980*, ed. Elaine Hedges (Old Westbury, N.Y.: Feminist Press, 1982), p. 34.

the American proletariat, women in particular. In her earlier fiction, the woman, as a spirit, struggles to find individuality within a bondage to the male, a bondage that is inevitable and not wholly undesirable. In later works, according to one of her biographers, the Persephone-Demeter myth becomes a strong influence,[2] causing Le Sueur to portray women as unwilling captives of dark forces from which they are freed by being reborn and reunited with their mothers or with other women.

Le Sueur's most recent stories move toward new and experimental formats, like her novel in progress: the words are written in three parallel columns rather than in traditional paragraphs. These works are largely centered on a philosophy that human bonding is essential to the psychological survival of each individual and that the bonding must reach backward and forward in time, linking people in the past and future as well as the present.

Because of her childbearing capability, the woman is more sensitive to the strength—and the necessity—of bonding, especially between mother and daughter. The bond reaches back into the past to a woman's mother and grandmother and great-grandmother and then reaches forward into the future through her daughter. In "Salutation to Spring," the protagonist fights to preserve this continuity, to keep her infant daughter alive. But she is not totally obsessed with it; she fully realizes the fulfillment to be found in sharing her husband's life.

The title character in Le Sueur's story "The Girl" is a spinster. She has no apparent bond with her mother and has no child. The story revolves around an opportunity to make love, which she rejects. She has a job and a nice car and can take a vacation, so we may infer that her life is much easier than that of the farm wife in "Salutation to Spring." We also realize, however, that she will never know the satisfaction of marriage and maternalism.

The Demeter-Persephone myth, one of Le Sueur's primary interests, is connected with the annual rebirth of grain. Le Sueur sees in it a parallel with certain myths of the American Indian, especially the spring corn rituals of the Hopi. An apparently dry and lifeless seed is buried in what appears to be barren earth, where the seed soon swells and bursts with life. Its vitality depends on the bonding of male, female, earth, water, and sun. It takes faith to plant the seed, faith that comes from a knowledge that at least some of the seeds of the past have borne fruit. In

2. Elaine Hedges discusses Le Sueur and the Persephone-Demeter myth in ibid., p. 252. Demeter was the Greek goddess of fertility and agriculture. When her daughter, Persephone (Proserpine), was kidnapped and taken to the underworld, Demeter's grief threatened the world with famine until Zeus arranged to let Persephone return to earth each summer. As Sir James Frazer points out in *The Golden Bough*, the Greeks used this myth to account for seasonal cycles of death and rebirth.

this mythic context, the ending of "Salutation to Spring" is optimistic rather than tragic.

▬

Salutation to Spring

For Mary Cotter

SHE TURNED off the squawking radio—the battery was running down—I want different news, I want to hear it, Lord, different news, she said out loud to herself as she went into the kitchen with the baby's bottle, thinking—her temperature seems better now and she wanted to hold the bottle herself—and seeing the land-locked, winter hills, snow-gripped, with the little black trees sticking out like the cross of our Lord.

The calendar above the stove said March, below a picture of a fat, naked baby. She reached up and tore the calendar down and tore the picture of the fat baby in two, and, as she poked up the fire, she threw the picture in.

Jim said—why did you do that? She started. She knew he had been sitting in the corner of the kitchen watching the thaw on the land, wishing for seed. Why did he sit in the corner like an old woman speaking out at her from the cold darkness?

He watched her fix the bottle. She was such a tiny woman. At first her tininess had seemed strange and wonderful to him, but now it seemed ominous. He could see his children Michael and Ruth, far down the road between the black winter oaks coming home from school. They went only in the morning now. It would take them half an hour to come up the road, but he could see them lift and fall beneath the waves of the lower forty, which was already rearing up black out of the snow, clear on top and slopes. Another week, if the sun came out, it would be ready for seeding. Is she better? he asked, and he felt his voice awkward with guilt between them.

She didn't want to answer. I don't know, she said, taking the bottle out of the pan of water and squirting some milk from the nipple to see if it was too hot. She didn't want to talk to him. She resented his sitting there and he knew it. She went out of the room and he looked out the window.

She gave the sick baby the bottle and it suckled feebly, its eyes half

First published in *Prairie Schooner* 12 (Fall 1938): 157–67. Reprinted in Meridel Le Sueur, *Salute to Spring, and Other Stories* (New York: International Publishers Co., 1940), pp. 144–58. Copyright © 1940 by International Publishers Co. Reprinted by permission of International Publishers.

open. She touched the open palm and the fingers curled around her finger. She had listened to the rasping breath night after night and now she was frightened by the quiet as the child looked at her from half closed eyes, voluptuously as if it did not have to fight now. Mary could see the hills out the window, her other children rising over the land and moving toward the house, toward food, toward her—the red cap of Michael rising on the wave crests and then disappearing as if he was drowning. She picked up the baby and held it as if those mounting wave crests were threatening, and she could feel the awful silence of the house, of the winter-locked land, that had gone on and on, day after day. The children would want food now when they got to the house and there was only the bread soaking in milk. The last of the store of potatoes had gone in last night's soup and Jim sitting in the kitchen like an idiot, in broad daylight, with no money to buy seed. A man got mad when seeding time was coming on and no seed.

She would find something, boil something; there would be something to eat. The child's head rolled back a little and the half-open eye revealed the pupil as if looking at her and she began to rub the child as if she could put her own will back into it. She had a lean strong face; Welsh by birth, she had a strong will. She would do it; nothing would stop her; she had a will like the crack of a whip. What else could have kept her going the years since her marriage: three babies, carrying water, baking, milking cows, as if you had put a sparrow to doing all these colossal tasks, but you could see her running in the yard, even after dark, after the babies were in bed, looking for eggs, darting, running like a sparrow from nest to nest, looking under boards as if she could never stop, or never could know fatigue or despair, as if her thin, wiry bones were made of steel. She had such fat babies and she liked having them if only there was not so much work. She had a passion for her children, for having them, for giving them birth.

She rubbed the twig legs of the child, the thin chest, and held the tiny feet in one palm. She lifted one foot and put it to her mouth, put the cold toes in her mouth and blew on them. She leaned over and blew her breath on the child and she knew that despite everything the child had no resistance; it had not had enough to eat. She opened her shawl and laid the child inside close to her body. If she'll live till spring, she promised someone, it will be all right, there will be food, carrots, tomatoes; I'll plant them myself.

The children came into the house crying Mama, and that meant hunger. She put the baby back into the crib and the lips smiled curiously at her, as if the baby were very old, understood something.

She gave the children the dried bread and they seemed silent and solemn as if they knew this was the last of the food. They ate, looking at their father in the corner until he got up, put on his coat, and went out.

Every move he made was like a knife cutting her. She felt him so keenly, shut in the house so long together, since harvest, his long thin body, his dark burnt face, both winter pallor and sunburn still on the neck and jowls. He was like a knife and every move cut her. Where you goin'? she cried out the door, and he went on down toward the barn. She threw her shawl over her head. The children watched her. She ran out after him, dogging his steps, crying, Where you goin', Jim? I'm goin' to town, he said back at her, walking fast to the barn and she after him, running to keep up with his scissor stride through the mud. Town, she cried; I'm goin' with you. She tugged at his coat. Naw, he said, ya better stay here lessen the baby needs ya.

She's better, she cried up at him; I got to get away from hereabouts. I got to get away too. He stopped by the pump and looked down at her where she stood in the wind, ready to fly at him like a black hen, her eyes snapping, her thin nervous body sharp-standing against the wind, full of that energy and zip that always pleased him. He grinned at her. All right, he said, we'll stop and get Janey to come and stay with the kids. I aim to go right away now. She turned and ran through the wind into the house like a girl.

Jim had a hard time getting the old tin can started. They hadn't used it all winter and they had saved the four gallons of gas since September. She and the children stood at the window watching him crank. When it began to shake, she told Janey to remember the hot blankets for the baby, kissed the upturned faces of the children, and ran out. She saw the flattened faces of the children at the window, saw the children waving and she waved back until she and Jim were clear down to the turn.

It was wonderful to see other land, to get out of the land-locked land-scape she saw from every window like a frozen sea. She knew Jim wouldn't say why he was going to town but she had read a letter, something about a meeting about seed loans at the fire hall, and she knew that must be where he was going, especially as they began to pass other farmers going to town. She knew everything he thought. He didn't have to tell her anything. She could feel his eye look at the land, calculate the seed, manure, lime needed. Fence posts down. She sat in her town hat and felt elegant to be driving to town. She didn't need much to feel wonderful. Life was brilliant in her and strong, and leaped up quickly in her blood for anything.

They drove through the lean strong hills she had known since her child-hood, and Jim didn't say anything until finally he said, How we gonna live till spring? If he hadn't been driving he wouldn't have said this. How we gonna do it?

It was a relief; it was the first he had spoken to her about it.

Why, she cried, why, Jim, of course we'll live till spring. Why, what's got into you? Why, certainly we will; surely, haven't we always? Is there ever a time when we haven't lived till spring?

Who's been complaining? I'm sure it's not me. Why, we'll do it; yes, sir. I aim to take those three sacks of wheat in the back seat old Dahl refused to take; I aim to get some money and a sack of meal and some credit this very day. I aim to get us something to eat all right. Why, it's a holy shame, a crying shame, crying to heaven, the way we been living in this town for years, had our younguns here, everything, and can't get more credit. It cries to high heaven; it does for a fact.

It's a hard time, he said.

A hard time, she cried. Ain't we always had hard times and those before us? Did ever anybody quit?

Quit having hard times?

She grinned, Well if you want to put it that way. Hard times ain't quit and we ain't quit.

He felt better. He looked at her out of the side of his eye—that cute old hat she'd had on their honeymoon sitting on her head with the black hair combed straight back and her nose so delicate and sharp, by gad, she didn't look old. She was like a pullet setten on a fence, by gad; she had spunk in her all right. He felt better and took out his tobacco and laughed.

Old lady, he said, you're full of vinegar all right.

Jim, she cried blushing, I told you—

He laughed and spit clean out the slit in the curtain.

The village street was full of men walking towards the fire hall. Yes, sir, she was right; that was what it was, a meeting on the seed loans which were due. She smiled and Jim looked away. They stopped in front of May's beer parlor and she got out and pulled down her old coat, looking to see who was in town. It looked like Saturday. Yes, sir, it was a meeting to see how they would get new seed. She saw Sadie Melthers across the street going into the grocery store. Jim said something that sounded like a grunt and went on down the street trying not to look like he was going to the fire hall to the meeting, and she ran across the street.

The sun had come up and everyone was moving down the tiny main street in the sun. Puddles of water stood in the street where the snow was still melting. The big Moline plant was closed. No more engines running. The men were slowly meeting down at the fire hall, trying not to let their women folk follow. All the women were looking out of the windows of the stores seeing what their men were up to.

Mary talked to Sadie, whose children had been sick, and they both kept watching the men go down the street to the fire hall, and Mary went back into the store, looking at the canned goods, the flour, the fresh vegetables. She didn't ask for credit; she thought she would wait until after the meeting. She spoke to several women who were looking at the fresh vegetables but not buying any. Then she went out and walked down the street and went into the fire hall and sat down. There weren't many women there. They were afraid to come. All the men looked at her, and she felt afraid.

Ole Hanson was standing on the floor and he was saying, We got the bitter experience of every-day life; we taste it every day. We got to begin to know it. We got to begin to go forward.

He must have been talking a long while. Sweat stood on his lip and brow. He stopped and stood there and then slowly walked to his seat, wiping his horny head.

She sat leaning forward as if driving a horse that was running away. She heard everything they said, as one man after another got up to testify how he was willing and ready to pay the seed loans incurred during the long drouth, but that if he did so he would not be able to seed the land in the present spring. She heard them: losses of early lambs in the drouth, losses of pigs last year, no word of the bones that wintered in the lime pits. Feed none too plentiful. The men testified with the sweat standing out on them from the pressures of speech. Hard to talk now. A stenographer, a pretty girl from the city, was taking it all down when they said it. It was awkward putting down all the thick and heavy suffering into little words. The chairman said they knew that the pressure of collectors was not coming from the government who held the loans, that no one understood what was happening and that was why they were there today.

Yes, she nodded to what they said. She wouldn't have known she knew all this, but now it was said she recognized the words fitting the happening. Farrowing season this year much less favorable than last: death, heavy losses. Yes, she nodded, yes, yes.

A professor from the university got up to talk. He was a pale man with a tall head and what he was saying was very sad. She sat back against it. He seemed sad and his white head hung down on the stalk of his body. She looked at the men sitting around her like the scarred and ruined machinery that sat out in their farm yards. You know the way, she thought; they test seed corn to see how it will germinate. You can test a man like that too. Educated people, she thought, have poor generative power sometimes; they don't believe in anything. No good for tomorrow's seeding. No good to look to them; so she stopped listening to the professor. She didn't hear a word he said.

And then she blushed; the sweat stood out on her, and she gripped her hands. It was Jim going forward, beginning to speak. He stood there looking at the floor. His hands hung down, a little longer than anything he could ever buy to cover them. The men all looked at him. It seemed a long time before he spoke. When he did, they were all startled. You could hear a car honk outside and the sound of the hoofs of horses, and the blacksmith in the next block shoeing.

What he said was—There's a noose around every man's throat. You can't see it this afternoon, but it's there just the same. No matter what we do there it is; we just wiggle around with the noose around our necks every single minute.

I believe in the Constitution, Jim said. I believe in America. She looked at him with new eyes. When he said that he believed in America the blood flushed into his face. He was a good speaker. You're a man, he said; you got the parts of a man; you got rights too, you and your chilluns. We want to do what's right. We want to pay our debts. We always pay our debts. It ain't us who don't pay our debts, brothers. It ain't that we want to get away from the seed loans; that ain't the ticket, not by a long shot. No, sir. We can't pay, brothers. We can't pay. We taken the food right out our children's mouths to pay what we already paid, and that's a fact nobody can't get around.

There was clapping and the pleasure of the men at a quick tongue. Jim wiped his hands on his handkerchief and went on—If we pay our seed loans now, we got from seven years' drouth, we ain't goin' to be able to plant any wheat this spring. It's now planting time and nary a man's got seed to plant. And these here collectors, it's got so you can't move the hay in your barn to feed a cow without uncovering a gol darn collector!

Men laughed and he continued, grinning—Yes, sir, you couldn't lift a bundle now without a collector popping out. It's getting worse, year in and year out; doggone, we all be put off like the rest been put off if we wait much longer. 1934 we had a crop failure. I cut 115 acres and put it into the silo and got a silo full of Russian thistles. During the fall I tried to get in on the feed loan and was refused that I was not able to get the waiver on the grounds I owed the bank. At that time I had 57 head of cattle and I begged the federal reserve not to sue me, which he promised me to leave me alone. I said I hadn't beat anybody and both federal reserve bank and receiver of the bank were witness to my hand that they would leave me alone.

Now she understood it better. She knew now how hard this was for him to tell it. He had never even told it to her. She had not known what was happening. She had only seen it happening.

He went on slowly—One week later the sheriff served papers on me and in twenty days to appear before a court before them and judgment was added onto me. When feed loans came on I was not able to get waivers. I had to get along with twenty-five a month and I had to shoot thirteen pigs and in that winter I lost eight head of cattle. And during the spring or summer when the alfalfa came to growth I lost three horses. When we opened them after they was dead we found alfalfa clots in the belly. Now I got a girl that's powerful sick.

A pang went through Mary as if she had forgotten about the baby.

Now we got to do something. We got to begin to go forward. These things got to be known.

He stopped and stood still and she got panicky and tried to motion for him to sit beside her, and the chairman said he thought they should appoint a committee to take what the secretary had put down and see that it got to the proper authorities so some action would be taken here, and he said I appoint Mary, Jim's wife, because there ought to be a woman on this here committee to sit on it, and everyone was smiling at her and she felt all her own energy in her, the whole world, as if it was all in her, the energy, belief, wisdom. She got up. They saw a little black Welsh woman, her hat awry on her head, lean as a young pullet and strong in anger and passion.

I rise to say, I want to speak, she said—I think the women should be here because it is important the women be here. We know these things and we suffer because of them every day. What I mean is that we know it, and every year when we are still alive in spring, still for another year we are surprised. We are still alive for another year, we say to ourselves, and count our children, and every year we are just a little different with what has happened. Seven years now like in the Bible this has been going on.[3] It isn't never over. It isn't never over. You say your children are an inch higher; you got one more—that's one thing we got no depression on; ain't no scarcity there! Alive yet; you are all alive! It's for hallelujah, sure enough. So that's what I rise to say. I never was on no committee, but I'll start being on one.

There was big applause. She sat down, surprised and happy. Ole Hanson got up and said that was a good speech and there ought to be more women there and he hoped they would be all together in unity, and go out of here with our arms around each other, and I hope half of us is women.

---

3. Genesis 41.

The fire hall cracked and split with laughter and the meeting was adjourned, and the pretty secretary ran down the aisle and put her hand on Mary's arm and said when would she come in and they could get the affidavits all together, and Mary looked at Jim and said tomorrow, and Jim nodded and took her arm and drew her close in to him and they walked out talking and smiling and nodding, with everyone excited and talking more than usual.

They got in the car and drove to the elevator. She put her hand on Jim's arm and said I'm a goin' this time. She got out and went into Mr. Dahl's office and said to him, I got three sacks of grain in the car, and I got to have something for my family. He said, I'm sorry but you can't sell it like that lessen you give one sack to the mill. All right, she said, you pay for two. Listen; you got to do it, hear? I got to have it and you got to do it elsen the committee will do something.

What committee is that? said Mr. Dahl. It's the seed loan committee, she said, big-like. Don't get excited, Mary, said Dahl. Mary said, Suppose you got four mouths to feed come supper and nothin' in the bin, nothin' on the shelves, nothin' in the cellar, nothin' anywhere. Well, he said, all right, I could do it, I reckon. All right, she said, do it. And he did.

They drove to the store and bought a sack of flour and she lost on the price of her wheat. She felt bitter and triumphant, and she said to Jim, Drive to the relief, I'm gonna get some hay too. He looked at her and drove to the relief. She went in and said to the girl there, Could we get a little bedding for our cattle? And the girl said they had all they could do to get straw to the animals. Mary said, Have you ever milked a cow? Why, no, the girl said. Well, then, Mary said, you don't know where the tits are on a cow. You know we could just as well wash our hands in manure, then wash the cow and that's the kind of milk that you and I are going to drink. I'm on the committee now, she said, and I want some straw for bedding. The girl said, All right, I'll do what I can. I'm a comin' in tomorrow, Mary said, and I want it then. I'll be gettin' it tomorrow. I'm a-comin' in then to set on the committee.

And Mary marched out.

They drove rapidly into the frozen hills. It was supper and they had the supper in the back seat. Mary was feeling full of talk. They drove through the cold rise and fall of hills, the black thickets, and she felt herself full of energy of the finest kind. She wanted to sing, to shout, to say more words that would be heard like in the afternoon. What was the good of silence, each man sitting on his farm silent as a turtle? You see, she said—sitting close to Jim's long flank—it's never over. She felt like crying, More life, more life, break these awful deathly silences and suffering. We are strong, she wanted to shout. She pressed against him—we are strong. Nothing is compared to us. We are tough and strong. She began to laugh.

I swan, for God's sake, what's so funny? If you ain't the damnedest woman.

All those who are dead this winter—all those who fought in Spain, in China, all over the world, everybody who struggled, who said something. . . . I read about a scientist and he kept a tick alive for seven years and put it on a dog and it hopped off to feed lively as all get out, hopped right off on the dog happy as could be.

He grinned, I'll be dogged, if you ain't the craziest—

A tick is nothing compared to us; it ain't a thing; it ain't got a thing on us: seven years drouth, grasshoppers, this and that, one thing and another. That air tick ain't got a thing on us, not a thing.

I'll be dogged, he laughed. She could feel the air draw into his long, strong body. I'll be doggone, ef it ain't the cat's whiskers. You would think of that. I'll be doggone if you ain't the sweetest craziest—and he slapped her thigh roundly and his big hand plundered her breasts.

Jim, you big fool, stop. What kind of goin's on in broad daylight on the road in plain sight? You'll run us plumb in the ditch! Jim, you almighty fool!

I'll be swan: I got me some old woman: full of vinegar, full of what it takes. I'll be doggone.

She smiled. The dusk was blue and birds were flying in it.

They turned off the highway and when she saw the house she knew something was wrong. Drive faster, she said, and she could see the children at the cold windows and the girl in the doorway waiting. Her heart sank.

She was out of the car before it stopped, and she saw the baby in the crib still as death. She snatched it up and tried to warm it, blowing on the hands, into the mouth. Jim came in and took the child. Its weight was light as a sick chicken's, the eyes drawn back. You know when an animal is dying you can feel it. He gave her back to Mary and took the children out of the room. The baby seemed so light as if she were disappearing. The breath stopped, and a terrible wrench came from Mary as if she gave the child birth again, and she walked to the door and to the window as if she would call someone. The other children were hungry in the kitchen. It was dark and cold. She laid the body down and smoothed out the limbs, closed the half dreaming eyes. The tiny arms were not made for crossing.

She went into the kitchen, got supper, and they ate it.

She put the children to bed. Jim went out to do the chores. The children were wide-eyed in bed and she lay down beside them to soothe their fright. She wanted to say something as if an upsurge of words lay buried beneath her skin. She could see the baby's head in the crib, disappearing in the deepening dusk. It seemed quiet now where it had been—no more fretting and fever and hunger.

The children sighed and murmured and touched her and went to sleep. She waited for Jim to come back into the house. She put out her hand and felt the legs of Michael, willful like his father, and the soft fair skull of Ruth. Spring and children's voices again.

She must have slept. The house was quiet; the dog walked softly in the kitchen. The honk of the ducks sounded far into the sky. She heard Jim approach the house, come in at the door. She saw him light the lamp and turn it low and look at the dead child. He covered her with an old coat and the light went out and she heard him get into bed.

She got up. She went past the dead child in the crib. No need to ever cover her now.

She got into bed beside him. He turned the strong scythe of his legs, the thrust and cleft of breast, and she turned into him, crying.

A. B. Guthrie, Jr.
b. 1901

▬

1947: *The Big Sky*
1949: *The Way West*
1956: *These Thousand Hills*
1960: *The Big It and Other Stories*
1971: *Arfive*
1975: *The Last Valley*
1982: *Fair Land, Fair Land*

▬

WE CAN *confidently proclaim A. B. Guthrie, Jr., the central literary figure of the "Big Sky" country. From automobile license plates to bills before the legislature, the title of Guthrie's novel can be found all over Montana. But the Big Sky region is even bigger than Montana: it dominates the top of the western United States, up where the Missouri River flows east from the Rockies and then makes a great, sweeping bend to flow due south. The wide, wild spirit of this high country nurtured Guthrie's artistic imagination. His writing captures not only its history, but its essence as well.*

Guthrie was born on January 13, 1901, in Bedford, Indiana; six months later, his parents moved to Choteau, Montana. At age fourteen, Guthrie started a newspaper career by taking a summer job as a printer's devil with the Choteau Acantha, *a local weekly. He left Choteau in 1919 to major in journalism at the University of Montana, and after finishing his degree he traveled and worked as a manual laborer in Mexico, California, and New York. He turned again to journalism in 1926, this time as a reporter in Kentucky with the* Lexington Leader.

After publishing a first novel in 1943, Guthrie reconsidered and bought and destroyed all the copies he could find. A year later, while recuperating in Montana from a bout with encephalitis, he began another novel and at the same time ap-

plied for a Nieman Fellowship. With the help of that award, he was able to spend a year at Harvard, where he finished his second novel, The Big Sky. *While teaching at the University of Kentucky, in the home state of his fictional hero Boone Caudill, he began work on a sequel,* The Way West, *which won the Pulitzer Prize in 1950.*

The Big Sky, The Way West, These Thousand Hills, Arfive, *and* Fair Land, Fair Land *tell a continuing story about five generations of people who came to live in the high plains and Rocky Mountain region. The basis for the series is the nineteenth-century opening of the West and the people who opened it, characters such as those described in the firsthand accounts of George F. Ruxton, L. H. Garrard, Francis Parkman, and Osborne Russell. Without violating history or disturbing any legends, Guthrie has brought his heroes to life by dramatizing them in mythic terms. Guthrie's trappers, scouts, plainsmen, and pioneers are as authentic as in the original accounts. His interpretation of them, however, adds a new dimension of psychological complexity. Like most modern characters of fiction, Guthrie's new mythic heroes act in ways that are not always admirable or socially acceptable, and they have weaknesses that they themselves are largely unaware of. These heroes can neither escape the results of their behavior nor find refuge from their innate flaws, even in the almost absolute freedom of the Big Sky frontier.*

In "Mountain Medicine," Guthrie re-creates the legendary footrace in which John Colter outran a band of Blackfoot Indians. Colter (c. 1774–1813) was a member of the 1804–6 Lewis and Clark expedition; near the end of the return trip, he asked permission to go back up the Missouri and into the Rockies with a pair of fur traders, Joseph Dickson and Forrest Hancock. Later, again returning down the river, Colter met Manuel Lisa, who offered him a job as a trader, trapper, and explorer for his trading fort, built in 1807 at the mouth of the Big Horn River. It was probably while trapping for Lisa that Colter and his partner, Daniel Potts, were captured by the Indians. Colter frequently retold the story of his "run," and several versions of it have survived.

━━

Mountain Medicine

THE MIST along the creek shone in the morning sun, which was coming up lazy and half-hearted, as if of a mind to turn back and let the spring season wait. The cottonwoods and quaking aspens were still bare and the needles of the pines old and dark with winter, but beaver were prime and beaver were plenty. John Clell made a lift and took the drowned animal quietly from the trap and stretched it in the dugout with three others.

Bill Potter said, "If 'tweren't for the Injuns! Or if 'tweren't for you and your notions!" For all his bluster, he still spoke soft, as if on the chance that there were other ears to hear.

Clell didn't answer. He reset the trap and pulled from the mud the twig that slanted over it and unstoppered his goat-horn medicine bottle, dipped the twig in it and poked it back into the mud.

"Damn if I don't think sometimes you're scary," Potter went on, studying Clell out of eyes that were small and set close. "What kind of medicine is it makes you smell Injuns with nary one about?"

"Time you see as many of them as I have, you'll be scary too," Clell answered, slipping his paddle into the stream. He had a notion to get this greenhorn told off, but he let it slide. What was the use? You couldn't put into a greenhorn's head what it was you felt. You couldn't give him the feel of distances and sky-high mountains and lonely winds and ideas spoken out of nowhere, ideas spoken into the head by medicines a man couldn't put a name to. Like now. Like here. Like this idea that there was brown skin about, and Blackfoot skin at that.

"I seen Blackfeet enough for both of us," he added. His mind ran back to Lewis and Clark and a time that seemed long ago because so much had come between; to days and nights and seasons of watching out, with just

First published in *Saturday Evening Post* 220 (August 16, 1947). Reprinted in A. B. Guthrie, Jr., *The Big It and Other Stories* (Boston: Houghton Mifflin Co., 1960), pp. 132–50. Copyright © 1960 by A. B. Guthrie, Jr. Reprinted by permission of Houghton Mifflin Company.

himself and the long silence for company; to last year and a hole that lay across the mountains to the south, where the Blackfeet and the Crows had fought, and he had sided with the Crows and got a wound in the leg that hurt sometimes yet. He could still see some of the Blackfeet faces. He would know them, and they would know him, being long-remembering.

He knew Blackfeet all right, but he couldn't tell Bill Potter why he thought some of them were close by. There wasn't any sign he could point to; the creek sang along and the breeze played in the trees, and overhead a big eagle was gliding low, and nowhere was there a footprint or a movement or a whiff of smoke. It was just a feeling he had, and Potter wouldn't understand it, but would only look at him and maybe smile with one side of his mouth.

"Ain't anybody I knows of carries a two-shoot gun but you," Potter said, still talking as if Clell was scared over nothing.

Clell looked down at it, where he had it angled to his hand. It had two barrels, fixed on a swivel. When the top one was fired, you slipped a catch and turned the other up. One barrel was rifled, the other bigger and smooth-bored, and sometimes he loaded the big one with shot, for birds, and sometimes with a heavy ball, for bear or buffalo, or maybe with ball and buck both, just for what-the-hell. There was shot in it this morning, for he had thought maybe to take ducks or geese, and so refresh his taste for buffalo meat. The rifle shone in the morning sun. It was a nice piece, with a patch box a man wouldn't know to open until someone showed him the place to press his thumb. For no reason at all, Clell called his rifle Mule Ear.

He said, "You're a fool, Potter, more ways than one. Injuns'll raise your hair for sure, if it don't so happen I do it myself. As for this here two-shooter, I like it, and that's that."

Bill Potter always took low when a man dared him like that. Now all he said was "It's heavy as all hell."

Slipping along the stream, with the banks rising steep on both sides, Clell thought about beaver and Indians and all the country he had seen— high country, pretty as paint, wild as any animal and lonesome as time, and rivers unseen but by him, and holes and creeks without a name, and one place where water spouted hot and steaming and sometimes stinking from the earth, and another where a big spring flowed with pure tar; and no one believed him when he told of them, but called him the biggest liar yet. It was all right, though. He knew what he knew, and kept it to himself now, being tired of queer looks and smiles and words that made out he was half crazy.

Sometimes, remembering things, he didn't see what people did or hear what they said or think to speak when spoken to. It was all right. It didn't matter what was said about his sayings or his doings or his ways of thinking. A man long alone where no other white foot ever had stepped got different. He came to know what the Indians meant by medicine. He got to feeling like one with the mountains and the great sky and the lonesome winds and the animals and Indians, too, and it was a little as if he knew what they knew, a little as if there couldn't be a secret but was whispered to him, like the secret he kept hearing now.

"Let's cache," he said to Potter. The mist was gone from the river and the sun well up and decided on its course. It was time, and past time, to slide back to their hidden camp.

"Just got one more trap to lift," Potter argued.

"All right, then."

Overhead the eagle still soared close. Clell heard its long, high cry.

He heard something else, too, a muffled pounding of feet on the banks above. "Injuns!" he said, and bent the canoe into the cover of an overhanging bush. "I told you."

Potter listened. "Buffalo is all. Buffalo trampin' around."

Clell couldn't be sure, except for the feeling in him. Down in this little canyon a man couldn't see to the banks above. It could be buffalo, all right, but something kept warning, "Injuns! Injuns!"

Potter said, "Let's git on. Can't be cachin' from every little noise. Even sparrers make noise."

"Wait a spell."

"Scary." Potter said just the one word, and he said it under his breath, but it was enough. Clell dipped his paddle. One day he would whip Potter, but right now he reckoned he had to go on.

It wasn't fear that came on him a shake later, but just the quick knowing he had been right all along, just the holding still, the waiting, the watching what to do, for the banks had broken out with Indians—Indians with feathers in their hair, and bows and war clubs and spears in their hands; Indians yelling and motioning and scrambling down to the shores on both sides and fitting arrows to their bow strings.

Potter's face had gone white and tight like rawhide drying. He grabbed at his rifle.

Clell said, "Steady!" and got the pipe that hung from around his neck and held it up, meaning he meant peace.

These were the Blackfeet sure enough. These were the meanest Indians living. He would know them from the Rees and Crows and Pierced Noses and any other. He would know them by their round heads and bent noses and their red-and-green leather shields and the moccasins mismatched in color, and their bows and robes not fancy, and no man naked in the bunch.

The Indians waved them in. Clell let go his pipe and stroked with his paddle. Potter's voice was shrill. "You fool! You gonna let 'em torment us to death?"

That was the way with a mouthy greenhorn—full of himself at first, and then wild and shaken. "Steady!" Clell said again. "I aim to pull to shore. Don't point that there rifle 'less you want a skinful of arrows."

There wasn't a gun among the Indians, not a decent gun, but only a few rusty trade muskets. They had battle axes, and bows taken from their cases, ready for business, and some had spears, and all looked itching for a white man's hair. They waited, their eyes bright as buttons, their faces and bare forearms and right shoulders shining brown in the sun. Only men were at the shore line, but Clell could see the faces of squaws and young ones looking down from the bank above.

An Indian splashed out and got hold of the prow of the canoe and pulled it in. Clell stepped ashore, holding up his pipe. He had to watch Potter. Potter stumbled out, his little eyes wide and his face white, and fear showing even for an Indian to see. When he stepped on the bank one of the Indians grabbed his rifle and wrenched it from him, and Potter just stood like a scared rabbit, looking as if he might jump back in the dugout any minute.

Clell reached out and took a quick hold on the rifle and jerked it away and handed it back to Potter. There was a way to treat Indians. Act like a squaw and they treated you bad; act like a brave man and you might have a chance.

Potter snatched the gun and spun around and leaped. The force of the jump carried the canoe out. He made a splash with the paddle. An arrow whispered in the air and made a little thump when it hit. Clell saw the end of it, shaking from high in Potter's back.

Potter cried out, "I'm hit! I'm hit, Clell!"

"Come back! Easy! Can't get away!"

Instead, Potter swung around with the rifle. There were two sounds, the crack of the powder and the gunshot plunk of a ball. Clell caught a glimpse of an Indian going down, and then the air was full of the twang of bow strings and the whispered flight of arrows, and Potter slumped slowly back in the canoe, his body stuck like a pincushion. An Indian splashed out to take the scalp. Two others carried the shot warrior up the bank. Already a squaw was beginning to keen.

Clell stood quiet as a stump, letting only his eyes move. It was so close now that his life was as good as gone. He could see it in the eyes around him, in the hungry faces, in the hands moving and the spears and the bows being raised. He stood straight, looking their eyes down, thinking the first arrow would come any time now, from anyplace, and then he heard the eagle scream. Its shadow lazed along the ground. His thumb slipped the barrel catch, his wrist twisted under side up. He shot without knowing he aimed. Two feathers puffed out of the bird. It went into a steep climb and faltered and turned head down and spun to the ground, making a thump when it hit.

The Indians' eyes switched back to him. Their mouths fell open, and slowly their hands came over the mouth holes in the sign of surprise. It was as he figured in that flash between life and death. They thought all guns fired a single ball. They thought he was big medicine as a marksman. One of them stepped out and laid his hand on Mule Ear, as if to draw some of its greatness into himself. A murmur started up, growing into an argument. They ordered Clell up the bank. When he got there, he saw one Indian high-tailing it for the eagle, and others following, so's to have plumes for their war bonnets, maybe, or to eat the raw flesh for the medicine it would give them.

There was a passel of Indians on the bank, three or four hundred, and more coming across from the other side. The man Clell took for the chief had mixed red earth with spit and dabbed it on his face. He carried a bird-wing fan in one hand and wore a half-sleeved hunting shirt made of bighorn skin and decorated with colored porcupine quills. His hair was a wild bush over his eyes and ears. At the back of it he had a tuft of owl feathers hanging. He yelled something and motioned with his hands, and the others began drifting back from the bank, except for a couple of dozen that Clell figured were head men. Mostly, they wore leggings and moccasins, and leather shirts or robes slung over the left shoulder. A few had scarlet trade blankets, which had come from God knew where. One didn't wear anything under his robe.

The squaws and the little squaws in their leather sacks of dresses, the naked boys with their potbellies and swollen navels, and the untried and middling warriors were all back now. The chief and the rest squatted down in a half circle, with Clell standing in front of them. They passed a pipe around. After a while they began to talk. He had some of the hang of Blackfoot, and he knew, even without their words, they were arguing what to do with him. One of them got up and came over and brought his face close to Clell's. His eyes picked at Clell's head and eyes and nose and mouth. Clell could smell grease on him and wood smoke and old sweat, but what came to his mind above all was that here was a man he had fought last season while siding with the Crows. He looked steadily into the black eyes and saw the knowing come into them, too, and watched the man turn back and take his place in the half circle and heard him telling what he knew.

They grunted like hogs, the Blackfeet did, like hogs about to be fed, while the one talked and pointed, arguing that here was a friend of their old enemies, the Crows. The man rubbed one palm over the other, saying in sign that Clell had to be rubbed out. Let them stand him up and use him for a target, the man said. The others said yes to that, not nodding their heads as white men would, but bowing forward and back from the waist.

Clell had just one trick left. He stepped over and showed his gun and pointed to the patch box and, waving one hand to catch their eyes, he sprang the cover with the other thumb. He closed the cover and handed the gun to the chief.

The chief's hands were red with the paint he had smeared on his face. Clell watched the long thumbnail, hooked like a bird claw, digging at the cover, watched the red fingers feeling for a latch or spring. While the others stretched their necks to see, the chief turned Mule Ear over, prying at it with his eyes. It wasn't any use. Unless he knew the hidden spot to press, he couldn't spring the lid. Clell took the piece back, opened the patch box again, closed it and sat down.

He couldn't make more medicine. He didn't have a glass to bring the sun down, and so to light a pipe, or even a trader's paper-backed mirror for the chief to see how pretty he was. All he had was the shot at the eagle and the patch box on Mule Ear, and he had used them both and had to take what came.

Maybe it was the eagle that did it, or the hidden cover, or maybe it was just the crazy way of Indians. The chief got up, and with his hands and with his tongue asked if the white hunter was a good runner.

Clell took his time answering, as a man did when making high palaver. He lighted his pipe. He said, "The white hunter is a bad runner. The other Long Knives think he runs fast. Their legs are round from sitting on a horse. They cannot run."

The chief grunted, letting the sign talk and the slow words sink into him. "The Long Knife will run." He pointed to the south, away from the creek. "He will run for the trading house that the whiteface keeps among the Crows. He will go as far as three arrows will shoot, and then he will run. My brothers will run. If my brothers run faster—" The chief brought his hand to his scalp lock.

The other Indians had gathered around, even the squaws and the young ones. They were grunting with excitement. The chief took Mule Ear. Other hands stripped off Clell's hunting shirt, the red-checked woolen shirt underneath, his leggings, his moccasins, his small-clothes, until he stood white and naked in the sun, and the squaws and young ones came up close to see what white flesh looked like. The squaws made little noises in their throats. They poked at his bare hide. One of them grabbed the red-checked shirt from the hands of a man and ran off with it. The chief made the sign for "Go!"

Clell walked straight, quartering into the sun. He walked slow and solemn, like going to church. If he hurried, they would start the chase right off. If he lazed along, making out they could be damned for all he cared, they might give him more of a start.

He was two hundred yards away when the first whoop sounded, the first single whoop, and then all the voices yelling and making one great whoop. From the corner of his eye he saw their legs driving, saw the uncovered brown skins, the feathered hair, the bows and spears, and then he was running himself, seeing ahead of him the far tumble and roll of high plains and hills, with buffalo dotting the distances and a herd of prairie goats sliding like summer mist, and everywhere, so that not always could his feet miss them, the angry knobs of cactus. South and east, many a long camp away where the Bighorn joined the Roche Jaune, lay Lisa's Fort, the trading house among the Crows.

He ran so as to save himself for running, striding long and loose through the new-sprouting buffalo grass, around the cactus, around the pieces of sandstone where snakes were likely to lie. He made himself breathe easy, breathe deep, breathe full in his belly. Far off in his feelings he felt the cactus sting him and the spines pull off to sting again. The sun looked him in the face. It lay long and warm on the world. At the sky line the heat sent up a little shimmer. There wasn't a noise anywhere except the thump of his feet and his heart working in his chest and his breath sucking in and out and, behind him, a cry now and then from the Indians, seeming not closer or farther away than at first. He couldn't slow himself with a look. He began to sweat.

A man could run a mile, or two or three, and then his breath wheezed in him. It grew into a hard snore in the throat. The air came in, weak and dry, and burned his pipes and went out in one spent rush while his lungs sucked for more. He felt as if he had been running on forever. He felt strange and out of the world, a man running in a dream, except that the ache in his throat was real and the fire of cactus in his feet. The earth spread away forever, and he was lost in it and friendless, and not a proper part of it any more; and it served him right. When a man didn't pay any mind to his medicine, but went ahead regardless, as he had done, his medicine played out on him.

Clell looked back. He had gained, fifty yards, seventy-five, half a musket shot; he had gained on all the Indians except one, and that one ran as swift and high-headed as a prairie goat. He was close and coming closer.

Clell had a quick notion to stop and fight. He had an idea he might dodge the spear the Indian carried and come to grips with him. But the rest would be on him before he finished. It took time to kill a man just with the hands alone. Now was the time for the running he had saved himself for. There was strength in his legs yet. He made them reach out, farther, faster, faster, farther. The pound of them came to be a sick jolting inside his skull. His whole chest fought for air through the hot, closed tunnel of his throat. His legs weren't a part of him; they were something to think about, but not to feel, something to watch and to wonder at. He saw them come out and go under him and come out again. He saw them weakening, the knees bending in a little as the weight came on them. He felt wetness on his face, and reached up and found his nose was streaming blood.

He looked over his shoulder again. The main body of Indians had fallen farther back, but the prairie goat had gained. Through a fog he saw the man's face, the chin set high and hard, the black eyes gleaming. He heard the moccasins slapping in the grass.

Of a sudden, Clell made up his mind. Keep on running and he'd get a spear in the back. Let it come from the front. Let it come through the chest. Let him face up to death like a natural man and to hell with it. His feet jolted him to a halt. He swung around and threw up his hands as if to stop a brute.

The Indian wasn't ready for that. He tried to pull up quick. He made to lift his spear. And then he stumbled and fell ahead. The spear handle broke as the point dug in the ground. Clell grabbed at the shaft, wrenched the point from the earth and drove it through the man. The Indian bucked to his hands and knees and strained and sank back. It was as easy as that.

Bending over him, Clell let his chest drink, let his numb legs rest, until he heard the yells of the Indians and, looking up, saw them strung out in a long file, with the closest of them so close he could see the set of their faces. He turned and ran again, hearing a sudden, louder howling as the Indians came on the dead one, and then the howling dying again to single cries as they picked up the chase. They were too many for him, and too close. He didn't have a chance. He couldn't fort up and try to stand them off, not with his hands bare. There wasn't any place to hide. He should have listened to his medicine when it was talking to him back there on the creek.

Down the slope ahead of him a river ran—the Jefferson Fork of the Missouri, he thought, while he made his legs drive him through a screen of brush. A beaver swam in the river, its moving head making a quiet V in the still water above a dam. As he pounded closer, its flat tail slapped the water like a pistol shot, the point of the V sank from sight, and the ripples spread out and lost themselves. He could still see the beaver, though, swimming under water, its legs moving and the black tail plain, like something to follow. It was a big beaver, and it was making for a beaver lodge at Clell's right.

Clell dived, came up gasping from the chill of mountain water, and started stroking for the other shore. Beaver lodge! Beaver lodge! It was as if something spoke to him, as if someone nudged him, as if the black tail pulled him around. It was a fool thing, swimming under water and feeling for the tunnel that led up into the lodge. A fool thing. A man got so winded and weak that he didn't know medicine from craziness. A fool thing. A man couldn't force his shoulders through a beaver hole. The point of his shoulder pushed into mud. A snag ripped his side. He clawed ahead, his lungs bursting. And then his head was out of water, in the dark, and his lungs pumped air.

He heard movement in the lodge and a soft churring, but his eyes couldn't see anything. He pulled himself up, still hearing the churring, expecting the quick slice of teeth in his flesh. There was a scramble. Something slid along his leg and made a splash in the water of the tunnel, and slid again and made another splash.

His hands felt sticks and smooth, dry mud and the softness of shed hair. He sat up. The roof of the lodge just cleared his head if he sat slouched. It was a big lodge, farther across than the span of his arms. And it was as dark, almost, as the inside of a plugged barrel. His hand crossing before his eyes was just a shapeless movement.

He sat still and listened. The voices of the Indians sounded far off. He heard their feet in the stream, heard the moccasins walking softly around the lodge, heard the crunch of dried grass under their steps. It was like something dreamed, this hiding and being able to listen and to move. It was like being a breath of air, and no one able to put a hand on it.

After a while the footsteps trailed off and the voices faded. Now Clell's eyes were used to blackness, the lodge was a dark dapple. From the shades he would know it was day, but that was all. He felt for the cactus spines in his feet. He had been cold and wet at first, but the wetness dried and the lodge warmed a little to his body. Shivering, he lay down, feeling the dried mud under his skin, and the soft fur. When he closed his eyes he could see the sweep of distances and the high climb of mountains, and himself all alone in all the world, and, closer up, he could see the beaver swimming under water and its flat tail beckoning. He could hear voices, the silent voices speaking to a lonesome man out of nowhere and out of everywhere, and the beaver speaking, too, the smack of its tail speaking.

He woke up later, quick with alarm, digging at his dream and the noise that had got mixed with it. It was night outside. Not even the dark dapple showed inside the lodge, but only such a blackness as made a man feel himself to make sure he was real. Then he heard a snuffling of the air, and the sound of little waves lapping in the tunnel, and he knew that a beaver had nosed up and smelled him and drawn back into the water.

When he figured it was day, he sat up slowly, easing his muscles into action. He knew, without seeing, that his feet were puffed with the poison of the cactus. He crawled to the tunnel and filled his lungs and squirmed into it. He came up easy, just letting his eyes and nose rise above the water. The sun had cleared the eastern sky line. Not a breath of air stirred; the earth lay still, flowing into spring. He could see where the Indians had flattened the grass and trampled an edging of rushes, but there were no Indians about, not on one side or the other, not from shore line to sky line. He struck out for the far shore.

✳ ✳ ✳

Seven days later a hunter at Fort Lisa spotted a figure far off. He watched it for a long spell, until a mist came over his eyes, and then he called to the men inside the stockade. A half dozen came through the big gate, their rifles in the crooks of their arms, and stood outside and studied the figure too.

"Man, all right. Somep'n ails him. Look how he goes."

"Injun, I say. A Crow, maybe, with a Blackfoot arrer in him."

"Git the glass."

One of them went inside and came back and put the glass to his eye. "Naked as a damn jay bird."

"Injun, ain't it?"

"Got a crop of whiskers. Never seed a Injun with whiskers yet."

"Skin's black."

"Ain't a Injun, though."

They waited.

"It ain't! Yes, I do believe it's John Clell! It's John Clell or I'm a Black-foot!"

They brought him in and put his great, raw swellings of feet in hot water and gave him brandy and doled out roast liver, and bit by bit, that day and the next, he told them what had happened.

They knew why he wouldn't eat prairie turnips afterward, seeing as he lived on raw ones all that time, but what they didn't understand, because he didn't try to tell them, was why he never would hunt beaver again.

John Steinbeck
1902-68

▬

1935: *Tortilla Flat*
1936: *In Dubious Battle*
1937: *Of Mice and Men*
The Red Pony
1938: *The Long Valley*
1939: *The Grapes of Wrath*
1941: *Sea of Cortez*
1945: *Cannery Row*
1952: *East of Eden*

▬

JOHN STEINBECK'S *biographers generally agree that three essential factors contributed to the novelist's success. First, the region in which Steinbeck was born and raised was rich in natural beauty and interesting people. Second, he had a strong childhood aspiration to become a writer, a desire that grew virtually unhindered. And finally, he was a person of intense and versatile intellect.*

Steinbeck was born in Salinas, California, in 1902, *when it was still a small farming community. The town lies in the valley of the Salinas River, the "long valley" that is the setting for much of Steinbeck's fiction. South of Salinas is a picturesque smaller valley where Steinbeck's aunt and uncle had a ranch. He was often their weekend guest, spending his days wandering and playing in the hills and his evenings listening to his aunt read to him. The whole Salinas region had a pulse and rhythm that nurtured Steinbeck's intellect; the human life of the valley was rich in color and variety. There he studied the characters that he would use in his novels, from the paisanos of* Tortilla Flat *to the father—his own—in* The Red Pony.

Steinbeck's determination to be a writer came partly from constant reading and partly from a discovery early in life that he could keep his friends entertained by telling them stories. This talent was sharpened by a series of excellent teachers and the discipline of long hours of writing. Steinbeck made a decision to live in New York because it was, he believed, the best place to find success as a writer. But his residence there was brief; in 1926, after a winter of struggling against the alien pace and climate of the East, he left, working his way back to California by ship.

Eventually, of course, Steinbeck's writing earned him a good living and considerable fame. Tortilla Flat *became a best seller, as did* The Grapes of Wrath, *which won him the Pulitzer Prize in 1940. He was awarded the Nobel Prize in literature in 1962, the fifth American to receive it. Many of his works became very successful dramatizations, such as the stage version of* Of Mice and Men *and the film of* The Grapes of Wrath.

The Red Pony *began as a simple two-part story about a boy growing up on a small family ranch in California. It was first published in 1937, then Steinbeck added two more parts to the story and it was republished in 1945, one of the parts being "The Leader of the People." When what he called "the pony story" was partially written, he wrote to his friend George Albee: "The whole thing is as simply told as though it came out of the boy's mind although there is no going into the boy's mind. It is an attempt to make the reader create the boy's mind for himself." Steinbeck also told Albee that he was writing the story more for discipline than for any other reason.*[1]

Other letters of Steinbeck's reveal a thematic link between "The Leader of the People" and Steinbeck's social theory about "group man" and the "phalanx." The group, Steinbeck wrote, is "as dependent on its units and as independent of its units' individual natures, as the human unit, or man, is dependent on his cells and yet is independent of them." He added: "The fascinating thing to me is the way the group has a soul, a drive, an intent, an end, a method, a reaction and a set of tropisms which in no way resembles the same things possessed by the men who make up the group. . . . They are beings in themselves, entities."[2]

Steinbeck had a term for this entity, this mass with its own vitality. He called it the phalanx, *and he saw it as the key to understanding the sum of human history. The phalanx is vital to the individual. "Man is lonely when he is cut off. He dies. From the phalanx he takes a fluid necessary to his life. In the mountains I saw men psychologically emaciated from being alone. You can't find a reason for doing certain things. You couldn't possibly find a reason."*[3] *For years Steinbeck*

1. "To George Albee," [1933], *Steinbeck: A Life in Letters*, ed. Elaine Steinbeck and Robert Wallsten (New York: Viking, 1975), p. 71.
2. "To Carlton A. Sheffield," June 21, 1933, *Steinbeck*, pp. 75, 76.
3. "To George Albee," [1933], *Steinbeck*, p. 81.

was fascinated by the phalanx idea, always exploring theories about its origin and meaning, always seeing new implications. He once wrote that his quest was to "find a fictional symbolism" that would "act as a vehicle" to express the meaning of the phalanx,[4] *a quest that undoubtedly influenced* The Grapes of Wrath *and* In Dubious Battle, *as well as "The Leader of the People."*

The Leader of the People

O N SATURDAY afternoon Billy Buck, the ranch-hand, raked together the last of the old year's haystack and pitched small forkfuls over the wire fence to a few mildly interested cattle. High in the air small clouds like puffs of cannon smoke were driven eastward by the March wind. The wind could be heard whishing in the brush on the ridge crests, but no breath of it penetrated down into the ranch-cup.

The little boy, Jody, emerged from the house eating a thick piece of buttered bread. He saw Billy working on the last of the haystack. Jody tramped down scuffing his shoes in a way he had been told was destructive to good shoe-leather. A flock of white pigeons flew out of the black cypress tree as Jody passed, and circled the tree and landed again. A half-grown tortoise-shell cat leaped from the bunkhouse porch, galloped on stiff legs across the road, whirled and galloped back again. Jody picked up a stone to help the game along, but he was too late, for the cat was under the porch before the stone could be discharged. He threw the stone into the cypress tree and started the white pigeons on another whirling flight.

Arriving at the used-up haystack, the boy leaned against the barbed wire fence. "Will that be all of it, do you think?" he asked.

The middle-aged ranch-hand stopped his careful raking and stuck his fork into the ground. He took off his black hat and smoothed down his hair. "Nothing left of it that isn't soggy from ground moisture," he said. He replaced his hat and rubbed his dry leathery hands together.

"Ought to be plenty mice," Jody suggested.

"Lousy with them," said Billy. "Just crawling with mice."

"Well, maybe, when you get all through, I could call the dogs and hunt the mice."

From John Steinbeck, *The Long Valley* (New York: Viking Press, 1938), pp. 283–303. Copyright © 1938, 1966 by John Steinbeck. Reprinted by permission of Viking Penguin, Inc.

4. "To Carlton A. Sheffield," June 21, 1933, *Steinbeck*, p. 75.

"Sure, I guess you could," said Billy Buck. He lifted a forkful of the damp ground-hay and threw it into the air. Instantly three mice leaped out and burrowed frantically under the hay again.

Jody sighed with satisfaction. Those plump, sleek, arrogant mice were doomed. For eight months they had lived and multiplied in the haystack. They had been immune from cats, from traps, from poison and from Jody. They had grown smug in their security, overbearing and fat. Now the time of disaster had come; they would not survive another day.

Billy looked up at the top of the hills that surrounded the ranch. "Maybe you better ask your father before you do it," he suggested.

"Well, where is he? I'll ask him now."

"He rode up to the ridge ranch after dinner. He'll be back pretty soon."

Jody slumped against the fence post. "I don't think he'd care."

As Billy went back to his work he said ominously, "You'd better ask him anyway. You know how he is."

Jody did know. His father, Carl Tiflin, insisted upon giving permission for anything that was done on the ranch, whether it was important or not. Jody sagged farther against the post until he was sitting on the ground. He looked up at the little puffs of wind-driven cloud. "Is it like to rain, Billy?"

"It might. The wind's good for it, but not strong enough."

"Well, I hope it don't rain until after I kill those damn mice." He looked over his shoulder to see whether Billy had noticed the mature profanity. Billy worked on without comment.

Jody turned back and looked at the side-hill where the road from the outside world came down. The hill was washed with lean March sunshine. Silver thistles, blue lupins and a few poppies bloomed among the sage bushes. Halfway up the hill Jody could see Doubletree Mutt, the black dog, digging in a squirrel hole. He paddled for a while and then paused to kick bursts of dirt out between his hind legs, and he dug with an earnestness which belied the knowledge he must have had that no dog had ever caught a squirrel by digging in a hole.

Suddenly, while Jody watched, the black dog stiffened, and backed out of the hole and looked up the hill toward the cleft in the ridge where the road came through. Jody looked up too. For a moment Carl Tiflin on horseback stood out against the pale sky and then he moved down the road toward the house. He carried something white in his hand.

The boy started to his feet. "He's got a letter," Jody cried. He trotted away toward the ranch house, for the letter would probably be read aloud and he wanted to be there. He reached the house before his father did, and ran in. He heard Carl dismount from his creaking saddle and slap the horse on the side to send it to the barn where Billy would unsaddle it and turn it out.

Jody ran into the kitchen. "We got a letter!" he cried.

His mother looked up from a pan of beans. "Who has?"

"Father has. I saw it in his hand."

Carl strode into the kitchen then, and Jody's mother asked, "Who's the letter from, Carl?"

He frowned quickly. "How did you know there was a letter?"

She nodded her head in the boy's direction. "Big Britches Jody told me."

Jody was embarrassed.

His father looked down at him contemptuously. "He *is* getting to be a Big-Britches," Carl said. "He's minding everybody's business but his own. Got his big nose into everything."

Mrs. Tiflin relented a little. "Well, he hasn't enough to keep him busy. Who's the letter from?"

Carl still frowned on Jody. "I'll keep him busy if he isn't careful." He held out a sealed letter. "I guess it's from your father."

Mrs. Tiflin took a hairpin from her head and slit open the flap. Her lips pursed judiciously. Jody saw her eyes snap back and forth over the lines. "He says," she translated, "he says he's going to drive out Saturday to stay for a little while. Why, this is Saturday. The letter must have been delayed." She looked at the postmark. "This was mailed day before yesterday. It should have been here yesterday." She looked up questioningly at her husband, and then her face darkened angrily. "Now what have you got that look on you for? He doesn't come often."

Carl turned his eyes away from her anger. He could be stern with her most of the time, but when occasionally her temper arose, he could not combat it.

"What's the matter with you?" she demanded again.

In his explanation there was a tone of apology Jody himself might have used. "It's just that he talks," Carl said lamely. "Just talks."

"Well, what of it? You talk yourself."

"Sure I do. But your father only talks about one thing."

"Indians!" Jody broke in excitedly. "Indians and crossing the plains!"

Carl turned fiercely on him. "You get out, Mr. Big-Britches! Go on, now! Get out!"

Jody went miserably out the back door and closed the screen with elaborate quietness. Under the kitchen window his shamed, downcast eyes fell upon a curiously shaped stone, a stone of such fascination that he squatted down and picked it up and turned it over in his hands.

The voices came clearly to him through the open kitchen window. "Jody's damn well right," he heard his father say. "Just Indians and crossing the plains. I've heard that story about how the horses got driven off about a thousand times. He just goes on and on, and he never changes a word in the things he tells."

When Mrs. Tiflin answered her tone was so changed that Jody, outside the window, looked up from his study of the stone. Her voice had become soft and explanatory. Jody knew how her face would have changed to match the tone. She said quietly, "Look at it this way, Carl. That was the big thing in my father's life. He led a wagon train clear across the plains to the coast, and when it was finished, his life was done. It was a big thing to do, but it didn't last long enough. Look!" she continued, "it's as though he was born to do that, and after he finished it, there wasn't anything more for him to do but think about it and talk about it. If there'd been any farther west to go, he'd have gone. He's told me so himself. But at last there was the ocean. He lives right by the ocean where he had to stop."

She had caught Carl, caught him and entangled him in her soft tone.

"I've seen him," he agreed quietly. "He goes down and stares off west over the ocean." His voice sharpened a little. "And then he goes up to the Horseshoe Club in Pacific Grove, and he tells people how the Indians drove off the horses."

She tried to catch him again. "Well, it's everything to him. You might be patient with him and pretend to listen."

Carl turned impatiently away. "Well, if it gets too bad, I can always go down to the bunkhouse and sit with Billy," he said irritably. He walked through the house and slammed the front door after him.

Jody ran to his chores. He dumped the grain to the chickens without chasing any of them. He gathered the eggs from the nests. He trotted into the house with the wood and interlaced it so carefully in the wood-box that two armloads seemed to fill it to overflowing.

His mother had finished the beans by now. She stirred up the fire and brushed off the stove-top with a turkey wing. Jody peered cautiously at her to see whether any rancor toward him remained. "Is he coming today?" Jody asked.

"That's what his letter said."

"Maybe I better walk up the road to meet him."

Mrs. Tiflin clanged the stove-lid shut. "That would be nice," she said. "He'd probably like to be met."

"I guess I'll just do it then."

Outside, Jody whistled shrilly to the dogs. "Come on up the hill," he commanded. The two dogs waved their tails and ran ahead. Along the roadside the sage had tender new tips. Jody tore off some pieces and rubbed them on his hands until the air was filled with the sharp wild smell. With a rush the dogs leaped from the road and yapped into the brush after a rabbit. That was the last Jody saw of them, for when they failed to catch the rabbit, they went back home.

Jody plodded on up the hill toward the ridge top. When he reached the little cleft where the road came through, the afternoon wind struck him and blew up his hair and ruffled his shirt. He looked down on the little hills and ridges below and then out at the huge green Salinas Valley. He could see the white town of Salinas far out in the flat and the flash of its windows under the waning sun. Directly below him, in an oak tree, a crow congress had convened. The tree was black with crows all cawing at once.

Then Jody's eyes followed the wagon road down from the ridge where he stood, and lost it behind a hill, and picked it up again on the other side. On that distant stretch he saw a cart slowly pulled by a bay horse. It disappeared behind the hill. Jody sat down on the ground and watched the place where the cart would reappear again. The wind sang on the hilltops and the puff-ball clouds hurried eastward.

Then the cart came into sight and stopped. A man dressed in black dismounted from the seat and walked to the horse's head. Although it was so far away, Jody knew he had unhooked the check-rein, for the horse's head dropped forward. The horse moved on, and the man walked slowly up the hill beside it. Jody gave a glad cry and ran down the road toward them. The squirrels bumped along off the road, and a road-runner flirted its tail and raced over the edge of the hill and sailed out like a glider.

Jody tried to leap into the middle of his shadow at every step. A stone rolled under his foot and he went down. Around a little bend he raced, and there, a short distance ahead, were his grandfather and the cart. The boy dropped from his unseemly running and approached at a dignified walk.

The horse plodded stumble-footedly up the hill and the old man walked beside it. In the lowering sun their giant shadows flickered darkly behind them. The grandfather was dressed in a black broadcloth suit and he wore kid congress gaiters and a black tie on a short, hard collar. He carried his black slouch hat in his hand. His white beard was cropped close and his white eyebrows overhung his eyes like moustaches. The blue eyes were sternly merry. About the whole face and figure there was a granite dignity, so that every motion seemed an impossible thing. Once at rest, it seemed the old man would be stone, would never move again. His steps were slow and certain. Once made, no step could ever be retraced; once headed in a direction, the path would never bend nor the pace increase nor slow.

When Jody appeared around the bend, Grandfather waved his hat slowly in welcome, and he called, "Why, Jody! Come down to meet me, have you?"

Jody sidled near and turned and matched his step to the old man's step and stiffened his body and dragged his heels a little. "Yes, sir," he said. "We got your letter only today."

"Should have been here yesterday," said Grandfather. "It certainly should. How are all the folks?"

"They're fine, sir." He hesitated and then suggested shyly, "Would you like to come on a mouse hunt tomorrow, sir?"

"Mouse hunt, Jody?" Grandfather chuckled. "Have the people of this generation come down to hunting mice? They aren't very strong, the new people, but I hardly thought mice would be game for them."

"No, sir. It's just play. The haystack's gone. I'm going to drive out the mice to the dogs. And you can watch, or even beat the hay a little."

The stern, merry eyes turned down on him. "I see. You don't eat them, then. You haven't come to that yet."

Jody explained, "The dogs eat them, sir. It wouldn't be much like hunting Indians, I guess."

"No, not much—but then later, when the troops were hunting Indians and shooting children and burning teepees, it wasn't much different from your mouse hunt."

They topped the rise and started down into the ranch cup, and they lost the sun from their shoulders. "You've grown," Grandfather said. "Nearly an inch, I should say."

"More," Jody boasted. "Where they mark me on the door, I'm up more than an inch since Thanksgiving even."

Grandfather's rich throaty voice said, "Maybe you're getting too much water and turning to pith and stalk. Wait until you head out, and then we'll see."

Jody looked quickly into the old man's face to see whether his feelings should be hurt, but there was no will to injure, no punishing nor putting-in-your-place light in the keen blue eyes. "We might kill a pig," Jody suggested.

"Oh, no! I couldn't let you do that. You're just humoring me. It isn't the time and you know it."

"You know Riley, the big boar, sir?"

"Yes. I remember Riley well."

"Well, Riley ate a hole into that same haystack, and it fell down on him and smothered him."

"Pigs do that when they can," said Grandfather.

"Riley was a nice pig, for a boar, sir. I rode him sometimes, and he didn't mind."

A door slammed at the house below them, and they saw Jody's mother standing on the porch waving her apron in welcome. And they saw Carl Tiflin walking up from the barn to be at the house for the arrival.

The sun had disappeared from the hills by now. The blue smoke from the house chimney hung in flat layers in the purpling ranch-cup. The puff-ball clouds, dropped by the falling wind, hung listlessly in the sky.

Billy Buck came out of the bunkhouse and flung a wash basin of soapy water on the ground. He had been shaving in mid-week, for Billy held Grandfather in reverence, and Grandfather said that Billy was one of the few men of the new generation who had not gone soft. Although Billy was in middle age, Grandfather considered him a boy. Now Billy was hurrying toward the house too.

When Jody and Grandfather arrived, the three were waiting for them in front of the yard gate.

Carl said, "Hello, sir. We've been looking for you."

Mrs. Tiflin kissed Grandfather on the side of his beard, and stood still while his big hand patted her shoulder. Billy shook hands solemnly, grinning under his straw moustache. "I'll put up your horse," said Billy, and he led the rig away.

Grandfather watched him go, and then, turning back to the group, he said as he had said a hundred times before, "There's a good boy. I knew his father, old Mule-tail Buck. I never knew why they called him Mule-tail except he packed mules."

Mrs. Tiflin turned and led the way into the house. "How long are you going to stay, Father? Your letter didn't say."

"Well, I don't know. I thought I'd stay about two weeks. But I never stay as long as I think I'm going to."

In a short while they were sitting at the white oilcloth table eating their supper. The lamp with the tin reflector hung over the table. Outside the dining-room windows the big moths battered softly against the glass.

Grandfather cut his steak into tiny pieces and chewed slowly. "I'm hungry," he said. "Driving out here got my appetite up. It's like when we were crossing. We all got so hungry every night we could hardly wait to let the meat get done. I could eat about five pounds of buffalo meat every night."

"It's moving around does it," said Billy. "My father was a government packer. I helped him when I was a kid. Just the two of us could about clean up a deer's ham."

"I knew your father, Billy," said Grandfather. "A fine man he was. They called him Mule-tail Buck. I don't know why except he packed mules."

"That was it," Billy agreed. "He packed mules."

Grandfather put down his knife and fork and looked around the table. "I remember one time we ran out of meat—" His voice dropped to a curious low sing-song, dropped into a tonal groove the story had worn for itself. "There was no buffalo, no antelope, not even rabbits. The hunters couldn't even shoot a coyote. That was the time for the leader to be on the watch. I was the leader, and I kept my eyes open. Know why? Well, just the minute the people began to get hungry they'd start slaughtering the team oxen. Do you believe that? I've heard of parties that just ate up their draft cattle. Started from the middle and worked toward the ends. Finally they'd eat the lead pair, and then the wheelers. The leader of a party had to keep them from doing that."

In some manner a big moth got into the room and circled the hanging kerosene lamp. Billy got up and tried to clap it between his hands. Carl struck with a cupped palm and caught the moth and broke it. He walked to the window and dropped it out.

"As I was saying," Grandfather began again, but Carl interrupted him. "You'd better eat some more meat. All the rest of us are ready for our pudding."

Jody saw a flash of anger in his mother's eyes. Grandfather picked up his knife and fork. "I'm pretty hungry, all right," he said. "I'll tell you about that later."

When supper was over, when the family and Billy Buck sat in front of the fireplace in the other room, Jody anxiously watched Grandfather. He saw the signs he knew. The bearded head leaned forward; the eyes lost their sternness and looked wonderingly into the fire; the big lean fingers laced themselves on the black knees. "I wonder," he began, "I just wonder whether I ever told you how those thieving Piutes drove off thirty-five of our horses."

"I think you did," Carl interrupted. "Wasn't it just before you went up into the Tahoe country?"

Grandfather turned quickly toward his son-in-law. "That's right. I guess I must have told you that story."

"Lots of times," Carl said cruelly, and he avoided his wife's eyes. But he felt the angry eyes on him, and he said, " 'Course I'd like to hear it again."

Grandfather looked back at the fire. His fingers unlaced and laced again.

Jody knew how he felt, how his insides were collapsed and empty. Hadn't Jody been called a Big-Britches that very afternoon? He arose to heroism and opened himself to the term Big-Britches again. "Tell about Indians," he said softly.

Grandfather's eyes grew stern again. "Boys always want to hear about Indians. It was a job for men, but boys want to hear about it. Well, let's see. Did I ever tell you how I wanted each wagon to carry a long iron plate?"

Everyone but Jody remained silent. Jody said, "No. You didn't."

"Well, when the Indians attacked, we always put the wagons in a circle and fought from between the wheels. I thought that if every wagon carried a long plate with rifle holes, the men could stand the plates on the outside of the wheels when the wagons were in the circle and they would be protected. It would save lives and that would make up for the extra weight of the iron. But of course the party wouldn't do it. No party had done it before and they couldn't see why they should go to the expense. They lived to regret it, too."

Jody looked at his mother, and knew from her expression that she was not listening at all. Carl picked at a callus on his thumb and Billy Buck watched a spider crawling up the wall.

Grandfather's tone dropped into its narrative groove again. Jody knew in advance exactly what words would fall. The story droned on, speeded up for the attack, grew sad over the wounds, struck a dirge at the burials on the great plains. Jody sat quietly watching Grandfather. The stern blue eyes were detached. He looked as though he were not very interested in the story himself.

When it was finished, when the pause had been politely respected as the frontier of the story, Billy Buck stood up and stretched and hitched his trousers. "I guess I'll turn in," he said. Then he faced Grandfather. "I've got an old powder horn and a cap and ball pistol down to the bunkhouse. Did I ever show them to you?"

Grandfather nodded slowly. "Yes, I think you did, Billy. Reminds me of a pistol I had when I was leading the people across." Billy stood politely until the little story was done, and then he said, "Good night," and went out of the house.

Carl Tiflin tried to turn the conversation then. "How's the country between here and Monterey? I've heard it's pretty dry."

"It is dry," said Grandfather. "There's not a drop of water in the Laguna Seca. But it's a long pull from '87. The whole country was powder then, and in '61 I believe all the coyotes starved to death. We had fifteen inches of rain this year."

"Yes, but it all came too early. We could do with some now." Carl's eye fell on Jody. "Hadn't you better be getting to bed?"

Jody stood up obediently. "Can I kill the mice in the old haystack, sir?"

"Mice? Oh! Sure, kill them all off. Billy said there isn't any good hay left."

Jody exchanged a secret and satisfying look with Grandfather. "I'll kill every one tomorrow," he promised.

Jody lay in his bed and thought of the impossible world of Indians and buffaloes, a world that had ceased to be forever. He wished he could have been living in the heroic time, but he knew he was not of heroic timber. No one living now, save possibly Billy Buck, was worthy to do the things that had been done. A race of giants had lived then, fearless men, men of a staunchness unknown in this day. Jody thought of the wide plains and of the wagons moving across like centipedes. He thought of Grandfather on a huge white horse, marshaling the people. Across his mind marched the great phantoms, and they marched off the earth and they were gone.

He came back to the ranch for a moment, then. He heard the dull rushing sound that space and silence make. He heard one of the dogs, out in the doghouse, scratching a flea and bumping his elbow against the floor with every stroke. Then the wind arose again and the black cypress groaned and Jody went to sleep.

He was up half an hour before the triangle sounded for breakfast. His mother was rattling the stove to make the flames roar when Jody went through the kitchen. "You're up early," she said. "Where are you going?"

"Out to get a good stick. We're going to kill the mice today."

"Who is 'we'?"

"Why, Grandfather and I."

"So you've got him in it. You always like to have someone in with you in case there's blame to share."

"I'll be right back," said Jody. "I just want to have a good stick ready for after breakfast."

He closed the screen door after him and went out into the cool blue morning. The birds were noisy in the dawn and the ranch cats came down from the hill like blunt snakes. They had been hunting gophers in the dark, and although the four cats were full of gopher meat, they sat in a semicircle at the back door and mewed piteously for milk. Doubletree Mutt and Smasher moved sniffing along the edge of the brush, performing the duty with rigid ceremony, but when Jody whistled, their heads jerked up and their tails waved. They plunged down to him, wriggling their skins and yawning. Jody patted their heads seriously, and moved on to the weathered scrap pile. He selected an old broom handle and a short piece of inch-square scrap wood. From his pocket he took a shoelace and tied the ends of the sticks loosely together to make a flail. He whistled his new weapon through the air and struck the ground experimentally, while the dogs leaped aside and whined with apprehension.

Jody turned and started down past the house toward the old haystack ground to look over the field of slaughter, but Billy Buck, sitting patiently on the back steps, called to him, "You better come back. It's only a couple of minutes till breakfast."

Jody changed his course and moved toward the house. He leaned his flail against the steps. "That's to drive the mice out," he said. "I'll bet they're fat. I'll bet they don't know what's going to happen to them today."

"No, nor you either," Billy remarked philosophically, "nor me, nor anyone."

Jody was staggered by this thought. He knew it was true. His imagination twitched away from the mouse hunt. Then his mother came out on the back porch and struck the triangle, and all thoughts fell in a heap.

Grandfather hadn't appeared at the table when they sat down. Billy nodded at his empty chair. "He's all right? He isn't sick?"

"He takes a long time to dress," said Mrs. Tiflin. "He combs his whiskers and rubs up his shoes and brushes his clothes."

Carl scattered sugar on his mush. "A man that's led a wagon train across the plains has got to be pretty careful how he dresses."

Mrs. Tiflin turned on him. "Don't do that, Carl! Please don't!" There was more of threat than of request in her tone. And the threat irritated Carl.

"Well, how many times do I have to listen to the story of the iron plates, and the thirty-five horses? That time's done. Why can't he forget it, now it's done?" He grew angrier while he talked, and his voice rose. "Why does he have to tell them over and over? He came across the plains. All right! Now it's finished. Nobody wants to hear about it over and over."

The door into the kitchen closed softly. The four at the table sat frozen. Carl laid his mush spoon on the table and touched his chin with his fingers.

Then the kitchen door opened and Grandfather walked in. His mouth smiled tightly and his eyes were squinted. "Good morning," he said, and he sat down and looked at his mush dish.

Carl could not leave it there. "Did—did you hear what I said?"

Grandfather jerked a little nod.

"I don't know what got into me, sir. I didn't mean it. I was just being funny."

Jody glanced in shame at his mother, and he saw that she was looking at Carl, and that she wasn't breathing. It was an awful thing that he was doing.

He was tearing himself to pieces to talk like that. It was a terrible thing to him to retract a word, but to retract it in shame was infinitely worse.

Grandfather looked sidewise. "I'm trying to get right side up," he said gently. "I'm not being mad. I don't mind what you said, but it might be true, and I would mind that."

"It isn't true," said Carl. "I'm not feeling well this morning. I'm sorry I said it."

"Don't be sorry, Carl. An old man doesn't see things sometimes. Maybe you're right. The crossing is finished. Maybe it should be forgotten, now it's done."

Carl got up from the table. "I've had enough to eat. I'm going to work. Take your time, Billy!" He walked quickly out of the dining-room. Billy gulped the rest of his food and followed soon after. But Jody could not leave his chair.

"Won't you tell any more stories?" Jody asked.

"Why, sure I'll tell them, but only when—I'm sure people want to hear them."

"I like to hear them, sir."

"Oh! Of course you do, but you're a little boy. It was a job for men, but only little boys like to hear about it."

Jody got up from his place. "I'll wait outside for you, sir. I've got a good stick for those mice."

He waited by the gate until the old man came out on the porch. "Let's go down and kill the mice now," Jody called.

"I think I'll just sit in the sun, Jody. You go kill the mice."

"You can use my stick if you like."

"No, I'll just sit here a while."

Jody turned disconsolately away, and walked down toward the old hay-stack. He tried to whip up his enthusiasm with thoughts of the fat juicy mice. He beat the ground with his flail. The dogs coaxed and whined about him, but he could not go. Back at the house he could see Grandfather sitting on the porch, looking small and thin and black.

Jody gave up and went to sit on the steps at the old man's feet.

"Back already? Did you kill the mice?"

"No, sir. I'll kill them some other day."

The morning flies buzzed close to the ground and the ants dashed about in front of the steps. The heavy smell of sage slipped down the hill. The porch boards grew warm in the sunshine.

Jody hardly knew when Grandfather started to talk. "I shouldn't stay here, feeling the way I do." He examined his strong old hands. "I feel as though the crossing wasn't worth doing." His eyes moved up the side-hill and stopped on a motionless hawk perched on a dead limb. "I tell those old stories, but they're not what I want to tell. I only know how I want people to feel when I tell them.

"It wasn't Indians that were important, nor adventures nor even getting out here. It was a whole bunch of people made into one big crawling beast. And I was the head. It was westering and westering. Every man wanted something for himself, but the big beast that was all of them wanted only westering. I was the leader, but if I hadn't been there, someone else would have been the head. The thing had to have a head.

"Under the little bushes the shadows were black at white noonday. When we saw the mountains at last, we cried—all of us. But it wasn't getting here that mattered, it was movement and westering.

"We carried life out here and set it down the way those ants carry eggs. And I was the leader. The westering was as big as God, and the slow steps that made the movement piled up and piled up until the continent was crossed.

"Then we came down to the sea, and it was done." He stopped and wiped his eyes until the rims were red. "That's what I should be telling instead of stories."

When Jody spoke, Grandfather started and looked down at him. "Maybe I could lead the people some day," Jody said.

The old man smiled. "There's no place to go. There's the ocean to stop you. There's a line of old men along the shore hating the ocean because it stopped them."

"In boats I might, sir."

"No place to go, Jody. Every place is taken. But that's not the worst—no, not the worst. Westering has died out of the people. Westering isn't a hunger any more. It's all done. Your father is right. It is finished." He laced his fingers on his knee and looked at them.

Jody felt very sad. "If you'd like a glass of lemonade I could make it for you."

Grandfather was about to refuse, and then he saw Jody's face. "That would be nice," he said. "Yes, it would be nice to drink a lemonade."

Jody ran into the kitchen where his mother was wiping the last of the breakfast dishes. "Can I have a lemon to make a lemonade for Grandfather?"

His mother mimicked—"And another lemon to make a lemonade for you."

"No, ma'am. I don't want one."

"Jody! You're sick!" Then she stopped suddenly. "Take a lemon out of the cooler," she said softly. "Here, I'll reach the squeezer down to you."

Frank Waters
b. 1902

——

1937: *Midas of the Rockies*
1941: *People of the Valley*
1942: *The Man Who Killed the Deer*
1946: *The Colorado*
1950: *Masked Gods*
1966: *The Woman at Otowi Crossing*
1971: *Pike's Peak*
1975: *Mexico Mystique:*
The Coming Sixth World of Consciousness
1986: *Flight From Fiesta*

——

FRANK WATERS *is exactly what you would expect a Taos novelist and historian to be. His speech is soft and slow, his face lean and sunbaked, his clothes the color of sage and sand. He knows the New Mexico Indians the way most people know their family, or better, and he has an encyclopedic knowledge of the Southwest's geography and history. If there is a single lesson in his work, it is that we must put ourselves in touch with our land despite the forces that draw us in other directions. The landscape, in Waters's works, is not something to be conquered, not something to be endured; it has its own rhythms and its own moods to be discovered. Before we can discover these, however, we must first reconcile our inner conflicts and resolve the dilemma of dualities in our lives.*

Born and raised in Colorado Springs, Colorado, where the mountains and canyons tugged at his imagination, Waters was pressured by his family to join the business community, to become a builder and entrepreneur like his grandfather. Waters's family was active in gold mining, so Frank went to college to learn mining technology. After three years as an engineering student, he went to work in the Wyoming oil fields and then took a job as a telephone company field engineer in California. There the dualities came into play. While striving to make good as a field engineer, he was also trying to become a novelist. He got his first novel, Fever Pitch, *published in 1930.*

Waters has also experienced dual loyalties of mixed blood, since his father had Indian ancestors. Waters found himself studying Native American cultures, and he was especially intrigued by the Indians' natural and nonexploitative acceptance of their environment. His own training, of course, had made him an expert in the exploitation of minerals. Many writers would simply have written about the contradictions of their own personal situation, but it is in Waters's nature to take the larger view of things. He realized that the problem of duality is universal and is probably one of mankind's central conflicts. Ever since he arrived at that belief, Waters has been on a philosophic quest, seeking a balance point between opposing forces, such as between technology and the spirit or between religion and materialism. His writings generally explore such opposites by dramatizing the spiritual and sometimes mystical dual relationship between the human soul and the physical conditions in which it finds itself. The Yogi of Cockroach Court *(1947), for example, is about the meditations of an Oriental philosopher who lives among the prostitutes of a shabby border village in Mexico. This man of peace and pure thought finds himself drawn into being a saloon owner and a smuggler, eventually ascending beyond the reach of any conflict. Waters's best-known novel,* The Man Who Killed the Deer, *is the story of a young man being pulled toward spiritual unity with his pueblo, a unity he resists because he has also learned the white ways. That book, and* People of the Valley, *represent Waters's long association with the region and people around Taos, New Mexico, where the author has lived since 1946. Today he is a leading authority on Southwest Indian mythology and spiritualism.* Masked Gods *and* Book of the Hopi *(1963) are significant contributions to cultural anthropology. Like Waters's neomythic fiction, they present fresh new perspectives on ancient legends.*

The central conflict of the "Doña Maria" novel, People of the Valley, *begins when government engineers want to build a dam across the valley in order to protect the people and stimulate the economy. The people of the valley have always accepted floods as a part of nature. They do not understand that the dam will mean the end of their way of life. Maria, wise and prophetic, becomes their guide to a solution that reconciles the inevitability of the dam with the integrity of the culture.*

"The Inheritors" is from Waters's superb history of the Colorado River, The Colorado. *He describes the new people of the new valleys, with their self-destructive belief that becoming a "part of the West" is simply a matter of materialism. Unlike the old people of the old valleys, "America on the whole has lived too fast to think," and as a result "we are still strangers to our earth." However, in other books by Waters, such as* The Woman at Otowi Crossing, *we find optimism and the hope*

that the western people will someday find enlightenment, will recognize their earth as a spiritual resource, and will discover the one balance point of life's multitude of polarities.

▬

Doña Maria de Valle

THE AGE of the beautiful blue valley and of Doña Maria is not, strictly speaking, a hundred years. Each is older, each echoing as they do one timeless and changeless pulse. But for a century they have been known by man—the valley ten years longer, Maria ten years less.

At the beginning of that short span six Hudson Bay trappers came warily down over the snowy pass hunting for beaver. On the banks of the frozen stream they found first three human skeletons left by Comanches, and so named the long blue crescent the valley of "L'Eau du Mort"—the Waters of the Dead.

All were Frenchmen. Roubidoux was one, and Ceran St. Vrain whose own skeleton lies yet beside the meandering stream, in the little Campo Santo rising out of the flat and covered by scrub oak. Their tongue still persists in the names of the little cañon settlements of Gascon and Ledoux, just over the hill; and it sounds at times in the general store of gruff, wooden-legged Pierre Fortier. In the church, behind, were French priests. The old linden in its courtyard, too, was a seedling brought by Father Guerin from France—one of the two which have rooted in these high western hills.

But it was up the Chihuahua Trail from Mexico, up the Rio Grande and over the Pecos, that the settlers came. Their soft fluent Spanish slurred the valley's name to "Lo de Mor," changed phonetically to "Lo de Mora," and finally shortened to "Demora." It was a place of berries, too, according to their translation: wild raspberries and strawberries thick along the streams and carpeting the clearings between thickets of chokecherry, gooseberry and wild plum. The steep, narrow cañon of Rio de la Caza, the place of the hunt, softened musically to Rio la Casa—and the beaver houses attested its change of name long after deer, wild turkey and bear grew scarce.

There were seventy-six settlers when they petitioned in the name of the Mexican nation for a land grant. Not only the long deep crescent was granted, but all the tributary cañons, the mountain uplands and the grassy plains below. And the beautiful blue valley to the north and to the south of the jutting cliffs which marked the handle of its curving bow, took two more names. The Valle de San Antonio above, and the Valle de Santa Gertrudes below.

The two villages were lifted slowly, a handful at a time, from the rich red-brown earth, roofed with vigas hand-hewn from the pines and interlaced with slim aspens. The adobes clustered thickly together for protection and according to the superior decree: "two hundred and fifty varas from East to West, leaving thirty varas outside for drippage and a common road and the meadow for the benefit of all, with its entrances and exits free."

But as the beautiful blue valley it persisted through its second name and tongue: more beautiful, more blue, as the thickets gave way to meadows of grass and the lower pine slopes to milpas of corn.

Yet little by little a third tongue, name and race crawled in. They came not over the pass from the north and west as had the first, nor up the Chihuahua Trail from the south as had the second. They came from the strange, unknown and barbaric east, over the vast buffalo plains. In great lumbering wains they came, with wheels high as a man and which left their traces forever imbedded in the soft limestone, with sheets drawn tight over the curving wagons bows—ships riding the pelagic plain. Men with eyes colder and bluer than the valley, in buckskin and with long emphatic rifles to punctuate their taciturnity. But where the wagons stopped to rest before the last climb, a fort grew up. Great walls it had, barracks and stables and courtyards where soldiers laughed, cursed, threw dice and shuffled cards. But they needed corn and wheat and oats, both men and horses—and the men wanted women and excitement.

So the beautiful blue valley over the hills prospered. For gold the village supplied liquor, gambling, horse races and cock fights. The people supplied the corn, wheat and oats for silver, and sometimes the women for a quicker exchange of lead and flashing steel. And duly, apathetically, they petitioned the new Jéfe, the Señor Presidente of the gringos, to confirm their title to their land. Again it was granted "with the stipulation that the United States herein expressly reserves to itself the buildings and improvements situated on the Fort Union Military and Timber Reservation, together with the possession and use of the same. . . ."

Save this, all the tributary cañons, the mountain uplands and the grassy plains below—a wilderness empire, remained theirs. But only the valley mattered.

New teams, new masters for the plow, but the land remains. The land that is mother to us all. An enduring truth that only her sons can know.

For the French disappeared with the beaver, leaving only their names and Pierre Fortier cursing and stamping his wooden leg. And soon the last of the gringo wagons passed over the trail, leaving the fort to crumble on the hillside and the colonel's grand piano to leer with a mouth of missing keys through the dusky parlor of the old inn.

Only the people remained rooted to their soil in a valley muy retirado, muy cerrado, that grew more isolated, more closed, within its mountain walls.

Through three tongues, three races and many names, then, the beautiful blue valley persisted; and yet it was but twenty years old when Doña Maria came. Old enough, but not too ripe, to be her mother.

$$* * *$$

Dawn-dusk drew the charcoal outline of a hut on the mountainside. Then the dirty gray light of day, like a soiled brush, thrust through the pines and smeared it with drabness. Its walls, waist-high, were heaped up stones chinked with adobe as were the gaping logs laid on top. The roof sagged with dirt and sprouted a growth of wild timothy.

A pig might have waddled out, but it was a woman who emerged into the clearing. She brought life and color into the drab monotone. About her bulging body she held a faded, striped, burnt-orange blanket. On her bare feet she wore sparse-beaded moccasins. Her long blue-black hair hung down around a smooth brown face slightly tinged red. The face was young but its pleasant immobility was marred by a strained expression of pain and anxiety. It was the look of a woman near childbirth, who watches for a man she knows will not return.

Without pausing she waddled across the flat stones in the stream and struggled up the trail. It rose through the gelid darkness of the pines into the pallid gray of scrub oak. Head down and breast heaving her protruding belly stretching the blanket in wrinkles across her broad hips, she climbed blindly, as if she had known it an incalculable number of ascents. Abruptly, across a face of frost-shattered granite, the path ended.

Below her the valley was rising out of a mist. She was standing on the tall weathered cliffs that jut out to separate the upper and lower halves of the one long valley so beautiful and blue. It curved like an Indian bow to left and right, as though the woman flexed it with her longing.

She looked toward the first mud clumps of Santa Gertrudes and San Antonio. Jets of pale smoke rose, adding blue to blue, but never the dust of a horse's hoofs from the plains below. Then the arrow of her gaze flew west to the wall of mountains.

She was Indian, Picuris, and the pueblo lay hidden behind the pass. Like her, others would be drawn out of its decaying, squalorous, mud-black walls to the tiny new settlements in the valley below. They would drift together to live about the hot springs, and be forgotten with the Mexican men who drew them hence. Only the faint red flush showing through the dark cheeks of their sons and grandsons would mark El Alto as different from the others—the rising end of the scale as Picuris lowered in oblivion.

But now, alone, she stood between them. It was day, and the rising sun marked her time on its dial.

She slumped down on her broad haunches, clasping her quivering belly, her face grown oily with sweat. Then with a last look over the precipice, she rose and stumbled weakly back down the trail.

The inside of the hut was growing gray with light. Its small room was windowless and without furniture save a deal table lashed together with rawhide, and a leather trunk. Patches of the dirt floor were hard and smooth and black with the goats' blood mixed in the adobe. In one corner was a small fireplace. Before it lay a straw mat and another blanket.

The woman pawed back the ashes, and blew the coals awake. In a nest of sticks she set a copper kettle, dropping fresh yerba buena into the water. From an earthen pot she drew out the last handful of parched corn and chewed a few kernels slowly. When the water boiled she drank the tea to ease the increasing pains of her pregnancy.

They kept mounting, bubbling up within her and sinking down, a geyser of cramps. She lay writhing on the sleeping mat, then rousing against the wall to wipe the sweat from her face.

A shaft of sunlight fell in the doorway and slowly revolved about the room. A blue jay screamed from a pine outside. Two magpies quarreled on the roof, dislodging a thin trickle of dirt between the smoke-stained vigas.

Shortly after noon the woman awoke from a sleep that was not a sleep. A deer was standing in the clearing outside of the door. The great petals of its ears were thrust forward, the sunlight glistened on its porous, rubber-black nose. Weakly the woman gathered up from the blanket a few dropped kernels of corn to toss outside. With the gesture the deer, stiff-legged, rose into the air and vanished with a twitch of its white tailpiece.

The woman's big body was now a volcano trying to erupt. Spasms of pain rolled her from side to side. From knots of cramps her arms and legs unraveled, twitching. Her face was no longer dark rose-brown. It was muddy orange. She chewed, as if starving, a corner of her blanket.

The tea was cold. It could not quench the fire within her. She rolled on her back and lay snorting through her wide nostrils.

After the next spasm she got up. The beaded moccasins she took off and laid away carefully in the old leather trunk. The blanket around her she removed, folded, and placed out of reach. Now barefooted, her wheat-sack body covered only by a loose, black cotton shift, she stood before the fireplace.

In the niche in the wall stood a small dusty Cristo carved out of cotton-wood. It had been lacquered with the gelatinous glue of cow's horns and gypsum, painted with egg yolk and ochre, and rubbed with mutton tallow. All this had soaked into the wood leaving a dark, muddy Rembrandt-brown figure with a long sharp nose, a bitter mouth and one broken leg. It was her man's Santo. The woman propped it up and lit a candle before it. She stared at it wonderingly in the vain attempt to discern power in such an inimical form.

Then she brought out a small buckskin sack, touching with it her nose and mouth, her breasts and belly, the secret parts of her body, after which she hung it back around her throat.

Another recurrent convulsion doubled her like a felled tree. She straight-ened slowly, her moon face glistening with sweat, and laboriously looped over a rafter a long horsehair rope which dangled to the center of the floor.

Now began her labor.

Hands above her sagging head, she hung and pulled on the rope. What she needed and wanted were the strong hands of her man or of midwives around her waist: dragging their weight on her bulging body, slipping down from breasts to broad hips, squeezing, compressing, forcing out the new little life clamoring within her for outlet.

Instead, she hung there alone, doggedly straining in the dusky hut be-fore the guttering candle. With one hand she prodded and pressed her belly and groin. Every few minutes fresh labor pains gripped her. Then she hung on with both hands. Her knees and feet twitched. Her hands slipped down the rope. Head down and moaning, her bare feet dragging in the dirt, she revolved more slowly, came to rest.

Little by little she hitched herself up, panting, waiting for the next spasm. The Cristo with his long sharp nose and bitter mouth looked on as if ironi-cally amused—an amusement that yet seemed to have in it the compassion derived from severer suffering.

By midafternoon the floor beneath the woman was a dark puddle of sweat. She could no longer hold herself up. She slipped down to her knees, legs outspread, and ripped off her soppy shift. Her long blue-black hair stuck to her broad back like a shadow.

Suddenly she rolled sideways upon the heap of blankets, howling. Her eyes filmed over. Her hands fought the air, fell and sought in the blankets something that was neither there or anywhere.

Time now had meaning. It hammered out its truth as if on a great drum. The pulse beats throbbed through her and through the earth below, they shook the mountains and the evening star in its socket above. It was her time and another's too, and all to which they were bound in unbroken sequence by the one pulsing beat which echoes dreamily and powerfully through the earth of the flesh and the flesh of the earth alike.

And so it passed. . . .

They found her that evening—Two goatherds passing the hut, who heard the child's cries.

"Mother of God! It is she. The India. The woman of that stranger who ran away again to join the great wagons of the gringos. She has been here all this time . . . Cristo Rey! What a mess, this of woman bearing children . . . Señora!"

This man's name, where had he come from, would he return . . . what does one do now with such a tiny babe . . . would the Señora like some tea, a scrap of fat meat and a cold tortilla? Señora! Señora India!

To all their questions, pleas and exhortations the woman made no answer. They got out of her a wild and frightened look, a last choking gasp and one intelligible "Maria."

It was the only name she spoke, and so it became the child's. Red and tiny, it lay on the edge of the stained blanket. One miniature hand was closed upon a bit of dirt. It was her birthright. Doña Maria never let it go.

Maria grew up with her goats. She was as scrawny and stringy-legged as they from scrambling up the rocky hillsides. Her hair too was long, coarse and tangled with burs and pine needles. Like theirs, her large, dark eyes could, in an instant, become wild and wary as though a pebble had been dropped into their placid depths. They were her only companions by day, her bedfellows at night. She drank their milk, ate their cheese and sometimes chewed a piece of their flesh. Their odor clung to her as if it were her own. Her life was like theirs save in one respect: she did not eat grass. At ten she was a little she-goat.

Their goatherds were two old philosophers. They kept back the mounting tide of life with a rampart of stones heaped across the narrow throat of a cañon. Behind it was an aspen fence and a roof of branches. To most of the valley below it looked like a corral. The inclosure did keep coyotes and an occasional bear from the flock at night; and interlaced with spruce branches in winter it kept out some snow and wind. But across the top of the high stone barricade gleamed a row of pale goat and sheep skulls. They were symbols of a school of thought, and its two exponents stared down between them into the valley with all the irreproachable dignity of their calling.

The older one sprouted on his long dark face a few gray chin whiskers like a he-goat's. Around his shoulders he wore a dirty sheepskin. He carried a staff and wielded it when pressed as Jove a thunderbolt. The other, scarcely over sixty, still betrayed a lingering worldliness by wearing a battered sombrero with its last tiny bell still dangling from its rim, brass earrings and leather leggings. It was obvious that he was conscious of his weakness. He kept wrinkling his seamed and weathered face as if he knew that the veneration accorded age and wisdom in men depended on their outward mien.

These two viejos lived in a small hut in back of the corral. Maria ate with them. On stormy nights she also slept with them on the floor. It was a privilege granted her with new-born kids, an ailing ewe or a goat maimed by wild beasts. During blizzards the whole flock was let in.

The kids whimpered, the ewes blatted. When warm grease was smeared on a lacerated leg a new voice added to the bedlam and muted the shrieking winds. Maria did the smearing. She sat on the goat's head and kept ducking back from its threshing legs.

The two old men squatted in front of the fire, watching. Generously they offered tidbits of advice from their feast of wisdom. They minded neither the stench, the noise nor the gusts of smoke that filled the hut. They were immersed in life yet never wetted; salved too, as it were, by the protective goose grease of their inherent aloofness.

Both had come up from the desert wastes of Chihuahua. The lush grass and innumerable streams of the beautiful blue valley they could never quite believe permanent. Twenty times a day, at every stream and rivulet they crossed, the older would stop and drink his fill.

"You will kill yourself with drinking, compadre," said the other, observing his companion's gasping red face and drum-tight belly.

"My son," replied he, "it is not thirst I indulge but safety. Fate has led us here, and without doubt it shall lead us back again into a desert wilderness where streams and water holes are a day apart. If here I grow lax and fail to drink my fill at every stream, thinking the next near by, I will surely perish there."

Thus they maintained caution.

Parsimony they practiced also, and tyranny over Maria. As the little herd under her care increased, her daily rations of tortillas and cheese decreased in wise proportion of her safety. A glutted child, they said, makes a careless climber.

This caution, parsimony and tyranny they regarded as custom, simplicity and benevolence, and so justified philosophy which is ever blind to the crass and superficial aspect of things seen by lesser men.

To prove it, Maria flourished. She often went out into the hills without food, and never asked for another covering when her old sheepskin wore through. The two viejos admitted satisfaction. "We are doing well by the child. She grows hardy as a weed."

Maria did not tell them that she sucked udders of milk from her herd, or that before entering the hut she hid the faded, burnt-orange blanket stolen from them. What they liked best about her was her silence.

This was the form of their lives. Its substance was impregnated by their peculiar philosophy whose symbols gleamed palely along the top of the high stone rampart, were stacked around the outside of the hut, and held their rapt gaze inside.

The men, by night, were always squatting down before the fire with a skull between their legs. With little twigs they measured the span between its eye sockets, from gaping mouth to top of head. These lineal measurements they recorded on the dirt floor. Little triangles and squares they drew in the flickering light, and these they compared with the seasonal patterns of moon and stars on the skull of the heaven above.

Often they rose and brought out from the corner a bundle of bound twigs. Each was marked by a knife cut, a strip of peeled bark or a broken branch. These too were laid out carefully on the floor to compare with a skull.

"Yes. The wild plum branch marked with the cut of a new moon. It is the one that shows where the water rose highest in the little stream to the west."

"Pues, brother. I remember this skull well. A lively young ram—he who climbed highest always. To the gray cliffs with moss so thick in the cracks. Observe these wrinkles, compadre. What a head!"

With such remarks they punctuated hours of silent study. Maria lay on the floor, belly down, watching their intent and timeless faces. Their sharp, shrewd eyes bored through the skulls at their feet. The vast skull of the heavens they probed, and added to the zodiacal signs read in the brittle bone. Even the earth they seemed to strip of its flesh to sound the depth of springs, of winter snows and underground streams.

To them, it was all one pattern endlessly repeated in magnitude and miniature. By goat skulls they read the record of floods and droughts, foretold heavy snows and drying springs, measured the movement of stars—and little by little as men ventured up from the valley, they began to prophesy love and illfortune, wealth and sickness, danger, drying wells, and to supply remedies for heavy hearts.

To the villagers below they were charlatans and greedy thieves, or men wise and learned in the ancient learning of the hills, depending upon the opinion of those badly cheated in trade, who slyly suspected where their missing goats had gone, or happened to seduce their chiquitas soon after purchasing a love charm. To all the beautiful blue valley they were at least markedly eccentric.

But to Maria they always remained philosophers.

She was a wild and wary little goat. She saw through their charlatanry and maintained silence. Their tyranny she endured for the spot of benevolence it contained. With simple, unsuspected guile she combated their parsimony, and was not above trading a kid to a passing stranger while excusing its loss by referring to a marauding bear.

Of it all nothing endured but the intent of their teachings. The great dome of the midnight skies, and the dome of the earth rounding from horizon to horizon: both forever repeated with the triangles and squares of stars, and with the wrinkled watermarks of freshets and spring thaws, upon the lesser, miniature skulls of beast and man. This was the lesson of her childhood. She never suspected it was philosophy. She only thought that she was learning about goats.

* * *

The two viejos, then, were wise men. In their wisdom they choked out life with a high stone wall across the throat of the cañon. It had one little gate. Out of it went Maria each day with her scrawny goats, and into it was permitted to pass an occasional visitor from the valley. Inside, the two old philosophers prophesied water and weather, attended personally to their precious sheep, and confounded all men with their alarming eccentricity.

They made only one mistake—one miscalculation of water and weather. It was as though the life they shut out in front crawled around and struck them from the unsuspected rear.

It came in the form of a flood down the steep-walled cañon. The thunderclouds broke against the face of the cliff, were transformed into great glacial boulders as round and gray and smooth as enormous skulls. They snapped pines, tore out dirt and brush, and swept down in a raging torrent that scarce thirty minutes before had been a twinkling little trout stream.

The high stone wall, shutting out the flow of life in front, had created something of a vacuum in the pocket in back. Now the flow from behind rushed in to fill it. It was a great lesson, this trite truth that nature abhors a vacuum, but the two philosophers had no time to learn it. In a twinkling they were immersed in a torrent six feet deep. The protective goose grease of their inherent aloofness was battered by rolling stones and twisting logs. Soon their heads were too.

The little hut unfolded like a flower, the aspen fence collapsed like straw. Men, sheep and a few goats, pitiously bleating and shrieking were dashed against the stone wall. For a minute it held. Then with a crash it collapsed, and the flood swept down into the valley to leave an apron of debris, a few bloated carcasses for the buzzards, and the bodies of the two viejos whose fate had perverted their philosophy by neither drawing them back into a desert wilderness nor developing their thirst in proportion to the water they received.

Maria, up in the hills with her goats, stumbled upon a half-collapsed hut in which they took up new quarters. It stood in a little clearing just below the tall weathered cliffs that jutted out to separate the upper and lower halves of the one long valley. Often she climbed the overgrown and almost imperceptible trail to the edge of the precipice. Here, immobile as one of her goats, her long hair blowing in the wind, she stood staring fixedly down into the beautiful blue valley.

Below, the great white-cloud wagons kept passing, the fort grew up. It was all very strange. But she was a stranger. Most people turn from the thing called life to the thing called philosophy. But Maria from philosophy was confronted by life.

——

The Inheritors

ALL THESE have made us what we are. The land we have inherited. And the human heritage of all those who have preceded us.

Human history is but the story of man's adaptation to his environment. The deepening relationship of a people to their earth. That is the essential truth we read here in this vast heart of America, the upland basin of the Colorado. In the conquerors, whom it defeated. In the padres, whom it rejected. In the trappers, who overcame the land physically and were caught by it psychically. The secret of its hold upon us is the treasure

From Frank Waters, *The Colorado* (New York: Rinehart, 1946), pp. 275–92. Copyright © 1946 by Frank Waters. Reprinted by permission of Joan Daves.

the prospectors sought. Until we find it—the profound and haunting secret of the reciprocal relationship that must exist between man and land—we will still remain outcasts. Outcasts like the Mormons from the rest of mankind in their time, and outcasts from the settlers in turn like the individual outlaws.

For to us, as to them, the haunting cry of space still and forever rings in our ears. The same vast loneliness engulfs us. We have spanned the horizons and the seas three thousand miles apart. Our towns dot the valleys, bestride the rivers, cling even to the mountainsides. Still tormented, we are driven forward and back by a gnawing restlessness. We can find no peace, no rest. The immense space conquered outside has only crawled inside us. The corrosive loneliness still eats within us. The shriek of a train whistle across the midnight cañon, like the shriek of a cougar—that is the voice we know best, and it is the voice of all wilderness America with its still unconquered space and our secret unassuaged loneliness.

Still the tension keeps mounting within us. Like the Mormons we are driven to a fanatical puritanism. Like the Penitentes to masochistic self-flagellation. And like both to sacrificial murder and crucifixion.

We cannot abide ourselves. How, then, have we lived with each other? With the development of our peculiar racial psychosis we killed off the red, enslaved the black, erected barriers against the yellow, discriminated against the brown, and now find it difficult to tolerate the Jewish race. Only to the white has Liberty held up her torch.

But instinctively we have felt the land to be at the root of all our trouble. A strange New World not to be wooed, won and finally understood. But a new wild land to be quickly overpowered, raped and gutted. Thus we have leapt to the one task by which we could expend the full force of our power, and find a momentary release from our constant nervous tension. To conquer the land and expend its riches.

It is done! We have sunk in it the foundations of the greatest materialistic-mechanistic civilization ever known. On it we have raised the highest triumphant towers ever built by man.

And now we but recoil upon ourselves. For of all men we are the only true killers. The most tolerant and good-natured, the slowest to be aroused, we are passionless, dispirited killers. Of what? Quién sabe? We only know that there lurks in all of us a cold murderous instinct that unannounced and unpremeditated lunges suddenly out of the easygoing shell of our lives. It strikes those we love as often as those we hate. Why not? It is undirected, impassionate, impersonal. The quality of a true half-breed, to strike *out,* not *at.*

And so we topple over our tall shining towers as soon as they are built. We claw down and stamp upon our idols the moment we have raised them to their brief acclaim. Nothing is safe, permanent and secure from our eventual knife thrust. It is as if at last we find even our success no more than a barrier across the path of our invisible destiny. Like the trappers, we are eternally driven by a strange compulsion from the known and loved to the feared unknown.

And deep in our hearts we know it. For all our vaunted practicality, we are the most mystical people on earth. From our souls we see, the pain is ever with us, and so we shout it down with a mammoth jest—the immense and ironic humor of America, to which nothing is long sacred.

Yet all the time the counterforces of salvation have been insidiously working in us against our will and knowledge. The strange and subtle forces of the land itself. Every anthropologist of merit, including the oft-quoted Ales Hrdlicka, has been pointing out for years how "climactic and other influences are gradually working to produce in us some of the facial characteristics they had already produced in the Indians." After a few generations here even the skull types of various pure Europeans change to that of the indigenous Indian. Not only physically but psychically a change is taking place. Jung has stated that when we reach the bottom of the American psyche, we find the Indian.

Slowly but ineluctably the land is rooting us to its soil. First the solitary trappers as individuals, then the isolated settlers as groups, and now us as a race. This is the real history of the vast heart of America, the upland basin of the Colorado. The story of man's adaptation, psychically as well as physically, to his environment. The deepening relationship of a people to their earth.

For a mere handful of men had confirmed us to a new destiny. They had wiped out the past. They had set us on a new trail, rooted deep in the immortal, impassionless American earth. But neither they nor those who followed them had gone far enough. They had not fully achieved that harmonic, reciprocal relationship with the land attained by the indigenous peoples whose trail to it they found.

The end of it is what we seek. This is what we know deep in our loneliness: that we are still strangers to our earth. Like the trappers we know it.

But they have set us on the trail—the long, long trail where the pony tracks go only one way. Nothing for long can hold us back. Neither our own materialistic-mechanistic success, our lofty towers, our own loves. Impassionate killers, we must at last destroy even the incompleteness that holds us back.

And so we look into the mirror to see the meek who have inherited the earth. We need such "a feeling of continuity in our experience as a people, a sense of the past as a living reality conditioning the present." But America on the whole has lived too fast to think.

The industrial East, quickly populated and still linked umbilically to Europe, has lost all perspective of time and place. Everything west of Chicago has seemed remote, irrelevant and provincial. At best it appears strangely picturesque—a romantic escape for a summer vacation.

Always the booming West Coast has been the end of a journey across empty, unregarded space. It still looks westward, not backward, with longing to continue the journey across more empty space.

The era of the Pacific is beginning, just as the era of Europe is ending.

But between them lies the crossroads of the world, America. And now, if ever, America must emerge: its full blossom, its final pattern, and its ideal of a completely synthesized people one at last with its own physical background.

In this final synthesis the vast hinterland—the still empty, backward, wilderness basin of the Colorado—must play its important part.

But let's face it. Cowboy boots and high-peaked Stetsons, as well as war bonnets, are out of style.

If there is anything that gives me a pain in the neck it's the professional Westerner. You know the type. The senator who insists on being photographed in a ten-gallon hat and astraddle the hood of his Packard limousine when he arrives in Washington. The strong, silent man of the open spaces always on the guest list for cocktails to parade his sunburn profile in front of visiting tourists. The artist who goes native in Mexican huaraches and a small adobe littered with expensive serapes but without a toilet. Particularly the writer who makes a cult of his sectional background. They are all phonies; you can spot them a mile away.

Concurrent with the recent world-wide war there has come inevitably a recurrent epidemic of nationalism. America, for its part, has been shaken to the roots. All the self-banished aesthetes have come scurrying home from the Riviera. Desperately we are hanging on against the high tide of change to what we are and to what, by Jesus, we intend to remain. Hence we are ready victims of the epidemic's most virulent attacks of rampant sectionalism.

Movies, radio and book publishers, theaters and slick-paper magazines are all afflicted. Anything American goes. Especially if it goes back far enough. What is it we want to see? Here in the Wide Open Spaces of God's Country we want to see ourselves as the rootin'-tootin'est, hell-roarin', God-fearin' sons-a-bitches that ever were suckled on panthers' milk and cactus juice or raked spurs in a hoss. Oh, but we have our tender side too! We sure do, ma'am, beggin' pardon. Why, when the old moon comes up over Pleasant Valley yonder, and the night breeze comes astealin' along the ridge like a pesky coyote, it makes a fellow think how good it is to be back here leadin' a noble simple life like his pappy and his ma afore him. A real American. Nothin' fancy. Just plain square-shooters, us folks.

Listen to the senator. Look at the movies. Hear the radio. Read almost any magazine, almost any book on the West. The same old stories. The same fictional vernacular. Pure, unadulterated hokum.

Why?

We insist on seeing ourselves as we like to think we were. We're afraid to see ourselves as we are.

Is it because we have lost our innate sense of direction? Or are we so afraid of the future that we cling to a false romantic past?

Let's face it. Cowboy boots, peaked Stetsons, war bonnets and huaraches are out of style. The professional Westerner is barking up the wrong tree. He's making a fool of himself and us too.

Dress, manner, vernacular and all the other affectations are all phony. Not the psychology of the Indian, Penitente, Mormon and all the others reflected in us. Let's keep this straight.

But even this latter is changing. The New Deal, Frank Sinatra, the Depression, the WPA, Clark Gable, the War, Coca-Cola, refrigerated beef, the Petty Girl and Donald Duck have left their ineradicable marks on our very souls. Not long ago I took some friends far up a remote mountain cañon to attend a Saturday night dance in a small Spanish-American village. I wanted them to see the old, graceful varsoviana. It was not danced. The people were too busy dancing to the boogie-woogie.

I was in California at the time of Pearl Harbor. A sudden telephone call sent me rushing to an Army Induction Center. An Indian boy who had been drafted had attacked a group of majors and colonels because they insisted on cutting off his hair. Imagine that indignity! Thousands of Indian boys have been bereft in an instant, by a clip of shears, of generations of tradition.

What about the old folks at home?

From one pueblo a group of old men came to call on a friend of mine. They wanted a letter written to President Roosevelt. "It is spring," they said. "It is time to plant our corn. But there is no one left to plant it. All our young men have gone to war. They have been gone a year. Now it is spring and time to plant our corn again. But they are not here to plant it. Please send us back our young men. They have been fighting long enough. It is the corn that must be planted, you understand. It is not us, their wives, their mothers, their own small sons. It is the corn, this you will say."

A year later they still sat, the corn unplanted, munching on the dollars the government sent them from their army sons in Guadalcanal, Tarawa, Burma, Iwo Jima, Normandy, Germany. When all these sons return, will it be back to hairbraids and the blanket, to finally plant the little milpas of squaw corn among the pines? Or will they have learned the possible persuasiveness of the vote, the almighty power of the dollar, a new trade, a larger brighter vision?

So it goes among Spanish-Americans and Anglos too.

Whoopee! *Beat Me Daddy Eight to the Bar* from a juke box instead of *La Paloma* on a guitar. Mother wants a high-altitude pressure cooker to can her own vegetables for winter. Father has bought another Ford; he's going to try this contour plowing. But brother is nuts about airplanes. Sister does her hair like the movie actress of the month. Baby doesn't believe in Santa Claus. Watch de cops when dey move in on de gang. Rat-a-tat-tat-tat-tat! Who the hell was Billy the Kid anyway? Give me Superman. *Rum and Coca-CO-la!* What! Me work my tail off for that damned little Schicklegruber for ten bucks a week like I been makin'? Who, ME? Not when I can grab off seventy-five over the hill. OH-oh! Where's the fire sale, honey? Nice pair of gams if they was gettin' you anywheres.

What's cookin' anyway?

It's about time the professional Westerner and all the rest of us were finding out.

Pyramid City

What is cooking, to be precise, is that the senator's half million constituents in 150 little towns and villages are building up the quarter million square miles of Pyramid City for occupation by, say, ten million future residents.

Don't get them wrong. There's nothing romantic about it, any more than there was about founding it some time back. The Stetson-hatted senator's still hell-bent on getting his proper cut. The huarache-clad artist is going to paint over the sweat and pain with a glossy finish of glamour. And inevitably the romantic-western writer is going to glorify the wrong heroes. But the people are going ahead with it just the same, taxes or not.

A great city is the most fascinating thing alive. Thomas Burke, who never set foot outside London, wrote twenty books on his travels through its streets. He did not begin to cover the surface of the subject. Since time immemorial youth has followed its dreams and ambitions to the turrets of Camelot, the garrets of Paris, the towers of New York. It is an idea rooted in every heart, a shadow cast upon the most remote peasant. The tremendous idea, the immense shadow of the city.

And so likewise has the city become the most corrupt, the most cancerous sore upon the body of civilization. All the strength of far provinces has been required to maintain it. Whole populations have been enslaved to stoke its furnaces. The land itself has been sucked dry. It is not enough! Inhuman and insatiable, a monster with a hide of concrete and guts of steel, it dominates humanity itself. It creates the slumdom of the poor and the boredom of the rich. It distorts all men equally, both those powerfully isolated in their tall towers and those groveling in the sunless gloom of their deep cañons below. Impartially it feeds on both their fears and their lusts. Still it keeps rearing, tier on tier, its towers clawing at the sky.

The metropolis, the megapolis, the city—beautiful, corrupt, entrancing, damned—the victory of height over space.

But nature—the mystery of that form of isostatic equilibrium we call nature eventually balances its scales with the mysterious phenomena we call wars, revolutions, catastrophes, plagues, shifts of centers of population, tides of economic change. The very forces that create the city destroy it. Carthage is plowed under. Rome is sacked. Berlin is bombed. London, anemically drained of world power, is a wax image. New York is dying on its feet with the last frenetic convulsions of a chicken with its head cut off. For the day of great cities as we have known them is ending.

The world has shrunk. Superhighways, giant air liners and the radio constrict it into a tiny ball. Helicopters and television will shrink the land still smaller. The great cities of the future will no longer consist of vast teeming populations concentrated in immense stone growths reaching into the skies. They will spread out, their great petals unfolding to light and air, enveloping suburbs miles away. Their tall towers will shrink and vanish. Space at last will have its victory over height.

For years I felt it sad and strange that we had no city in our own vast domain to compare with those I knew in books. The lack was only in my own imagination. We were already citizens of a great city—Pyramid City.

A character named Half-Pint Petey, who had wandered up for work in the mine, assured me solemnly it was so. He had been everywhere, done everything; he had been a mule skinner, a railroad surveyor on the U.P., a cook for Theodore Roosevelt on his western jaunts, was a good hand with an ax, could turn out blindfolded a pan of breakfast biscuits that shamed Mother's, and swore by *Gulliver's Travels*. A capable and talented man.

Now, son, he said, don't you be grievin' none about never seein' no city. We got one here. A proper world wonder. Naturally it was new. There was plenty of time to get in on the ground floor. This of course was Petey's main obsession. He would propose that we expend the proceeds of the mine for the purchase of an entire valley at two bits an acre; that we secure squatters' rights to a whole plain; establish the water rights to a mountain watershed. Watch her boom then!

Under his eloquent persuasiveness we could see a prairie-dog town metamorphose overnight into a right handsome human town. This, he warned, was but the beginning. Soon all the spaces in-between, all the valleys, plains and parks would be filled. All one vast city extending from the mountains to the river. Pyramid City—the whoppin'est big city in the whole plumb world. Pulling his handle-bar mustaches, Petey would continue.

The Colorado ran right through it. Well, he'd put locks on it like in the Panama Canal. Big ships, by cracky, would sail right up to Pikes Peak and we could buy our tea fresh from China. Another thing, son. We'll have us Moffat Tunnels running through all the mountains. Just ring a bell at a likely ore showing and get off and mine. What's the use of paradin' around on top the hills with a jackass and drivin' separate shafts? And the desert— God Almighty!—put her under glass. Make one big hothouse of her. Grow your own bananas and coconuts. Have parrots squawkin' in the trees, and monkeys climbin' around. It'll be a zoo to boot, where people can go on Sunday afternoons whizzin' in the subway.

Well, we failed him miserably. Half-Pint Petey one day washed out his extra shirt, stuffed his week's wages in his tattered trousers and wandered over the range to seek a better place to begin. But I never forgot his inspired words. Today there is a paved street where we hunted rabbits, a corner drugstore on the site of the campfire where we cooked them. A part of Pyramid City, no less.

First there's the boroughs, all seven: named Wyoming, Utah, Colorado, New Mexico, Arizona, Nevada and California.

Then properly laid out to avoid congestion are the public parks: Grand Cañon, Bryce Cañon, Zion, Petrified Forest, Cañon de Chelly, Mesa Verde, Grand Teton, Natural Bridges and a dozen others.

Main Street now is labeled Highway 66; it runs east and west through the southern half of Pyramid City. The upper half is more full of hills than Rome or Kansas City. Huge mountains in fact, though residents on one side refer to those on the other as merely living "over the hill." Central Avenue spans the lot; the Pikes Peak Ocean-to-Ocean Highway is its present name. Between these two are a thousand cross streets to suit the fancy of every dweller—wide-paved boulevards, narrow dirt roads, tree-lined lanes. Pick your house to suit the weather and the neighborhood: log cabin, adobe or ramada, or a de luxe copy of either.

Like Budapest, Pyramid City is split lengthwise by a river. You can't forget the red Colorado any more than you can the blue Danube. But here we let it sing its own song, being more orchestral than melodic.

Geographically our 42nd and Broadway lies exactly in the center of Pyramid City. Like Times Square, it has its popular name—Lee's Ferry. For nearly four centuries everybody has eventually showed up here at the confluence of the Colorado and the Paria. John D. Lee, the Mormon renegade, built its huge ferryboat from pine hauled sixty miles by ox team. Now, since 1929, the Navajo Bridge spans the river. It has the same deathless quality as Brooklyn Bridge; one cannot love one without loving the other. Some 480 feet above water, this is the highest steel-arch bridge in the United States; the only highway bridge crossing the Colorado between Moab, Utah, and Boulder Cañon, a thousand-mile stretch.

Talk about interurbans! Pyramid City's got elevateds, inclines, surface trams, subways and Toonerville Trolleys galore. Its greatest traditions stem from these lines of steel rails. A man could spend a lifetime chasing down the legends and lives of its railroads. The old Colorado Midland elevated that crawled over the roof of the continent. The Mount Manitou and Red Rock inclines that were yanked up the peaks by cables, to say nothing of the Pikes Peak Cog Road with its greasy cogged third rail and an engine on stilts which pushed its single car up the peak. The T.C. & G.B., officially labeled the Tucson, Cornelia and Gila Bend, but better known as the Tough Coming and Worse Going Back. The Denver and Salt Lake—that's a subway for you! Through the Moffat Tunnel, six miles long, it burrows clear through James Peak and the Continental Divide; shortens the distance between Denver and Salt Lake 173 miles; and also brings water through the Rockies from the western slope to the eastern slope. For Toonerville Trolleys we've got a dozen miniatures of trains, complete to detail, high in the Rockies. There's the narrow-gauge lines of the D. & R.G.— "Through the Rockies, Not Over Them"—twisting around the peaks and creeping through the gorges; the little narrow-gauge spur running down from San Luis Valley, lately transported bodily to Burma. And for surface trams the U.P., the San Diego and Arizona, the Santa Fe, the crack fliers with the wonderful names—the Mountaineer, the Colorado Eagle, the Chief, the Navajo, El Capitán, and Grand Cañon Limited.

From the historic Santa Fe stems that wholly American legend and incomparable institution which alone in all America compares with the traditional wayside inn of Europe—the Fred Harvey House. No boy who has ever known one but scoffs at a mere diner and hotel.

Spaced mealtimes apart, they spanned our whole wilderness domain. Each was at once an oasis for all travelers and the focus of life for miles around. Not only were they richly named—Castaneda, Alvarado, Escalante, Fray Marcos and Garces after our earliest travelers; El Navajo and Havasu after our first citizens; La Posada and Casa del Desierto as proper names of inns. Their architecture and decoration were distinctly original and distinctive. Nothing phony, scrumptious or Grand Rapids about them. Hung with Navajo blankets, their walls painted with Indian designs, selling Hopi and Pueblo pottery, Navajo silver, and folders of Scenic Views of the Region, they were deeply rooted in our homeland as perhaps no other institution and proud of it—an astounding, isolated fact in the days of their prime.

When The Train Came In!—that was the event for which the Fred Harvey House was expressly built and nobly planned. Before the wheels stopped turning the great brass gong began its deep-toned musical summons. Trainmen and passengers poured off—everyone on board. And everything was ready. In the small dining room hot soup was already steaming on white tablecloths. At the long horseshoe lunch counter of green marble tidy packets of ham sandwiches wrapped in tissue and tied with green paper bands were stacked high, with doughnuts, cakes and pies. Huge polished urns, like the pipes of an organ, played the aromatic tune of Fred Harvey coffee, sweet as the strains of a calliope. Along the walls outside squatted Indian squaws with their pots and baskets and beads spread out on the brick platform. Beyond stood a row of buckboards, the town hack, Studebaker wagons; a line of shouting tourist drivers. And all around milled the townspeople and the countryfolk come in for the mail. . . . When The Train Came In.

In twenty-five minutes to the second it was over. With a last haunting shriek, pouring sand on the rails, the train and all we knew of the World Beyond swung round the curve and vanished from sight.

There was still the Fred Harvey House. On birthdays and gala Sundays we had dinner there, playing we were travelers. At night a cup of coffee, the talk of grimy railroad men, and the rich acrid smell of coal smoke and hot cinders. The Fred Harvey Girls were perpetual attractions. Those in the dining room dressed completely in starched white; those at the lunch counter wore black blouses and black stockings. All were paragons of virtue. They lived upstairs, were up at six and were checked in at ten. The first girl I ever took to a dance was a Fred Harvey Girl. On this occasion she was allowed to remain out till eleven. The romance was short-lived. She married a fireman on the Long Run. Who could compete with such a man? The turnover in all Fred Harvey Girls was terrific, they were in such demand. Always they chose the best—engineers, firemen, brakemen, yardmen, even conductors, all railroad men who neither drank nor smoked, and received the highest and steadiest pay in town.

The Fred Harvey House! At Las Vegas, just below the mouth of our lonely cañon. At Lamy, where the train winds through the pine mountains and the piñons and the patches of bright red adobe. At Albuquerque, down past the old pueblos along the Rio Grande. At Gallup, where you race across the wide, wind-swept plateau. At Winslow, Williams, Ash Fork, Seligman. At Needles, where you cross the river. On the desert at Barstow and San Bernardino. . . . All with their long portales or patios, their great open fireplaces, and their cool clean rooms where you could lie abed at night and listen to the ceaseless prowling of the goat bucking empties along the spurs, and wait for the haunting shriek of the midnight Chief as it swept in out of immeasurable empty space. America's modern mission and only true inn, compounded at once of its rooted past and its ceaseless longing and unrest.

What strange and diverse neighborhoods there are in Pyramid City. Like those of any great city they seem like different towns: Spanish, Anglo, Indian, Mormon, even Chinatowns; foreign quarters, Old Towns, new subdivisions; industrial, agrarian, commercial, arty or merely indolent as Mayfair; yet whose citizenry are linked as closely as any others living round closer corners from one another.

Ouray, snowbound months out of the year in the high San Juans. At night starving herds of elk and deer steal down to eat the hay stacked in the square by townspeople. Lying quietly in bed you can watch their ghostly antlered shapes glide past the window in moonlight.

Gallup, marooned on the high sandy plateaus with more kinds of weather per hour than any other place I know. You can be stuck there any day by wind, rain, dust or snow. A railroad town, a coal-mining town, a center for Indian trading, and one of the toughest towns in the country, it is yet so desolate and lonely that I have heard it has the highest suicide rate in the United States. Stalled drummers, they say, just can't survive a weekend.

Yuma, on the Arizona side of the Colorado, and the old territorial fort prisons crumbling on the bluff overhanging the great bending river. The hottest town in the country. With its sign on the depot lunch room, "Free Meals Every Day the Sun Doesn't Shine."

Bisbee, built on the cliffsides of Mule Pass and Brewery Gulch. The only town of its size in the country where postmen don't deliver letters to the door; the wooden stairs are too high and steep.

Calipatria, Imperial, Brawley, huddling beneath the desert sun of the Colorado Desert in the shadow of their scraggly palms and bougainvillaea vines. The lowest towns in the country.

Such are the strange neighborhoods of our city. The coldest, hottest, highest, lowest, driest, steepest, most desolate and lonely towns in the United States. And precious few at that. What makes them also the most interesting, the most individual, and certainly for many of us, travelers and residents alike, the most loved ones we know? Quién sabe? It is not worth the shrug. But they are the odd street corners, the surveyor stakes between which Pyramid City is building up into one of the great cities of the future. Not into another megapolis, as we have known them, with their dense urban concentrations. But into a new form, with all the solidarity that modern technology implies.

But there is no need to steal Half-Pint Petey's thunder and embroider his analogy further. We can only bow to his prophetic wisdom and say devoutly of his visionary city, "I knew her when."

For in one of its immense and deserted valleys, worth much less than two bits an acre, already had begun work on the superduper waterworks that are to mushroom Pyramid City into the future.

Dorothy Johnson
1905-84

—

1953: *Indian Country*
1957: *The Hanging Tree*
1967: *Some Went West*
1977: *Buffalo Woman*
1979: *All the Buffalo Returning*
1982: *When You and I Were Young,*
Whitefish

—

D OROTHY MARIE JOHNSON *was born in Iowa, but it was Montana that held her imagination for seventy years and became both the core of her life and the essence of her fiction. Even during the two decades she spent working in Wisconsin and New York City, it was to Montana that her mind and spirit kept returning. Although Johnson occasionally wrote about other places and other people, her best works are about the people of the Big Sky country.*

Johnson was four years old when her parents moved from Iowa to Great Falls, seven when they moved again to the northern Montana town of Whitefish. Her father died two years later, leaving nine-year-old Dorothy and her mother to make a living at whatever jobs they could find. By the time she was fourteen Dorothy was a telephone operator. She graduated to newspaper reporter and eventually entered Montana State University as a premed student. Medicine seemed a likely career in which a determined young woman could rise to independence and success. Unfortunately, Johnson and medicine did not get along; she could hardly bring herself to do even experimental dissections. Realizing that story writing was her first love, she transferred to the University of Montana and majored in English.

After college, and on through the depression years, Johnson kept on writing stories, and managed to have most of them published. Nine years of her eastern residency was spent in New York City, doing staff work for the Business Education World. *Even so, her best stories always turned out to be Westerns, such as "The Man Who Shot Liberty Valance" (*Cosmopolitan Magazine, *1949). It became obvious to her that her heart lay somewhere out West, and so in 1950 she left the world of business journalism and took a reporting job back home at the* Whitefish Pilot.

There may not be many readers who recognize Dorothy Johnson's name, but her colleagues in literature have honored her with significant tributes. From the University of Montana, she received the Distinguished Service Award as well as an honorary Doctor of Letters degree. Her story "Lost Sister" won the 1956 Spur Award from the Western Writers of America as Best Western Short Story. In 1976, the WWA also gave Johnson the Golden Saddleman Award for "significant contribution to Western literature." The Cowboy Hall of Fame conferred their Wrangler Award on her for Buffalo Woman *in 1977, and in 1981 she received the Western Literature Association's Distinguished Service Award.*

Professor Barbara Meldrum has a term for Johnson's contribution to the new western myth. She calls it part of the "rugged realm" of the "wild pastoral," a genre about the reconciliations that have to take place when an ideal pastoral world is in conflict with the necessities of reality.[1] In "The Hanging Tree," for example, Elizabeth takes psychological refuge from the real world by becoming a passive recluse. But when an angry crowd threatens to hang her friend Joe Frail, she is forced to come out of her "hidden life" to save him. The white man who is captured by the Crow Indians in "A Man Called Horse" is treated like an animal by his captors. He plans to escape back to a world where life is easy and perfect, but when the opportunity comes, he finds that he cannot bring himself to abandon the Indian woman who loves him.

"The Man Who Shot Liberty Valance" is a study of a man without purpose. He uses the West as a refuge because it is an ideal place for doing nothing, a place where he can drift "from one shack town to another," with "no aim in life at all." Typical of Johnson's characters, Ransome Foster does not "develop" in the usual sense. At the beginning of the story, we learn that he dislikes being indebted to anyone, whether it is a debt of vengeance or of gratitude. By the end of the story, that trait has not changed. Foster owes Bert Barricune his life, and spends the rest of his life paying for it, but that does not change his basic character. He becomes reconciled to the demands of reality, but is not altered by them.

———

1. Barbara Howard Meldrum, "Dorothy M. Johnson's Short Fiction: The Pastoral and the Uses of History," *Western American Literature* 17 (November 1982): 214.

The Man Who Shot Liberty Valance

ERT BARRICUNE died in 1910. Not more than a dozen persons showed up for his funeral. Among them was an earnest young reporter who hoped for a human-interest story; there were legends that the old man had been something of a gunfighter in the early days. A few aging men tiptoed in, singly or in pairs, scowling and edgy, clutching their battered hats—men who had been Bert's companions at drinking or penny ante while the world passed them by. One woman came, wearing a heavy veil that concealed her face. White and yellow streaks showed in her black-dyed hair. The reporter made a mental note: Old friend from the old District. But no story there—can't mention that.

One by one they filed past the casket, looking into the still face of Bert Barricune, who had been nobody. His stubbly hair was white, and his lined face was as empty in death as his life had been. But death had added dignity.

One great spray of flowers spread behind the casket. The card read, "Senator and Mrs. Ransome Foster." There were no other flowers except, almost unnoticed, a few pale, leafless, pink and yellow blossoms scattered on the carpeted step. The reporter, squinting, finally identified them: son of a gun! Blossoms of the prickly pear. Cactus flowers. Seems suitable for the old man—flowers that grow on prairie wasteland. Well, they're free if you want to pick 'em, and Barricune's friends don't look prosperous. But how come the Senator sends a bouquet?

There was a delay, and the funeral director fidgeted a little, waiting. The reporter sat up straighter when he saw the last two mourners enter.

Senator Foster—sure, there's the crippled arm—and that must be his wife. Congress is still in session; he came all the way from Washington. Why would he bother, for an old wreck like Bert Barricune?

After the funeral was decently over, the reporter asked him. The Sena-

From Dorothy Johnson, *Indian Country* (New York: Ballantine, 1949), pp. 89–107. Copyright © 1949, 1977 by Dorothy Johnson. Reprinted by permission of McIntosh and Otis, Inc.

tor almost told the truth, but he caught himself in time. He said, "Bert Barricune was my friend for more than thirty years."

He could not give the true answer: He was my enemy; he was my conscience; he made me whatever I am.

* * *

Ransome Foster had been in the Territory for seven months when he ran into Liberty Valance. He had been afoot on the prairie for two days when he met Bert Barricune. Up to that time, Ranse Foster had been nobody in particular—a dude from the East, quietly inquisitive, moving from one shack town to another; just another tenderfoot with his own reasons for being there and no aim in life at all.

When Barricune found him on the prairie, Foster was indeed a tenderfoot. In his boots there was a warm, damp squidging where his feet had blistered, and the blisters had broken to bleed. He was bruised, sunburned, and filthy. He had been crawling, but when he saw Barricune riding toward him, he sat up. He had no horse, no saddle and, by that time, no pride.

Barricune looked down at him, not saying anything. Finally Ranse Foster asked, "Water?"

Barricune shook his head. "I don't carry none, but we can go where it is."

He stepped down from the saddle, a casual Samaritan, and with one heave pulled Foster upright.

"Git you in the saddle, can you stay there?" he inquired.

"If I can't," Foster answered through swollen lips, "shoot me."

Bert said amiably, "All right," and pulled the horse around. By twisting its ear, he held the animal quiet long enough to help the anguished stranger to the saddle. Then, on foot—and like any cowboy Bert Barricune hated walking—he led the horse five miles to the river. He let Foster lie where he fell in the cottonwood grove and brought him a hat full of water.

* * *

After that, Foster made three attempts to stand up. After the third failure, Barricune asked, grinning, "Want me to shoot you after all?"

"No," Foster answered. "There's something I want to do first."

Barricune looked at the bruises and commented, "Well, I should think so." He got on his horse and rode away. After an hour he returned with bedding and grub and asked, "Ain't you dead yet?"

The bruised and battered man opened his uninjured eye and said, "Not yet, but soon." Bert was amused. He brought a bucket of water and set up camp—a bedroll on a tarp, an armload of wood for a fire. He crouched on his heels while the tenderfoot, with cautious movements that told of pain, got his clothes off and splashed water on his body. No gunshot wounds, Barricune observed, but marks of kicks, and a couple that must have been made with a quirt.

After a while he asked, not inquisitively, but as one who has a right to know how matters stood, "Anybody looking for you?"

Foster rubbed dust from his clothes, being too full of pain to shake them.

"No," he said. "But I'm looking for somebody."

"I ain't going to help you look," Bert informed him. "Town's over that way, two miles, when you get ready to come. Cache the stuff when you leave. I'll pick it up."

Three days later they met in the town marshal's office. They glanced at each other but did not speak. This time it was Bert Barricune who was bruised, though not much. The marshal was just letting him out of the one-cell jail when Foster limped into the office. Nobody said anything until Barricune, blinking and walking not quite steadily, had left. Foster saw him stop in front of the next building to speak to a girl. They walked away together, and it looked as if the young man were being scolded.

The marshal cleared his throat. "You wanted something, Mister?"

Foster answered, "Three men set me afoot on the prairie. Is that an offense against the law around here?"

The marshal eased himself and his stomach into a chair and frowned judiciously. "It ain't customary," he admitted. "Who was they?"

"The boss was a big man with black hair, dark eyes, and two gold teeth in front. The other two—"

"I know. Liberty Valance and a couple of his boys. Just what's your complaint, now?" Foster began to understand that no help was going to come from the marshal.

"They rob you?" the marshal asked.

"They didn't search me."

"Take your gun?"

"I didn't have one."

"Steal your horse?"

"Gave him a crack with a quirt, and he left."

"Saddle on him?"

"No. I left it out there."

The marshal shook his head. "Can't see you got any legal complaint," he said with relief. "Where was this?"

"On a road in the woods, by a creek. Two days' walk from here."

The marshal got to his feet. "You don't even know what jurisdiction it was in. They knocked you around; well, that could happen. Man gets in a fight—could happen to anybody."

Foster said dryly, "Thanks a lot."

The marshal stopped him as he reached the door. "There's a reward for Liberty Valance."

"I still haven't got a gun," Foster said. "Does he come here often?"

"Nope. Nothing he'd want in Twotrees. Hard man to find." The marshal looked Foster up and down. "He won't come after you here." It was as if he had added, *Sonny!* "Beat you up once, he won't come again for that."

And I, Foster realized, am not man enough to go after him.

"Fact is," the marshal added, "I can't think of any bait that would bring him in. Pretty quiet here. Yes sir." He put his thumbs in his galluses and looked out the window, taking credit for the quietness.

Bait, Foster thought. He went out thinking about it. For the first time in a couple of years he had an ambition—not a laudable one, but something to aim at. He was going to be the bait for Liberty Valance and, as far as he could be, the trap as well.

At the Elite Cafe he stood meekly in the doorway, hat in hand, like a man who expects and deserves to be refused anything he might ask for. Clearing his throat, he asked, "Could I work for a meal?"

The girl who was filling sugar bowls looked up and pitied him. "Why, I should think so. Mr. Anderson!" She was the girl who had walked away with Barricune, scolding him.

The proprietor came from the kitchen, and Ranse Foster repeated his question, cringing, but with a suggestion of a sneer.

"Go around back and split some wood," Anderson answered, turning back to the kitchen.

"He could just as well eat first," the waitress suggested. "I'll dish up some stew to begin with."

Ranse ate fast, as if he expected the plate to be snatched away. He knew the girl glanced at him several times, and he hated her for it. He had not counted on anyone's pitying him in his new role of sneering humility, but he knew he might as well get used to it.

When she brought his pie, she said, "If you was looking for a job . . ."

He forced himself to look at her suspiciously. "Yes?"

"You could try the Prairie Belle. I heard they needed a swamper."

Bert Barricune, riding out to the river camp for his bedroll, hardly knew the man he met there. Ranse Foster was haughty, condescending, and cringing all at once. He spoke with a faint sneer, and stood as if he expected to be kicked.

"I assumed you'd be back for your belongings," he said. "I realized that you would change your mind."

Barricune, strapping up his bedroll, looked blank. "Never changed it," he disagreed. "Doing just what I planned. I never give you my bedroll."

"Of course not, of course not," the new Ranse Foster agreed with sneering humility. "It's yours. You have every right to reclaim it."

Barricune looked at him narrowly and hoisted the bedroll to sling it up behind his saddle. "I should have left you for the buzzards," he remarked.

Foster agreed, with a smile that should have got him a fist in the teeth. "Thank you, my friend," he said with no gratitude. "Thank you for all your kindness, which I have done nothing to deserve and shall do nothing to repay."

Barricune rode off, scowling, with the memory of his good deed irritating him like lice. The new Foster followed, far behind, on foot.

Sometimes in later life Ranse Foster thought of the several men he had been through the years. He did not admire any of them very much. He was by no means ashamed of the man he finally became, except that he owed too much to other people. One man he had been when he was young, a serious student, gullible and quick-tempered. Another man had been reckless and without an aim; he went West, with two thousand dollars of his own, after a quarrel with the executor of his father's estate. That man did not last long. Liberty Valance had whipped him with a quirt and kicked him into unconsciousness, for no reason except that Liberty, meeting him and knowing him for a tenderfoot, was able to do so. That man died on the prairie. After that, there was the man who set out to be the bait that would bring Liberty Valance into Twotrees.

Ranse Foster had never hated anyone before he met Liberty Valance, but Liberty was not the last man he learned to hate. He hated the man he himself had been while he waited to meet Liberty again.

The swamper's job at the Prairie Belle was not disgraceful until Ranse Foster made it so. When he swept floors, he was so obviously contemptuous of the work and of himself for doing it that other men saw him as contemptible. He watched the customers with a curled lip as if they were beneath him. But when a poker player threw a white chip on the floor, the swamper looked at him with half-veiled hatred—and picked up the chip. They talked about him at the Prairie Belle, because he could not be ignored.

At the end of the first month, he bought a Colt .45 from a drunken cowboy who needed money worse than he needed two guns. After that, Ranse went without part of his sleep in order to walk out, seven mornings a week, to where his first camp had been and practice target shooting. And the second time he overslept from exhaustion, Joe Mosten of the Prairie Belle fired him.

"Here's your pay," Joe growled, and dropped the money on the floor.

A week passed before he got another job. He ate his meals frugally in the Elite Cafe and let himself be seen stealing scraps off plates that other diners had left. Lillian, the older of the two waitresses, yelled her disgust, but Hallie, who was young, pitied him.

"Come to the back door when it's dark," she murmured, "and I'll give you a bite. There's plenty to spare."

The second evening he went to the back door, Bert Barricune was there ahead of him. He said gently, "Hallie is my girl."

"No offense intended," Foster answered. "The young lady offered me food, and I have come to get it."

"A dog eats where it can," young Barricune drawled.

Ranse's muscles tensed and rage mounted in his throat, but he caught himself in time and shrugged. Bert said something then that scared him: "If you wanted to get talked about, it's working fine. They're talking clean over in Dunbar."

"What they do or say in Dunbar," Foster answered, "is nothing to me."

"It's where Liberty Valance hangs out," the other man said casually. "In case you care."

Ranse almost confided then, but instead said stiffly, "I do not quite appreciate your strange interest in my affairs."

Barricune pushed back his hat and scratched his head. "I don't understand it myself. But leave my girl alone."

"As charming as Miss Hallie may be," Ranse told him, "I am interested only in keeping my stomach filled."

"Then why don't you work for a living? The clerk at Dowitts' quit this afternoon."

Jake Dowitt hired him as a clerk because nobody else wanted the job.

"Read and write, do you?" Dowitt asked. "Work with figures?"

Foster drew himself up. "Sir, whatever may be said against me, I believe I may lay claim to being a scholar. That much I claim, if nothing more. I have read law."

"Maybe the job ain't good enough for you," Dowitt suggested.

Foster became humble again. "Any job is good enough for me. I will also sweep the floor."

"You will also keep up the fire in the stove," Dowitt told him. "Seven in the morning till nine at night. Got a place to live?"

"I sleep in the livery stable in return for keeping it shoveled out."

Dowitt had intended to house his clerk in a small room over the store, but he changed his mind. "Got a shed out back you can bunk in," he offered, "You'll have to clean it out first. Used to keep chickens there."

"There is one thing," Foster said. "I want two half-days off a week."

Dowitt looked over the top of his spectacles. "Now what would you do with time off? Never mind. You can have it—for less pay. I give you a discount on what you buy in the store."

The only purchase Foster made consisted of four boxes of cartridges a week.

In the store, he weighed salt pork as if it were low stuff but himself still lower, humbly measured lengths of dress goods for the women customers. He added vanity to his other unpleasantnesses and let customers discover him combing his hair admiringly before a small mirror. He let himself be seen reading a small black book, which aroused curiosity.

It was while he worked at the store that he started Twotrees' first school. Hallie was responsible for that. Handing him a plate heaped higher than other customers got at the café, she said gently, "You're a learned man, they say, Mr. Foster."

With Hallie he could no longer sneer or pretend humility, for Hallie was herself humble, as well as gentle and kind. He protected himself from her by not speaking unless he had to.

He answered, "I have had advantages, Miss Hallie, before fate brought me here."

"That book you read," she asked wistfully, "what's it about?"

"It was written by a man named Plato," Ranse told her stiffly. "It was written in Greek."

She brought him a cup of coffee, hesitated for a moment, and then asked, "You can read and write American, too, can't you?"

"English, Miss Hallie," he corrected. "English is our mother tongue. I am quite familiar with English."

She put her red hands on the café counter. "Mr. Foster," she whispered, "will you teach me to read?"

He was too startled to think of an answer she could not defeat.

"Bert wouldn't like it," he said. "You're a grown woman besides. It wouldn't look right for you to be learning to read now."

She shook her head. "I can't learn any younger." She sighed. "I always wanted to know how to read and write." She walked away toward the kitchen, and Ranse Foster was struck with an emotion he knew he could not afford. He was swept with pity. He called her back.

"Miss Hallie. Not you alone—people would talk about you. But if you brought Bert—"

"Bert can already read some. He don't care about it. But there's some kids in town." Her face was so lighted that Ranse looked away.

He still tried to escape. "Won't you be ashamed, learning with children?"

"Why, I'll be proud to learn any way at all," she said.

He had three little girls, two restless little boys, and Hallie in Twotrees' first school sessions—one hour each afternoon, in Dowitt's storeroom. Dowitt did not dock his pay for the time spent, but he puzzled a great deal. So did the children's parents. The children themselves were puzzled at some of the things he read aloud, but they were patient. After all, lessons lasted only an hour.

"When you are older, you will understand this," he promised, not looking at Hallie, and then he read Shakespeare's sonnet that begins:

> No longer mourn for me when I am dead
> Than you shall hear the surly sullen bell

and ends:

> Do not so much as my poor name rehearse,
> But let your love even with my life decay,
>   Lest the wise world should look into your moan
>   And mock you with me after I am gone.

Hallie understood the warning, he knew. He read another sonnet, too:

> When in disgrace with Fortune and men's eyes,
> I all alone beweep my outcast state,

and carefully did not look up at her as he finished it:

> For thy sweet love rememb'red such wealth brings
> That then I scorn to change my state with kings.

Her earnestness in learning was distasteful to him—the anxious way she grasped a pencil and formed letters, the little gasp with which she always began to read aloud. Twice he made her cry, but she never missed a lesson.

* * *

He wished he had a teacher for his own learning, but he could not trust anyone, and so he did his lessons alone. Bert Barricune caught him at it on one of those free afternoons when Foster, on a horse from the livery stable, had ridden miles out of town to a secluded spot.

Ranse Foster had an empty gun in his hand when Barricune stepped out from behind a sandstone column and remarked, "I've seen better."

Foster whirled, and Barricune added, "I could have been somebody else—and your gun's empty."

"When I see somebody else, it won't be," Foster promised.

"If you'd asked me," Barricune mused, "I could've helped you. But you didn't want no helping. A man shouldn't be ashamed to ask somebody that knows better than him." His gun was suddenly in his hand, and five shots cracked their echoes around the skull-white sandstone pillars. Half an inch above each of five cards that Ranse had tacked to a dead tree, at the level of a man's waist, a splintered hole appeared in the wood. "Didn't want to spoil your targets," Barricune explained.

"I'm not ashamed to ask you," Foster told him angrily, "since you know so much. I shoot straight but slow. I'm asking you now."

Barricune, reloading his gun, shook his head. "It's kind of late for that. I come out to tell you that Liberty Valance is in town. He's interested in the dude that anybody can kick around–this here tenderfoot that boasts how he can read Greek."

"Well," said Foster softly. "Well, so the time has come."

"Don't figure you're riding into town with me," Bert warned. "You're coming all by yourself."

Ranse rode into town with his gun belt buckled on. Always before, he had carried it wrapped in a slicker. In town, he allowed himself the luxury of one last vanity. He went to the barbershop, neither sneering nor cringing, and said sharply, "Cut my hair. Short."

The barber was nervous, but he worked understandably fast.

"Thought you was partial to that long wavy hair of yourn," he remarked.

"I don't know why you thought so," Foster said coldly.

Out in the street again, he realized that he did not know how to go about the job. He did not know where Liberty Valance was, and he was determined not to be caught like a rat. He intended to look for Liberty.

Joe Mosten's right-hand man was lounging at the door of the Prairie Bell. He moved over to bar the way.

"Not in there, Foster," he said gently. It was the first time in months that Ranse Foster had heard another man address him respectfully. His presence was recognized—as a menace to the fixtures of the Prairie Belle.

When I die, sometime today, he thought, they won't say I was a coward. They may say I was a damn fool, but I won't care by that time.

"Where is he?" Ranse asked.

"I couldn't tell you that," the man said apologetically. "I'm young and healthy, and where he is is none of my business. Joe'd be obliged if you stay out of the bar, that's all."

Ranse looked across toward Dowitt's store. The padlock was on the door. He glanced north, toward the marshal's office.

"That's closed, too," the saloon man told him courteously. "Marshal was called out of town an hour ago."

Ranse threw back his head and laughed. The sound echoed back from the false-fronted buildings across the street. There was nobody walking in the street; there were not even any horses tied to the hitching racks.

"Send Liberty word," he ordered in the tone of one who has a right to command. "Tell him the tenderfoot wants to see him again."

The saloon man cleared his throat. "Guess it won't be necessary. That's him coming down at the end of the street, wouldn't you say?"

Ranse looked, knowing the saloon man was watching him curiously.

"I'd say it is," he agreed. "Yes, I'd say that was Liberty Valance."

"I'll be going inside now," the other man remarked apologetically. "Well, take care of yourself." He was gone without a sound.

This is the classic situation, Ranse realized. Two enemies walking to meet each other along the dusty, waiting street of a western town. What reasons other men have had, I will never know. There are so many things I have never learned! And now there is no time left.

He was an actor who knew the end of the scene but had forgotten the lines and never knew the cue for them. One of us ought to say something, he realized. I should have planned this all out in advance. But all I ever saw was the end of it.

Liberty Valance, burly and broad-shouldered, walked stiff-legged, with his elbows bent.

When he is close enough for me to see whether he is smiling, Ranse Foster thought, somebody's got to speak.

He looked into his own mind and realized, This man is afraid, this Ransome Foster. But nobody else knows it. He walks and is afraid, but he is no coward. Let them remember that. Let Hallie remember that.

Liberty Valance gave the cue. "Looking for me?" he called between his teeth. He was grinning.

Ranse was almost grateful to him; it was as if Liberty had said, The time is now!

"I owe you something," Ranse answered. "I want to pay my debt."

Liberty's hand flashed with his own. The gun in Foster's hand exploded, and so did the whole world.

Two shots to my one, he thought—his last thought for a while.

He looked up at a strange, unsteady ceiling and a face that wavered like a reflection in water. The bed beneath him swung even after he closed his eyes. Far away someone said, "Shove some more cloth in the wound. It slows the bleeding."

He knew with certain agony where the wound was—in his right shoulder. When they touched it, he heard himself cry out.

The face that wavered above him was a new one. Bert Barricune's.

"He's dead," Barricune said.

Foster answered from far away, "I am not."

Barricune said, "I didn't mean you."

Ranse turned his head away from the pain, and the face that had shivered above him before was Hallie's, white and big-eyed. She put a hesitant hand on his, and he was annoyed to see that hers was trembling.

"Are you shaking," he asked, "because there's blood on my hands?"

"No," she answered. "It's because they might have been getting cold."

He was aware then that other people were in the room; they stirred and moved aside as the doctor entered.

"Maybe you're gonna keep that arm," the doctor told him at last. "But it's never gonna be much use to you."

The trial was held three weeks after the shooting, in the hotel room where Ranse lay in bed. The charge was disturbing the peace; he pleaded guilty and was fined ten dollars.

When the others had gone, he told Bert Barricune, "There was a reward, I heard. That would pay the doctor and the hotel."

"You ain't going to collect it," Bert informed him. "It'd make you too big for your britches." Barricune sat looking at him for a moment and then remarked, "You didn't kill Liberty."

Foster frowned. "They buried him."

"Liberty fired once. You fired once and missed. I fired once, and I don't generally miss. I ain't going to collect the reward, neither. Hallie don't hold with violence."

Foster said thoughtfully, "That was all I had to be proud of."

"You faced him," Barricune said. "You went to meet him. If you got to be proud of something, you can remember that. It's a fact you ain't got much else."

Ranse looked at him with narrowed eyes. "Bert, are you a friend of mine?"

Bert smiled without humor. "You know I ain't. I picked you up off the prairie, but I'd do that for the lowest scum that crawls. I wisht I hadn't."

"Then why—"

Bert looked at the toe of his boot. "Hallie likes you. I'm a friend of Hallie's. That's all I ever will be, long as you're around."

Ranse said, "Then I shot Liberty Valance." That was the nearest he ever dared come to saying "Thank you." And that was when Bert Barricune started being his conscience, his Nemesis, his lifelong enemy and the man who made him great.

"Would she be happy living back East?" Foster asked. "There's money waiting for me there if I go back."

Bert answered, "What do you think?" He stood up and stretched. "You got quite a problem, ain't you? You could solve it easy by just going back alone. There ain't much a man can do here with a crippled arm."

He went out and shut the door behind him.

There is always a way out, Foster thought, if a man wants to take it. Bert had been his way out when he met Liberty on the street of Twotrees. To go home was the way out of this.

I learned to live without pride, he told himself. I could learn to forget about Hallie.

When she came, between the dinner dishes and setting the tables for supper at the café, he told her.

She did not cry. Sitting in the chair beside his bed, she winced and jerked one hand in protest when he said, "As soon as I can travel, I'll be going back where I came from."

She did not argue. She said only, "I wish you good luck, Ransome. Bert and me, we'll look after you long as you stay. And remember you after you're gone."

"How will you remember me?" he demanded harshly.

As his student she had been humble, but as a woman she had her pride. "Don't ask that," she said, and got up from the chair.

"Hallie, Hallie," he pleaded, "how can I stay? How can I earn a living?"

She said indignantly, as if someone else had insulted him, "Ranse Foster, I just guess you could do anything you wanted to."

"Hallie," he said gently, "sit down."

He never really wanted to be outstanding. He had two aims in life: to make Hallie happy and to keep Bert Barricune out of trouble. He defended Bert on charges ranging from drunkenness to stealing cattle, and Bert served time twice.

Ranse Foster did not want to run for judge, but Bert remarked, "I think Hallie would kind of like it if you was His Honor." Hallie was pleased but not surprised when he was elected. Ranse was surprised but not pleased.

He was not eager to run for the legislature—that was after the territory became a state—but there was Bert Barricune in the background, never urging, never advising, but watching with half-closed, bloodshot eyes. Bert

Barricune, who never amounted to anything, but never intruded, was a living, silent reminder of three debts: a hat full of water under the cotton-woods, gunfire in a dusty street, and Hallie, quietly sewing beside a lamp in the parlor. And the Fosters had four sons.

All the things the opposition said about Ranse Foster when he ran for the state legislature were true, except one. He had been a lowly swamper in a frontier saloon; he had been a dead beat, accepting handouts at the alley entrance of a café; he had been despicable and despised. But the accusation that lost him the election was false. He had not killed Liberty Valance. He never served in the state legislature.

When there was talk of his running for governor, he refused. Handy Strong, who knew politics, tried to persuade him.

"That shooting, we'll get around that. 'The Honorable Ransome Foster walked down a street in broad daylight to meet an enemy of society. He shot him down in a fair fight, of necessity, the way you'd shoot a mad dog—but Liberty Valance could shoot back, and he did. Ranse Foster carries the mark of that encounter today in a crippled right arm. He is still paying the price for protecting law-abiding citizens. And he was the first teacher west of Rosy Buttes. He served without pay.' You've come a long way, Ranse, and you're going further."

"A long way," Foster agreed, "for a man who never wanted to go any-where. I don't want to be governor."

When Handy had gone, Bert Barricune sagged in, unwashed, unshaven. He sat down stiffly. At the age of fifty, he was an old man, an unwanted relic of the frontier that was gone, a legacy to more civilized times that had no place for him. He filled his pipe deliberately. After a while he remarked. "The other side is gonna say you ain't fitten to be governor. Because your wife aint fancy enough. They're gonna say Hallie didn't even learn to read till she was growed up."

Ranse was on his feet, white with fury. "Then I'm going to win this election if it kills me."

"I don't reckon it'll kill you," Bert drawled. "Liberty Valance couldn't."

"I could have got rid of the weight of that affair long ago," Ranse reminded him, "by telling the truth."

"You could yet," Bert answered. "Why don't you?"

Ranse said bitterly, "Because I owe you too much. . . . I don't think Hallie wants to be the governor's lady. She's shy."

"Hallie don't never want nothing for herself. She wants things for you. The way I feel, I wouldn't mourn at your funeral. But what Hallie wants, I'm gonna try to see she gets."

"So am I," Ranse promised grimly.

"Then I don't mind telling you," Bert admitted, "that it was me reminded the opposition to dig up that matter of how she couldn't read."

As the Senator and his wife rode out to the airport after old Bert Barricune's barren funeral, Hallie sighed. "Bert never had much of anything. I guess he never wanted much."

He wanted you to be happy, Ranse Foster thought, and he did the best he knew how.

"I wonder where those prickly-pear blossoms came from," he mused.

Hallie glanced up at him, smiling. "From me," she said.

Henry Nash Smith

1906-86

▬

1950: *Virgin Land: The American West
as Symbol and Myth*
1962: *Mark Twain: The Development
of a Writer*
1964: *Mark Twain's Fable of Progress*
1978: *Democracy and the Novel:
Popular Resistance to
Classic American Writers*

▬

H ENRY NASH SMITH *was one of the West's leading interpreters
and one of western literature's most influential critics. Analyzing
America's nineteenth- and twentieth-century intellectual evolution,
Smith took a fresh look at the frontier phenomenon. The frontier, or "virgin
land," he concluded, had exerted a powerful influence over this nation's beliefs and
attitudes.*

*Smith was a native of the West and a Harvard Ph.D. He was born in Dallas
and began his college teaching at Southern Methodist University. Smith later
taught at the University of Texas, the University of Minnesota, and ultimately at
the University of California, Berkeley, where he retired in* 1974. *He was a highly
respected scholar, particularly as the writer of* Virgin Land *and as a leading
authority on Mark Twain. He was also one of the more influential (and controversial) editors of the* Southwest Review *and helped to establish the* American
Quarterly.

*In "The Myth of the Garden and Turner's Frontier Hypothesis," Smith ex-
plored—from the humanist standpoint—one of the central documents of American history. He did not set out to prove that Turner was right, or that he was
wrong. Instead, Smith examined the myth that lay* behind *Turner's hypothe-*

sis. That myth made two basic assumptions. The first assumption was that the "empty" West was to be a new garden for America, a kind of promised land for the people. The second assumption was that a society of farmers, living in democratic freedom, would be the ideal form of civilization for this new land. Such democracy, according to Turner, comes about because of the existence of free land; it grows stronger as the agricultural settlements conquer the wilderness, moving the line of civilization westward. The frontier *is any place where democracy and civilization confront primitive living conditions and savagery.*

Smith demonstrated that Turner did not use history or economics as the basis of his argument; Turner's terminology, Smith maintained, is actually the language of myth. Furthermore, Turner's theories about democracy and the frontier lead toward philosophical dilemmas. For example, if free land promotes democracy, what happens to democracy after the land is closed? And if the ideal society consists of farmers living on their own land, what becomes of the idea that a civilized society is always evolving and progressing? Will society civilize the frontier to a certain point, at which all change and progress will halt? In Smith's words, "As we have had occasion to observe in studying the literary interpretation of the agricultural West, the theory of social progress through a uniform series of stages was poor equipment for any observer who wished to understand Western farmers."

Smith issues a clear challenge to writers who interpret the meaning of the West and who create new western myths: they must find a "new intellectual system" that is not based on the "paired but contradictory ideas of nature and civilization." To some, the debate over the validity of Turner's thesis may seem to be only a regional or an academic question. But according to Smith, the argument "concerns the image of themselves which many—perhaps most—Americans of the present day cherish, an image that defines what Americans think of their past, and therefore what they propose to make of themselves in the future." [1]

―――

1. Henry Nash Smith, *Virgin Land: The American West as Symbol and Myth* (Cambridge, Mass.: Harvard University Press, 1950), p. 4.

The Myth of the Garden and Turner's Frontier Hypothesis

B Y FAR the most influential piece of writing about the West produced during the nineteenth century was the essay on "The Significance of the Frontier in American History" read by Frederick Jackson Turner before the American Historical Association at Chicago in 1893.
The "frontier hypothesis" which he advanced on that occasion revolution-
ized American historiography and eventually made itself felt in economics
and sociology, in literary criticism, and even in politics.[2]

Turner's central contention was that "the existence of an area of free land,
its continuous recession, and the advance of American settlement westward
explain American development."[3] This proposition does not sound novel
now because it has been worked into the very fabric of our conception of
our history, but in 1893 it was a polemic directed against the two dominant
schools of historians: the group interpreting American history in terms of
the slavery controversy, led by Hermann Edouard von Holst, and the group
headed by Turner's former teacher, Herbert B. Adams of Johns Hopkins,

From Henry Nash Smith, *Virgin Land: The American West as Symbol and Myth* (Cambridge, Mass.: Harvard University Press, 1950), pp. 250–60. Copyright © 1950 by the
President and Fellows of Harvard College; © 1978 by Henry Nash Smith. Reprinted by
permission of Harvard University Press.

2. *References on the Significance of the Frontier in American History*, compiled by Everett
E. Edwards (United States Department of Agriculture Library, Bibliographical Contributions, No. 25, 2nd ed. [April, 1939]. Mimeographed), lists 124 items bearing on the
subject, ranging in date from Franklin's "Observations on the Peopling of Countries"
(1751) to 1939. A passage from a radio address by Franklin D. Roosevelt in 1935 which
Dr. Edwards quotes in his excellent Introduction illustrates the political application of
Turner's ideas: "Today we can no longer escape into virgin territory. We must master
our environment. . . . We have been compelled by stark necessity to unlearn the too
comfortable superstition that the American soil was mystically blessed with every kind of
immunity to grave economic maladjustments . . ." (p. 3). [Smith's note]

3. "The Significance of the Frontier in American History," in *The Early Writings of
Frederick Jackson Turner, with a List of All His Works Compiled by Everett E. Edwards and an
Introduction by Fulmer Mood* (Madison, Wisconsin, 1938), p. 186. [Smith's note]

who explained American institutions as the outgrowth of English, or rather ancient Teutonic germs planted in the New World. Turner maintained that the West, not the proslavery South or the antislavery North, was the most important among American sections, and that the novel attitudes and institutions produced by the frontier, especially through its encouragement of democracy, had been more significant than the imported European heritage in shaping American society.

To determine whether Turner's hypothesis is or is not a valid interpretation of American history forms no part of the intention of this book.[4] The problem here is to place his main ideas in the intellectual tradition that has been examined in earlier chapters. Whatever the merits or demerits of the frontier hypothesis in explaining actual events, the hypothesis itself developed out of the myth of the garden. Its insistence on the importance of the West, its affirmation of democracy, and its doctrine of geographical determinism derive from a still broader tradition of Western thought that would include Benton and Gilpin as well, but its emphasis on agricultural settlement places it clearly within the stream of agrarian theory that flows from eighteenth-century England and France through Jefferson to the men who elaborated the ideal of a society of yeoman farmers in the Northwest from which Turner sprang. Turner's immersion in this stream of intellectual influence had an unfortunate effect in committing him to certain archaic assumptions which hampered his approach to twentieth-century social problems. But one must not forget that the tradition was richer than these assumptions, and that it conferred on him the authority of one who speaks from the distilled experience of his people.[5] If the myth

4. A growing body of scholarship is being devoted to this challenging question. George W. Pierson has called attention to inconsistencies in Turner's doctrines and has inquired into the extent of their currency among historians at the present time: "The Frontier and Frontiersman of Turner's Essays: A Scrutiny of the Foundations of the Middle Western Tradition," *Pennsylvania Magazine of History and Biography*, LXIV, 449–478 (October, 1940); "The Frontier and American Institutions: A Criticism of the Turner Theory," *New England Quarterly*, XV, 224–255 (June, 1942); "American Historians and the Frontier Hypothesis in 1941," *Wisconsin Magazine of History*, XXVI, 36–60, 170–185 (September, December, 1942). I am indebted to Professor Pierson for many ideas, especially the remark he quotes from a colleague to the effect that Turner's frontiersman closely resembles the stock eighteenth-century picture of the small farmer of Britain (*Wisconsin Magazine of History*, XXVI, 183–184) and the suggestion that Turner's "poetic interpretations" revived "the grandest ideas that had gone to make up the American legend" (*idem*). [Smith's note]

5. James C. Malin points out that most of Turner's ideas were "in the air." He remarks that great thinkers are normally "the beneficiaries of the folk process and are probably seldom so much true creators as channels through which the folk process finds its fullest

of the garden embodied certain erroneous judgments made by these people concerning the economic forces that had come to dominate American life, it was still true to their experience in the large, because it expressed beliefs and aspirations as well as statistics. This is not the only kind of historical truth, but it is a kind historians need never find contemptible.

Turner's most important debt to his intellectual tradition is the ideas of savagery and civilization that he uses to define his central factor, the frontier. His frontier is explictly "the meeting point between savagery and civilization."[6] For him as for his predecessors, the outer limit of agricultural settlement is the boundary of civilization, and in his thought as in that of so many earlier interpreters we must therefore begin by distinguishing two Wests, one beyond and one within this all-important line.

From the standpoint of economic theory the wilderness beyond the frontier, the realm of savagery, is a constantly receding area of free land. Mr. Fulmer Mood has demonstrated that Turner derived this technical expression from a treatise on economics by Francis A. Walker used as a text by one of his teachers at Johns Hopkins, Richard T. Ely. In Walker's analysis Turner found warrant for his belief that free land had operated as a safety valve for the East and even for Europe by offering every man an opportunity to acquire a farm and become an independent member of society. Free land thus tended to relieve poverty outside the West, and on the frontier itself it fostered economic equality. Both these tendencies made for an increase of democracy.[7] Earlier writers from the time of Franklin had noted that the West offered freedom and subsistence to all,[8] but Turner restated the idea in a more positive form suggested by his conviction that democracy, the rise of the common man, was one of the great movements of modern history.

In an oration delivered in 1883 when he was still an undergraduate he

---

expression in explicit language . . ." ("Space and History: Reflections on the Closed-Space Doctrines of Turner and Mackinder and the Challenge of Those Ideas by the Air Age," *Agricultural History*, XVIII, 67–68, April, 1944). [Smith's note]

6. *Early Writings*, p. 187. [Smith's note]

7. Fulmer Mood, "The Development of Frederick Jackson Turner as a Historical Thinker," *Publications of the Colonial Society of Massachusetts*, XXXIV: *Transactions 1937–1942* (Boston, 1943), pp. 322–325. [Smith's note]

8. Turner copied into a Commonplace Book that he kept in 1886, during his first year of teaching, a quotation ascribed to Franklin: "The boundless woods of America which are sure to afford freedom and subsistence to any man who can bait a hook or pull a trigger" (Commonplace Book [II], p. [1]. Turner Papers, Henry E. Huntington Library). The idea occurs often in Franklin but I have not been able to find these words. [Smith's note]

had declared: "Over all the world we hear mankind proclaiming its existence, demanding its rights. Kings begin to be but names, and the sons
of genius, springing from the people, grasp the real sceptres. The reign of
aristocracy is passing; that of humanity begins."[9] Although "humanity" is
a broad term, for Turner it referred specifically to farmers. He conceived
of democracy as a trait of agricultural communities. About this time, for
example, he wrote in his Commonplace Book that historians had long occupied themselves with "noble warriors, & all the pomp and glory of the
higher class—But of the other phase, of the common people, the lowly
tillers of the soil, the great mass of humanity . . . history has hitherto said but
little." And he fully accepted the theory of small landholdings that underlay
the cult of the yeoman. He planned to develop the idea in an "Oration on
Peasant Proprietors in U. S." (by which he meant small farmers tilling their
own land).

> . . . the work of the Cobden Club on Land Tenure [he wrote] giving
> the systems of the various countries the paper on America—opens by
> showing how uninteresting is the subject being as it is purely peasant
> proprietorship—In this simplicity of our land system lies one of the
> greatest factors in our progress. Enlarge on the various systems &
> show the value of it here—point out the fact that if our lands in the
> west had not been opened to & filled with foreign emigrant it is not
> unlikely that they would have fallen into the hands of capitalists &
> hav been made great estates—e.g. Dalrymple farm—Show effects of
> great estates in Italy—in Eng.[10]

In systems of land tenure, he felt, lay the key to the democratic upsurge
that had reached a climax in the nineteenth century:

> It is not by Contrat Socials that a nation wins freedom & pros-
> perity for its people—; it is by attention to minor details—like this—
> it is by evolution—
> Show place of F. R. [French Revolution]—ring in Shelleys Pro-
> metheus this was an awakening but now—in our own age is the
> real revolution going on which is to raise *man* from his low estate

9. "The Poet of the Future," delivered at the Junior Exhibition, University of Wisconsin, May 25, 1883, and reported in full in the Madison *University Press* (May 26, 1883),
p. 4 (clipping in Turner Papers, Henry E. Huntington Library). [Smith's note]

10. Commonplace Book [I], 1883, pp. [25–27]. Turner Papers, Henry E. Huntington
Library. [Smith's note]

to his proper *dignity* (enlarge from previous oration)—in this grand conception it is not an anticlimax to urge the value—the essential necessity of such institutions as the peasant proprietors—a moving force, all the stronger that it works quietly in the great movement.[11]

This is the theoretical background of the proposition in the 1893 essay that "democracy [is] born of free land,"[12] as well as of the celebrated pronouncement made twenty years later: "American democracy was born of no theorist's dream; it was not carried in the Susan Constant to Virginia, nor in the Mayflower to Plymouth. It came stark and strong and full of life out of the American forest, and it gained new strength each time it touched a new frontier."[13]

But while economic theory still underlies this later statement, the change of terminology has introduced new and rich overtones. We have been transferred from the plane of the economist's abstractions to a plane of metaphor, and even of myth—for the American forest has become almost an enchanted wood, and the image of Antaeus has been invoked to suggest the power of the Western earth. Such intimations reach beyond logical theory. They remind us that the wilderness beyond the limits of civilization was not only an area of free land; it was also nature. The idea of nature suggested to Turner a poetic account of the influence of free land as a rebirth, a

11. *Ibid.*, pp. [49–53]. [Smith's note]

12. *Early Writings*, p. 221. [Smith's note]

13. "The West and American Ideals," an address delivered at the University of Washington, June 17, 1914, *Washington Historical Quarterly*, V, 245 (October, 1914). When Turner revised this address for inclusion in the volume of collected papers *The Frontier in American History* in 1920, he omitted the words "stark and strong and full of life" (New York, 1920, reprint ed., 1931, p. 293). Although Turner repudiated the "germ theory" of constitutional development in his 1893 essay (*Early Writings*, p. 188), he had accepted it for a time after he left Herbert B. Adams' seminar at Johns Hopkins. Reviewing the first two volumes of Theodore Roosevelt's *The Winning of the West* in the Chicago *Dial* in August of 1889 (X, 72), he remarked that "the old Germanic 'tun'" reappeared in the "forted village" of early Kentucky and Tennessee, the "folkmoot" in popular meetings of the settlers, and the "witenagemot" in representative assemblies like the Transylvania legislature. "These facts," he added, "carry the mind back to the warrior-legislatures in the Germanic forests, and forward to those constitutional conventions now at work in our own newly-made states in the Far West; and they make us proud of our English heritage." In an undergraduate address he had asserted that "The spirit of individual liberty slumbered in the depths of the German forest" from the time of the barbarian invasions of Rome until it burst forth in the American and French Revolutions (Madison *University Press* [May 26, 1883], p. 4). Turner's discovery of the American frontier as a force encouraging democracy may exhibit some imaginative persistence of this association between desirable political institutions and a forest. [Smith's note]

regeneration, a rejuvenation of man and society constantly recurring where civilization came into contact with the wilderness along the frontier.[14]

Rebirth and regeneration are categories of myth rather than of economic analysis, but ordinarily Turner kept his metaphors under control and used them to illustrate and vivify his logical propositions rather than as a structural principle or a means of cognition: that is, he used them rhetorically not poetically. The nonpoetic use of a vivid metaphor is illustrated in a speech he delivered in 1896:

> Americans had a safety valve for social danger, a bank account on which they might continually draw to meet losses. This was the vast unoccupied domain that stretched from the borders of the settled area to the Pacific Ocean. . . . No grave social problem could exist while the wilderness at the edge of civilizations [*sic*] opened wide its portals to all who were oppressed, to all who with strong arms and stout heart desired to hew out a home and a career for themselves. Here was an opportunity for social development continually to begin over again, wherever society gave signs of breaking into classes. Here was a magic fountain of youth in which America continually bathed and was rejuvenated.[15]

14. A characteristic phrase is the reference to "this rebirth of American society" that has gone on, decade after decade, in the West (from an essay in the *Atlantic*, 1896, reprinted in *The Frontier in American History*, p. 205). In his undergraduate Commonplace Book Turner had jotted down, among notes for an oration, "See Emerson's preface to 'Nature' . . ." and had added part of a sentence: ". . . let us believe in the eternal genesis, the freshness & value of things present, act as though, just created, we stood looking a new world in the face and investigate for ourselves and act regardless of past ideas" (Commonplace Book [I], p. [3]). This is quite Emersonian; it might well be a paraphrase of the familiar first paragraph of Emerson's essay: "Why should not we also enjoy an original relation to the universe? Embosomed for a season in nature, whose floods of life stream around and through us, and invite us, by the powers they supply, to action proportioned to nature, why should we grope among the dry bones of the past, or put the living generation into masquerade out of its faded wardrobe?" (*Complete Works*, Volume I: *Nature, Addresses, and Lectures* [Boston, 1903], p. [3]). Turner said in 1919 that he had been impressed with Woodrow Wilson's emphasis on Walter Bagehot's idea of growth through "breaking the cake of custom" (Frederick Jackson Turner to William E. Dodd, Cambridge, Mass., October 7, 1919, copy in Turner Papers, Henry E. Huntington Library). The phrase appears in the *Atlantic* essay (*The Frontier in American History*, p. 205). [Smith's note]

15. Address at the dedication of a new high school building at Turner's home town of Portage, Wisconsin, January 1, 1896, reported in the Portage *Weekly Democrat*, January 3, 1896 (clipping in Turner Papers, Henry E. Huntington Library). [Smith's note]

The figure of the magic fountain is merely a rhetorical ornament at the end of a paragraph having a rational structure and subject to criticism according to recognized canons. But sometimes, especially when the conception of nature as the source of occult powers is most vividly present, Turner's metaphors threaten to become themselves a means of cognition and to supplant discursive reasoning. This seems to happen, for example, in an essay he wrote for the *Atlantic* in 1903. After quoting a clearly animistic passage from Lowell's Harvard Commemoration Ode on how Nature had shaped Lincoln of untainted clay from the unexhausted West, "New birth of our new soil, the first American," Turner builds an elaborate figurative structure:

> Into this vast shaggy continent of ours poured the first feeble tide of European settlement. European men, institutions, and ideas were lodged in the American wilderness, and this great American West took them to her bosom, taught them a new way of looking upon the destiny of the common man, trained them in adaptation to the conditions of the New World, to the creation of new institutions to meet new needs; and ever as society on her eastern border grew to resemble the Old World in its social forms and its industry, ever, as it began to lose faith in the ideal of democracy, she opened new provinces, and dowered new democracies in her most distant domains with her material treasures and with the ennobling influence that the fierce love of freedom, the strength that came from hewing out a home, making a school and a church, and creating a higher future for his family, furnished to the pioneer.[16]

It would be difficult to maintain that all these metaphors are merely ornamental. Is it wholly meaningless, for example, that the West, the region close to nature, is feminine, while the East, with its remoteness from nature and its propensity for aping Europe, is neuter?

In the passage just quoted, a beneficent power emanating from nature is shown creating an agrarian utopia in the West. The myth of the garden is constructed before our eyes. Turner is asserting as fact a state of affairs that on other occasions he recognized as merely an ideal to be striven for. Earlier in the same essay, for example, he had summarized Jefferson's "platform of political principles" and his "conception that democracy should have an agricultural basis."[17] The "should" easily becomes "did": Jefferson's

16. *The Frontier in American History*, pp. 255, 267. [Smith's note]
17. *Ibid.*, p. 250. [Smith's note]

agrarian ideal proves to be virtually identical with the frontier democracy that Turner believed he had discovered in the West. To imagine an ideal so vividly that it comes to seem actual is to follow the specific procedure of poetry.

The other member of the pair of ideas which defined the frontier for Turner was that of civilization. If the idea of nature in the West provided him with a rich and not always manageable store of metaphorical coloring, his use of the idea of civilization had the equally important consequence of committing him to the theory that all societies, including those of successive Wests, develop through the same series of progressively higher stages. Mr. Mood has traced this conception also to Ely and to Walker, and back of them to the German economic theorist Friedrich List.[18] But, as we have had occasion to notice earlier in this study, the idea had been imported into the United States from France soon after 1800 and by the 1820's had become one of the principal instruments for interpreting the agricultural West.

Turner's acceptance of this theory involved him in the difficulties that it had created for earlier observers of frontier society, such as Timothy Flint. For the theory of social stages was basically at odds with the conception of the Western farmer as a yeoman surrounded by utopian splendor. Instead, it implied that the Western farmer was a coarse and unrefined representative of a primitive stage of social evolution. Turner's adoption of these two contradictory theories makes it difficult for him to manage the question of whether frontier character and society, and frontier influence on the rest of the country, have been good or bad. As long as he is dealing with the origins of democracy in the West he evidently considers frontier influence good. A man who refers to "the familiar struggle of West against East, of democracy against privileged classes"[19] leaves no doubt concerning his own allegiance. This attitude was in fact inevitable as long as one maintained the doctrine that frontier society was shaped by the influence of free land, for free land was nature, and nature in this system of ideas is unqualifiedly benign. Indeed, it is itself the norm of value. There is no way to conceive possible bad effects flowing from the impact of nature on man and society.

But when Turner invokes the concept of civilization, the situation be-

18. *Publications of the Colonial Society of Massachusetts*, XXXIV, 304–307. Mr. Mood says that the idea of applying the theory of evolution to social phenomena was the "fundamental, unifying concept" of Turner's early writings (p. 304), but adds that the *a priori* idea of a sequence of social stages "can be asserted to be, as a universal rule . . . fallacious . . . . It is one component element in Turner's [1893] essay that will not now stand the test of inspection" (p. 307n.). [Smith's note]

19. *The Frontier in American History*, p. 121 (1908). [Smith's note]

comes more complex. His basic conviction was that the highest social values were to be found in the relatively primitive society just within the agricultural frontier. But the theory of social stages placed the highest values at the other end of the process, in urban industrial society, amid the manufacturing development and city life which Jefferson and later agrarian theorists had considered dangerous to social purity. Turner wavered between the two views. In the 1893 essay, to take a minute but perhaps significant bit of evidence, he referred to the evolution of each successive region of the West "into a higher stage"—in accord with the orthodox theory of civilization and progress. When he revised the essay for republication in 1899, he realized that such an assumption might lead him into inconsistency and substituted "a different industrial stage."[20]

But he could not always maintain the neutrality implied in this revision. For one thing, he strongly disapproved of the Western love of currency inflation, which he considered a consequence of the primitive state of frontier society. "The colonial and Revolutionary frontier," he asserted in the 1893 essay, "was the region whence emanated many of the worst forms of an evil currency," and he pointed out that each of the periods of lax financial integrity in American history had coincided with the rise of a new set of frontier communities. The Populist agitation for free coinage of silver was a case in point.

> Many a state that now declines any connection with the tenets of the Populists [he wrote] itself adhered to such ideas in an earlier stage of the development of the state. A primitive society can hardly be expected to show the intelligent appreciation of the complexity of business interests in a developed society.[21]

In his revision of the essay in 1899 Turner noted with satisfaction that Wisconsin had borne out his principles:

> Wisconsin, to take an illustration, in the days when it lacked varied agriculture and complex industrial life, was a stronghold of the granger and greenback movements; but it has undergone an industrial transformation, and in the last presidential contest Mr. Bryan carried but one county in the state.[22]

Here the evolution of society from agrarian simplicity toward greater complexity is assumed to bring about improvement.

20. *Early Writings*, pp. 199, 285. [Smith's note]
21. *Ibid.*, p. 222. [Smith's note]
22. *Ibid.*, p. 285. [Smith's note]

Yet if Turner could affirm progress and civilization in this one respect, the general course of social evolution in the United States created a grave theoretical dilemma for him. He had based his highest value, democracy, on free land. But the westward advance of civilization across the continent had caused free land to disappear. What then was to become of democracy? The difficulty was the greater because in associating democracy with free land he had inevitably linked it also with the idea of nature as a source of spiritual values. All the overtones of his conception of democracy were therefore tinged with cultural primitivism, and tended to clash with the idea of civilization. In itself this was not necessarily a disadvantage; the conception of civilization had been invoked to justify a number of dubious undertakings in the course of the nineteenth century, including European exploitation of native peoples all over the world. Furthermore, as we have had occasion to observe in studying the literary interpretation of the agricultural West, the theory of social progress through a uniform series of stages was poor equipment for any observer who wished to understand Western farmers. But Turner had accepted the idea of civilization as a general description of the society that had been expanding across the continent, and with the final disappearance of free land this idea was the only remaining principle with which he could undertake the analysis of contemporary American society.

Since democracy for him was related to the idea of nature and seemed to have no logical relation to civilization, the conclusion implied by his system was that postfrontier American society contained no force tending toward democracy. Fourierists earlier in the century, reaching a conclusion comparable to this, had maintained that civilization was but a transitory social stage, and that humanity must transcend it by advancing into the higher stage of "association." Henry George in Turner's own day had announced that progress brought poverty, that civilization embodied a radical contradiction and could be redeemed only by a revolutionary measure, the confiscation of the unearned increment in the value of natural resources. But Turner did not share the more or less revolutionary attitude that lay back of these proposals.[23] On the contrary, he conceived of social progress as taking place within the existing framework of society, that is, within civilization. Whatever solution might be found for social problems would have to be developed according to the basic principles already accepted by society. This meant that his problem was to find a basis for democracy in

23. Frederick Jackson Turner to Merle E. Curti, San Marino, Cal., January 5, 1931. Copy in Turner Papers, Henry E. Huntington Library. Turner says he had not read George before writing the 1893 essay and that he had never accepted the single-tax idea. [Smith's note]

some aspect of civilization as he observed it about him in the United States. His determined effort in this direction showed that his mind and his standards of social ethics were subtler and broader than the conceptual system within which the frontier hypothesis had been developed, but he was the prisoner of the assumptions he had taken over from the agrarian tradition.[24] He turned to the rather unconvincing idea that the Midwestern state universities might be able to save democracy by producing trained leaders,[25] and later he placed science beside education as another force to which men might turn for aid in their modern perplexity. But these suggestions were not really satisfying to him, and he fell back at last on the faith he had confided to his Commonplace Book as an undergraduate—a faith neither in nature nor in civilization but simply in man, in the common people. In 1924, after reviewing the most urgent of the world's problems, Turner declared with eloquence and dignity:

> I prefer to believe that man is greater than the dangers that menace him; that education and science are powerful forces to change these tendencies and to produce a rational solution of the problems of life on the shrinking planet. I place my trust in the mind of man seeking solutions by intellectual toil rather than by drift and by habit, bold to find new ways of adjustment, and strong in the leadership that spreads new ideas among the common people of the world; committed to peace on earth, and ready to use the means of preserving it.[26]

This statement is an admission that the notion of democracy born of free land, colored as it is by primitivism, is not an adequate instrument for dealing with a world dominated by industry, urbanization, and international conflicts. The first World War had shaken Turner's agrarian code of values as it destroyed so many other intellectual constructions of the nineteenth century. He continued to struggle with the grievous problems of the modern world, but his original theoretical weapons were no longer useful.

24. Professor Malin has emphasized the fact that in his later career Turner was "baffled by his contemporary world and had no satisfying answer to the closed-frontier formula in which he found himself involved" (*Essays on Historiography*, Lawrence, Kansas, 1946, p. 38). [Smith's note]

25. *The Frontier in American History*, p. 285 (1910). [Smith's note]

26. "Since the Foundation," an address delivered at Clark University, February 4, 1924, *Publications of the Clark University Library*, VII, No. 3, p. 29. After the words "dangers that menace him" Turner has indicated in his personal copy in the Henry E. Huntington Library (No. 222544) the addition of the following words: "that there are automatic adjustments in progress." [Smith's note]

Turner's predicament illustrates what has happened to the tradition within which he worked. From the time of Franklin down to the end of the frontier period almost a century and a half later, the West had been a constant reminder of the importance of agriculture in American society. It had nourished an agrarian philosophy and an agrarian myth that purported to set forth the character and destinies of the nation. The philosophy and the myth affirmed an admirable set of values, but they ceased very early to be useful in interpreting American society as a whole because they offered no intellectual apparatus for taking account of the industrial revolution. A system which revolved about a half-mystical conception of nature and held up as an ideal a rudimentary type of agriculture was powerless to confront issues arising from the advance of technology. Agrarian theory encouraged men to ignore the industrial revolution altogether, or to regard it as an unfortunate and anomalous violation of the natural order of things. In the restricted but important sphere of historical scholarship, for example, the agrarian emphasis of the frontier hypothesis has tended to divert attention from the problems created by industrialization for a half century during which the United States has become the most powerful industrial nation in the world.[27] An even more significant consequence of the agrarian tradition has been its effect on politics. The covert distrust of the city and of everything connected with industry that is implicit in the myth of the garden has impeded coöperation between farmers and factory workers in more than one crisis of our history, from the time of Jefferson to the present.

The agrarian tradition has also made it difficult for Americans to think of themselves as members of a world community because it has affirmed that the destiny of this country leads her away from Europe toward the agricultural interior of the continent. This tendency is quite evident in Turner.[28] Although he devoted much attention to the diplomatic issues

27. Charles A. Beard makes this point in what seems to me a convincing manner in "The Frontier in American History," *New Republic*, XCVII, 359–362 (February 1, 1939). Professor Malin asserts vigorously that "among other things, the frontier hypothesis is an agricultural interpretation of American history which is being applied during an industrial urban age . . ." ("Mobility and History," *Agricultural History*, XVII, 177, October, 1943). [Smith's note]

28. Benjamin F. Wright has a similar comment in his review of *The Significance of Sections in American History, New England Quarterly*, VI, 631 (September, 1933). Professor Malin calls the frontier hypothesis "an isolationist interpretation in an international age" (*Agricultural History*, XVII, 177). "It seemed to confirm the Americans," he remarks elsewhere, "in their continental isolationism. Was not their United States a unique civilization; was it not superior to that of Europe and Asia?" (*ibid.*, XVIII, 67, April, 1944). [Smith's note]

arising out of westward expansion, the frontier hypothesis implied that it would be a last misfortune for American society to maintain close connections with Europe. The frontier which produced Andrew Jackson, wrote Turner with approval in 1903, was "free from the influence of European ideas and institutions. The men of the 'Western World' turned their backs upon the Atlantic Ocean, and with a grim energy and self-reliance began to build up a society free from the dominance of ancient forms."[29] It was only later, when he was trying to find a theoretical basis for democracy outside the frontier, that Turner criticized the American attitude of "contemptuous indifference" to the social legislation of European countries.[30]

But if interpretation of the West in terms of the idea of nature tended to cut the region off from the urban East and from Europe, the opposed idea of civilization had even greater disadvantages. It not only imposed on Westerners the stigma of social, ethical, and cultural inferiority, but prevented any recognition that the American adventure of settling the continent had brought about an irruption of novelty into history. For the theory of civilization implied that America in general, and the West *a fortiori*, were meaningless except in so far as they managed to reproduce the achievements of Europe. The capital difficulty of the American agrarian tradition is that it accepted the paired but contradictory ideas of nature and civilization as a general principle of historical and social interpretation. A new intellectual system was requisite before the West could be adequately dealt with in literature or its social development fully understood.

29. *The Frontier in American History*, p. 253 (1903). [Smith's note]

30. *Ibid.*, p. 294 (1914). In the 1903 article Turner had emphasized the contrast between American democracy, which was "fundamentally the outcome of the experiences of the American people in dealing with the West," and the "modern efforts of Europe to create an artificial democratic order by legislation" (*ibid.*, p. 266). The implication is clearly that American democracy is the opposite of artificial, i.e., natural, and that this natural origin establishes its superiority. [Smith's note]

Jack Schaefer

b. 1907-91

—

1949: *Shane*
1953: *The Canyon*
1959: *The Kean Land, and Other Stories*
1963: *Monte Walsh*
1967: *Mavericks*
1978: *Conversations with
a Pocket Gopher*

—

THE SUMMERS *of 1885 and 1886 in Wyoming were ominously dry; as grass became scarce, more cattle were put onto the range in an attempt to combat the falling price of beef. The fierce winter of 1886–87, still known as "the big die-up," decimated the herds, sending ranchers into bankruptcy while creating an opportunity for homesteaders. The resulting conflict between cattlemen and farmers became the background for a novel titled* Shane, *written by a Virginia newspaper editor who had never set foot west of Ohio.*

The little book was a tremendous success. It has been translated into more than two dozen languages, was made into a western film that has become a classic, and is often used as a standard for measuring other western novels.

Jack Warner Schaefer was born in Cleveland, Ohio. He became interested in creative writing and Greek and Latin literature while attending Oberlin College, and he went on to Columbia University for graduate study, intending to concentrate in eighteenth-century drama. Soon after entering Columbia, however, Schaefer had an intriguing change of interests and told the university's thesis committee that he wanted to research the development of motion pictures. The committee laughed at the idea, and that was the end of the relationship.

Schaefer held several jobs in newspaper work after that, eventually ending up in Norfolk, Virginia, where he wrote Shane. *From then on, he was a western writer, as readers of* Monte Walsh, Mavericks, The Kean Land, The Canyon, *or any of his short stories and novels can tell you. In a biography of Schaefer, Gerald Haslam concluded: "Schaefer seems to be a writer who found the West in himself, and then himself in the West. . . . he has explored Western experiences with the skill and depth of one who is a part of his own subject matter."* [1]

*Schaefer moved to New Mexico in 1955. His writing since that time has included biography (Adolphe Francis Bandelier, 1966) and western history (*The Great Endurance Horse Race, 1963, *and* Heroes without Glory, 1965*). More recently, he has turned to natural history; in* An American Bestiary *(1975) and* Conversations with a Pocket Gopher *(1978), Schaefer studied animal behavior while also offering provocative insights into human conduct.*

Hugo Kertchak, Builder

IN AMERICA, people said, there was work for anyone willing to work. A man with a trade could make his way there and freedom would be a real thing freshening the air he breathed.

Four years Hugo Kertchak saved for the passage money. He had the few coins that remained from his mother's burial fund and the small amount that had been left to him by his father. He had the smaller amount that had come to him with his wife. He had the gold piece given to him by his uncle at the birth of the first child because it was a son and would bear the uncle's name. He had these and he saved in many ways. He saved though he had work only about one week in three. He put away his pipe, out of sight and out of mind. He drank only one mug of beer and that only on Sunday and after a time none at all. He fed himself and his family on bread and potatoes and occasional green vegetables. The money that would have bought meat joined the rest in the old leather purse that had been his father's and that was kept behind a stone of the fireplace.

After four years and two months he had enough. He sold the few pieces of furniture that were his in the rented cottage. He led the way for his family. Under his left arm he carried the long narrow toolbox that had been his father's and his grandfather's. His right hand held the small hand

From Jack Schaefer, *The Collected Stories of Jack Schaefer* (Boston: Houghton Mifflin, 1966), pp. 299–317. Copyright © 1953, 1981 by Jack Schaefer. Reprinted by permission of Don Congdon Associates, Inc.

    1. Gerald Haslam, *Jack Schaefer,* Boise State University Western Writers Series, no. 20 (Boise, Idaho: Boise State University, 1975), p. 43.

of his seven-year-old son. Behind him came his wife. On her left shoulder she carried the bundle of extra clothing wrapped in a blanket with a strap around it. Her right hand held the small hand of their five-year-old daughter. They walked the nine miles to the station, where they waited for the train that took them west across Europe to the port and to the ship that took them west across the Atlantic.

Hugo Kertchak walked the streets of New York. He left his wife and children in the boardinghouse run by a man from the old country and walked the streets of the strange city. He knew fifty-three words of English, useful words learned the last days of the crossing from another steerage passenger on the ship. He could not learn them as fast as his wife, for she was quick at such things, but he was learning more each day, learning them slowly and thoroughly so that he would never lose them and so that he could pronounce them clearly, with only a small trace of accent. He walked the streets and times were hard. Even in America times could be hard. There was no work.

✳ ✳ ✳

There was plenty of work in the new lands, people said, in the new settlements westward with the afternoon sun. A country was growing and a man could grow with it, even a man already in his middle thirties.

Hugo Kertchak talked to the boardinghouse man, who could speak to him in his native tongue. He talked to a patient man at the railroad station, using the words he had learned, and had difficulty arranging in right order. He counted what was left of the money. It was enough.

Hugo Kertchak and his wife and two children rode upright on stiff railroad coach cushions west to Chicago. All one day and one night they rode. They walked across the sprawling city to the other station. They carried the toolbox and the bundle and they walked asking directions. They rode upright on other slat-backed seats west across Iowa into Nebraska. They leaned against each other and slept in snatches as the train jolted through the darkness of night. The sun rose and they sat up straighter and divided and ate the last loaf of bread and the last piece of the cheese bought in Chicago. They looked out the train windows and saw the wide miles reach and run past them. It was a new and a strange and a big country. But in the side pocket of Hugo Kertchak's jacket was a letter from the boardinghouse man addressed to a friend out in this new and strange and big country.

The train stopped at the town. Hugo Kertchak and his wife and two children stepped down into the dust of the road that was the town's one street, flanked on one side by the single line of track, on the other by a brief row of false-fronted frame buildings. The wind that blew over the wide country, tireless and unending, swirled the dust stirred up around their legs and made the children cough. The train moved on and the sun beat down and the wind blew and they were alone in the road dust. The few sparse buildings of the town seemed lost in a circling immensity. Distance stretched outward and on and beyond grasp of the eyes in every direction. They walked through the swirling dust across the road and up the two steps to the platform along the front of the building whose sign said "Store & Post Office." Hugo Kertchak set the toolbox down on the platform and went into the building.

At the rear of the store two men sat hunched on stools playing checkers on the squared-off top of a barrel. They raised their heads and looked at him. Behind a counter at the right another man leaned back in an old chair with his feet up on the counter reading a newspaper. This one lowered the paper and looked over at him like the others. Hugo Kertchak took the letter from his pocket. He went to the counter and held the letter out so that the name on it could be seen. "You know?" he said.

The man behind the counter raised his feet and set them carefully down on the floor. He folded the newspaper and laid it carefully on the counter. He leaned forward and took the letter and held it at arm's length to read the name. He handed the letter back. "Sure I know," he said. "Or aiming it a mite better I'd offer I used to know. That there particular person ain't inhabiting these parts any more."

Hugo Kertchak frowned in the effort to understand. "You say what?"

The man behind the counter smacked a hand down upon it. "I say high-tailed out of the county. Skedaddled. Vamoosed. To put it pretty, he ain't here any more. He's gone."

Hugo Kertchak understood the final words. "You say where?"

The man behind the counter shouted a question at the checker players. "Back east somewheres," one of them said. "Didn't name a place." The man behind the counter shrugged his shoulders and spread out his hands. "Reckon that's that. Anything else, stranger?"

Hugo Kertchak shook his head. He could think of nothing else, only the fact that confronted him. Slowly he turned and went out again to the front platform. He stood staring into the far reaches of distance. He tore the letter into many small pieces and let these fall fluttering around his feet. Slowly he sat down on the platform edge with his feet on the lower step and his head sank forward until it was almost between his knees. In the old leather purse in his pocket there was thirty-seven cents of the strange American money. And a woman and two children were staring at him in a stricken silence.

The tireless wind of the wide country blew upon him, hot and dry. The wind brought with it a sound, the sound of a hammer driving a nail.

Hugo Kertchak's head rose. He stood, erect on the step. He reached and took the toolbox. "Anna," he said to his wife, "here you wait."

Hugo Kertchak walked along the road through the swirling dust. The sound led him to the last building westward. Around the far side, out of sight before, a man was constructing a small shed. The framework was already up, the rafters for the flat, slightly sloping roof already in place. There was a pile of lumber on the ground with a small keg of nails beside it. The man had cut several side lengths of board and was nailing them to the corner posts. He stopped and turned to look at Hugo Kertchak. He seemed glad of an excuse to stop.

"Am carpenter," Hugo Kertchak said. That was wrong. He made the correction. "I am carpenter."

"Be damned if I am," the man said. "This beswoggled hammer has a mind of its own. Likes my thumb better'n the nails."

Hugo Kertchak was not certain what all the words meant. But here was work, the work he knew. "I show," he said. He laid down the toolbox and opened it. He took out the hammer with the new handle that he had whittled and sanded long hours on the journey until the balance was exactly right for his broad, square hand. He dropped some nails from the keg into his jacket pocket. He lifted the next side board and set it in position. He swung the hammer in smooth, steady strokes, short arcs with clean power in them. It was good to be using a good tool again. But the framework was not solid. The whole skeletal structure quivered under the strokes.

Hugo Kertchak forgot the man watching him. He was intent upon the problem before him. He walked around the framework, examining it from each side. The joints were not well fitted. They did not lap each other so that they would share and subdue the strains. The braces were in the wrong places. This America needed good workmen.

Hugo Kertchak took his wooden rule from the toolbox and unsnapped it to full length. He made his measurements. He selected several boards and marked them off, using a nail to scratch the lines. The saw was in his hands, the saw that had been his father's and that he had filed and refiled on the long journey until its teeth yearned for good wood to cut. It sliced through this wood swiftly and sweetly. Here were his braces. He nailed these into place. He put a shoulder against a corner post and heaved. The framework stood solid. It was not as firm as it would have been if it had been built right from the beginning, but it was much better. He reached for the next board and stopped. The man was making a noise.

"Hey!" the man was saying again and again, each time louder, trying to catch his attention. "Hey, carpenter. What'd you stick me to polish off this thing?"

"Stick?" Hugo Kertchak said. "Polish off?"

"How much to finish it?" the man said. "Do the job up right."

Hugo Kertchak looked at the framework again. The shed would have no windows. There would be only a door to make. This work was nothing, just nailing boards in place. He tried to estimate a price, one that would not be too low because this was America and yet would not be so high that the man would be unwilling to bargain. "Four dollar," he said.

"Well, now," the man said, rubbing a hand up and down along one side of his chin. "That's a reasonable fair price, I reckon. But cash is mighty scarce in these parts around about now. Tell you what. I'll make it two dollars cash and toss in whatever stuff's left, boards and nails and the like."

Hugo Kertchak's mind worked slowly over the words. "I can do," he said. "Done," the man said. "Reckon all else you'll need is some hinges and a latch for the door. I'll go rustle some." The man swung away and Hugo Kertchak stared after him in amazement. There was no arguing back and forth. There was no talk about how much wood he should use and how many nails. There was no talk about how good the work must be for the price or how long he must wait for the money. There was no writing about the business on paper so that there could be no argument afterwards over what had been said and promised. A man said "done" and it was settled. Hugo Kertchak shed his jacket in the warm sun and began sawing board lengths and the endless wind of the wide country sent the sawdust swirling as he sawed.

The sun climbed high overhead and the shed sides climbed with it. The man came back with a pair of big hinges and a latch and screws to go with them. He set these down by the lumber. "Lunchtime," he said. "Better go wrastle yourself some food." He disappeared into the nearby building.

Lunchtime. Suddenly Hugo Kertchak remembered his wife and two children alone on the store platform. Thirty-seven cents would buy bread if bread could be found in this strange place. He started toward the road. He had not gone ten steps when around the corner of the last building came his wife. She walked proudly with her head high. In one hand she carried two fat sandwiches made of thick slices of bread with meat between them and in the other hand she carried a tin pitcher of cool water. "The store man gives," she said in English and then she began talking rapidly in their native tongue, but she had no chance to say much because the store man himself came around the corner close behind her and he was talking so loudly that he almost shouted. He talked straight at Hugo Kertchak. He was very angry. He thought that Hugo Kertchak was closely related to an animal called a polecat with maybe a dose of rattlesnake thrown in. What kind of a horned toad was Hugo Kertchak anyway to leave a woman and two kids in the hot sun breathing road dust when decent neighbors were around that would let them come in and sit a spell and stay as long as they liked? Why hadn't he spoken up like a man with a chunk of backbone and said he had a family with him and was flat busted and didn't have a place to stay? What brand of mangy miscreants did he think people in that state were that they couldn't provide food and shelter for a family that needed same till they could provide their own? He, the store man, was going to tell this Hugo Kertchak or whatever crazy name he called himself what he, this Hugo Kertchunkhead, was going to do and he'd better do it. This ring-tailed baboon of a Hugo crazyname was going to set himself and his family down in the extra room of the living quarters back of the store and he was going to pay a stiff price. How? He was supposed to be a carpenter, wasn't he? So his wife said anyway. Well, he was going to prove that. He was going to slap some decent shelves in the store to take the place of the rickety ones there and they'd better be good shelves or he'd find himself with a sore backside from being kicked all over a quarter section. And maybe he wasn't such a hollow-head of a bohunk as he looked because he seemed to have rustled himself a hammer-and-saw job already but the shelf proposition still stood and was he man enough to rear up on his hind legs and say would he do it?

Hugo Kertchak understood only part of the words. But he understood that the store man's anger was a good anger and that there was more work for him to do. What exactly it was did not matter. It was carpenter's work. He was a good carpenter, almost as good a carpenter as his father had been. He looked straight at the store man. "Done," he said.

The store man was not angry any more. He chuckled. "Talking American already," he said. "When you're through here, come on down to my place." He turned abruptly and disappeared around the corner of the building.

Hugo Kertchak nailed the last roof board in position. He was worried about the roof. It should have some other covering to make it waterproof. He would talk to the man about that. He slid to the ground and cut and shaped the last side boards to fit up snugly under the eaves. He ran neat finishing strips down the corners. There was still a nice pile of wood left and the keg of nails was only half empty. It was not really fair. All this good

wood and all these nails and two dollars too for a little sawing and hammering finished with the afternoon only half gone. There was still a door
to make. It should be a good door.

He selected the wood carefully. The door grew under his hands. He cut
and mortised the pieces for the outer rim. He planed and fitted the pieces
to be set in these and give a paneled effect. The wind of the wide country
set the shavings dancing. This was the kind of work that showed what a
good carpenter could do. He was so intent on it that he did not hear the
hooves approaching, the sound softened in the dust. He was startled when
he looked up and saw a man, a new man, watching him about thirty feet
away. It was a horseman and he had a pistol in a leather holder on his hip.
Hugo Kertchak saw the horse and the pistol and was afraid. It was an instinctive fear out of old memories deep in his mind. Then he saw the face of
the horseman and he was no longer afraid. It was a young face, serious and
sunburned, with many small wrinkles around the eyes from much squinting
into the endless wind, and the expression in the eyes and on the face was
wide and open like the country around.

"Man oh man," the horseman said. He pushed his hat up from his forehead and wiped at the dust there. "You sure can wrangle those tools." He
turned his horse and went out of sight around the building.

Hugo Kertchak fastened the hinges to the door. He set the door in the
doorway and slipped thin shavings under it for clearance and fastened the
hinges to the door frame. He pulled out the shavings and tried the door.
It hung true and swung easily out and back to fit snug and flat in line with
the frame. He began work on the latch. This time he heard the hooves. The
horseman appeared around the building. A tied bundle of letters and newspapers hung from his saddlehorn. He stopped his horse and leaned forward
in the saddle inspecting the shed. "Man oh man," he said. "That's what I
call a door. Kind of like a fancy beaver on a roadside bum but there ain't no
mistaking it's a door." He clucked to the horse and moved on, straight on
out into the wide country, riding easily and steadily into the far distance.

Hugo Kertchak stood on the small rear platform or porch of the store
building and saw the last tinges of almost unbelievable color fading out of
the western horizon and the clear clean darkness claiming the land. There
were two silver dollars with the thirty-seven cents in the old leather purse
in his pocket. Behind him in the lamplit kitchen his wife and the store
man's wife were clearing dishes from the table and rattling them in a tin
washbasin. The two voices made a gentle humming. It was remarkable how
women did not need to know many of each other's words to talk so much
together. But there had been much talk too with the store man himself,

who was still sitting by the table reading his newspaper as if he had to cover every word in it. This was only a small town, a very small town, the store man said, but it would not always be small. It would change, and quickly. Now there were only wide stretches of land around where men raised cattle for meat and leather and let them wander without fences to hold them. But soon the government would open the land for farmers and their families. They would come. Whole trainloads of them would be coming. They would settle all around and the town would grow and business would be good and there would be more work than men to do it.

Hugo Kertchak could hardly believe that what was happening was true. In one day he had new money and some materials for his trade and a friend who could be angry at him for his own good. This was a strange country and the people were strange but theirs was not an alien strangeness. It was only a difference that a man could learn to understand.

His wife was on the porch beside him. "Hugo. Think of it. In the cold time, in the winter, they have a school. Free for all people's children." She put a hand on his arm. She had not complained very much through the four years of saving. She had followed where he led on the long journeying. "We stay here?" she said.

The tireless wind of the wide country blew full in Hugo Kertchak's face. It was still hot and it was still dry. But there was a freshness in it that was not just the beginning of the evening cool. Hugo Kertchak put an arm around his wife's shoulders. "We stay," he said.

✳ ✳ ✳

Hugo Kertchak was the town carpenter. He helped the town get ready for the coming land boom. He built new shelves in the store and a long new counter and racks for farm tools. He built and polished to a shining finish a bar in the biggest of the buildings that was a saloon and would be a dance hall. He patched the blacksmith shop roof and extended it out to form a lean-to addition where wagons could be kept waiting repairs. He built stalls in the broad shedlike structure that would be a livery stable. These were honest jobs well done and he could pay the store man board money and even save a little for the house he would build for himself with the materials he was assembling. But they did not satisfy him. They seemed so small in the bigness of the land.

He sat on the front steps with the store man and watched the western color fading out of the sky. A man on a horse came along the road, hurrying, stirring the dust for the tireless wind to whirl. It was the young horseman. He stopped and looked down at the two on the steps.

"Howdy, Cal," the store man said. "Climb off that cayuse and sit a spell. Could be there's a bottle of beer hanging to cool in the well out back."

"Man oh man," the horseman said, "you would think of that when I ain't got the time." He looked straight at Hugo Kertchak. "Reckon me and the other hands ain't so hot with our hammers. Barn we built's in bad shape. Haymow's collapsed with hardly no hay in it at all. And everybody's pulling out early morning for fall roundup. So I tell the boss how you wrangle those tools. So he sends me to put a rope on you for repairs."

Hugo Kertchak picked out the important words here and there as he had learned to do with these Americans. "Done," he said. "Where is barn?"

It was a big barn, casting a long shadow in the morning sun. Hugo Kertchak drove toward it, perched on the seat of the store man's light wagon. All the last miles he could see the barn bumping up out of the wide flat land and he did not like what he saw. It was too high for its width. It leaned a little as if the bottom timbers on one side had not been set right on a firm foundation. There were no neat slatted windows high up under the pointed eaves to give proper ventilation. The doors sagged and could not be closed all the way. Hugo Kertchak shook his head and muttered to himself.

He stood inside the doors and saw the remains of the haymow and listened to the boss, the ranchman, speak many words about propping it up again and perhaps strengthening it some. He did not listen to catch the important words. He was looking up at the fine big timbers that should have been cut to lap each other and fastened with stout wooden pegs and instead were simply butted against each other and tortured with long spikes driven in at angles that had already started splittings in the good wood. He did not even wait for the ranchman to stop talking. "No," he said in a loud voice. "Sorry is it to me I said 'done.' This work no." He sought for the words that would say what he meant and found them and as always in excitement he forgot the pronouns. "Is America," he said. "Has freedom."

The ranchman's eyes narrowed. His voice was soft and gentle. "What in hell has freedom got to do with my barn?"

"Freedom," Hugo Kertchak said. "Freedom for work right." He waved his arms at the walls around. "You see? Bad work. Not strong. Cold weather come. Snow. On roof. All the time wind blow. One year. Two year. Not no more. Everything down."

The ranchman's eyes were wide open again. He sucked in one end of his mustache and chewed on it. "That bad, eh? I know it was slapped together in a hell of a hurry. Couldn't you fix it up some?"

"Fix bad work," Hugo Kertchak said, "makes better. But all the time still bad."

The ranchman chewed more on his mustache. He remembered that the range would be shrinking as homesteaders came in and he would have to depend more and more on winter feeding. He couldn't take chances on a rickety barn. The old days were slipping away and he would have to plan closer for the future. "Maybe," he said, "maybe you could build me a good barn?" He saw Hugo Kertchak's eyes begin to shine. "Whoa, now," he said. "Take it slow. I don't mean the best damn barn in the country. And no fancy doors. Just a good solid dependable barn. Knocking this one apart and using as much of it as you can for the new one."

Hugo Kertchak no longer said "I am carpenter." He said "I am builder." The land boom arrived and the trainloads and wagonloads of settlers and they fanned out over the wide land and with them for miles in all directions went word that when it came to building, Hugo Kertchak, builder, could do a job right. Most of the homesteaders threw up their own shacks. Many of them simply squatted on their claims in tents and flimsy tarpapered huts waiting to prove title and sell out for a quick profit. Many others were too shiftless even to do that and drifted away. But here and there were a few and their number gradually increased who had capital or the competence to acquire it and could meet the conditions of the new land. They looked forward and they built for the future and Hugo Kertchak built for them. They paid what and when they could and sometimes he waited months and a year or more and longer for the last of the money but that did not matter because there was work for every working day and he was building and he had enough.

He built toolsheds and wagonsheds, sturdy and unshakable. He built barns, strong and solid, that seemed to grow out of the earth itself and settled firmly to the long competition with wind and weather. He built houses, small ones at first and then larger when times were flush and money plentiful and small ones again when that was all people could afford. No roof on these houses sagged when snow was heavy on it. The tireless wind found no chinks to whip through and widen. Sometimes he hired a helper or even two, but mostly he worked alone or when there was no school with his growing son as helper because that was the way to be certain that all work was done right.

The town grew and spread out on both sides of the railroad track and other builders came, men who underbid each other on jobs and hired many men and had the work done rapidly, sometimes good and sometimes not good. They built a town hall and a hotel and a jail and a railroad station and some store blocks and some fine-looking houses and other things and how they built them was their own business. Always there was someone out across the wide land who needed a shed or a barn or a house built as Hugo Kertchak could build it.

Hugo Kertchak's son was a good carpenter. He worked on Saturdays and during vacations with his father and was paid what a helper would have been paid. Sometimes he seemed to think more of the money to be earned than of the job to be done and he had a tendency to hurry his work. But when his father was there to watch he was a good carpenter. When he graduated from high school, he did not work as a carpenter any more. He worked at many jobs in the town, only a week or two at each. He was restless and irritable in the home. He talked with his father. He wanted to go to the state university and study to be an architect. "That is right," Hugo Kertchak said. "In America the son should do more and better than the father. Work with me until the school begins and save the money." His son did and when the school began again what he had with what Hugo Kertchak had in the town bank was enough.

Hugo Kertchak's daughter was a good cook like her mother, fine-colored and well-rounded as her mother had been at the same age. She was quick with words, too, like her mother and did well in her studies. She won a scholarship to go to the state normal school and study to be a teacher. But in the first year at the school she met a mining engineer who was leaving soon to work for a mining company in western Montana. She wanted to marry him and go with him. Hugo Kertchak comforted his wife. "Is she different than you?" he said. "Is it not she should go where her man goes?" There was only a little money in the bank now but there was enough for a wedding.

Times were slack. The town was very quiet. The opening of new lands had long since moved far on farther westward. The population of the town dwindled and dropped to a stable level. There was no more building.

Hugo Kertchak became a maker of barrels. He made them of all sizes for many purposes, from small kegs to big hogsheads. He made them firm and tight. He shaped the staves and fitted them together as he had shaped and fitted the timbers of his barns and houses. On most of them he used iron hoops, but he liked to make some completely of wood with wooden hoops fitted and shrunk so that they held better than the iron itself. He made them outdoors in the back yard of his house, where his wife could see him from the window, working under the high sky while the endless wind blew through his graying hair and made the shavings dance around his feet.

He had a broad shed there for a workshop but he worked in it only when the weather was bad. He was building outdoors in the open, using his tools on good wood with the skill he had brought with him to this new land. He was building good barrels. But he did not call himself Hugo Kertchak, builder, any more.

* * *

Hugo Kertchak's son was home for the summer vacation. After one more school year he would have the parchment that would say he was an architect. Now during the summer he worked with his father, making barrels. He talked as a young American talked, fast and with much enthusiasm, and his talk was big with his plans for his profession. Hugo Kertchak listened and thought of the time when men who worked with steel and stone and concrete as he worked with wood would build the fine structures his son would design for them. And Hugo Kertchak's wife sat on the small back porch in the summer sun and watched the father and the son making barrels together.

Hugo Kertchak's son went back to the university and the winter was long and hard and when the spring arrived Hugo Kertchak's son and other young men at the university were given their degrees early so that they could enlist and fight in the war with Spain. There would be time enough for him to be an architect when the war was finished. But there was no time. The telegram came telling that he died in Cuba of the yellow fever. Hugo Kertchak tried to comfort his wife and she tried to comfort him. He at least had his work, his barrels to make, and she had nothing. Even her daughter was far away to the west in Montana. She sat on the small back porch and watched him work where their son had worked with him. She sat there too often and too late in the endless wind with no shawl over her shoulders and no scarf around her head. It was pneumonia with complications, the doctor said. Four days after she took to her bed she died quietly in the night. Hugo Kertchak stood by the bed a long time in the early morning light. He cranked the handle on the telephone in the hall and called the undertaker and made the arrangements. He went out to the back yard to his tools, old and worn but still serviceable like himself. Only with them in his hands did he feel alive now.

Two days after the funeral the letter came from his daughter telling why she herself had not come. Her husband had been hurt in the mine. His left leg was crushed and he would not walk again. The company was paying for the doctor and the hospital but even so there was no extra money. Her husband would not be able to do mine work any more but in time perhaps with his training he could do office work of some kind. Meanwhile they thought of establishing a small store which she could run. The local bank might loan her the money she would need.

Hugo Kertchak sold his house. He kept the workshop and a small bit of land with it bordering on the rear alley and moved a bed and a table and some chairs and a bureau into the shop. It had a coal stove that gave good heat and on which he could do his small cooking. There was a mortgage on the house and the price he received was not high but when the mortgage was paid there was enough. He sent the money to his daughter and her crippled husband. He did not need it. He had a workshop and he had his tools.

Hugo Kertchak made barrels but they did not sell as they used to sell. They stood in rows and on top of each other along the side of the workshop and he had no orders for them. Tin and galvanized-iron containers were being used more and more. These were cheaper and more convenient and more easily handled. Hugo Kertchak became a maker of coffins.

The coffins Hugo Kertchak made were good coffins, built as the houses and the barns and the barrels had been built, shaped and fitted, firm and solid. Always, as he worked on them, he remembered that one he had made for his wife and worried about the one someone else had made for his son far off in Cuba. He did not make many, most of them only on order from the town undertaker, because good wood was becoming expensive and he could not have a big supply on hand and because working was harder now. He moved more slowly and there was a stiffness at times in the muscles. But the skill was unchanged, the sure strong touch with the tools.

People he had known in the first years died and were buried in Hugo Kertchak's coffins. People he did not know were buried in them too. The town was changing. New people and new generations walked the streets. Electric lights brightened many houses. Horseless carriages began to cough along the roads and their owners talked about the paving of streets. The new ways of the new century changed old habits. The undertaker came to see Hugo Kertchak. He could use no more of the coffins. People wanted the shiny decorated models that came from the manufacturing places in the cities. People wanted these and there was a nice profit in them. That was business.

Hugo Kertchak puttered around town with any little jobs he could find. Sometimes he built bookcases or pantry shelves or flower trellises when he found people who wanted these. Most of the jobs were tending people's yards, planting bulbs in the spring, cutting grass in the summer, raking leaves in the fall. His daughter wrote to him regularly, once a month. She sent him snapshots taken by a neighbor of the two grandchildren he had never seen. She wanted him to come and live with her. He could help in the store. There was not much money but it would be enough. But he could not do that. The thought of going so far now and of living in the mountains frightened him. He could not leave the town and the wide flat country that had welcomed him and the quiet grave in its half of the small plot in a corner of the town cemetery. Regularly he wrote back, laboring hours over his broad rounded script, careful of his spelling and to put in all the pronouns. He was well. There was plenty of work. Someday soon he would come on a visit, in the fall perhaps when the rush of summer work was done, or in the spring when the winter cold was past. And sometimes he managed to put several dollar bills in the envelope for the grandchildren. He did not need much for himself.

Days when there was no work and the weather was pleasant he liked to sit in the sun on one of the benches by the town hall and watch the two morning trains go past on the track across the way, the express that roared through without stopping and the local that puffed to a stop by the station for a flurry of activity there. Always people were arriving and people were leaving and new faces were around and things were changing and that was America. He could remember when a train could stop and only a single small family step down from it into a dusty little town that seemed deserted and yet they would find friendship springing up around them as if from the wide land itself. That too was America. He sat on the bench and remembered and people smiled at him as they passed and sometimes stopped to talk to him because he was a part of the town and of the past that had made the town and he did not know it but he was America too.

A woman from one of the county boards came to see Hugo Kertchak in his shop. She sat on the edge of one of his old chairs and talked in a self-consciously kind voice. She had a card in her hand that told her facts about him and she did not know these were not the important facts. He was an old man, living alone, with no regular work. The card told her that. It would be much better for him if he would turn over to the county any small property he still had and let the county take care of him. The county had a nice old folks' home where he would have companionship and would not have to worry about anything.

The woman saw the tightening of the old muscles of Hugo Kertchak's face and she hurried to say more. That would not be charity. Oh, good heavens, no. He had been one of the early settlers and he had helped the community grow. The county owed it to him to take care of him. "Wrong," Hugo Kertchak said. "All wrong. This America owes me nothing at all.

It gave what a man needs. A home without fear. Good friends. A chance to work. Freedom to work right. If there is owing, it is for me. To take care of myself." He was indignant and this made his voice sharp and the woman flushed and stood up and turned to go. Hugo Kertchak was a little ashamed. "I have thanks that you think of me," he said. "It is good that you help people. But for me there is no need."

Hugo Kertchak sat on the bench by the town hall and the tireless wind of the plains country ruffled the dwindling gray hair on his bare head. People nodded at him as they passed but few people talked to him any more. That was his fault. He talked too much. He said the same things over and over. He wanted to talk about the weather or politics or prospects for the year's crops or anything else another person wanted to talk about. But inevitably his voice rose, shriller and more querulous, and he would be doing most of the talking, telling about the old days when a man got angry at another man for his own good and a man said "done" and a thing was settled and a young horseman remembered a man he saw doing good work and people appreciated work that was done right, not slipshod and in a hurry, but right with every beam and board shaped and fitted and fastened to join its strength with the strength of the others in the solid firmness of the whole structure.

Hugo Kertchak remembered. His old hands remembered the feel of his good tools. He began going home by different and roundabout routes, walking along the roads and alleys and looking for stray pieces of wood. He gathered what he could find, pieces of old shingles, broken boards, boxes and crates thrown away. He carried them to his workshop. Day after day he worked in the old shop. Two days a week he did gardening and that paid for his food. The rest of the time he stayed in the shop and worked. When the wife of the man who had bought the house went out to hang her wash in the back yard near the shop, she heard the sounds of old tools in use, the steady striking of a hammer, the soft swish of a plane, the rhythmic stroke of a saw.

The day came when she hung out her wash and heard no sounds in the shop. When she took down the dry clothes in late afternoon there was no sign of activity. In the evening, when she stood on the back porch and peered into the darkness, there was no lamplight showing through the shop window. Her husband refused to leave his newspaper. "So what?" he said. "The old windbag can take care of himself. He's been doing it for years, hasn't he?" But in the morning, after a worrying night, she insisted and her husband went out to investigate. He came in again quickly and to the telephone and called the coroner's office.

The coroner and a deputy sheriff found the body of Hugo Kertchak on the floor where he had toppled from a chair in the last struggle for breath as his heart failed. The old pen he had been using was still tight in the fingers of his right hand. They picked the body up and laid it on the old bed. "Sometime yesterday," the coroner said. "That's the way it is with these old ones. One day they're fussing around. Next day they're gone."

The deputy sheriff was looking around the shop. "What d'you know," he said. "Take a look at these things." On a shelf above the workbench was a row of little buildings, small birdhouses, each delicately made yet sturdy with every piece of the old wood shaped and fitted and fastened with skillful care. The deputy sheriff put his hands on his hips and stared at the tiny buildings. "I'll be damned," he said. "You never know what these old bums'll be doing next, fussing around with things like that when anyone's a mind for one can get it for a quarter or maybe fifty cents at a hardware store. Wasting his time on those when likely he didn't have a nickel. Now the town'll have to bury him."

"Shut up," the coroner said. He was holding the unfinished letter that had been lying on the old table. He was reading the last words: "The town people will sell my shop and the land that is left and send the money to you. They are good people. It is for the boy. For help with a school. To study it may be for an architect . . ." The coroner folded the paper and put it in his pocket. He moved around the foot of the bed and pulled an old blanket from what lay between the bed and the wall. It was a coffin, firm and strongly built, the once rough planks cut and fitted and planed smooth and polished to a good finish. On the top lay an old cigar box. In the box were a title form for a small lot in the town cemetery and an old leather purse. In the purse were some crumbled dollar bills and a handful of coins. "No," the coroner said. "Not this one. He paid his score to the end."

The man filling in the grave in a corner of the cemetery shivered a bit in the chill sunny air. He finished the job, piling the dirt in a mound so that when it settled it would be level with the ground around. He leaned a moment on the shovel while he took a scrap of paper from his pocket and looked at the name on it. "Kertchak," he muttered to himself. "Seems like I remember that. Made barrels when I was a kid." He lifted the shovel over one shoulder and went away.

An automobile approached and stopped by the cemetery and two men stepped from it. One was the editor of the local newspaper. The other was tall and erect with the heaviness of late middle-age beginning to show in a once lean body. He wore a wide-brimmed hat and under it his face with the many wrinkles about the eyes was windburned and wide and open like the country around. Under his arm he carried a cross made of two pieces of wood. "Man oh man," he said to the editor, "I'd never have known if it wasn't for that article in your paper. Started me remembering things." He went to the mound of dirt and stuck the wooden cross into the ground at the upper end. He stood silent a moment, staring at the wooden cross. The upright was a piece of new two-by-four. The crossbar was an old board found in the old shop that had once been nailed over the doorway of the house in front of the shop. Carved into it in square solid letters were the words: Hugo Kertchak, Builder.

The automobile moved away and silence settled over the cemetery. The endless wind blew and whipped some of the dried earth of the mound in tiny dust whirls around the base of the cross and blew in soft whispers on out over the wide land where they stood, strong against weather and time, the sheds and the barns and the houses Hugo Kertchak had built.

Loren Eiseley

1907-77

<hr/>

1957: *The Immense Journey*
1970: *The Invisible Pyramid*
1971: *The Night Country*
1972: *Notes of an Alchemist*
1973: *The Innocent Assassins*
1973: *The Man Who Saw Through Time*
1975: *All the Strange Hours:*
The Excavation of a Life

<hr/>

I N H I S *autobiography,* All the Strange Hours, *Loren Eiseley described how he rode the rails as a teenager, hopping freight trains that took him all the way across the United States. Once, after he had been severely beaten by a brakeman, he was told by an older hobo that the beating was a lesson to remember about politics and society. "The capitalists beat men into line. The communists beat men into line. Men beat men, that's all. That's all there is." The experience, Eiseley wrote, left his life "henceforward free of mobs and movements."* [1]

Riding the roofs of the freight cars and watching the landscape spin past, Eiseley also experienced something of a revelation; he realized he was fascinated with the tyranny of time. For the rest of his life, as an anthropologist, naturalist, writer, poet, professor, and philosopher, Eiseley studied the meanings hidden in time's faint traces.

Eiseley's work is both abstract and theoretical, but his life was marked by hard realities. He was the late child of a second marriage, and throughout his boyhood in Lincoln, Nebraska, his parents moved from house to house as his father tried to

1. Loren Eiseley, *All the Strange Hours* (New York: Charles Scribner's Sons, 1975), p. 12.

find work. His autobiography recalls a very lonely childhood and how he took to riding the rails during his high school years, hopping freights and living in hobo camps. In 1928, he returned home from such a journey after getting a wire that his father was dying of cancer; that same year, the ailment that had been nagging Eiseley was diagnosed as tuberculosis. He went to Colorado for his "cure" and within a couple of years was back to riding freight trains, supporting himself with whatever manual labor he could find as he traveled. Eventually, Eiseley settled down long enough to earn his B.A. in 1933 and his Ph.D. four years later. From then on, he was a teacher and an anthropologist—but never an orthodox member of either profession. Eiseley's biographers agree with his descriptions of himself as a changeling, a fugitive, and an intellectual drifter of the middle border.

The Immense Journey *was published in 1957, and its success quickly changed Eiseley's life, transforming him from a rather obscure professor into a noted writer and sought-after public speaker, who now occupied an honorary faculty position at the University of Pennsylvania. According to the figures of the biographer Andrew J. Angyal,* The Immense Journey *has sold over a half a million copies, has been through eight printings, and has been translated into nine languages.[2] It is a book of anthropological adventures as well as a book of personal history; it is a collection of essays about time, Darwin, visitors from space, evolution and revolution.*

"The Flow of the River"—like the other chapters in The Immense Journey— *was written in what Eiseley called the "concealed essay" format. He had recognized that, as a scientist, he was expected to write scientific-sounding, technical articles; but he had also realized that he had "an attachment for the personal essay." The respectability of the personal essay dates back to 1580 and Montaigne's publication of* Essays, *but Eiseley's colleagues viewed the genre as "subjective" and unsuitable for science. Knowing this, Eiseley nevertheless set out to include his experiences and personal philosophies in "scientific" prose. The result was the "concealed essay, in which personal anecdote was allowed gently to bring under observation thoughts of a more purely scientific nature."[3]*

In "The Flow of the River," Eiseley puts himself in touch with timelessness, learning to flow along with the river, without resistance. He realizes his similarity to the catfish. "We were both projections out of that timeless ferment and locked as well in some greater unity that lay incalculably beyond us." Eiseley's almost extrasensory journey is proof of a universal organizing principle, a vast and mysterious order of things that includes each of us. His journey offers, momentarily, an escape

---

2. Andrew J. Angyal, *Loren Eiseley* (Boston: Twayne, 1983), p. 26.
3. Eiseley, *Strange Hours*, p. 182.

*from the tyranny of time, against which Eiseley again rebels in the poem "In the
Fern Forest of All Time I Live."*

> I would prefer, like all my reptile kind, the still
> space between clock ticks, sandbars in silent rivers;
> man's first mistake was ever to see time pointed
> somewhere beyond us. Break the spell then,
>   stop the pendulum, sign
> this document with a scaled hand and no
>   dateline.[4]

The Flow of the River

I F THERE IS magic on this planet, it is contained in water. Its least stir
even, as now in a rain pond on a flat roof opposite my office, is enough
to bring me searching to the window. A wind ripple may be translating
itself into life. I have a constant feeling that some time I may witness that
momentous miracle on a city roof, see life veritably and suddenly boiling
out of a heap of rusted pipes and old television aerials. I marvel at how
suddenly a water beetle has come and is submarining there in a spatter of
green algae. Thin vapors, rust, wet tar and sun are an alembic remarkably
like the mind; they throw off odorous shadows that threaten to take real
shape when no one is looking.

One in a lifetime, perhaps, one escapes the actual confines of the flesh.
Once in a lifetime, if one is lucky, one so merges with sunlight and air and
running water that whole eons, the eons that mountains and deserts know,
might pass in a single afternoon without discomfort. The mind has sunk
away into its beginnings among old roots and the obscure tricklings and
movings that stir inanimate things. Like the charmed fairy circle into which
a man once stepped, and upon emergence learned that a whole century
had passed in a single night, one can never quite define this secret; but it
has something to do, I am sure, with common water. Its substance reaches
everywhere; it touches the past and prepares the future; it moves under

From Loren Eiseley, *The Immense Journey* (New York: Random House, 1957), pp. 15–27.
Copyright © 1953 by Loren Eiseley. Reprinted by permission of Random House, Inc.
    4. Loren Eiseley, "In the Fern Forest of All Time I Live," *The Innocent Assassins* (New
York: Charles Scribner's Sons, 1973), p. 91.

the poles and wanders thinly in the heights of air. It can assume forms of exquisite perfection in a snowflake, or strip the living to a single shining bone cast up by the sea.

Many years ago, in the course of some scientific investigations in a remote western county, I experienced, by chance, precisely the sort of curious absorption by water—the extension of shape by osmosis—at which I have been hinting. You have probably never experienced in yourself the meandering roots of a whole watershed or felt your outstretched fingers touching, by some kind of clairvoyant extension, the brooks of snow-line glaciers at the same time that you were flowing toward the Gulf over the eroded debris of worn-down mountains. A poet, MacKnight Black, has spoken of being "limbed . . . with waters gripping pole and pole." He had the idea, all right, and it is obvious that these sensations are not unique, but they are hard to come by; and the sort of extension of the senses that people will accept when they put their ear against a sea shell, they will smile at in the confessions of a bookish professor. What makes it worse is the fact that because of a traumatic experience in childhood, I am not a swimmer, and am inclined to be timid before any large body of water. Perhaps it was just this, in a way, that contributed to my experience.

As it leaves the Rockies and moves downward over the high plains towards the Missouri, the Platte River is a curious stream. In the spring floods, on occasion, it can be a mile-wide roaring torrent of destruction, gulping farms and bridges. Normally, however, it is a rambling, dispersed series of streamlets flowing erratically over great sand and gravel fans that are, in part, the remnants of a mightier Ice Age stream bed. Quicksands and shifting islands haunt its waters. Over it the prairie suns beat mercilessly throughout the summer. The Platte, "a mile wide and an inch deep," is a refuge for any heat-weary pilgrim along its shores. This is particularly true on the high plains before its long march by the cities begins.

The reason that I came upon it when I did, breaking through a willow thicket and stumbling out through ankle-deep water to a dune in the shade, is of no concern to this narrative. On various purposes of science I have ranged over a good bit of that country on foot, and I know the kinds of bones that come gurgling up through the gravel pumps, and the arrowheads of shining chalcedony that occasionally spill out of water-loosened sand. On that day, however, the sight of sky and willows and the weaving net of water murmuring a little in the shallows on its way to the Gulf stirred me, parched as I was with miles of walking, with a new idea: I was going to float. I was going to undergo a tremendous adventure.

The notion came to me, I suppose, by degrees. I had shed my clothes and was floundering pleasantly in a hole among some reeds when a great desire to stretch out and go with this gently insistent water began to pluck at me. Now to this bronzed, bold, modern generation, the struggle I waged with timidity while standing there in knee-deep water can only seem farcical; yet actually for me it was not so. A near-drowning accident in childhood had scarred my reactions; in addition to the fact that I was a nonswimmer, this "inch-deep river" was treacherous with holes and quicksands. Death was not precisely infrequent along its wandering and illusory channels. Like all broad wastes of this kind, where neither water nor land quite prevails, its thickets were lonely and untraversed. A man in trouble would cry out in vain.

I thought of all this, standing quietly in the water, feeling the sand shifting away under my toes. Then I lay back in the floating position that left my face to the sky, and shoved off. The sky wheeled over me. For an instant, as I bobbed into the main channel, I had the sensation of sliding down the vast tilted face of the continent. It was then that I felt the cold needles of the alpine springs at my fingertips, and the warmth of the Gulf pulling me southward. Moving with me, leaving its taste upon my mouth and spouting under me in dancing springs of sand, was the immense body of the continent itself, flowing like the river was flowing, grain by grain, mountain by mountain, down to the sea. I was streaming over ancient sea beds thrust aloft where giant reptiles had once sported; I was wearing down the face of time and trundling cloud-wreathed ranges into oblivion. I touched my margins with the delicacy of a crayfish's antennae, and felt great fishes glide about their work.

I drifted by stranded timber cut by beaver in mountain fastnesses; I slid over shallows that had buried the broken axles of prairie schooners and the mired bones of mammoth. I was streaming alive through the hot and working ferment of the sun, or oozing secretively through shady thickets. I *was* water and the unspeakable alchemies that gestate and take shape in water, the slimy jellies that under the enormous magnification of the sun writhe and whip upward as great barbeled fish mouths, or sink indistinctly back into the murk out of which they arose. Turtle and fish and the pinpoint chirpings of individual frogs are all watery projections, concentrations— as man himself is a concentration—of that indescribable and liquid brew which is compounded in varying proportions of salt and sun and time. It has appearances, but at its heart lies water, and as I was finally edged gently against a sand bar and dropped like any log, I tottered as I rose. I knew once more the body's revolt against emergence into the harsh and unsupporting air, its reluctance to break contact with that mother element which still, at this late point in time, shelters and brings into being nine tenths of everything alive.

As for men, those myriad little detached ponds with their own swarming corpuscular life, what were they but a way that water has of going about beyond the reach of rivers? I, too, was a microcosm of pouring rivulets and floating driftwood gnawed by the mysterious animalcules of my own creation. I was three fourths water, rising and subsiding according to the hollow knocking in my veins: a minute pulse like the eternal pulse that lifts Himalayas and which, in the following systole, will carry them away.

Thoreau, peering at the emerald pickerel in Walden Pond, called them "animalized water" in one of his moments of strange insight. If he had been possessed of the geological knowledge so laboriously accumulated since his time, he might have gone further and amusedly detected in the planetary rumblings and eructations which so delighted him in the gross habits of certain frogs, signs of that dark interior stress which has reared sea bottoms up to mountainous heights. He might have developed an acute inner ear for the sound of the surf on Cretaceous beaches where now the wheat of Kansas rolls. In any case, he would have seen, as the long trail of life was unfolded by the fossil hunters, that his animalized water had changed its shapes eon by eon to the beating of the earth's dark millennial heart. In the swamps of the low continents, the amphibians had flourished and had their day; and as the long skyward swing—the isostatic response of the crust— had come about, the era of the cooling grasslands and mammalian life had come into being.

A few winters ago, clothed heavily against the weather, I wandered several miles along one of the tributaries of that same Platte I had floated down years before. The land was stark and ice-locked. The rivulets were frozen, and over the marshlands the willow thickets made such an array of vertical lines against the snow that tramping through them produced strange optical illusions and dizziness. On the edge of a frozen backwater, I stopped and rubbed my eyes. At my feet a raw prairie wind had swept the ice clean of snow. A peculiar green object caught my eye; there was no mistaking it.

Staring up at me with all his barbels spread pathetically, frozen solidly in the wind-ruffled ice, was a huge familiar face. It was one of those catfish of the twisting channels, those dwellers in the yellow murk, who had been about me and beneath me on the day of my great voyage. Whatever sunny dream had kept him paddling there while the mercury plummeted downward and that Cheshire smile froze slowly, it would be hard to say. Or perhaps he was trapped in a blocked channel and had simply kept swimming until the ice contracted around him. At any rate, there he would lie till the spring thaw.

At that moment I started to turn away, but something in the bleak, whiskered face reproached me, or perhaps it was the river calling to her children. I termed it science, however—a convenient rational phrase I reserve for such occasions—and decided that I would cut the fish out of the ice and take him home. I had no intention of eating him. I was merely struck by a sudden impulse to test the survival qualities of high-plains fishes, particularly fishes of this type who get themselves immured in oxygenless ponds or in cut-off oxbows buried in winter drifts. I blocked him out as gently as possible and dropped him, ice and all, into a collecting can in the car. Then we set out for home.

Unfortunately, the first stages of what was to prove a remarkable resurrection escaped me. Cold and tired after a long drive, I deposited the can with its melting water and ice in the basement. The accompanying corpse I anticipated I would either dispose of or dissect on the following day. A hurried glance had revealed no signs of life.

To my astonishment, however, upon descending into the basement several hours later, I heard stirrings in the receptacle and peered in. The ice had melted. A vast pouting mouth ringed with sensitive feelers confronted me, and the creature's gills labored slowly. A thin stream of silver bubbles rose to the surface and popped. A fishy eye gazed up at me protestingly.

"A tank," it said. This was no Walden pickerel. This was a yellow-green, mud-grubbing, evil-tempered inhabitant of floods and droughts and cyclones. It was the selective product of the high continent and the waters that pour across it. It had outlasted prairie blizzards that left cattle standing frozen upright in the drifts.

"I'll get the tank," I said respectfully.

He lived with me all that winter, and his departure was totally in keeping with his sturdy, independent character. In the spring a migratory impulse or perhaps sheer boredom struck him. Maybe, in some little lost corner of his brain, he felt, far off, the pouring of the mountain waters through the sandy coverts of the Platte. Anyhow, something called to him, and he went. One night when no one was about, he simply jumped out of his tank. I found him dead on the floor next morning. He had made his gamble like a man—or, I should say, a fish. In the proper place it would not have been a fool's gamble. Fishes in the drying shallows of intermittent prairie streams who feel their confinement and have the impulse to leap while there is yet time may regain the main channel and survive. A million ancestral years had gone into that jump, I thought as I looked at him, a million years of climbing through prairie sunflowers and twining in and out through the pillared legs of drinking mammoth.

"Some of your close relatives have been experimenting with air breathing," I remarked, apropos of nothing, as I gathered him up. "Suppose we meet again up there in the cottonwoods in a million years or so."

I missed him a little as I said it. He had for me the kind of lost archaic glory that comes from the water brotherhood. We were both projections out of that timeless ferment and locked as well in some greater unity that lay incalculably beyond us. In many a fin and reptile foot I have seen myself passing by—some part of myself, that is, some part that lies unrealized in the momentary shape I inhabit. People have occasionally written me harsh letters and castigated me for a lack of faith in man when I have ventured to speak of this matter in print. They distrust, it would seem, all shapes and thoughts but their own. They would bring God into the compass of a shopkeeper's understanding and confine Him to those limits, lest He proceed to some unimaginable and shocking act—create perhaps, as a casual afterthought, a being more beautiful than man. As for me, I believe nature capable of this, and having been part of the flow of the river, I feel no envy—any more than the frog envies the reptile or an ancestral ape should envy man.

Every spring in the wet meadows and ditches I hear a little shrilling chorus which sounds for all the world like an endlessly reiterated "We're here, we're here, we're here." And so they are, as frogs, of course. Confident little fellows. I suspect that to some greater ear than ours, man's optimistic pronouncements about his role and destiny may make a similar little ringing sound that travels a small way out into the night. It is only its nearness that is offensive. From the heights of a mountain, or a marsh at evening, it blends, not too badly, with all the other sleepy voices that, in croaks or chirrups, are saying the same thing.

After a while the skilled listener can distinguish man's noise from the katydid's rhythmic assertion, allow for the offbeat of a rabbit's thumping, pick up the autumnal monotone of crickets, and find in all of them a grave pleasure without admitting any to a place of preëminence in his thoughts. It is when all these voices cease and the waters are still, when along the frozen river nothing cries, screams or howls, that the enormous mindlessness of space settles down upon the soul. Somewhere out in that waste of crushed ice and reflected stars, the black waters may be running, but they appear to be running without life toward a destiny in which the whole of space may be locked in some silvery winter of dispersed radiation.

It is then, when the wind comes straitly across the barren marshes and the snow rises and beats in endless waves against the traveler, that I remember best, by some trick of the imagination, my summer voyage on the river. I remember my green extensions, my catfish nuzzlings and minnow wrigglings, my gelatinous materializations out of the mother ooze. And as I walk on through the white smother, it is the magic of water that leaves me a final sign.

Men talk much of matter and energy, of the struggle for existence that molds the shape of life. These things exist, it is true; but more delicate, elusive, quicker than the fins in water, is that mysterious principle known as "organization," which leaves all other mysteries concerned with life stale and insignificant by comparison. For that without organization life does not persist is obvious. Yet this organization itself is not strictly the product of life, nor of selection. Like some dark and passing shadow within matter, it cups out the eyes' small windows or spaces the notes of a meadow lark's song in the interior of a mottled egg. That principle—I am beginning to suspect—was there before the living in the deeps of water.

The temperature has risen. The little stinging needles have given way to huge flakes floating in like white leaves blown from some great tree in open space. In the car, switching on the lights, I examine one intricate crystal on my sleeve before it melts. No utilitarian philosophy explains a snow crystal, no doctrine of use or disuse. Water has merely leapt out of vapor and thin nothingness in the night sky to array itself in form. There is no logical reason for the existence of a snowflake any more than there is for evolution. It is an apparition from that mysterious shadow world beyond nature, that final world which contains—if anything contains—the explanation of men and catfish and green leaves.

Walter Van Tilburg Clark

1909-71

1940: *The Ox-Bow Incident*
1945: *The City of Trembling Leaves*
1949: *The Track of the Cat*
1950: *The Watchful Gods
and Other Stories*

NEVADA *can claim Walter Van Tilburg Clark as one of its finest novelists, but critics agree that his work consistently transcends any such regional setting. Somewhere, whether it was as a student at the University of Nevada or as a teacher in Vermont and New York, Clark developed an acute perception of mythic and universal themes. The hunting of the black mountain lion in* The Track of the Cat *becomes a struggle between evil and man's lack of understanding; the lynching in* The Ox-Bow Incident *dramatizes how segments of society can be led to "use authoritarian methods to oppose authoritarian methods." Clark termed this "a kind of American Naziism."* [1]

In protest against what he regarded as an autocratic administration at the University of Nevada, Clark left his professorship there and accepted a series of appointments at other universities, including Reed College, the University of Oregon, and the University of Montana. In this way, he expanded his western experience. He also earned a reputation for being an outstanding teacher. Eventually, Clark taught on both coasts—at San Francisco State College and at Wesleyan University in Connecticut—before returning to the University of Nevada as its writer-in-residence in 1962.

Many readers recognize Clark's short stories, such as "Hook," "The Portable

---

1. As quoted by Walter Prescott Webb, Afterword to *The Ox-Bow Incident*, by Walter Van Tilburg Clark (1940; reprint, New York: New American Library, 1960), pp. 223–24.

Phonograph," and "The Wind and the Snow of Winter." Many more, however, have read The Ox-Bow Incident, *a novel that critics call a masterpiece of sharp, clean style and a perceptive diagnosis of universal social ailments—a novel that is remarkable for having dozens of fully drawn characters while lacking a hero.*

The Track of the Cat, a haunting story of men in vengeful pursuit of a mysterious black mountain lion, has been compared to Herman Melville's Moby Dick. *Other critics can find no novel at all with which to compare it. It is an example of "novel of place," based on the theme that the West's natural world exerts a powerful psychological impact on the human intruders.*

In his biography of Clark, Max Westbrook calls "The Indian Well" a "paradigmatic version of The Track of the Cat."[2] *The dominant feature is not the man but the setting, the life and landscape surrounding the well. Clark focuses our attention on the natural, timeless cycles of life at the oasis. The fawn and the calf learn lessons of both fear and joy; nearby, an old coyote takes his food as best he can, while a young coyote hunts with almost vicious enthusiasm. The intrusive human species too has had its rhythm of life in this desert place. The most recent of these, Jim Suttler, simply perpetuates the human presence, playing a small part in one brief scene of nature's drama.*

—

The Indian Well

I N T H I S dead land the only allegiance was to sun. Even night was not strong enough to resist; earth stretched gratefully when night came, but had no hope that day would not return. Such living things as hoarded a little juice at their cores were secret about it, and only the most ephemeral existences, the air at dawn and sunset, the amethyst shadows in the mountains, had any freedom. The Indian Well alone, of lesser creations, was in constant revolt. Sooner or later all minor breathing rebels came to its stone basin under the spring in the cliff, and from its overflow grew a tiny meadow delta and two columns of willows and aspens, holding a tiny front against the valley. The pictograph of a starving, ancient journey, cut in rock above the basin, a sun-warped shack on the south wing of the canyon, and an abandoned mine above it, were the only tokens of man's participation in the well's cycles, each of which was an epitome of centuries, and perhaps of the wars of the universe.

From *Accent* 3 (Spring 1943): 131–43. Reprinted by permission of International Creative Management, Inc. Copyright © 1950 by Walter Van Tilburg Clark.
    2. Max Westbrook, *Walter Van Tilburg Clark* (New York: Twayne, 1969), p. 135.

The day before Jim Suttler came up, in the early spring, to take his part in one cycle, was a busy day. The sun was merely lucid after four days of broken showers, and, under the separate cloud shadows sliding down the mountain and into the valley, the canyon was alive. A rattler emerged partially from a hole in the mound on which the cabin stood, and having gorged in the darkness, rested with his head on a stone. A road-runner, stepping long and always about to sprint, came down the morning side of the mound, and his eye, quick to perceive the difference between the live and the inanimate of the same color, discovered the coffin shaped head on the stone. At once he broke into a reaching sprint, his neck and tail stretched level, his beak agape with expectation. But his shadow arrived a step before him. The rattler recoiled, his head scarred by the sharp beak but his eye intact. The road-runner said nothing, but peered warily into the hole without stretching his neck, then walked off stiffly, leaning forward again as if about to run. When he had gone twenty feet he turned, balanced for an instant, and charged back, checking abruptly just short of the hole. The snake remained withdrawn. The road-runner paraded briefly before the hole, talking to himself, and then ran angrily up to the spring, where he drank at the overflow, sipping and stretching his neck, lifting his feet one at a time, ready to go into immediate action. The road-runner lived a dangerous and exciting life.

In the upper canyon the cliff swallows, making short harp notes, dipped and shot between the new mud under the aspens and their high community on the forehead of the cliff. Electrical bluebirds appeared to dart the length of the canyon at each low flight, turned up tilting. Lizards made unexpected flights and stops on the rocks, and when they stopped did rapid push-ups, like men exercising on a floor. They were variably pugnacious and timid.

Two of them arrived simultaneously upon a rock below the road-runner. One of them immediately skittered to a rock two feet off, and they faced each other, exercising. A small hawk coming down over the mountain, but shadowless under a cloud, saw the lizards. Having overfled the difficult target, he dropped to the canyon mouth swiftly and banked back into the wind. His trajectory was cleared of swallows, but one of them, fluttering hastily up, dropped a pellet of mud between the lizards. The one who had retreated disappeared. The other flattened for an instant, then sprang and charged. The road-runner was on him as he struck the pellet, and galloped down the canyon in great, tense strides, on his toes, the lizard lashing the air from his beak. The hawk stooped at the road-runner, thought better of it, and rose against the wind to the head of the canyon, where he turned back and coasted over the desert, his shadow a little behind him and farther and farther below.

The swallows became the voice of the canyon again, but in moments when they were all silent, the lovely smaller sounds emerged, their own feathering, the liquid overflow, the snapping and clicking of insects, a touch of wind in the new aspens. Under these lay still more delicate tones, erasing, in the most silent seconds, the difference between eye and ear, a white cloud shadow passing under the water of the well, a dark cloud shadow on the cliff, the aspen patterns on the stones. Silentest of all were the rocks, the lost on the canyon floor, and the strong, thinking cliffs. The swallows began again.

At noon a red and white cow with one new calf, shining and curled, came slowly up from the desert, stopping often to let the calf rest. At each stop the calf would try vigorously to feed, but the cow would go on. When they reached the well the cow drank slowly for a long time; then she continued to wrinkle the water with her muzzle, drinking a little and blowing, as if she found it hard to leave. The calf worked under her with spasmodic nudgings. When she was done playing with the water, she nosed and licked him out from under her and up to the well. He shied from the surprising coolness and she put him back. When he stayed, she drank again. He put his nose into the water too, and bucked up as if bitten. He returned, got water up his nostrils and took three jumps away. The cow was content and moved off towards the canyon wall, tonguing grass tufts from among the rocks. Against the cliff she rubbed gently and continuously with a mild voluptuous look, occasionally lapping her nose with a serpent tongue. The loose winter shag came off in tufts on the rock. The calf lost her, became panicked and made desperate noises which stopped prematurely, and when he discovered her, complicated her toilet. Finally she led him down to the meadow where, moving slowly, they both fed until he was full and went to sleep in a ball in the sun. At sunset they returned to the well, where the cow drank again and gave him a second lesson. After this they went back into the brush and northward into the dusk. The cow's size and relative immunity to sudden death left an aftermath of peace, rendered gently humorous by the calf.

Also at sunset, there was a resurgence of life among the swallows. The thin golden air at the cliff tops, in which there were now no clouds so that the eastern mountains and the valley were flooded with unbroken light, was full of their cries and quick maneuvres among a dancing myriad of insects. The direct sun gave them, when they perched in rows upon the cliff, a dramatic significance like that of men upon an immensely higher promontory. As dusk rose out of the canyon, while the eastern peaks were still lighted, the swallows gradually became silent. At twilight, the air was full of velvet, swooping bats.

In the night jack-rabbits multiplied spontaneously out of the brush of the valley, drank in the rivulet, their noses and great ears continuously searching the dark, electrical air, and played in fits and starts on the meadow, the many young ones hopping like rubber, or made thumping love among the aspens and the willows.

A coyote came down canyon on his belly and lay in the brush with his nose between his paws. He took a young rabbit in a quiet spring and snap, and went into the brush again to eat it. At the slight rending of his meal the meadow cleared of leaping shadows and lay empty in the star-light. The rabbits, however, encouraged by new-comers, returned soon, and the coyote killed again and went off heavily, the jack's great hind legs dragging.

In the dry-wash below the meadow an old coyote, without family, profited by the second panic, which came over him. He ate what his loose teeth could tear, leaving the open remnant in the sand, drank at the basin and, carefully circling the meadow, disappeared into the dry wilderness.

Shortly before dawn, when the stars had lost lustre and there was no sound in the canyon but the rivulet and the faint, separate clickings of mice in the gravel, nine antelope in loose file, with three silently flagging fawns, came on trigger toe up the meadow and drank at the well, heads often up, muzzles dripping, broad ears turning. In the meadow they grazed and the fawns nursed. When there was as much gray as darkness in the air, and new wind in the canyon, they departed, the file weaving into the brush, merging into the desert, to nothing, and the swallows resumed the talkative day shift.

Jim Suttler and his burro came up into the meadow a little after noon, very slowly, though there was only a spring-fever warmth. Suttler walked pigeon-toed, like an old climber, but carefully and stiffly, not with the loose walk natural to such a long-legged man. He stopped in the middle of the meadow, took off his old black sombrero, and stared up at the veil of water shining over the edge of the basin.

"We're none too early, Jenny," he said to the burro.

The burro had felt water for miles, but could show no excitement. She stood with her head down and her four legs spread unnaturally, as if to postpone a collapse. Her pack reared higher than Suttler's head, and was hung with casks, pans, canteens, a pick, two shovels, a crowbar, and a rifle in a sheath. Suttler had the cautious uncertainty of his trade. His other burro had died two days before in the mountains east of Beatty, and Jenny and he bore its load.

Suttler shifted his old six-shooter from his rump to his thigh, and studied the well, the meadow, the cabin and the mouth of the mine as if he might choose not to stay. He was not a cinema prospector. If he looked like one of the probably mistaken conceptions of Christ, with his red beard and red hair to his shoulders, it was because he had been away from barbers and without spare water for shaving. He was unlike Christ in some other ways.

"It's kinda run down," he told Jenny, "but we'll take it."

He put his sombrero back on, let his pack fall slowly to the ground, showing the sweat patch in his bleached brown shirt, and began to unload Jenny carefully, like a collector handling rare vases, and put everything into one neat pile.

"Now," he said, "we'll have a drink." His tongue and lips were so swollen that the words were unclear, but he spoke casually, like a club-man sealing a minor deal. One learns to do business slowly with deserts and mountains. He picked up a bucket and started for the well. At the upper edge of the meadow he looked back. Jenny was still standing with her head down and her legs apart. He did not particularly notice her extreme thinness, for he had seen it coming on gradually. He was thinner himself, and tall, and so round-shouldered that when he stood his straightest he seemed to be peering ahead with his chin out.

"Come on, you old fool," he said. "It's off you now."

Jenny came, stumbling in the rocks above the meadow, and stopping often as if to decide why this annoyance recurred. When she became interested, Suttler would not let her get to the basin, but for ten minutes gave her water from his cupped hands, a few licks at a time. Then he drove her off and she stood in the shade of the canyon wall watching him. He began on his thirst in the same way, a gulp at a time, resting between gulps. After ten gulps he sat on a rock by the spring and looked up at the meadow and the big desert, and might have been considering the courses of the water through his body, but noticed also the antelope tracks in the mud.

After a time he drank another half dozen gulps, gave Jenny half a pail full, and drove her down to the meadow, where he spread a dirty blanket in the striped sun and shadow under the willows. He sat on the edge of the blanket, rolled a cigarette and smoked it while he watched Jenny. When she began to graze with her rump to the canyon, he flicked his cigarette onto the grass, rolled over with his back to the sun and slept until it became chilly after sunset. Then he woke, ate a can of beans, threw the can into the willows and led Jenny up to the well, where they drank together from the basin for a long time. While she resumed her grazing, he took another blanket and his rifle from the pile, removed his heel-worn boots, stood his rifle against a fork, and rolling up in both blankets, slept again.

In the night many rabbits played in the meadow in spite of the strong sweat and tobacco smell of Jim Suttler lying under the willows, but the antelope, when they came in the dead dark before dawn, were nervous, drank less, and did not graze but minced quickly back across the meadow and began to run at the head of the dry wash. Jenny slept with her head hanging, and did not hear them come or go.

Suttler woke lazy and still red-eyed, and spent the morning drinking at the well, eating and dozing on his blanket. In the afternoon, slowly, a few things at a time, he carried his pile to the cabin. He had a bachelor's obsession with order, though he did not mind dirt, and puttered until sundown, making a brush bed and arranging his gear. Much of this time, however, was spent studying the records on the cabin walls of the recent human life of the well. He had to be careful, because among the still legible names and dates, after Frank Davis, 1893, Willard Harbinger, 1893, London, England, John Mason, June 13, 1887, Bucksport, Maine, Mathew Kenling, from Glasgow, 1891, Penelope and Martin Reave, God Guide Us, 1885, was written Frank Hayward, 1492, feeling my age. There were other wits too. John Barr had written, Giv it back to the injuns, and Kenneth Thatcher, two years later, had written under that, Pity the noble redskin, while another man, whose second name was Evans, had written what was already a familiar libel, since it was not strictly true, Fifty miles from water, a hundred miles from wood, a million miles from God, three feet from hell. Someone unnamed had felt differently, saying, God is kind. We may make it now. Shot an antelope here July 10, 188——and the last number blurred. Arthur Smith, 1881, had recorded, Here berried my beloved wife Semantha, age 22, and my soul. God let me keep the child. J.M. said cryptically, Good luck, John, and Bill said, Ralph, if you come this way, am trying to get to Los Angeles. B. Westover said he had recovered from his wound there in 1884, and Galt said, enigmatically and without date, Bart and Miller burned to death in the Yellow Jacket. I don't care now. There were poets too, of both parties. What could still be read of Byron Cotter's verses, written in 1902, said,

> .   .   .   . here alone
> Each shining dawn I greet,
> The Lord's wind on my forehead
> And where he set his feet
> One mark of heel remaining
> Each day filled up anew,

To keep my soul from burning,
With clear, celestial dew.
Here in His Grace abiding
The mortal years and few
I shall. . .

but you can't tell what he intended, while J. A. had printed,

My brother came out in '49
I came in '51
At first we thought we liked it fine
But now, by God, we're done.

Suttler studied these records without smiling, like someone reading a funny paper, and finally, with a heavy blue pencil, registered, Jim and Jenny Suttler, damn dried out, March—and paused, but had no way of discovering the day—1940.

In the evening he sat on the steps watching the swallows in the golden upper canyon turn bats in the dusk, and thought about the antelope. He had seen the new tracks also, and it alarmed him a little that the antelope could have passed twice in the dark without waking him.

Before false dawn he was lying in the willows with his carbine at ready. Rabbits ran from the meadow when he came down, and after that there was no movement. He wanted to smoke. When he did see them at the lower edge of the meadow, he was startled, yet made no quick movement, but slowly pivoted to cover them. They made poor targets in that light and backed by the pale desert, appearing and disappearing before his eyes. He couldn't keep any one of them steadily visible, and decided to wait until they made contrast against the meadow. But his presence was strong. One of the antelope advanced onto the green, but then threw its head up, spun, and ran back past the flank of the herd, which swung after him. Suttler rose quickly and raised the rifle, but let it down without firing. He could hear the light rattle of their flight in the wash, but had only a belief that he could see them. He had few cartridges, and the ponderous echo under the cliffs would scare them off for weeks.

His energies, however, were awakened by the frustrated hunt. While there was still more light than heat in the canyon, he climbed to the abandoned mine tunnel at the top of the alluvial wing of the cliff. He looked at the broken rock in the dump, kicked up its pack with a boot toe, and went into the tunnel, peering closely at its sides, in places black with old smoke smudges. At the back he struck two matches and looked at the jagged dead end and the fragments on the floor, then returned to the shallow beginning of a side tunnel. At the second match here he knelt quickly, scrutinized a portion of the rock, and when the match went out at once lit another. He lit six matches, and pulled at the rock with his hand. It was firm.

"The poor chump," he said aloud.

He got a loose rock from the tunnel and hammered at the projection with it. It came finally, and he carried it into the sun on the dump.

"Yessir," he said aloud, after a minute.

He knocked his sample into three pieces and examined each minutely.

"Yessir, yessir," he said with malicious glee, and, grinning at the tunnel, "the poor chump."

Then he looked again at the dump, like the mound before a gigantic gopher hole. "Still, that's a lot of digging," he said.

He put sample chips into his shirt pocket, keeping a small black, heavy one that had fallen neatly from a hole like a borer's, to play with in his hand. After trouble he found the claim pile on the side hill south of the tunnel, its top rocks tumbled into the shale. Under the remaining rocks he found what he wanted, a ragged piece of yellowed paper between two boards. The writing was in pencil, and not diplomatic. "I hearby clame this hole damn side hill as far as I can dig in. I am a good shot. Keep off. John Barr, April 11, 1897."

Jim Suttler grinned. "Tough guy, eh?" he said.

He made a small ceremony of burning the paper upon a stone from the cairn. The black tinsel of ash blew off and broke into flakes.

"O.K., John Barr?" he asked.

"O.K., Suttler," he answered himself.

In blue pencil, on soiled paper from his pocket, he slowly printed, "Becus of the lamented desease of the late clamant, John Barr, I now clame these diggins for myself and partner Jenny. I can shoot too." And wrote, rather than printed, "James T. Suttler, March—" and paused.

"Make it an even month," he said, and wrote, "11, 1940." Underneath he wrote, "Jenny Suttler, her mark," and drew a skull with long ears.

"There," he said, and folded the paper, put it between the two boards, and rebuilt the cairn into a neat pyramid above it.

In high spirit he was driven to cleanliness. With scissors, soap, and razor he climbed to the spring. Jenny was there, drinking.

"When you're done," he said, and lifted her head, pulled her ears and scratched her.

"Maybe we've got something here, Jenny," he said.

Jenny observed him soberly and returned to the meadow.

"She doesn't believe me," he said, and began to perfect himself. He sheared off his red tresses in long hanks, then cut closer, and went over yet a third time, until there remained a brush, of varying density, of stiff red bristles, through which his scalp shone whitely. He sheared the beard likewise, then knelt to the well for mirror and shaved painfully. He also shaved his neck and about his ears. He arose younger and less impressive, with jaws as pale as his scalp, so that his sunburn was a red domino. He burned tresses and beard ceremoniously upon a sage bush, and announced, "It is spring."

He began to empty the pockets of his shirt and breeches onto a flat stone, yelling, "In the spring a young man's fancy," to a kind of tune, and paused, struck by the facts.

"Oh yeah?" he said. "Fat chance."

"Fat," he repeated with obscene consideration. "Oh, well," he said, and finished piling upon the rock notebooks, pencil stubs, cartridges, tobacco, knife, stump pipe, matches, chalk, samples, and three wrinkled photographs. One of the photographs he observed at length before weighting it down with a .45 cartridge. It showed a round, blonde girl with a big smile on a stupid face, in a patterned calico house dress in front of a blossoming rhododendron bush.

He added to this deposit his belt and holster with the big .45.

Then he stripped himself, washed and rinsed his garments in the spring, and spread them upon stones and brush, and carefully arranged four flat stones into a platform beside the trough. Standing there he scooped water over himself, gasping, made it a lather, and at last, face and copper bristles also foaming, gropingly entered the basin and submerged, flooding the water over in a thin and soapy sheet. His head emerged at once. "My God," he whispered. He remained under, however, till he was soapless, and goose pimpled as a file, he climbed out cautiously onto the rock platform and performed a dance of small, revolving patterns with a great deal of up and down.

At one point in his dance he observed the pictograph journey upon the cliff, and danced nearer to examine it.

"Ignorant," he pronounced. "Like a little kid," he said.

He was intrigued, however, by some more recent records, names smoked and cut upon the lower rock. One of these, in script, like a gigantic handwriting deeply cut, said ALVAREZ BLANCO DE TOLEDO, Anno Di 1624. A very neat, upright cross was chiselled beneath it.

Suttler grinned. "Oh yeah?" he asked, with his head upon one side. "Nuts," he said, looking at it squarely.

But it inspired him, and with his jack-knife he began scraping beneath the possibly Spanish inscription. His knife, however, made scratches, not incisions. He completed a bad Jim and Jenny and quit, saying, "I should kill myself over a phoney wop."

Thereafter, for weeks, while the canyon became increasingly like a furnace in the daytime and the rocks stayed warm at night, he drove his tunnel farther into the gully, making a heap of ore to be worked, and occasionally adding a peculiarly heavy pebble to the others in his small leather bag with a draw string. He and Jenny thrived upon this fixed and well-watered life. The hollows disappeared from his face and he became less stringy, while Jenny grew round, her battle-ship gray pelt even lustrous and its black markings distinct and ornamental. The burro found time from her grazing to come to the cabin door in the evenings and attend solemnly to Suttler playing with his samples and explaining their future.

"Then, old lady," Suttler said, "you will carry only small children, one at a time, for never more than half an hour. You will have a bedroom with French windows and a mattress, and I will paint your feet gold.

"The children," he said, "will probably be red-headed, but maybe blonde. Anyway, they will be beautiful.

"After we've had a holiday, of course," he added. "For one hundred and thirty-three nights," he said dreamily. "Also," he said, "just one hundred and thirty-three quarts. I'm no drunken bum.

"For you, though," he said, "for one hundred and thirty-three nights a quiet hotel with other old ladies. I should drag my own mother in the gutter." He pulled her head down by the ears and kissed her loudly upon the nose. They were very happy together.

Nor did they greatly alter most of the life of the canyon. The antelope did not return, it is true, the rabbits were fewer and less playful because he sometimes snared them for meat, the little, clean mice and desert rats avoided the cabin they had used, and the road-runner did not come in daylight after Suttler, for fun, narrowly missed him with a piece of ore from the tunnel mouth. Suttler's violence was disproportionate perhaps, when he used his .45 to blow apart a creamy rat who did invade the cabin, but the loss was insignificant to the pattern of the well, and more than compensated when he one day caught the rattler extended at the foot of the dump in a drunken stupor from rare young rabbit, and before it could recoil held it aloft by the tail and snapped its head off, leaving the heavy body to turn slowly for a long time among the rocks. The dominant voices went undisturbed, save when he sang badly at his work or said beautiful things to Jenny in a loud voice.

There were, however, two more noticeable changes, one of which, at least, was important to Suttler himself. The first was the execution of the range cow's calf in the late fall, when he began to suggest a bull. Suttler felt a little guilty about this because the calf might have belonged to somebody, because the cow remained near the meadow bawling for two nights, and because the calf had come to meet the gun with more curiosity than challenge. But when he had the flayed carcass hung in the mine tunnel in a wet canvas, the sensation of providence overcame any qualms.

The other change was more serious. It occurred at the beginning of such winter as the well had, when there was sometimes a light rime on the rocks at dawn, and the aspens held only a few yellow leaves. Suttler thought often of leaving. The nights were cold, the fresh meat was eaten, his hopes had diminished as he still found only occasional nuggets, and his dreams of women, if less violent, were more nostalgic. The canyon held him with a feeling he would have called lonesome but at home, yet he probably would have gone except for this second change.

In the higher mountains to the west, where there was already snow, and at dawn a green winter sky, hunger stirred a buried memory in a cougar. He had twice killed antelope at the well, and felt there had been time enough again. He came down from the dwarfed trees and crossed the narrow valley under the stars, sometimes stopping abruptly to stare intently about, like a house-cat in a strange room. After each stop he would at once resume a quick, noiseless trot. From the top of the mountain above the spring he came down very slowly on his belly, but there was nothing at the well. He relaxed, and leaning on the rim of the basin, drank, listening between laps. His nose was clean with fasting, and he knew of the man in the cabin and Jenny in the meadow, but they were strange, not what he remembered about the place. But neither had his past made him fearful. It was only his habitual hunting caution which made him go down into the willows carefully, and lie there head up, watching Jenny, but still waiting for antelope, which he had killed before near dawn. The strange smells were confusing and therefore irritating. After an hour he rose and went silently to the cabin, from which the strangest smell came strongly, a carnivorous smell which did not arouse appetite, but made him bristle nervously. The tobacco in it was like pins in his nostrils. He circled the cabin, stopping frequently. At the open door the scent was violent. He stood with his front paws up on the step, moving his head in serpent motions, the end of his heavy tail furling and unfurling constantly. In a dream Suttler turned over without waking, and muttered. The cougar crouched, his eyes intent, his ruff lifting. Then he swung away from the door again and lay in the willows, but where he could watch the cabin also.

When the sky was alarmingly pale and the antelope had not come, he crawled a few feet at a time, behind the willows, to a point nearer Jenny. There he crouched, working his hind legs slowly under him until he was set, and sprang, raced the three or four jumps to the drowsy burro, and struck. The beginning of her mortal scream was severed, but having made an imperfect leap, and from no height, the cat did not at once break her neck, but drove her to earth, where her small hooves churned futilely in the sod, and chewed and worried until she lay still.

Jim Suttler was nearly awakened by the fragment of scream, but heard nothing after it, and sank again.

The cat wrestled Jenny's body into the willows, fed with uncertain relish, drank long at the well, and went slowly over the crest, stopping often to look back. In spite of the light and the beginning talk of the swallows, the old coyote also fed and was gone before Suttler woke.

When Suttler found Jenny, many double columns of regimented ants were already at work, streaming in and out of the interior and mounting like bridge workers upon the ribs. Suttler stood and looked down. He desired to hold the small muzzle in the hollow of his hand, feeling that this familiar gesture would get through to Jenny, but couldn't bring himself to it because of what had happened to that side of her head. He squatted and lifted one hoof on its stiff leg and held that. Ants emerged hurriedly from the fetlock, their lines of communication broken. Two of them made disorganized excursions on the back of his hand. He rose, shook them off, and stood staring again. He didn't say anything because he spoke easily only when cheerful or excited, but a determination was beginning in him. He followed the drag to the spot torn by the small hoofs. Among the willows again, he found the tracks of both the cougar and the coyote, and the cat's tracks again at the well and by the cabin doorstep. He left Jenny in the willows with a canvas over her during the day, and did not eat.

At sunset he sat on the doorstep, cleaning his rifle and oiling it until he could spring the lever almost without sound. He filled the clip, pressed it home, and sat with the gun across his knees until dark, when he put on his sheepskin, stuffed a scarf into the pocket, and went down to Jenny. He removed the canvas from her, rolled it up and held it under his arm.

"I'm sorry, old woman," he said. "Just tonight."

There was a little cold wind in the willows. It rattled the upper branches lightly.

Suttler selected a spot thirty yards down wind, from which he could see Jenny, spread the canvas and lay down upon it, facing towards her. After an hour he was afraid of falling asleep and sat up against a willow clump.

He sat there all night. A little after midnight the old coyote came into the dry-wash below him. At the top of the wash he sat down, and when the mingled scents gave him a clear picture of the strategy, let his tongue loll out, looked at the stars for a moment with his mouth silently open, rose and trotted into the desert.

At the beginning of daylight the younger coyote trotted in from the north, and turned up towards the spring, but saw Jenny. He sat down and looked at her for a long time. Then he moved to the west and sat down again. In the wind was only winter, and the water, and faintly the acrid bat dung in the cliffs. He completed the circle, but not widely enough, walking slowly through the willows, down the edge of the meadow and in again not ten yards in front of the following muzzle of the carbine. Like Jenny, he felt his danger too late. The heavy slug caught him at the base of the skull in the middle of the first jump, so that it was amazingly accelerated for a fraction of a second. The coyote began it alive, and ended it quite dead, but with a tense muscular movement conceived which resulted in a grotesque final leap and twist of the hind-quarters alone, leaving them propped high against a willow clump while the head was half buried in the sand, red welling up along the lips of the distended jaws. The cottony underpelt of the tail and rump stirred gleefully in the wind.

When Suttler kicked the body and it did not move, he suddenly dropped his gun, grasped it by the upright hind legs, and hurled it out into the sage-brush. His face appeared slightly insane with fury for that instant. Then he picked up his gun and went back to the cabin, where he ate, and drank half of one of his last three bottles of whiskey.

In the middle of the morning he came down with his pick and shovel, dragged Jenny's much-lightened body down into the dry-wash, and dug in the rock and sand for two hours. When she was covered, he erected a small cairn of stone, like the claim post, above her.

"If it takes a year," he said, and licked the salt sweat on his lips.

That day he finished the half bottle and drank all of a second one, and became very drunk, so that he fell asleep during his vigil in the willows, sprawled wide on the dry turf and snoring. He was not disturbed. There was a difference in his smell after that day which prevented even the rabbits from coming into the meadow. He waited five nights in the willows. Then he transferred his watch to a niche in the cliff, across from and just below the spring.

All winter, while the day wind blew long veils of dust across the desert, regularly repeated, like waves or the smoke of line artillery fire, and the rocks shrank under the cold glitter of night, he did not miss a watch. He learned to go to sleep at sundown, wake within a few minutes of midnight, go up to his post, and become at once clear headed and watchful. He talked to himself in the mine and the cabin, but never in the niche. His supplies ran low, and he ate less, but would not risk a startling shot. He rationed his tobacco, and when it was gone worked up to a vomiting sickness every three days for nine days, but did not miss a night in the niche. All winter he did not remove his clothes, bathe, shave, cut his hair or sing. He worked the dead mine only to be busy, and became thin again, with sunken eyes which yet were not the eyes he had come with the spring before. It was April, his food almost gone, when he got his chance.

There was a half moon that night, which made the canyon walls black, and occasionally gleamed on wrinkles of the overflow. The cat came down so quietly that Suttler did not see him until he was beside the basin. The animal was suspicious. He took the wind, and twice started to drink, and didn't, but crouched. On Suttler's face there was a set grin which exposed his teeth.

"Not even a drink, you bastard," he thought.

The cat drank a little though, and dropped again, softly, trying to get the scent from the meadow. Suttler drew slowly upon his soul in the trigger. When it gave, the report was magnified impressively in the canyon. The cougar sprang straight into the air and screamed outrageously. The back of Suttler's neck was cold and his hand trembled, but he shucked the lever and fired again. This shot ricocheted from the basin and whined away thinly. The first, however, had struck near enough. The cat began to scramble rapidly on the loose stone, at first without voice, then screaming repeatedly. It doubled upon itself, snarling and chewing in a small furious circle, fell and began to throw itself in short, leaping spasms upon the stones, struck across the rim of the tank and lay half in the water, its head and shoulders raised in one corner and resting against the cliff. Suttler could hear it breathing hoarsely and snarling very faintly. The soprano chorus of swallows gradually became silent.

Suttler had risen to fire again, but lowered the carbine and advanced, stopping at every step to peer intently and listen for the hoarse breathing, which continued. Even when he was within five feet of the tank the cougar did not move, except to gasp so that the water again splashed from the basin. Suttler was calmed by the certainty of accomplishment. He drew the heavy revolver from his holster, aimed carefully at the rattling head, and fired again. The canyon boomed, and the east responded faintly and a little behind, but Suttler did not hear them, for the cat thrashed heavily in the tank, splashing him as with a bucket, and then lay still on its side over the edge, its muzzle and forepaws hanging. The water was settling quietly in the tank, but Suttler stirred it again, shooting five more times with great deliberation into the heavy body, which did not move except at the impact of the slugs.

The rest of the night, even after the moon was gone, he worked fiercely, slitting and tearing with his knife. In the morning, under the swallows, he dragged the marbled carcass, still bleeding a little in places, onto the rocks on the side away from the spring, and dropped it. Dragging the ragged hide by the neck, he went unsteadily down the canyon to the cabin, where he slept like a drunkard, although his whiskey had been gone for two months.

In the afternoon, with dreaming eyes, he bore the pelt to Jenny's grave, took down the stones with his hands, shoveled the earth from her, covered her with the skin, and again with earth and the cairn.

He looked at this monument. "There," he said.

That night, for the first time since her death, he slept through.

In the morning, at the well, he repeated the cleansing ritual of a year before, save that they were rags he stretched to dry, even to the dance upon the rock platform while drying. Squatting naked and clean, shaven and clipped, he looked for a long time at the grinning countenance, now very dirty, of the plump girl in front of the blossoming rhododendrons, and in the resumption of his dance he made singing noises accompanied by the words, "Spring, spring, beautiful spring." He was a starved but revived and volatile spirit. An hour later he went south, his boot soles held on by canvas strips, and did not once look back.

The disturbed life of the spring resumed. In the second night the rabbits loved in the willows, and at the end of the week the rats played in the cabin again. The old coyote and a vulture cleaned the cougar, and his bones fell apart in the shale. The road-runner came up one day, tentatively, and in front of the tunnel snatched up a horned toad and ran with it around the corner, but no farther. After a month the antelope returned. The well brimmed, and in the gentle sunlight the new aspen leaves made a tiny music of shadows.

Wallace Stegner
b. 1909

1943: *The Big Rock Candy Mountain*
1954: *Beyond the Hundredth Meridian:*
John Wesley Powell and the
Second Opening of the West
1962: *Wolf Willow: A History,*
a Story, and a Memory
of the Last Plains Frontier
1969: *The Sound of Mountain Water*
1971: *Angle of Repose*
1976: *The Spectator Bird*

N OT EVEN *the Pulitzer Prize, which Wallace Stegner won in 1972 for*
Angle of Repose, *can sufficiently acknowledge Stegner's contribution to American literature. His books include more than a dozen volumes of fiction and a dozen more of nonfiction; he has had editorial responsibility for another eighteen volumes of literary scholarship. Stegner's short stories have appeared in* Harper's *and* New Yorker; *over a hundred of his articles on literature, history, nature, and the American West have occupied pages in* Atlantic, Saturday Review of Literature, American Heritage, *and other magazines. The* Spectator Bird *won the National Book Award for fiction in 1977.*

Stegner's restless, wide-ranging intellect reflects a life of movement and variety. "Since I was born in Iowa in 1909," he wrote, "I have lived in twenty places in eight different states, besides a couple of places in Canada, and in some of these places we lived in anywhere from two to ten different houses and neighborhoods." [1]

1. Wallace Stegner, *The Sound of Mountain Water* (1969; reprint, Lincoln: University of Nebraska Press, 1985), p. 158.

He studied at the University of Iowa, then taught in Utah and Wisconsin and at Breadloaf and Harvard before joining Stanford's creative writing program. Stegner's knowledge of history, biography, sociology, and psychology, together with his forceful personal style, made him an effective teacher. He was also a controversial teacher, at times. Early in his academic life, between 1940 and 1945, Stegner leaped into a major literary battle against a group of scholars who had followed Sinclair Lewis in an attack on Bernard DeVoto's critical views. By the time Stegner was hired to teach at Stanford in 1945, he had a reputation for being an outspoken critic and advocate of the western heritage. An example is "Wilderness Letter," published in 1969 as the coda to part 1 of Stegner's collection of essays The Sound of Mountain Water. *Addressing a commission formed to assess public use of the nation's wilderness, Stegner forcefully argues that an intangible, spiritual "resource" exists in the wilderness, a force that helped form the national character; without the wilderness, the American identity as we know it will vanish. Stegner makes his thesis so clear that he seems to simplify the conflict between wilderness and civilization. In fact, these two forces are complex, and the tension between them is even more complex. Stegner's* Beyond the Hundredth Meridian *explores the effect of such "simplifiers" as William Gilpin, portrayed as an archromantic with a view of the West as a vast garden, in contrast to the realistic perspective of John Wesley Powell.*

When it comes to fiction, Stegner employs history in more personal ways. His intimate use of Mary Hallock Foote's letters and stories in Angle of Repose, *for instance, led some critics to attack him.[2] In* The Big Rock Candy Mountain, *Stegner's family provides the basis for much of the story. And one biography has pointed out that the people in "The Blue-Winged Teal" are "recognizable descendants" of Stegner's parents. However true that may be, the fact does not affect the larger symbolism of the characters. In his essay "History, Myth, and the Western Writer," Stegner himself pointed out parallels between the mother and the women in* The Virginian *and "The Bride Comes to Yellow Sky," the women representing sensitivity and domesticity in contrast to coarse masculinity.[3]*

---

2. See Mary Ellen Williams Walsh, "*Angle of Repose* and the Writings of Mary Hallock Foote: A Source Study," in *Critical Essays on Wallace Stegner*, ed. Anthony Arthur (Boston: G. K. Hall, 1982), pp. 184–209.

3. Forrest G. Robinson and Margaret G. Robinson, *Wallace Stegner* (Boston: Twayne, 1977), p. 79; Stegner, "History, Myth, and the Western Writer," *Mountain Water*, p. 195.

Wilderness Letter

David E. Pesonen   Los Altos, Calif.
Wildland Research Center   Dec. 3, 1960
Agricultural Experiment Station
243 Mulford Hall
University of California
Berkeley 4, Calif.

Dear Mr. Pesonen:

I believe that you are working on the wilderness portion of the Out-door Recreation Resources Review Commission's report. If I may, I should like to urge some arguments for wilderness preservation that involve recreation, as it is ordinarily conceived, hardly at all. Hunting, fishing, hiking, mountain-climbing, camping, photography, and the enjoyment of natural scenery will all, surely, figure in your report. So will the wilderness as a genetic reserve, a scientific yardstick by which we may measure the world in its natural balance against the world in its man-made imbalance. What I want to speak for is not so much the wilderness uses, valuable as those are, but the wilderness *idea*, which is a resource in itself. Being an intangible and spiritual resource, it will seem mystical to the practical-minded—but then anything that cannot be moved by a bulldozer is likely to seem mystical to them.

I want to speak for the wilderness idea as something that has helped form our character and that has certainly shaped our history as a people. It has no more to do with recreation than churches have to do with recreation, or than the strenuousness and optimism and expansiveness of what historians call the "American Dream" have to do with recreation. Nevertheless, since it is only in this recreation survey that the values of wilderness are being compiled, I hope you will permit me to insert this idea between the leaves, as it were, of the recreation report.

From Wallace Stegner, *The Sound of Mountain Water* (New York: Doubleday and Co., 1969), pp. 145–53. Copyright © 1969 by Wallace Stegner. Reprinted by permission of Doubleday and Company, Inc.

Something will have gone out of us as a people if we ever let the remaining wilderness be destroyed; if we permit the last virgin forests to be turned into comic books and plastic cigarette cases; if we drive the few remaining members of the wild species into zoos or to extinction; if we pollute the last clear air and dirty the last clean streams and push our paved roads through the last of the silence, so that never again will Americans be free in their own country from the noise, the exhausts, the stinks of human and automotive waste. And so that never again can we have the chance to see ourselves single, separate, vertical and individual in the world, part of the environment of trees and rocks and soil, brother to the other animals, part of the natural world and competent to belong in it. Without any remaining wilderness we are committed wholly, without chance for even momentary reflection and rest, to a headlong drive into our technological termite-life, the Brave New World of a completely man-controlled environment. We need wilderness preserved—as much of it as is still left, and as many kinds—because it was the challenge against which our character as a people was formed. The reminder and the reassurance that it is still there is good for our spiritual health even if we never once in ten years set foot in it. It is good for us when we are young, because of the incomparable sanity it can bring briefly, as vacation and rest, into our insane lives. It is important to us when we are old simply because it is there—important, that is, simply as idea.

We are a wild species, as Darwin pointed out. Nobody ever tamed or domesticated or scientifically bred us. But for at least three millennia we have been engaged in a cumulative and ambitious race to modify and gain control of our environment, and in the process we have come close to domesticating ourselves. Not many people are likely, any more, to look upon what we call "progress" as an unmixed blessing. Just as surely as it has brought us increased comfort and more material goods, it has brought us spiritual losses, and it threatens now to become the Frankenstein that will destroy us. One means of sanity is to retain a hold on the natural world, to remain, insofar as we can, good animals. Americans still have that chance, more than many peoples; for while we were demonstrating ourselves the most efficient and ruthless environment-busters in history, and slashing and burning and cutting our way through a wilderness continent, the wilderness was working on us. It remains in us as surely as Indian names remain on the land. If the abstract dream of human liberty and human dignity became, in America, something more than an abstract dream, mark it down at least partially to the fact that we were in subtle ways subdued by what we conquered.

The Connecticut Yankee, sending likely candidates from King Arthur's unjust kingdom to his Man Factory for rehabilitation, was over-optimistic, as he later admitted. These things cannot be forced, they have to grow. To make such a man, such a democrat, such a believer in human individual dignity, as Mark Twain himself, the frontier was necessary, Hannibal and the Mississippi and Virginia City, and reaching out from those the wilderness; the wilderness as opportunity and as idea, the thing that has helped to make an American different from and, until we forget it in the roar of our industrial cities, more fortunate than other men. For an American, insofar as he is new and different at all, is a civilized man who has renewed himself in the wild. The American experience has been the confrontation by old peoples and cultures of a world as new as if it had just risen from the sea. That gave us our hope and our excitement, and the hope and excitement can be passed on to newer Americans, Americans who never saw any phase of the frontier. But only so long as we keep the remainder of our wild as a reserve and a promise—a sort of wilderness bank.

As a novelist, I may perhaps be forgiven for taking literature as a reflection, indirect but profoundly true, of our national consciousness. And our literature, as perhaps you are aware, is sick, embittered, losing its mind, losing its faith. Our novelists are the declared enemies of their society. There has hardly been a serious or important novel in this century that did not repudiate in part or in whole American technological culture for its commercialism, its vulgarity, and the way in which it has dirtied a clean continent and a clean dream. I do not expect that the preservation of our remaining wilderness is going to cure this condition. But the mere example that we can as a nation apply some other criteria than commercial and exploitative considerations would be heartening to many Americans, novelists or otherwise. We need to demonstrate our acceptance of the natural world, including ourselves; we need the spiritual refreshment that being natural can produce. And one of the best places for us to get that is in the wilderness where the fun houses, the bulldozers, and the pavements of our civilization are shut out.

Sherwood Anderson, in a letter to Waldo Frank in the 1920's, said it better than I can. "Is it not likely that when the country was new and men were often alone in the fields and the forest they got a sense of bigness outside themselves that has now in some way been lost . . . Mystery whispered in the grass, played in the branches of trees overhead, was caught up and blown across the American line in clouds of dust at evening on the prairies . . . I am old enough to remember tales that strengthen my belief in a deep semi-religious influence that was formerly at work among our people. The flavor of it hangs over the best work of Mark Twain . . . I can remember old fellows in my home town speaking feelingly of an evening spent on the big empty plains. It had taken the shrillness out of them. They had learned the trick of quiet . . ."

We could learn it too, even yet; even our children and grandchildren could learn it. But only if we save, for just such absolutely non-recreational, impractical, and mystical uses as this, all the wild that still remains to us.

It seems to me significant that the distinct downturn in our literature from hope to bitterness took place almost at the precise time when the frontier officially came to an end, in 1890, and when the American way of life had begun to turn strongly urban and industrial. The more urban it has become, and the more frantic with technological change, the sicker and more embittered our literature, and I believe our people, have become. For myself, I grew up on the empty plains of Saskatchewan and Montana and in the mountains of Utah, and I put a very high valuation on what those places gave me. And if I had not been able periodically to renew myself in the mountains and deserts of western America I would be very nearly bughouse. Even when I can't get to the back country, the thought of the colored deserts of southern Utah, or the reassurance that there are still stretches of prairie where the world can be instantaneously perceived as disk and bowl, and where the little but intensely important human being is exposed to the five directions and the thirty-six winds, is a positive consolation. The idea alone can sustain me. But as the wilderness areas are progressively exploited or "improved," as the jeeps and bulldozers of uranium prospectors scar up the deserts and the roads are cut into the alpine timberlands, and as the remnants of the unspoiled and natural world are progressively eroded, every such loss is a little death in me. In us.

I am not moved by the argument that those wilderness areas which have already been exposed to grazing or mining are already deflowered, and so might as well be "harvested." For mining I cannot say much good except that its operations are generally short-lived. The extractable wealth is taken and the shafts, the tailings, and the ruins left, and in a dry country such as the American West the wounds men make in the earth do not quickly heal. Still, they are only wounds; they aren't absolutely mortal. Better a wounded wilderness than none at all. And as for grazing, if it is strictly controlled so that it does not destroy the ground cover, damage the ecology, or compete with the wildlife it is in itself nothing that need conflict with the wilderness feeling or the validity of the wilderness experience. I have known enough range cattle to recognize them as wild animals; and the people who herd them have, in the wilderness context, the dignity of rareness; they belong on the frontier, moreover, and have a look of rightness. The invasion they make on the virgin country is a sort of invasion that is as old as Neolithic man, and they can, in moderation, even emphasize a man's feeling of belonging to the natural world. Under surveillance, they can belong; under control, they need not deface or mar. I do not believe that in wilderness areas where grazing has never been permitted, it should be permitted; but I do not believe either that an otherwise untouched wilderness should be eliminated from the preservation plan because of limited existing uses such as grazing which are in consonance with the frontier condition and image.

Let me say something on the subject of the kinds of wilderness worth preserving. Most of those areas contemplated are in the national forests and in high mountain country. For all the usual recreational purposes, the alpine and forest wildernesses are obviously the most important, both as genetic banks and as beauty spots. But for the spiritual renewal, the recognition of identity, the birth of awe, other kinds will serve every bit as well. Perhaps, because they are less friendly to life, more abstractly non-human, they will serve even better. On our Saskatchewan prairie, the nearest neighbor was four miles away, and at night we saw only two lights on all the dark rounding earth. The earth was full of animals—field mice, ground squirrels, weasels, ferrets, badgers, coyotes, burrowing owls, snakes. I knew them as my little brothers, as fellow creatures, and I have never been able to look upon animals in any other way since. The sky in that country came clear down to the ground on every side, and it was full of great weathers, and clouds, and winds, and hawks. I hope I learned something from knowing intimately the creatures of the earth; I hope I learned something from looking a long way, from looking up, from being much alone. A prairie like that, one big enough to carry the eye clear to the sinking, rounding horizon, can be as lonely and grand and simple in its forms as the sea. It is as good a place as any for the wilderness experience to happen; the vanishing prairie is as worth preserving for the wilderness idea as the alpine forests.

So are great reaches of our western deserts, scarred somewhat by prospectors but otherwise open, beautiful, waiting, close to whatever God you want to see in them. Just as a sample, let me suggest the Robbers' Roost country in Wayne County, Utah, near the Capitol Reef National Monument. In that desert climate the dozer and jeep tracks will not soon melt back into the earth, but the country has a way of making the scars insignificant. It is a lovely and terrible wilderness, such a wilderness as Christ and the prophets went out into; harshly and beautifully colored, broken and worn until its bones are exposed, its great sky without a smudge or taint from Technocracy, and in hidden corners and pockets under its cliffs the sudden poetry of springs. Save a piece of country like that intact, and it does not matter in the slightest that only a few people every year will go into it. That is precisely its value. Roads would be a desecration, crowds would ruin it. But those who haven't the strength or youth to go into it and live can simply sit and look. They can look two hundred miles, clear into Colorado; and looking down over the cliffs and canyons of the San Rafael Swell and the Robbers' Roost they can also look as deeply into themselves as anywhere I know. And if they can't even get to the places on the Aquarius Plateau where the present roads will carry them, they can simply contemplate the *idea*, take pleasure in the fact that such a timeless and uncontrolled part of earth is still there.

These are some of the things wilderness can do for us. That is the reason we need to put into effect, for its preservation, some other principle than the principles of exploitation or "usefulness" or even recreation. We simply need that wild country available to us, even if we never do more than drive to its edge and look in. For it can be a means of reassuring ourselves of our sanity as creatures, a part of the geography of hope.

Very sincerely yours,
Wallace Stegner

—

The Blue-Winged Teal

STILL IN WADERS, with the string of ducks across his shoulder, he stood hesitating on the sidewalk in the cold November wind. His knees were stiff from being cramped up all day in the blind, and his feet were cold. Today, all day, he had been alive; now he was back ready to be dead again.

Lights were on all up and down the street, and there was a rush of traffic and a hurrying of people past and around him, yet the town was not his own, the people passing were strangers, the sounds of evening in this place were no sounds that carried warmth or familiarity. Though he had spent most of his twenty years in the town, knew hundreds of its people, could draw maps of its streets from memory, he wanted to admit familiarity with none of it. He had shut himself off.

From Wallace Stegner, *The City of the Living and Other Stories* (Boston: Houghton Mifflin Co., 1956), pp. 1–22. Copyright © 1956 by Wallace Stegner. Copyright renewed © 1984 by Wallace Stegner. Reprinted by permission of Brandt and Brandt Literary Agents, Inc.

Then what was he doing here, in front of this poolhall, loaded down with nine dead ducks? What had possessed him in the first place to borrow gun and waders and car from his father and go hunting? If he had wanted to breathe freely for a change, why hadn't he kept right on going? What was there in this place to draw him back? A hunter had to have a lodge to bring his meat to and people who would be glad of his skill. He had this poolhall and his father, John Lederer, Prop.

He stepped out of a woman's path and leaned against the door. Downstairs, in addition to his father, he would find old Max Schmeckebier, who ran a cheap blackjack game in the room under the sidewalk. He would find Giuseppe Sciutti, the Sicilian barber, closing his shop or tidying up the rack of *Artists and Models* and *The Nudist* with which he lured trade. He would probably find Billy Hammond, the night clerk from the Windsor Hotel, having his sandwich and beer and pie, or moving alone around a pool table, whistling abstractedly, practicing shots. If the afternoon blackjack game had broken up, there would be Navy Edwards, dealer and bouncer for Schmeckebier. At this time of evening there might be a few counter customers and a cop collecting his tribute of a beer or that other tribute that Schmeckebier paid to keep the cardroom open.

And he would find, sour contrast with the bright sky and the wind of the tule marshes, the cavelike room with its back corners in darkness, would smell that smell compounded of steam heat and cue-chalk dust, of sodden butts in cuspidors, of coffee and meat and beer smells from the counter, of cigarette smoke so unaired that it darkened the walls. From anywhere back of the middle tables there would be the pervasive reek of toilet disinfectant. Back of the counter his father would be presiding, throwing the poolhall light switch to save a few cents when the place was empty, flipping it on to give an air of brilliant and successful use when feet came down the stairs past Sciutti's shop.

The hunter moved his shoulder under the weight of the ducks, his mind full for a moment with the image of his father's face, darkly pale, fallen in on its bones, and the pouched, restless, suspicious eyes that seemed always looking for someone. Over the image came the face of his mother, dead now and six weeks buried. His teeth clicked at the thought of how she had held the old man up for thirty years, kept him at a respectable job, kept him from slipping back into the poolroom-Johnny he had been when she married him. Within ten days of her death he had hunted up this old failure of a poolhall.

In anger the hunter turned, thinking of the hotel room he shared with his father. But he had to eat. Broke as he was, a student yanked from his studies, he had no choice but to eat on the old man. Besides, there were the ducks. He felt somehow that the thing would be incomplete unless he brought his game back for his father to see.

His knees unwilling in the stiff waders, he went down the steps, descending into the light shining through Joe Sciutti's door, and into the momentary layer of clean bay rum smell, talcum smell, hair tonic smell, that rose past the still-revolving barber pole in the angle of the stairs.

Joe Sciutti was sweeping wads of hair from his tile floor, and hunched over the counter beyond, their backs to the door, were Schmeckebier, Navy Edwards, Billy Hammond, and an unknown customer. John Lederer was behind the counter, mopping alertly with a rag. The poolroom lights were up bright, but when Lederer saw who was coming he flipped the switch and dropped the big room back into dusk.

As the hunter came to the end of the counter their heads turned toward him. "Well I'm a son of a bee," Navy Edwards said, and scrambled off his stool. Next to him Billy Hammond half stood up so that his pale yellow hair took a halo from the backbar lights. "Say!" Max Schmeckebier said. "Say, dot's goot, dot's pooty goot, Henry!"

But Henry was watching his father so intently he did not turn to them. He slid the string of ducks off his shoulder and swung them up onto the wide walnut bar. They landed solidly—offering or tribute or ransom or whatever they were. For a moment it was as if this little act were private between the two of them. He felt queerly moved, his stomach tightened in suspense or triumph. Then the old man's pouchy eyes slipped from his and the old man came quickly forward along the counter and laid hands on the ducks.

He handled them as if he were petting kittens, his big white hands stringing the heads one by one from the wire.

"Two spoonbill," he said, more to himself than to others crowding around. "Shovelducks. Don't see many of those any more. And two, no three, hen mallards and one drake. Those make good eating."

Schmeckebier jutted his enormous lower lip. Knowing him for a stingy, crooked, suspicious little man, Henry almost laughed at the air he could put on, the air of a man of probity about to make an honest judgment in a dispute between neighbors. "I take a budderball," he said thickly. "A liddle budderball, dot is vot eats goot."

An arm fell across Henry's shoulders, and he turned his head to see the hand with red hairs rising from its pores, the wristband of a gray silk shirt with four pearl buttons. Navy Edwards' red face was close to his. "Come clean now," Navy said. "You shot 'em all sitting, didn't you, Henry?"

"I just waited till they stuck their heads out of their holes and let them have it," Henry said.

Navy walloped him on the back and convulsed himself laughing. Then his face got serious again, and he bore down on Henry's shoulder. "By God you could've fooled me," he said. "If I'd been makin' book on what you'd bring in I'd've lost my shirt."

"Such a pretty shirt, too," Billy Hammond said.

Across the counter John Lederer cradled a little drab duck in his hand. Its neck, stretched from the carrier, hung far down, but its body was neat and plump and its feet were waxy. Watching the sallow face of his father, Henry thought it looked oddly soft.

"Ain't that a beauty, though?" the old man said. "There ain't a prettier duck made than a blue-wing teal. You can have all your wood ducks and redheads, all the flashy ones." He spread a wing until the hidden band of bright blue showed. "Pretty?" he said, and shook his head and laughed suddenly, as if he had not expected to. When he laid the duck down beside the others his eyes were bright with sentimental moisture.

So now, Henry thought, you're right in your element. You always did want to be one of the boys from the poolroom pouring out to see the elk on somebody's running board, or leaning on a bar with a schooner of beer talking baseball or telling the boys about the big German Brown somebody brought in in a cake of ice. We haven't any elk or German Browns right now, but we've got some nice ducks, a fine display along five feet of counter. And who brought them in? The student, the alien son. It must gravel you.

He drew himself a beer. Several other men had come in, and he saw three more stooping to look in the door beyond Sciutti's. Then they too came in. Three tables were going; his father had started to hustle, filling orders. After a few minutes Schmeckebier and Navy went into the card room with four men. The poolroom lights were up bright again, there was an ivory click of balls, a rumble of talk. The smoke-filled air was full of movement.

Still more people dropped in, kids in high school athletic sweaters and bums from the fringes of skid road. They all stopped to look at the ducks, and Henry saw glances at his waders, heard questions and answers. John Lederer's boy. Some of them spoke to him, deriving importance from contact with him. A fellowship was promoted by the ducks strung out along the counter. Henry felt it himself. He was so mellowed by the way they spoke to him that when the players at the first table thumped with their cues, he got off his stool to rack them up and collect their nickels. It occurred to him that he ought to go to the room and get into a bath, but he didn't want to leave yet. Instead he came back to the counter and slid the nickels toward his father and drew himself another beer.

"Pretty good night tonight," he said. The old man nodded and slapped his rag on the counter, his eyes already past Henry and fixed on two youths coming in, his mouth fixing itself for the greeting and the "Well, boys, what'll it be?"

Billy Hammond wandered by, stopped beside Henry a moment. "Well, time for my nightly wrestle with temptation," he said.

"I was just going to challenge you to a game of call-shot."

"Maybe tomorrow," Billy said, and let himself out carefully as if afraid a noise would disturb someone—a mild, gentle, golden-haired boy who looked as if he ought to be in some prep school learning to say "Sir" to grownups instead of clerking in a girlie hotel. He was the only one of the poolroom crowd that Henry half liked. He thought he understood Billy Hammond a little.

He turned back to the counter to hear his father talking with Max Schmeckebier. "I don't see how we could on this rig. That's the hell of it, we need a regular oven."

"In my room in back," Schmeckebier said. "Dot old electric range."

"Does it work?"

"Sure. Vy not? I t'ink so."

"By God," John Lederer said. "Nine ducks, that ought to give us a real old-fashioned feed." He mopped the counter, refilled a coffee cup, came back to the end and pinched the breast of a duck, pulled out a wing and looked at the band of blue hidden among the drab feathers. "Just like old times, for a change," he said, and his eyes touched Henry's in a look that might have meant anything from a challenge to an apology.

Henry had no desire to ease the strain that had been between them for months. He did not forgive his father the poolhall, or forget the way the old man had sprung back into the old pattern, as if his wife had been a jailer and he was now released. He neither forgot nor forgave the red-haired woman who sometimes came to the poolhall late at night and waited on a bar stool while the old man closed up. Yet now when his father remarked that the ducks ought to be drawn and plucked right away, Henry got to his feet.

"I could do ten while you were doing one," his father said.

The blood spread hotter in Henry's face, but he bit off what he might have said. "All right," he said. "You do them and I'll take over the counter for you."

So here he was, in the poolhall he had passionately sworn he would never do a lick of work in, dispensing Mrs. Morrison's meat pies and tamales smothered in chile, clumping behind the counter in the waders which had been the sign of his temporary freedom. Leaning back between orders, watching the Saturday night activity of the place, he half understood why he had gone hunting, and why it had seemed to him essential that he bring his trophies back here.

That somewhat disconcerted understanding was still troubling him when his father came back. The old man had put on a clean apron and brushed his hair. His pouched eyes, brighter and less houndlike than usual, darted along the bar, counting, and darted across the bright tables, counting again. His eyes met Henry's, and both smiled. Both of them, Henry thought, were a little astonished.

* * *

Later, propped in bed in the hotel room, he put down the magazine he had been reading and stared at the drawn blinds, the sleazy drapes, and asked himself why he was here. The story he had told others, and himself, that his mother's death had interrupted his school term and he was waiting for the new term before going back, he knew to be an evasion. He was staying because he couldn't get away, or wouldn't. He hated his father, hated the poolhall, hated the people he was thrown with. He made no move to hobnob with them, or hadn't until tonight, and yet he deliberately avoided seeing any of the people who had been his friends for years. Why?

He could force his mind to the barrier, but not across it. Within a half minute he found himself reading again, diving deep, and when he made himself look up from the page he stared for a long time at his father's bed, his father's shoes under the bed, his father's soiled shirts hanging in the open closet. All the home he had any more was this little room. He could not pretend that as long as he stayed here the fragments of his home and family were held together. He couldn't fool himself that he had any function in his father's life any more, or his father in his, unless his own hatred and his father's uneasy suspicion were functions. He ought to get out and get a job until he could go back to school. But he didn't.

Thinking made him sleepy, and he knew what that was, too. Sleep was another evasion, like the torpor and monotony of his life. But he let drowsiness drift over him, and drowsily he thought of his father behind the counter tonight, vigorous and jovial, Mine Host, and he saw that the usual fretful petulance had gone from his face.

He snapped off the bed light and dropped the magazine on the floor. Then he heard the rain, the swish and hiss of traffic in the wet street. He felt sad and alone, and he disliked the coldness of his own isolation. Again he thought of his father, of the failing body that had once been tireless and bull-strong, of the face before it had sagged and grown dewlaps of flesh on the square jaws. He thought of the many failures, the jobs that never quite worked out, the schemes that never quite paid off, and of the eyes that could not quite meet, not quite hold, the eyes of his cold son.

Thinking of this, and remembering when they had been a family and when his mother had been alive to hold them together, he felt pity, and he cried.

His father's entrance awakened him. He heard the fumbling at the door, the creak, the quiet click, the footsteps that groped in darkness, the body that bumped into something and halted, getting its bearings. He heard the sighing weight of his father's body on the bed, his father's sighing breath as he bent to untie his shoes. Feigning sleep, he lay unmoving, breathing deeply and steadily, but an anguish of fury had leaped in him as sharp and sudden as a sudden fear, for he smelled the smells his father brought with him: wet wool, stale tobacco, liquor; and above all, more penetrating than any, spreading through the room and polluting everything there, the echo of cheap musky perfume.

The control Henry imposed upon his body was like an ecstasy. He raged at himself for the weak sympathy that had troubled him all evening. One good night, he said to himself now, staring furiously upward. One lively Saturday night in the joint and he can't contain himself, he has to go top off the evening with his girl friend. And how? A drink in her room? A walk over to some illegal after-hours bar on Rum Alley? Maybe just a trip to bed, blunt and immediate?

His jaws ached from the tight clamping of his teeth, but his orderly breathing went in and out, in and out, while the old man sighed into bed and creaked a little, rolling over, and lay still. The taint of perfume seemed even stronger now. The sow must slop it on by the cupful. And so cuddly. Such a sugar baby. How's my old sweetie tonight? It's been too long since you came to see your baby. I should be real mad at you. The cheek against the lapel, the unreal hair against the collar, the perfume like some gaseous poison tainting the clothes it touched.

The picture of his mother's bureau drawers came to him, the careless simple collection of handkerchiefs and gloves and lace collars and cuffs, and he saw the dusty blue sachet packets and smelled the faint fragrance. That was all the scent she had ever used.

My God, he said, how can he stand himself?

After a time his father began to breathe heavily, then to snore. In the little prison of the room his breathing was obscene—loose and bubbling, undisciplined, animal. Henry with an effort relaxed his tense arms and legs, let himself sink. He tried to concentrate on his own breathing, but the other dominated him, burst out and died and whiffled and sighed again. By now he had a resolution in him like an iron bar. Tomorrow, for sure, for good, he would break out of his self-imposed isolation and see Frank, see Welby. They would lend him enough to get to the coast. Not another day in this hateful relationship. Not another night in this room.

He yawned. It must be late, two or three o'clock. He ought to get to sleep. But he lay uneasily, his mind tainted with hatred as the room was tainted with perfume. He tried cunningly to elude his mind, to get to sleep before it could notice, but no matter how he composed himself for blankness and shut his eyes and breathed deeply, his mind was out again in a half minute, bright-eyed, lively as a weasel, and he was helplessly hunted again from hiding place to hiding place.

Eventually he fell back upon his old device.

He went into a big dark room in his mind, a room shadowy with great half-seen tables. He groped and found a string above him and pulled, and light fell suddenly in a bright cone from the darker cone of the shade. Below the light lay an expanse of dark green cloth, and this was the only lighted thing in all that darkness. Carefully he gathered bright balls into a wooden triangle, pushing them forward until the apex lay over a round spot on the cloth. Quietly and thoroughly he chalked a cue: the inlaid handle and the smooth taper of the shaft were very real to his eyes and hands. He lined up the cue ball, aimed, drew the cue back and forth in smooth motions over the bridge of his left hand. He saw the balls run from the spinning shock of the break, and carom, and come to rest, and he hunted up the yellow 1-ball and got a shot at it between two others. He had to cut it very fine, but he saw the shot go true, the 1 angle off cleanly into the side pocket. He saw the cue ball rebound and kiss and stop, and he shot the 2 in a straight shot for the left corner pocket, putting drawers on the cue ball to get shape for the 3.

Yellow and blue and red, spotted and striped, he shot pool balls into pockets as deep and black and silent as the cellars of his consciousness. He was not now quarry that his mind chased, but an actor, a willer, a doer, a man in command. By an act of will or of flight he focused his whole awareness on the game he played. His mind undertook it with intent concentration. He took pride in little two-cushion banks, little triumphs of accuracy, small successes of foresight. When he had finished one game and the green cloth was bare he dug the balls from the bin under the end of the table and racked them and began another.

Eventually, he knew, nothing would remain in his mind but the clean green cloth traced with running color and bounded by simple problems, and sometime in the middle of an intricately-planned combination shot he would pale off into sleep.

✳ ✳ ✳

At noon, after the rain, the sun seemed very bright. It poured down from a clearing sky, glittered on wet roofs, gleamed in reflection from pavements and sidewalks. On the peaks beyond the city there was a purity of snow.

Coming down the hill Henry noticed the excessive brightness and could not tell whether it was really as it seemed, or whether his plunge out of the dark and isolated hole of his life had restored a lost capacity to see. A slavery, or a paralysis, was ended; he had been for three hours in the company of a friend; he had been eyed with concern; he had been warmed by solicitude and generosity. In his pocket he had fifty dollars, enough to get him to the coast and let him renew his life. It seemed to him incredible that he had alternated between dismal hotel and dismal poolroom so long. He could not understand why he had not before this moved his legs in the direction of the hill. He perceived that he had been sullen and morbid, and he concluded with some surprise that even Schmeckebier and Edwards and the rest might have found him a difficult companion.

His father too. The fury of the night before had passed, but he knew he would not bend again toward companionship. That antipathy was too deep. He would never think of his father again without getting the whiff of that perfume. Let him have it; it was what he wanted, let him have it. They could part without an open quarrel, maybe, but they would part without love. They could part right now, within an hour.

Two grimy stairways led down into the cellar from the alley he turned into. One went to the furnace room, the other to the poolhall. The iron rail was blockaded with filled ash cans. Descent into Avernus, he said to himself, and went down the left-hand stair.

The door was locked. He knocked, and after some time knocked again. Finally someone pulled on the door from inside. It stuck, and was yanked irritably inward. His father stood there in his shirt sleeves, a cigar in his mouth.

"Oh," he said. "I was wondering what had become of you."

The basement air was foul and heavy, dense with the reek from the toilets. Henry saw as he stepped inside that at the far end only the night light behind the bar was on, but that light was coming from Schmeckebier's door at this end too, the two weak illuminations diffusing in the shadowy pool-room, leaving the middle in almost absolute dark. It was the appropriate time, the appropriate place, the stink of his prison appropriately concentrated. He drew his lungs full of it with a kind of passion, and he said, "I just came down to—"

"Who is dot?" Schmeckebier called out. He came to his door, wrapped to the armpits in a bar apron, with a spoon in his hand, and he bent, peering out into the dusk like a disturbed dwarf in an underhill cave. "John? Who? Oh, Henry. Shust in time, shust in time. It is not long now." His lower lip waggled, and he pulled it up, apparently with an effort.

Henry said, "What's not long?"

"Vot?" Schmeckebier said, and thrust his big head far out. "You forgot about it?"

"I must have," Henry said.

"The duck feed," his father said impatiently.

They stood staring at one another in the dusk. The right moment was gone. With a little twitch of the shoulder Henry let it go. He would wait a while, pick his time. When Schmeckebier went back to his cooking, Henry saw through the doorway the lumpy bed, the big chair with a blanket folded over it, the roll-top desk littered with pots and pans, the green and white enamel of the range. A rich smell of roasting came out and mingled oddly with the chemical stink of toilet disinfectant.

"Are we going to eat in here?" he asked.

His father snorted. "How could we eat in there? Old Maxie lived in the ghetto too damn long. By God I never saw such a boar's nest."

"Vot's duh matter? Vot's duh matter?" Schmeckebier said. His big lip thrust out, he stooped to look into the oven, and John Lederer went shaking his head up between the tables to the counter. Henry followed him, intending to make the break when he got the old man alone. But he saw the three plates set up on the bar, the three glasses of tomato juice, the platter of olives and celery, and he hesitated. His father reached with a salt shaker and shook a little salt into each glass of tomato juice.

"All the fixings," he said. "Soon as Max gets those birds out of the oven we can take her on."

Now it was easy to say, "As soon as the feed's over I'll be shoving off." Henry opened his mouth to say it, but was interrupted this time by a light tapping at the glass door beyond Sciutti's shop. He swung around angrily and saw duskily beyond the glass the smooth blond hair, the even smile.

"It's Billy," he said. "Shall I let him in?"

"Sure," the old man said. "Tell him to come in and have a duck with us."

But Billy Hammond shook his head when Henry asked him. He was shaking his head almost as he came through the door. "No thanks, I just ate. I'm full of chow mein. This is a family dinner anyway. You go on ahead."

"Got plenty," John Lederer said, and made a motion as if to set a fourth place at the counter.

"Who is dot?" Schmeckebier bawled from the back. "Who come in? Is dot Billy Hammond? Set him up a blate."

"By God his nose sticks as far into things as his lip," Lederer said. Still holding the plate, he roared back, "Catch up with the parade, for Christ sake, or else tend to your cooking." He looked at Henry and Billy and chuckled.

Schmeckebier had disappeared, but now his squat figure blotted the lighted doorway again. "Vot? Vot you say?"

"Vot?" John Lederer said. "Vot, vot, vot? Vot does it matter vot I said? Get the hell back to your kitchen."

He was, Henry saw, in a high humor. The effect of last night was still with him. He was still playing Mine Host. He looked at the two of them and laughed so naturally that Henry almost joined him. "I think old Maxie's head is full of duck dressing," he said, and leaned on the counter. "I ever tell you about the time we came back from Reno together? We stopped off in the desert to look at a mine, and got lost on a little dirt road so we had to camp. I was trying to figure out where we were, and started looking for stars, but it was clouded over, hard to locate anything. So I ask old Maxie if he can see the Big Dipper anywhere. He thinks about that maybe ten minutes with his lip stuck out and then he says, 'I t'ink it's in duh water bucket.'"

He did the grating gutturals of Schmeckebier's speech so accurately that Henry smiled in spite of himself. His old man made another motion with the plate at Billy Hammond. "Better let me set you up a place."

"Thanks," Billy said. His voice was as polite and soft as his face, and his eyes had the ingenuous liquid softness of a girl's. "Thanks, I really just ate. You go on, I'll shoot a little pool if it's all right."

Now came Schmeckebier with a big platter held in both hands. He bore it smoking through the gloom of the poolhall and up the steps to the counter, and John Lederer took it from him there and with a flourish speared one after another three tight-skinned brown ducks and slid them onto the plates set side by side for the feast. The one frugal light from the backbar shone on them as they sat down. Henry looked over his shoulder to see Billy Hammond pull the cord and flood a table with a sharp-edged cone of brilliance. Deliberately, already absorbed, he chalked a cue. His lips pursed, and he whistled, and whistling, bent to take aim.

Lined up in a row, they were not placed for conversation, but John Lederer kept attempting it, leaning forward over his plate to see Schmeckebier or Henry. He filled his mouth with duck and dressing and chewed, shaking his head with pleasure, and snapped off a bite of celery with a crack like a breaking stick. When his mouth was clear he leaned and said to Schmeckebier, "Ah, das schmecht gut, hey Maxie?"

"Ja," Schmeckebier said, and sucked grease off his lip and only then turned in surprise. "Say, you speak German?"

"Sure, I speak German," Lederer said. "I worked three weeks once with an old squarehead brickmason that taught me the whole language. He taught me about sehr gut and nicht wahr and besser I bleiben right hier, and he always had his frau make me up a lunch full of kalter aufschnitt and gemixte pickeln. I know all about German."

Schmeckebier stared a moment, grunted, and went back to his eating. He had already stripped the meat from the bones and was gnawing the carcass.

"Anyway," John Lederer said, "es schmecht God damn good." He got up and went around the counter and drew a mug of coffee from the urn. "Coffee?" he said to Henry.

"Please."

His father drew another mug and set it before him. "Maxie?"

Schmeckebier shook his head, his mouth too full for talk. For a minute, after he had set out two little jugs of cream, Lederer stood as if thinking. He was watching Billy Hammond move quietly around the one lighted table, whistling. "Look at that sucker," Lederer said. "I bet he doesn't even know where he is."

By the time he got around to his stool he was back at the German. "*Schmeckebier,*" he said. "What's that mean?"

"Uh?"

"What's your name mean? Tastes beer? Likes beer?"

Schmeckebier rolled his shoulders. The sounds he made eating were like sounds from a sty. Henry was half sickened, sitting next to him, and he wished the old man would let the conversation drop. But apparently it had to be a feast, and a feast called for chatter.

"That's a hell of a name, you know it?" Lederer said, and already he was up again and around the end of the counter. "You couldn't get into any church with a name like that." His eyes fastened on the big drooping greasy lip, and he grinned.

"Schmeckeduck, that ought to be your name," he said. "What's German for duck? Vogel? Old Man Schmeckevogel. How about number two?"

Schmeckebier pushed his plate forward and Lederer forked a duck out of the steam table. Henry did not take a second.

"You ought to have one," his father told him. "You don't get grub like this every day."

"One's my limit," Henry said.

For a while they worked at their plates. Back of him Henry heard the clack of balls hitting, and a moment later the rumble as a ball rolled down the chute from a pocket. The thin, abstracted whistling of Billy Hammond broke off, became words:

> Annie doesn't live here any more.
> You must be the one she waited for.
> She said I would know you by the blue in your eye—

"Talk about one being your limit," his father said. "When we lived in Nebraska we used to put on some feeds. You remember anything about Nebraska at all?"

"A little," Henry said. He was irritated at being dragged into reminiscences, and he did not want to hear how many ducks the town hog could eat at a sitting.

"We'd go out, a whole bunch of us," John Lederer said. "The sloughs were black with ducks in those days. We'd come back with a buggyful, and the womenfolks'd really put us on a feed. Fifteen, twenty, thirty people. Take a hundred ducks to fill 'em up." He was silent a moment, staring across the counter, chewing. Henry noticed that he had tacked two wings of a teal up on the frame of the backbar mirror, small, strong bows with a band of bright blue half hidden in them. The old man's eyes slanted over, caught Henry's looking at the wings.

"Doesn't seem as if we'd had a duck feed since we left there," he said. His forehead wrinkled; he rubbed his neck, leaning forward over his plate, and his eyes met Henry's in the backbar mirror. He spoke to the mirror, ignoring the gobbling image of Schmeckebier between his own reflection and Henry's.

"You remember that set of china your mother used to have? The one she painted herself? Just the plain white china with the one design on each plate?"

Henry sat stiffly, angry that his mother's name should even be mentioned between them in this murky hole, and after what had passed. Gabble, gabble, gabble, he said to himself. If you can't think of anything else to gabble about, gabble about your dead wife. Drag her through the pool-room too. Aloud he said, "No, I guess I don't."

"Blue-wing teal," his father said, and nodded at the wings tacked to the mirror frame. "Just the wings, like that. Awful pretty. She thought a teal was about the prettiest little duck there was."

His vaguely rubbing hand came around from the back of his neck and rubbed along the cheek, pulling the slack flesh and distorting the mouth. Henry said nothing, watching the pouched hound eyes in the mirror.

It was a cold, skin-tightening shock to realize that the hound eyes were cloudy with tears. The rubbing hand went over them, shaded them like a hatbrim, but the mouth below remained distorted. With a plunging movement his father was off the stool.

"Oh, God damn!" he said in a strangling voice, and went past Henry on hard, heavy feet, down the steps and past Billy Hammond, who neither looked up nor broke the sad thin whistling.

Schmeckebier had swung around. "Vot's duh matter? Now vot's duh matter?"

With a short shake of the head, Henry turned away from him, staring after his father down the dark poolhall. He felt as if orderly things were breaking and flying apart in his mind; he had a moment of white blind terror that this whole scene upon whose reality he counted was really only a dream, something conjured up out of the bottom of his consciousness where he was accustomed to comfort himself into total sleep. His mind was still full of the anguished look his father had hurled at the mirror before he ran.

The hell with you, the look had said. The hell with you, Schmeckebier, and you, my son Henry. The hell with your ignorance, whether you're stupid or whether you just don't know all you think you know. You don't know enough to kick dirt down a hole. You know nothing at all, you know less than nothing because you know things wrong.

He heard Billy's soft whistling, saw him move around his one lighted table—a well-brought-up boy from some suburban town, a polite soft gentle boy lost and wandering among pimps and prostitutes, burying himself for some reason among people who never even touched his surface. Did he shoot pool in his bed at night, tempting sleep, as Henry did? Did his mind run carefully to angles and banks and englishes, making a reflecting mirror of them to keep from looking through them at other things?

Almost in terror he looked out across the sullen cave, past where the light came down in an intense isolated cone above Billy's table, and heard the lugubrious whistling that went on without intention of audience, a re-current and deadening and only half-conscious sound. He looked toward the back, where his father had disappeared in the gloom, and wondered if in his bed before sleeping the old man worked through a routine of little jobs: cleaning the steam table, ordering a hundred pounds of coffee, jacking up the janitor about the mess in the hall. He wondered if it was possible to wash yourself to sleep with restaurant crockery, work yourself to sleep with chores, add yourself to sleep with columns of figures, as you could play yourself to sleep with a pool cue and a green table and fifteen colored balls. For a moment, in the sad old light with the wreckage of the duck feast at his elbow, he wondered if there was anything more to his life, or his father's life, or Billy Hammond's life, or anyone's life, than playing the careful games that deadened you into sleep.

Schmeckebier, beside him, was still groping in the fog of his mind for an explanation of what had happened. "Vere'd he go?" he said, and nudged Henry fiercely. "Vot's duh matter?"

Henry shook him off irritably, watching Billy Hammond's oblivious bent head under the light. He heard Schmeckebier's big lip flop and heard him sucking his teeth.

"I tell you," the guttural voice said. "I got somet'ing dot fixes him if he feels bum."

He too went down the stairs past the lighted table and into the gloom at the back. The light went on in his room, and after a minute or two his voice was shouting, "John! Say, come here, uh? Say, John!"

Eventually John Lederer came out of the toilet and they walked together between the tables. In his fist Schmeckebier was clutching a square bottle. He waved it in front of Henry's face as they passed, but Henry was watch-ing his father. He saw the crumpled face, oddly rigid, like the face of a man in the grip of a barely controlled rage, but his father avoided his eyes.

"Kümmel," Schmeckebier said. He set four ice cream dishes on the counter and poured three about a third full of clear liquor. His squinted eyes lifted and peered toward Billy Hammond, but Henry said, on an impulse, "Let him alone. He's walking in his sleep."

So there were only the three. They stood together a moment and raised their glasses. "Happy days," John Lederer said automatically. They drank.

Schmeckebier smacked his lips, looked at them one after another, shook his head in admiration of the quality of his kümmel, and waddled back toward his room with the bottle. John Lederer was already drawing hot water to wash the dishes.

In the core of quiet which was not broken even by the clatter of crockery and the whistling of Billy Hammond, Henry said what he had to say. "I'll be leaving," he said. "Probably tonight."

But he did not say it in anger, or with the cold command of himself that he had imagined in advance. He said it like a cry, and with the feeling he might have had on letting go the hand of a friend too weak and too exhausted to cling any longer to their inadequate shared driftwood in a wide cold sea.

Wright Morris
b. 1910

■

1942: *My Uncle Dudley*
1948: *The Home Place*
1956: *The Field of Vision*
1958: *The Territory Ahead*
1960: *Ceremony in Lone Tree*
1980: *Plains Song: For Female Voices*
1985: *A Cloak of Light:*
Writing My Life

■

WRIGHT MORRIS'S *biographers spend relatively little time telling us the details of the author's life. We learn that Morris grew up in small Nebraska towns, left college early to travel through Europe, and punctuated his remarkable writing career with extended tours of the United States, Europe, and Mexico. In 1963 he began teaching at San Francisco State College, where he retired in 1975. But the best account of Wright Morris's life comes from his fiction, which presents us with one fascinating semiautobiographical situation after another, each of them undertaken, studied, and written about with extraordinary intensity. Each book or story manages to enlarge on Morris's experiences, from the trips, taken with his father, that inspired* My Uncle Dudley *to the small-town scenery details that set the stage for* Ceremony in Lone Tree.

One biographical encyclopedia lists Morris as an American novelist, short story writer, essayist, critic, memoirist, and photographer who has successfully tried his hand at all of these genres—and others—in his thirty-five books and in scores of stories and articles. One biographer, David Madden, says of Morris, "In vision and content, he is, I believe, the most thoroughly American contemporary writer." Leon Howard's biography praises Morris as "the most consistently original of American novelists for a quarter of a century," and calls his art "as sophisticated as that of Henry James." According to Granville Hicks, the writings of Wright Morris make up "one of the most imposing edifices on the contemporary literary horizon. When anyone sets out to list the best living novelists, his name is usually mentioned." [1]

"What is Morris' field of vision?" David Madden asks. "Bringing into focus a representative part of America, he has sought the meaning of the legends, myths and realities of America as they survive and prevail today in the minds of common men; the uncommon exist for the edification of the common. We are conditioned to think of action when we think of the West. Born when the short-lived era of action, the conflict with the Indians and such, had passed away, Morris became interested in what he observed himself—the monotony of everyday life. . . . what interests him is the impression left on the imagination—the internal rather than the external drama." [2]

Ceremony in Lone Tree *opens with "The Scene." Old man Scanlon usually sits all alone in the ghost town's decaying hotel; today, however, his daughters and their husbands and a middle-aged ne'er-do-well named Gordon Boyd are coming to celebrate his ninetieth birthday. Scanlon, a relic from the western farming boom, actually lives in the past, "remembering" events that happened even before he was born. The hotel faces east, but Scanlon spends his time looking toward the West through a flaw in a windowpane. The flaw, like his memories, transforms the dry, dead world into a "metaphysical landscape" of activity and wonderful sights. Perhaps the old man represents the point where East meets West; perhaps he is merely a survivor of that great collision when manifest destiny and the Great American Dream ran headfirst into the dust bowl and the Great Depression.*

Morris's black-and-white photography captures Scanlon's world in another medium. His vivid portraits of the era when the "promised land" first fell into ruin supplement his novel The Home Place; *other photos supplement his lyrical memoirs in* God's Country and My People *(1968), and still others lend extra dimension to* The Inhabitants *(1946). Like the flaw in the old man's window, Morris's photographs seem to offer us a glimpse of a reality that is older than our life, but not beyond our remembering.*

▬

1. David Madden, *Wright Morris* (New York: Twayne Publishers, 1964), p. 171; Leon Howard, *Wright Morris* (Minneapolis: University of Minnesota Press, 1968), pp. 5, 6; Granville Hicks, ed., *Wright Morris: A Reader* (New York: Harper and Row, 1970), p. ix.

2. Madden, *Morris*, pp. 28–29.

The Scene

COME TO THE WINDOW. The one at the rear of the Lone Tree Hotel. The view is to the west. There is no obstruction but the sky. Although there is no one outside to look in, the yellow blind is drawn low at the window, and between it and the pane a fly is trapped. He has stopped buzzing. Only the crawling shadow can be seen. Before the whistle of the train is heard the loose pane rattles like a simmering pot, then stops, as if pressed by a hand, as the train goes past. The blind sucks inward and the dangling cord drags in the dust on the sill.

At a child's level in the pane there is a flaw that is round, like an eye in the glass. An eye to that eye, a scud seems to blow on a sea of grass. Waves of plain seem to roll up, then break like a surf. Is it a flaw in the eye, or in the window, that transforms a dry place into a wet one? Above it towers a sky, like the sky at sea, a wind blows like the wind at sea, and like the sea it has no shade: there is no place to hide. One thing it is that the sea is not: it is dry, not wet.

Drawn up to the window is a horsehair sofa covered with a quilt. On the floor at its side, garlanded with flowers, is a nightpot full of cigar butts and ashes. Around it, scattered like seed, are the stubs of half-burned kitchen matches, the charcoal tips honed to a point for picking the teeth. They also serve to aid the digestion and sweeten the breath. The man who smokes the cigars and chews on the matches spends most of the day on the sofa; he is not there now, but the sagging springs hold his shape. He has passed his life, if it can be said he has lived one, in the rooms of the Lone Tree Hotel. His coat hangs in the lobby, his shoes are under the stove, and a runner of ashes marks his trail up and down the halls. His hat, however, never leaves his head. It is the hat, with its wicker sides, the drayman's license at the front, that comes to mind when his children think of him. He has never run a dray, but never mind. The badge is what they see, through the hole

From Wright Morris, *Ceremony in Lone Tree* (New York: Atheneum Publishers, 1960), pp. 3–21. Copyright © 1960 by Wright Morris, renewed 1988 by Wright Morris. Reprinted by permission of Russell and Volkening, Inc., as agents for the author.

where his sleeve has smudged the window, on those rare occasions when they visit him. If the hat is not there, they look for him in the lobby, dozing in one of the hardwood rockers or in one of the beds drawn to a window facing the west. There is little to see, but plenty of room to look.

Scanlon's eyes, a cloudy phlegm color, let in more light than they give out. What he sees are the scenic props of his own mind. His eye to the window, the flaw in the pane, such light as there is illuminates Scanlon, his face like that of a gobbler in the drayman's hat. What he sees is his own business, but the stranger might find the view familiar. A man accustomed to the ruins of war might even feel at home. In the blowouts on the rise are flint arrowheads, and pieces of farm machinery, half buried in sand, resemble nothing so much as artillery equipment, abandoned when the dust began to blow. The tidal shift of the sand reveals one ruin in order to conceal another. It is all there to be seen, but little evidence that Tom Scanlon sees it. Not through the clouded eye he puts to the glass. The emptiness of the plain generates illusions that require little moisture, and grow better, like tall stories, where the mind is dry. The tall corn may flower or burn in the wind, but the plain is a metaphysical landscape and the bumper crop is the one Scanlon sees through the flaw in the glass.

Nothing irked him more than to hear from his children that the place was empty, the town deserted, and that there was nothing to see. He saw plenty. No matter where he looked. Down the tracks to the east, like a headless bird, the bloody neck still raw and dripping, a tub-shaped water tank sits high on stilts. Scanlon once saw a coon crawl out the chute and drink from the spout. Bunches of long-stemmed grass, in this short-grass country, grow where the water drips between the rails, and Scanlon will tell you he has seen a buffalo crop it up. A big bull, of course, high in the shoulders, his short tail like the knot in a whip, walking on the ties like a woman with her skirts tucked up. Another time a wolf, half crazed by the drought, licked the moisture from the rails like ice and chewed on the grass like a dog out of sorts. On occasion stray geese circle the tank like a water hole. All common sights, according to Scanlon, where other men squinted and saw nothing but the waves of heat, as if the cinders of the railbed were still on fire.

It seldom rains in Lone Tree, but he has often seen it raining somewhere else. A blue veil of it will hang like the half-drawn curtain at Scanlon's window. Pillars of cloud loom on the horizon, at night there is much lightning and claps of thunder, and from one window or another rain may be seen falling somewhere. Wind from that direction will smell wet, and Scanlon will complain, if there is someone to listen, about the rheumatic pains in his knees. He suffered greater pains, however, back when he had neighbors who complained, of all things, about the lack of rain.

In the heat of the day, when there is no shadow, the plain seems to be drawn up into the sky, and through the hole in the window it is hard to be sure if the town is still there. It takes on, like a sunning lizard, the colors of the plain. The lines drawn around the weathered buildings smoke and blur. At this time of day Scanlon takes his nap, and by the time he awakes the town is back in its place. The lone tree, a dead cottonwood, can be seen by the shadow it leans to the east, a zigzag line with a fishhook curve at the end. According to Scanlon, Indians once asked permission to bury their dead in the crotch of the tree, and while the body was there the tree had been full of crows. A small boy at the time, Scanlon had shot at them with his father's squirrel gun, using soft lead pellets that he dug out of the trunk of the tree and used over again.

From the highway a half mile to the north, the town sits on the plain as if delivered on a flatcar—as though it were a movie set thrown up during the night. Dry as it is, something about it resembles an ark from which the waters have receded. In the winter it appears to be locked in a sea of ice. In the summer, like the plain around it, the town seems to float on a watery surface, stray cattle stand knee-deep in a blur of reflections, and waves of light and heat flow across the highway like schools of fish. Everywhere the tongue is dry, but the mind is wet. According to his daughters, who should know, the dirt caked around Tom Scanlon's teeth settled there in the thirties when the dust began to blow. More of it can be seen, fine as talcum, on the linoleum floor in the lobby, where the mice raised in the basement move to their winter quarters in the cobs behind the stove.

* * *

To the east, relatively speaking, there is much to see, a lone tree, a water tank, sheets of rain and heat lightning: to the west a strip of torn screen blurs the view. The effect is that of now-you-see-it, now-you-don't. As a rule, there is nothing to see, and if there is, one doubts it. The pane is smeared where Scanlon's nose has rubbed the glass. The fact that there is little to see seems to be what he likes about it. He can see what he pleases. It need not please anybody else. Trains come from both directions, but from the east they come without warning, the whistle blown away by the wind. From the west, thin and wild or strumming like a wire fastened to the building, the sound wakes Scanlon from his sleep before the building rocks. It gives him time, that is, to prepare himself. The upgrade freights rock the building and leave nothing but the noise in his head, but the downgrade trains leave a vacuum he sometimes raises the window to look at. A hole? He often thought he might see one there. A cloud of dust would veil the caboose, on the stove one of the pots or the lids would rattle, and if the lamp was lit, the flame would blow as if in a draft.

One day as the dust settled he saw a team of mares, the traces dragging, cantering down the bank where the train had just passed. On the wires above the tracks, dangling like a scarecrow, he saw the body of Emil Bickel, in whose vest pocket the key-wound watch had stopped. At 7:34, proving the train that hit him had been right on time.

* * *

To the west the towns are thin and sparse, like the grass, and in a place called Indian Bow the white faces of cattle peer out of the soddies on the slope across the dry bed of the river. They belong to one of Scanlon's grandchildren who married well. On the rise behind the soddies are sunken graves, one of the headstones bearing the name of Will Brady, a railroad man who occasionally stopped off at Lone Tree. Until he married and went east, Scanlon thought him a sensible man.

Down the grade to the east the towns are greener and thicker, like the grass. The town of Polk, the home of Walter McKee, who married Scanlon's eldest daughter, Lois, has elm-shaded streets and a sign on the highway telling you to slow down. There is also a park with a Civil War cannon, the name of Walter McKee carved on the breech and that of his friend, Gordon Boyd, on one of the cannon balls. In the house where Walter McKee was born grass still grows between the slats on the porch, and the neighbor's chickens still lay their eggs under the stoop. At the corner of the porch a tar barrel catches and stores the rain from the roof. At the turn of the century, when McKee was a boy, he buried the white hairs from a mare's tail in the rain barrel, confident they would turn up next as garter snakes. In the middle of the century that isn't done, and a TV aerial, like a giant Martian insect, crouches on the roof as if about to fly off with the house. That is a change, but on its side in the yard is a man's bicycle with the seat missing. The small boy who rides it straddles it through the bars: he never sits down. He mounts it slantwise, like a bareback rider, grease from the chain rubbing off on one leg and soiling the cuff of the pants leg rolled to the knee. Gordon Boyd still bears the scar where the teeth of the sprocket dug into his calf. Bolder than McKee, he liked to ride on the gravel around the patch of grass in the railroad station, leaning forward to hold a strip of berry-box wood against the twirling spokes.

The short cut in the yard, worn there by McKee, still points across the street to a wide vacant lot and to the tree where McKee, taunted by Boyd, climbed to where the sway and the height made him dizzy. He fell on a milk-can lid, breaking his arm. Mrs. Boyd, a white-haired woman, had put his arm to soak in a cold tub of water while Gordon went for the doctor on McKee's new bike. Over that summer Boyd had grown so fast he could pump it from the seat.

The Boyd house, having no basement, had a storm cave at the back of the yard where McKee smoked corn silk and Boyd smoked Fourth of July punk. The white frame house still has no basement, and the upstairs bedroom, looking out on the porch, is still heated by a pipe that comes up from the stove below. When McKee spent the night with Boyd, Mrs. Boyd would rap a spoon on the pipe to make them quiet, or turn down the damper so the room would get cold. The old coke burner, with the isinglass windows through which Boyd and McKee liked to watch the coke settle, now sits in the woodshed, crowned with the horn of the Victrola. The stove board, however, the floral design worn away where Boyd liked to dress on winter mornings, is now in the corner where the floor boards have sagged, under the new TV. Since the house has no porch high enough to crawl under, Boyd kept his sled and Irish Mail under the porch of a neighbor. Along with Hershey bar tinfoil, several pop bottles, a knife with a woman's leg for a handle, and a tin for condoms, thought to be balloons and blown up till they popped on the Fourth of July, the sled is still there. The boys don't use the ones with wooden runners any more. The chain swing no longer creaks on the porch or spends the winter, cocoonlike, drawn to the ceiling, but the paint still peels where it grazed the clapboards and thumped on the railing warm summer nights. Long after it was gone Mrs. Boyd was kept awake by its creak.

* * *

The people change—according to a survey conducted by a new supermarket—but the life in Polk remains much the same. The new trailer park on the east edge of town boasts the latest and best in portable living, but the small fry still fish, like McKee, for crawdads with hunks of liver, and bring them home to mothers who hastily dump them back in the creek. The men live in Polk, where there is plenty of room, and commute to those places where the schools are overcrowded, the rents inflated, but where there is work. At the western edge of town an air-conditioned motel with a stainless-steel diner blinks at night like an airport, just across the street from where McKee chipped his front teeth on the drinking fountain. Once or twice a year on his way to Lone Tree, McKee stops off in Polk for what he calls a real shave, in the shop where he got his haircuts as a boy. The price for a shave and a haircut has changed, but the mirror on the wall is the same. In it, somewhere, is the face McKee had as a boy. Stretched out horizontal, his eyes on the tin ceiling, his lips frothy with the scented lather, he sometimes fancies he hears the mocking voice of Boyd:

> Walter McKee,
> Button your fly.
> Pee in the road
> And you'll get a sty.

Although he comes from the south, McKee goes out of his way to enter town from the west, passing the water stack with the word POLK like a shadow under the new paint. Just beyond the water stack is the grain elevator, the roof flashing like a mirror in the sun, the name T. P. CRETE in black on the fresh coat of aluminum. The same letters were stamped like a legend on McKee's mind. The great man himself was seldom seen in the streets of Polk, or in the rooms of his mansion, but his name, in paint or gold leaf, stared at McKee from walls and windows and the high board fence that went along the lumberyard. T. P. Crete's wife, like a bird in a cage, sometimes went by in her electric car, making no more noise than the strum of the wires on the telephone poles. It was this creature who deprived McKee of his friend Boyd. She sent him, when he proved to be smart, to those high-toned schools in the East that indirectly led to the ruin he made of his life. Destiny manifested itself through the Cretes, and the sight of the name affected McKee like a choir marching in or the sound of his mother humming hymns.

Beyond the grain elevator is the railroad station, the iron wheels of the baggage truck sunk in the gravel, an OUT OF ORDER sign pasted on the face of the penny scales in the lobby. On the east side of the station is a patch of grass. Around it is a fence of heavy wrought iron, the top rail studded to discourage loafers, pigeons and small fry like McKee and Boyd. Polk is full of wide lawns and freshly cropped grass healthy enough for a boy to walk on, but for McKee the greenest grass in the world is the patch inside the wrought-iron fence. He never enters town without a glance at it. If it looks greener than other grass it might be due to the cinder-blackened earth, and the relative sparseness and tenderness of the shoots. But the secret lies in McKee, not in the grass. No man raised on the plains, in the short-grass country, takes a patch of grass for granted, and it is not for nothing they protect it with a fence or iron bars. When McKee thinks of spring, or of his boyhood, or of what the world would be like if men came to their senses, in his mind's eye he sees the patch of green in the cage at Polk. Tall grass now grows between the Burlington tracks that lead south of town to the bottomless sand pit where Boyd, before the eyes of McKee, attempted to walk on water for the first time. But not the last. Nothing seemed to teach him anything.

Southeast of Polk is Lincoln, capital of the state, the present home of McKee and his wife Lois, as well as of Lois's sister Maxine and her family. Tom Scanlon's youngest girl, Edna, married Clyde Ewing, an Oklahoma horse breeder, who found oil on his farm in the Panhandle. The view from their modern air-conditioned house is so much like that around Lone Tree, Edna Ewing felt sure her father would feel right at home in it. Tom Scanlon, however, didn't like the place. For one thing, there were no windows, only those gleaming walls of glass. He had walked from room to room as he did outside, with his head drawn in. Although the floor and walls radiated heat, Scanlon felt cold, since it lacked a stove with an oven door or a rail where he could put his feet. Only in the back door was there something like a window, an opening about the size of a porthole framing the view, with a flaw in the glass to which he could put his eye. Through it he saw, three hundred miles to the north, the forked branches of the lone tree like bleached cattle horns on the railroad embankment that half concealed the town, the false fronts of the buildings like battered remnants of a board fence. Even the hotel, with its MAIL POUCH sign peeling like a circus poster, might be taken for a signboard along an abandoned road. That is how it is, but not how it looks to Scanlon. He stands as if at the screen, gazing down the tracks to where the long-stemmed grass spurts from the cinders like leaks in a garden hose. The mindless wind in his face seems damp with the prospect of rain.

Three stories high, made of the rough-faced brick brought out from Omaha on a flatcar, the Lone Tree Hotel sits where the coaches on the westbound caboose once came to a stop. Eastbound, there were few who troubled to stop. In the westbound caboose were the men who helped Lone Tree to believe in itself. The hotel faces the south, the empty pits that were dug for homes never erected and the shadowy trails, like Inca roads, indicating what were meant to be streets. The door at the front, set in slantwise on the corner, with a floral design in the frosted glass, opens on the prospect of the town. Slabs of imported Italian marble face what was once the bank, the windows boarded like a looted tomb, the vault at the rear once having served as a jail. A sign:

$5. FINE FOR TALKING
TO
PRISONERS

once hung over one of the barred windows, but a brakeman who was something of a card made off with it.

The lobby of the hotel, level with the hitching bar, affords a view of the barbershop interior, the mirror on the wall and whoever might be sitting in the one chair. Only the lower half of the window is curtained, screening off the man who is being shaved but offering him a view of the street and the plain when he sits erect, just his hair being cut. Tucked into the frame of the mirror are the post cards sent back by citizens who left or went traveling to those who were crazy enough to stay on in Lone Tree. The incumbent barber usually doubled as the postmaster. In the glass razor case, laid out on a towel still peppered with his day-old beard, is the razor that shaved William Jennings Bryan. In Lone Tree, at the turn of the century, he pleaded the lost cause of silver, then descended from the platform of the caboose for a shampoo and a shave. On that day a balloon, brought out on a flatcar, reached the altitude of two hundred forty-five feet with Edna Scanlon, who was something of a tomboy, visible in the basket that hung beneath. The century turned that memorable summer, and most of the men in Lone Tree turned with it; like the engines on the roundhouse platform they wheeled from west to east. But neither Scanlon, anchored in the lobby, nor the town of Lone Tree turned with it. The century went its own way after that, and Scanlon went his.

From a rocker in the lobby Scanlon can see the gap between the barbershop and the building on the west, the yellow blind shadowed with the remaining letters of the word MIL NE Y. On the floor above the millinery is the office of Dr. Twomey, where a cigar-store Indian with human teeth guards the door. He stands grimacing, tomahawk upraised, with what are left of the molars known to drop out when the building is shaken by a downgrade freight. When Twomey set up his practice, the barber chair served very nicely as an operating table, a place for lancing boils, removing adenoids or pulling teeth. A flight of wooden steps without a railing mounted to his office on the second floor, but they collapsed within a week or so after he died. He was a huge man, weighing some three hundred pounds, and it took four men to lower his body to the casket on the wagon in the street. The stairs survived the strain, then collapsed under their own weight.

A hand-cranked gas pump, the crank in a sling, sits several yards in front of the livery stable, as if to disassociate itself from the horses once stabled inside. At the back of the stable, inhabited by bats, is the covered wagon Scanlon was born in, the bottom sloped up at both ends like a river boat. Strips of faded canvas, awning remnants, partially cover the ribs. Until the hotel was built in the eighties, the Scanlon family lived in the rear of the millinery, and the covered wagon, like a gypsy encampment, sat under the lone tree. Before the railroad went through, the pony express stopped in the shade of the tree for water. Scanlon remembers the sweat on the horses, and once being lifted to the pommel of the saddle, but most of the things he remembers took place long before he was born.

In the weeds behind the stable are a rubber-tired fire-hose cart without the hose, two short lengths of ladder and the iron frame for the fire bell. When the water-pressure system proved too expensive, the order for the hose and the fire bell was canceled. On the east side of the stable, the wheels sunk in the sand, a water sprinkler is garlanded with morning glories and painted with the legend VISIT THE LYRIC TONITE. The Lyric, a wooden frame building, has a front of galvanized tin weathered to the leaden color of the drainpipes on the hotel. It stands like a souvenir book end at the east end of the town, holding up the row of false-front stores between it and the bank. Most of the year these shops face the sun, the light glaring on the curtained windows, like a row of blindfolded Confederate soldiers lined up to be shot. A boardwalk, like a fence blown on its side, is half concealed by the tidal drift of the sand—nothing could be drier, but the look of the place is wet. The wash of the sand is rippled as if by the movement of water, and stretches of the walk have the look of a battered pier. The town itself seems to face what is left of a vanished lake. Even the lone tree, stripped of its foliage, rises from the deck of the plain like a mast, and from the highway or the bluffs along the river, the crows'-nest at the top might be that on a ship. The bowl of the sky seems higher, the plain wider, because of it.

A street light still swings at the crossing corner but in the summer it casts no shadow, glowing like a bolthole in a stove until after nine o'clock. The plain is dark, but the bowl of the sky is full of light. On his horsehair sofa, drawn up to the window, Scanlon can see the hands on his watch until ten o'clock. The light is there after the sun has set and will be there in the morning before it rises, as if a property of the sky itself. The moon, rather than the sun, might be the source of it. In the summer the bats wing in and out of the stable as if it were dark, their radar clicking, wheel on the sky, then wing into the stable again. At this time of the evening coins come out to be found. The rails gleam like ice in the cinders, and the drayman's badge on Scanlon's hat, bright as a buckle, can be seen through the hole he has rubbed in the glass.

If a grass fire has been smoldering during the day you will see it flicker on the plain at night, and smoke from these fires, like Scanlon himself, has seldom left the rooms of the Lone Tree Hotel. It is there in the curtains like the smell of his cigars. His daughter Lois, the moment she arrives, goes up and down the halls opening the windows, and leaves a bottle of Air Wick in the room where she plans to spend the night. For better or worse—as she often tells McKee—she was born and raised in it.

✱ ✱ ✱

The last time Lois spent a night in Lone Tree was after her father had been found wrapped up like a mummy, his cold feet in a colder oven, and paraded big as life on the front page of the Omaha *Bee*. The caption of the story read:

MAN WHO KNEW BUFFALO BILL
SPENDS LONELY XMAS

although both his daughter and McKee were out there in time to spend part of Christmas with him. The story brought him many letters and made him famous, and put an end to his Lone Tree hibernation. To keep him entertained, as well as out of mischief, his daughter and her husband took him along the following winter on their trip to Mexico. There he saw a bullfight and met McKee's old friend, Gordon Boyd.

In Claremore, Oklahoma, on their way back, they stopped to see Edna and Clyde Ewing. Clyde claimed to be one fifth Cherokee Indian and an old friend of Will Rogers, whoever that might be. Although they had this new modern home, the Ewings spent most of their time going up and down the country in a house trailer just a few feet shorter than a flatcar. It had two bedrooms, a shower and a bath, with a rumpus room said to be soundproof. In the rumpus room, since they had no children, they kept an English bulldog named Shiloh, whose daddy had been sold for thirty thousand dollars. Scanlon never cared for dogs, and being too old to ride any of the Ewings' prize horses he was put in a buggy, between Ewing and McKee, and allowed to hold the reins while a white mare cantered. It made him hmmmphh. The Ewings were having a family reunion, but Scanlon saw no Cherokees present.

While they were there, they got on the Ewings' TV the report of a tragedy in Lincoln: a high-school boy with a hot-rod had run down and killed two of his classmates. An accident? No, he had run them down as they stood in the street, taunting him. On the TV screen they showed the boy's car, the muffler sticking up beside the windshield like a funnel, the fenders dented where he had smashed into the boys. Then they showed the killer, a boy with glasses, looking like a spaceman in his crash helmet. His name was Lee Roy Momeyer—pronounced *Lee* Roy by his family—the son of a Calloway machine-shop mechanic, and related to Scanlon by marriage. At the time he ran down and killed his classmates, he was working in a grease pit at the gasoline station where Walter McKee had used his influence to get him the job. Eighteen years of age, serious-minded, studious-looking in his thick-lensed glasses, Lee Roy was well intentioned to the point that it hurt—but a little slow. Talking to him, McKee fell into the habit of repeating himself.

"Mr. McKee," Lee Roy would say, "what can I do you for?" and McKee never quite got accustomed to it. And there he was, famous, with his picture on TV. In the morning they had a telegram from Lois's sister, Maxine Momeyer, asking if McKee would go his bail, which he did. Two days later, as they drove into Lincoln, coming in the back way so nobody would see them, there was no mention of Lee Roy Momeyer on the radio. A man and his wife had just been found murdered, but it couldn't have been Lee Roy. They had *him,* as the reporter said, in custody. Before that week was out there had been eight more, shot down like ducks by the mad-dog killer, and then he was captured out in the sand hills not far from Lone Tree. His name was Charlie Munger, and he was well known to Lee Roy Momeyer, who often greased his car. Between them they had killed twelve people in ten days.

Why did they do it?

When they asked Lee Roy Momeyer he replied that he just got tired of being pushed around. Who was pushing *who*? Never mind, that was what he said. The other one, Charlie Munger, said that he wanted to be somebody. Didn't everybody? Almost anybody, that is, but who he happened to be? McKee's little grandson thought he was Davy Crockett, and wore a coonskin hat with a squirrel's tail dangling, and Tom Scanlon, the great-grandfather, seemed to think he was Buffalo Bill. But when McKee read that statement in the paper there was just one person he thought of. His old boyhood chum, Gordon Boyd. Anybody could run over people or shoot them, but so far as McKee knew there was only one other man in history who had tried to walk on water—and He had got away with it.

McKee filed his clippings on these matters in a book entitled THE WALK ON THE WATER, written by Boyd after he had tried it himself. When it came to wanting to be somebody, and wanting, that is, to be it the hard way, there was no one in the same class as Boyd.

William Stafford

b. 1914

1960: *West of Your City*
1962: *Traveling Through the Dark*
1973: *Someday, Maybe*
1977: *Stories That Could Be True:*
New and Collected Poems
1983: *Smoke's Way*

WILLIAM STAFFORD'S *achievements include thirty volumes of poems, essays, conversations, and lectures; the National Book Award for* Traveling Through the Dark; *and the title of poet laureate of Oregon. Stafford has given poetry readings and lectures throughout the United States, and in 1972 he made a lecture tour of India, Egypt, Iran, and Pakistan.*

Born and brought up in Kansas, Stafford went to Iowa to earn his Ph.D., then migrated up to Oregon. And he stayed there, from 1948 until his retirement in 1980, as a professor of creative writing at Lewis and Clark College. Considering his western roots, far from the large cities and always in close proximity to either the Great Plains or the Pacific Northwest, it seems correct to call Stafford a western pastoral poet. This does not mean that he is an idealist, however; he simply prefers landscapes over cityscapes. Like pastoral poets everywhere, he likes to let his imagination travel back in time, visiting those earlier eras when life was more primitive.

> I put my foot in cold water
> and hold it there; early mornings
> they had to wade through broken ice
> to find the traps in the deep channel
> with their hands, drag up the chains and

the drowned beaver. That slow current
of their life below tugs at me all day.
When I dream at night, they save a place for me,
no matter how small, somewhere by the fire.[1]

Stafford's thoughts consistently transcend his superficial subject matter, giving his poetry a dimension beyond that which we generally see in pastoral works. In "Ferns" and "Witness," he perceives his own life as part of an infinite pattern, a pattern as delicate as lace and as tough as the Missouri or the Rockies. Humans have a responsibility to that pattern because they are part of it and it is part of them; they need to nurture their sympathy for life, even forms of life that will never be born and forms that stand on the verge of extinction. The moments that Stafford catches in "Traveling Through the Dark" and "Report to Crazy Horse" also transcend their pastoral settings and expose some of life's most insidious enemies.

Throughout his many poems—there are 350 of them just in Stories That Could Be True—*Stafford envisions a "new western myth," according to J. Russell Roberts, Sr. The heroes of that myth are ordinary people, but "while they are not divinities they are surrounded by something greater than man."[2] Their heroism does not lie in performing deeds of battle or in conquering the land. It comes from the willingness to understand, sympathize, and endure.*

Ferns

After the firestorms that end history,
a fern may print on the rock
some pattern about chance, and
the reaching for it, and the odds.

Already they are prints for us:
lace in the dusk, thin

From William Stafford, *Smoke's Way* (Port Townsend, Wash.: Graywolf Press, 1983), p. 60. Copyright © 1983 by William Stafford. Reprinted by permission of Graywolf Press.

1. William Stafford, "Remembering Mountain Men," *Concerning Poetry* 13 (Fall 1980): 4. Reprinted by permission of William Stafford.

2. J. Russell Roberts, Sr., "William Stafford," in *A Literary History of the American West*, ed. J. Golden Taylor and Thomas J. Lyon (Fort Worth: Texas Christian University Press, 1987), p. 459.

stem, wide hand, faint presence; and
I know something fainter, fern:

The map under this country
that shows where we are while
we wander lost and the sun pulls
and our thought swims into the air.

Witness

This is the hand I dipped in the Missouri
above Council Bluffs and found the springs.
All through the days of my life I escort
this hand. Where would the Missouri
meet a kinder friend?

On top of Fort Rock in the sun I spread
these fingers to hold the world in the wind;
along that cliff, in that old cave
where men used to live, I grubbed in the dirt
for those cool springs again.

Summits in the Rockies received this diplomat.
Brush that concealed the lost children yielded
them to this hand. Even on the last morning
when we all tremble and lose, I will reach
carefully, eagerly through that rain, at the end—

Toward whatever is there, with this loyal hand.

This and the following selections of William Stafford's verse are from *Someday, Maybe* (New York: Harper and Row, 1973), p. 73 (copyright © 1973 by William Stafford); *Stories That Could Be True: New and Collected Poems* (New York: Harper and Row, 1977), p. 61 (copyright © 1960 by William Stafford); *Someday, Maybe*, pp. 45–46 (copyright © 1971 by William Stafford). All reprinted by permission of Harper and Row, Publishers, Inc.

Traveling Through the Dark

Traveling through the dark I found a deer
dead on the edge of the Wilson River road.
It is usually best to roll them into the canyon:
that road is narrow; to swerve might make more dead.

By glow of the tail-light I stumbled back of the car
and stood by the heap, a doe, a recent killing;
she had stiffened already, almost cold.
I dragged her off; she was large in the belly.

My fingers touching her side brought me the reason—
her side was warm; her fawn lay there waiting,
alive, still, never to be born.
Beside that mountain road I hesitated.

The car aimed ahead its lowered parking lights;
under the hood purred the steady engine.
I stood in the glare of the warm exhaust turning red;
around our group I could hear the wilderness listen.

I thought hard for us all—my only swerving—,
then pushed her over the edge into the river.

———

Report to Crazy Horse

All the Sioux were defeated. Our clan
got poor, but a few got richer.
They fought two wars. I did not
take part. No one remembers your vision
or even your real name. Now

the children go to town and like
loud music. I married a Christian.

Crazy Horse, it is not fair
to hide a new vision from you.
In our schools we are learning
to take aim when we talk, and we have
found out our enemies. They shift when
words do; they even change and hide
in every person. A teacher here says
hurt or scorned people are places
where real enemies hide. He says
we should not hurt or scorn anyone,
but help them. And I will tell you
in a brave way, the way Crazy Horse
talked: that teacher is right.

I will tell you a strange thing:
at the rodeo, close to the grandstand,
I saw a farm lady scared by a blown
piece of paper; and at that place
horses and policemen were no longer
frightening, but suffering faces were,
and the hunched-over backs of the old.
Crazy Horse, tell me if I am right:
these are the things we thought we were
doing something about.

In your life you saw many strange things,
and I will tell you another: now I salute
the white man's flag. But when I salute
I hold my hand alertly on the heartbeat
and remember all of us and how we depend
on a steady pulse together. There are those
who salute because they fear other flags
or mean to use ours to chase them:
I must not allow my part of saluting
to mean this. All of our promises,
our generous sayings to each other, our
honorable intentions—these I affirm

when I salute. At these times it is like
shutting my eyes and joining a religious
colony at prayer in the gray dawn
in the deep aisles of a church.

Now I have told you about new times.
Yes, I know others will report
different things. They have been caught
by weak ways. I tell you straight
the way it is now, and it is our way,
the way we were trying to find.

The chokecherries along our valley
still bear a bright fruit. There is good
pottery clay north of here. I remember
our old places. When I pass the Musselshell
I run my hand along those old grooves in the rock.

PART 4

The Neowestern Period

1915-present

Introduction

—

B ACK AT THE TURN of the twentieth century, the West still seemed
young. World War I came along, however, and then the subsequent
depressions, droughts, and wars. Growth and prosperity also came,
and the West advanced rapidly in population and in economic and political stature. And among the complexities of twentieth-century American
life, the old frontier West seemed to be "closed," just as Frederick Jackson
Turner had said. In Willa Cather's novel *The Professor's House*, Tom Outland
represents exuberance and youth and seems to be symbolic of the spirit of
the nineteenth-century West. Outland dies in World War I; his teacher and
friend, Godfrey St. Peter, wonders whether the romantic cowboy-explorer
actually existed. "You know, Tom isn't very real to me any more. Sometimes
I think he was just a—a glittering idea." [1]

Fifty years of domestic peacelessness followed the Great War: ambiguous
values went to war against each other in virtually every arena of American
life. The hawks and the doves fought for control of the national policy;
the bears and the bulls both claimed to know what was best for the economy; the atheists and the born-agains began competing to see who would
win the souls of the humanists. American literature, some critics have said,
entered an era of unprecedented decay; others hailed this time as a golden
age of letters. Edward Wagenknecht, in *Cavalcade of the American Novel*,
noted that the American society was in a state of "moral bankruptcy" and
"surpassing folly," and he found a "widespread sickness of soul" among
young writers. At the same time, he called this period a brilliant time in
literary history. [2] Other critics have echoed Wagenknecht, viewing the post-
WWI period as a "literary revolution," an "awakening," and a "renaissance."

1. Willa Cather, *The Professor's House* (New York: Grosset and Dunlap, 1925), p. 111.
2. Edward Wagenknecht, *Cavalcade of the American Novel* (New York: Holt, Rinehart
and Winston, 1952), pp. 451, 454.

Fiction of these fifty years performed daring experiments in bold, clean prose; poetry reached new intellectual depths and learned to speak with forceful impact; drama became adventurous and honest.

In spite of wars and depression and dust bowls, the West managed to grow and prosper in the twentieth century. According to the historian Gerald Nash, "more than 40 million Americans and at least 8 million foreigners" poured into the trans-Mississippi region between 1898 and 1973.[3] They brought with them most of the advances—and drawbacks—of eastern economics, social patterns, culture, and technology. Since the turn of the century, urban areas in the West had been more populous than rural regions; in comparatively little time, these cities became sophisticated, modern, and politically powerful. Farming technology brought industrial agriculture to California and was also instrumental in creating the dust bowl in drier areas. Even though the results were mixed benefits at best, the West continued to exploit its resources as it grew toward affluence and stability.

Gerald Nash wrote of three "fundamental weaknesses of American society" that appeared in the twentieth-century West. One was a widespread feeling of non-belonging, or "loss of community," among people. The second was the disjunction of Indian, Spanish-American, and Anglo cultures within the western community, not to mention other cultures that lay outside the majority. The third weakness, an inability to populate the land without spoiling it, was seen in the plethora of environmental problems, some of which had their beginnings with the first pioneers. "Continuity as much as change has been a central theme of Western development since 1890, and if we are to understand some of the major problems of the twentieth-century West, we must approach them in their historical context. These problems grew out of a complicated web of past experience, and in that sense the past provides a mirror for the future."[4]

Some of our writers still write about that West of "once upon a time," just as a few modern English writers still write about the never-never days of King Arthur. But whether western authors portray the fur trappers, the gunfighters, or urban gangs and astronauts, they are acutely sensitive to the stereotypes; they sense the thinness of the romantic facade and feel responsible for preserving history with accuracy. Either they consciously avoid the

3. Gerald D. Nash, *The American West in the Twentieth Century* (Englewood Cliffs, N.J.: Prentice-Hall, 1973), p. 2.

4. Ibid., pp. 304–5; Gerald D. Nash, "Mirror for the Future: The Historical Past of the Twentieth-Century West," in *The Twentieth Century American West*, ed. Thomas G. Alexander and John F. Bluth (Provo, Utah: Brigham Young University, Charles Redd Center for Western Studies, 1983), p. 2.

stereotypes altogether or they innovate new uses for that same old material. But they cannot be content to use the material as it was used by the earlier writers because this is a new generation of western civilization. The purple sage has given way to wheat fields and bluegrass lawns, while the rose-colored sunsets are dark with windblown desiccated topsoil and urban air pollution.

The writers of the Neowestern Period grew up as children and students in a society that, in the words of Wallace Stegner, has assumed "a reality whose past and present do not match."[5] This mismatch has caused contemporary authors to take a second look at some basic concepts, starting with the idea of manifest destiny, the premise stemming from the assumption that nothing is impossible, no problem insoluble. Courage and endurance would settle the frontier wilderness; strength and ingenuity would conquer the land and bring forth fruit; religion and civilized systems would tame the Wild West. But after fifty years of increasingly frustrating wars, five decades of an unmanageable economy, and the perpetual threat of environmental disaster, the manifest destiny idea underwent major revisions. New writers had to accept the possibility that such problems as drought, depression, and racial conflict might not be solvable.

Another attitude shift affected the "promised land" image of the West as a garden waiting to be cultivated—and then harvested—by the right people. Tom Outland, in *The Professor's House*, learns that the government regards his Mesa Verde discovery only as a resource for exploitation. In another example, Leslie Marmon Silko's *Ceremony* dramatizes the ugliness of military industrialism: sacred earth is taken from Laguna land and is used to destroy strangers halfway around the world. Laguna sacred earth, the government explains, contains uranium.

Along with losing control of its own resources, the New West has also lost significant parts of its nineteenth-century image and cannot seem to decide what to do with the image it has left. Earlier writers of the West felt free to write about romantic ideals as if these were everyday verities, as Owen Wister did in *The Virginian*. They could also write about the struggles and the realism, or the glamour, or the stoicism, or they could lament the passing of the old days or hail the coming of the new. But whether they dealt in romanticism, realism, nostalgia, or futurism, they rarely took an ambivalent stance. With the advent of the postwar period in literature, this changed. Ambiguities began springing up like weeds in an overworked field.

5. Wallace Stegner, "Who Are the Westerners?" *American Heritage* 38 (December 1987): 35.

In 1981, a fourth-generation Coloradoan, Russell Martin, raised a few eyebrows and blood pressures among the western literati when he published an article in the *New York Times Magazine*. He discussed the ambivalence between myth and actuality "out West," and what he said about the neo-West itself irritated quite a few westerners. Contemporary western writers, according to Martin, "have had the most difficulty dealing with the power of the myth. They had to come to terms with it, or at least get it out of their way, before they could attempt to mold an artistic sense of their lives lived out, out West, before they could take a critical view of a region that had become, in many ways, a parody of itself."[6]

To explain what *self-parody* means, Wallace Stegner has referred again to the romantic quality inherent in the western image. "The outside never got over its heightened and romantic notion of the West," he wrote, using *outside* to mean everyone outside of the West. "The West never got over its heightened and romantic notion of itself." When Russell Martin and Mark Barasch brought out their anthology of neowestern writers, their preface repeated much of what Martin had said in the *New York Times Magazine* article. "Westerners nowadays," Martin and Barasch said, "live in a brash and often chaotic present that has little to do with the past that was limned by the mythic stories. . . . the new Western writers are chronicling this uneasy shift, the sometimes melancholy slide of one epoch into another, the emergence of the West as a region that extends beyond its myths."[7]

The idea that we see ourselves unrealistically is not exactly new. Frank Waters put his finger on it forty years ago.

> Read almost any magazine, almost any book on the West. The same old stories. The same fictional vernacular. Pure, unadulterated hokum.
>
> Why?
>
> We insist on seeing ourselves as we like to think we were. We're afraid to see ourselves as we are.
>
> Is it because we have lost our innate sense of direction? Or are we so afraid of the future that we cling to a false romantic past?[8]

Imagine yourself as a writer who has grown up in this period, caught between heritage and hokum, between history and parody. Wallace Stegner offers you a way out of your dilemma when he suggests that things really

6. Russell Martin, "Writers of the Purple Sage," *New York Times Magazine*, December 27, 1981, p. 20.

7. Stegner, "Who Are the Westerners?" p. 36; Russell Martin and Mark Barasch, *Writers of the Purple Sage* (New York: Penguin, 1984), pp. xii, xiii.

8. Frank Waters, *The Colorado* (New York: Rinehart and Co., 1946), p. 280.

haven't changed that much. The neowesterner still has many of the old frontier personality traits. "A high degree of mobility, a degree of ruthlessness,
a large component of both self-sufficiency and self-righteousness mark the
historical pioneer, the lone-riding folk hero, and the modern businessman
intent on opening new industrial frontiers and getting his own in the process."[9] If, as a novelist, you create characters on *that* model, you violate a
romantic western myth that most of your neowestern readers have grown
up believing.

Writers faced with the postwar western world have several options. First,
they can stay with the myth and keep writing romances in the manner of
Max Brand or Louis L'Amour or Jeanne Williams (who has written more
than forty romantic western novels). Second, they can take the approach
pioneered by A. B. Guthrie, Jr., and Walter Van Tilburg Clark and Wallace
Stegner, authors who breathe new life into the old stereotypes. As Martin
and Barasch have noted: "In the imaginations of the Western-born writers
at work in the postwar 1940's and 1950's, the pervasive frontier myths hung
like a late spring storm over the scrublands, limiting vision and obscuring
opportunities to give literary shape to contemporary lives and surroundings. [They] had to confront the myths head on, to retell the Western stories
in anti-mythological terms, to by God set the record straight."[10] Third, neowestern writers can resort to writing individualistic poetry and prose, or
extremely character-centered fiction, and thereby sidestep the whole mythic
question.

In some instances, writers find the forces too strong to ignore and too
traditional to modify. For such deeply rooted influences we use the term
heritage, rather than *myth* or *history.* For the best examples of heritage-
centered writers, look at the Chicano literary movement; there, the sense
of cultural heritage governs even the most innovative imaginations. In
an autobiographical article written for *Contemporary Authors,* Rudolfo A.
Anaya said: "If I am to be a writer, it is the ancestral voices of these people
who will form a part of my quest, my search. They taught me that life is fragile, that there are signs given to us, signs that we must learn to interpret."
Jimmy Santiago Baca called his 1987 volume of poems an "epic," part of an
inherited Hispanic genre dating back to 1598 when Gaspar Perez de Villa-
gra wrote his epic, *Historia de la Nueva Mexico.*[11] Likewise, the plays of El

9. Stegner, "Who Are the Westerners?" p. 39.

10. Martin and Barasch, *Writers of the Purple Sage,* p. xi.

11. Rudolfo A. Anaya, in *Contemporary Authors Autobiography Series,* ed. Adele Sarkissian (Detroit: Gale Research, 1986), vol. 4, p. 16; Jimmy Santiago Baca, letter to the
author, February 8, 1988.

Teatro Campesino, which began in 1965, belong to a heritage that begins, in America, with a play titled *Moros y cristianos*, also presented in 1598.

Whether coming from a long literary lineage or having newly arrived on the western scene, each writer of the neowestern generation seems to have a conflict of values lurking somewhere behind each story, play, or poem. Anaya and Baca, for example, represent the bicultural difficulty; they are sensitive to two different cultures and must of necessity deal with two separate value systems, driven all the while by an impulse to seek some kind of unity. N. Scott Momaday and Leslie Marmon Silko, both prominent Native American writers, want their literature to preserve the rapidly vanishing traditions of their people, yet they recognize that many of those traditions are archaic. Native Americans must learn their history and the traditional ways of thinking, but they cannot live as did their ancestors. In James Welch we have a Native American writer who successfully combines ageless lore and legends with his own contemporary reflections.

Nature writers such as Ann Zwinger and Edward Abbey might seem to be free from such cross-purposes. Yet they probably have the most poignant dilemma of all. Their books and articles promote an understanding of the landscape and publicize places of isolation and beauty; therefore, if their writing is successful, nature writers actually attract more people to the very places they set out to defend. Ironically, they are lovers of nature who make their living through literary exploitation of nature. Like the rest of the postwar writers, they get caught with one foot in the world they like and one foot in the world they must deal with. Other examples include John Sterling Harris and Gary Snyder, both of whom are poets with a profound lyric impulse and a gentle understanding of beauty yet who often must write about the hammering realities of life and death.

Whatever their individual dilemmas, and whatever their literary genres, contemporary writers continue to be intrigued by one subject—the environment. The natural environment determined the history of society in the West and shaped the lives of the early people. Indian legends tell of a deeply mystical relationship with the land; today, centuries later, novels and short stories still feature the land as a spiritual protagonist or antagonist. In Indian legend, nature is a great mystery full of supernatural forces. Early American writers dramatized the land as a challenge, a barrier, an opponent; with the coming of industrialism and urbanization, landscape came to be viewed as an unguarded treasure of "resources." Today's neowestern writers challenge that resource concept, asking us whether the rivers were meant to be dammed, the forests to be harvested, and the minerals to be stripped from the ground. The majority of westerners now live and work and play in cities, largely out of touch with the wild; however, the non-urban natural environment cannot be mistreated or ignored without consequences.

The resource concept is complex, offering endless issues to consider. Some say, for instance, that we have too much open and government-owned land. Wallace Stegner wrote: "It is public land, partly theirs, and that space is a continuing influence on their minds and senses. It encourages a fatal carelessness and destructiveness because it seems so limitless and because what is everybody's is nobody's responsibility."[12] Frank Waters fears the potential of human technology, a technology that is now capable of causing serious climatic changes in the earth's atmosphere.

> For all our technological achievements, our very lives tremble upon the delicate scales of nature. We are as ultimately dependent upon the ancient verities of land and sky as were the prehistoric cliff dwellers. Man has not yet completed the full circle toward a realization that his own laws of life must conform in the long view with those greater laws to which he still and forever owes allegiance.[13]

In much of their fiction, Edward Abbey, Max Evans, James Welch, and N. Scott Momaday blame modern western problems on one basic cause: society has lost touch with the earth. Their protagonists recognize the loss as they struggle to regain contact, but society inevitably frustrates their efforts. This theme in literature, the editor and critic John R. Milton tells us, dramatizes the consequences of the West's traditional belief in mobility, the tendency of each generation to "move on" without gaining a sense of place anywhere. "It is a hard contemporary realization that a nonlanded society which is continually separating itself from the lessons of the past and from intuitive knowledge may soon destroy itself in a welter of mistaken values."[14]

That would be a bleak analysis if it applied to all authors. But here and there throughout the New West are still writers who see the past for what it was, the present for what it is, and the future for what it can be. Gerald Haslam, a fiction writer and critic from California, does not hesitate to admit that his generation has heard more than one discouraging word. Because of modern media, we have a generation of authors who witnessed the mindless assassination of national leaders, viewed the humiliating vio-

12. Stegner, "Who Are the Westerners?" p. 41.

13. Waters, *The Colorado*, p. 370.

14. John R. Milton, *The Novel of the American West* (Lincoln: University of Nebraska Press, 1980), p. 324.

lence against people seeking their civil rights, saw live close-ups of a war that would not be resolved, and got the bird's-eye view of brown chemical clouds hovering over every major western city. Over everything, including the fine arts, hangs the general threat of nuclear wipeout. Writers like William Eastlake, realizing that the prospects look gloomy and that literature cannot save the world, demonstrate optimism in the way that they continue to refine the craft of writing. "Finally," Haslam has written, "it is the questing of Eastlake and his peers, not their conclusions, that is most important, their questing and their willingness to employ contemporary philosophy and literary techniques to examine a region always in danger of romanticization." [15]

Somewhere, this New West generation of questing writers may find some conclusions. If not, perhaps the next generation will. The few writers presented here—Snyder and Harris, Zwinger and Anaya, Silko and Baca and the rest—represent hundreds of other writers who have also begun to explore options and potentials for western America. Somewhere, it seems certain, people with that kind of insight will eventually succeed in struggling through the dilemmas and contradictions, the paradoxical social impulses, the random value and philosophy shifts that have characterized the years since World War I. They might even arrive at a realization like that of Doña Maria de Valle, the central character of Frank Waters's 1941 novel, *People of the Valley*.

> Maria believed neither in the majority nor in the minority. She believed in all men. Good for the strong at the expense of the weak she saw as a natural inevitability. But also she saw that intentional wrong dealt the few can never be paid for by the right derived from it by the many. Maria believed in fulfillment instead of progress. Fulfillment is individual evolution. It requires time and patience. Progress, in haste to move mass, admits neither. [16]

The literature of the American West continues to evolve, gaining more and more individuality as it goes. The neowestern writers, our most recent literary generation, are finding fulfillment in three distinct ways: as individual expressive artists, as interpretive ambassadors of their various cultural communities, and—perhaps most important of all—as western people with a true sense of place.

15. Gerald W. Haslam, "Introduction: Rediscovering the West," in *A Literary History of the American West*, ed. J. Golden Taylor and Thomas J. Lyon (Fort Worth: Texas Christian University Press, 1987), p. 1019.

16. Frank Waters, *People of the Valley* (1941; reprint, Chicago: Swallow Press, 1969), p. 134.

Ann Zwinger
b. 1925

———

1970: *Beyond the Aspen Grove*
1972: *Land Above the Trees:*
A Guide to American Alpine Tundra
1975: *Run, River, Run*
1978: *Wind in the Rock*
1983: *A Desert Country Near the Sea*
1989: *The Mysterious Lands*

———

CAREFUL SKETCHES *of plants, insects, fossils, and artifacts illustrate Ann Zwinger's nature books, supplementing her graphic descriptions of landscape. Together, her illustrations and her prose invite readers to look at everyday objects with new interest, to see surroundings as if for the first time. In* Wind in the Rock, *the author looks back at a desert canyon. "I turn away with regret, feeling freshly molted. Down in the canyon I grew a little, understood a little more, perceived even more, and in so doing split the carapace of time and place I commonly wear. Split it, wriggled out of it, left it there, a stiff and empty shell to be blown away by a canyon wind. The new skin was extra-sensitive, and so I perceived the canyon about me with new eyes, more sensitive touch, emotions closer to the surface."* [1]

Zwinger's books reflect the influence of other American nature writers, such as John Muir, John Burroughs, and Henry David Thoreau; however, her careful research and details give her writing a unique freshness and individuality. Beyond the Aspen Grove *methodically surveys a high-country ecosystem, taking an inventory of Rocky Mountain flora and fauna. It also describes Zwinger's very personal love affair with a mountain valley.*

Zwinger is sometimes compared to Edward Abbey, her contemporary. Like

———

1. Ann Zwinger, *Wind in the Rock* (Tucson: University of Arizona Press, 1978), p. 51.

Abbey, Zwinger excels at intimate anecdotes that educate her readers while giving them fresh ways of looking at familiar landscapes. Abbey's Desert Solitaire *does this with shock and polemic; Zwinger's books rely on the inherent appeal of meticulous detail, organized for maximum intellectual effect.* Beyond the Aspen Grove *exemplifies this; the book resembles a painting that deliberately leads the observer's eye from point to point. The opening chapter is panoramic, providing a sweeping overview of Zwinger's mountain property. The next chapter draws attention to the ecology of the lake, which is the most visible feature; Zwinger then lets us examine the lake's sources of water, two small streams abounding with plants and microscopic life-forms. Our perspective next moves naturally toward the meadows, then to the meadow-fringing aspen, and finally beyond into the deeper, surrounding forests.*

This structured sequence in Beyond the Aspen Grove *also leads from the man-made to the natural, from the lake to the forest. Therefore it is fitting that Zwinger's closing chapter returns to the lake, where a large natural rock sits in the artificial reservoir. Here, natural life-forms have survived by exploiting the man-made change in their environment. "Beginning to know these mountain acres has been to discover a puzzle with a million pieces already set out on a table," Zwinger wrote in her opening chapter. "Occasionally a few pieces fit together and we gain another awareness of the land's total pattern of existence, of its intricate interdependencies, enhanced by knowing that the puzzle will never be completed. . . . Humans are but intruders who have presumed the right to be observers, and who, out of observation, find understanding."* [2]

—

The Lake Rock

WHEN I NEED my sense of order restored, I sit on the lake rock. It sums up all I have learned about this mountain world. Connected to the shore by a narrow, somewhat unstable catwalk, the rock is just big enough to sit on comfortably. It is a pebble dropped into the water, the center of widening rings of montane life, beginning with the life of the lake itself and culminating in the evergreen forests, where the succession that is taking place is mapped in the communities that I can see. The rock is a place of order, reason, and bright mountain air.

From Ann Zwinger, *Beyond the Aspen Grove* (New York: Harper and Row, 1970), pp. 295–309. Copyright © 1970, 1981 by Ann Zwinger. Reprinted by permission of the author.

    2. Ann Zwinger, *Beyond the Aspen Grove* (New York: Harper and Row, 1970), pp. 8–9.

Encircling the rock is the community of plants and animals which can survive only in the water. Small motes of existence, they float with its currents, cling to underwater supports, or burrow in the brown silt of the lake bottom. Some I can see as I sit here. Others have to be corralled under a microscope lens. I watch a fat trout lurking in the fringed shadows of the sedges. All around the edges of the lake, where water meets land, grow willows, sedges, and rushes, predicting a time when amber water will be green plant, the lapping sound of small waves the sly whisper of grass stems.

It is a busy place with a constant spin of insects, punctuated by the pursuing green arcs of leopard frogs. The south stream enters the lake through willows and cow parsnip and a pile of logs placed there when the lake was built to prevent silting. The north stream's entrance is hidden in elephant-foot-sized clumps of bulrush which change sheen in every breeze. Tangles of willows forecast spring in their catkins. Yellow or red branches identify them even in winter. The streams are the one constant in this landscape.

The circle widens. Behind the lake edge, to the north and west, the land rises into the lake meadow, drying as it slopes upward. Blue grass and brome grass crowd every square inch. I see chipmunk and ground-squirrel burrows, haloed with dandelions. Hundreds of wildflowers grow in this meadow, perennials whose coming I look for each year. A few aspens tentatively grow along its edge.

The established young aspen community between the two streams contains small slender trees, growing almost a foot a year. Still gangling and adolescent, they will in a short time obscure the view of the mature grove behind them. Leaves flicker celadon in spring, viridian in summer, clinquant in fall, tallying the sovereign seasons, graying and greening to reiterate the message of snow and sun.

Wider still, the north edge of the lake meadow steps upward over its granite base. Where it levels off, the ponderosas grow, big and sturdy and full of cones. They stand staunch, widely spaced, allowing sunlight to filter through for wild geranium and kinnikinnik and tiny wild candytuft that crosses the dusky duff.

The south slope of the lake curves away from the shore, becoming more spruce-shaded as it retreats. This area is the first to be snow-covered, the last to be clear. Shade-tolerant plants root in the precipitous hillside; from here I can see a few late orange-red Indian paintbrush and the stalks of monkshood and larkspur. Dark-red strawberry blite ties down an old log with the help of raspberry and rose bushes. A few last aspens mingle with the spruces, their trunks thin and pallid, most of their branches down from insufficient light. Above them the Douglas-firs and spruces grow close together, presenting a solid wall of black-green.

The ever-widening circles of montane life culminate in these evergreens which intrude visually into the lake. Even in winter, when the India-ink reflections are gone, the uncompromising contrast of black and white still commands the eye. In the spring, when the air is heavy and laden with late snows, the lake reflects their pendent spires, solid as a German Expressionist woodcut. In the summer the reflections shimmer in the breeze, slotted with blue sky, an animate Monet. In the fall they form a moving mosaic with the aspen when the wind fragments the surface to create tesserae of emerald and gold leaf—a Byzantine pavement.

It is impossible to look at the land and not be aware of the evergreens. In all seasons they dominate, unchanging in color, towering in size. Their spires crenelate the sky. Their opacity of color, depth, and density create a background against which are measured the brightness of aspen leaf, iridescence of dragonfly wing, scarlet of gilia, and gleam of lake. The ponderosa, spruce, and Douglasfir are the reminders of an end point of succession for this land, for there is no other vegetation that will replace them, short of catastrophic climate change.

These trees change the environment to fit their needs, making an acid soil which is inhospitable to other plants, attracting rain by the massiveness of their own transpiration. At the beginning of succession, moss and lichen grow a few centimeters above the ground and a few below. At the end of succession, for this land, trees tower many feet into the air and send their roots through the ground, demanding the most that the environment can give. These conifers will be there in decades, in centuries, to come. They will shade out other trees and brighter flowers, intrude into the deepening soil of the meadows. Succession is an inexorable progression which may be altered or disrupted but which will eternally begin again and again to achieve the same end. No emotional pleas or moral inducements will change it; to understand this is to accept the irrevocableness of nature.

The knob of granite forming my tiny island rises three feet above the water on the lake side, stepping and sloping down to a few inches above on the land side. The surface breaks off and crumbles into sharp gravel in my hand with the ease of Pikes Peak granite. Near the waterline on the east, the plants grow in independent patches, on a nearly vertical face. On the rise and tread of the protected step they grow more thickly. Green pincushions of moss are softer to sit on than the gravel. At my feet, on top of one mat of moss, are a few square inches of blue grass, neatly trimmed by the wind. Through this nest of stolons and roots and rhizomes grow cinquefoils, wild strawberry, white clover, an ubiquitous dandelion, asters, wild chrysanthemum, rosettes of scarlet gilia and bright pink wild geranium.

Strawberry and geranium seeds may have arrived via the droppings of a gluttonous chickadee. The tiny leaves, replicas of normal-sized leaves on shore, bear the imprint of limitation. Composite seeds came on efficient parachutes, sometimes air-borne, sometimes as a flotilla sailing across the water and snagging in a crack. Porter's asters and wild chrysanthemums give the final touch of yellow and white to the rock; golden asters are one of the most tolerant plants of the mountains, flourishing in a wide variety of habitats in a wide variety of altitudes.

Bush cinquefoil cliff-hangs at the southernmost edge of the rock; fully exposed, they set brilliant blooms against the darkness of the lake's pine-tree reflections. Although the bushes are small, their leaf and blossom size are the same as those of shore plants. Looking around the lake shore, I can see these same flowers and shrubs in the meadow or the aspen grove, usually where there is some protection and, at the very least, more soil.

I take a mental walk along the rim of the parent rocks of this island which form the south-facing slope at the edge of the lake. There, large boulders of Pikes Peak granite form a crumbling cliff with the ponderosa grove at the top and the lake at the base. Below the dam, the rim of granite drops sharply to the runoff stream. Facing almost due south, the slope receives the full intensity of mountain sunlight, especially in the winter when the low sun hits at a ninety-degree angle and keeps the slope snow-free.

In the weathered gravel which forms talus-like patches between the rocks, some plants have rooted. Water drains most quickly from a gravel slope, making colonization exceedingly difficult. Decomposed rock has little stability, and the steepness of the slope causes it to roll easily. Nonetheless there is a fairly even growth of penny-cress, shepherd's-purse, butter-and-eggs, amaranth, and buckwheat. Considered as being noxious weeds at lower elevations, they provide soil hold here, and even their propensity for forming myriads of seeds has not given them unchallenged progress. They simply find the growing conditions too difficult to make nuisances of themselves.

Towering over the annuals are the exclamation points of mullein, huge stalks of this year's green reiterated in the browned stalks of last year's pods. *Candelaria* is the descriptive Spanish name, and indeed they seem like huge candelabra, verdigris in summer, bronze in winter. With a few scarlet gilia, some small-flowered blue gilia, and white thistles, these are the only biennials. An early narrow-leafed mertensia is the only perennial herb. There are some rose twigs, but to call them shrubs would be presumptuous.

Farther down this same slope, on top of a large level rock which the children used to use for a stage, are a few pincushion cacti. Some also grow in the loose gravel nearby, tucked at the foot of another boulder near sprigs of pin cherry. Cacti have extremely shallow and spreading root systems, which cover such a large area that they can take full advantage of even a light rainfall. Leaves, like those of the conifers, have been narrowed to needles; stems are thickened to a sphere covered with a heavy cuticle. The stomata are closed during the day when evaporation is high and opened in the cool of the night. These devices hinder water loss so effectively that cacti are most common in desert areas. And this is very nearly just that: there is no shade, the rocks catch and radiate the full heat and glare of high-intensity altitude sunlight, and solid rock lies just beneath the surface. Growing conditions are hard indeed; the delicacy of the early pink flowers is almost incongruous.

Still farther down the slope, on another large rock table, is a cluster of stonecrop. Like the cactus, its succulent leaves are thickly cuticled and the root system is shallow and wide. Tolerant of a wide soil range, stonecrop grows on many montane rocks and dry slopes. It blooms profusely in June and July, brilliant six-pointed stars visible as puddles of yellow many feet away although no single blossom exceeds half an inch in diameter. Its vitality is in no way diminished by conditions other plants would find impossible.

✳ ✳ ✳

To compare these rock environments with the lake rock is to see what water can do to alter the vegetational pattern. Cactus, stonecrop, and mullein could not grow on the lake rock, for they require a dry situation. Other conditions are the same: Pikes Peak granite base, exposed site, close enough to receive identical amounts of sun and rain. The difference in vegetation is caused by the surrounding water, and is indicated not only in the type but the increased variety of plants. The measured relative humidity on the rock is consistently nearly double that of the shore rocks. In the winter the rock is ice-locked and generally snow-covered over the plant line, protecting the plants from the extremes of thaw and freeze and desiccation that the shore plants must endure.

Water is the most important single factor in this succession. The lake has made possible a local condition with local vegetation, just as the stream running through the dry prairie makes possible the phalanx of trees along its banks. The two extremes exist side by side.

The lake-rock community has progressed as far, in terms of plant succession, as the meadow community, and in a measurably short time—since the lake was built some seventeen years ago. It had and still has many aspects of a pioneer community. Much of the growth is isolated, a hand-span or more apart. The soil is minimal and undifferentiated. Layering is narrow, and the environmental factors almost totally control the plant life. The predominant growth here is that of perennial herbs, characteristic of a more advanced stage of succession than that which exists on the shore rocks before me. None of these plants are limited in range or in need of special conditions on this rock. Tolerance and hardiness mark the pioneers.

A succession of animal life accompanies the succession of plant life. The animals who busy themselves by the lake rock are insects, mostly transients who can fly. No mice burrow here, no deer browse, no birds perch. The blue damselfly frequents the rock as a passer-by. Flies make a noisy nuisance of themselves but lay their eggs elsewhere. Only wolf spiders leave dots of white cotton egg cases. The lake rock is isolated from the shore, the water as effective a barrier as if it were a mile across, and the sparse plant cover provides no shelter for larger animals.

But when the lake has finally been absorbed, and the rock is surrounded and covered by soil, then perhaps larger animals will come padding and pawing and nosing about, their ancestors even now roaming the woods. I would like to think so. But perhaps they will not, for by then they may already be gone from here, as the wolves, wolverines, and grizzly bears are already gone, pushed to extinction by man's narrowing of the wilderness.

We have tried to understand the patterns of the land at Constant Friendship. We have hoped to change it as little as possible. After all, we are only visitors to this mountain land. But to keep this land untouched has meant that we have had to partially fence it, with a fence almost as much psychological as physical. And this, incongruously, seems to be the only way in which wilderness lands can be saved. Only within the periphery of the fence is there time to learn, to understand, to cherish. My interest in the vast world of nature began when we came to this land, with the finding of a new world, a sense of discovery, a sharing. But somewhere in the learning came commitment, the realization that in the understanding of this natural world comes the maintenance of it, that with knowledge comes responsibility.

At Constant Friendship we chop down a dead aspen that might fall on the cabin during a wind storm, destroying the chance for it to be home for bird or insect or weasel. It makes good firewood, we say, thinking of our creature comforts. But we have cut down no masses of trees, leaving open scars to erode. We have polluted no streams, shot no marauding bobcat for bounty, no deer for sport. But by our presence we do cause the balances of nature to be readjusted.

Because we can and do manipulate our environment, we are then charged with the responsibility of our acts, for if we are to survive we must insure that this best of all possible worlds survives with us.

The lake rock is a microcosm, and here I find stability and order, and an understanding of my own place in an impeccable design. From here I can reach out to my less orderly world beyond. From here I can see the seasons chain together in a continuity that runs through our lives. Each one of us has sat here, at one time or another, almost as much a part of the landscape as the lake rock itself, absorbing a sense of strength from the granite and a sense of freedom from the sky.

This rock in winter is a handy place for Sara to put her ice skates on or for me to rest from the altitudinal exertions of shoveling snow to make a rink. I can look down and down through pellucid ice into a silent deep world where air bubbles are trapped in crystal. It is so cold that the snow creaks and crunches with our footsteps and sparkles as if it had mica in it. If there is no wind and the sky is clear, the sun shining through the thin atmosphere is gloriously warm. But if there is a January wind cutting out of the north, the rock is untenable. The warmth of the cabin is more than welcome; it is a necessity.

The lake rock awakens to spring in small ways. Tiny wolf spiders spew out from under the moss cover which is just greening underneath. A ladybug staggers along the unbalanced boulders of gravel on top of the rock. Among the deep-red strawberry leaves of last year is a cocoon of unfurled fuzzy leaves, not yet ready to face the frosted mornings. Clover leaves are folded in *origami* patterns of pale green. The lichen, usually dry as a cornflake, is pliable with the moisture of spring. I look up to see a flight of robins leafing the aspen below the dam. By now a wide rim of black water circles the rock, contrasting with the milky rotting ice. The snow patches at the edge of the lake are granulated and shiny on top from daytime thaw and nighttime freeze. Herman stands on the dam, listening to the spring runoff pour down the standpipe, reassured to know that the lake is coming alive again, and that the rainbow trout are getting fresh oxygen.

In summer the sun is hot on the rock, but the persistent mountain breeze and high altitude keep the air cool. If you sit very quietly and dangle your feet in the sun-warmed surface of the water, a rainbow trout, nibbling from the submerged rock ledge, may also nibble upon a toe. I watch Susan watching the world beneath, finding her own order in her own way. Iridescent dragonflies, bluer than the blue lettuce or the penstemons flowering in the lake meadow, dart a busy halo above her head. A horizontal line of golden banner is a band of sunshine marching across the dam.

As soon as she leaves, Graf brings out three precisely equal sticks, of a significant length known only to him. He lines them up neatly and pushes them one by one into the water. Then he dashes down the catwalk, around the shore, and plunges in to capture each of the flotilla in turn. Sometimes he tries to reach the floating sticks from the lake rock itself, feet slipping on the loose graveled surface of the south side, barking hysterically when the currents edge the sticks just out of reach. He finally tires of his game and goes in search of Herman, who is chopping firewood and will welcome him not at all.

Folly trots out to watch one of her beloved humans in the rowboat. Jane rows over and coaxes her to jump in. Folly ducks and bobs her head in basset indecision and cries and whines, but she won't jump. She stands woebegone and forlorn when Jane rows away.

One summer's day when I came out to the rock, a large creamy-white crab spider, with two handsome maroon racing stripes on her back, lay in wait in a chokecherry bush near the catwalk. Half an hour later when I returned, a butterfly dangled from her clutches.

On a warm sunny autumn day I sun on the lake rock like a turtle. A damselfly wings by, late-starting and slow-flying. The chill nights cramp its style. Having escaped trout and swift, the damselfly will not escape the predation of winter. Its hesitant flight tells of summer's going.

I pull up the swimming ladder and it smells like the back corner of a Florida beach, pungent and fishy. Plumatella are clustered on the underside of some of the steps. Caddisfly cases are attached to another. Snail eggs glisten gelatinously along the side. Algae and green protozoa enliven the yellow-brown of the underwater growth. Flies appear immediately, busily exploring the rapidly drying surface.

A small snail makes its way down the still-damp ladder into a puddle formed by dripping water, and insinuates itself over the edge of the rock and down the side into the water. The snail will survive, but not the minutiae attached to the steps. They seem to retreat within themselves as the sheen of the water evaporates. They will be dead within the day, the heat from the sun drying them into lifeless crusts. But they are preserved in the statoblasts and seeds and spores and bits of pieces of continuity drifting slowly to the lake bottom.

The late asters and wild chrysanthemums bend and twist in the sharp freshening wind. Fireweed's cottony seeds skitter across the lake's surface, diagramming the darting gusts. The chillness of the wind stiffens my hands and tugs at the page of the paper, so that I cannot draw. An aster seed blows into the lake, joining a fleet of aspen leaves. Cinquefoil, geranium, and strawberry leaves are burnished bronze-red. On the south shore a few aspens hold the last golden leaves. The rhythm of their quavering is doubled to semiquavers by the lake's reflections. The year is on its way to ending.

It is time to go back, light the wood stove, and begin supper.

Edward Abbey
1927-89

1956: *The Brave Cowboy*
1962: *Fire on the Mountain*
1968: *Desert Solitaire*
1975: *The Monkey Wrench Gang*
1979: *Abbey's Road*
1982: *Down the River*
1984: *Slumgullion Stew*
1988: *The Fool's Progress*

E DWARD ABBEY'S *preface to* Slumgullion Stew *summarizes a theme found in all of his work, the theme of "the traditional conflict between our instinctive urge toward fraternity, community, and freedom, and the opposing demands of discipline and the state. The human versus human institutions—a conflict as old as the development of agriculture, urbanism, militarism, and hierarchy."* [1] *It is best to think of Abbey as a writer with a recurrent theme, for he is not always a writer with a story to tell. His writing, in fact, defies categorization. His followers—and there are many—generally see him playing a dual role: Abbey is a novelist with the anarchistic inclinations of George Hayduke, the saboteur of* The Monkey Wrench Gang, *and he is also a slightly hermitic naturalist playing a game of desert solitaire.*

Abbey grew up in Pennsylvania, but his soul came of age in the Southwest. After a hitch in the U.S. Army, he began to do some serious wandering in that region of enchantment; before long he had quietly appointed himself the advocate of deserts, of mountains, of unspoiled people, and of sanity in general. Abbey enjoyed his role as knight-errant to helpless causes; shortly before his untimely death, he

1. Edward Abbey, *Slumgullion Stew* (New York: E. P. Dutton, 1984), p. ix.

inscribed a copy of The Fool's Progress: *"There* are *a lot of windmills [signed] Ed "Don Q." Abbey.*

In The Fool's Progress, *Henry Holyoak Lightcap and his dying dog, Solstice, leave Tucson and head out on their last trip, an odyssey back to Henry's backwater home in West Virginia. The trip is also a progress backward in time as Henry recalls the events of his life. Some of his memories are humorous, some passionate, some tragic; Abbey's theme of humans versus institutions makes an appearance in each one.*

"Rites of Spring" recounts the spring in which Henry awakened to love. Like the young William Wordsworth of "Tintern Abbey," Henry experiences the confusing, aching, wholly physical passion for everything, from nature to the farmyard to Wilma Fetterman. His principal passion, baseball, offers him camaraderie and freedom. The baseball game against Blacklick marks Henry Lightcap's passage from innocence to experience. He enters the game in a state of thoughtless emotional enthusiasm for the sounds and the smells and the feel of bats and gloves and good pitches; about "five thousand years" later, he realizes that the baseball game was also his initiation into the realities of a much bigger game.

April 1942: The Rites of Spring

I

THE WAR? WHAT WAR? Henry Lightcap, fifteen years old and lean as a willow sapling, had deeper things in mind. Henry loved the chant of the spring peepers, ten thousand tiny titillated frogs chanting in chorus from the pasture, down in the marshy bottoms by the crick, that music of moonlight and fearful desire, that plainsong, that Te Deum Laudamus, that Missa Solemnis deep as creation that filled the twilight evenings with a song as old (at least) as the carboniferous coal beds beneath his homeland. (Grandfather Lightcap had signed a broadform deed to the mineral rights in 1892 but nothing ever came of it. Or ever would, thought Paw.)

Henry detested high school with a hatred keen as his knifeblade but loved getting on the bus behind Wilma Fetterman, watching as she climbed the high steps, her skirt riding high, his eyes fixed on the tendons behind her knees, the sweet virgin untouchable gloss of her forever inaccessible thighs. Henry, virgin himself, thought that he understood the mechanical principle of the human sexual connection but also believed, with the hopeless sorrow of youth, that he himself would never, never be capable of the act because—well, because his penis, when excited and erect, rose hard and rigid as bone against his belly button. There was no room in there, no space whatsoever, for a female of his own species. The thing could not be forced down to a horizontal approach, as he assumed was necessary, without breaking off like the joint of a cornstalk. He told no one of his deformity. Not even his mother. But though it was hopeless, he continued to love watching Wilma Fetterman climb the school-bus steps.

He loved the lament of the mourning doves, echoing his own heartache, when they returned each spring from wherever they went in winter. He loved the soft green of the linwood trees, the bright green of the Osage orange against the morning sun. He loved the red-dog dirt road that meandered through the smoky hills beside the sulfur-colored creek, into and through the covered bridge and up the hollow that led, beyond the last split-rail fence, toward the barn, the forge, the pigpen, the wagon shed, the icehouse, the springhouse and the gray good gothic two-story clapboard farmhouse that remained, after a century, still the Lightcap family home.

He loved his Berkshire pigs. He loved the beagle hounds that ran to meet him each evening. He loved—but intuitively not consciously—the sight of the family wash hanging from the line, the sound of his father's ax in the woodyard as the old man split kindling for the kitchen stove. He even loved the arrogant whistling of his older brother, Will—hated rival—as Will brought the horses up from the half-plowed cornfield, the team harnessed but unhitched, traces dragging, chains jingling, over the stony lane to the barn.

But most of all and above all and always in April Henry loved the sound of a hardball smacking into leather. The WHACK! of a fat bat connecting with ball. And better yet, when he was pitching, he loved the swish of air and grunt of batter lunging for and cleanly missing Henry's fast one, low and outside, after he's brushed the hitter back with two consecutive speedballs to the ear.

He loved his brand-new Joe "Ducky" Medwick glove, personally autographed (at the Spalding factory) by Joe himself. He loved the feel and heft and fine-grained integrity of his sole uncracked Louisville Slugger, autographed by baseball's one and only active .400 hitter, the great and immortal Ted Williams.

Brother Will liked the game too, in his calm complacent way, but never lay awake at night dreaming about it, never dawdled away hours composing elaborate box scores of imaginary games in a fantasy league that existed only in the mind of Henry Lightcap.

Henry had his reasons. He had a real team also. And real opponents. The Blacklick team was coming to Stump Creek for the first contest of the season.

Henry and Will picked their lineup, writing names down on a ruled paper tablet. Henry would take over the mound, Will, as usual, handle the catching. Their little brother Paul could play right field where he'd be mostly out of the way, not in a position to do much harm. Their best player and one genuine athlete, the sharp-eyed clean-cut Eagle Scout Chuck Tait, would sparkplug the team at shortstop or take over first or relieve the pitcher, wherever needed. That made four players, the solid core of the Stump Creek nine. But where to find the other five? Stump Creek, West Virginia, population 120 (counting dogs and girls), clumped in a lump beside County Road 14, did not offer much talent.

They brooded over the problem and decided the best they could do was have the Adams brothers, Clarence thirteen and Sonny twelve, play second and third base, and let the Fetterman boys, Junior (his baptized, Christian name) age thirteen and Elman age eleven, play the outfield. That Elman, says Will, he couldn't hit a cow's ass with a snow shovel. But we need him.

We're still one player short, Henry pointed out; we need somebody at first base. They thought about that for a while. Finally Will mentioned the name of Ginter.

No, said Henry. Who else? Not Red Ginter. Who else we got? But Red, said Henry, Red's seventeen. Yeah but he's still in fourth grade. That was three years ago. Well that's where he was last time he went to school. Blacklick would have a fit. We promised no players over sixteen. Besides . . . Besides what? Red won't play. Ask him. Who else we got? He can't play, says Henry. He's big but he won't move, he won't run.

He'll catch the ball if you throw it to him. He'll do for first base.

Can't hit the ball. Undercuts—swings his bat like it's a golf club. Strikes out every time.

Yeah but he takes a mighty powerful cut at the ball. Will smiled, his dark eyes musing. I saw him hit a ball four hundred feet on a line drive one time.

I saw that. A fluke hit and anyway it went foul.

He's the only one we have left, Henry.

Henry thought about it. What about Red's little brother? Leroy? Maybe he could play.

Christ, muttered Will, making a rotating motion with his forefinger close by his right ear. Leroy's crazy as a moon-eyed calf. We don't even want him around.

They were silent for a minute, sitting there in the kitchen at the oilcloth-covered table, under the amber glow of the kerosene lamp, staring at their paper lineup of eight ball players, five of them children. Then it has to be Red, says Henry.

I I

Swinging out from the school bus late in the afternoon, Henry and Will walked half a mile homeward up the red-dog road, under the trees, then cut off over the hill through the Big Woods toward the next cove on the south. Once called Crabapple Hollow, it became known as Hardscrabble when the Ginter family, coming from no one knew where, made it their family seat in the late 1800s, soon after the end of the War Between the States.

They tramped through the ruins of Brent's sawmill, abandoned half a century before, and struck a footpath leading down the steep side of the ridge toward the corn patches and pastures of Ginter's farm. Halfway down they passed the tailings pile of a small coal mine, unworked for years. A dribble of sulfurous water leaked from the portal; decayed locust props, warped by the overburden, shored up the roof of the tunnel. There were many such workings in the area; in one of these old Jefferson Davis Ginter kept his distilling equipment.

The farm buildings came in view, ramshackle structures with sagging roofbeams. The main house was a one-story slab shack with rusted tin roof; built by Ginter, it leaned for support against a much older but far steadier pine-log cabin. Ginter's coon hounds, smelling the Lightcap brothers from afar, began to bay, tugging at their chains.

The path to the back porch of the house—their goal—was wide enough for two but Henry let Will walk before him. Will was both bigger and older, a dark stolid solid fellow, broad at the shoulders and thick in the arms, built—as everyone agreed—like a brick shithouse. Even as a freshman he had played first-string tackle on the varsity football team at Shawnee High School.

The back door stood wide open to the mellow April afternoon, revealing a dark interior. There was no screendoor. Ginter chickens wandered in and out of the house, pausing to shit on the doorstep, pecking at cockroaches, ticks, ants, June bugs, dead flies, fallen shirt buttons, crumbs of tobacco, whatever looked edible. A string of blue smoke from the kitchen stovepipe rose straight up in the still air.

The four dogs chained beneath the porch barked with hoarse and passionate intensity as Will and Henry approached the house. From inside came voices—angry, outraged.

They're fightin' again, says Henry. Maybe we should come back later.

They're always fightin', Will says. Come on. He marched firmly forward. Then stopped at the sound of a shriek.

There was an explosion of hens from the open doorway followed by a stub-tailed yellow dog, airborne, as if propelled by a mighty kick. The dog cleared the porch without touching the planks, landed running on the bare dirt of the yard—something pale and soft clamped in its jaws—and scuttled like a wounded rat toward the nearest outbuilding.

Will hesitated; Henry stopped behind him.

Old Jeff Ginter appeared in the doorway holding a pint Mason jar in one hand. He roared after the dog: You ever come back in here again you docktail misbegotten yellowback mutt I'll fill your hinder end with birdshot so goldamn stiff you'll be shittin' B-Bs through your teeth for a month.

And then the old man saw Will and Henry, two schoolboys in bright sport shirts and fresh blue jeans staring at him from fifty feet away across the beaten grassless dung-spotted yard. Ginter wore bib overalls, frayed at the knee, unpatched and unwashed; instead of a shirt he wore a long-sleeved union suit buttoned to the neck, once white but aged to a grayish blend of sweat, dust, woodsmoke and ashes. He was barefoot. He squinted at the boys through bloodshot eyes. What're you two a-doin' here?

Will gazed calmly at Ginter, waiting for Henry to speak. Henry was pitcher, scorekeeper, self-appointed manager of the Stump Creek baseball team.

Henry swallowed and said, We're lookin' for Red.

What you want him for?

We need him for the ball team, Mr. Ginter. We got a game with Blacklick Saturday.

The old man swayed a little on the porch, took a languid sip from his pint, raised the jar to the light and checked the bead. He glowered at Henry. When's this here game a-gonna be?

Saturday, Henry said.

Hain't the Sunday?

No sir, Saturday.

Any child of mine plays that baseball game on Sunday I'll peel the hide off his back with a drawknife, hang him by the ears to yon ole snag. Ginter gestured toward the dead butternut tree in the yard. Like I would a blacksnake. Till he stops wigglin'. Ain't Christian to play games on the Sunday.

No sir, it's Saturday.

Old Jeff relented. They're out at the pigpen sloppin' the sow, him and Leroy. Leroy's name suggested an afterthought. Now you mind and let Leroy play too or by God Red don't play.

Will and Henry glanced at each other. Will shrugged. They had no choice.

Yes sir, Henry said.

Behind the barn they found Red Ginter leaning on the pigpen fence, watching his little brother Leroy. Red was six feet six inches tall, weighed 240 pounds, had a small red-haired skull that tapered to a point between his ears. Like his father he wore bib overalls, long-sleeved gray underwear, no shoes.

Henry said hello. Red ignored him, ignored Will who said nothing but stood close by, ready for trouble. Will never did talk much—but then like Red Ginter he didn't have to. They stared at young Leroy.

Leroy, crouched on hands and knees inside the pen, was creeping over the muck toward a three-hundred-pound sow. The sow lay on her side, eyes closed, giving suck to a litter of eight. Leroy, twelve years old, was playing piglet. Ernk, ernk, he grunted, lowering his belly to the ground, wriggling forward, ernk, ernk, mumma. . . . Leroy's pink harelip formed what he understood as an ingratiating, shoatlike appeal.

Red encouraged him. Keep a-goin', Leroy. No sign of malice in Red's pale, dull eyes. And don't settle for hind tit neither.

Leroy squirmed closer. Ernk, ernk, mumma, gimme suck too. He was barefoot; his ragged bleached-out overalls seemed two sizes too small. The reddish hair on his head was thin, fine, short, giving him a half-bald look. Ernk, mumma, he crooned in begging tones, ernk, ernk. . . .

The great sow, lying peacefully in the April sun, at ease in the cool mud, opened one tiny red eye and saw Leroy inching toward her and her children. She grunted.

Leroy hesitated. Ernk . . . ? He raised his head.

The sow grunted again and scrambled to her feet. Leroy rose to his hands and knees. The sow squealed with outrage and charged. Her brood hung swinging from her tough teats, unwilling to let go. Leroy jumped up, turned. Nom nam nun of a nitch! he yelled, I gotta get the nom nam outa here! He leaped for the fence and rolled over, falling to the ground outside. The sow crashed into the planks and stopped, backed off and shook her head. She glared at Leroy.

Red Ginter, bland-eyed and unmoved, turned his face to Will and Henry. Henry explained the purpose of the visit.

I play first or nothin', Red says.

That's okay, Red.

Bat first too.

Will and Henry looked at each other. No options.

Leroy bats second, Red went on.

What? says Henry. Not Leroy!

You heard me, Red says. He picked up a wooden bucket full of skim milk, potato peelings, turnip greens, muskrat entrails, chicken heads, eggshells, bacon rinds. He emptied the bucket into the wooden trough inside the fence. The sow shuffled to the trough, snorted, plunged her snout into the swill. Red thumped the bucket on her head, clearing the bottom. The sow twitched her ears and kept on feeding. The piglets hung from her udders, still suckling.

III

Henry and Will tramped homeward over the ridge, into the Big Woods, past the forgotten sawmill, through the gloom of the trees. A hoot owl hooted from the darkness of a hollow sycamore, calling for its mate. Another answered from a faraway pine.

You hear that, Henry? says Will, as they paused before the split-rail fence that marked the Lightcap frontier.

Henry listened carefully. The owls called again, first one, then after a few moments of thought, the second.

Will grinned at his little brother; the bright teeth shone in his brown honest face. Will said, They're a boy owl and a girl owl.

Baloney. How do you know?

Because the first owl says, Hoo hoo, wanna screw? And the second owl she says, Hoo hoo, not with you.

Bull-loney.

They went down the hill into Lightcap's Hollow. While poor Henry, nursing in silence the secret of his desolate, hopeless incapacity, thought of Wilma Fetterman climbing into the school bus, of Betsy Kennedy draping her splendid cashmere-sweatered breasts over the back of her chair as she turned to tease him, of Donna Shoemaker turning cartwheels in her cheerleader uniform at the pregame pep rally. A pang of agony coursed upward through Henry's aching core, from the misaligned piston rod of his groin to the undifferentiated longing in his heart. Never, never with a girl.

The owls hooted softly after him through the soft green cruelty of April, down the hills of the Allegheny. The ghosts of Shawnee warriors watched from the shadows of the red oaks.

IV

A light rain fell Saturday morning, leaving pools of water on the base paths, but the sun appeared on time at noon. Henry and Will and little Paul filled burlap sacks with sand and paced off the bases. Chuck Tait came soon after with a bag of lime to mark the batter's boxes, the base lines, the coaching positions. They built up the pitcher's mound, chased Prothrow's cows into deep left field and shoveled the fresh cow patties off the infield. They filled in the pools with dry dirt, creating deceptive mudholes which only the home team need know about. They patched the backstop with chicken wire and scrap lumber. The Fetterman boys came with their gloves and a new bat, then the Adams brothers with gloves and two fractured, taped bats. (Both were cross-handed hitters.) No sign of the Ginters. There was time for a little practice; Will batted hot grounders to Chuck and the Adams boys, high-flying fungos to Paul and Elman and Junior in the outfield.

Henry felt he was ready; he'd spent an hour every day for six months throwing a tennis ball at a strike zone painted on the barn door, scooping up the ball one-handed as it bounced down the entrance ramp. Precision control, that was his secret. He only had three pitches: an overhand fastball, not very fast; a sidearm curve that sometimes broke and sometimes didn't; and his newly developed Rip Sewell blooper, a high floating change of pace which he lofted forward with the palm of his hand, a tempting mushball of a pitch that rose high in the air and drifted toward the plate like a sinking balloon. Weak pitches—but he had control. He could hit the center of Will's mitt whenever Will called for it.

The Blacklick team arrived an hour late, Tony Kovalchick the captain driving his father's twelve-cylinder 1928 Packard sedan. The three smallest boys sat in the trunk holding up the lid with a bat. The Blacklick players fingered rosaries; they wore sacred medals. Stump Creek surrendered the field to the visitors for a ten-minute warm-up.

Tony and Henry compared scorecards.

Your guys are too old, Henry complained. Those are all senior high school guys.

That's our team, Tony says. You wanta play baseball or you wanta go home and cry?

Carci, Watta, Jock Spivak—those are football players.

You got Will and Chuck, they're varsity. And who's this Red Ginter? Ain't he the one nearly killed some coal miner in the fight at Rocky Glen Tavern Saturday night?

Not Red, you got him mixed up with somebody else. Henry pointed to the Packard. A pale little fellow with strabismic eyes sat on the running board. Who's he? He's not in your lineup.

That's Joe Glemp. He's our umpire.

Umpire? He's cross-eyed!

Yeah, don't make fun of him. He's kind of sensitive. He can't play ball worth a shit. But he's a good ump.

You're crazy. He can't see anything but his own nose. Anyhow Mr. Prothrow's gonna be umpire. Henry looked around; old Frank Prothrow was nowhere in sight.

The visiting team always brings the umpire, Tony said complacently. You know that, Lightcap.

You're nuts.

It's in the rule book. Black and white.

Not in any rule book I ever saw. Let's see this rule book.

Let's see this Mr. Prothrow.

Henry looked again. No Prothrow in view. But there came the Ginters, Red and Leroy, tramping up the dirt road, Red carrying his ax-hewn homemade hickory bat on his shoulder. The one with the square shaft, like a tapered four-by-four. Henry appointed little Paul the field umpire. The Stump Creek nine took the field, Red Ginter on first nonchalantly catching Chuck Tait's rifle-shot throws from short, Henry on the mound, the children at second, third and scattered across the outfield among the grazing milk cows.

Play ball! hollered little Joe Glemp with harsh authority, masked and armored, crouching behind the broad back of Will Lightcap hunkered down at home plate. Tony Kovalchick, batting right-handed, stepped into the box, tapped mud from his cleated shoes, made the sign of the cross and dug in for the first pitch.

Henry, glove in armpit, rubbed the sweet new Spalding between moist palms and surveyed his team. All were in place except Leroy in deep right yelling obscenities at a cow.

Henry faced the batter, noticing at once that Tony choked his bat by three inches. Will gave Henry the sign, fastball wide and low. Henry wound up and threw exactly where Will wanted it, cutting the outside corner. Tony let it go by.

Ball one! shouted the umpire.

Will held the ball for a few moments to indicate contempt for the call, then without rising tossed it back to Henry. Tony crowded the plate a little more. Will asked for another fastball, high and inside. Ball—began the umpire as Tony tipped it foul. One ball, one strike, little Joe Glemp conceded.

He can't see but he can hear pretty good, thought Henry, rubbing the ball like a pro. Will called for the sidearm curve, low and outside. Backing off slightly (weakness!), Tony swung and tipped the pitch off the end of the bat. Two strikes. He scowled at the pitcher. Now we got him, Henry thought, he's getting mad. Will called for the floater, mixing them up, and Tony waited, watching the ball sail in a high arc toward him, and lost patience and swung furiously much too soon, nearly breaking his spine. He picked himself up, brushing mud from his knees, and stormed back to the visitors' bench.

A fat Italian boy named Frank Carci now stood in the box, anxious, tense, well away from the plate. A second-string center, he was better known as Snotrag: both on and off the field, the entire football team used the tail of Carci's jersey for noseblowing. Henry and Will struck out Snotrag with three fastballs high and inside, the batter drawing away from the plate as he swung, each time missing the ball by a foot.

Big Stan Watta came to bat. Stan was big but the next batter, Jock Spivak, fullback, was bigger. After a brief conference Henry and Will agreed to pitch to Watta and then, if necessary, walk Jock. Will called for the side-arm slider, low and outside. Henry threw it, the ball failed to slide, Watta trotted into second base with a stand-up double.

Jock Spivak took his stance deep in the batter's box, measuring the plate with his slugger's bat. Will and Henry stuck with their plan: a free pass to first for the big man. On deck was the easy third out Mike Spivak, Jock's kid brother, a weak hitter.

Henry checked the runner at second, then threw the pitchout high and outside into Will's guiding mitt. Ball one. Watta returned to second. Henry repeated the pitch, Will standing away from the plate to catch it. Ball two. Quickly now, impatient to get at the easy batter, Henry threw ball three. Jock Spivak spat on the plate, moved forward a step and grinned like a tiger.

Henry threw the ball neck high and a foot outside. Laughing, Jock stepped across the plate—Ball four! shouted Glemp—and smacked the pitch true, hard and high into far right field. Leroy Ginter dreamed out there, wiggling bare toes in a fresh cowpie. The Stump Creek team hollered for attention. Leroy wiped the drool from his chin and ran three steps to the left, four to the right, slipped in another pile of cowshit and fell to his knees. Nom nam nun of a nitch! he screamed, throwing his glove at the ball. Missed. The ball bounced into the weeds along the fence. Leroy made no move to retrieve it. Stan Watta crossed home plate. Laughing all the way, Jock Spivak jogged toward third. Junior Fetterman found the ball and pegged it to Chuck Tait at short, who relayed it to Sonny Adams at third. Sonny dropped the ball. Half sick with laughter, Spivak headed for home. Sonny threw the ball to Will, trapping Spivak between home plate and third. Spivak stopped but couldn't stop laughing. Will ran him down and tagged him out.

Backlick 1, Stump Creek 0, bottom of the first. The home team came to bat.

Red Ginter slouched into the batter's box with the squared-off log on his shoulder. He took a few underhand practice swings, like a golfer at the tee, spat on the ground and waited for the pitch. He wore the same greasy bib overalls, the same grime-gray flannel underwear he'd been wearing all winter and would not remove till May. Like his old man, Red knew only two seasons, winter and summer. Let the weather change, not him. He waited, cheek bulging, peering at the pitcher from beneath his dangling, reddish forelock, a sloping, pale and freckled brow. His small eyes, set close together, betrayed no gleam of human light.

The pitcher, Tony Kovalchick, raised both arms above his head and began an elaborate windup.

Ginter waited, legs far apart, rotating the bulk of his club in slow ominous circles behind his shoulder. The first pitch sped in like a bullet straight down the middle. Ginter reared back and took an awkward but vicious cut at the ball, swinging eighteen inches beneath it. His bat scraped a groove through the dirt behind the plate.

Sta-rike! yells Glemp, jabbing the air with his thumb.

The Blacklick catcher—squat square massive Dominic Del Poggio— chuckled as he flipped the ball to Tony. The pitcher allowed himself a smile. Both could see already that this game was going to be such a laugher they might not make it through the fifth inning.

Untroubled, Red awaited the second pitch. It came: a repeat of the first. He let it go by. No balls, two strikes.

Teasing the batter this time—anything for a laugh—Tony threw a careless slider inside and too low, almost on the ground. Red swung down and up, digging another furrow through the dirt, and golfed the ball foul in a drive of flat trajectory toward deep left, where it struck a cow on the head and caromed into the weeds. The cow sank to its knees, then fell on its side, where it lay comatose for half an hour. The count at the plate remained the same: no balls, two strikes.

Red Ginter waited, pale eyes bland and empty. The pitcher and catcher— after brief talk—played the next pitch safe: a fastball chest-high across the center of the plate. The long-ball hitter's dream pitch. Red watched it go by. Three strikes and out. Leroy Ginter, second batter, took his place.

As Red shuffled back to the bench Chuck Tait rose to meet him. Look, Red, Chuck says, you're swinging way under the ball. He imitated Red's underhand swing. Now watch: you have to level your stroke. Watch. He demonstrated a swift beautifully smooth perfectly level swing, in the manner of Williams and DiMaggio. See? Like that. He gave a second demonstration, pure grace, sweet perfection.

Chewing on his plug of Red Man, leaning on his four-by-four, Red stared down at Chuck from ten superior inches, some eighty extra pounds, and spat a jet of tobacco juice onto Chuck's shoe. You bat your way, baby face, he says, and I'll bat mine. He tramped past Chuck and sat on the bench.

Chuck stared at the dirty splotch on his clean new sneakers and said nothing. But to Henry and Will, later, he grumbled, No team spirit. None of your guys have the real team spirit.

Clowning at the plate, Leroy struck out in three wild swings, two from the left side and one from the right. He slammed his taped bat on the plate— Nom nam nun of a nitch!—broke it again, and ran off toward the elderberry bushes beside the creek, where two heifers browsed on the shrubbery.

Chuck Tait stepped up and cracked the first pitch between first and second, a clean single. He danced back and forth on the base path as Will came to bat. Will let the first pitch go by and Chuck stole second. Will waited out a second pitch, then doubled Chuck home with a drive over third base. Henry Lightcap came to bat, anxious and eager, aware of Wilma Fetterman and the other girls watching from the sidelines. Trying hard to be a hero, he popped out to second base.

Blacklick 1, Stump Creek 1, top of the second. Hating himself, Henry took his place on the mound, threw a few warmup pitches and checked his fielders. Nobody in right field. Leroy had disappeared. Thank God. He signaled little Paul to take Leroy's place and faced the batter, Mike Spivak. Henry pitched carefully, following Will's instructions; Mike hit an easy grounder to second. But Clarence Adams bobbled the ball and Mike slid safely into first base. He always slid into first; nobody knew why.

Now the dangerous Dominic Del Poggio waited at the plate, ready for the pitch. Will, keeping one eye on Spivak edging off first base, called for an outside pitch. Henry threw it, Spivak ran for second, Will hurled the ball precisely to Chuck, covering the base, for what should have been an easy out. But Clarence, thinking the throw was meant for him, leaped for the ball and got run over by the base runner, piling them both in the mud. Chuck tagged the runner out. A discussion followed.

Joe Glemp, peering sternly at his own nose, declared the runner safe on grounds of interference; furthermore he penalized the home team by awarding Mike Spivak free passage to third base. The decision led to more discussion, bitter, prolonged, hectic. But the umpire stood firm. Dominic waited, grinning.

Concentrating on the batter, Henry threw two strikes low and inside, then jammed him with an inside curveball. Dominic swung and hit the ball with the handle of his bat, an easy slow roller toward Red Ginter at first base. Red waited for it, waited and waited, one foot on the bag; the runner got there before the ball.

Blacklick scored another five runs. The cow hoisted herself erect and staggered into center field. The game, like the cow, lurched into the shadows of the afternoon. The visiting team led, inning after inning, but not by much: Chuck Tait, Will Lightcap and Henry (after the first inning) managed to single, double or triple each time they came to bat, for Kovalchick's pitching turned out to be steady and predictable: nothing but fastballs down the middle. By the end of the fifth inning every player on the Stump Creek team had got on base at least once. Even Elman. Even Paul, the baby.

Everyone but Red Ginter. Never lifting his bat from his shoulder, he waited for the pitch he wanted. Which never came. Red went down on called strikes every time, spat in the dirt and said nothing.

At the end of the fifth inning the score stood 14 to 12, Blacklick leading. The sun hovered close to the roof of Prothrow's barn on the hill to the west. Henry and Tony agreed to end the game after seven innings.

In the sixth inning each team batted around the order, scoring on fumbled grounders, dropped fly balls, wild throws, doubles by Stan Watta, Jock Spivak, Tony Kovalchick, Chuck Tait, Will Lightcap and Henry. As he waited on second, wiping his brow with the felt of his cap, Henry thought for a moment he saw Wilma smiling at him. But he couldn't be certain, she sat so far away in the encroaching twilight among a cluster of other girls, all of them smiling, laughing, talking. Laughing at me? he wondered—the pride in his two-base hit sank before the pain in his lonely heart.

Red Ginter struck out again, letting three fat pitches float past through the center of the strike zone.

Blacklick scored five runs in the top of the seventh, taking advantage of fly balls to the Fetterman boys, bouncing grounders to the Adams brothers, a throw to first a little wide that Red would not reach for, and an intentional walk to the left-handed Dominic Del Poggio, who replayed Jock Spivak's stunt by stepping across the plate to hit the pitch-out into far left field.

Nobody on either team hit a true bona fide home run. The pasture fence stood four hundred feet away at the nearest point. Beyond the fence and a row of trees ran the creek and beyond the creek lay Prothrow's cornfield, twenty-five acres of stubble and weeds.

In gathering darkness and deepening gloom, Blacklick ahead 21 to 16, the home team came to bat. Last of the seventh. Last chance. Chuck Tait, leading off, intense and eager as always, hit the first pitch inside first and down the foul line for a triple. His fifth hit of the game. Tony Kovalchick, still pitching, sighed wearily and faced Will Lightcap. Will doubled again, scoring Chuck, and Henry singled, scoring Will. He took second then third on wild throws by Panatelli in left and Carci at second. Blacklick 21, Stump Creek 18, man on third and nobody out. Sonny Adams walked. Clarence popped to second. Junior Fetterman popped to the pitcher for the second out, Henry holding on third. The end was near: Elman Fetterman, Stump Creek's last and poorest hitter, the final hope, stood limp at the plate. But Elman tried, he went down swinging, and the catcher—massive nerveless impassive Dominic—let the third strike get past him. He groped for the ball while Stump Creek hollered at Elman:

Run Elman run!

Elman ran. Dominic found the ball, whipped it toward first and hit Elman on the rump, spurring the child facedown into the base. Henry raced home, Sonny took second and Elman stood up on first smiling happily with his second big hit of the day. Two runners on base, two outs and the score now 21 to 19.

Top of the order, Red Ginter. Hope—stifled by reality. Henry had to call him in from far left field, where he'd been hunting for Leroy. Red slouched toward the batter's box, holding his private bat by its rough-cut, heavy end. He spat in the dirt, inverted the bat, took his stance. Feet far apart, shoulders hunched, towering like an impotent Goliath over the plate, Red stared blank as a zombie at Kovalchick and waited for the first pitch, the inevitable but slowing fastball down the middle.

Will rose from his squatting position beyond third, where he was coaching the runners, and contemplated the tiring, exasperated pitcher. Henry, watching from the bench, saw Tony Kovalchick touch the silver medal at his neck—St. Anthony—make the sign of the cross and begin his final windup. Red stopped chewing.

Kovalchick leaned back, one leg high in the air, about to rock forward and lob the pitch—

Fuck the Pope! shouted Will, loud and clear.

—released the pitch, awkwardly, his body rigid, off-balance, and threw weakly into the dirt halfway between the pitcher's mound and home plate. The ball dribbled crookedly toward the batter in little rabbity bounces.

Ball one! yelped the umpire as Red stepped forward this time, confidently, and swung down like Sam Snead with a driving iron and caught the ball with his slashing club as it made its last pathetic hop toward the plate. A flurry of dirt rose in the air, as if Red had dug too deep and missed, but every ear present heard the sharp *crack!* of hickory meeting hardball with magnum impact.

There is a certain special unmistakable sound that ballplayer and fan recognize instantly, as if engraved on memory and soul among those clouds of glory on the other side of birth, beyond the womb, long ago before conception when even God Himself was only a gleam in a witch doctor's eye.

The sound of the long ball.

All faces turned toward the sky, toward the far-flung splendor of an Appalachian sunset, and saw Red's departing pellet of thread, cork, rubber and frazzled leather rise like a star into the last high beams of the sun, saw it ascending high, higher and still higher over Jock Spivak's outstretched despairing arms in the remotest part of center field, far above the fence, over the trees and beyond the creek, where it sank at last into twilight and disappeared (for two weeks) in the tangled fodder of Mr. Prothrow's cornfield.

Sonny Adams followed by Elman Fetterman came trotting across home plate, dancing in delight. Blacklick 21, Stump Creek 20, Stump Creek 21. The home team swarmed with joy around the runners, waiting for the last and winning run.

But where exactly was it? that winning run? Where was Red? Red was nowhere. Red was everywhere. Red stood in front of home plate leaning on his bat, watching his first hit of the game vanish into immortality somewhere southwest of Stump Crick. Run? he said. What the hell you mean, run? Hit's a *home* run, hain't it? What the hell I gotta run round them goldamn bases fer? He spat a filthy gob of tobacco juice into the trenched soil at his feet, shouldered his bat in disgust and strode down the red-dog road, headed for Ginter's hollow.

Blacklick claimed a tie, 21–21. Stump Creek claimed a victory *de jure,* 22 to 21. The discussion never was settled to the satisfaction of anybody except maybe Red Ginter. And Leroy, who didn't care one way or the other. Old man Prothrow found Leroy that night bedded down in a stall on cowshit and straw, between two heifers, when he checked his cow barn before turning in.

The fight between Will Lightcap and Tony Kovalchick, Stan Watta and Jock Spivak also ended, more or less, in a draw. Called on account of darkness.

V

No team spirit, Chuck Tait complained. I don't think I'll play with you guys anymore. You hillbillies just don't have the right team spirit. Chuck was a town boy; he lived in the heart of Stump Creek in a brick house with coal furnace, plumbing and electricity. His father was village postmaster, owned the general store, drove a new Buick. Chuck joined the Army Air Corps in 1943, learned to fly a Mustang P-51, and would return from the Pacific Theater with captain's bars and a chest covered with ribbons. He started an insurance business and later evaporated, forever, into the state legislature. Red Ginter joined the U.S. Army and rose to the rank of master sergeant for life. Leroy joined the Salvation Army and became a major general.

And Henry? Henry Lightcap fell in love. He fell in love that year with Wilma, with Betsy, with Donna and eleven other girls. He knew his cause was hopeless but he tried. Though it was not Wilma or Betsy or Donna or the others but Mary, Tony Kovalchick's little sister, who provided the needed succor. One rainy night in May, in the backseat of Will's 1935 Hudson Terraplane, Mary Kovalchick showed Henry Lightcap a thing or two. Henry joined Mary. She conjoined him. For a number of times. He never again went back, after that, to throwing tennis balls at barn doors or baseballs at Roman Catholics.

Will Lightcap, he stayed with the farm.

So it was and so it all really happened down there in that Shawnee County, in the Allegheny Mountains of West Virginia, about five thousand years ago.

John Sterling Harris

b. 1929

———

1974: *Barbed Wire*

———

S OME POETS *travel from place to place, recording their impressions and experiences as they go, while others stay put. These latter, the firmly rooted writers, develop an acute chronological and ecological perspective of one particular region, identifying themselves with that land's history and spirit.*

One such western poet is John Sterling Harris, who began with an outdoor boyhood in Tooele, Utah, and went on to become a professor of English at Brigham Young University, leaving Utah long enough to do graduate studies at the University of Texas and to serve in the U.S. Army. He edited and coauthored several technical-writing publications, acted as technical consultant to government and industry, and founded the Association of Teachers of Technical Writing. Harris's interest in technology even led him to build and fly his own experimental aircraft.

As a writer, Harris studies ordinary people, people who reflect essential human characteristics. In their everyday lives there is a certain universality of feelings and behaviors; to capture these requires a poet possess an above-average sensitivity to simple surroundings and intense moments. Harris's keen awareness of unembellished symbolism, for example, leads into the tension and sorrow of "Hay Derrick." The derrick, the unfinished haystack, and the unhooked hay hoist, like parts of a pastoral eulogy, express the father's silent grief.

"Fallow" also utilizes unsophisticated symbolism. It gives the reader the uncomfortable feeling of overhearing two people awkwardly trying to express their feelings and struggling to cope with their barrenness, speaking to each other in sad riddles. They are regional characters: they live on a farm, in an era of blacksmiths and woodstoves and gossiping neighbors. The riddle, however, the thing that they must try to understand and accept, is universal and timeless.

"The Gate" and "The Unhobbled Mare," in the same narrative style, estab-

lish characters and conflicts in efficient phrases. Harris conveys his settings with a minimum of detail, but vividly. Like "Hay Derrick," these poems transcend the region and the time of their settings. They deal with human beings whose immediate circumstances serve merely to sharpen the poignancy of their fundamental emotions. The simple elements of their ordinary daily lives—a sewing basket, a barbed-wire gate, a tool shed, and a glass vase—become emblems of deep and seemingly irreconcilable feelings.

Hay Derrick

You can see the derrick there
In the lower meadow by the marsh
Where there's a low stack
Of hay against the pale sky.

The father made them unhook the chain
That linked the pole to base
And lowered the end
To rest upon the ground.

But the big pine pole
Used to point toward the sun like a dial
And swing across the summer sky
To raise the loads of meadow hay

That creaking wagons brought to stack—
The Jackson hanging from the block,
With four curved tines like blades of scythes
Dropping down and sinking in the load,

Then hoisting high with cable taut,
Turning slowly in the air,
And swinging over the stack
With the screek of straining blocks—

The selections of John Sterling Harris's verse included here are from *Barbed Wire* (Provo, Utah: Brigham Young University Press, 1974), pp. 171–72, 46–49, 24–26, and *Dialogue: A Journal of Mormon Thought* 3 (Winter 1968): 94–96, respectively. Reprinted by permission of John Sterling Harris.

Then the shout of *yo* to pull
The trip rope and dump the hay,
Returning then to the wagon—
Eight forkfuls for the load.

So they were that August day,
The father pushing the fork into the load,
His son carefully building the stack,
And a child on the plodding derrick horse

That drew the cable up
Then backed to let it down,
In easy rhythm of lower
And hoist and swing and drop.

Then there came a shift of wind
That made the derrick horse start.
The child tried to pull the reins,
But the horse bolted fast.

The empty fork flew to the block
But stopped and then plunged down
Where one tine pinned the son to the stack
And the broken cable covered him with coils.

They left the stack unfinished
To bleach in the summer sun,
And the autumn winds stirred the hay
Like unkempt hair on the head of a boy.

—

Fallow

She eased herself into the bed beside him,
His farmer's heavy sleep
Was lighter now with dawning near.
At the creak of springs
He stirred

And turned to reach her hand, holding it,
Carefully as his calloused fingers would allow.

Have you been up to make the fire, Jennie?
She caught her breath and held her answer,
But in a moment said,
I rose to find the crop you planted failed
Like the others—this field lies fallow still.

He took his turn at delay
And reached to pull her in before reply.
Perhaps I planted too shallow
Or in the wrong time of moon
Or worse, the seed was old and weak—
You haven't yourself to blame for that.
A man can't really know the cause in this.
I've wondered at it though,

If it came from a boyhood fever—
The men at the blacksmith shop
Would call it shooting blanks
Or some such thing,
And laugh and say that
If a man's father had no sons,
It's likely he won't either.
I've never thought it could be you—
Not with your sister's brood,
And your twin brother's wife
Is walking heavy now.

Stop, she said, Can't you see.
A freemartin heifer never calves.
Some places, you know, you could
Send me back like faulty goods,
And well you should.
I've seen you envy other men their sons.
And I know about that shiny
Pony saddle in the barn.
If you had another woman—

A Hagar to dam an heir, he said.
And watch you go to quiltings
So you can tend the children there
And have to listen to
The smug complaints of overbearing wives,
And then return to your
Own quiet house to weep.

No, I'll not have that.
We need not wait for spring,
And if the field does not reject
The plow, we'll plant again.

The field does not reject the plow
Till gulls no longer follow in the furrow,
But with this latest loss
The plowing seems a ritual now
Of some forgotten faith
Or a prayer to a departed god.
But it comforts those that live,
When all the meaning's gone.

The Gate

She heard her brother's horse outside
And hurried to see the parlor showed no trace,
Then moved to the rocker by the kitchen stove,
Picked up her work from the basket,
And was sewing when he came in.

Nettie, he said, Did you see anyone
Ride this way over the hill?
I found the lower gate
Down again today.

No, she answered,
Without looking up from her needle.
I haven't left the house today—

Nor had a chance to
Leave the ranch for a month.

I'll have to lock it up, he said,
Before our breeding stock
Gets out and strays away.
That's the way with a barbed wire gate—
Likely somebody rode by
And slipped the wire loop
Off the gate top from his horse
And let the dancers lay where they fell—
Not taking the trouble
To get down and hook it up.
How a man could leave a gate that way—

Yes, she said, it's always easier
To let the gate down
Than close it up again—
Ward, she said, as if to change the talk,
Why can't I go and live
In town like Annie does.
This empty house and empty land
Oppress me so
I feel a prisoner here
Inside your fences,
And a woman can't live this way.

Nettie, I've told you many times,
I cannot let you go.
I can't tend the ranch and the house too.
Besides, who would watch over you in town.
You'd not be safe with that pretty face
And all those men.
We'll talk no more about it.
And as if to dismiss her,
He drank from the dipper
And went out.

Left there, she sat in the rocker watching
The stitches of her thread

And wondered when the gate
Would be down again.

—

The Unhobbled Mare

From a lace-curtained upstairs window,
She absently watched the cluttered farmyard below.
In the shadow of the shed she saw his cold forge,
His heavy hammers, his grindstone and his powerful vise—
Beyond this the sheds and pens for his gentle cows and mares
And the high, strong corrals for his bull and stallion.

Her husband appeared around the corner of the barn,
Pumped water over his hands at the horse trough,
Splashed his face and wiped his mouth
On the rough cloth of his sleeve.
Seeing him, her shoulders drooped a bit more,
And she tried to bite loose a small hangnail
From a hand made rough with scrubbing floors.
She turned to descend the stairs reluctantly, but stopped
To straighten a milk-glass vase on a small mahogany table.

He stood in his boots on her kitchen floor,
Smelling of soil, horsesweat, silage and sour milk.
His hands reached for her as she passed.
She quickly turned toward the icebox,
Making it seem her first destination.
Efficiently, she laid a proper supper on the table.

He ate quickly, as one long starved, and
As he finished her competent blueberry pie,
Pushed back and picked a reluctant bit of meat
From his teeth with his longbladed stock knife.
She cleared the dishes from the table
And when her hands were deep in dishsuds
Felt his heavy arms encircle from behind
His breath in her tight-braided hair.

"Don't" she said, "Why must you always do that?"
He backed away. "Ellie, why don't you?"
He started to say. Then left it.
Not looking at his eyes with their half anger, half hurt,
And knowing what he wanted to say,
But had left unsaid, she left it unanswered.

Perhaps it could be avoided and eventually die.
Her only hope was to borrow strength from tomorrow,
When perhaps—but no he could never know,
And if he didn't know, he could not be told.
He knew his livestock, but all he knew of women
Was what he learned from the Holy Bible
And the Sears Roebuck Catalog.

Not like Arnold who had courted her
With poetry and praise—who once had bared
Her shoulder and gently kissed her milk-white skin,
And she'd wept in delight—or even like Jed
Who had carried her across a stream then clear
To the top of the hill for a picnic, laughing confidently
At his own strength and youth and her susceptibility.

He broke the silence, starting for the door,
Saying he had to bed down the stock,
That he would probably sleep in the barn that night—
The bay mare was due to foal, and might need help.
So he went out, and she breathed again.

Outside he clenched his jaws
And banged his fist into the granary door,
Savoring the pain.
Must it always be so with women to invert
The Golden Rule and return love with hate?

While he was horny as Jim Marshall's stud horse
That, kept in the barn, could smell the mares pass
In the lane, neighing high and long and
Stamping the wooden floor, until, they say,

He found a knothole he could see through,
And went cross-eyed trying to see
With both eyes at once.

He remembered old Padriac, the Army Remount stud.
They'd brought a mare to him, but not hobbled,
As regulations required.
And at the crucial, vulnerable moment,
She kicked with both hind feet.
And Padriac had died.
The man hit the wall again saying,
"The poor son of a bitch, the poor son of a bitch."

Gary Snyder
b. 1930

——

1960: *Myths and Texts*
1969: *Earth House Hold*
1970: *Regarding Wave*
1974: *Turtle Island*
1983: *Axe Handles*

——

I N 1955, *Jack Kerouac and other hipsters organized a poetry reading at San Francisco's Six Gallery. Participants included Philip Whalen, Michael McClure, Allen Ginsberg (doing his "Howl" for the first time), and Gary Snyder. That reading gave California its first good look at members of the beat movement, an artistic tremor that still reverberates throughout American poetry. Gary Snyder's poetry soon took on a shape of its own, independent of the beat culture, and earned him a reputation as a San Francisco intellectual and leading West Coast writer.*

Jack Kerouac's On the Road, *the bible of the beats, describes a life of restless impatience with long-term obligations. Snyder, however, eventually turned his back on the road-trip lifestyle and committed himself to a serious intellectual vocation: to know himself, to understand the human species, and to discover the ideal relationship between the earth and humankind. Snyder has studied social and philosophical systems thoroughly. At Reed College, in Oregon, his bachelor's thesis explored myths and legends of the Northwest Indians; after a semester of graduate study in linguistics, he transferred to the University of California at Berkeley as a student of Japanese and Chinese culture, majoring in Oriental languages. Snyder's youthful love for the forested mountains of Washington and Oregon gradually grew until it became a mystic affinity. Many of his poems, like "Piute Creek" and "Milton by Firelight," stem from living and working outdoors. Some, such as "Hay for the Horses," also draw upon his close association with work-*

men of the forests and fields. He sees his subjects in terms of Oriental philosophy, thanks to his knowledge of Zen and Buddhism. Just after the 1955 poetry reading in San Francisco, Snyder won a scholarship to study in Japan. When his study ended, he worked his way back to San Francisco on the ship Sappa Creek. *In 1959 he returned to Japan to spend six years learning Zen from the teacher Oda Sesso. "No poet in American literature has made Buddhist psychology so completely his own," wrote Snyder's biographer, Bob Steuding.*[1]

Snyder now speaks out in defense of ecology, emphasizing a oneness with nature that his Buddhist training has reaffirmed and expanded. His poetry readings feature verbal attacks against nuclear power plants, industrial pollution, or any *manifestation of ecological irresponsibility. Life, Snyder believes, cannot be divided into "living" and "nonliving" entities: all is one. As he said in his introduction to* Turtle Island*: "Each living being is a swirl in the flow, a formal turbulence, a 'song.' The land, the planet itself, is also a living being—at another pace."*[2]

Critics compare Snyder to the imagists, including Ezra Pound, Hilda Doolittle (H.D.), and Carl Sandburg. Following Oriental criteria, the imagists believed (1) that poetry should not state a complete thought but should suggest one, (2) that all subjects for poetry are of equal value, (3) that clichés should be avoided altogether, (4) that poets should use ordinary language, with precision, (5) that poets can use their own rhythms—not the traditional ones—to suit their own subjects, (6) that a poem should concentrate much meaning into few words, and (7) that poets should strive for clear, vivid, thought-provoking, memorable images.

These precepts underlie the following poems. Rhythm shares the meaning, for example, in Snyder's American Indian song-story "This Poem Is for Bear," together with language that conveys the flavor of a tribal legend. Vivid images are everywhere, from the "bubble of a heart" in "Piute Creek" to the "flecks of alfalfa / Whirling through shingle-cracks of light" in "Hay for the Horses." As in the Buddhist way of learning, some thoughts remain for the reader to finish. Consider, for example, the responsibilities implied by "Axe Handles." Or, after having read Snyder's "The Call of the Wild," consider Jack London's comment that Charles Darwin's idea of the survival of the fittest seemed to fit the facts but was not necessarily a comforting revelation.

———

1. Bob Steuding, *Gary Snyder* (Boston: Twayne, 1976), p. 167.
2. Gary Snyder, *Turtle Island* (New York: New Directions, 1974), introductory note.

The Call of the Wild

*

The heavy old man in his bed at night
Hears the Coyote singing
            in the back meadow.
All the years he ranched and mined and logged.
A Catholic.
A native Californian.
      and the Coyotes howl in his
Eightieth year.
He will call the Government
Trapper
Who uses iron leg-traps on Coyotes,
Tomorrow.
My sons will lose this
Music they have just started
To love.
                  *

The ex acid-heads from the cities
Converted to Guru or Swami,
Do penance with shiny
Dopey eyes, and quit eating meat.
In the forests of North America,
The land of Coyote and Eagle,
They dream of India, of
      forever blissful sexless highs.
And sleep in oil-heated
Geodesic domes, that
Were stuck like warts
In the woods.

From Gary Snyder, *Turtle Island* (New York: New Directions, 1974), pp. 21–23. Copyright © 1974 by Gary Snyder. Reprinted by permission of New Directions Publishing Corporation.

And the Coyote singing
    is shut away
    for they fear
    the call
    of the wild.

And they sold their virgin cedar trees,
    the tallest trees in miles,
To a logger
Who told them,

"Trees are full of bugs."

✳

The Government finally decided
To wage the war   all-out. Defeat
    is Un-American.
And they took to the air,
Their women beside them
    in bouffant hairdos
    putting nail-polish on the
    gunship cannon-buttons.
And they never came down,
    for they found,
    the ground
is pro-Communist. And dirty.
And the insects side with the Viet Cong.

So they bomb and they bomb
Day after day, across the planet
    blinding sparrows
    breaking the ear-drums of owls
    splintering trunks of cherries
    twining and looping
    deer intestines
    in the shaken, dusty, rocks.
All these Americans up in special cities in the sky
Dumping poisons and explosives
Across Asia first,
And next North America,

A war against earth.
When it's done there'll be
        no place

A Coyote could hide.

envoy

I would like to say
Coyote is forever
Inside you.

But it's not true.

—

Axe Handles

One afternoon the last week in April
Showing Kai how to throw a hatchet
One-half turn and it sticks in a stump.
He recalls the hatchet-head
Without a handle, in the shop
And go gets it, and wants it for his own.
A broken-off axe handle behind the door
Is long enough for a hatchet,
We cut it to length and take it
With the hatchet head
And working hatchet, to the wood block.
There I begin to shape the old handle
With the hatchet, and the phrase
First learned from Ezra Pound
Rings in my ears!
"When making an axe handle
        the pattern is not far off."
And I say this to Kai
"Look: We'll shape the handle

From Gary Snyder, *Axe Handles* (San Francisco: North Point Press, 1983), pp. 5–6.
Copyright © 1983 by Gary Snyder. Reprinted by permission of North Point Press.

By checking the handle
Of the axe we cut with—"
And he sees. And I hear it again:
It's in Lu Ji's *Wên Fu*, fourth century
A.D. "Essay on Literature"—in the
Preface: "In making the handle
Of an axe
By cutting wood with an axe
The model is indeed near at hand."
My teacher Shih-hsiang Chen
Translated that and taught it years ago
And I see: Pound was an axe,
Chen was an axe, I am an axe
And my son a handle, soon
To be shaping again, model
And tool, craft of culture,
How we go on.

———

Piute Creek

One granite ridge
A tree, would be enough
Or even a rock, a small creek,
A bark shred in a pool.
Hill beyond hill, folded and twisted
Tough trees crammed
In thin stone fractures
A huge moon on it all, is too much.
The mind wanders. A million
Summers, night air still and the rocks
Warm. Sky over endless mountains.
All the junk that goes with being human
Drops away, hard rock wavers
Even the heavy present seems to fail

This and the following selection of Gary Snyder's verse are from *Riprap and Cold Mountain Poems* (San Francisco: Grey Fox Press, 1980), pp. 6, 13. Reprinted by permission of Gary Snyder.

This bubble of a heart.
Words and books
Like a small creek off a high ledge
Gone in the dry air.

A clear, attentive mind
Has no meaning but that
Which sees is truly seen.
No one loves rock, yet we are here.
Night chills. A flick
In the moonlight
Slips into Juniper shadow:
Back there unseen
Cold proud eyes
Of Cougar or Coyote
Watch me rise and go.

Hay for the Horses

He had driven half the night
From far down San Joaquin
Through Mariposa, up the
Dangerous mountain roads,
And pulled in at eight a.m.
With his big truckload of hay
            behind the barn.
With winch and ropes and hooks
We stacked the bales up clean
To splintery redwood rafters
High in the dark, flecks of alfalfa
Whirling through shingle-cracks of light,
Itch of haydust in the
            sweaty shirt and shoes.
At lunchtime under Black oak
Out in the hot corral,
—The old mare nosing lunchpails,
Grasshoppers crackling in the weeds—
"I'm sixty-eight" he said,

"I first bucked hay when I was seventeen.
I thought, that day I started,
I sure would hate to do this all my life.
And dammit, that's just what
I've gone and done."

———

This Poem Is for Bear

"As for me I am a child of the god of the mountains."

A bear down under the cliff.
She is eating huckleberries.
They are ripe now
Soon it will snow, and she
Or maybe he, will crawl into a hole
And sleep. You can see
Huckleberries in bearshit if you
Look, this time of year
If I sneak up on the bear
It will grunt and run

The others had all gone down
From the blackberry brambles, but one girl
Spilled her basket, and was picking up her
Berries in the dark.
A tall man stood in the shadow, took her arm,
Led her to his home. He was a bear.
In a house under the mountain
She gave birth to slick dark children
With sharp teeth, and lived in the hollow
Mountain many years.
                    snare a bear: call him out:
honey-eater
forest apple

From Gary Snyder, *Myths and Texts* (1960; reprint, New York: New Directions, 1978), pp. 23–25. Copyright © 1978 by Gary Snyder. Reprinted by permission of New Directions Publishing Corporation.

light-foot
Old man in the fur coat, Bear! come out!
Die of your own choice!
Grandfather black-food!
           this girl married a bear
Who rules in the mountains, Bear!
              you have eaten many berries
              you have caught many fish
              you have frightened many people

Twelve species north of Mexico
Sucking their paws in the long winter
Tearing the high-strung caches down
Whining, crying, jacking off
(Odysseus was a bear)

Bear-cubs gnawing the soft tits
Teeth gritted, eyes screwed tight
              but she let them.
Til her brothers found the place
Chased her husband up the gorge
Cornered him in the rocks.
Song of the snared bear:
        "Give me my belt.
        "I am near death.
        "I came from the mountain caves
        "At the headwaters,
        "The small streams there
        "Are all dried up.

—I think I'll go hunt bears.
        "hunt bears?
Why shit Snyder,
You couldn't hit a bear in the ass
        with a handful of rice!"

N. Scott Momaday
b. 1934

▬

1968: *House Made of Dawn*
1969: *The Way to Rainy Mountain*
1974: *Angle of Geese, and Other Poems*
1976: *The Gourd Dancer*
1976: *The Names: A Memoir*

▬

T HE WAY TO RAINY MOUNTAIN *tells the story of the Kiowas' migration toward the dawn. The journey began in the northern mountains,
lasted through many generations, and ended in the late 1800s, when the
Kiowas were deprived of their buffalo, forbidden to follow their religion, and confined to a reservation near Anadarko, Oklahoma. A high knoll there, called Rainy
Mountain, stands apart from the Wichita Range. N. Scott Momaday entered
life at Anadarko and began his individual journey, one that eventually led to
the Pulitzer Prize and beyond. The first stage of his life-journey took him to the
Navaho reservation near Shiprock, New Mexico, where his parents had accepted
teaching positions. In 1946, the family moved to Jemez Pueblo, remaining there
throughout Momaday's adolescent years. The traditions of Jemez, including the
footrace toward the sun, became the basis for Momaday's most successful novel,*
House Made of Dawn.

*After graduation from the University of New Mexico in 1958, Momaday
began teaching at the Jicarilla Apache reservation at Dulce, New Mexico. His
professional odyssey then took him to Stanford University. Yvor Winters, a widely
known writer, critic, and Stanford professor of poetry, had nominated Momaday
for the Wallace Stegner Creative Writing scholarship "in recognition of his respect
for, control of, and enjoyment in using language."*[1] *Winters believed that lan-*

---

1. Matthias Schubnell, *N. Scott Momaday: The Cultural and Literary Background* (Norman: University of Oklahoma Press, 1985), p. 22.

guage should be used well, and sparingly. With his assistance, Momaday prepared House Made of Dawn *for publication; unfortunately, Winters died shortly before his student's novel won the Pulitzer Prize.*

Momaday earned his M.A. and Ph.D. at Stanford and taught writing at Stanford and elsewhere until his 1981 professorial appointment to the University of Arizona. A succinct account of his status comes from the biographer and critic Matthias Schubnell. "In recent years he has lectured and given readings from his work on four continents; taught at Stanford, Princeton, and Columbia; and received the Pulitzer Prize and a score of other literary awards as well as eight honorary doctorates. His work has been translated into Russian, Polish, German, Italian, Norwegian, and Japanese." [2]

Momaday's talents include painting and poetry, but his reputation largely rests on two prose works, The Way to Rainy Mountain *and* House Made of Dawn. *The former is an account of the Kiowas' migration from the mountain headwaters of the Yellowstone River to the Oklahoma prairie, recording the birth, life, and death of a whole culture. Momaday called it "the history of an idea" and an evocation of "a landscape that is incomparable, a time that is gone forever, and the human spirit, which endures."* [3] The Way to Rainy Mountain *is a tribal epic told through personal, historical, and cultural stories.*

Abel, in House Made of Dawn, *lives in two worlds, his soul split between his Indian culture and the white man's ways. Searching for unity, Abel goes to the Los Angeles "city Indian" neighborhood, where poverty, crime, drugs, and alcohol abound. The Priest of the Sun, John Big Bluff Tosamah, operates a basement mission church there, preaching his "hip" version of the Native American heritage. Tosamah's sermon has unique meaning for Abel because Abel has lost his own power over words, and can no longer find language with which to re-create himself.*

Momaday believes that people are made of words, that "our very existence consists in our imagination of ourselves." Abel's distorting experiences in the army and in prison have warped his self-image beyond all focus. He needs Tosamah's uncluttered way of understanding, achieved through the power of simple words. In The Way to Rainy Mountain, *Momaday's arrowmaker illustrates the same concept. As Momaday explains in his* Indian Voices *essay: "The arrowmaker is preeminently the man made of words. He has consummate being in language; it is the world of his origin and of his posterity, and there is no other. But it is a world of definite reality and of infinite possibility."* [4]

———

2. Ibid., p. 38.

3. N. Scott Momaday, *The Way to Rainy Mountain* (Albuquerque: University of New Mexico Press, 1969), p. 4.

4. N. Scott Momaday, "The Man Made of Words," in *Indian Voices: The First Convoca-*

The Word

January 26

THERE IS A SMALL silversided fish that is found along the coast of southern California. In the spring and summer it spawns on the beach during the first three hours after each of the three high tides following the highest tide. These fishes come by the hundreds from the sea. They hurl themselves upon the land and writhe in the light of the moon, the moon, the moon; they writhe in the light of the moon. They are among the most helpless creatures on the face of the earth. Fishermen, lovers, passers-by catch them up in their bare hands.

The Priest of the Sun lived with his disciple Cruz on the first floor of a two-story red-brick building in Los Angeles. The upstairs was maintained as a storage facility by the A. A. Kaul Office Supply Company. The basement was a kind of church. There was a signboard on the wall above the basement steps, encased in glass. In neat, movable white block letters on a black field it read:

LOS ANGELES
HOLINESS PAN-INDIAN RESCUE MISSION
Rev. J. B. B. Tosamah, Pastor & Priest of the Sun
Saturday 8:30 P.M.
"The Gospel According to John"
Sunday 8:30 P.M.
"The Way to Rainy Mountain"
Be kind to a white man today

From N. Scott Momaday, *House Made of Dawn* (New York: Harper and Row, 1968), pp. 89–98. Copyright © 1966, 1967, 1968 by N. Scott Momaday. Reprinted by permission of Harper and Row.

tion of American Indian Scholars, ed. Rupert Costo (San Francisco: Indian Historian Press, 1970), pp. 55, 61. See also Schubnell, "The Man Made of Words," chapter 2 in *Momaday*, pp. 40–62.

The basement was cold and dreary, dimly illuminated by two 40-watt bulbs which were screwed into the side walls above the dais. This platform was made out of rough planks of various woods and dimensions, thrown together without so much as a hammer and nails; it stood seven or eight inches above the floor, and it supported the tin firebox and the crescent altar. Off to one side was a kind of lectern, decorated with red and yellow symbols of the sun and moon. In back of the dais there was a screen of purple drapery, threadbare and badly faded. On either side of the aisle which led to the altar there were chairs and crates, fashioned into pews. The walls were bare and gray and streaked with water. The only windows were small, rectangular openings near the ceiling, at ground level; the panes were covered over with a thick film of coal oil and dust, and spider webs clung to the frames or floated out like smoke across the room. The air was heavy and stale; odors of old smoke and incense lingered all around. The people had filed into the pews and were waiting silently.

Cruz, a squat, oily man with blue-black hair that stood out like spines from his head, stepped forward on the platform and raised his hands as if to ask for the quiet that already was. Everyone watched him for a moment; in the dull light his skin shone yellow with sweat. Turning slightly and extending his arm behind him, he said, "The Right Reverend John Big Bluff Tosamah."

There was a ripple in the dark screen; the drapes parted and the Priest of the Sun appeared, moving shadow-like to the lectern. He was shaggy and awful-looking in the thin, naked light: big, lithe as a cat, narrow-eyed, suggesting in the whole of his look and manner both arrogance and agony. He wore black like a cleric; he had the voice of a great dog:

" '*In principio erat Verbum.*' Think of Genesis. Think of how it was before the world was made. There was nothing, the Bible says. 'And the earth was without form, and void; and darkness was upon the face of the deep.' It was dark, and there was nothing. There were no mountains, no trees, no rocks, no rivers. There was nothing. But there was darkness all around, and in the darkness something happened. *Something happened!* There was a single sound. Far away in the darkness there was a single sound. Nothing made it, but it was there; and there was no one to hear it, but it was there. It was there, and there was nothing else. It rose up in the darkness, little and still, almost nothing in itself—like a single soft breath, like the wind arising; yes, like the whisper of the wind rising slowly and going out into the early morning. But there was no wind. There was only the sound, little and soft. It was almost nothing in itself, the smallest seed of sound—but it took hold of the darkness and there was light; it took hold of the stillness and there was motion forever; it took hold of the silence and there was sound. It was almost nothing in itself, a single sound, a word—a word broken off at the darkest center of the night and let go in the awful void, forever and forever. And it was almost nothing in itself. It scarcely was; but it was, and everything began."

Just then a remarkable thing happened. The Priest of the Sun seemed stricken; he let go of his audience and withdrew into himself, into some strange potential of himself. His voice, which had been low and resonant, suddenly became harsh and flat; his shoulders sagged and his stomach protruded, as if he had held his breath to the limit of endurance; for a moment there was a look of amazement, then utter carelessness in his face. Conviction, caricature, callousness: the remainder of his sermon was a going back and forth among these.

"Thank you *so* much, Brother Cruz. Good evening, blood brothers and sisters, and welcome, welcome. Gracious me, I see lots of new faces out there tonight. *Gracious me!* May the Great Spirit—can we knock off that talking in the back there?—be with you always.

"'In the beginning was the Word.' I have taken as my text this evening the almighty Word itself. Now get this: 'There was a man sent from God, whose name was John. The same came for a witness, to bear witness of the Light, that all men through him might believe.' Amen, brothers and sisters, *Amen*. And the riddle of the Word, 'In the beginning was the Word. . . .' Now what do you suppose old John *meant* by that? That cat was a preacher, and, well, you know how it is with preachers; he had something big on his mind. Oh my, it was big; it was the *Truth,* and it was heavy, and old John hurried to set it down. And in his hurry he said too much. 'In the beginning was the Word, and the Word was with God, and the Word was God.' It was the Truth, all right, but it was more than the Truth. The Truth was overgrown with fat, and the fat was God. The fat was *John's* God, and God stood between John and the Truth. Old John, see, he got up one morning and caught sight of the Truth. It must have been like a bolt of lightning, and the sight of it made him blind. And for a moment the vision burned on in back of his eyes, and he *knew* what it was. In that instant he saw something he had never seen before and would never see again. That was the instant of revelation, inspiration, Truth. And old John, he must have fallen down on his knees. Man, he must have been shaking and laughing and crying and yelling and praying—all at the same time—and he must have been drunk and delirious with the Truth. You see, he had lived all his life waiting for that one moment, and it came, and it took him by surprise, and it was gone. And he said, 'In the beginning was the Word. . . .' And, man, right then and there he should have stopped. There was nothing more to say, but he went on. He had said all there was to say, everything, but he went on. 'In the beginning was the Word. . . .' Brothers and sisters, *that* was the Truth, the whole of it, the essential and eternal Truth, the bone and blood and muscle of the Truth. But he went on, old John, because he was a preacher. The perfect vision faded from his mind, and he went on. The instant passed, and then he had nothing but a memory. He was desperate and confused, and in his confusion he stumbled and went on. 'In the beginning was the Word, and the Word was with God, and the Word was God.' He went on to talk about Jews and Jerusalem, Levites and Pharisees, Moses and Philip and Andrew and Peter. Don't you see? Old John *had* to go on. That cat had a whole lot at stake. He couldn't let the Truth alone. He couldn't see that he had come to the end of the Truth, and he went on. He tried to make it bigger and better than it was, but instead he only demeaned and encumbered it. He made it soft and big with fat. He was a preacher, and he made a complex sentence of the Truth, two sentences, three, a paragraph. He made a sermon and theology of the Truth. He imposed his idea of God upon the everlasting Truth. 'In the beginning was the Word. . . .' And that is all there was, and it was enough.

"Now, brothers and sisters, old John was a white man, and the white man has his ways. Oh gracious me, he has his ways. He talks about the Word. He talks through it and around it. He builds upon it with syllables, with prefixes and suffixes and hyphens and accents. He adds and divides and multiplies the Word. And in all of this he subtracts the Truth. And, brothers and sisters, you have come here to live in the white man's world. Now the white man deals in words, and he deals easily, with grace and sleight of hand. And in his presence, here on his own ground, you are as children, mere babes in the woods. You must not mind, for in this you have a certain advantage. A child can listen and learn. The Word is sacred to a child.

"My grandmother was a storyteller; she knew her way around words. She never learned to read and write, but somehow she knew the good of reading and writing; she had learned how to listen and delight. She had learned that in words and in language, and there only, she could have whole and consummate being. She told me stories, and she taught me how to listen. I was a child and I listened. She could neither read nor write, you see, but she taught me how to live among her words, how to listen and delight. 'Storytelling; to utter and to hear . . .' And the simple act of listening is crucial to the concept of language, more crucial even than reading and writing, and language in turn is crucial to human society. There is proof of that, I think, in all the histories and prehistories of human experience.

When that old Kiowa woman told me stories, I listened with only one ear. I was a child, and I took the words for granted. I did not know what all of them meant, but somehow I held on to them; I remembered them, and I remember them now. The stories were old and dear; they meant a great deal to my grandmother. It was not until she died that I knew how *much* they meant to her. I began to think about it, and then I knew. When she told me those old stories, something strange and good and powerful was going on. I was a child, and that old woman was asking me to come directly into the presence of her mind and spirit; she was taking hold of my imagination, giving me to share in the great fortune of her wonder and delight. She was asking me to go with her to the confrontation of something that was sacred and eternal. It was a timeless, *timeless* thing; nothing of her old age or of my childhood came between us.

"Children have a greater sense of the power and beauty of words than have the rest of us in general. And if that is so, it is because there occurs— or reoccurs—in the mind of every child something like a reflection of all human experience. I have heard that the human fetus corresponds in its development, stage by stage, to the scale of evolution. Surely it is no less reasonable to suppose that the waking mind of a child corresponds in the same way to the whole evolution of human thought and perception.

"In the white man's world, language, too—and the way in which the white man thinks of it—has undergone a process of change. The white man takes such things as words and literatures for granted, as indeed he must, for nothing in his world is so commonplace. On every side of him there are words by the millions, an unending succession of pamphlets and papers, letters and books, bills and bulletins, commentaries and conversations. He has diluted and multiplied the Word, and words have begun to close in upon him. He is sated and insensitive; his regard for language—for the Word itself—as an instrument of creation has diminished nearly to the point of no return. It may be that he will perish by the Word.

"But it was not always so with him, and it is not so with you. Consider for a moment that old Kiowa woman, my grandmother, whose use of language was confined to speech. And be assured that her regard for words was always keen in proportion as she depended upon them. You see, for her words were medicine; they were magic and invisible. They came from nothing into sound and meaning. They were beyond price; they could neither be bought nor sold. And she never threw words away.

"My grandmother used to tell me the story of Tai-me, of how Tai-me came to the Kiowas. The Kiowas were a sun dance culture, and Tai-me was their sun dance doll, their most sacred fetish; no medicine was ever more powerful. There is a story about the coming of Tai-me. This is what my grandmother told me:

Long ago there were bad times. The Kiowas were hungry and there was no food. There was a man who heard his children cry from hunger, and he began to search for food. He walked four days and became very weak. On the fourth day he came to a great canyon. Suddenly there was thunder and lightning. A Voice spoke to him and said, "Why are you following me? What do you want?" The man was afraid. The thing standing before him had the feet of a deer, and its body was covered with feathers. The man answered that the Kiowas were hungry. "Take me with you," the Voice said, "and I will give you whatever you want." From that day Tai-me has belonged to the Kiowas.

"Do you see? There, far off in the darkness, something happened. Do you see? Far, far away in the nothingness something happened. There was a voice, a sound, a word—and everything began. The story of the coming of Tai-me has existed for hundreds of years by word of mouth. It represents the oldest and best idea that man has of himself. It represents a very rich literature, which, because it was never written down, was always but one generation from extinction. But for the same reason it was cherished and revered. I could see that reverence in my grandmother's eyes, and I could hear it in her voice. It was that, I think, that old Saint John had in mind when he said, 'In the beginning was the Word. . . .' But he went on. He went on to lay a scheme about the Word. He could find no satisfaction in the simple fact that the Word was; he had to account for it, not in terms of that sudden and profound insight, which must have devastated him at once, but in terms of the moment afterward, which was irrelevant and remote; not in terms of his imagination, but only in terms of his prejudice.

"Say this: 'In the beginning was the Word. . . .' There was nothing. There was *nothing!* Darkness. There was darkness, and there was no end to it. You look up sometimes in the night and there are stars; you can see all the way to the stars. And you begin to know the universe, how awful and great it is. The stars lie out against the sky and do not fill it. A single star, flickering out in the universe, is enough to fill the mind, but it is nothing in the night sky. The darkness looms around it. The darkness flows among the stars, and beyond them forever. In the beginning that is how it was, but there were no stars. There was only the dark infinity in which nothing was. And something happened. At the distance of a star something happened, and everything began. The Word did not come into being, but *it was.* It did not break upon the silence, but *it was older than the silence and the silence was made of it*.

"Old John caught sight of something terrible. The thing standing before him said, 'Why are you following me? What do you want?' And from that day the Word has belonged to us, who have heard it for what it is, who have lived in fear and awe of it. In the Word was the beginning; *'In the beginning was the Word. . . .'*"

The Priest of the Sun appeared to have spent himself. He stepped back from the lectern and hung his head, smiling. In his mind the earth was spinning and the stars rattled around in the heavens. The sun shone, and the moon. Smiling in a kind of transport, the Priest of the Sun stood silent for a time while the congregation waited to be dismissed.

"Good night," he said, at last, "and get yours."

Rudolfo A. Anaya
b. 1937

▬

1972: *Bless Me, Ultima*
1976: *Heart of Aztlan*
1979: *Tortuga*
1980: *Cuentos: Tales from the*
Hispanic Southwest
1986: *A Chicano in China*
1987: *Lord of the Dawn,*
The Legend of Quetzalcoatl

▬

O NE HUNDRED *miles east of Albuquerque, in the direction of the*
Texas Panhandle, the main highway crosses the valley of the Pecos
River. The windy plains, which natives call the llano, seem to stretch
without end, but in the Pecos Valley, fertile green hollows hide between low hills
and mesas. The inheritors of a three-hundred-year-old culture live here, descended
from vaqueros and conquistadores. Rudolfo A. Anaya was born here, in the village
of Pastura. His mother's family farmed in Puerto De Luna, and his father worked
livestock on the llano. This lineage, like other aspects of Anaya's boyhood, closely
parallels Anaya's best-known novel, Bless Me, Ultima. *Reaching high school age,*
Anaya took the highway to Albuquerque, where he earned three degrees at the
University of New Mexico and where his writing talent matured.

Anaya's reputation, which extends across the United States and into Europe,
grew quickly after the publication of his popular trilogy. In the first segment,
Bless Me, Ultima, *an adolescent boy struggles for self-identity and maturity. His*
mother cherishes a hope that he will become a priest, but his father expects him to
become a vaquero. The second book of Anaya's trilogy, Heart of Aztlan, *continues*
the search for personal and cultural identity, moving from a contemporary barrio
to the legend of an ancient Aztec empire in North America. Tortuga *concludes*

the trilogy in a hospital that is "an existential hell," as Anaya has described it. In this setting, his characters plunge "to the depths of despair and human suffering, and they find in their hellish existence the faith they need to survive." [1]

Bless Me, Ultima *gives literature of the Chicano movement a benchmark against which to measure subsequent fiction. The movement's first literature came from El Teatro Campesino, organized in 1965 to write and produce plays dramatizing the labor struggles of Cesar Chávez's farm workers' union. In 1967, the Quinto Sol publishing company was formed to publish works by Mexican-American writers;* Bless Me, Ultima *is one of their best-selling publications. Anaya and writers such as Luis Valdez of El Teatro Campesino, Sandra Cisneros, Lorna Dee Cervantes, Gary Soto, Rolando Hinojosa, and Tomas Rivera have reawakened the rich, distinctive, and extensive intellectual culture of Mexican-Americans. It had lain dormant for too long. "The movement changed the destiny of the Chicanos," wrote Anaya, "changed in small part the way the society looks at this cultural group. The country was not completely changed, but a significant beginning was made. A feeling of renewed pride flowed in the people."* [2]

"B. Traven Is Alive and Well in Cuernavaca" is from Anaya's short-story collection, The Silence of the Llano *(1982). The title raises an immediate question: who is "B. Traven"? Many scholars have searched for the mysterious B. Traven, each writing a different account of the man.* [3] *Dozens of articles and a half-dozen books have been devoted to exposing the true identity of Traven, who wrote* The Death Ship, The Treasure of the Sierra Madre, *and other novels. As Anaya's story tells us, Traven was a writer who shunned all publicity and used several names to conceal his whereabouts. The dates of his birth and death are uncertain, although a death date of March 26, 1969, is often mentioned. He wrote in German, claimed to have been born in America, and lived in Mexico. Many of his stories reflect an impressive knowledge of Mexico.*

In B. Traven's The Treasure of the Sierra Madre, *Anglo treasure hunters and native Indians have opposite sets of cultural values. In Anaya's story, the narrator discovers a similar difference between the values of his host and those of the Indian gardener. He also discovers, through firsthand experience, that "time recycles in Mexico. Time returns to the past." And in this* poco tiempo *country where people still have faith that Quetzalcoatl will someday return, why can't B. Traven still be alive and well?*

——

1. Rudolfo A. Anaya, in *Contemporary Authors Autobiography Series*, ed. Adele Sarkissian (Detroit: Gale Research, 1986), vol. 4, p. 26.

2. Ibid., p. 25.

3. One such account is Will Wyatt's *The Secret of the Sierra Madre* (Garden City, N.Y.: Doubleday and Co., 1980).

B. Traven Is Alive and Well
in Cuernavaca

I DIDN'T GO to Mexico to find B. Traven. Why should I? I have enough to do writing my own fiction, so I go to Mexico to write, not to search out writers. B. Traven? you ask. Don't you remember THE TREASURE OF THE SIERRA MADRE? A real classic. They made a movie from the novel. I remember seeing it when I was a kid. It was set in Mexico, and it had all the elements of a real adventure story. B. Traven was an adventurous man, traveled all over the world, then disappeared into Mexico and cut himself off from society. He gave no interviews and allowed few photographs. While he lived he remained unapproachable, anonymous to his public, a writer shrouded in mystery.

He's dead now, or they say he's dead. I think he's alive and well. At any rate, he has become something of an institution in Mexico, a man honored for his work. The cantineros and taxi drivers in Mexico City know about him as well as the cantineros of Spain knew Hemingway, or they claim to. I never mention I'm a writer when I'm in a cantina, because inevitably some aficionado will ask, "Do you know the work of B. Traven?" And from some dusty niche will appear a yellowed, thumb-worn novel by Traven. Then if the cantinero knows his business, and they all do in Mexico, he is apt to say, "Did you know that B. Traven used to drink here?" If you show the slightest interest, he will follow with, "Sure, he used to sit right over here. In this corner. . . ." And if you don't leave right then you will wind up hearing many stories about the mysterious B. Traven while buying many drinks for the local patrons.

Everybody reads his novels, on the buses, on street corners, if you look closely you'll spot one of his titles. One turned up for me, and that's how this story started. I was sitting in the train station in Juarez, waiting for the train to Cuernavaca, which would be an exciting title for this story ex-

From Rudolfo A. Anaya, *The Silence of the Llano* (Berkeley: Tonatiuh–Quinto Sol International, 1982), pp. 129–46. Copyright © 1982 by Rudolfo A. Anaya. Reprinted by permission of the author.

cept that there is no train to Cuernavaca. I was drinking beer to kill time, the erotic and sensitive Mexican time which is so different from the clean-packaged, well-kept time of the Americanos. Time in Mexico is at times cruel and punishing, but it is never indifferent. It permeates everything, it changes reality. Einstein would have loved Mexico because there time and space are one. I stare more often into empty space when I'm in Mexico. The past seems to infuse the present, and in the brown, wrinkled faces of the old people one sees the presence of the past. In Mexico I like to walk the narrow streets of the cities and the smaller pueblos, wandering aimlessly, feeling the sunlight which is so distinctively Mexican, listening to the voices which call in the streets, peering into the dark eyes which are so secretive and proud. The Mexican people guard a secret. But in the end, one is never really lost in Mexico. All streets lead to a good cantina. All good stories start in a cantina.

At the train station, after I let the kids who hustle the tourists know that I didn't want chewing gum or cigarettes, and I didn't want my shoes shined, and I didn't want a woman at the moment, I was left alone to drink my beer. Luke-cold Dos Equis. I don't remember how long I had been there or how many Dos Equis I had finished when I glanced at the seat next to me and saw a book which turned out to be a B. Traven novel, old and used and obviously much read, but a novel nevertheless. What's so strange about finding a B. Traven novel in that dingy little corner of a bar in the Juarez train station? Nothing, unless you know that in Mexico one never finds anything. It is a country that doesn't waste anything, everything is recycled. Chevrolets run with patched up Ford engines and Chrysler transmissions, busses are kept together, and kept running, with baling wire and home-made parts, yesterday's Traven novel is the pulp on which tomorrow's Fuentes story will appear. Time recycles in Mexico. Time returns to the past, and the Christian finds himself dreaming of ancient Aztec rituals. He who does not believe that Quetzalcoatl will return to save Mexico has little faith.

So the novel was the first clue. Later there was Justino. "Who is Justino?" you want to know. Justino was the jardinero who cared for the garden of my friend, the friend who had invited me to stay at his home in Cuernavaca while I continued to write. The day after I arrived I was sitting in the sun, letting the fatigue of the long journey ooze away, thinking nothing, when Justino appeared on the scene. He had finished cleaning the swimming pool and was taking his morning break, so he sat in the shade of the orange tree and introduced himself. Right away I could tell that he would rather be a movie actor or an adventurer, a real free spirit. But things didn't work out for him. He got married, children appeared, he took a couple of mistresses, more children appeared, so he had to work to support his family. "A man is like a rooster," he said after we talked awhile, "the more chickens he has the happier he is." Then he asked me what I was going to do about a woman while I was there, and I told him I hadn't thought that far ahead, that I would be happy if I could just get a damned story going. This puzzled Justino, and I think for a few days it worried him. So on Saturday night he took me out for a few drinks and we wound up in some of the bordellos of Cuernavaca in the company of some of the most beautiful women in the world. Justino knew them all. They loved him, and he loved them.

I learned something more of the nature of this jardinero a few nights later when the heat and an irritating mosquito wouldn't let me sleep. I heard music from a radio, so I put on my pants and walked out into the Cuernavacan night, an oppressive, warm night heavy with the sweet perfume of the dama de la noche bushes which lined the wall of my friend's villa. From time to time I heard a dog cry in the distance, and I remembered that in Mexico many people die of rabies. Perhaps that is why the walls of the wealthy are always so high and the locks always secure. Or maybe it was because of the occasional gunshots which explode in the night. The news media tells us that Mexico is the most stable country in Latin America, and with the recent oil finds the bankers and the oil men want to keep it that way. I sense, and many know, that in the dark the revolution does not sleep. It is a spirit kept at bay by the high fences and the locked gates, yet it prowls the heart of every man. "Oil will create a new revolution," Justino had told me, "but it's going to be for our people. Mexicans are tired of building gas stations for the Gringos from Gringolandia." I understood what he meant: there is much hunger in the country.

I lit a cigarette and walked toward my friend's car which was parked in the driveway near the swimming pool. I approached quietly and peered in. On the back seat with his legs propped on the front seatback and smoking a cigar sat Justino. Two big, luscious women sat on either side of him running their fingers through his hair and whispering in his ears. The doors were open to allow a breeze. He looked content. Sitting there he was that famous artist on his way to an afternoon reception in Mexico City, or he was a movie star on his way to the premiere of his most recent movie. Or perhaps it was Sunday and he was taking a Sunday drive in the country, towards Tepoztlan. And why shouldn't his two friends accompany him? I had to smile. Unnoticed I backed away and returned to my room. So there was quite a bit more than met the eye to this short, dark Indian from Ocosingo.

In the morning I asked my friend, "What do you know about Justino?"

"Justino? You mean Vitorino."

"Is that his real name?"

"Sometimes he calls himself Trinidad."

"Maybe his name is Justino Vitorino Trinidad," I suggested.

"I don't know, don't care," my friend answered. "He told me he used to be a guide in the jungle. Who knows? The Mexican Indian has an incredible imagination. Really gifted people. He's a good jardinero, and that's what matters to me. It's difficult to get good jardineros, so I don't ask questions."

"Is he reliable?" I wondered aloud.

"As reliable as a ripe mango," my friend nodded.

I wondered how much he knew, so I pushed a little further. "And the radio at night?"

"Oh, that. I hope it doesn't bother you. Robberies and break-ins are increasing here in the colonia. Something we never used to have. Vitorino said that if he keeps the radio on low the sound keeps thieves away. A very good idea, don't you think?"

I nodded. A very good idea.

"And I sleep very soundly," my friend concluded, "so I never hear it."

The following night when I awakened and heard the soft sound of the music from the radio and heard the splashing of water, I had only to look from my window to see Justino and his friends in the pool, swimming nude in the moonlight. They were joking and laughing softly as they splashed each other, being quiet so as not to awaken my friend, the patrón who slept so soundly. The women were beautiful. Brown skinned and glistening with water in the moonlight they reminded me of ancient Aztec maidens, swimming around Chac, their god of rain. They teased Justino, and he smiled as he floated on a rubber mattress in the middle of the pool, smoking his cigar, happy because they were happy. When he smiled the gold fleck of a filling glinted in the moonlight.

"¡Qué cabrón!" I laughed and closed my window.

Justino said a Mexican never lies. I believed him. If a Mexican says he will meet you at a certain time and place, he means he will meet you sometime at some place. Americans who retire in Mexico often complain of maids who swear they will come to work on a designated day, then don't show up. They did not lie, they knew they couldn't be at work, but they knew to tell the señora otherwise would make her sad or displease her, so they agree on a date so everyone would remain happy. What a beautiful aspect of character. It's a real virtue which Norteamericanos interpret as a fault in their character, because we are used to asserting ourselves on time and people.

We feel secure and comfortable only when everything is neatly packaged in its proper time and place. We don't like the disorder of a free-flowing life.

Some day, I thought to myself, Justino will give a grand party in the sala of his patrón's home. His three wives, or his wife and two mistresses, and his dozens of children will be there. So will the women from the bordellos. He will preside over the feast, smoke his cigars, request his favorite beer-drinking songs from the mariachis, smile, tell stories and make sure everyone has a grand time. He will be dressed in a tuxedo, borrowed from the patrón's closet of course, and he will act gallant and show everyone that a man who has just come into sudden wealth should share it with his friends. And in the morning he will report to the patrón that something has to be done about the poor mice that are coming in out of the streets and eating everything in the house.

"I'll buy some poison," the patrón will suggest.

"No, no," Justino will shake his head, "a little music from the radio and a candle burning in the sala will do."

And he will be right.

I liked Justino. He was a rogue with class. We talked about the weather, the lateness of the rainy season, women, the role of oil in Mexican politics. Like other workers, he believed nothing was going to filter down to the campesinos. "We could all be real Mexican greasers with all that oil," he said, "but the politicians will keep it all."

"What about the United States?" I asked.

"Oh, I have traveled in the estados unidos to the north. It's a country that's going to the dogs in a worse way than Mexico. The thing I liked the most was your cornflakes."

"Cornflakes?"

"Sí. You can make really good cornflakes."

"And women?"

"Ah, you better keep your eyes open, my friend. Those gringas are going to change the world just like the Suecas changed Spain."

"For better or for worse?"

"Spain used to be a nice country," he winked.

We talked, we argued, we drifted from subject to subject. I learned from him. I had been there a week when he told me the story which eventually led me to B. Traven. One day I was sitting under the orange tree reading the B. Traven novel I had found in the Juarez train station, keeping one eye on the ripe oranges which fell from time to time, my mind wandering as it worked to focus on a story so I could begin to write. After all, that's why I had come to Cuernavaca, to get some writing done, but nothing was coming, nothing. Justino wandered by and asked what I was reading and I replied it was an adventure story, a story of a man's search for the illusive pot of gold at the end of a make-believe rainbow. He nodded, thought awhile and gazed toward Popo, Popocatepetl, the towering volcano which lay to the south, shrouded in mist, waiting for the rains as we waited for the rains, sleeping, gazing at his female counterpart, Itza, who lay sleeping and guarding the valley of Cholula, there, where over four-hundred years ago Cortés showed his wrath and executed thousands of Cholulans.

"I am going on an adventure," he finally said and paused. "I think you might like to go with me."

I said nothing, but I put my book down and listened.

"I have been thinking about it for a long time, and now is the time to go. You see, it's like this. I grew up on the hacienda of Don Francisco Jimenez, it's to the south, just a day's drive on the carretera. In my village nobody likes Don Francisco, they fear and hate him. He has killed many men and he has taken their fortunes and buried them. He is a very rich man, muy rico. Many men have tried to kill him, but Don Francisco is like the devil, he kills them first."

I listened as I always listen, because one never knows when a word or a phrase or an idea will be the seed from which a story sprouts, but at first there was nothing interesting. It sounded like the typical patrón-peón story I had heard so many times before. A man, the patrón, keeps the workers enslaved, in serfdom, and because he wields so much power soon stories are told about him and he begins to acquire super-human powers. He acquires a mystique, just like the divine right of old. The patrón wields a mean machete, like old King Arthur swung Excaliber. He chops off heads of dissenters and sits on top of the bones and skulls pyramid, the king of the mountain, the top macho.

"One day I was sent to look for lost cattle," Justino continued. "I rode back into the hills where I had never been. At the foot of a hill, near a ravine, I saw something move in the bush. I dismounted and moved forward quietly. I was afraid it might be bandidos who steal cattle, and if they saw me they would kill me. When I came near the place I heard a strange sound. Somebody was crying. My back shivered, just like a dog when he sniffs the devil at night. I thought I was going to see witches, brujas who like to go to those deserted places to dance for the devil, or la Llorona."

"La Llorona," I said aloud. My interest grew. I had been hearing Llorona stories since I was a kid, and I was always ready for one more. La Llorona was that archetypal woman of ancient legends who murdered her children, then repentant and demented she has spent the rest of eternity searching for them.

"Sí, la Llorona. You know that poor woman used to drink a lot. She played around with men, and when she had babies she got rid of them by throwing them into la barranca. One day she realized what she had done and went crazy. She started crying and pulling her hair and running up and down the side of cliffs of the river looking for her children. It's a very sad story."

A new version, I thought, and yes, a sad story. And what of the men who made love to the woman who became la Llorona, I wondered? Did they ever cry for their children? It doesn't seem fair to have only her suffer, only her crying and doing penance. Perhaps a man should run with her, and in our legends we would call him "El Mero Chingón," he who screwed up everything. Then maybe the tale of love and passion and the insanity it can bring will be complete. Yes, I think someday I will write that story.

"What did you see?" I asked Justino.

"Something worse than la Llorona," he whispered.

To the south a wind mourned and moved the clouds off Popo's crown. The bald, snow-covered mountain thrust its power into the blue Mexican sky. The light glowed like liquid gold around the god's head. Popo was a god, an ancient god. Somewhere at his feet Justino's story had taken place.

"I moved closer, and when I parted the bushes I saw Don Francisco. He was sitting on a rock, and he was crying. From time to time he looked at the ravine in front of him, the hole seemed to slant into the earth. That pozo is called el Pozo de Mendoza. I had heard stories about it before, but I had never seen it. I looked into the pozo, and you wouldn't believe what I saw."

He waited, so I asked, "What?"

"Money! Huge piles of gold and silver coins! Necklaces and bracelets and crowns of gold, all loaded with all kinds of precious stones! Jewels! Diamonds! All sparkling in the sunlight that entered the hole. More money than I have ever seen! A fortune, my friend, a fortune which is still there, just waiting for two adventurers like us to take it!"

"Us? But what about Don Francisco? It's his land, his fortune."

"Ah," Justino smiled, "that's the strange thing about this fortune. Don Francisco can't touch it, that's why he was crying. You see, I stayed there, and I watched him closely. Every time he stood up and started to walk into the pozo the money disappeared. He stretched out his hand to grab the gold, and poof, it was gone! That's why he was crying! He murdered all those people and hid their wealth in the pozo, but now he can't touch it. He is cursed."

"El Pozo de Mendoza," I said aloud. Something began to click in my mind. I smelled a story.

"Who was Mendoza?" I asked.

"He was a very rich man. Don Francisco killed him in a quarrel they had over some cattle. But Mendoza must have put a curse on Don Francisco before he died, because now Don Francisco can't get to the money."

"So Mendoza's ghost haunts old Don Francisco," I nodded.

"Many ghosts haunt him," Justino answered. "He has killed many men."

"And the fortune, the money. . . ."

He looked at me and his eyes were dark and piercing. "It's still there. Waiting for us!"

"But it disappears as one approaches it, you said so yourself. Perhaps it's only an hallucination."

Justino shook his head. "No, it's real gold and silver, not hallucination money. It disappears for Don Francisco because the curse is on him, but the curse is not on us." He smiled. He knew he had drawn me into his plot. "We didn't steal the money, so it won't disappear for us. And you are not connected with the place. You are innocent. I've thought very carefully about it, and now is the time to go. I can lower you into the pozo with a rope, in a few hours we can bring out the entire fortune. All we need is a car. You can borrow the patrón's car, he is your friend. But he must not know where we're going. We can be there and back in one day, one night." He nodded as if to assure me, then he turned and looked at the sky. "It will not rain today. It will not rain for a week. Now is the time to go."

He winked and returned to watering the grass and flowers of the jardín, a wild Pan among the bougainvillea and the roses, a man possessed by a dream. The gold was not for him, he told me the next day, it was for his women, he would buy them all gifts, bright dresses, and he would take them on a vacation to the United States, he would educate his children, send them to the best colleges. I listened and the germ of the story cluttered my thoughts as I sat beneath the orange tree in the mornings. I couldn't write, nothing was coming, but I knew that there were elements for a good story in Justino's tale. In dreams I saw the lonely hacienda to the south. I saw the pathetic, tormented figure of Don Francisco as he cried over the fortune he couldn't touch. I saw the ghosts of the men he had killed, the lonely women who mourned over them and cursed the evil Don Francisco. In one dream I saw a man I took to be B. Traven, a grey-haired distinguished looking gentleman who looked at me and nodded approvingly. "Yes, there's a story there, follow it, follow it. . . ."

In the meantime, other small and seemingly insignificant details came my way. During a luncheon at the home of my friend, a woman I did not know leaned toward me and asked me if I would like to meet the widow of B. Traven. The woman's hair was tinged orange, her complexion was ashen grey. I didn't know who she was or why she would mention B. Traven to me. How did she know Traven had come to haunt my thoughts? Was she a clue which would help unravel the mystery? I didn't know, but I nodded. Yes, I would like to meet her. I had heard that Traven's widow, Rosa Elena, lived in Mexico City. But what would I ask her? What did I want to know? Would she know Traven's secret? Somehow he had learned that to keep his magic intact he had to keep away from the public. Like the fortune in the pozo, the magic feel for the story might disappear if unclean hands reached for it. I turned to look at the woman, but she was gone. I wandered to the terrace to finish my beer. Justino sat beneath the orange tree. He yawned. I knew the literary talk bored him. He was eager to be on the way to el Pozo de Mendoza.

I was nervous, too, but I didn't know why. The tension for the story was there, but something was missing. Or perhaps it was just Justino's insistence that I decide whether I was going or not that drove me out of the house in the mornings. Time usually devoted to writing found me in a small cafe in the center of town. From there I could watch the shops open, watch the people cross the zócalo, the main square. I drank lots of coffee, I smoked a lot, I daydreamed, I wondered about the significance of the pozo, the fortune, Justino, the story I wanted to write and B. Traven. In one of these moods I saw a friend from whom I hadn't heard in years. Suddenly he was there, trekking across the square, dressed like an old rabbi, moss and green algae for a beard, and followed by a troop of very dignified Lacandones, Mayan Indians from Chiapas.

"Victor," I gasped, unsure if he was real or a part of the shadows which the sun created as it flooded the square with its light.

"I have no time to talk," he said as he stopped to munch on my pan dulce and sip my coffee. "I only want you to know, for purposes of your story, that I was in a Lacandonian village last month, and a Hollywood film crew descended from the sky. They came in helicopters. They set up tents near the village, and big-bossomed, bikined actresses emerged from them, tossed themselves on the cut trees which are the atrocity of the giant American lumber companies, and they cried while the director shot his film. Then they produced a grey-haired old man from one of the tents and took shots of him posing with the Indians. Herr Traven, the director called him."

He finished my coffee, nodded to his friends and they began to walk away.

"B. Traven?" I asked.

He turned. "No, an imposter, an actor. Be careful for imposters. Remember, even Traven used many disguises, many names!"

"Then he's alive and well?" I shouted. People around me turned to stare.

"His spirit is with us," were the last words I heard as they moved across the zócalo, a strange troop of near naked Lacandon Mayans and my friend the Guatemalan Jew, returning to the rain forest, returning to the primal, innocent land.

I slumped in my chair and looked at my empty cup. What did it mean? As their trees fall the Lacandones die. Betrayed as B. Traven was betrayed. Does each one of us also die as the trees fall in the dark depths of the Chiapas jungle? Far to the north, in Aztlan, it is the same where the earth is ripped open to expose and mine the yellow uranium. A few poets sing songs and stand in the way as the giant machines of the corporations rumble over the land and grind everything into dust. New holes are made in the earth, pozos full of curses, pozos with fortunes we cannot touch, should not touch. Oil, coal, uranium, from holes in the earth through which we suck the blood of the earth.

There were other incidents. A telephone call late one night, a voice with a German accent called my name, and when I answered the line went dead. A letter addressed to B. Traven came in the mail. It was dated March 26, 1969. My friend returned it to the post office. Justino grew more and more morose. He sat under the orange tree and stared into space, my friend complained about the garden drying up. Justino looked at me and scowled. He did a little work then went back to daydreaming. Without the rains the garden withered. His heart was set on the adventure which lay at el pozo. Finally I said yes, dammit, why not, let's go, neither one of us is getting anything done here, and Justino cheering like a child, ran to prepare for the trip. But when I asked my friend for the weekend loan of the car he reminded me that we were invited to a tertulia, an afternoon reception, at the home of Señora Ana R. Many writers and artists would be there. It was in my honor, so I could meet the literati of Cuernavaca. I had to tell Justino I couldn't go.

Now it was I who grew morose. The story growing within would not let me sleep. I awakened in the night and looked out the window, hoping to see Justino and women bathing in the pool, enjoying themselves. But all was quiet. No radio played. The still night was warm and heavy. From time to time gunshots sounded in the dark, dogs barked, and the presence of a Mexico which never sleeps closed in on me.

Saturday morning dawned with a strange overcast. Perhaps the rains will come, I thought. In the afternoon I reluctantly accompanied my friend to the reception. I had not seen Justino all day, but I saw him at the gate as we drove out. He looked tired, as if he, too, had not slept. He wore the white shirt and baggy pants of a campesino. His straw hat cast a shadow over his eyes. I wondered if he had decided to go to the pozo alone. He didn't speak as we drove through the gate, he only nodded. When I looked back I saw him standing by the gate, looking after the car, and I had a vague, uneasy feeling that I had lost an opportunity.

The afternoon gathering was a pleasant affair, attended by a number of affectionate artists, critics, and writers who enjoyed the refreshing drinks which quenched the thirst.

But my mood drove me away from the crowd. I wandered around the terrace and found a foyer surrounded by green plants, huge fronds and ferns and flowering bougainvillea. I pushed the green aside and entered a quiet, very private alcove. The light was dim, the air was cool, a perfect place for contemplation. At first I thought I was alone, then I saw the man sitting in one of the wicker chairs next to a small, wrought iron table. He was an elderly white-haired gentleman. His face showed he had lived a full life, yet he was still very distinguished in his manner and posture. His eyes shone brightly.

"Perdón," I apologized and turned to leave. I did not want to intrude.

"No, no, please," he motioned to the empty chair, "I've been waiting for you." He spoke English with a slight German accent. Or perhaps it was Norwegian, I couldn't tell the difference. "I can't take the literary gossip. I prefer the quiet."

I nodded and sat. He smiled and I felt at ease. I took the cigar he offered and we lit up. He began to talk and I listened. He was a writer also, but I had the good manners not to ask his titles. He talked about the changing Mexico, the change the new oil would bring, the lateness of the rains and how they affected the people and the land, and he talked about how important a woman was in a writer's life. He wanted to know about me, about the Chicanos of Aztlan, about our work. It was the workers, he said, who would change society. The artist learned from the worker. I talked, and sometime during the conversation I told him the name of the friend with whom I was staying. He laughed and wanted to know if Vitorino was still working for him.

"Do you know Justino?" I asked.

"Oh, yes, I know that old guide. I met him many years ago, when I first came to Mexico," he answered. "Justino knows the campesino very well. He and I traveled many places together, he in search of adventure, I in search of stories."

I thought the coincidence strange, so I gathered the courage and asked, "Did he ever tell you the story of the fortune at el Pozo de Mendoza?"

"Tell me?" the old man smiled. "I went there."

"With Justino?"

"Yes, I went with him. What a rogue he was in those days, but a good man. If I remember correctly I even wrote a story based on that adventure. Not a very good story. Never came to anything. But we had a grand time. People like Justino are the writer's source. We met interesting people and saw fabulous places, enough to last me a lifetime. We were supposed to be gone for one day, but we were gone nearly three years. You see, I wasn't interested in the pots of gold he kept saying were just over the next hill, I went because there was a story to write."

"Yes, that's what interested me," I agreed.

"A writer has to follow a story if it leads him to hell itself. That's our curse. Ay, and each one of us knows our own private hell."

I nodded. I felt relieved. I sat back to smoke the cigar and sip from my drink. Somewhere to the west the sun bronzed the evening sky. On a clear afternoon, Popo's crown would glow like fire.

"Yes," the old man continued, "a writer's job is to find and follow people like Justino. They're the source of life. The ones you have to keep away from are the dilettantes like the ones in there." He motioned in the general direction of the noise of the party. "I stay with people like Justino. They may be illiterate, but they understand our descent into the pozo of hell, and they understand us because they're willing to share the adventure with us. You seek fame and notoriety and you're dead as a writer."

I sat upright. I understood now what the pozo meant, why Justino had come into my life to tell me the story. It was clear. I rose quickly and shook the old man's hand. I turned and parted the palm leaves of the alcove. There, across the way, in one of the streets that led out of the maze of the town towards the south, I saw Justino. He was walking in the direction of Popo, and he was followed by women and children, a rag-tail army of adventurers, all happy, all singing. He looked up to where I stood on the terrace, and he smiled as he waved. He paused to light the stub of a cigar. The women turned, and the children turned, and all waved to me. Then they continued their walk, south, towards the foot of the volcano. They were going to the Pozo de Mendoza, to the place where the story originated.

I wanted to run after them, to join them in the glorious light which bathed the Cuernavaca valley and the majestic snow-covered head of Popo. The light was everywhere, a magnetic element which flowed from the clouds. I waved as Justino and his followers disappeared in the light. Then I turned to say something to the old man, but he was gone. I was alone in the alcove. Somewhere in the background I heard the tinkling of glasses and the laughter which came from the party, but that was not for me. I left the terrace and crossed the lawn, found the gate and walked down the street. The sounds of Mexico filled the air. I felt light and happy. I wandered aimlessly through the curving, narrow streets, then I quickened my pace because suddenly the story was overflowing and I needed to write. I needed to get to my quiet room and write the story about B. Traven being alive and well in Cuernavaca.

James Welch
b. 1940

■

1971: *Riding the Earthboy 40*
1974: *Winter in the Blood*
1979: *The Death of Jim Loney*
1986: *Fools Crow*

■

PRIOR TO THE 1960s *surge of ethnic awareness, most Native American fiction was out of print. The standard canon of Native American literature included Oliver La Farge's* Laughing Boy *(1929), John G. Neihardt's* Black Elk Speaks *(1932), D'Arcy McNickle's* The Surrounded *(1936), and Frank Waters's* The Man Who Killed the Deer *(1942). Most readers could not tell you whether these classics had been written by Indians, by people with some measure of Indian blood in their ancestry, or by whites.*

Around 1970, new works by Native Americans began appearing, focusing attention on contemporary Indian life. Four leading books appeared within ten years of each other: N. Scott Momaday's House Made of Dawn *(1968); Vine Deloria, Jr.'s* Custer Died for Your Sins *(1969); Leslie Silko's* Ceremony *(1977); and James Welch's* Winter in the Blood *(1974).*

In 1870, just 101 years before Welch published Riding the Earthboy 40, *federal troops all but exterminated his Blackfeet ancestors in the Marias Massacre. Novels of the mountain men generally portray the Blackfeet as the most savage, bloodthirsty, fearsome tribe in North America. The Lewis and Clark expedition killed two Piegans of the Blackfeet nation in 1806, the opening act of a conflict that lasted for eighty years. Half the Blackfeet population died from smallpox; some of the survivors fled to Canada to escape the epidemic, abandoning their traditional lands. Those who remained behind had to face starvation, thanks to the virtual extinction of the northern buffalo.*

Today, the central headquarters of the Blackfeet Indian Reservation is in

Browning, Montana, where James Welch was born. He attended the University of Minnesota and Northern Montana College and finished his baccalaureate degree at the University of Montana. He continues to live, write, and teach in Montana.

Welch's first two novels portray young men living dead lives in towns deeply scarred by poverty, apathy, alcoholism, and desperation. They are modern Indians with little knowledge of their heritage and no hope of a future. By contrast, his 1986 historical novel, Fools Crow, *ends on a positive note. Both* Winter in the Blood *and* The Death of Jim Loney *come to bleak, wintry conclusions, with the frozen earth seeming to mock the dead and dying alike.* Fools Crow, *in contrast, ends in early spring. The people feast and talk of moving to fresh campsites; new grass sprouts for the buffalo. Children—new people—play in the mud.*

Welch's fiction has earned him a place among significant western writers. However, readers should also pay attention to his remarkable poetry, which demonstrates Welch's artistic versatility. His richly complex, original imagery can be startling. And some of his metaphors are actually puzzles, as in his semi-ironic use of the term Thanksgiving *in* "Thanksgiving at Snake Butte." *In other places, the clarity of his language lets us see through it and into it at the same time, like looking at a landscape through a spider's web.*

> I saw your spiders weaving threads
> to bandage up the day. And more,
> those webs were filled with words
> that tumbled meaning into wind.

Snow Country Weavers

A time to tell you things are well.
Birds flew south a year ago.
One returned, a blue-wing teal
wild with news of his mother's love.

Mention me to friends. Say
wolves are dying at my door,
the winter drives them from their meat.
Say this: say in my mind

The selections of James Welch's verse included here are from *Riding the Earthboy 40* (New York: Harper and Row, 1971), pp. 47, 32, 4, 40, and 64, respectively. Copyright © 1971 by James Welch. Reprinted by permission of Elaine Markson Literary Agency, Inc.

I saw your spiders weaving threads
to bandage up the day. And more,
those webs were filled with words
that tumbled meaning into wind.

—

Riding the Earthboy 40

Earthboy: so simple his name
should ring a bell for sinners.
Beneath the clowny hat, his eyes
so shot the children called him
dirt, Earthboy farmed this land
and farmed the sky with words.

The dirt is dead. Gone to seed
his rows become marker to a grave
vast as anything but dirt.
Bones should never tell a story
to a bad beginner. I ride
romantic to those words,

those foolish claims that he
was better than dirt, or rain
that bleached his cabin
white as bone. Scattered in the wind
Earthboy calls me from my dream:
Dirt is where the dreams must end.

—

Verifying the Dead

We tore the green tree down
searching for my bones.
A coyote drove the day back
half a step until we killed
both him and it. Our knives
became a bed for quick things.

It's him all right
I heard old Nine Pipe say.
As we turned away,
a woman blue as night
stepped from my bundle,
rubbed her hips and sang
of a country like this far off.

Thanksgiving at Snake Butte

In time we rode that trail
up the butte as far as time
would let us. The answer to our time
lay hidden in the long grasses
on the top. Antelope scattered

through the rocks before us, clattered
unseen down the easy slope to the west.
Our horses balked, stiff-legged,
their nostrils flared at something unseen
gliding smoothly through brush away.

On top, our horses broke, loped through
a small stand of stunted pine, then jolted
to a nervous walk. Before us lay
the smooth stones of our ancestors, the fish,
the lizard, snake and bent-kneed

bowman—etched by something crude,
by a wandering race, driven by their names
for time: its winds, its rain, its snow
and the cold moon tugging at the crude figures
in this, the season of their loss.

Grandma's Man

That day she threw the goose over the roof
of the cowshed, put her hand to her lips
and sucked, cursing, the world ended. In blood
her world ended though these past twenty years
have healed the bite and that silly goose
is preening in her favorite pillow.

Her husband was a fool. He laughed too long
at lies told by girls whose easy virtue disappeared
when he passed stumble-bum down the Sunday street.
Baled hay in his every forty, cows on his allotted range,
his quick sorrel quarter-horse, all neglected for
the palms of friends. Then, he began to paint LIFE.

His first attempt was all about a goose that bit
the hand that fed it. The obstacles were great.
Insurmountable. His fingers were too thick to grip
the brush right. The sky was always green
and hay spoiled in the fields. In wind,
the rain, the superlative night, images came, geese
skimming to the reservoir. This old man listened.
He got a bigger brush and once painted the cry
of a goose so long, it floated off the canvas
into thin air. Things got better. Sky turned white.
Winter came and he became quite expert at snowflakes.
But he was growing wise, Lord, his hair white as snow.

Funny, he used to say, how mountains are blue
in winter and green in spring. He never ever
got things quite right. He thought a lot about the day
the goose bit Grandma's hand. LIFE seldom came
the shade he wanted. Well, and yes, he died well,
but you should have seen how well his friends took it.

Leslie Marmon Silko
b. 1948

1974: *Laguna Woman: Poems*
1977: *Ceremony*
1981: *Storyteller*

... it is together—
all of us remembering what we have heard together—
that creates the whole story
the long story of the people.[1]

THE PEOPLE *in Leslie Marmon Silko's* Storyteller *inhabit the Laguna Pueblo of New Mexico, with the Navajo, Hopi, Zuni, Acoma, and Apache Indians as neighbors. A native of Laguna, Silko grew up in a family that cherished the storytelling tradition. After earning her B.A. in English at the University of New Mexico, she spent a short time in law school and then took a teaching position at Navajo Community College in Tsaile, Arizona. From there, Silko went to Alaska for two years, where she began writing* Ceremony.

Ceremony, *according to* American Women Writers, *made Silko "the first Native American woman to publish a full length novel."* [2] *Unlike the majority of contemporary Native American novels,* Ceremony *does not end pessimistically; moreover, it challenges three general assumptions about Native Americans and literature. First, it denies the idea that a ceremony is a fixed, unchangeable ritual. Second, it shows that legends and oral literature also change while being carefully handed down from generation to generation. And finally, like N. Scott Momaday's* House Made of Dawn, *Silko's* Ceremony *displays artistic dexterity,*

---

1. Leslie Marmon Silko, *Storyteller* (New York: Seaver Books, 1981), p. 7.
2. Edith Blicksilver, "Leslie Marmon Silko," in *American Women Writers*, ed. Lina Mainiero (New York: Frederick Ungar, 1982), vol. 4, p. 82.

disproving the old hypothesis that the novel, a European invention, is an "alien form" of fiction for Native American writers.

The Laguna oral historians—storytellers—gave Silko the key to narrative technique. "The story was the important thing and little changes here and there were really part of the story. There were even stories about the different versions of stories and how they imagined these differing versions came to be." [3] *Tayo, in* Ceremony, *lives his own story over and over until he finds one version that contains his identity.*

"Lullaby" resembles a familiar song, changing slightly each year yet always coming back to the themes of life and loss. Images of pattern and repetition reoccur in the woolen clouds, the woven blankets, the sheltering rock of the timeless mountain, and the garden that the old people plant every year, "not because anything would survive the summer dust, but because it was time to do this." Faith in the pattern, even with its variations, brings a moment of peace, a reason to smile at the storm, and a serenity amid the rhythm of the pains.

—

Lullaby

THE SUN had gone down but the snow in the wind gave off its own light. It came in thick tufts like new wool—washed before the weaver spins it. Ayah reached out for it like her own babies had, and she smiled when she remembered how she had laughed at them. She was an old woman now, and her life had become memories. She sat down with her back against the wide cottonwood tree, feeling the rough bark on her back bones; she faced east and listened to the wind and snow sing a high-pitched Yeibechei song. Out of the wind she felt warmer, and she could watch the wide fluffy snow fill in her tracks, steadily, until the direction she had come from was gone. By the light of the snow she could see the dark outline of the big arroyo a few feet away. She was sitting on the edge of Cebolleta Creek, where in the springtime the thin cows would graze on grass already chewed flat to the ground. In the wide deep creek bed where only a trickle of water flowed in the summer, the skinny cows would wander, looking for new grass along winding paths splashed with manure.

3. Silko, *Storyteller*, p. 227.

Ayah pulled the old Army blanket over her head like a shawl. Jimmie's blanket—the one he had sent to her. That was a long time ago and the green wool was faded, and it was unraveling on the edges. She did not want to think about Jimmie. So she thought about the weaving and the way her mother had done it. On the tall wooden loom set into the sand under a tamarack tree for shade. She could see it clearly. She had been only a little girl when her grandma gave her the wooden combs to pull the twigs and burrs from the raw, freshly washed wool. And while she combed the wool, her grandma sat beside her, spinning a silvery strand of yarn around the smooth cedar spindle. Her mother worked at the loom with yarns dyed bright yellow and red and gold. She watched them dye the yarn in boiling black pots full of beeweed petals, juniper berries, and sage. The blankets her mother made were soft and woven so tight that rain rolled off them like birds' feathers. Ayah remembered sleeping warm on cold windy nights, wrapped in her mother's blankets on the hogan's sandy floor.

The snow drifted now, with the northwest wind hurling it in gusts. It drifted up around her black overshoes—old ones with little metal buckles. She smiled at the snow which was trying to cover her little by little. She could remember when they had no black rubber overshoes; only the high buckskin leggings that they wrapped over their elkhide moccasins. If the snow was dry or frozen, a person could walk all day and not get wet; and in the evenings the beams of the ceiling would hang with lengths of pale buckskin leggings, drying out slowly.

She felt peaceful remembering. She didn't feel cold any more. Jimmie's blanket seemed warmer than it had ever been. And she could remember the morning he was born. She could remember whispering to her mother, who was sleeping on the other side of the hogan, to tell her it was time now. She did not want to wake the others. The second time she called to her, her mother stood up and pulled on her shoes; she knew. They walked to the old stone hogan together, Ayah walking a step behind her mother. She waited alone, learning the rhythms of the pains while her mother went to call the old woman to help them. The morning was already warm even before dawn and Ayah smelled the bee flowers blooming and the young willow growing at the springs. She could remember that so clearly, but his birth merged into the births of the other children and to her it became all the same birth. They named him for the summer morning and in English they called him Jimmie.

It wasn't like Jimmie died. He just never came back, and one day a dark blue sedan with white writing on its doors pulled up in front of the box-car shack where the rancher let the Indians live. A man in a khaki uniform trimmed in gold gave them a yellow piece of paper and told them that Jimmie was dead. He said the Army would try to get the body back and then it would be shipped to them; but it wasn't likely because the helicopter had burned after it crashed. All of this was told to Chato because he could understand English. She stood inside the doorway holding the baby while Chato listened. Chato spoke English like a white man and he spoke Spanish too. He was taller than the white man and he stood straighter too. Chato didn't explain why; he just told the military man they could keep the body if they found it. The white man looked bewildered; he nodded his head and he left. Then Chato looked at her and shook his head, and then he told her, "Jimmie isn't coming home anymore," and when he spoke, he used the words to speak of the dead. She didn't cry then, but she hurt inside with anger. And she mourned him as the years passed, when a horse fell with Chato and broke his leg, and the white rancher told them he wouldn't pay Chato until he could work again. She mourned Jimmie because he would have worked for his father then; he would have saddled the big bay horse and ridden the fence lines each day, with wire cutters and heavy gloves, fixing the breaks in the barbed wire and putting the stray cattle back inside again.

She mourned him after the white doctors came to take Danny and Ella away. She was at the shack alone that day they came. It was back in the days before they hired Navajo women to go with them as interpreters. She recognized one of the doctors. She had seen him at the children's clinic at Cañoncito about a month ago. They were wearing khaki uniforms and they waved papers at her and a black ball-point pen, trying to make her understand their English words. She was frightened by the way they looked at the children, like the lizard watches the fly. Danny was swinging on the tire swing on the elm tree behind the rancher's house, and Ella was toddling around the front door, dragging the broomstick horse Chato made for her. Ayah could see they wanted her to sign the papers, and Chato had taught her to sign her name. It was something she was proud of. She only wanted them to go, and to take their eyes away from her children.

She took the pen from the man without looking at his face and she signed the papers in three different places he pointed to. She stared at the ground by their feet and waited for them to leave. But they stood there and began to point and gesture at the children. Danny stopped swinging. Ayah could see his fear. She moved suddenly and grabbed Ella into her arms; the child squirmed, trying to get back to her toys. Ayah ran with the baby toward Danny; she screamed for him to run and then she grabbed him around his chest and carried him too. She ran south into the foothills of juniper trees and black lava rock. Behind her she heard the doctors running, but they had been taken by surprise, and as the hills became steeper and the cholla cactus were thicker, they stopped. When she reached the top of the hill, she stopped to listen in case they were circling around her. But in a few minutes she heard a car engine start and they drove away. The children had been too surprised to cry while she ran with them. Danny was shaking and Ella's little fingers were gripping Ayah's blouse.

She stayed up in the hills for the rest of the day, sitting on a black lava boulder in the sunshine where she could see for miles all around her. The sky was light blue and cloudless, and it was warm for late April. The sun warmth relaxed her and took the fear and anger away. She lay back on the rock and watched the sky. It seemed to her that she could walk into the sky, stepping through clouds endlessly. Danny played with little pebbles and stones, pretending they were birds eggs and then little rabbits. Ella sat at her feet and dropped fistfuls of dirt into the breeze, watching the dust and particles of sand intently. Ayah watched a hawk soar high above them, dark wings gliding; hunting or only watching, she did not know. The hawk was patient and he circled all afternoon before he disappeared around the high volcanic peak the Mexicans called Guadalupe.

Late in the afternoon, Ayah looked down at the gray boxcar shack with the paint all peeled from the wood; the stove pipe on the roof was rusted and crooked. The fire she had built that morning in the oil drum stove had burned out. Ella was asleep in her lap now and Danny sat close to her, complaining that he was hungry; he asked when they would go to the house. "We will stay up here until your father comes," she told him, "because those white men were chasing us." The boy remembered then and he nodded at her silently.

If Jimmie had been there he could have read those papers and explained to her what they said. Ayah would have known then, never to sign them. The doctors came back the next day and they brought a BIA policeman with them. They told Chato they had her signature and that was all they needed. Except for the kids. She listened to Chato sullenly; she hated him when he told her it was the old woman who died in the winter, spitting blood; it was her old grandma who had given the children this disease. "They don't spit blood," she said coldly. "The whites lie." She held Ella and Danny close to her, ready to run to the hills again. "I want a medicine man first," she said to Chato, not looking at him. He shook his head. "It's too late now. The policeman is with them. You signed the paper." His voice was gentle.

It was worse than if they had died: to lose the children and to know that somewhere, in a place called Colorado, in a place full of sick and dying strangers, her children were without her. There had been babies that died soon after they were born, and one that died before he could walk. She had carried them herself, up to the boulders and great pieces of the cliff that long ago crashed down from Long Mesa; she laid them in the crevices of sandstone and buried them in fine brown sand with round quartz pebbles that washed down the hills in the rain. She had endured it because they had been with her. But she could not bear this pain. She did not sleep for a long time after they took her children. She stayed on the hill where they had fled the first time, and she slept rolled up in the blanket Jimmie had sent her. She carried the pain in her belly and it was fed by everything she saw: the blue sky of their last day together and the dust and pebbles they played with; the swing in the elm tree and broomstick horse choked life from her. The pain filled her stomach and there was no room for food or for her lungs to fill with air. The air and the food would have been theirs.

She hated Chato, not because he let the policeman and doctors put the screaming children in the government car, but because he had taught her to sign her name. Because it was like the old ones always told her about learning their language or any of their ways: it endangered you. She slept alone on the hill until the middle of November when the first snows came. Then she made a bed for herself where the children had slept. She did not lie down beside Chato again until many years later, when he was sick and shivering and only her body could keep him warm. The illness came after the white rancher told Chato he was too old to work for him anymore, and Chato and his old woman should be out of the shack by the next afternoon because the rancher had hired new people to work there. That had satisfied her. To see how the white man repaid Chato's years of loyalty and work. All of Chato's fine-sounding English talk didn't change things.

It snowed steadily and the luminous light from the snow gradually diminished into the darkness. Somewhere in Cebolleta a dog barked and other village dogs joined with it. Ayah looked in the direction she had come, from the bar where Chato was buying the wine. Sometimes he told her to go on ahead and wait; and then he never came. And when she finally went back looking for him, she would find him passed out at the bottom of the wooden steps to Azzie's Bar. All the wine would be gone and most of the money too, from the pale blue check that came to them once a month in a government envelope. It was then that she would look at his face and his hands, scarred by ropes and the barbed wire of all those years, and she would think, this man is a stranger; for forty years she had smiled at him and cooked his food, but he remained a stranger. She stood up again, with the snow almost to her knees, and she walked back to find Chato.

It was hard to walk in the deep snow and she felt the air burn in her lungs. She stopped a short distance from the bar to rest and readjust the blanket. But this time he wasn't waiting for her on the bottom step with his old Stetson hat pulled down and his shoulders hunched up in his long wool overcoat.

She was careful not to slip on the wooden steps. When she pushed the door open, warm air and cigarette smoke hit her face. She looked around slowly and deliberately, in every corner, in every dark place that the old man might find to sleep. The bar owner didn't like Indians in there, especially Navajos, but he let Chato come in because he could talk Spanish like he was one of them. The men at the bar stared at her, and the bartender saw that she left the door open wide. Snowflakes were flying inside like moths and melting into a puddle on the oiled wood floor. He motioned to her to close the door, but she did not see him. She held herself straight and walked across the room slowly, searching the room with every step. The snow in her hair melted and she could feel it on her forehead. At the far corner of the room, she saw red flames at the mica window of the old stove door; she looked behind the stove just to make sure. The bar got quiet except for the Spanish polka music playing on the jukebox. She stood by the stove and shook the snow from her blanket and held it near the stove to dry. The wet wool smell reminded her of new-born goats in early March, brought inside to warm near the fire. She felt calm.

In past years they would have told her to get out. But her hair was white now and her face was wrinkled. They looked at her like she was a spider crawling slowly across the room. They were afraid; she could feel the fear. She looked at their faces steadily. They reminded her of the first time the white people brought her children back to her that winter. Danny had been shy and hid behind the thin white woman who brought them. And the baby had not known her until Ayah took her into her arms, and then Ella had nuzzled close to her as she had when she was nursing. The blonde woman was nervous and kept looking at a dainty gold watch on her wrist. She sat on the bench near the small window and watched the dark snow clouds gather around the mountains; she was worrying about the unpaved road. She was frightened by what she saw inside too: the strips of venison drying on a rope across the ceiling and the children jabbering excitedly in a language she did not know. So they stayed for only a few hours. Ayah watched the government car disappear down the road and she knew they were already being weaned from these lava hills and from this sky. The last time they came was in early June, and Ella stared at her the way the men in the bar were now staring. Ayah did not try to pick her up; she smiled at her instead and spoke cheerfully to Danny. When he tried to answer her, he could not seem to remember and he spoke English words with the Navajo. But he gave her a scrap of paper that he had found somewhere and carried in his pocket; it was folded in half, and he shyly looked up at her and said it was a bird. She asked Chato if they were home for good this time. He spoke to the white woman and she shook her head. "How much longer?" he asked, and she said she didn't know; but Chato saw how she stared at the boxcar shack. Ayah turned away then. She did not say good-bye.

She felt satisfied that the men in the bar feared her. Maybe it was her face and the way she held her mouth with teeth clenched tight, like there was nothing anyone could do to her now. She walked north down the road, searching for the old man. She did this because she had the blanket, and there would be no place for him except with her and the blanket in the old adobe barn near the arroyo. They always slept there when they came to Cebolleta. If the money and the wine were gone, she would be relieved because then they could go home again; back to the old hogan with a dirt roof and rock walls where she herself had been born. And the next day the old man could go back to the few sheep they still had, to follow along behind them, guiding them, into dry sandy arroyos where sparse grass grew. She knew he did not like walking behind old ewes when for so many years he rode big quarter horses and worked with cattle. But she wasn't sorry for him; he should have known all along what would happen.

There had not been enough rain for their garden in five years; and that was when Chato finally hitched a ride into the town and brought back brown boxes of rice and sugar and big tin cans of welfare peaches. After that, at the first of the month they went to Cebolleta to ask the postmaster for the check; and then Chato would go to the bar and cash it. They did this as they planted the garden every May, not because anything would survive the summer dust, but because it was time to do this. The journey passed the days that smelled silent and dry like the caves above the canyon with yellow painted buffaloes on their walls.

He was walking along the pavement when she found him. He did not stop or turn around when he heard her behind him. She walked beside him and she noticed how slowly he moved now. He smelled strong of woodsmoke and urine. Lately he had been forgetting. Sometimes he called her by his sister's name and she had been gone for a long time. Once she had found him wandering on the road to the white man's ranch, and she asked him why he was going that way; he laughed at her and said, "You know they can't run that ranch without me," and he walked on determined, limping on the leg that had been crushed many years before. Now he looked at her curiously, as if for the first time, but he kept shuffling along, moving slowly along the side of the highway. His gray hair had grown long and spread out on the shoulders of the long overcoat. He wore the old felt hat pulled down over his ears. His boots were worn out at the toes and he had stuffed pieces of an old red shirt in the holes. The rags made his feet look like little animals up to their ears in snow. She laughed at his feet; the snow muffled the sound of her laugh. He stopped and looked at her again. The wind had quit blowing and the snow was falling straight down; the southeast sky was beginning to clear and Ayah could see a star.

"Let's rest awhile," she said to him. They walked away from the road and up the slope to the giant boulders that had tumbled down from the red sandrock mesa throughout the centuries of rainstorms and earth tremors. In a place where the boulders shut out the wind, they sat down with their backs against the rock. She offered half of the blanket to him and they sat wrapped together.

The storm passed swiftly. The clouds moved east. They were massive and full, crowding together across the sky. She watched them with the feeling of horses—steely blue-gray horses startled across the sky. The powerful haunches pushed into the distances and the tail hairs streamed white mist behind them. The sky cleared. Ayah saw that there was nothing between her and the stars. The light was crystalline. There was no shimmer, no distortion through earth haze. She breathed the clarity of the night sky; she smelled the purity of the half moon and the stars. He was lying on his side with his knees pulled up near his belly for warmth. His eyes were closed now, and in the light from the stars and the moon, he looked young again.

She could see it descend out of the night sky: an icy stillness from the edge of the thin moon. She recognized the freezing. It came gradually, sinking snowflake by snowflake until the crust was heavy and deep. It had the strength of the stars in Orion, and its journey was endless. Ayah knew that with the wine he would sleep. He would not feel it. She tucked the blanket around him, remembering how it was when Ella had been with her; and she felt the rush so big inside her heart for the babies. And she sang the only song she knew to sing for babies. She could not remember if she had

ever sung it to her children, but she knew that her grandmother had sung
it and her mother had sung it:

> The earth is your mother,
>   she holds you.
> The sky is your father,
>   he protects you.
> Sleep,
> sleep.
> Rainbow is your sister,
>   she loves you.
> The winds are your brothers,
>   they sing to you.
> Sleep,
> sleep.
> We are together always
> We are together always
> There never was a time
> when this
> was not so.

Jimmy Santiago Baca
b. 1952

—

1979: *Immigrants in Our Own Land*
1982: *What's Happening*
1987: *Martín and Meditations
on the South Valley*

—

I PRETTY MUCH GOT MY SCHOOLING FROM LIFE, *wrote Jimmy Santiago Baca, who taught himself to read and write in several languages after dropping out of school in the eighth grade. "Then one day I decided to keep a journal of my observations."* [1] *That journal became his first poetry, published in* Mother Jones. *A native of Santa Fe, New Mexico, Baca represents the latest generation of Chicano artists. He illustrates a trait that this group generally has in common, namely a remarkable balance between political and personal incentives, between the voice of the Hispanic spokesperson and the voice of the private writer.*

The poet in Baca's early volume, Immigrants in Our Own Land, *is a prison inmate. He speaks about a life that is not really life and about a daily form of death that is not really death. Existence revolves around detached guards and disinterested friendships between prisoners, all following a daily cycle of brutality and hopelessness. He arrives at the prison hoping for rehabilitation but learns that there is no vocational training, no counseling, nothing but stifling silence.*

> I am the broken reed in this deathly organ,
> I am those mad glazed eyes staring from bars,
> the silent stone look . . . [2]

1. Jimmy Santiago Baca, letter to the author, March 7, 1988.
2. Jimmy Santiago Baca, "How We Carry Ourselves," *Immigrants in Our Own Land* (Baton Rouge: Louisiana State University Press, 1979), p. 43.

The prison is a walled microcosm of the Southwest, where a century and a half of cultural oppression turned Spanish-speaking descendants of the first Europeans into immigrants in their own land. Like the Southwest, the prison is a place where "time gets lost."

> In this land there is a graveness, of color
> and heart. Here the white sands cannot absorb the rich blood
> that sun sponges light from.
> Here wounds open in the heart like cracks
> in a mountainside, here there is a solitude in each person,
> like a cave where a portion of the person sits and thinks.[3]

Martín and Meditations on the South Valley, *Baca's personal epic, is a poem of deep insight. In* Chicano Literature, *Charles M. Tatum described an "introspective current" in Chicano poetry, "dominated by a search for meaning in self."* [4] *In "Meditations," Baca finds that meaning.*

> I dream
> myself maiz root
> swollen in pregnant earth,
> rain seeping into my black bones
> sifting red soil grains of my heart
> into earth's hungry mouth.

> I am part of the earth.[5]

Denise Levertov's introduction to Martín and Meditations on the South Valley *calls attention to Baca's skill with language. "It is not only his responsive sensibility that, at the very opening of* Martín, *enters presences that linger in the air of an abandoned pueblo like the former presence of a picture on a wall; it is the donative articulation with which he can transmit experience. How rich the spare, mostly monosyllabic cadences can be!"* [6]

▬

3. Jimmy Santiago Baca, "In My Land," *Immigrants in Our Own Land* (Baton Rouge: Louisiana State University Press, 1979), p. 23.

4. Charles M. Tatum, *Chicano Literature* (Boston: Twayne, 1982): p. 164.

5. Jimmy Santiago Baca, "Meditations," *Martín and Meditations on the South Valley* (New York: New Directions, 1987), p. 70.

6. Denise Levertov, Introduction to *Martín and Meditations*, by Jimmy Santiago Baca, p. xvii.

II

Forced by circumstances
to live in this Heights apartment—
how strangely clean and new
these white walls are,
thin orange carpet
that sprawls through every room
like a rat's
red faded wrinkled brain
pulsating noises
from tenants below.
The ceramic faces of women
who live here,
and buddha-cheeked men
who all wear straw hats
to walk their poodles,
manicured and clipped elegant
as heirloom dinnerware
glittering beneath chandeliers—

               I don't want
to live here
among the successful. To the South Valley
the white dove of my mind flies,
searching for news of life.

The selections of Jimmy Santiago Baca's verse included here are from *Martín and Meditations on the South Valley* (New York: New Directions, 1987), pp. 55, 58, 59–60, 63–66, and 91–93. Copyright © 1986, 1987 by Jimmy Santiago Baca. Reprinted by permission of New Directions Publishing Corporation.

V

Sunset over the black water of the Río Grande.
It means something to me.
My soul flutters like a black wing
every time I cross the Río Grande bridge.
Crows in cottonwoods
form a long black waving path,
rustling along the horizon.
An old drunk squirms under the bridge
to drink his quart of COORS.
Pack dogs roam—Chicanos cruise in Monte Carlos—
the dead eavesdrop at windows
on women talking at kitchen tables—
children holler in dusty games on dirt roads—
the moon blazes warmly on black water
of the Río Grande.

—

VI

Cruising back from 7–11
esta mañana
in my '56 Chevy truckita,
beat up ranckled
farm truck,
clanking between rows
of new shiny cars—

"Hey fella! Trees need pruning
and the grass needs trimming!"

A man yelled down to me
from his 3rd-story balcony.

       "Sorry, I'm not the gardener,"
       I yelled up to him.

Funny how in the Valley
an old truck symbolizes prestige
and in the Heights, poverty.

Worth is determined in the Valley
by age and durability,
and in the Heights, by newness
and impression.

In the Valley,
the atmosphere is soft and worn,
things are shared and passed down.
In the Heights,
the air is blistered with the glaze
of new cars and new homes.

How many days of my life
I have spent fixing up
rusty broken things,
charging up old batteries,
wiring pieces of odds and ends together!
Ah, those lovely bricks
and sticks I found in fields
and took home with me
to make flower boxes!
The old cars I've worked on
endlessly giving them tune-ups,
changing tires, tracing
electrical shorts,
cursing when I've been stranded
between Laguna pueblo and Burque.
It's the process of making-do,
of the life I've lived between

breakdowns and break-ups, that has made life
worth living.

I could not bear a life
with everything perfect.

—

IX

Eddie blew his head off
playing chicken
with his brother. Para proof
he was man,
he blew his head off.
Don't toll the bell brother,
'cuz he was not religious.
The gray donkey he liked to talk to
at Dead-Man's Corner
grazes sadly. Eddie's gone, its black-lashed dark eyes
mourn. His tío Manuel shatters a bottle
of La Copita wine against the adobe wall
where he and his compas drink every afternoon,
and Manuel weeps for Eddie.

> "He was the kid without a coat
> during winter. 'Member he stole
> those gloves from SEARS, you 'member,
> he stole those gloves? Nice gloves.
> He gave 'em to me ese."

Blew his head off.
The explosion of the gun
was the golden flash of his voice
telling us *no more, no more, no more.*
His last bloody words
water the dried weeds
where his hefa threw the stucco fragments
out. Sparrows peck his brains outside
by the fence posts.

Flaco said, "Don't give him no eulogy!
He was for brothers and sisters
in struggle. You know I saw him
in court one day, when they handcuffed
his older brother to take his brother
to prison, you know Eddie jumped the
benches, and grabbed his brother's
handcuffs, yelling, don't take my brother
he is not a bad man!"

Everybody in Southside knew Eddie,
little Eddie, bad little Eddie.
He treated everybody with respect and honor.
With black-board classroom attention
he saw injustice, hanging out en las calles,
sunrise 'til sunset, with the bros and sisters.

Don't ring the bell, brother.
Let it lie dead.
Let the heavy metal rust.
Let the rope fray and swing mutely
in the afternoon dust and wind.

How many times they beat you Eddie?
How many police clubs
are smeared with your blood,
Switch blade en bolsa,
manos de piedra,
en la linia con sus carnales,[7]
to absorb the tire-jack beatings from other locotes,
    billy-club beatings de la hoda—
your blood Eddie spotted
sidewalks,
smeared shovel handles,
coated knife blades,
blurred your eyes and painted your body

7. "Switch blade in his pocket, / hands of stone, / standing the line with his brothers."
[Baca's translation]

in a tribal-barrio dance
to set yourself free,
to know what was beyond the boundaries
you were born into,

> in your own way,
> in your own sweet way, taking care
> of grandma, her room giving off the aura
> of a saintly relic,
> old wood floors and walls
> smoothed by the continual passing of her body,
> burnished to an altar of sorts,
> in which she was your saint,
> you cared for,

eating with her each evening,
sharing the foodstamps she had,
walking her to la tiendita,
whose walls were scribbled with black paint
your handwriting and initials,
your boundary marker, deadly symbol to other chavos
entering your barrio—the severe, dark stitches of letters
on the walls
healed your wound at being illiterate—
the white adobe wall with your cholo symbols
introduced you to the world,

> as Eddie

who leaned on haunches in the sun,
back against a wall,
talking to 11, 13, 15, 17 year old vatos
sniffing airplane glue
from a paper bag,
breathing in typing correction fluid,
smoking basucon, what Whites call crack,
smoking pelo rojo sinsemilla:

> You listened to their words,
> chale
> simon
> wacha bro
> me importa madre
> ni miedo de la muerta

ni de la pinta
ni de la placa,[8]

and you cried out
hijo de la chingada madre,
cansao
de retablos de calles
pintao con sangre de sus gente,[9]

you cried out

to stop it!
Quit giving the wind our grief stricken voices
at cemeteries,
quit letting the sun soak up our blood,
quit dropping out of high school,
in the center of the storm,
you absorbing the feeling of worthlessness,
caught in your brown skin
and tongue that could not properly pronounce English words,
caught like a seed unable to plant itself,
you picked up God's blue metal face
and scattered the seed of your heart
across the afternoon air,
among the spiked petals of a cactus,
and elm leaves,

your voice whispered
in the dust and weeds,

a terrible silence,
not to forget your death.

XXV

Benny drowned today in the Río Grande.
After drinking a few beers
with Louey y Fernando,

8. "no / yes / look at this man / I don't give a damn / nor am I afraid of death / nor of prison / nor of the badge." [Baca's translation]

9. "son of the cursed mother, / I'm tired / of street altars / painted with the blood of your people." [Baca's translation]

caulando on la playa como vatos do,
he swam out poco pedo.[10]
El Agua was in a mood of lust.
Mean shadowy crevices of moss
yearned,
tree-roots and shag-grass
blackened hair on the Water's face,
as it became a gold mask
with two obsidian eyes,
                    opening its mouth to swallow Benny,
crushing his young brown body
in its swaying-blue claws,
clawing it to the bottom with sledge-hammer hits.

El Agua drank him in deliriously,
adopted Benny as part of its familia,
gasping at the murky bottom,
until the last small bubbles throbbed to the top,
hung limp on surface and swayed away on gray currents.

They found him downstream
days later by Belen, swollen, at a bank
slushing in swamp twigs, grass, and weeds.
Packs of wild perros
feasted on him, and gnawed the puffy white tortilla
of his belly, arms and neck.
He dreamed in the mud and water.
Staggering away with grief
and anger, his hefito Benito Chavez screamed
at El Agua of the Río Grande,
raised his arms pleading with the water
to give back his only son.

Pero el Benny murio hoy
todo el barrio was saying
the day they found him dead.
On porches guitaristas sang death songs,
and old viejas prayed for his soul

---

10. "horsing around on the beach the way guys do, / he swam out a little drunk."
[Baca's translation]

before their small altars in bedrooms,
At paint & body shops
vatos locos milling outside were saying,

> ". . . el vato thought
> he could swim across,
> y luego un current
> le pesco y le tumbo." [11]

At Casa Armijo Community Center,
el Ernie said,

> ". . . el Agua was switching
> Benny back and forth like a rag
> shook out after dusting."

At gas stations & auto parts stores
that litter Isleta, la gente were saying,

> "Estaba gacho, More he hit and kicked el Agua,
> mas que la Muerte le garro. Bien gacho bro,
> te digo."

> ". . . lo que flipio el swiche, fue cuando
> we were standing on the playa, ese. Benny
> yelled ayudame! ayudame! The air turned cold,
> cold ese, bien frio." [12]

At St. Ann's church, los vatos that knew
el Benny, and came for his rosario,
said,

> ". . . bien firme el Benny, muy 'uena gente
> el vato. His cora y alma will be with warriors
> under the earth. He was chosen to be sacrificed
> ese, como los Aztecas al sol, pues,
> al Agua. Asina es, asina es, our lives I mean." [13]

11. "and then a current / picked him up and turned him over." [Baca's translation]

12. "It was bad, the more he hit and kicked the water, / the more Death clutched him. Cold blooded bro, / I tell you. /

". . . what changed it was when / we were standing on the beach, man. Benny / yelled help me! help me! The air turned cold, / it was cold, very cold." [Baca's translation]

13. ". . . Benny was strong, he was good / people. His heart and soul will be with warriors / under the earth. He was chosen to be sacrificed / man, like the Aztecs to the sun, well, / to the water. That's the way it is, that's the way it is, our lives I mean." [Baca's translation]

Day after his funeral,
viejas hung laundry together
and sighed about his death,
viejos hoed their weeds
and felt sorry for Benny's hefe.
Graffiti on grocery-store walls
and laundry mats
warned others away from el Agua,
". . . es donde vive La Muerte . . ."

And on and on
the Río Grande flows,
a fast spinning roulette wheel,
spinning past lives
until, it points a brown fingering wave
to another body, and drops it
like a black marble
into its silver swirling mouth.

Index of Authors, Titles, and First Lines of Poems